William Shakespeare

HIS WORLD · HIS WORK
HIS INFLUENCE

A Midsummer Night's Dream, by Arthur Rackham (1908).

All credits for illustrations are included in Volume III in the *List of Illustrations.*

Copyright © 1985 Charles Scribner's Sons

Library of Congress Cataloging in Publication Data

Main entry under title:

William Shakespeare: his world, his work, his influence.

Includes bibliographies and index.
Contents: v. 1. His world—v. 2. His work—
v. 3. His influence.
1. Shakespeare, William, 1564–1616—Criticism and
interpretation.   2. Shakespeare, William, 1564–1616—
Contemporary England.   3. Shakespeare, William, 1564–1616
—Influence.   4. Great Britain—Civilization—16th
century.   5. Great Britain—Civilization—17th century.
I. Andrews, John, 1942–
PR2976.W5354   1985   822.3′3   85-8305
ISBN 0-684-17851-6 (Set)
ISBN 0-684-18773-6 (Volume 1)
ISBN 0-684-18774-4 (Volume 2)
ISBN 0-684-18775-2 (Volume 3)

3 5 7 9 11 13 15 17 19   V/C   20 18 16 14 12 10 8 6 4

PRINTED IN THE UNITED STATES OF AMERICA

90-0912

Contents

CONTENTS

VOLUME II
hIS WORK

VOLUME III

his INFLUENCE

CONTENTS

ix

William Shakespeare

HIS WORLD · HIS WORK
HIS INFLUENCE

The Life: A Survey

S. SCHOENBAUM

In November 1582 the eighteen-year-old Shakespeare was given a special dispensation to marry a local girl from Shottery, a hamlet about one mile west of Stratford. The facts about the marriage are well known, although their significance has been much debated. Less familiar are the verses addressed by Anne Hathaway to her spouse, which Richard Fenton—attorney, poet, topographer, and historian of the Welsh counties—reported in 1811 having found in a manuscript quarto volume that he had acquired at auction in Wales. One goes like this:

> From my throne in Willie's love,
> Whilst more than royal state I prove,
> Circled proud with myrtle crown,
> I on England's queen look down.
>
> And proud thy Anna well may be,
> For queens themselves might envy me,
> Who scarce in palaces can find
> My Willie's form, with Willie's mind.

These sentiments, no doubt true, are expressed in "To Her own Loving Willie Shakspere" and are signed "Anna Hathaway. By Avon's Side." From another source (William Henry Ireland) we learn that "Willie" was not remiss in reciprocating this ardent effusion. Verses that he addressed to her include this stanza:

> Is there in heaven aught more rare
> Than thou sweet nymph of Avon fair?

> Is there on earth a man more true
> Than Willy Shakspeare is to you?

With this tribute Willy thoughtfully included a lock of his hair, which has been preserved and is now in a splendid private collection in New Jersey. The lock is, as one may have suspected, fake, just as Willy's verses are. They belong with the various exhibits that have been offered from time to time to a public avid for those intimate revelations which the authentic documents, being mostly arid legal instruments, cannot provide.

If forgers have sought to re-create a life for Shakespeare, so too have playwrights and novelists. One example is Edward Bond's play *Bingo* (1973), dealing with Shakespeare's life after his retirement from the stage. The play centers on a crisis in Stratford, where Shakespeare passed his last years. During this last phase of Shakespeare's life, several powerful local landowners moved to reorganize the agricultural system of the neighborhood by converting small farms run by tenants into large expanses of sheep-grazing pasturage, surrounded by ditches and hedges. This development, a manifestation of the enclosure movement, dispossessed the poorer farmers and added to the wealth of already rich landholders; naturally it aroused fierce emotions. Shakespeare, a man of property and influence in the affected fields, was drawn into the controversy. His cousin, the town clerk Thomas Greene, whose property was also involved, sought Shakespeare's advice; we know this from Greene's diary, which is now to be found in the Stratford Records Office. *Bingo* dramatizes Shakespeare's response to this challenge to the daily life of Stratford. Bond depicts the dramatist who had sympathized with the poor naked wretches in *King Lear* as siding with the ruthless landholder William Combe for the sake of increased profits, even though, as a result, the poor rolls would be swelled with the names of the dispossessed. In a crucial scene, Shakespeare, after driving a strict bargain, signs the document that signifies his acquiescence in the landowners' scheme. "Pity you didn't go into business before," Combe says admiringly. "You can bargain."

Mostly, however, in this play Shakespeare broods in his garden; his wife keeps to her bed and hides from him. "She doesn't know who she is, or what she's supposed to do, or who she married," his daughter Judith upbraids him. Later, in a Stratford tavern Shakespeare has a reunion with his friend and archrival Ben Jonson. As they drink together, Shakespeare slumps over the table, spilling his wine. The greatest poet and playwright of the English stage moves through *Bingo* like a sleepwalker, depressed and dissatisfied with his achievement, which, however great as art, has done nothing to alleviate the poverty, cruelty, and injustice of his world. Shakespeare ends his life by swallowing poison. His last despairing words—"Was anything done?"—have a resonance that would be impossible if spoken by any other character.

In his own life Shakespeare no doubt knew disappointment, but there is no evidence that, like Hamlet, he ever contemplated suicide. The earliest report of his mood during his last years comes from Nicholas Rowe (1709).

> The latter part of his life was spent, as all men of good sense will wish theirs may be, in ease, retirement, and the conversation of his friends. He had the good fortune to gather an estate equal to his occasion, and, in that, to his wish; and is said to have spent some years before his death at his native Stratford.

No hint of despair here; rather, at twilight, the afterglow of a life well spent. Nor is the evidence clear that Shakespeare sided with the landowners in the dispute over the enclosure. Bond, however, is not a biographer but a playwright. In *Bingo,* which he subtitles "Scenes of Money and Death," he wants to give expression to some passionately held convictions about the role of a writer in society. "I

admit," he says in the introduction to the printed text of his play, "that I'm not really interested in Shakespeare's true biography in the way a historian might be."

Whatever Bond's conception of his task, some people have gone to see *Bingo* in the expectation of gaining biographical enlightenment—mistakenly, as it turns out; but curiosity about the lives of great men is neither unnatural nor ignoble. To what extent may curiosity be legitimately satisfied? How much do we really know about that monumental figure carved in the Mount Rushmore of bardolatry? Little, according to popular wisdom. We are told that all the facts can be written on a postcard—with plenty of room for the address. George Steevens summed up Shakespeare's life (1778) in a single memorable sentence: "All that is known with any degree of certainty concerning Shakespeare is—that he was born at Stratford upon Avon,—married and had children there,—went to London, where he commenced actor, and wrote poems and plays,—returned to Stratford, made his will, died, and was buried. . . ."

Much has been learned since Steevens wrote these words. And the facts of any life, unless it is of a public figure, can be boiled down to an irreducible minimum. Actually, as a result of the indefatigable research of scholars over more than two centuries, we know more about Shakespeare than we do about any other playwright of his age except Ben Jonson, whose assertive personality engraved a powerful imprint on contemporary records. For Shakespeare it is mainly the nature of the record that leaves us dissatisfied: there are no letters or diaries, no verses from "Anna Hathaway, by Avon's Side," to her beloved Willy. Yet what we can glean raises, for the biographer, historical questions of some interest. We learn something about how sixteenth-century people recorded their births and went to school and got married, how they acquired property and bequeathed it, and how, in general, they ordered their personal and professional lives. As all—or most—of us do these things ourselves, temporal variations hold their own interest. And if we allow ourselves to read between the lines of the ostensibly impersonal record, we find that that figure, out-topping knowledge (in Matthew Arnold's phrase), was not carved from stone after all but was made of flesh and blood.

The essential facts, if not the circumstantial details, of the life may be economically set forth. The playwright's grandfather was probably the Richard

Shakespeare who farmed on two manors of Snitter-field, some three miles north of Stratford, renting his lands from one Robert Arden. Richard's son John married the well-to-do Arden's youngest daughter, Mary. After moving to Stratford, he set himself up as a glover and whittawer, a curer or whitener of skins, a trade requiring a seven-year apprenticeship. He and Mary had four sons and four daughters. Meanwhile, John prospered and rose up the ladder of civic preferment, becoming bailiff (mayor) in 1568, a post with a one-year term of office. The bailiff presided over the court of record and at council meetings and served his borough as justice of the peace. He set the weekly price of grain—and therefore of bread and ale. Yet this respected townsman witnessed corporation minutes with his mark—a cross or pair of glover's compasses. Apparently he was illiterate; not surprisingly, for as a tenant farmer's son in a country village without a school, few educational opportunities were available to him.

John Shakespeare acquired properties and leased them. As early as 1552 he was residing in the western wing of the large double house in Henley Street, the wing that would become known as the Birthplace. He also engaged in subsidiary wool dealings and moneylending, as has recently come to light. These transactions were deemed illegal, and in the early 1570s he faced prosecution four times in the Exchequer for such offenses, which were widespread. (In buying wool John Shakespeare had violated legislation restricting such purchases to manufacturers or merchants of the Staple. In the sixteenth century, as in later periods, trade depended upon the availability of credit, but anachronistic legal practices held usury "a vice most odious and detestable" and hence subject to prosecution.)

The first of the Shakespeares' eight offspring were daughters: Joan in 1558 and Margaret in 1562; their christenings are recorded in the Stratford parish register. The first son, William, was baptized on 26 April 1564. Posterity has elected to celebrate his birth on the 23rd, which happens to be the feast of St. George, England's patron saint. Shakespeare may indeed have been born on that day, but it is not factually established that he was. Rowe tells us that the poet's father educated him "for some time at a free school," which would have been the King's New School of Stratford-upon-Avon, an excellent institution of its kind. Here William would have acquired the "small Latin and less

Greek" with which the formidably learned Ben Jonson credits him in his celebrated eulogy. The youth did not proceed to university. In 1582, he took a wife, "Anne Hathwey of Stratford," as the bishop of Worcester's bond describes her. A daughter, Susanna, was christened on 26 May 1583, and two years later Anne gave birth to twins, Hamnet and Judith, named after lifelong Stratford friends, Hamnet and Judith Sadler. (Sadler was by trade a baker.) Hamnet Shakespeare died young; the Stratford register lists his burial, at the age of eleven, on 11 August 1596.

The seven years that passed between the birth of the twins and the first mention of Shakespeare in London are biographically virtually a void and are accordingly known as the Lost Years. In such vacancies speculation flourishes. During this period did Shakespeare spend some years as a lawyer's clerk? So distinguished barristers have thought. Or did he see military service in the Low Countries, or stand behind the mast at sea? Perhaps he traveled in Italy. Special interest attaches to the will devised in 1581 for Alexander Hoghton of Lea in Lancashire. In this deathbed testament Hoghton, a wealthy Catholic landholder, made provision for his musical instruments and play clothes and asked his half brother Thomas, or failing that, his brother-in-law Sir Thomas Hesketh, "to be friendly unto Fulk Gillom and William Shakeshafte now dwelling with me and either to take them unto his service or else to help them to some good master." Might this Shakeshafte be our Shakespeare under a variant name? Perhaps he doubled as household player and an assistant schoolmaster for the Lancashire magnate. The Hoghton will has for long been known, but its claims on attention have been revived, on the basis of original archival researches, by E. A. J. Honigmann in *Shakespeare: The "Lost Years"* (1985). The Lancashire connection represents an intriguing, if remote, possibility.

We next hear of him in 1592, when a rival playwright, Robert Greene, in his deathbed pamphlet *A Groatsworth of Wit,* enviously referred to him as an "upstart crow, beautified with our feathers." The disparagement evoked a protest from Henry Chettle, a printer and later a prolific dramatist, in the prefatory epistle to his *Kind-Heart's Dream.* "I am as sorry as if the original fault had been my fault," Chettle wrote, "because myself have seen his demeanor no less civil than he excellent in the quality [acting] he professes. Besides, divers of worship [sundry gentlemen] have reported his uprightness of dealing, which argues his honesty, and his facetious grace in writing, that approves his art.''

The names of the "divers of worship" have not come down, but we do know that in 1593 Shakespeare addressed his long narrative poem on an erotic theme, *Venus and Adonis,* with a signed dedication, to Henry Wriothesley, the third earl of Southampton, nine years his junior. The poet diffidently offered his "unpolished lines" to his patron. The next year Shakespeare presented *The Rape of Lucrece* to the same nobleman. This time a warmer note may be discerned in the dedication: "What I have done is yours," he avouches, "what I have to do is yours; being part in all I have, devoted yours.'' Shakespeare may have composed his sonnet sequence mainly during this period, say, from 1592 to 1595; the earl is thought by many to have inspired the Fair Youth of these poems, although both chronology and identification resist conclusive determination. We do not again hear of Southampton in a Shakespearean context, although he outlived the poet by eight years.

Nondramatic writing occupied Shakespeare during the outbreak of plague that closed down the theaters during most of the period between June 1592 and May 1594. When the playhouses reopened, Shakespeare lost no time in returning to his primary endeavors of art. During the 1594 Christmas season the Lord Chamberlain's Men played twice before Queen Elizabeth at her royal palace at Greenwich, and on 15 March 1595 William Shakespeare, with the actors William Kempe and Richard Burbage—all three "servants to the Lord Chamberlain"—were listed as joint payees for an honorarium of £20. This notice, the first to connect Shakespeare with an acting company, shows him, at thirty, a leading member of the most prestigious troupe in England.

A document recovered in 1931 shows one William Wayte in 1596 petitioning for sureties of the peace, in the court of Queen's Bench, against William Shakespeare, Francis Langley, Dorothy Soer, wife of John Soer, and Anne Lee, *ob metum mortis* [for fear of death], the conventional legal phrase used in such writs. Normal procedure called for the magistrate to command the sheriff to produce the accused person or persons, who then had to post bond to keep the peace, on penalty of forfeiting the security. Another document describes Wayte as "a certain loose person of no reckoning or value.'' Dorothy Soer and Anne Lee are otherwise un-

known, but Langley had sponsored the building of the Swan Theatre in the manor of Paris Garden on Bankside. How Shakespeare was drawn into this minor imbroglio remains unclear.

In 1597 the company's lease on the Theatre in Shoreditch expired, and efforts at renewal failed. The playhouse was razed and the timber ferried across the Thames to Bankside, where by 1599 the Globe had opened its doors. For their new setup the players instituted a species of proprietorship in which Shakespeare, along with the other principal shareholders, was entitled to 10 percent of the profits. The value of shares fluctuated, depending on earnings and the number of holders, so estimations of Shakespeare's income vary; but a reasonable guess would be (on average) £200 per year at a time when a decently paid schoolmaster might earn £10. With the accession of James I in 1603, the Lord Chamberlain's Men became, by royal patent, the King's Men; in the warrant Shakespeare's name appears second on the list. During the next thirteen years the King's Men gave more performances before the sovereign at Whitehall Palace or Greenwich than all other theatrical companies combined.

In 1604 Shakespeare was one of nine players allowed scarlet red cloth for participation, as grooms of the chamber, in the coronation procession. That August members of the king's company attended the new Spanish ambassador and his train at Somerset House, the queen's palace. The Declared Accounts of the King's Chamber records the disbursement, for the occasion, of £21 12s. to Augustine Phillips and John Heminges and "ten of their fellows''; as the senior member of the troupe, Shakespeare was almost certainly one of those rewarded. Although the leading playwright for the age's leading troupe, he did not disdain such ephemeral employments as devising the *impresa*—an insignia, allegorical or mythological, with appropriate mottoes, the whole painted on a paper shield—to be borne by Francis Manners, the sixth earl of Rutland, on the King's Accession Day (24 March) in 1613. For his services Shakespeare received 44s.

Shakespeare required lodgings near the theaters at which he worked. Tax assessments show him dwelling first in St. Helen's, Bishopsgate, and later in Bankside, close to the theaters. In 1604 he lodged for a time at the Silver Street house of Christopher Mountjoy, a French Huguenot manufacturer of women's ornamental headdresses, and he played a role, as well-wisher, in the marriage settlement worked out for the Mountjoys' daughter

Mary. In 1612 Shakespeare was called upon to testify when Mary's husband, Stephen Belott, a former apprentice in Silver Street, sued his father-in-law over the dowry and a promised legacy. The case shows Shakespeare in a very human situation, and his deposition contains one of his six surviving, authenticated signatures.

Preserved at the Heralds' College in London are two rough drafts of a document, dated 1596, granting the application of John Shakespeare for a coat of arms. Many years earlier, the elder Shakespeare had made a preliminary approach, but nothing came of the move, for he had fallen upon hard times. He had stopped attending council meetings and in 1578 was excused from paying his weekly tax for poor relief. In 1592 his name appears in a list of those who stayed away from divine services "for fear of process for debt." Most likely the successful 1596 application was made by William in his father's name; Shakespeare nurtured his roots in the town of his birth. Thus was the family's social standing enhanced five years before John Shakespeare's death in 1601 (Mary Shakespeare lived on until 1608).

In 1597 the dramatist bought New Place, the great house of three stories and five gables at the corner of Chapel Street and Chapel Lane, opposite the Guild Chapel, in Stratford. Not long afterward, on 25 October 1598, Richard Quiney, a local businessman, wrote to his "loving good friend and countryman" to request a loan of £30 on good security. It is the only extant letter addressed to Shakespeare. Shakespeare's other investments include payment in 1602 of £320 in cash to William Combe for 107 acres of arable land in Old Stratford, a nearby farming area, and, in 1605, of £440 for a half-interest in a lease of tithes of corn, hay, and the like in the hamlets of Old Stratford, Welcombe, and Bishopton, along with most of the small tithes of the whole of Stratford parish. His last investment (1613) was the purchase in London of the Blackfriars gatehouse, situated close to the company's enclosed winter playhouse.

In 1607 Shakespeare's elder daughter Susanna had married John Hall, a respected Stratford physician of Puritan leanings. They had one child, Elizabeth. Judith had married late for those days, at thirty-one, in February 1616, and her husband, Thomas Quiney, promptly disgraced himself in an affair with a local woman, Margaret Wheeler, who died in childbirth that March. For this delinquency Quiney was summoned before the ecclesiastical court, where he was punished with a small fine. How his father-in-law reacted to the scandal is not known, although his last will and testament is in this respect suggestive.

By this time Shakespeare was dying. Around 1660 John Ward, the Stratford vicar and physician, noted in his diary that "Shakespeare, Drayton, and Ben Jonson had a merry meeting, and it seems drank too hard, for Shakespeare died of a fever there contracted." The story is not wholly implausible: Shakespeare might well have gathered with his old theatrical comrades for a drinking party, and Judith's wedding would have furnished a suitable pretext for such conviviality. Ward, moreover, was in touch with a living tradition; as his diary indicates, he knew Judith Quiney, who dwelled nearby in Stratford.

In late March 1616, Shakespeare revised the page of his will making provision for Judith and her husband. The bulk of his estate was bequeathed to his firstborn daughter, Susanna, and her husband. His sister Joan, married to the hatter William Hart, was permitted to stay on with her family in the western wing of the family house in Henley Street. She was the sole surviving sibling. His youngest brother, Edmund (born in 1580), had most taken after the playwright, following William to London and becoming a professional actor; but he had died at the age of twenty-seven and was buried in the cemetery of St. Giles Church without Cripplegate within the city limits. In his will Shakespeare mentioned his wife once to make sure she received their second-best bed. To Burbage, John Heminges, and Henry Condell, friends from his days with the King's Men, he left sums for memorial rings.

On 23 April 1616 Shakespeare died, the Stratford register records his burial two days later. Presumably one or more adult family members engaged Gheerart Janssen, whose stonemason's shop stood not far from the Globe on Bankside, to fashion the white marble monument, with half-length effigy, in Holy Trinity Church. It must have been in place by 1623, for it is mentioned in Digges's commendatory poem, which precedes *Mr. William Shakespeares Comedies, Histories, & Tragedies,* the folio collection that Heminges and Condell brought together to honor their worthy friend and fellow.

Those records that we have for Shakespeare both answer questions and pose them. It is, for example, miraculous that Richard Quiney's letter to Shakespeare should have survived. Measuring, when folded, only three by two inches, it was turned up in 1793 in a bundle of Quiney papers by Edmond Malone while he was going through 3,000 documents in the Stratford archives. We are grateful for the recovery, but why was the letter found among the Quiney correspondence? The natural inference is that it was never delivered to Shakespeare. Various explanations have been offered, but, in the last resort, we do not know why. As in other instances in Shakespearean biography, we must fall back on speculation.

The circumstances surrounding the poet's marriage furnish an ideal illustration of the problems faced by the biographer. In the sixteenth century a marriage license was not normally required to certify a legally binding union. All that was needed was the proclamation of the banns in church on three successive Sundays or holy days. But Shakespeare's marriage involved special considerations. He was only eighteen and therefore subject to the laws affecting minors; and his bride, some eight years older, was pregnant. Shakespeare specialists have referred to Shakespeare's marriage license; in fact no such document now exists, although in this special case a license would have been required. Instead we have a marriage-license bond, dated 28 November 1582, in which two farmers from the bride's neighborhood swore to indemnify the bishop of Worcester or his ecclesiastical officers in the event that any legal action arose from the granting of the license. These sureties were friends of the bride's family. Although her name is given as "Anne Hathwey of Stratford," she came from the village of Shottery, which was in Stratford parish. This bond grants a special dispensation allowing the couple to marry with only one, instead of the usual three, readings of the banns. The day before this bond was furnished, the clerk of the ecclesiastical court recorded in the bishops' register the granting of a marriage license to William Shakespeare and Anne Whateley—not Hathaway—of Temple Grafton. We know from other sources that Shakespeare married Anne Hathaway. These curious discrepancies have given rise to a good deal of confusion and misunderstanding.

Biographers have noted that only the bride's interests were represented by the two bondsmen. What of the young groom, a mere youth of eighteen? Was this, as many have concluded, a shotgun marriage, with the unwilling boy, helpless before irate parents and their brawny yeoman supporters, brought to account for a passionate indiscretion one summer night in the fields near Stratford? And what of the mysterious Anne Whateley, who appears only in this record and nowhere else? Was she Shakespeare's true, chaste sweetheart, the maiden he yearned to marry and was indeed about to marry when the Hathaways forced his hand?

William Shakespeare could not have married Anne Hathaway without his father's consent; so the law, protective of minors, provided. And it was customary for the guarantors of such marriage bonds to be friends of the bride's, not the groom's, family; unmarried heiresses rather than their prospective husbands stood most in need of legal safeguards against unscrupulous fortune hunters. As for Anne Whateley, about whom so much ink has been spilled, she probably never existed but was created merely by an erring clerk's substitution of the wrong name. He had been seeing Whateleys earlier that day, and they were much on his mind; by a process of unconscious association he had unwittingly exchanged one name for another. The bride's pregnancy did indeed present a problem: her condition called for matrimony as early as possible. Unfortunately the church prohibited the reading of the banns during certain seasons, and the couple had missed the last opportunity for proceeding with their marriage in the customary way. Hence the necessity for a special dispensation.

To sum up: there is no evidence that Shakespeare at this stage of his life had any sweetheart besides Anne Hathaway. Later, in his sonnets, he would express in impassioned lyric verse his tortured love for a Dark Lady, but we have no reason to believe that she had yet made her appearance when Shakespeare was courting Anne. Nor is there any evidence that Shakespeare married Anne unwillingly.

But was the marriage happy? The proverb holds, "Marry in haste, repent at leisure." Did he repent his "o'erhasty marriage"? Biographers, conscious of the eight-year discrepancy between husband and wife, have combed Shakespeare's works for some clue to his feelings.

In *Twelfth Night,* the Duke speaks thus to the disguised Viola:

> *Duke.* Let still the woman take
> An elder than herself: so wears she to him,
> So sways she level in her husband's heart;
> For, boy, however we do praise ourselves,
> Our fancies are more giddy and unfirm,
> More longing, wavering, sooner lost and won,
> Than woman's are.
> *Viola.* I think it well, my lord.

Duke. Then let thy love be younger than thyself.
Or thy affection cannot hold the bent;
For women are as roses, whose fair flow'r,
Being once displayed, doth fall that very hour.

(II. iv. 28–38)

The difficulty, of course, is that such passages occur in plays, not in autobiographical memoirs, and the writer speaks not in his own voice but with the lips of creatures of his dramatic imagination; the theater is, after all, a public forum. Shakespeare's sonnets, on the other hand, are more intimate, and perhaps we may feel on safer ground there in discerning reflections on his personal situation. ("With this key," Wordsworth said of the sonnets, "Shakespeare unlocked his heart.") As they deal, in part, with an intense and unhappy liaison with a married woman, they suggest that for Shakespeare the marital bed was not always a contented one. The identity of the other woman, the so-called Dark Lady, has stirred fierce academic passions. However, in the sonnets, too, experience is shaped by the poet's transfiguring imagination, and it is at our peril that we read these wonderfully wrought poems as straightforward autobiographical testimony.

The bed mentioned in Shakespeare's will provides a clue. The document contains only one reference to the woman whom Shakespeare had married thirty-three years before. "Item: I give unto my wife my second best bed with the furniture"—that is, with the hangings, bed linen, and the like, that make up this elaborate item of Renaissance domestic furnishing. That is it; not a word more. What are we to make of this bequest? Some biographers see it as derisive, a husband's scornful dismissal of his wife. As far back as 1780, Edmond Malone commented on this provision of Shakespeare's will: "His wife had not wholly escaped his memory; he had forgot her,—he had recollected her,—but he had already (as is vulgarly expressed) cut her off, not indeed with a shilling, but with an old bed." That is one way to look at it, and this view still has supporters. But another interpretation is possible. May not the best bed have been kept in a special room, reserved out of gracious hospitality for overnight visitors to the splendid house in Stratford? If so, it would have been regarded as an heirloom and would naturally have formed part of the estate that he wished to keep together for his legal heir. The second-best bed, according to this interpretation, would then have been the matrimonial bed, with a

special, intimate significance. Other wills of this period refer to such beds with tender associations. We do not know what Shakespeare was thinking when he made this bequest; but he did not have to provide otherwise in order for his wife to be looked after properly. By English common law, reinforced by local custom, a widow was entitled to a life interest of one-third of her husband's estate.

We really cannot say with any confidence whether Shakespeare's marital life was contented, miserable, or any of the innumerable shades between those polarities. We can say that he married only once and that his wife bore him three children early in the marriage. His professional obligations as the leading playwright for his acting company required his presence in London, the hub of the nation's theatrical life, through most of the year. We do not know who, if anyone, shared his bed in his London lodgings, but it was probably not his wife, for she had the house and children to look after in Stratford. As a rule, long separations do not encourage marital harmony. Yet Shakespeare, according to a reliable tradition expressed by John Aubrey in 1681, returned regularly to Stratford each year. So the domestic ties were maintained—though in what fashion we cannot, with any assurance, say.

In the aggregate the facts concerning Shakespeare's life would require a very large postcard indeed. But what of the man who emerges from them? The mass of material is prosaic indeed; many of these documents could chronicle the life of any Elizabethan man of property who pursued a successful career in the metropolis and celebrated his triumph by spending his last years in comfortable backwater retirement. How are we to reconcile the banality of the records with the impassioned genius that finds expression in the sonnets and in the great tragedies that harrow us with pity and dread? Where in these records will we find echoes of the laughter that sparkles in *As You Like It* or *Much Ado About Nothing* and bursts the sides of propriety with Falstaff? Nowhere.

Yet his last will and testament, while anything but poetic, tells us a good deal about Shakespeare's position in the world—not as an artist, but as a Jacobean gentleman whose art had brought him material rewards and social prominence in his native town (which apparently mattered to him). The will also tells us about the family members and friends, mostly townsmen, whom he valued most, and teases us with its bequest of a second-best bed.

What is omitted can sometimes be as intriguing as what is included: Shakespeare makes no reference to the earl of Southampton, to whom he dedicated his two early poems, or to any other aristocrat. But we would not have expected him to do so. It would have been presumptuous—and anyway they already had enough. Nor does the will mention the Hathaways, although they farmed in the neighborhood.

The testament is a bourgeois document that records a success story. Shakespeare amassed a considerable estate that he took pains to hold together for his heirs. In the later documents he never fails to use the honorific title of "Gentleman," and his monument is emblazoned with the family arms. Little in his will accords with latter-day, romantic ideas of the poet. Whatever pain he might have experienced, the will and other documents fail to convey.

We can only guess what he felt when his only son, Hamnet, was buried. Shakespeare could not have foreseen that with the death of his granddaughter Elizabeth in 1670 his entire direct line would be extinct; nor, if he still bedded his wife, could he have known that she would fail to give him another son, although, as she was already past forty, he may have reckoned that to be unlikely. Presumably Shakespeare was present for the burial of Hamnet, but even that we can only infer. Such facts as we have simply do not help us in fathoming the inner wellsprings of genius.

Yet what we know about Shakespeare the man has a special value by virtue of its very ordinariness, for conveying by its very starkness and in such manifold ways that ordinariness. Shakespeare must have been in many ways like other people. His personality, when he rubbed shoulders in the taverns with the wits and witlings of his day, made no such forcible impression as did Jonson's. True, Thomas Fuller's report (1662) has come down describing the combats of wit between Shakespeare and Jonson, the latter likened to a Spanish great galleon, "built far higher in learning; solid, but slow in his performances." According to this account, Shakespeare is the English man-of-war who, "lesser in bulk, but lighter in sailing, could turn with all tides, tack about and take advantage of all winds, by the quickness of his wit and invention." The comparison is nicely made, and maybe there is something to it. However, it belongs not to the biographical record but to the accretion of legend, to what has been called the mythos that springs up around remarkable figures after they and their circle are gone.

Yet, surely the ordinariness, which the mythos fails to dwell on, belongs to the fabric of the achievement. For Shakespeare's plays express, more profoundly than any of Jonson's or the others, the bread and cheese of life: fundamental human relationships between sovereign and subject, parent and child, husband and wife, and lovers. It may be that he found literary inspiration in Ovid or Holinshed or Plutarch, or that royal blood courses through many of his characters' veins, or that he chooses for his setting Ephesus or Illyria or Rome; but the men and women Shakespeare portrays experience such passions as he himself must have known or seen.

And if the biographical record fails to express what was extraordinary in the life, in one respect it does so. The documents reveal strikingly Shakespeare's professional commitment to the stage— first to the Lord Chamberlain's Men when they played at the Theatre in Shoreditch, then to the same company when it became known as the King's Men and performed at the Globe on Bankside and the Blackfriars near St. Paul's. Shakespeare served his company as actor, playwright, and shareholder for almost two decades. As part-owner, he would have had a voice in company policy, and he probably helped to stage his own plays and those of others. He also acted in other dramatists' plays; Ben Jonson lists him in the cast of *Every Man in His Humour* (1598) and *Sejanus* (1603), and in the First Folio he has pride of place in the list of the "Principall Actors in all of these Playes." As his company's regular playwright, or "ordinary poet," he would normally have furnished two plays a year. Shakespeare was, as Gerald E. Bentley has observed, "the most complete man of the theatre of his time." Every now and then we encounter a playwright who also acts; Harold Pinter, in our own time, comes to mind. But to be involved as a principal voice of the management side in addition to these other commitments is now extremely rare. One thinks of Molière—but then one thinks again for a long time. That professional dedication reminds us, as we continually have to be reminded, of the special nature of Shakespeare's literary achievement. It also helps to explain why he apparently took no interest in giving his unpublished plays the permanence of print.

For over two decades the men who eventually edited the 1623 Folio had been Shakespeare's colleagues in the same acting company. Together with Shakespeare, John Heminges and Henry Condell joined the Lord Chamberlain's Men when the troupe was formed in 1594. They were in the company in 1597 when it lost the lease of the Theatre and when, shortly thereafter, the Globe was built. They were with the troupe when its playhouse burned to the ground in 1613 during one of the first performances of *Henry VIII.* Heminges was in the playhouse that fatal day:

> Then with swol'n eyes, like drunken Flemings,
> Distressed stood old stuttering Heminges.

Thus ran a ballad commemorating the occasion. Through these vicissitudes Heminges, Condell, and Shakespeare had no call to resist the temptation to move on to greener pastures. There were no greener pastures.

An actor's claim to remembrance, especially if he is not of the first rank, is transient. Heminges and Condell live in fame because they served letters by bringing together Shakespeare's plays in the First Folio. "For such a task," Bentley remarked in 1941, "no two men in the company, and possibly no two men in London, were so well qualified by their long personal and professional acquaintance with the author and by their knowledge of his services to the company." But then Shakespeare was always fortunate in his career, and we are fortunate in his good fortune.

It was fitting that such a grand volume as the First Folio be dedicated to a noble lord or lords. It is interesting that Heminges and Condell passed over the third earl of Southampton, choosing as their dedicatees the earls of Pembroke and Montgomery. They had good—indeed compelling—reasons. A very large and therefore very expensive book, the First Folio required a patron of generous means and disposition. William Herbert, the third earl of Pembroke, fitted the bill. Moreover, as Lord Chamberlain, and thus in charge of all entertainments presented before the monarch, he was in a position to do the King's Men some service. Pembroke's younger brother Philip, the first earl of Montgomery, was constantly in a state of financial embarrassment and had powerful enemies; but word had got round that he was in line for higher office and that he was prepared to relinquish his Chamberlain's staff to his brother. By dedicating the First Folio to these noble brothers who had "beene pleas'd to thinke these trifles some-thing heeretofore; and

have prosequuted both them, and their Authour living, with so much favour," Heminges and Condell offered appreciation for past benevolences and looked prudentially to the future.

The trifles thus assembled numbered thirty-six. Heminges and Condell failed to include *Venus and Adonis* and *The Rape of Lucrece,* the only works that Shakespeare himself had seen fit to offer to the public, and works which in the period went through numerous editions—a measure of their popularity. Nor did Shakespeare's first editors reprint Shakespeare's cycle of 154 "sugared sonnets" (as his contemporary Francis Meres characterized them), although "this poor rime"—so the poet himself had proclaimed—would still live "when tyrants' crests and tombs of brass are spent" (Sonnet 107). The poet whom the First Folio celebrates is the poet of the London stage. Fully half of the volume's plays appear between covers for the first time. Had Heminges and Condell let pass the opportunity to publish them, it is not inconceivable that *Twelfth Night, Antony and Cleopatra,* and *The Winter's Tale*—not to mention *Julius Caesar* and *Macbeth*—would have vanished like the Globe itself on whose boards they had been performed, leaving not a rack behind. "We have but collected them," Heminges and Condell allow in their dedicatory epistle, "and done an office to the dead, to procure his Orphanes, Guardians; without ambition either of selfe-profit, or fame: onely to keepe the memory of so worthy a Friend, & Fellow alive, as was our Shakespeare."

The storm from which Heminges and Condell sheltered the orphans broke on 30 January 1649 when Charles I knelt on the executioner's improvised scaffold. A new dispensation, the Commonwealth under the protector Oliver Cromwell, now held sway. By then the playhouses, once the glory of England, had been closed for seven years, casualties, like Charles I himself, of the Puritan revolution. They would not reopen until the restoration of the Crown in 1660.

Through this tumultuous era and after, the volume of Shakespeare's plays made its magisterial progress, being thrice reprinted, in 1685 for the last time. By then the Folio had acquired numerous minute textual variations—some of them corrections, others new errors—and had been augmented by seven additional plays. All of these, save one, scholarship has deemed apocryphal. That one is *Pericles, Prince of Tyre,* which completes the roster of the thirty-seven plays of the traditional canon.

The plays have been continually reedited as textual understanding has progressed, and greater numbers of spectators with each succeeding age have seen them performed. The Royal Shakespeare Company plays in Stratford and London and on tour abroad. Hundreds of university productions and Shakespeare festivals dot the landscape. Filmed and televised versions bring to an audience of many millions the comedies, histories, and tragedies that Shakespeare's acting colleagues collected in a handsome folio volume to keep their friend's memory alive.

BIBLIOGRAPHY

John Quincy Adams, *A Life of William Shakespeare* (1923). George P. V. Akrigg, *Shakespeare and the Earl of Southampton* (1968). Peter Alexander, *Shakespeare* (1964). Gerald E. Bentley, *Shakespeare: A Biographical Handbook* (1961). Edmund K. Chambers, *William Shakespeare: A Study of Facts and Problems,* 2 vols. (1930) and *A Short Life of Shakespeare with the Sources,* abridged by Charles Williams (1933). John Henry de Groot, *The Shakespeares and "The Old Faith"* (1946). Mark Eccles, *Shakespeare in Warwickshire* (1961). Charles Isaac Elton, *William Shakespeare, His Family and Friends* (1904). Edgar I. Fripp, *Shakespeare, Man and Artist,* 2 vols. (1938).

Joseph William Gray, *Shakespeare's Marriage* (1905). James O. Halliwell-Phillipps, *Outlines of the Life of Shakespeare,* 7th ed., 2 vols. (1887). E. A. J. Honigmann, *Shakespeare: The "Lost Years"* (1985). Benjamin Roland Lewis, *The Shakespeare Documents,* 2 vols. (1941). Max Meredith Reese, *Shakespeare: His World and His Work,* (rev. ed., 1980). A. L. Rowse, *William Shakespeare: A Biography* (1963). S. Schoenbaum, *Shakespeare's Lives* (1970); *William Shakespeare: A Compact Documentary Life* (1977); and *William Shakespeare: Records and Images* (1981). Charlotte Stopes, *Shakespeare's Warwickshire Contemporaries,* new ed. (1907) and *Shakespeare's Environment* (1914). Frank W. Wadsworth, *The Poacher from Stratford* (1958).

Thinking About Shakespeare's Thought

J. LEEDS BARROLL

None of us has met William Shakespeare, but often we think we know him so well that personal acquaintance seems superfluous. We think we know, for instance, that Shakespeare believed that lilies festering smell far worse than weeds. And we feel that Polonius speaks for the author of *Hamlet* with his sage advice: "To thine own self be true." And we are inclined to believe that for Shakespeare, as well as for Hamlet, "to be, or not to be" was indeed the question.

These sentiments seem universal and true because they happen to be our own favorites—the thoughts from Shakespeare that we ourselves have found most appealing, most personally moving. And because Hamlet or Othello or Romeo or other great Shakespearean creations are the sources for these sentiments, we have no doubt that their thoughts (or at least those we approve of) are Shakespeare's own.

We assume we know, then, what Shakespeare thought, and we know we like what he thought. Thus we journey through Shakespeare's work on the way to a personal encounter with him. Sensing his sincerities, we weave a skein of ideas and desirings from his poetry into the whole cloth that becomes the thought and sensibility of the man Shakespeare, a human being who lived and died four centuries ago.

However, certain difficulties attend upon this psychological swimming party. For even though we immerse ourselves in Shakespeare's oeuvre, we do not necessarily become part of that element. In the end, as Archimedes—and Joseph Conrad—might have predicted, we only displace. Walking up on the beach from our bath in Shakespeare, we claim to be the spirit of the sea itself, but we merely stand sparkled with drops.

If we are not content with this floating, if we wish not to displace but to become steeped in Shakespeare's great sea, we must, paradoxically, step back from it. If we want to think about Shakespeare's "thoughts," we must first consider how they may be captured. On the one hand, there are Shakespeare's personal emotions—his individual psychology, if we like—and, on the other hand, there are his acts of artistic creation. The personal emotions died with the man; the art is our only entrée. More accessible than the irretrievable dust that is all that remains of the living, speaking, and confiding human who was Shakespeare, his art is the medium through which we must strive to reach his spirit. Reading his work is easier for us than trying to talk with the dead.

Not easy: merely easier. For the remains of Shakespeare are artifacts that need to be handled with care, with due regard for their nature and shape. They are not diaries or personal mementoes. They are artistic creations intended as drama for a sixteenth-century English stage. And they are available to us only in their scripts: all that remains, in the end, is the written word.

I

Michael Riffaterre speaks more truly than he may realize when he observes that literary history has validity "only if it is a history of words." Even at this most accessible level, the printed page—where we first encounter Shakespeare's remains—we find that what we call his thought is inevitably delineated in the language of his time-defined culture. Shakespeare wrote in what students of the period term Early Modern English. When Hamlet says that "conscience does make cowards of us all," linguistic history tells us that *conscience* meant consciousness, awareness, or even rationality primarily, and conscience in our modern sense only secondarily, if at all. Yet, as we think of Shakespeare thinking and find we do not especially like "awareness does make cowards of us all," will we continue to accept the sentiment as one of Shakespeare's thoughts? Or will we allow the dramatist only those personal opinions that to us seem appropriate?

Elementary linguistic errors stemming from historical naïveté are easy enough to avoid. And perhaps those meanings that we discover through our understanding of Early Modern English will even enhance our favorite statements from the plays and poems. The clearest and most compelling of these utterances may, in fact, remain unaltered, easily outnumbering those instances in which linguistic relativities have sharply altered sense. "To thine own self be true" is a thought that can still stand as it did in Shakespeare's time, "true" being no more nor less ambiguous in 1601 or 1602 than now. So one can know that Shakespeare had this particular thought and be fairly clear about what the sentiment is.

Yet as we again immerse ourselves in the element, the temperature of the water suddenly seems to change for the worse. "To thine own self be true. . . ." Why must *Polonius* be the presenter of this favorite Shakespearean thought? Must we really attend when this obsequious, daughter-castrating, romance-infatuated voyeur dumps into his profligate discourses Universal Truths of which he is not even the purveyor but procuror? It is even a temptation to refuse being "true" to oneself simply because Polonius counsels the opposite! And are we also supposed to believe that persons such as Hamlet go mad from unrequited love, as Polonius thinks they do, and that the best way to find out about one's sons is to spread rotten little lies about them to see whether or not fellow barflies agree?

Perhaps, then, we should not listen to Polonius as the voice of Shakespeare. Perhaps we should insist, in drama, upon distinguishing between what a character expresses in a work and what the work as a whole seems to convey. But even so, a recent writer on the subject of "thought" in drama, Leon Rosenstein, suggests that we should operate in traditional fashion when we wish to infer the sentiments of a dramatist from what his characters say. In most dramas, goes the suggestion, we can find a statement that "by its very nature, the universality of its language" reaches out not only "beyond the given character, the given context, the given tragedy" to other characters, contexts, and tragedies but also "to life and extra-artistic reality in general." Such statements have the ring of truth, we are assured, and, it would seem, by these tones we shall know them. Such statements tell us what the author truly thinks.

But the trouble with Shakespeare is that everybody in his plays seems to ring. Polonius, Iago, Edmund, Othello, Gloucester—all in their own ways speak astoundingly. How can we sift one magnificence from all the others until only the authentically magnificent Shakespeare remains, clinking like a nugget?

Profound sounds are dangerous attractions as we search for Shakespeare's opinions. We cannot expect that a Shakespearean villain whose statements we are inclined to disbelieve, discount, or reject is necessarily going to mouth these statements so that they have a ring of squalor rather than a ring of grandeur. If dramatic convention in Shakespeare's day shaped the speeches of both hero and villain into iambic pentameter—rather than into the accents of everyday speech—such convention seems to have been little concerned with making evil talk aesthetically repellent. The thoughts of evil or dastardly characters would hardly be composed in "villainous" cadences, in broken English, in faulty grammar, or in other naturalistic imitations of moral unworthiness. In life, villainous talk has that appalling gray mediocrity of ignorant sadism or of uncontrolled lustings poured forth in boring fragments—the newspapers are full of such talk, as were the criminal reports of Shakespeare's time. But art can hardly be asked to emulate the drabness of horror, and certainly Renaissance art did not. Iago is eloquent, and so is Goneril.

If we assume, instead, that Shakespeare's

thoughts will be uttered only by characters who present what we regard as "good" sentiments, we encounter another difficulty: what we might term the "Polonius syndrome"—noble words by an ignoble speaker. A villain, a wretch, or a bore will seem to convey to us Shakespeare's innermost thoughts as readily as does a hero. The only way to avoid the dilemma is to abandon Rosenstein's view of profound truths rising to the top like cream and to think instead in terms of dramatic context. For, as Charles Altieri has reminded us in the case of Troilus, magnificent rhetoric even in a Shakespearean hero may still describe only the hero's, not the poet's, viewpoint. And certainly it is on this scale that we must weigh the homiletic power of artful observations such as Iago's. Here he is talking to Roderigo:

> . . . we have reason to cool
> our raging motions, our carnal stings, our
> unbitted lusts; whereof I take this that you call
> love to be a sect or scion.
> *Roderigo.* It cannot be.
> *Iago.* It is merely a lust of the blood and a permission
> of the will.

(Othello, I. iii. 329–334)

Roderigo has been ready to drown himself from love of Desdemona, and most spectators would describe the situation in something like these words: Iago is attempting to persuade his dupe Roderigo not to kill himself over his passion for Desdemona. So Iago is saying whatever he can to talk Roderigo out of the shallow despair that, if left to run its course, could go dangerously deep and ruin all of the ensign's plans. At the same time, however, there is always the possibility that Iago may be more than half sincere in the thoughts he utters to dissuade Roderigo.

But if all this is so, may we take Iago's statement about love—a statement written, after all, by Shakespeare—as reflecting the playwright's sentiments on the subject? Did Shakespeare think that love was nothing but lechery? Few viewers or readers of the play would wish to embrace this conclusion.

Therefore it is not necessarily to Iago that we should go if we search in *Othello* for thoughts that will bring us nearer to Shakespeare's personal sentiments. We must consult other characters in the play: and this is where the problem comes in. For if we continue to claim that Shakespeare's thoughts

about love are expressed in *Othello* but that Iago does not voice them, then which character (or characters) does speak for the poet? If, in our quest for Shakespeare's mind, we are not to be allowed to collect notions from the first fine-sounding thoughts available—Iago's—how can we determine which characters' speeches to listen to, say, about love? Is there a rule?

If so, it should be, like all good rules, impartial. What I mean is this. Suppose you admire Iago, yet because of the angry clamor of other viewers you are not allowed to advance his sentiments as the true feelings of Shakespeare. Then—and here is the impartiality of the rule—you can forbid other readers and viewers from using the method that they have forbidden to you. They cannot seek out the true Shakespeare in the speeches, say, of Cassio just because they like what Cassio says. For why is Cassio any better than Iago? After all, his behavior causes almost as many problems as does that of Iago. Must you abandon your liking for Iago at the mere bidding of those who have their own subjective liking for Cassio, Roderigo, Desdemona? Or Othello? If the rule for finding Shakespeare's personal sentiments is to judge by your subjective reactions, then what is fair for Cassio-lovers is also fair for Iago-lovers.

Nor will it do to suggest that some viewers have better "subjectivities" than others, that only those who admire, say, Othello have reliable instinctive reactions about who speaks for Shakespeare. It is all rather grand for Othello to say, over the sleeping Desdemona, "This sorrow's heavenly; It strikes where it doth love." But to ask us to see this sentiment as reflecting Shakespeare's personal understanding of the nature of heavenly sorrow or of love—that it punishes its objects out of sexual jealousy—is to ask us to accept nothing much different in moral quality from Iago's love-as-scion-of-lust approach.

But let us grant, for the sake of argument, that Othello's exclamation is superior to Iago's statement about love. Why then is that alleged qualitative superiority the grounds for attributing those particular sentiments, but not Iago's, to Shakespeare the man? Is it not at least theoretically possible that Shakespeare the man resembled Edmund, Iago, and Richard III rather than such characters as Romeo, Coriolanus, and Timon of Athens?

An immediate response to this question might be that Shakespeare was bound to hold the more attractive, not the less attractive, sentiments that we come upon in his plays. But even waiving the definition of "attractive," if we subscribe to such a theory, why should we even bother to winnow out Shakespeare's personality from his writings? For adherents of this "theory of the attractive" will already have found their Shakespeare in some golden land where angels informed them which moral sentiments were the most attractive, and informed them, furthermore, that Shakespeare the man held only those and no other kinds of feelings.

Most readers do not go to such extremes. More common—and somewhat more rational—are those who work with some witting or unwitting theory of "Expression," as Alan Tormey has described the term. Because an author expresses himself only through his work, one seeks the author via some aesthetic assumption about that work. One such tacit assumption is that it is tragedy that most often reveals the genuine Shakespeare. Through the dignity of his suffering, the tragic hero becomes a Shakespearean spokesman, and his magnificent speeches and attitudes become the inevitable indices of Shakespeare's own thoughts.

> Who would fardels bear,
> To grunt and sweat under a weary life,
> But that the dread of something after death,
> The undiscovered country, from whose bourn
> No traveller returns, puzzles the will,
> And makes us rather bear those ills we have
> Than fly to others that we know not of?
> Thus conscience does make cowards of us all.
>
> (III. i. 76–83)

So says Hamlet in what is certainly an eloquent statement. But here is another speech by the same tragic hero.

> O, that this too too sullied flesh would melt,
> Thaw, and resolve itself into a dew,
> Or that the Everlasting had not fixed
> His canon 'gainst self-slaughter. O God, God,
> How weary, stale, flat, and unprofitable
> Seem to me all the uses of this world!
> Fie on't, ah, fie, 'tis an unweeded garden
> That grows to seed. Things rank and gross in nature
> Possess it merely.
>
> (I. ii. 129–137)

Was Shakespeare as skeptical as would appear from the first set of lines quoted above? Or was the dramatist suicidal, as the first two lines in the latter speech seem to suggest? Is Hamlet, in other words, the poet's spokesman? If we say so, then we must puzzle over the fact that the very critics for whom these contradictory statements are expressions of Shakespeare's own sentiments will warn us elsewhere against reading Shakespeare out of dramatic context. Put the case where, standing over the praying Claudius, Hamlet says to himself:

> A villain kills my father, and for that
> I, his sole son, do this same villain send
> To heaven.
> Oh, this is hire and salary, not revenge.
> 'A took my father grossly, full of bread,
> With all his crimes broad blown, as flush as May;
> And how his audit stands, who knows save heaven?
> But in our circumstance and course of thought,
> 'Tis heavy with him; and am I then revenged,
> To take him in the purging of his soul,
> When he is fit and seasoned for his passage?
> No.
>
> (III. iii. 76–87)

A proper revenge lies in trying to send the soul of one's enemy to hell. So thinks Shakespeare? No, the answer will be. And the reason we are not allowed to take this speech as the expression of Shakespeare's own convictions is the dramatic situation. Far from reflecting Shakespeare's own ideas about revenge, Hamlet's lines here are merely the expressions of a certain character in a certain situation.

Such a dualism implies not one but two classes of speaking, two levels of discourse, in Shakespeare's dramas. On the one hand, in the foregoing speech, Shakespeare wrote lines intended to disclose Hamlet's thoughts about revenge—thoughts that may differ significantly from Shakespeare's own. On the other hand, we should presumably understand that, in other instances, lines written by Shakespeare—even in the same play—are indeed indicative of Shakespeare's personal feelings. It is as if, in a tragedy, one kind of speech by the hero presents us with the thoughts of the hero only, while another kind of speech reveals the thoughts not only of the hero but of his creator as well.

In the end, such an approach reveals a concept not merely about Shakespeare but about drama in general. It is a curious and difficult notion, too. We observe a figure on the stage. He is the hero of a Shakespearean tragedy: he is Hamlet or Othello or Macbeth. And it seems that he and he alone among all the people in the drama has been endowed with a double task. Sometimes when he speaks he will in our imaginations be Othello talking with Iago, or

King Lear dealing with his daughters, or Macbeth plotting against Duncan. But at other times, he will not only say the things we might expect of or accept from a Macbeth: he will also express the private opinions of William Shakespeare.

What is curious about this aesthetic theory is that, in the end, it drops away, leaving the interpreter without that guidance which theory is usually understood to furnish: the predicting of consequences. If you have a theory that the earth is round, and if you live in the fifteenth century, you are, among other things, predicting that if I sail far enough in the same direction I will eventually return to the point from which I started. That is a "consequence" of your theory that the earth is round. Another consequence is that if I am sailing away from another ship, going in the opposite direction, that ship eventually will seem to drop below the "horizon" as the earth's curvature begins to hide the vessel from me. That is, you can explain this "dropping" too in terms of your round-earth theory.

Now, if I have a theory that the tragic hero in a drama written by William Shakespeare sometimes utters the hero's sentiments but sometimes utters Shakespeare's, should I not be able to predict when it is Shakespeare's voice that comes through? Or more specifically, should not a theory about what one might call the two voices of drama be able to say definitely to whom we should ascribe such a speech as this:

> To-morrow, and to-morrow, and to-morrow
> Creeps in this petty pace from day to day
> To the last syllable of recorded time,
> And all our yesterdays have lighted fools
> The way to dusty death. Out, out, brief candle!
> Life's but a walking shadow, a poor player
> That struts and frets his hour upon the stage
> And then is heard no more. It is a tale
> Told by an idiot, full of sound and fury,
> Signifying nothing.
>
> (V. v. 19–28)

Do we take these sentiments as an expression of Shakespeare's despondency when he was writing *Macbeth,* of his opinion about life at that time? If so, then these lines are not the opinions of Macbeth, who has much to be disturbed about at this point in his tragedy. And if these words are indeed not Macbeth's opinions, how are we to understand *him* to be feeling when he is speaking/not speaking here? Macbeth has just learned that his wife has died, and many critics have understood these lines to be his response to the news. But if we see Macbeth as the bearer of Shakespeare's personal sentiments, are we to take this moment as the anachronistic equivalent of a television commercial? Macbeth does a quick fade-out while William Shakespeare, in a voice-over, winks on to tell us how he personally feels about life.

Perhaps this moment in *Macbeth* is shared—the lines doing a kind of double duty. Do they project two sets of emotions, Macbeth's despair and Shakespeare's too? If this is the case, then the situation raises even more theoretical difficulties. At the beginning of the play Macbeth has some exultant lines. Toward the middle of the play he has many fearful and worried lines. And then after that he begins to speak despairingly, and so forth. Is it possible that Shakespeare the man mirrored Macbeth's developing frame of mind over the course of writing the play, sharing his character's emotional journey? Surely not. Surely Shakespeare was not, say, afraid of Banquo; surely he did not wish to kill himself at the end of one of his plays, as do such characters as Romeo and Juliet, Brutus, Othello, and Antony and Cleopatra. Surely Shakespeare did not gradually become mad as he wrote *King Lear.*

Once this particular interpretational bag has been opened, why should we confine Shakespeare to speaking through the mouths of only certain characters? Because Shakespeare wrote the speeches of all the characters in all his plays, his innermost self could be revealed not only through the heroes and heroines of the tragedies but also through the main characters of the comedies, histories, and romances. And why should Shakespeare not speak through the mouths of his walk-ons as well as his heroes? In the end, the theory that Shakespeare the man can be discovered through the speeches of his tragic heroes is not useful because it is, paradoxically, too specific. Of course Macbeth in some way "expresses" Shakespeare the man. The trick is to find out just what aspects of that human being, the poet, Macbeth expresses—or can express.

II

There are other ways to think when we set out to differentiate Shakespeare the man from the problematical evidence of his written work. Even if the plays cannot offer us direct access to him, his writing does make available certain kinds of knowledge about him. For example, in *Hamlet,* although much of the main business of the play is wrapped up in the hero's response to his father's murder, other subjects are also presented: the spectacle of a young woman driven mad; the conversations of gravediggers about old bones; the fearful encounter of realistic soldiers and their superiors with a horrifyingly supernatural apparition. These subjects seem to draw attention to themselves beyond their bearing on the hero's responses; they seem to exist above and beyond the limited outlooks of individual characters.

When we read or see or speak of a Shakespearean tragedy, we accordingly find ourselves thinking in such a way as to imagine not only "characters" but something besides characters—something that exists in addition to them. These motifs, as they may be called, seem to have lives of their own because they do not appear to be confined to the observations of any one figure in the play. For example, we can identify ideas about suicide in *Hamlet* that go beyond the hero's own thoughts on the subject. For the tragedy shows a good deal of activity in which Hamlet is not concerned but in which suicide is still offered as a topic. Ophelia, in her madness, wanders into the water and is helpless to keep herself from drowning, we are told. But her death is called a suicide by the Church which buries her. What is more, we observe Laertes arguing fiercely with the priest over the point. The gravediggers have been playing with the suicide problem before Ophelia's funeral procession comes on stage. (They think, we remember, that Ophelia's high rank as Polonius' daughter circumvented Church law so that she is granted at least a simple ceremony, rather than the suicide's barren interment.) Earlier, Horatio worries that the ghost will draw Hamlet to the cliff where the very height puts "toys of desperation" in the brain. At the end of the play, Horatio attempts suicide in the "Roman" fashion and is stopped not by reflection but by Hamlet—"Absent thee from felicity awhile." Suicide is dwelled on throughout *Hamlet,* then, not merely as a personal possibility for Hamlet, but as a general idea.

In *Measure for Measure,* to suggest examples from another play, we do not know whether even the Duke shares the perspective that the play offers regarding the difference between external indications of piety and true inner holiness. The stage lives of Angelo and Isabella have presented the distinction for our inspection; similarities between the two figures have long been perceived by viewers and readers of the play. The motif of godliness thus acquires a conceptual existence that goes beyond the thinking of Isabella alone or of Angelo. The strength of this motif asserts itself in the suspense surrounding Isabella's resistance to Mariana's entreaty for help in begging the Duke to forgive Angelo. And Isabella's eventual response to Mariana's request, actually sinking to her knees to plead for Angelo's life, relates as much to "idea" as it does to "character." For by this point godliness has become focused on the concept of mercy and forgiveness, the core of Christian doctrine as it was understood in Shakespeare's time.

In the past, the word *theme* has been overused to describe situations that seem, in a Shakespearean play, to extend beyond the purview of any one character. In the minds of many critics, "themes" in the dramatist's works were the keys that could unlock the mind of Shakespeare the man. Thus "Shakespeare and Murder," "Shakespeare and the Law," and similar topics appeared as the titles of many an essay. Yet this approach to the search for Shakespeare the man, while evading the redundancy posed by simply identifying the dramatist with any one of his heroes or heroines, offers complications of its own.

This time the difficulty is not a result of our inability to read the mind of the author by identifying him with one character; it stems instead from the matter of definition. For example, in *Othello* the protagonist is associated with some ideas or even themes about witchcraft. There are Brabantio's reiterated accusations, for example, that Othello has employed witchcraft to win his daughter's love. And there is Othello's magic handkerchief, which he describes in great detail to Desdemona. Thus we might say that witchcraft, for whatever reason, has become an "idea" or a "theme" in the tragedy. But may we therefore conclude that the presence of witchcraft as a concept in *Othello* argues Shakespeare's personal belief in witches? May we infer from the presence of "themes" of madness in *King Lear* and *Hamlet* that Shakespeare was personally preoccupied with mental instability?

Let us finally generalize the question. Can we abstract some sense of Shakespeare's private emotions by using any elements at all in his dramas as evidence? We might insist that the very stories are directly informative—that they tell us something about the nature of Shakespeare's preoccupations as a person. Shakespeare wrote one tragedy about a figure confronted with the idea of revenge, another about a warrior whose mother gravely affected his life, and another about a man and woman in history who tried to make their love affair more important than the Roman Empire. Did all these scenarios replicate Shakespeare's personal concerns? Was he haunted by the stories that energized his plots? Two young persons from feuding families but in love with each other; unappreciated loyal retainers; men continually outwitted by women?

Certainly modern psychodynamics might wish to explore the preoccupations of an author who twice wrote of sea-separated twins and, on several occasions, created men who wanted to kill their masters. Post-Freudian psychologists could also argue that the developmental configuration of a play like *Macbeth* mirrors the tension-and-release processes of Shakespeare's personal psychological dynamics. Or for the idea that the images of blackness and chaos associated with Macbeth's murder of a nourishing king mirror the anxieties triggered in Shakespeare the man as he wrote about something very much like father-killing. The psychologically oriented reader might even suspect Shakespeare's preoccupations in his association of Venus/Venice with daughters marrying against their fathers' wishes, as do the Venetian women Jessica and Desdemona, who both flee to husbands who seem to their fathers to be alien threats to all they hold dear. Similarly, *Timon of Athens* and *King Lear* can be interpreted as revealing certain intimate characteristics of their author. Because Lear and Timon both spend much of their time inveighing against those who they suppose have put them in positions of helplessness, and because these protagonists never take practical steps to remedy their situations, they might seem psychologically suggestive in their paralyses. Their paralyses have been caused by their own evasive bids for a love and attention supposedly earned not by interpersonal relating but by bribery. Thus we might ask why Shakespeare constructed sequences in which bribery as a mode of evading love results in disaster and consequent passivity. Such a question might produce an interesting (although inconclusive) essay in psychobiography, especially for those philosophers who, like D. W. Hamlyn, are interested in "unconscious intention."

Yet since Shakespeare was a professional dramatist, we can never know which scenarios already

used by a lesser playwright for one version of the script it was merely his job to improve upon. Furthermore, how is the critic to respond when such scenarios, whether inherited or original, begin to seem psychologically contradictory? In *Cymbeline,* Imogen's "dead" brothers in turn seem to "bury" her, while in *Twelfth Night* a "dead" brother delivers a sister from a buried identity. A woman, Coriolanus' mother, helps to destroy him; but Macbeth seems to help destroy his wife. We have thus returned to a familiar-sounding question. But now, instead of asking which characters speak for Shakespeare, we are asking which *elements,* contradictory as they are, may be taken from the plays to guide us back to Shakespeare the man.

For the biographer the problem about "ideas" or "themes" in Shakespeare's dramas is that the ideas Shakespeare uses to develop a particular dramatic situation cannot necessarily furnish material for analyzing Shakespeare's unconscious associations. Shakespeare might have had theories about appropriateness, for example, that were formulated more for aesthetic purposes than for the fulfillment of a psychological need. Having chosen a Moor for a tragedy, Shakespeare's decision in *Othello* to present images of blackness and of Africa, and concepts of inner beauty versus outer appearance, probably had little to do with personal and compulsive associations. For, when writing another tragedy with a nonwhite African protagonist, Shakespeare ignored blackness, Africa, and the idea of internal versus external. In *Antony and Cleopatra,* skin color is not an issue at all, let alone a trait associated with ideas of the devil. Moreover, we encounter in that same play a motif—that of the vanity of human wishes—that has no parallel in *Othello.* Again, if the loss of personal power in *King Lear* evokes dramatic suggestions about nakedness and madness, there is little or no reference to those ideas in *Antony and Cleopatra,* a play in which the loss of personal power is also a crucial element.

Meeting the ghost of one's father who calls for revenge will naturally evoke questions about the legitimacy of ghosts as advisers. But the appearance of a ghost need not precipitate discussions about madness or suicide. Dividing a kingdom among one's daughters and being wrong about their responses may easily give rise to concepts of fathering, ingratitude, or even bastardy, but such an act does not necessarily lead to meditations on fidelity, folly/fools, or demonic possession (the role Edgar pretends). And it is these particular connections—

these themes, if we like—that seem to differ from play to play in Shakespeare's work.

The working principle is this: if there are linkings of ideas in Shakespeare's plays—whether obvious or obscure—we must allow their use for artistic purposes before we, as Shakespeare's biographers, immediately see them as unconscious associations of personal psychological significance. Part of what we find in *Othello,* which features an easily jealous husband, is a "theme" having to do with the social complexity of wifehood. In Act I, Desdemona has definite thoughts about wifehood; so does Iago, as he makes clear while they all await Othello's arrival in Cyprus. Emelia has much to say on the subject, dwelling on the problem presented by her wife's status before she exposes Iago at the end of the play. And even Bianca is termed a certain kind of housewife. Why such emphasis on the concept of wifehood? An examination of the play as an aesthetic, not a psychological, document will answer the question more readily than will a hypothesis that at this time in his life Shakespeare was having trouble with his own wife, Anne Hathaway.

Part of what *Macbeth* offers is the motif of "murdered sleep." Lady Macbeth sleepwalks restlessly; Macbeth has insomnia; before the murder, Banquo walks around the castle when everyone else seems asleep. Those who sleep well—the Porter and the grooms—do so because they are drunk. But in *Hamlet,* even though the hero's father was murdered in *his* sleep, sleeplessness—let alone "murdered sleep"—is not a motif at all. Both Claudius and Hamlet kill people, but neither strikes us as an insomniac, nor do we hear of the violation of sleep as an idea. It is as if the philosophizings that we are often tempted to attribute to Shakespeare are no other than the special, separate, and appropriate means of ornamentation he chooses for particular dramatic offerings.

We may sense, we may feel, that no matter what has been said here, Shakespeare the man was indeed saying for himself that murder relates to sleeplessness, that abdication relates to madness, or that murder and revenge and despair, as in *Hamlet,* relate to madness and suicide. These themes really might be tantamount to utterances by Shakespeare the person. Perhaps. But we ought to remind ourselves, if we search for Shakespeare's obsessions in his themes, that neither the man Shakespeare nor we ourselves need always say the same thing in the same way, time after time, even about the same subject.

I cannot know, from the many things you will say about murder in your various conversations with me, what is the one thing that you personally hate the most about, or most profoundly associate with, the idea of murder. For if the two of us should happen, over several years, to talk casually about murder and about how evil it is, we may variously speak of it in the terms appropriate to the contexts of our many different conversations. Talking about peace of mind, you may raise the subject of crime (for example, murder) and its effects upon the conscience. But if we are discussing a revenge bombing we have read about in the newspaper, we may wonder about the morality of "paying back" when it also hurts or kills innocent bystanders. And although we may have discussed murder in these various contexts from time to time, neither your remarks nor mine may have had a great deal to do with our own personal, subjective reactions to the idea of murder in general. It would be unfair to you if I were to claim that your biggest problem with murder was worry about a guilty conscience. For all I know, you may once have killed a child with your car, or been in a war, so that the term "murder" always evoked for you a special kind of nightmare that I can never deduce from your talking with me.

By the same token, the various "topics" or "themes" associated with one idea in various of Shakespeare's plays—murder as broken sleep in one tragedy, as social code in another—may not reveal Shakespeare's personal thinking on that one idea. The variations the poet rings on such concepts are, rather, part of the moral rhetoric of a particular drama. They are ornamental, in that paradoxically organic mode of the baroque period of which Shakespeare's age was the precursor. Themes in the tragedies may not be the personal convictions of Shakespeare the man so much as they are the embellishments of Shakespeare the artist.

III

Can Shakespeare's plays ever reveal to us his personal thoughts? The answer to this question is, I think, "yes" provided that we limit ourselves to matters suggested by the plays themselves. But we must first think about what we mean by a writer's thoughts. In one class are the elements that a writer takes to be facts—those things that seem to him to possess verifiable existence: the firmness of the earth, the change of the seasons, the events recorded in history. And in this connection we must be flexible about how we envision Shakespeare in his approach to fact. He was obviously less well informed than we are about physical science. Atoms were not a fact for him; angels may have been. It is beside the present point whether what Shakespeare actually believed to be a fact was indeed so.

If one class of a person's thoughts are those things he believes to be facts, the unyielding realities that one cannot avoid, then shining at the other end of the spectrum is the most tenuous of the fancies that wishing might illuminate. At one end is Shakespeare's understanding of fact; at the other end is what he desires as fact. His personal leanings can make him believe that certain ideas are indeed facts: the inevitability of retribution, the triumph of goodness, and so forth. On this end of the spectrum reside an author's feelings about what is desirable or hateful, good or bad.

When we consider the problem of Shakespeare's thought, we are interested primarily in this second end of the spectrum. Unconcerned about whether the poet knew that Mercury is the planet closest to the sun, we inquire about what he likes or dislikes, what he approves or disapproves, what he admires and detests. When we search for Shakespeare's thought, we are searching for his personal ethical system.

Can we discover Shakespeare's value system in his plays? We cannot. Despite the position of many advocates of deconstructivist views about literature and drama, dramatic material is by its very nature intractable to such purposes. What we can perhaps find out is how we, as an audience, are meant to feel —what ethical evaluations we are supposed to make—while watching one of Shakespeare's dramas.

It is as though we have two authors for one play. There is the human being, with his personal hopes, fears, and thoughts. And there is, if we use John Hospers' term for the phenomenon, an "implied" author who adheres not to the values he holds dear in real life but to the values expressed by the form of his work. This understanding, while it may not give us useful and reliable information about Shakespeare's own thoughts, can offer us equally important data. For knowing how we are expected to feel about the events and characters in each of his tragedies or comedies reveals to us the moral postures Shakespeare has adopted from play to play.

Why do I say posture? Why not use a term such

as *implication,* as Hospers does, when thinking about how literature conveys meaning and information to us? By posture I do not mean fraudulent activity. I am thinking, rather, of posture as it might apply to ballet, where it is part of the art. A certain kind of posture is part of the art of the drama, too, for comedy and tragedy actually require a standard of ethics against which the activity on stage is to be measured. One could call this standard the drama's ethical posture.

When a dramatist fills the stage with characters enacting a story, and when this stage situation requires us to understand the words of the characters as descriptive not of the author's personal desires and values but instead of the desires and values of the figure who is speaking, then the audience needs guidance. We must have some way of knowing how we are to respond to what these stage people are saying and doing. When Hamlet tells us he would like to kill himself, we cannot immediately approve of his desire, even if we sympathize with his frame of mind. For the playwright may want us to be dismayed at this talk of self-slaughter. In the same play Laertes plots to kill Hamlet in revenge for the slaying of his father. How are we to take this? Are we to cheer for him to kill Hamlet? Why not, if we are cheering for Hamlet to kill Claudius? What are we supposed to feel about murder, anyhow? When we have finally determined how the author of the play means us to respond morally or ethically—when we feel that we know what values we ought to hold as we judge whom to support— then we have, as I would phrase it, determined the drama's ethical posture.

"Christianity," "atheism," "unkindness," "love," "dictatorship," "cruelty," and "murder" are words that refer to ethical systems. As Aristotle and others remind us, patterns of behavior, whether attractive to us or not, stem from assumptions about what is or is not desirable in life. A play that seems to be favorable to, say, fascism has an ethical posture or an ethical system in that its assumptions are based on principles considered valuable by fascists. Fascism may be repellent to most audiences, but it is still a system of ethics in the sense that it is held by its adherents to be a guide about how to behave.

It is in this sense that comedy and tragedy can be described as having ethical postures. Comedies and tragedies are inevitably structured upon one set of values or another. And from the viewpoint of ethics it is even possible to differentiate tragedy from comedy. To avoid reviewing here the innumerable definitions of tragedy and comedy that have evolved since the time of Aristotle, let us simply agree upon one stipulation, that in tragedy spectators are to respond differently from the way they respond in comedy at one particular point. In tragedy they do not take pleasure in, but are dismayed at, what finally happens to the hero, no matter how much aesthetic satisfaction they may take in the unfolding of the drama. In comedy, on the other hand, spectators not only take delight in the architectonics of the comedy, they also take pleasure in the outcome of events. In other words, the ethical posture of a tragedy induces us to feel that certain things should not have happened, whereas that of a comedy induces us to agree that certain things should have happened just as they did. We can say that the emotions elicited by the events we witness in comedy and tragedy—pleasure and dismay—have their origins in a standard of morality, a value system. In tragedy we are expected to be dismayed by the hero's fall because the hero has some "value." In comedy we are expected to be pleased by the hero's success because, again, he has value.

Why speak of the value system as something that resides in the play? Because we are quite capable of suspending for the moment our personal values when we read a novel or watch a play or go to the cinema. We watch a Kurosawa film, and we learn that in a particular situation, a Samurai warrior can achieve a kind of victory only if he commits suicide. We may not believe in suicide as an ideal under any circumstances; indeed, we may be so hostile to suicide as to dislike the Kurosawa film. But if so, we dislike it because we know that it is the film that supports suicide. We are sensing the ethical structure, the ethical posture, of the film; and from what we can observe, this posture seems to support, seems to expect us to believe in, the moral validity of suicide.

Tragedy, from the viewpoint of ethical posture, is more complex than comedy. In comedy, being rewarded for good behavior is a straightforward ethical proposition; because he wins out in the end, we understand, in comedy, that the hero is the hero. He is the hero because he wins, and he will win because he is the hero. But because a tragedy presents a hero who is good and then does not reward him for being good, the audience demands some kind of explanation. For it is in the nature of ethics as a philosophical activity to generate two premises: actions in accordance with the ethical system produce "happiness," however it is defined, and actions not in accordance with the ethical system produce "unhappiness," however defined. So a playwright who creates a tragedy must offer some acceptable resolution to the ethical paradox of an attractive hero who suffers unhappiness. Accordingly, Shakespeare had to adopt ethical postures which may or may not have coincided with his own personal convictions, for he had to make understandable to the audience why the (ethically attractive) hero had to suffer. Undertaking to write a Renaissance "tragedy" required this. Anyone could write a "hard luck" story in which, for example, a pious virgin at prayer was run down by a team of horses or hit by a falling brick. But to write a tragedy, one had to offer a satisfactory account of what might at first appear to be nothing more than very bad luck.

Because ethical postures were required by the forms of comedy and tragedy in which Shakespeare worked, understanding the postures that he created will bring us as near as we can come to discovering something like Shakespeare's thought. We will not emerge with a description of Shakespeare's psyche, but we may come away with a delineation of the ethical structures he considered appropriate to the stories he selected. There is some value for us, I think, in knowing this, even if we know nothing else about the private person who was the early seventeenth-century man named William Shakespeare.

But again a difficulty arises. Even though we are refraining from a search in his plays for Shakespeare's private moral convictions, we may continue to be tempted by what may be called the Johnsonian maneuver. With regard to the values he perceived as operating in Shakespeare's works, the great eighteenth-century critic Samuel Johnson constantly reverted to a moral touchstone. This was the old idea of the *consensus gentium,* a body of decent feelings that people like Doctor Johnson believed to be shared by all mankind throughout the ages. It was as if the human race had a collective and accurate sense of what was good and what was evil. And for Samuel Johnson, living in 1743, such an English consensus may indeed have approached more closely than do our twentieth-century opinions the values embraced by Shakespeare and his contemporaries a century and a half earlier. But in the end neither we nor Johnson, when viewing Shakespeare's plays, can afford the luxury of invoking one universal morality. The nature of drama forbids us to assume that one character, or even several, who voice what we take to be universal principles, are necessarily the normative voices of a play. If we wish to discover the moral posture of a particular play, we are forced to other measures. Rather than use our own morality as a criterion, we must try to infer the morality operating in the play itself.

Since no one character is inherently believable as the moral center of a drama, the playwright must adopt something beyond didactic speech to construct the ethical posture. Shakespeare seems to have done so, and the general principle underlying the devices he arrived at is hinted at in the controversy over a single and rather simple device, that of the bed trick in the problem comedies. What bothers modern critics about these bed tricks is not the tricks themselves so much as the fact that their instigators seem to be rewarded. In *All's Well That Ends Well,* Helena gains her husband through a bed trick. In *Measure for Measure,* through a similar subterfuge, Isabella gets even with Angelo, receives a proposal of marriage from the Duke, and regains her brother. Accordingly, many critics sense that whether we like it or not, we are in fact expected to applaud these substitutions of sexual partners, because the tricksters are rewarded for their efforts. And because this rewarding occurs in a comedy, not a tragedy, it is of great significance in our effort to understand how the ethical posture of a Shakespearean drama is presented. It reveals to us an element in a play separate from characterization, from theme, from imagery, or from plot sequence.

For something like the rewarding of a character in a play operates independently. The characters in a drama may try to persuade us that they are morally justified in playing bed tricks. We may or may not believe them. But for the author to allow these bed tricks to redound to the undisputed benefit of the tricksters is for the dramatist, godlike, to create a reality in which bed tricking is the way to happiness. And happiness, after all, is the subject and object of ethics.

The effect upon an audience of this "Godhood" of the dramatist, since the dramatist is not truly a god, can sometimes be different from what he intends. A member of the audience says to herself something like this: "I know I am supposed to think that Helena tricked Bertram fairly with the bed business, and I know that I am supposed to be happy about it. But I am not happy. I am repelled. Besides, Bertram was not worth gaining in the first

place." This critic is saying not that some intrinsically good or evil thing is happening in the play, but that something in the play's ethical structure is pushing her to an acceptance that she is not willing to grant. It is as if the play has a will of its own, forcing us away from our personal moral standards to accept another set of values merely so that we can make sense of the play. This will is the ethical structure of the play.

IV

No playwright of any age can assume that his audience has uniform morals, that all the people watching his play have the same values. If, on a given date, all the spectators are citizens of the same city —say, early seventeenth-century London—even then they will not respond identically to the situations they observe on the stage. Viewing *Hamlet,* some of those Londoners might have favored a good, thorough revenge; others might have abhorred any bloodshed or despised princes who seem to trifle with young women they would never be allowed to marry; still others might have thought it quite reasonable for a widow to remarry, especially when the stability of a kingdom could be involved.

If we accept the premise of authorial artistic intention—the assumption that Shakespeare meant to write a tragedy—then it is reasonable to suppose that he also wanted a particular tragedy to be responded to in a certain way. To take an obvious case, the poet must have assumed, for *King Lear,* that we would pity the old King's suffering, dislike Edmund, and come to detest Goneril and Regan.

But if we concur on these large points, we do not as easily come to agreement about the details. We argue about whether the tragedy is pessimistic or optimistic, whether Lear is more sinned against than sinning, whether Cordelia should have been so frank, considering what this frankness brought upon them all, whether the tragedy is that Lear remains uncomprehending about life's requirements until the end or that his world mercilessly hounds him and his daughter to their graves. When it comes to determining what set of ethical preferences we should temporarily assume in order to make sense of the play, we are rather like that unpredictable seventeenth-century audience of *Hamlet.*

One way out of this interpretive predicament is

to make an assumption about Shakespeare's ethical plans for the tragedy. We can assume that he wanted to spread ethical confusion in his audience, to spin a kaleidoscope of meanings that crystallizes at different times to dozens of different understandings of what *King Lear* is about. But showing that a particular work of art is confused and showing that this confusion is deliberate can be quite difficult as logical procedures. It is easier to begin by assuming order: in the case of a tragedy such as *King Lear,* by assuming that Shakespeare's plans for the drama included a coherent context for the basic situation of an old king who experiences appalling misery. This is as much as to say that the playwright intended his audience to respond to *King Lear* along particular ethical lines.

Certainly Shakespeare did not want spectators to laugh at King Lear or at Cordelia. How then did he want them to respond? To phrase the matter differently, what values, what ethical framework, does an audience have to adopt in order to understand what Shakespeare presents in *King Lear?* To pose this question is to ask not about the characterization and not about the imagistic or dramatic technique of the play, but about still another of its aesthetic characteristics, namely its ethical structure.

In Shakespearean tragedy, such a structure is an intricate phenomenon: viewers of *Hamlet* can attest to that. It would be unacceptably simplistic to say that *Hamlet,* insofar as it deals with values, flatly tells us that it is wrong—or right—to take revenge. *Hamlet* and Shakespeare's other tragedies are difficult because they force us to confront a complex seventeenth-century artistic mind accustomed to approaching ethical matters in a way that was familiar to his contemporary poets or dramatists, but that is no longer familiar to us.

In Shakespeare's time, as readers of Edmund Spenser's *Faerie Queene* will affirm, poets were used to the idea that ethical questions do not always admit of simple answers. *Macbeth,* seen by some as a comparatively straightforward drama, illustrates the point as far as Shakespeare is concerned. We do not come away from this tragedy with the smug conclusion that crime does not pay or that all murderers are monsters. For enveloped as we may become in this simple and particular sense of righteousness, we are still a bit uncomfortable in the final scene. After Macduff carries Macbeth's severed head on stage, Malcolm concludes the play speaking of "this dead butcher and his fiend-like queen." All of this may be applicable as name-

calling, but in fact we have not experienced Macbeth and Lady Macbeth merely as butcher and fiend. Indeed, much of the tension the tragedy evokes in us has resulted from the fact that the two characters deteriorate because they lack just that cold-blooded devilishness of which others accuse them. We have only to compare them with Goneril and Regan. Macbeth and Lady Macbeth, though they become butcher and fiend, have lived through a great deal of torment. And we should remember that Malcolm's father, King Duncan, was much taken, in the second scene of the play, with Macbeth's butcherlike qualities, which a bloody captain described in admiring detail to approving listeners.

If we were to be asked about the ethical posture of *Macbeth,* in other words, we might feel an extended answer to be necessary. For what comes across is not a simple moral but an ethical exploration. A person more nearly contemporaneous with Shakespeare, Martin Luther, simply assumed that those who wrote drama in his time began with a well-defined moral plan (Bacon). In *Macbeth* it seems clear that we are not simply being told that crime does not pay. Rather, the play's message is more like the following: "*Macbeth,* insofar as it is concerned with ethics, argues that a man accustomed to professional killing is naïve if his devotion to some burning sense of ambition leads him to pretend that civil murder will leave him as emotionally untouched as does killing enemy warriors. And such ambition is particularly perilous if its naïve goal is some shallowly conceived notion of kingship that ignores monarchy as a profound social contract." *Macbeth's* ethical posture cannot be summed up in a moral one-liner. It requires an essay.

The effect of a Shakespearean play is like that of an essay. But the means to that effect are not at all those employed in an essay. A moral or philosophical essay about a king giving his kingdom to his daughters, if it is to make statements that enforce our intellectual agreement, must adopt a method of argumentation compared to which the claims of a *King Lear* to be similarly "philosophical" and analytical would seem absurd. (But then the claim of any philosophical treatise to be as moving as *King Lear* would be equally absurd.) Shakespeare's great tragedy is not a disquisition on kings, problems of succession, family relationships, social programs for the poor, sick, and insane, nor a treatise on how these problems should be handled in 1606. Nor does it purport to be. *King Lear* has been structured so that our emotions will make us accept the tragedy's rendered and implicitly stated values without question. Thus when we ask how we are supposed to feel about a play, we are, in effect, undertaking to discover not how the author has persuaded us by logic, but how he has conditioned our feelings and attitudes.

How is this conditioning achieved? Certainly a discussion of the ethical structure of a specific drama would be useful here, but space can hardly permit. In another place I have written at length on the "ethical structure" of *Antony and Cleopatra* and several chapters in my *Shakespearean Tragedy* must serve as my detailed example. Here I would prefer to advert to several underlying techniques and to the principles that Shakespeare employed continually to establish the ethical postures of his plays. Small and sometimes trivial-seeming items in themselves, yet just as $2+2=4$, though seemingly trivial, forms the basis for a system of mathematics, so Shakespeare deploys these small dramatic patterns throughout a drama to build a structure of moral discussion that will condition our response.

The very story the poet selected would have provided an early tracing of the ethical vector. Those listening to the story, simply by the act of giving it their attention, would have promised (as Sidney and later Coleridge noted) to believe for the moment in the actuality of the events narrated or enacted. On the most elementary level they would have promised to believe that Macbeth quelled rebels, that he was therefore rewarded by his king, that he was then tempted by witches to murder his king and take the crown, and that he never knew a moment of peace afterward, dying unloved at the hands of an army half filled with rebellious subjects.

Here lay the aesthetic trap, for when the spectators accepted all the details of the Macbeth story, they were not merely believing that events took place: they were accepting a version of cause and effect. They were accepting a version of life in which the murderer of a king fails to reap the expected harvest. They were seeing that the result of murder turns out instead to be the agonies of fear and sleeplessness, the suicide of a wife, and ultimately despair. The story's "bare facts" point the moral. As Sir Philip Sidney noted, fiction is morally more persuasive than history. If poets were faithful to factual history, they would report the horrible things that have happened to good men and the good things that have happened to evil men. His-

tory, unaltered and unedited, can indeed be seen as a discouragement from "well-doing." But poetry invents "histories" that are, in effect, moral—histories that are ethical equations. Macbeth murders, but he suffers for it. Poetry can mold history into the moral example that history alone could never be.

Story itself is thus the most elementary means of creating an ethical stance, and Shakespeare's particular method is suggested by his treatment of the historical story of King Lear. As received by Shakespeare's contemporaries who knew ancient British history and as it exists in the well-constructed play known as *King Leir,* acted on the London stage before Shakespeare's tragedy was written, King Lear's traditional story differed from Shakespeare's version. The events in Shakespeare's and in the older play are generally similar until Cordelia returns from France to rescue her father. In the old chronicles and in *King Leir,* Cordelia is successful. She defeats the armies of her sisters and places her old father back on the throne. *King Leir* ends here. In the old chronicles, the story goes on to Lear's eventual and peaceful death while still king, with Cordelia succeeding to the throne of England before ultimately being deposed by her nephew.

Shakespeare changed the traditional version of King Lear as drastically as if he had molded the old history of Macbeth in Holinshed to show Macbeth and his wife living happily ever after. More importantly, by changing the old Lear plot, Shakespeare established a story, a cause-and-effect sequence different from what was traditional. We can derive from both *Leir* and the ancient English chronicles a rough-hewn moral lesson such as this: "If you are going to give your kingdom away, you had better be careful to whom you give it, and you had better be sure you know who loves you, because if you are careful, you can be happy." But the shape of events in Shakespeare's tragedy implies that surrendering a kingdom is a much more catastrophic error than it appears to be in *King Leir*—indeed, it is irretrievable—and that a daughter's love can bring intense pain as well as happiness. Yet, before Shakespeare, the legend of the chronicles and the old play was the accepted history; Shakespeare's *King Lear* was a fiction shaped to configure an equation that the historical facts did not exemplify. According to Shakespeare, when Lear gives away his kingdom, his favorite daughter is killed and he dies in misery. This recital of "facts" is as much a moral equation as "Macbeth kills his king and as a consequence seldom sleeps at night."

By such dim lights we hardly pierce through to the intricacies in the moral postures of *Macbeth* or *King Lear.* But we are alerted to the principle on which ethical posturing relies, a principle akin to the idea underlying *consideratio* in late medieval poetry (Allen). As with the medieval concept of *consideratio,* by which the embracing ethical principle is knowingly built into a work, so the ethical premise or premises, in Shakespeare's approach to drama, are built into a dramatic structure without the use of specifically didactic speeches. These principles are initially embodied in the shape of the story. We have, in effect, been enticed to participate in a real-life happening in which certain principles triumph over others.

The equation established by the bare plot of a tragedy is far short of a complex ethical statement. It is rather like the theme in a symphonic movement. Once a simple key is established, a development section follows. In a symphony the development consists of a process of building new relationships among the notes and among portions of the thematic line. In a Shakespearean drama we observe a similar deployment of sequences, many of which are based on the same manner of equation as that underlying the original story. These sequences are pictures, large or small, of success or failure—depictions of efforts by various characters in the play to gratify their wishes.

Like the main plot in the tragedy of which they are a part, these sequences are no more a rendering of real life than is the blank verse through which the conversations are conveyed in a Shakespearean play. In life, if great or small persons fail to achieve desperately desired goals, the reasons may range from personal enemies, to luck, to the world economic situation, to accidental death. In Shakespeare's dramatic fictions, failures to attain goals are not allowed to partake of such randomness. In Shakespeare, when a figure is depicted as frustrated in the attainment of wishes, the frustration is morally crucial. It indicates that we must reject the values held or voiced by the person frustrated. Failure is no longer a question of content but of form. Frustration in life can be attributed to all sorts of external agencies. When depicted in Shakespearean drama, frustrations are always to be attributed primarily to the person failing. The grounds for failure become in themselves small or large statements of value. All these

statements, great or small, accrue in turn into a substructure that helps delineate the outlines of the ethical argument.

The cumulative power of such small sequences is illustrated by the scenes depicting Portia's unsuccessful suitors in *The Merchant of Venice.* Each has a specific goal: to win Portia. She will be won when a suitor chooses the correct casket. But except for Bassanio, all the suitors fail in their choices and therefore in their goals. What makes the sequence meaningful is that we can see a connection between the characters of the suitors and their frustrations. Morocco is proud and thinks he is a gift for Portia. Arragon is literal-minded and materialistic—rather like Shylock. Having these traits leads to failure in the world of *The Merchant of Venice,* just as having wisdom about risk-taking, losing, and love, as does Bassanio, leads to success. We are the wiser for attending to these small sequences because we now know something more about what values to reject and what values to accept if we are to make sense of the play. A proper ethical analysis of *The Merchant of Venice* would have to go much further than these small incidents, but of such small stuff will much of the analysis have to be made.

In these respects, tragedy is much more intricate than comedy. For example, in *Antony and Cleopatra,* Enobarbus, Antony's confidante and a blunt soldier, sees Antony's fortunes decline and thus contemplates desertion. Finally he does desert to better his condition. In doing so, he illustrates a variation on the Shakespearean sequence of wanting something and not getting it: wanting something, getting it, and then regretting that one has attained it. Shakespeare offers us a later scene in which Enobarbus, now on Caesar's side of the front lines, observes that nothing good is happening to those who have deserted to Caesar. Then Enobarbus is informed that Antony has sent all of his former soldier's possessions after him in an act of great generosity. Enobarbus now knows his heart will break. Later the guards hear his dying words as he regrets having become a "master leaver," a deserter.

Clearly, we have here a statement that desertion and infidelity are not to be approved of in the ethical context of this tragedy. But this is where the tragedies are more complex than the comedies. On reflection, few who see *Antony and Cleopatra* will assume that its putative moral lesson is primarily concerned with desertion. The tragedy seems to convey something about the nature of love, the nature of empire, the nature of greed, and the nature of narcissism, and, in the context, military desertion is not the most compelling of problems. Perhaps then we need to consider the principle underlying Enobarbus' frustration: it is somewhat more complex than fidelity per se. Enobarbus dies of regret because he has made the mistake of thinking that prudence must take precedence over love. His common sense has told him to go; his heart has told him to stay. By following his common sense, he dies of a broken heart. According to this episode, then, we find that we ignore our feelings at our peril. Despite the trouble that Antony's relationship with Cleopatra has brought him, *Antony and Cleopatra,* through the experience of Enobarbus, puts forth the statement that love is more important than political success or material well-being.

Elsewhere in the play, Antony, though he loves Cleopatra, rages over his loss of the world. And Caesar's loveless character is shown as the cause of his immense success in garnering up the Roman Empire as his personal domain. Meanwhile, Octavia's loyalty to Antony seems to be repaid only by his desertion and humiliation of her. The tragedy makes no simple, all-embracing ethical announcement: the most it offers is an ethical process. That is to say, its ethical structure is an evolving argument, something we sense to be true of *Hamlet* and *King Lear* as well.

If this form for ethical argument in Shakespearean drama seems strange now, it would not have seemed so to readers or audiences familiar with the ways of Sidney's *Arcadia* or of Edmund Spenser's *Faerie Queene* or of Ben Jonson's *Volpone.* In all these works, the idea of plot involves a consistent and considered series of interwoven ethical statements. The special techniques of these other authors may differ from those of Shakespeare, but Ben Jonson's Tribulation Wholesome does not differ as greatly from Enobarbus as he might seem to. Both characters experience a failure, a frustration that is meant to instruct. People who desert, people who are religious Puritans, get into trouble. Whether the trouble is serious or comic depends on the demands of the play in question.

It is impossible to deal here with the ethical complexities of Shakespeare's individual tragedies, beyond pointing out a series of devices through which small indications of the thrust of the ethical argument can be inferred. For in addition to sequences depicting gratification or frustration, Shakespeare also adduces other modes. As a dramatist Shakespeare offered no ostensibly didactic statements; he created didactic actions. These, when joined to the shapes of the ethical propositions that were his plots and subplots, helped to shape his dramatic statements of values.

One such device, used early on, is activity that employs metaphors traditionally associated with particular moral arguments among Shakespeare's contemporaries. The sequence is from *Henry VI, Part 3:*

> *Alarum. Enter a Son that hath killed his father, at one door,*
>   [*bearing the body in his arms*].
> *Son.* Ill blows the wind that profits nobody.
> This man whom hand to hand I slew in fight
> May be possessèd with some store of crowns;
> And I that, haply, take them from him now
> May yet, ere night, yield both my life and them
> To some man else, as this dead man doth me.
> Who's this? O God! It is my father's face,
> Whom in this conflict I, unwares, have killed.
> O heavy times, begetting such events.
>   . . .
> *King Henry.* O piteous spectacle! O bloody times!
>   . . .
> *Enter, at another door, a Father that hath killed his son,*
>   *bearing of his son.*
> *Father.* Thou that so stoutly hast resisted me,
> Give me thy gold, if thou hast any gold;
> For I have bought it with an hundred blows.
> But let me see. Is this our foeman's face?
> Ah, no, no, no! It is mine only son!
> Ah, boy, if any life be left in thee,
> Throw up thine eye. See, see what show'rs arise,
> Blown with the windy tempest of my heart
> Upon thy wounds, that kills mine eye and heart.
> O, pity, God, this miserable age!

                           (II. v. 55–88)

These self-absorbed figures do not state that civil war and rebellion are morally equivalent to patricide and filicide. Instead they enact metaphors that were associated, among Shakespeare's contemporaries, with a condemnation of civil war—as a form of political, not familial, "unnaturalness."

Ten years later Shakespeare would employ this same metaphorical technique in the account in *Macbeth* of the behavior of King Duncan's horses. The horse under the rider was a conventional symbol of man's passionate nature under the control of his reason, and, in the play, these horses, these controlled servants of man, break out of their stalls "as they would make war with mankind"; they revert to their basic nature as wild beasts, even going so far as to "eat each other." They remind us of Macbeth, another servant who has slipped out of control and gone wild. They imply that Macbeth's rebellion is also to be viewed as unnatural, like that of cannibalistic horses. In other words, the play's account of a strange event conveys a conventional moral metaphor.

More complex are allusive sequences suggesting scenes from well-known moral arguments. In *Antony and Cleopatra* Shakespeare included an imitation of Alexander the Great's reputed encounter with a pirate, a story traditionally used to suggest that world politics was merely theft on a grand scale. In *King Lear*, Edgar stages the "miracle" of Gloucester's inability to kill himself. This event recalls Christ's Temptation in the Wilderness (later to be a subject of Milton's *Paradise Regained*). When Satan tempted Christ to hurl himself from the top of the temple, he urged him to prove he was the son of God by calling angels to save him as he hurtled to the ground. Christ answered that this seeking of miracles was a form of trying to tempt God. Gloucester's attempt at suicide is transformed by Edgar into an episode in which Gloucester jumps from a cliff and is saved by a miracle. There was even a devil, Edgar tells Gloucester, standing next to him on the cliff. Thus, tempted by a Devil to jump, Gloucester sees himself as also saved by God's miracle. As a consequence, he resolves (for a time) never to be in despair again. The ethical significance of the episode depends on the traditional idea that belief through miracle is an inferior kind of spirituality. This strand of thought, in turn, has its place in the ethical structure of a tragedy depicting characters as concerned with the absence of justice in the universe.

Another device Shakespeare used to suggest the ethical posture of his plays was the vatic figure—the soothsayer. Such figures foretell the future, but unlike the simple predicting of Caesar's seer who warns of the Ides of March, these visionaries convey ethical principles. Leontes is "a jealous tyrant," according to the oracle of Delphi in *The Winter's Tale*. "You shall be yet far fairer than you are," says the mysterious soothsayer to the laughing Charmian and Iras in Cleopatra's Egyptian court: he is speaking not about their faces but about the manner of their deaths in their fidelity to Cleopatra. We recall Enobarbus, and we continue to be reminded about the importance of fidelity in the ethical argument of this Roman tragedy.

Prophecy was not Shakespeare's favorite means of sketching ethical lines in his plays. He also featured other mysterious figures who spoke in ambiguous and allusive terms. These words are often taken by their onstage auditors as nonsense, madness, or irrelevance. Lear's Fool is famous in this respect. Less famous but equally significant is the Clown in *Othello* who points out the sexual symbolism of the wind instruments that the apologetic Cassio hired to be played before Othello's palace to placate his commander. When the Clown associates these instruments with venereal disease and other scatalogical topics, he implies some comment on the quality of Cassio's behavior, as Cassio follows Iago's advice to return to his commander's good graces by ingratiating himself with Othello's wife.

The mad Ophelia's remark, "Lord, we know what we are, but know not what we may be," is a statement of the same quality as that of Cleopatra's Clown. An ostensibly simple mind generates an utterance of great cultural resonance. Most familiar in this mode is the Porter who plays the doorkeeper to hell in *Macbeth*. The use of madness, foolery, or ambiguity as signals of ethical relevance was part of a long-standing cultural tradition inherited by Shakespeare and his contemporaries. This tradition had to do with the sometimes misleading nature of the sources from which ultimate truth emanates —hovels in Bethlehem, to take an archetypal example.

I should obscure the point if I seemed to imply that if we only listen to the Clown in *Othello*, or to the simple countryman bearing figs to Cleopatra, all will be known—the ethical statements in these tragedies served up to us in nutshells. Far from it. Shakespeare used many ethical modes—so many because in each play he was delineating a complex *argumentum*. In tragedy especially, when he set out to establish ethical posture, Shakespeare seems to have had an artistic predisposition to work out this posture through process. Thus no one utterance, such as Ophelia's remark about knowing ourselves, is necessarily definitive. Rather, Ophelia's mad words take their place alongside other such exterior statements; and their cumulative and intermodifying effects, by the end, have traced for us the detailed ethical argument of the play.

A number of such devices indicates that the ethical posture of *Hamlet* transcends any simple argument that one must avenge one's father. For if we wish to trace the moral of *Hamlet* we must take a number of statements into account. Much is said in this play, for instance, about the relevance of the circumstances of death to the welfare of the soul. We are asked to think about death by suicide, death while sleeping, death while at prayer, death when insane. Do the circumstances in which our lives end have a bearing on the afterlife? The states of death seem to be a subject of discussion, too: whether corpses walk again as ghosts; whether one dreams within the sleep of death; whether flights of angels immediately convey one to heaven.

Far from the subject of death in *Hamlet,* theories of honor come in for consideration. We are told of Hamlet's father and his duel with Fortinbras' father over honor; we hear of Fortinbras the son and his vengeful war against Denmark to recover honor; and we witness Laertes' successful revenge as he seeks to redeem his honor. And why does Fortinbras succeed where Laertes and Hamlet fail?

Stoicism is another subject in *Hamlet* (Horatio and his "philosophy," as well as his gesture toward Roman suicide and "felicity"), as is the status of women. Gertrude and Ophelia, the most heavily shielded ladies in Shakespeare, are nevertheless destroyed—and by those who shield them. The ethical posture of *Hamlet,* beyond the hero's own tragedy, is a complex and far-ranging discourse, and one that transcends the mere rubric "murder should not go unpunished." Ethically, *Hamlet* is an argument that considers such consequences as the trivializing of death, the trivializing of women, and the trivializing of ethical systems—for those who do this trivializing encounter fundamental and obvious failures.

If we attend to a Shakespearean play we may not be able to know Shakespeare the man, insofar as his own personal thoughts and sentiments are concerned, but we may be able to infer how Shakespeare the man wished us to react morally to *Hamlet, Othello, Antony and Cleopatra,* and his other plays. But how, one may ask, can we be moved to hold the various ethical positions that are reflected in the individual tragedies? Does a sense of the ethical posture of a play require a more profound response than an ordinary "emotional reaction" to the drama? A play such as *Hamlet* or *King Lear* can only seem rich and complex as the result of a calculated complexity of effect. The playwright's cold calculation, as it were, evokes the audience's passion. Whether our passion is to be any the less because it has a complicated focus is a function of our theory of art. The most complex symphonies are not the least moving.

Passion can be choked in the modern viewer simply by the diachronic nature of the subject. I have assumed throughout a reader who is interested in how Shakespeare's contemporaries might have responded to him or how Shakespeare himself might have wished his contemporaries to respond to him. I have not assumed a reader who feels that we must deal with each Shakespearean play as if it were a structure of words springing up spontaneously in the twentieth century and thus requiring analysis by someone with no chronological presuppositions. The parochial view may be more difficult than the view that takes a play as existing in a timeless matrix in which we can discuss the twentieth-century quality of Ophelia's neuroses and the contrapuntal relationships among the rhythms of her speeches. The reader I have assumed attempts to imagine a sixteenth- or early-seventeenth-century Shakespearean drama acting upon an audience of those times. Trying for this view, the reader must always reckon on being left out in certain ways—especially in the matter of immediate and subjective reactions. For we must also face the possibility that only the wiser sort among Shakespeare's contemporaries would have been able truly to appreciate what he was doing aesthetically.

We can attempt to reconstruct certain qualities in those Renaissance presentations, but we can never be certain that we have recovered emotional appeals that might not affect us now. The issues that mattered in Shakespeare's time may no longer be our issues. Questions about life and death in the sense in which they are dealt with in *Hamlet* may not vex us as they vexed Shakespeare and his contemporaries even though this play may still speak to us in other ways. The Bible may not be as electric or urgent a repository of knowledge for us as it was for them. History itself may not speak to us as it spoke to the people of Shakespeare's times. But we must attempt some such reconstruction from the evidence of Shakespeare's plays, because otherwise we can never hope to know his thoughts as a man or his emotions as a human being.

For we can only reach Shakespeare through his preserved dramas and poems. As a man, he no longer exists beyond his work, even though he did once exist for his contemporaries, for his family, for his lovers, for his parents, for his friends. We play with the idea of the man who created the art, but perhaps it was one of that man's achievements that in the art he created we do not find the frail human being he was but the human being he might have wanted to be. He may have been easily jealous, but I do not think he communicated to us that jealousy was a good thing. He may have easily despaired, but I do not think that he communicated to us that despair was a mature attitude. He may have been easily moved by glamor, but I do not know whether he felt that glamor was an ultimate value. So what we have in the end are not necessarily the thoughts and sentiments that were Shakespeare's, but those that he felt were worth communicating, those, perhaps, that he might have wished were his own.

BIBLIOGRAPHY

Judson Boyce Allen, *The Ethical Poetic of the Later Middle Ages* (1982). Charles Altieri, *Act and Quality: A Theory of Literary Meaning and Humanistic Understanding* (1981). Gertrude E. M. Anscombe, *Intention* (1957). Thomas I. Bacon, *Martin Luther and the Drama* (1976). J. Leeds Barroll, *Artificial Persons* (1974) and *Shakespearean Tragedy* (1984). Monroe C. Beardsley, *Aesthetics: Problems in the Philosophy of Criticism* (1958). Wayne C. Booth, *The Rhetoric of Fiction*, 2nd ed. (1983). Jonathan D. Culler, *Structuralist Poetics* (1975). Paul De Man, *Blindness and Insight: Essays in the Rhetoric of Contemporary Criticism* (1971). Marcia M. Eaton, "Liars, Ranters, and Dramatic Speakers," in Benjamin R. Tilghman, ed., *Language and Aesthetics* (1973).

Käte Hamburger, *The Logic of Literature*, 2nd rev. ed., Marilyn J. Rose, trans. (1973). D. W. Hamlyn, "Unconscious Intentions," in *Philosophy*, 46 (1971). Gilbert Highet, *The Classical Tradition* (1949). Eric Donald Hirsch, *Validity in Interpretation* (1967). John Hospers, "Implied Truths in Literature," in *Journal of Aesthetics and Art Criticism*, 19 (1960). Roman Ingarden, *The Literary Work of Art*, George G. Grabowicz, trans. (1973). Peter D. Juhl, *Interpretation: An Essay in the Philosophy of Literary Criticism* (1980). Harry Levin, "Thematics and Criticism," in Peter Demetz et al., eds., *The Discipline of Criticism* (1968). Richard McKeon, "Literary Criticism and the Concept of Imitation in Antiquity," in Ronald Salmon Crane et al., eds., *Critics and Criticism* (1952).

Michael Riffaterre, *Text Production*, Terese Lyons, trans. (1983). Leon Rosenstein, "On Aristotle and Thought in the Drama," in *Critical Inquiry*, 3 (1977). Alan J. Tormey, *The Concept of Expression* (1971). Bernard Weinberg, *A History of Literary Criticism in the Renaissance*, 2 vols. (1961). Morris Weitz, *Hamlet and the Philosophy of Literary Criticism* (1964). Ludwig Wittgenstein, *Philosophical Investigations*, G. E. M. Anscombe, trans. (1968).

Shakespeare's Professional Career: Poet and Playwright

DAVID BEVINGTON

We do not know precisely when Shakespeare went to London from Stratford or when he was first employed by a dramatic company. We do know that one of his first professional ambitions was to publish nondramatic poetry. His narrative poems *Venus and Adonis* and *The Rape of Lucrece* were published in 1593 and 1594 by the printer Richard Field, son of a Stratford associate of Shakespeare's father, and were dedicated to the earl of Southampton. Both were carefully seen through the press. Never again, during his productive lifetime, would Shakespeare take such care with the publication of his work. Paradoxically, the greatest of English dramatists never troubled himself about his plays as printed works, though he seems to have cared about his early reputation as a poet.

One reason for this attitude is clear enough. Playwriting in the 1590s offered employment for talented young writers, but it brought little status in the literary world of London. Shakespeare, in his early bid for literary fame, directed his attention instead to the fashionable genres of Ovidian erotic poetry, in the vein of Christopher Marlowe's *Hero and Leander* (1593), and of the poetic "complaint," in the tradition of *A Mirror for Magistrates* and Samuel Daniel's *Complaint of Rosamond.* Nor was Shakespeare wrong in his appraisal of Elizabethan taste in poetry. His published poems went through numerous editions during his lifetime (*Venus and Adonis,* nine, and *Lucrece,* five) and were handsomely praised by his contemporaries.

Shakespeare must also have written at least some of his sonnets during the early 1590s, for a number of them reflect his relationship to Southampton's family. Sonneteering was then de rigueur for any serious poet, in the wake of Sir Philip Sidney's *Astrophel and Stella* (1591), Samuel Daniel's *Delia* (1591–1592), Edmund Spenser's *Amoretti* (1595), and others. Francis Meres in 1598 praised Shakespeare's "sugared Sonnets among his private friends," indicating that some sonnets were in private circulation by this time. Two sonnets were printed in 1599 in William Jaggard's *The Passionate Pilgrim.* Full publication, when it came in 1609, seems not to have had Shakespeare's authorization; in any case, it was too late for the sonnet vogue of the 1590s. Whatever the reasons for this delay in publication, Shakespeare does appear to have regarded himself as a serious nondramatic poet in the 1590s and to have won the assent of his contemporaries to this distinction.

How did this ambitious young poet from Stratford begin his career in the theater? The details of his early affiliations with particular acting companies are obscure. In the 1580s, he could have joined Leicester's Men, led by James Burbage, who had built in 1576 England's first permanent building for the commercial performance of plays, called simply the Theatre, in the northeast suburbs of London. (Burbage's son Richard later became Shakespeare's leading man.) This company disbanded in 1588 upon the death of its patron. Some of its prominent members, who later became

Shakespeare's associates, joined Lord Strange's company, known as Derby's Men after 1593, when Lord Strange was granted the earldom of Derby. Perhaps Shakespeare joined this group when it was amalgamated with the Admiral's Men some time between 1590 and 1594. Or he may have belonged to Pembroke's Men, since that company evidently owned some of his early plays. The early 1590s were difficult years for the players; unusually bad outbreaks of the plague and the death of the fifth earl of Derby in 1594 led to a reshuffling of the London companies. One of the few things we know for certain is that Shakespeare emerged in 1594 as an established member of the Lord Chamberlain's Men, along with Richard Burbage and William Kemp.

Shakespeare acted in his own and in other plays mounted by the repertory companies to which he belonged. He became an "actor-sharer," or joint owner, of this successful company along with some eight or nine other sharers. And from his earliest professional years Shakespeare was evidently prized as a dramatist. As such he enjoyed an unusual status; few dramatists belonged to the companies for which they wrote. So valued was Shakespeare as a playwright that eventually he was privileged to retire from acting (in which he had never taken the most important roles). We know of his early success as a playwright from the testimony of Thomas Nash, whose *Pierce Pennilesse* (1592) celebrates the popularity of Lord Talbot in Shakespeare's *Henry VI, Part 1.* How it would "have joyed brave Talbot, (the terror of the French)," wrote Nash, "to think that after he had lain two hundred years in his tomb, he should triumph again on the stage, and have his bones new embalmed with the tears of ten thousand spectators at least (at several times) who in the tragedian that represents his person imagine they behold him fresh bleeding." Shakespeare's first history play seems to have been a tremendous hit.

The English history play was indeed an essential part of Shakespeare's early success. His arrival in London coincided with an outburst of national pride in the aftermath of England's defeat of the Spanish Armada (July 1588). Three decades of prosperity and peace under Queen Elizabeth had given Protestant England the strength to face the threat of Catholic Spain under Philip II. A new edition of Holinshed's *Chronicles* had appeared in 1587, as an important updating of Edward Hall's *Union of the Two Noble and Illustre Families of Lancas-*

ter and York, John Foxe's *Acts and Monuments of Martyrs, A Mirror for Magistrates,* and other chronicle writings. Materials were at hand for the exploration of England's national identity, and the burgeoning new commercial popular theater was a perfect forum.

Nor was Shakespeare the only professional writer whose talents were drafted to satisfy the new hunger for drama based on English history. Marlowe wrote *Edward II* (ca. 1591–1593), from which Shakespeare learned a great deal that he was able to use in *Richard II.* An anonymous *Edward III* (ca. 1590–1595) may have been written in part by Shakespeare; so, too, with *Sir Thomas More* (ca. 1593–1601). George Peele contributed *Edward I* (1590–1593), and Robert Greene wrote a fanciful romantic history called *The Scottish History of James IV* (ca. 1590–1591). The anonymous play *Thomas of Woodstock* (1591–1595) relates the tragic events of Richard II's reign prior to the point at which Shakespeare takes up the story. Thomas Heywood and perhaps others wrote two plays on Edward IV (1591–1599). All of English history was open territory for dramatists, except for the recent, controversial years of the English Reformation. The crucial era was the late fourteenth century and the fifteenth century, when England's greatness was tested by civil war.

Shakespeare was regarded at one time as a follower or imitator in the genre of the history play. His genius, according to conventional interpretations, was in perfecting dramatic forms devised by others rather than in innovating. Recent evidence has challenged this assumption and has argued the case for Shakespeare as one of the great creators of the genre of English history on the popular stage. Only a raw and chauvinistic anonymous play called *The Famous Victories of Henry V* (1583–1588), from which Shakespeare drew material for his later plays on Henry IV and Henry V, is definitely earlier in date than Shakespeare's three-play sequence *Henry VI,* performed between 1590 and 1592. (Dates for Shakespeare's plays in this essay are those of performance.) The playwright Robert Greene's outburst against Shakespeare as an "upstart crow, beautified with our feathers" (*Groatsworth of Wit,* 1592) seems the outcry of a disappointed rival.

Certainly Shakespeare perceived, far more acutely than Greene, the serious purpose to which a dramatization of England's recent past could be put. Shakespeare saw England's great civil wars of the fifteenth century, the so-called Wars of the

Roses, as a testing of national mettle, a time of divisiveness and of decline in military authority abroad from which England had nonetheless emerged, under the Tudors, as a unified nation able to face the challenges of Reformation and Counter-Reformation. Shakespeare and his audience were attuned to the political and social lessons that their history might teach them.

From the start of his trilogy of plays about Henry VI, Shakespeare directs attention to the painful consequences of division at home and military indecisiveness abroad. Henry VI, as the inexperienced and underage son of the mighty Henry V, whose funeral begins the first play in the series, finds himself surrounded with uncles and kinsmen ready to exploit his youth and inexperience as well as his uncertain genealogical claims to the throne. The servingmen of two such uncles, Humphrey, Duke of Gloucester, and the Bishop of Winchester, war openly at the Tower of London. The Earl (later Duke) of Somerset and his allies, sporting the red rose of Lancaster, are at enmity with Richard Plantagenet, whose white rose symbolizes the claim of the York dynasty to the throne that the Lancastrian Henry occupies. Plantagenet can urge a line of succession back to Edward III; so can Henry VI, but his claim is vitiated by his grandfather Henry IV's usurpation of the crown from Richard II. Weakened by these internal quarrels, England is in no position to defend a deteriorating military position in France. Joan of Arc and her lover, the French Dauphin, find it all too easy to vanquish England's great general, Lord Talbot. The moral issues are starkly clear, for Joan of Arc traffics with evil spirits and bargains for temporary success by selling her body and soul.

Shakespeare's play sees something profoundly unnatural in the Dauphin's surrender to the charms of a woman like Joan of Arc. Female domination infects the English court as well, for by the end of *Part 1* King Henry VI is ready to give away most of his remaining claims to France in order to marry the powerless but ambitious Margaret of Anjou.

The subsequent plays in this series offer similarly painful lessons about civil conflict and unbridled personal ambition. In *Part 2*, the Duke of Suffolk, who as Margaret's lover has arranged the disastrous royal marriage, heads a conspiracy against the good Duke Humphrey of Gloucester. Humphrey, as King Henry's one loyal stay against opportunism and backbiting, must be removed by his self-serving enemies so that they can operate without re-straint. Richard Plantagenet, duke of York, joins the conspiracy and encourages a rabble-rouser named Jack Cade to mount open rebellion in the streets of London. *Part 2* is thus much concerned with the increasingly ominous restiveness of the common people, who, deprived of stable leadership, turn on their aristocratic masters in senseless slaughter. Rebellion is eventually brought under control, but not before York's forces have attained an unstoppable momentum.

By the opening of *Part 3,* civil war has erupted and York is temporarily in possession of the English throne. Shakespeare portrays the agony of a seesawing conflict in which ordinary Englishmen find themselves slaughtering their own fathers, sons, and brothers. A horrifying result of the civil war is that the two leading families, York and Lancaster, engage in a senseless feud in which one death must repay another. York is slaughtered in a savage ritual murder by his Lancastrian captors; King Henry VI is murdered in the Tower by York's youngest son, Richard of Gloucester. Many of the mourners are women—widowed, powerless, and bound together only by their hatred and desire for vengeance. York's eldest son, Edward IV, survives for a time as England's victorious king, but he is crippled by illness and by a fatal weakness for women—the same kind of imprudence that had earlier brought disaster to King Henry VI.

Richard III, performed around 1593 as a conclusion to the *Henry VI* series, is another of Shakespeare's huge early successes, in good part because the character of Richard so brilliantly epitomizes the evils of civil conflict. Borrowing stage mannerisms from the resourceful Vice of the popular morality plays, Richard takes the audience into his confidence while he boasts, leers, and conspires. His gloating soliloquies reveal the brilliance of a man determined to gain total mastery in the wake of anarchy. He is the genius of divisiveness and civil discord, a product of England's lack of fidelity to its best interests. Indeed, the language of the play suggests that Richard is a scourge, an evil man sent by Providence to punish the English for their waywardness. Richard induces the factional members of the court to turn against one another and then disposes of them in ways appropriate to their perjuries. In doing so, he thinks that he is simply furthering his own mad ambitions and proving that anyone can be seduced to his will. Eventually, however, the joke turns against Richard. His schemes are, in ways that he cannot realize, a necessary part of the all-encompassing destruction through which England will paradoxically be renewed. Richard's nemesis, the future Henry VII, arrives on England's shores blessed by the force of some providential will before which Richard's guilty conscience is abashed and thrown down. In this final play of the series, Shakespeare offers comforting signs of providential meaning in history. The path by which he has explored the realities of civil conflict is nonetheless troubling and full of solemn warning. In this early series of plays, Shakespeare nicely balances the lessons of history with a belief in national purpose and a ringing oratory that seems to have been just what his audiences were looking for.

King John (ca. 1594) moves to an even earlier period of English history, the thirteenth century. It, too, employs history as a means of warning contemporary society. King John faces political problems that are by now familiar as dramatic subject matter: an uncertain dynastic claim; a rival in Arthur, the son of John's older brother; a restless baronage; and a continental papal power that stands ready to exploit England's inner division. John was seen by sixteenth-century historians both as a proto-Protestant hero in the struggle against Catholicism (as in Foxe's *Acts and Monuments*) and as a betrayer of his people. Shakespeare endorses neither of these extreme views. Instead, he dramatizes a dilemma of power not unlike that faced by Queen Elizabeth in her troubled relations with her cousin and rival, Mary, Queen of Scots.

The English history play typified by *King John* and Shakespeare's other early histories is a genre unto itself, not distinctively comic or tragic in the classical senses of those terms but usually a mixture of the two. Structurally it is episodic, crowded with incidents and characters. Its action is dominated by scenes of confrontation and struggle. Its mode of enactment is gymnastic. The open Elizabethan stage frequently becomes the ground before a castle or a city under siege, the walls of which are represented by the gallery above the main stage and the city gates by a door in the theater facade. Lacking theoretical or generic precedent, the English history play evolved as a practical form of entertainment in response to popular enthusiasm and strong national feeling. Shakespeare was at once the originator of its distinctive form and its leading exemplar.

In his early comedies, Shakespeare proved no less an innovator. He did learn from classical and English models, and in comedy he found more models than were available for historical drama. The years before 1594 can properly be regarded as experimental for Shakespearean comedy. Nonetheless, the experimentation quickly resulted in a kind of romantic comic play that was distinctively Shakespeare's own, foreshadowing his great comic romances of the later 1590s.

The Comedy of Errors (1590–1593) is based on Plautus' New Comedy *Menaechmi.* Both plays concern long-separated twins who are farcically mistaken for one another when one twin comes to his brother's city. Both plays rely on a classical theatrical set picturing the street in front of two houses, one of them belonging to a twin who is locked out by his wife. As in his model, Shakespeare confines the action of the play to a single day; never again does the playwright observe the so-called unities of time, place, and action with such care. Yet even in this elaborately plotted neoclassical comedy, Shakespeare's English sensibility and his romantically comic vision are unmistakably present. With newly invented characters to enhance the love interest, the morality is identifiably English in its emphasis on marriage and fidelity. Shakespeare deepens the farce of mistaken identity by adding a framing story of separation, threatened execution, and eventual reunion. The narrative pattern of journey, loss at sea, and recovery through nearly miraculous revelation or intervention generates a sense of wonder and rebirth that will endure into his latest comic plays.

The Taming of the Shrew (1592–1594) is an even clearer illustration of the way Shakespeare combines neoclassical models with English comic spirit. In this play, Shakespeare closely follows a neoclassical source for one plot and turns for the other to broad fabliau humor. The story of Bianca and her suitors, taken from Ariosto's *I suppositi* (1509) as translated into English by George Gascoigne (1566), is a conventional love contest in which fatherly tyrannies and the unwelcome attentions of rich old men are foiled by resourceful young lovers. The characters are stock types from classical comedy, including the pantaloon, the narrow prying father, and the clever servant, though Shakespeare invests them with a vitality all his own. His chief originality is in the wooing of Petruchio and Kate, the wife-tamer and the shrew. Despite the antifeminist premises of the humorous tradition upon which Shakespeare drew, these lovers are intent upon a mature self-discovery that will fashion a relationship at once unconventional and enduring. They stand in contrast to the conventional wooers of the Bianca plot, for whom marriage offers the unhappy prospect of willfulness and a struggle for domination. A third, framing plot of a tinker, Christopher Sly, tricked into thinking himself a lord for a day, enriches the perspective of illusion and mistaken identity with which this play, like most early Shakespearean comedy, is so much involved.

The Two Gentlemen of Verona (1590–1594) is highly romantic in its expectations. *Romantic* in this Shakespearean context can mean at least two things: first, a love story in which the lovers face parental opposition, misunderstanding, enforced separation, and even physical dangers before they are blissfully reunited; and second, a saga of wandering in which the journey from one location to another signifies a love quest that is long frustrated and eventually fulfilled. Shakespeare's main source for the play, a romance in Spanish called *Diana* by the Portuguese writer Jorge de Montemayor (ca. 1559), provided the requisite romantic elements. The obstructions to love in Shakespeare's version are both external and internal: Proteus and his Julia are separated by parental decree, but Proteus' perfidy in falling for Silvia, the lady fair of his best friend, Valentine, poses the more serious complication. Only a journey to a forest near Mantua, the first of what Northrop Frye (1948) calls Shakespeare's "green worlds," can provide a restorative landscape in which the lovers are brought into self-knowledge. The forest is improbably outfitted with outlaws and is a place of equally improbable conversions. It is a foreshadowing of the sylvan landscapes in *As You Like It* and similar plays in which improbability is so much a part of the rejuvenation. Society needs an idealized landscape like this, a magical place controlled by the artist, as a corrective for social injustice. A major contribution of Shakespearean comedy is in providing just such a place of retreat and amelioration.

Love's Labor's Lost (1588–1597) opens in a make-believe world of sexual innocence. The blithe, young noblemen of this play have chosen to devote their lives to study in a rural academy, far from worldly concerns and, more to the point, from the wiles of attractive women. Their attempt is comically doomed to fail. The real world of passion and even of death is not to be denied; the brittle love-games of the young swains and their female visitors are broken off by the sobering news that the Prin-

cess' father is dead. The concluding song of Spring and Winter takes the form of a debate between Carnival and Lent, love and death, to remind us of the necessary return to reality from the artist's visionary landscape.

A Midsummer Night's Dream (1594–1595), like *Love's Labor's Lost,* is derived from no single identifiable source and thus reveals with particular clarity the characteristics of early Shakespearean romantic comedy. The green world of this play is a wood near Athens, with fairies, a nocturnal atmosphere, farcical mix-ups and sudden alterations of affection caused by a magical drug, metamorphoses of men into beasts, and, above all, a sense of dreamlike unreality. The journey made by the lovers in their attempt to evade the "sharp Athenian law" is a transforming experience from which they eventually awaken as though from an improbable and even nightmarish dream. They have been led through jealousies, mutual recriminations, and terror to reconciliation and a sense that their experience of passionate misunderstanding has been chimerical. Bottom, too, awakens as though from a dream, which he will set down in a ballad. Only Theseus and his courtly associates have been untouched by the poet's magic, and even Theseus sees that dreaming and love resemble the artist's imaginative vision, in which "airy nothing" is given "a local habitation and a name." Dreaming comes to represent the transforming experience of the theater itself—from which, as Puck observes, we will awaken as though we have "but slumb'red here," yet sensing that what we have undergone in the artist's world will renew us no less than it has renewed the lovers. By the time he wrote this splendid comedy, Shakespeare had truly begun to master the art of expressing philosophic vision in a sublimely entertaining form, at once serious and festive, profound and lighthearted.

Not coincidentally, perhaps, this was the point at which Shakespeare found himself securely established in his profession. By late 1594, he had become a sharer in the Lord Chamberlain's Men and was on the verge of considerable financial success. During the later 1590s, this company achieved a reputation as the best London had to offer, in good part because of the plays Shakespeare wrote for them. His plays began to appear in print, with his name on the title page as a drawing card. He acquired property in Stratford and London and was granted the privilege of a coat of arms. His success in the theater was unrivaled and uninterrupted, with one or two brilliant plays every year. At the top of his form in romantic comedy, he continued to exploit this distinctively Shakespearean genre with increasing subtlety. *The Merchant of Venice* was performed between 1594 and 1597, *Much Ado About Nothing* in 1598 or 1599, *The Merry Wives of Windsor* between 1597 and 1601, *As You Like It* between 1598 and 1600, and *Twelfth Night* between 1600 and 1602. The subtitle of this last comedy, *What You Will,* like the titles *As You Like It* and *Much Ado About Nothing,* suggests the author's characteristic modesty in offering comic masterpieces as apparent trifles for the entertainment of his audience.

In *The Merchant of Venice,* the familiar polarity between civilized and green worlds takes the form of a contrast between Venice and Belmont. Venice, seen mainly by day, is a place of law courts and commercial rivalry, presided over by men interested in wealth and power. Belmont—far away, mountainous, reachable only by a journey—is a place of nighttime and magic. Many of its inhabitants are women. Bassanio's voyage to Portia's Belmont is a quest, like that for the Golden Fleece, involving danger and romantic excitement. From Belmont, Portia descends into the frenetic arena of Venice to offer mercy and forgiveness as a corrective to man's competitive social ills and vengeful plottings. The polarity is, in fact, more complex than any such schematic can suggest, for Shylock is at once the embodiment of vengeful legalism and the victim of an inequitable social order. To equate his overthrow with the triumph of comedy is to oversimplify the play's ironies and difficult questions. Still, an important sense of comic renewal in the play does reside in Bassanio's and Portia's belief in risk for the sake of friendship, in hazarding all one has not to gain "what many men desire" but to achieve the paradoxical renewal of a selfless commitment. Portia and Bassanio are romantic protagonists because they are prepared to lose the world in order to gain the world, and in their fellowship at Belmont they are joined by like-minded Christians who spurn both moral and financial usury.

Much Ado About Nothing dispenses with any literal journey to a green world, exploring instead the metaphor of masking and unmasking as an expression of self-delusion and self-discovery in love. The action of the comedy revolves on scenes of masking, overhearing, deceptively staged appearances at windows, and a marriage ceremony in which the bride masks as her own cousin. Claudio and Hero, in the conventional love plot, know one another only slenderly. Because Claudio is all too ready to depend on such superficial manifestations of value as fair appearance and respectability, he is easily misled by false appearances into denouncing his innocent bride-to-be. This melodramatic plot is derived ultimately from Italian sources. Benedick and Beatrice, the less conventional couple, belong to a more English and original plot, one that features a comic battle of the sexes like that in *The Taming of the Shrew.* Benedick and Beatrice also wear defensive masks toward one another, but, because they are intent on real self-knowledge in love, their discovery of mutual compatability is firmly based on realistic expectations. The contrast between the two plots exposes the dangers of conventionality in human relationships. Since Shakespeare has repeated his double-plot strategy of the earlier *Taming of the Shrew,* we are able to measure his increased mastery of the comedy of manners. (The sprightly *Much Ado* influenced the work of later comic writers, such as Wycherley in *The Way of the World* and Shaw in *Man and Superman.*) By this point in his career, Shakespeare has demonstrated that his comic vision is by no means limited to fairy magic, journeys to improbable sylvan worlds, and the recognition of long-lost siblings, though to be sure even the more socially realistic comedy of *Much Ado* lays romantic stress on identity renewed through the setting aside of disguise and on a wondrous sense of rebirth.

The Merry Wives of Windsor is sometimes dismissed as a minor diversion in the Shakespearean canon, a jeu d'esprit written at the command of Queen Elizabeth, who, according to an eighteenth-century tradition, wished to see Falstaff in love. The dramatist John Dennis is responsible for this story, which also states that Shakespeare wrote the play in fourteen days. Dennis' account has encouraged critics to regard *Merry Wives* as occasional and farcical, a play in which the comic greatness of Falstaff has been trivialized. The resourceful jokester of the *Henry IV* plays is, in fact, a comic butt in this work. Nevertheless, *The Merry Wives of Windsor* is significant in any account of Shakespeare's development. For one thing, it shows his fascination with the new comedy of humors, just then becoming the rage in the London theater, in plays like Ben Jonson's *Every Man In His Humour* (1598) and George Chapman's *An Humourous Day's Mirth* (1597). Shakespeare's play abounds in "humorous" types—that is, characters dominated by a noted eccentricity or obsession. The Welsh Parson Evans and the French Doctor Caius exaggerate, with their verbal traits and mannerisms, the supposed characteristics of their respective countries. Justice Shallow is the caricature of a meddlesome country justice; Slender, an idiotic bumpkin ill fitted to woo a lady; Pistol, a ranter and swaggerer; Bardolph, a drunkard with an inflamed face; and Ford, a jealous husband. We learn about each character only what is required for comic caricature; the plot is designed to sustain the farcical interchange of feuding humorous types. In such a context, Falstaff is reduced from the complexity of the *Henry IV* plays to something of a type. He is a boastful would-be seducer, tricked by the merry wives into a series of compromising and hilarious situations, and, at the last, he is made the scapegoat, embodying all that Windsor wishes to expunge. Still, even he is forgiven and included in the characteristically Shakespearean generosity of the play's ending. The plan of Mistress Anne Page to outwit her parents and unwelcome wooers in favor of the attractive young Fenton is no less typical of much Shakespearean romantic comedy. The very real comic success of this critically ignored play is attested to by its triumph on the nineteenth-century operatic stage, in the versions of Nicolai and Verdi.

With *As You Like It,* Shakespeare returns once again to the vision of the green world. In contrasting Duke Frederick's envious court with the Forest of Arden, Shakespeare offers a splendidly varied and rich view of the differences between city and country, nurture and nature, civilization and wildness. At first, the contrast appears one-sidedly in favor of the natural order, for Frederick's court is a place of suspicion, tyranny, and danger. Those who love virtue must escape or be driven into exile, banding together in a sylvan landscape where their only enemy is winter and rough weather. "Sweet are the uses of adversity," muses Duke Senior, as he and his cohorts extol a Robin Hood kind of social equality and rejoice in their escape from "painted pomp." Yet the issue is more complex. Jaques points out that the forest has its own inequalities in that animals must be hunted and eaten for human sustenance. Touchstone the clown is no less iconoclastic in his exploration of customs that divide city from country. Young Orlando, driven into the forest by Frederick's enmity, discovers that the harsh necessity of survival can best be alleviated by man's humanity to man. In his longing

to be worthy of Rosalind, moreover, he learns that "nature" has ill provided him with the breeding to court a lady and that "nurture" must therefore come to his aid. Rosalind, disguised as a young man, counsels Orlando in the ways of wooing and tutors him in realistic expectations as a corrective to the fashionable, courtly, Petrarchan style of wooing.

The forest is a place of magical and improbable events, like all of Shakespeare's green worlds. It even casts its spell on Orlando's envious brother Oliver—not to mention Duke Frederick, who has usurped Duke Senior's title and banished his elder brother. Yet the sudden conversions through which Oliver and Duke Frederick are made better men are not the end of the story. The artist's imaginative world draws characters and audience alike into its curative orbit, but both must be returned to society. They move, in Victor Turner's model, from a highly structured, hierarchical, and often unjust society into a world of "communitas" that is relatively unstructured and undifferentiated, but eventually they return to a "societas" that has been renewed and enlightened by exposure to the liberating values of communitas. The interplay between country and city is a necessary and continuing one, through which human beings achieve maturity and self-knowledge. *As You Like It* depicts this movement as essentially comic, not only because it delights and entertains but also because it affirms. Even man's darker self, in this comic vision, is contained within a pattern of hopeful expectation, since the characters at Duke Frederick's envious court search for a better way. The very quality of their envy bespeaks a longing for what Le Beau calls "a better world than this."

Nowhere is Shakespeare's concern with mature self-discovery in love better expressed than in *Twelfth Night,* perhaps his last comedy in this festive vein. The repetition of a plot device from *The Comedy of Errors,* the mistaken identity of twins, underscores Shakespeare's fascination with a self-discovery that (as Marjorie Garber has observed) must go beyond the lack of individuation characteristic of a close sibling pairing to friendship and then to a marriage in which the self is compared with, and differentiated from, others. Viola's disguise as a young man enables her to fashion her identity through several relationships. She is the twin of her brother, Sebastian, supposedly lost at sea, and so like him that farcical complications are inevitable when Viola and then Sebastian arrive in Illyria.

When Viola, in male attire, becomes the object of the Countess Olivia's infatuation, the plot sorts out this inappropriate bonding by providing Olivia with a a male identical in appearance to the person she thinks she loves. In her growing acquaintance with Orsino, Viola progresses through the close identity of a supposedly male friendship to one in which sexual differentiation makes possible the fullest of human relationships.

This quest for self-knowledge based on identity and differentiation is part of a larger celebration in this festive comedy that proceeds "through release to clarification" (Barber, 1959). Feste the clown sounds the note of holiday release in his song urging that "present mirth hath present laughter" and reminding us that "in delay there lies no plenty." Viola makes a similar point when she rebukes Olivia for withdrawing her beauty from the world in self-indulgent isolation: "Lady, you are the cruell'st she alive / If you will lead these graces to the grave, / And leave the world no copy." Orsino, too, must be instructed to abandon his self-pitying posture as a rejected suitor so that instead he can find fulfillment through mutual fondness. On a more broadly comic level, Sir Toby Belch and Sir Andrew Aguecheek are apostles of the doctrine that "care's an enemy to life." The comeuppance delivered to Malvolio for his assumption that, because he is virtuous, "there shall be no more cakes and ale" identifies that ill-willing person as the enemy to any hedonistic seizing of the moment. Malvolio is "a kind of Puritan," in Maria's phrase, and he is subjected to an uncharacteristically satirical plot of comic exposure in punishment for his self-righteousness and his insistence on spoiling the pleasure of others. Despite Olivia's urging of reconciliation, the issue remains sharply divided, reflecting a split in the London public of Shakespeare's day between those pursuing entertainment in the theater and those who objected to the theater's licentiousness. In his literary search for self-identity in love, Shakespeare does battle with dark and oppressive forces both within the self and outside it, in a hostile social environment. Part of what makes Shakespeare's festive and romantic comedies so endearing is that the triumph of comedy is so fragile and so preciously won.

In much the same way that Shakespeare in the later 1590s perfected the form of the romantic comedy he had developed in the early part of the decade, he also brought to its culmination the form of the history play. As a successor to his early tetralogy from *Henry VI* to *Richard III,* Shakespeare wrote another four-play series from *Richard II* (1595–1596), through the two parts of *Henry IV* (1596–1598), to *Henry V* (1599). In doing so, he turned to the beginnings of England's civil wars, to Henry IV's usurpation of the throne from Richard II, and to a chain of events leading up to the civil conflicts of Henry VI. The outline of this series resembles that of *Henry VI* and *Richard III,* for both sequences begin with weak kings and end with strong ones. Henry V, at the end of this second tetralogy, is a mirror of all Christian kings, just as Henry VII, at the end of the earlier series, is the first successful Tudor monarch and grandfather of Queen Elizabeth.

The series that culminates in the reign of Henry V is sometimes called the Henriad, since Henry is its protagonist. His education as Christian prince provides an enduring focus, and it parallels in a political context the quest for self-discovery in personal relationships that we see in the love comedies. Yet Henry is not presented in any simplistic apologia for the English monarchy; what he and the audience learn about political conflict and war is complex and sobering. The Henriad celebrates the necessity and the sometimes distasteful reality of a process through which all mature humans must pass, that of putting away childish innocence and accepting mature responsibility.

Richard II concerns Prince Henry (Hal) only indirectly, though he is mentioned as the "unthrifty son" of his father and a "plague" hanging over Henry IV's new reign. What this play dramatizes is a kind of political immaturity that Hal must learn to eschew. However attractive Richard may be as a man of poetic sensibility and undeniably royal bearing, his rule is disastrous. Like the young Henry VI of the earlier historical series, Richard has inherited the throne in his immaturity because of the untimely death of his father. He spends recklessly on his favorites and neglects matters of national concern. Surrounded by officious uncles, he quarrels with them and is even implicated in the death of the youngest, Thomas of Woodstock, duke of Gloucester. He refuses to heed the counsel of his uncles York and John of Gaunt, duke of Lancaster. Henry Bolingbroke, who is Gaunt's son and Richard's cousin, presses the attack against Richard's apparent surrogate in the murder, the Duke of Norfolk, and then returns from imposed exile when Richard illegally seizes the dukedom of Lancaster after Gaunt's death. Richard's illegal act nearly alienates the Duke of York, for it violates the very charter upon which the King's own claims of allegiance must rest, the concept of inherited rank and property. Yet Bolingbroke's return is also manifestly illegal. Older and more experienced men like York preach forbearance and the need to leave all to God, but what are English subjects to do when both Richard and Bolingbroke have offended against the law? Once Bolingbroke has proved his military superiority to Richard, there can be no turning back, and York uncomfortably acquiesces in the new necessity. So do most Englishmen, and a reign of charismatic irresponsibility yields place to one of pragmatism and Machiavellian efficiency. The ironies are stark as the bravely dying Richard earns our admiration in a way he never did as king. By the same token, Henry IV assumes the unattractive role of usurper and murderer of his own kinsman, like Cain in the biblical story. A heavy mood of unfinished business hangs over Richard's irregular funeral procession as the play ends. England has somehow survived, but what will be the long-term consequences of de facto rule?

The first part of *Henry IV* opens on an ominous note that seems to confirm Henry's worst fears. The allies who have helped him to the throne, the Percy clan of the north, now regard with increasing suspicion the man they had hoped to control but who instead insists on his royal prerogative. It is as though Henry, by his rebellion against Richard, has taught others to rebel against him. The fact that his authority has been acquired by usurpation invites rival claims, and the Percys have married into a dynastic line of descent through an older brother of Henry IV's father. Hotspur, the charismatic spokesman for the Percy family, soon learns from his wary kinsmen to despise Henry IV as a "vile politician" and as the murderer of his royal cousin Richard.

As if the Percys were not enough to contend with, King Henry confronts a seeming rebellion in his own family, for the Prince of Wales spends his time carousing with a debauched fat knight, Sir John Falstaff, and his crew of highwaymen and tavern mates. The alternation of scenes between court and tavern reinforces the parallel of rebellion in the land and in the royal family. As King Henry sees it, "riot and dishonor" stain the brow of his own son. The King wishes the chivalrous Hotspur were his son instead, but finds this relationship cut off by the Percys' rebellion.

Hal is not as irredeemable as his father fears, however. He speaks in soliloquy, at the end of his first scene with Falstaff, promising to redeem the time by throwing off his loose behavior at the appropriate moment. He studies his companions, learning their mannerisms of speech and their views on the English commonwealth. He learns much from Falstaff, whose youthful joie de vivre comically belies his age and corporeality. Falstaff is doubtless a drunkard, a boastful coward, and a counselor to sin, but he is also the genius of Hal's youth, a figure to whom Hal clings as any young man must do when faced with the stern role model of such a father as Henry IV. Yet Hal studies his father as well, listening carefully as the careworn, aging politician coaches his son in the art of orchestrating public appearances and dealing with recalcitrant foes. The "skipping" King Richard lives on in rueful memory as an example of the shallow capering from which Hal must recoil.

No less important to Hal's schooling is the example of his rival, Hotspur, a dutiful youth of chivalrous honor who is yet so fanatical and humorless in his ambition that he, too, is a negative model as well as a person to be emulated and bested. Hal's triumphant moment in this play is his overcoming of Hotspur in personal combat, taking from him the honorable title the two had been too proud to share. Hal's victory also constitutes his separation from Falstaff, for, although the resourceful liar rises as though from the dead to claim Hotspur as his prize, Hal is no longer intimate with his former companion. He has embraced his responsibility as Prince of Wales and has proved himself to be his father's son on the field of battle.

Henry IV, Part 2, suggests that Hal has more to learn. The lesson of reputation, introduced by the allegorical Rumor in the play's induction, is more distasteful than the lesson of honor, for it deals in deceiving appearances and in lingering suspicions. After the battle of Shrewsbury, false rumors of Hotspur's military success intensify the painful truth when Hotspur's father learns of his death. By a similarly devious process, Falstaff comes away from Shrewsbury with a reputation for bravery earned at Hal's expense. Hal, meantime, having assumed that his reformation would end all uneasiness between father and son, discovers the perversity of reputation: no one credits him with a sincere regard for his father. Everyone assumes that he is simply awaiting his father's death, and that when it occurs he will seize authority with unfeeling suddenness to usher in a reign of license. Hal's lack of concern for appearances intensifies this misperception and leads to a second painful interview between father and son in which the old suspicions are still much in evidence. Hal has, in fact, visited Falstaff at the tavern once more, although under very different circumstances from those of the first play; he has not seen Falstaff in some time, scarcely knows of his whereabouts, and is dismayed by what he finds. Falstaff seems older, less self-aware, and more given to self-pity. His current companions are swaggerers like Pistol and whores like Doll Tearsheet. Hal hastens from his tavern encounter as much distressed by the waste of his time as by Falstaff's lack of wit. Yet others will not believe that Hal has truly reformed, and a public renunciation of Falstaff at the time of Hal's coronation will prove necessary as a means of political reassurance. A reputation as a wastrel dies hard.

Part 2 also abounds in lessons of justice for Prince Hal. Falstaff's opposite number is the Lord Chief Justice, a man of utter probity and public responsibility. In *Part 1,* Hotspur was a rebel and a fanatic; his extreme view of honor needed the correction provided by Falstaff's humorously wise catechism on honor. In *Part 2,* the Lord Chief Justice is simply right about justice, whereas Falstaff is wrong. Falstaff remains a step ahead of the law for a time, associating with venal country justices of the peace who hope to profit from his expected rise to prominence, until finally reputation and justice catch up with him in the person of the stern yet wise official to whom King Henry V entrusts the administration of his laws. The choice of the Lord Chief Justice is Hal's answer to those who have feared the elevation of Falstaff to a position of influence.

Less obviously, Hal must choose whether to model himself on his younger brother John, who, in negotiating with the rebels at Gaultree Forest, encourages them to disband their forces under the seeming promise of amnesty and redress of grievances, only to arrest the leaders on charges of high treason. To the question "Is this proceeding just and honorable?" comes the response "Is your assembly so?" The ends are used to justify the means. Hal does not repudiate his brother's conduct, but he had been far away from Gaultree Forest during the negotiations there, and his own conduct avoids such open displays of duplicity. Hal's stratagem is to win by assent and inspirational leadership what

his father and brother have achieved by close dealing.

The education of Hal and his emergence as successful king are not achieved without a price. His use of Falstaff and his companions, followed by his rejection of them, savors too much of the calculated exploitation of acquaintances for personal and political advantage. His turning away from the pleasures of his boyhood is a difficult choice, and the rejection of Falstaff is for him a compassionate act that also involves his rejection of a private self. Even so, the choice carries with it some significant diminution of character. As the Hal of *Henry V* becomes king, his identity becomes absorbed in the role of leader. When, on the night before the battle of Agincourt, he converses incognito with his soldiers or when he plays practical jokes on a soldier who quarrels with him, we recognize the playful Hal; but his games are now directed toward the winning of loyal subjects and the defeat of the French. Even when he woos Katharine of France, dazzling her with the skillful rhetoric of one who affects to be no polished wooer, Hal is playing for a kingdom. Private affections now serve the public personality.

King Henry V is the successful king that most of Shakespeare's earlier history plays have lacked. His politically wise marriage contrasts with the disastrous unions of Henry VI and Edward IV. His victories in France offset the decline of England's greatness in the civil wars depicted in the earlier cycle of history plays. Henry V is a master of public rhetoric, of learning, of statesmanship, and of "policy"—that is, of astute political control. Even his enemies are forced to admire him, and the Chorus, as unabashed apologist, sings the praises of "a largess universal, like the sun." Henry unifies a diverse and even quarrelsome nation of Welshmen, Scotsmen, Irishmen, and Englishmen. He avoids both Richard II's irresponsible megalomania and Henry IV's joyless wariness, so apt to awaken resentment in others. Although Henry IV's claim to the throne was dynastically flawed, like that of King John, Henry V wins ready consent for his plan to press a wider dynastic claim in the heart of France. In short, the former Prince Hal has resolved the conflicts of maturation, or at least buried them in his enigmatic inner self, and he has now become the king his father hoped him to be. In all these ways, *Henry V* is the culminating dramatic statement of Shakespeare's interest in English history. It was to be his last play in the genre until some fourteen years later, when, perhaps in partial retirement, he would write *Henry VIII.*

By and large, Shakespeare devoted his first decade of professional activity to perfecting the genres of romantic comedy and the English history play, genres in which other successful dramatists of those years also wrote. He seems to have been comfortable with the models of romantic comedy available to him and was inspired to write history plays by an upsurge of national feeling. Because these two genres lent themselves to explorations of self-discovery and maturation in love and in political life, they must have offered congenial material to a dramatist who was himself still young and newly successful.

Yet the questions raised by *Henry V* suggest unfinished business. The uncertain morality of Henry's war against the French, with its obscure claims of dynastic right and its basis in Henry's political need to settle differences at home—not to mention his rousing speeches condoning rapine and the slaughter of the French prisoners—points to larger difficulties in the very institution of kingship. Henry is successful as a king and as a man, but at what price? One senses that Shakespeare, while seeming to provide confident answers, has come upon new questions so challenging that they require expression in the genre of tragedy, which he has hitherto largely ignored. And what is true of the histories is also true of the comedies. Shakespeare's comic writing has offered apparently definitive statements about maturation in personal relationships, only to reveal new threats requiring the investigation that tragedy provides. Meanwhile, some of the Sonnets, written perhaps in the late 1590s, offer a candid and frightening view of similar problems. If we can begin to understand what led Shakespeare from the Sonnets, *Twelfth Night,* and *Henry V* to *Julius Caesar, Hamlet,* and the problem plays of the early 1600s, we will have some sense of the way in which progression from one dramatic genre to another was a factor in Shakespeare's development.

In one sense, Shakespeare did write "tragedies" on the subject of English history during the 1590s. *Richard II* was called *The Tragedy of King Richard the Second* on the original quarto title page of 1597. The word was similarly applied to *Richard III* in the same year, and an early "bad" quarto of *Henry VI, Part 3,* was entitled *The True Tragedy of Richard,*

Duke of York. Still, these works were chronicles in form, relating the political events of a particular reign, as one would infer from such a title as *The Life and Death of King John.* To the extent that tragic events were depicted, they were treated as part of a larger pattern of history, the eventual outcome of which might well be fortunate, as in *Richard III* and *Henry V.* Shakespeare's history plays are structurally closer to the medieval cycles of religious plays, with their overarching form of "divine comedy," than to classical tragedy. Henry VI is not a tragic protagonist in the mold of Oedipus or Agamemnon. Indeed, the title figures of the history plays are scarcely protagonists at all in some instances.

When Shakespeare did turn to writing tragedies in a generically recognizable sense of the term, he seems to have been less sure of his models than he was when writing comedy. Shakespeare's few tragedies written in the 1590s are remarkably unlike the great tragedies he wrote after 1599. They offer a hesitant pattern of development: *Titus Andronicus* (by 1594) is as unlike *Romeo and Juliet* (1594–1596) as both are unlike the plays that followed.

Tragedy was of course not unknown on the London stage of the 1580s and 1590s. One notoriously successful play, *The Spanish Tragedy* by Thomas Kyd (ca. 1587), left an indelible mark on Shakespeare's first attempt in the genre, *Titus Andronicus.* Shakespeare's play, like Kyd's, is a declamatory revenge tragedy in the Senecan mode. In both plays, a father seeks to avenge wrongs done to his family and finds that the corrupt state has turned against him. He proceeds to a private vengeance, employing deception, the disguise of mad behavior, and the device of a play within the play. Both plays end in a scene of wholesale slaughter, with the avenger dying alongside his victims.

Many of these features will later appear in *Hamlet,* and indeed *Titus* is a significant bridge between the work of Kyd (supposed author of an Ur-*Hamlet*) and Shakespeare's later tragedy. The villainous Queen Tamora is a stark adumbration of the devouring women of later Shakespearean tragedy, such as Lady Macbeth, Goneril, or Regan. Aaron the Moor, a resourceful and gloating Machiavel, resembles later Vice-like villains such as Iago and Edmund. The enormity of evil in human life is vividly, even garishly, presented. Shakespeare's company seems to have succeeded with *Titus* in the theater; three early quartos

(1594, 1600, 1611) attest to its continued popularity. Ultimately, however, the play seems unconvincing. It lacks any deep psychic motivation for so much violence and horror, as well as the sense of tragic greatness in its protagonist that we associate with later Shakespearean tragedy.

The extraordinarily different character of Shakespeare's next tragedy, *Romeo and Juliet,* suggests the dramatist's unreadiness to address tragedy and the fearsome confrontations that the genre can provoke. Even though it ends with the deaths of the lovers, *Romeo and Juliet* is sheltered from tragic vision by an insistently comic view of love. The play has more in common with its contemporary, *A Midsummer Night's Dream,* than it does with the later tragedies. In its unhappy outcome, *Romeo and Juliet* uncannily resembles the sad story of Pyramus and Thisbe as played by Bottom and his cohorts. Both love stories deal, as do many of the romantic comedies, with lovers seeking to escape parental restraints and an unfeeling social order. Romeo and Juliet experience no inner difficulties in their relationship; the obstacles are all external. Romeo is a comic wooer, like Orlando, mouthing Petrarchan nonsense and at first believing himself to be in love with an unresponsive woman named Rosaline. He is much in need of Juliet's tutelage in the realities of courtship and marriage. Romeo and Juliet are paired with comic companions, Mercutio and the Nurse, whose bawdy and even sardonic view of love offsets the innocence and idealism of the young protagonists.

Romeo and Juliet are not tragic protagonists in the later Shakespearean sense. Nothing is remarkable about them but the intensity of their mutual attachment, and they can scarcely be said to embody a tragic flaw. Their haste to woo and wed is but part of the evocation of love's exquisite brevity. Tragedy follows not as a consequence of their actions but because of a senseless family feud, the lovers' ironic inability to tell their families what has happened, and simple bad luck (for example, the failure of Friar Laurence's letter to reach Romeo in his banishment). Any sense of tragic confrontation between parents and children is blunted by our perception of the many misunderstandings that impair communication; thus, Juliet is denounced by her parents only because they find her refusal to wed the handsome Count Paris inexplicable. The play's final scene of discovery stresses the parents' new awareness of what they have unwittingly done and their resolve to bury hate in their children's tomb. Romeo and Juliet are innocent sacrifices, not tragic protagonists suffering the consequences of a destructive passion. Their fate holds little sense of man's tragic destiny. Instead, it is a testimonial to the perishable quality of young love. The catastrophe serves to confirm our perception that anything so intensely beautiful cannot last.

With *Julius Caesar* (1599), issues of tragic conflict begin to be more fully addressed and to be manifested in the characters themselves in a way that we do not find in Shakespeare's earlier tragedies. Standing at midpoint in Shakespeare's career, this play is transitional in a number of ways. It represents an important step beyond the English history plays. Though still historical in scope and subject and concerned as before with civil unrest and usurpation, *Julius Caesar* is freed of the restraints of Christian morality and of English monarchical norms. Caesar's single rule can claim no divine sanction; by the same token, the senatorial and republican tradition championed by Brutus is very different from the mob rule of a figure like Jack Cade. In such a morally neutral environment, Shakespeare's presentation seems dispassionate and detached. We are invited less to take sides than to appraise the consequences of an ambivalent struggle.

Caesar and Brutus are remarkably alike. Both are proud men, prone to flattery and suggestion, especially when they are told that they detest flattery. We see them in adjoining scenes in their private homes, each turning a deaf ear to his wife's counsel, each being worked upon by the conspirators, each insisting on going forth to what will prove his doom. Caesar, for all his command and firmness of purpose, is plagued with physical frailties, is notably superstitious, and is fatally ambitious for the crown. Hubris overwhelms his better judgment and the warnings of the gods. Brutus meanwhile, despite his intense disapproval of Caesar's ambition, deals autocratically with his fellow conspirators and sees himself as the savior of Rome's liberties. The argument through which Cassius successfully tempts Brutus is really one of emulation: " 'Brutus,' and 'Caesar.' What should be in that 'Caesar'? / Why should that name be sounded more than yours?"

Part of Brutus' tragic conflict is that he feels compelled to kill a man who is at once his rival and fatherly figure of authority. Brutus does so in a bloody ceremonial that he prefers to think of as a sacrifice rather than a butchery. The ironic outcome suggests how chimerical is the illusion of gain. Brutus himself supplants the authority figure he has slain, but he does so most unwillingly. He accordingly disables the revolution by insisting that Antony be spared and that no oaths be allowed to coarsen the conspirators' sense of mission. Increasingly, Brutus will brook no rivalry, whether from Cicero or later from Cassius. His insistence on making military decisions at Philippi (disregarding Cassius' greater experience as a soldier) leads to defeat and suicide. Only in such an expiatory death can Brutus find reconciliation with his rival and brother-officer Cassius and with the spirit of the Caesar that he has unsuccessfully tried to usurp.

The play thus centers on Brutus' personal failure, but it also reflects in a sardonic vein the political anarchy that follows from such a flawed attempt at revolution. The ultimate victors are Antony and Octavius, though they too are divided by a rivalry that bodes ill for the future. Their matter-of-fact dispatching of their enemies eloquently reveals what has happened to liberty through Brutus' attempt to secure liberty for all. Rome's republican greatness is brought low by the very man who has symbolized its long and noble tradition. The rise and fall of great men in ancient Rome is a process that insistently reminds us of the brevity of human glory. Because they know so little about themselves, men blindly repeat the errors of the past. Tragic destiny is framed in a political context, but its human dimension is no less painfully revealed. Brutus' fate is to be overcome at Philippi by the spirit of the fatherly man he has slain, and he resolutely proceeds to this self-destroying fatal engagement as though he has no other choice. Prince Hal's successful supplanting of his father in the Henriad has here given way to a tragic exploration of the issues latent in that earlier rivalry.

For all its boldness in treating such issues as rebellion versus authority, as C. L. Barber and Richard Wheeler show, *Julius Caesar* does not deal with the threat of female sexuality. As in the English history plays (though Queen Margaret of Anjou and Joan of Arc are exceptions), males interact with males; Portia and Calphurnia are powerless and stoically chaste in the conventional image of the Roman matron. In *Hamlet* (1599–1601), on the other hand, the protagonist faces his mother's threatening carnality and, by extension, that of Ophelia, along with the unspeakable deeds of his uncle-father, the King of Denmark. Claudius stands in Hamlet's way at every turn: he has murdered

Hamlet's father, secretly gained the throne to which Hamlet should have been elected, and whored Hamlet's mother. As a brother-murderer, usurper, and incestuous drunkard, Claudius has offended against blood relationship, marriage, and every other sacred obligation of civilized life. The imperatives demanding his death are irresistible. Yet Hamlet's shock in his intense family crisis is no less powerful, and his irresolution is plain to see. At one moment he longs to "sweep" to his revenge "with wings as swift / As meditation or the thoughts of love"; on other occasions he berates himself for being "pigeon-livered" and for lacking gall "to make oppression bitter."

Still, Hamlet's tragedy cannot be explained simply by an inner flaw of hesitation, for his world is a profoundly corrupt one that cannot be easily cured. Claudius' secret crime is a poison infecting all Denmark. Hamlet must exercise care in becoming sure of Claudius' guilt and in tracking down such a wary foe. As Hamlet compares himself with others who have lost fathers, he sees that the problem of what to do will not yield easy answers. Laertes acts in a rage against Hamlet, whom he considers responsible for the murder of his father, Polonius; in doing so, he plays into the hands of the villain most responsible for Denmark's malaise. Fortinbras, the son of a dead father and the most successful pursuer of action in the play, gambles his fortunes on an "eggshell," a "straw," a piece of Polish ground that "hath in it no profit but the name." Hamlet's skeptical attitude toward unconsidered action is philosophical, not merely a personal flinching, and it is confirmed by the absurdity of what Laertes and Fortinbras have achieved. The opposite alternative of passivity shows an attractive aspect in the stoicism of Horatio, "a man that Fortune's buffets and rewards / Hast ta'en with equal thanks." But passivity, too, has its manifest dangers. The acquiescence of Ophelia to her father's rule leads to her break with Hamlet and contributes to her suicide, the ultimate choice of passivity that Hamlet considers but rejects. Gertrude's compliance, too, has disastrous consequences.

How then are action and passivity to be reconciled? Hamlet is torn by the question until his return from England, when he unfolds to Horatio a newfound understanding in which "rashness" and "indiscretion" play a part (as in the exchange of the letters ordering Hamlet's execution) and in which "the readiness is all." Convinced that "there's a divinity that shapes our ends, / Rough-hew them how we will," and that "there is special providence in the fall of a sparrow," Hamlet feels ready to act when providence shall dictate. "Indiscretion" will serve him well when his own "deep plots" have palled. And so it comes about, for the play's catastrophe is one in which Hamlet acts unpremeditatively. He avenges his father's death without the kind of conniving treachery that fittingly undoes Laertes and Claudius; Hamlet comes to the end of his troubled existence, moreover, without committing suicide. *Hamlet* thus provides a kind of resolution to its protagonist's dilemma, but it is a resolution possible only by means of several deaths; and it leaves in its wake a devastating image of human weakness in the incestuous royal marriage.

Shakespeare's exploration of seemingly intractable family conflicts can be traced in three so-called problem plays performed at about the time of *Hamlet: All's Well That Ends Well* (1601–1604), *Measure for Measure* (1603–1604), and *Troilus and Cressida* (1601–1602). These forays into bitter comedy and dark satire are no less akin to Shakespeare's tragedies than to the preceding romantic comedies. Helena's pluckiness and nurturing steadfastness in *All's Well* remind us of Rosalind and other earlier heroines, but in this play such a heroine is a threat to the male protagonist. Bertram prefers the company of his fellow soldiers and attaches himself to the empty braggart Parolles. This *miles gloriosus* is all too ready to urge Bertram to go to the wars instead of "spending his manly marrow" in the arms of the young woman he has unwillingly married. As a consequence, Helena must force Bertram's male role upon him through trickery; she takes the place in bed of Diana, a woman of presumed easy virtue with whom Bertram finds it possible to couple. Once Helena has presented Bertram with a child he has fathered and once Bertram has been forced to recognize the falseness of Parolles, with whom he has so closely identified, all is well at last. Yet this maturation comes about so belatedly and perfunctorily that we remain wary of the young man's callowness. For a comedy, the play is surprisingly generous toward mature and managerial figures like the French King and Bertram's mother, the Countess of Rossillion; it also celebrates the strength of the young woman. What remains problematical is the young man's resistance, his lack of self-knowledge.

Fear of sexuality seems an odd choice of emphasis in comedy. Yet in *Measure for Measure* it characterizes both sexes. Isabella is, when we first see her,

on the verge of sisterhood in a convent, seeking even greater restraints than the votarists of Saint Clare demand. Angelo, newly appointed deputy of Vienna in the puzzling absence of the Duke, seeks to restrain the licentiousness of Vienna's citizens with a cold severity that bespeaks a mistrust of his own submerged feelings. Vienna encourages these extreme responses to sexuality, for its moral climate has become lax, and even the Duke (who remains on the scene disguised as a friar) applauds efforts at social control. Yet dispassionate observers find Angelo's puritanical measures unfair when they lead to the arrest of Isabella's brother, Claudio, for getting his fiancée with child. The irony of the injustice becomes apparent when Angelo himself guiltily desires Isabella as she pleads for Claudio's life. That Angelo should lust after one so pure is a torture to his soul, and it presents in nearly tragic dimensions the psychic agony of one whose attitudes toward sexuality are in such violent conflict. The gap between licentiousness and renunciation in Angelo, as in Vienna, leaves no middle ground; women to him are whores or saints, and something in him longs to seduce the saint who pleads for him to emulate divine mercy.

The disguised Duke's role becomes crucial at this point, for only he can save Isabella, Angelo, and Claudio from their own fears. The Duke tests them in turn. As friar, he prepares Claudio for death, only to have Claudio undo any progress he has made by begging for life at the expense of his sister's shame. Isabella's response to this dishonorable plea for life is hysterical, however motivated in deep religious belief, as she declares her intention to do nothing more to save her brother. Yet the Duke has witnessed this outburst, and under his guidance the painful revelations of self-hatred and conflict are ultimately curative. Isabella must be taught to accept her human weakness and that of others. At the end of the play, she is tested again by the Duke in one of his many virtuous deceptions: thinking that her brother has been executed by Angelo, she must find the charity in herself to forgive Angelo and thereby provide a husband for the abandoned Mariana.

Angelo, too, must be led through an illusion of tragic failure so that he can find self-knowledge. Hoodwinked by a bed trick like that in *All's Well,* he thinks that he has slept with Isabella and therefore that he must order her brother's execution in violation of his promise to her. Angelo's spiritual fall is very real, but his offense in this dark comedy is largely a stage illusion contrived by the omniscient Duke. The most salutary revelation for Angelo, in fact, is that the Duke, "like power divine," has looked upon his trespasses. Freed from the nightmare of his sinful intent and even more from his attempts to hide his lust and murder through corrupt authority, Angelo is brought face to face simultaneously with his openly revealed guilt and with the nurturing pardon of the woman he had sought to violate. Isabella's coming to terms with the human condition is signaled by her doffing of religious garb and her presumed readiness to accept the Duke's proposal of marriage. As in *All's Well,* a comic resolution is at last perilously achieved, but not without a problematic sense of the conflicts with which it has had to contend.

Troilus and Cressida does not even attempt a comic resolution; it ends with Cressida's desertion of Troilus and the brutal slaying of Hector by Achilles. More than any other Shakespearean play, it refuses to fulfill conventional expectations of genre. Its lack of generic regularity seems symptomatic of Shakespeare's search for new forms with which to express personal and political conflict. Despite Hector's death, the play is not a tragedy, for its title figures suffer nothing more fatal than disillusionment. The leering, scabrous chortlings of Pandarus and Thersites invite at times the sardonic laughter of "black" comedy, and the love story of the play is anything but conventional romantic comedy. The play is called a "historie" on its early title page; the Trojan war is part of the story, but it functions chiefly to provide an ironic perspective on the disastrous interconnections of love and war. *Troilus and Cressida* is perhaps best described as a satire, in which Shakespeare responded to a vogue current in the plays of Ben Jonson, George Chapman, and John Marston.

The war provides the context in which we are to understand, and perhaps pity, personal failure. Its heroes are the greatest that history can provide, and yet their quarrel is trivial and obscure. Even as they muster arms to force the return of Helen, the Greek leaders contemptuously laugh at Menelaus' cuckoldry. The disaffection that demoralizes the Greek camp encourages Achilles and Ajax to pout like prima donnas. Among the Trojans, open skepticism about the moral defensibility of keeping Helen contends with a blustering chauvinism that insists upon the maintenance of Troy's "honor." Troilus is one of those who argue in the Trojan council that Helen must be kept at all costs. The

ironic consequence is that he is asked to consent to Cressida's return to the Greeks in exchange for the captured Antenor. Troilus realizes that his commitment to the war logically obliges him to accept this sacrifice but perceives injustice in his doing so in order to allow his brother Paris to lie with the indolent and sybaritic Helen. Cressida, for her part, having long resisted Troilus' love suit out of a wariness of emotional commitment, sees Troilus' consent to her return as an act of abandonment. His willingness to agree to the plan confirms her worst fears of male insincerity. And, indeed, Troilus is a callow young man, able to see only the degree to which he has been wronged by Cressida. In his eyes, her behavior, once she has reached the Greek camp, confirms the widespread male apprehension that all women will turn whores. She does in fact yield to Diomedes, but who has deserted whom?

The Trojan war is both an exciting circumstance and a symbol of universal surrender to opportunism and depraved appetite. In the sordid interplay of love and war, men and women seem destined to become their worst selves—as, for example, when Achilles slaughters the unarmed Hector. All self-pitying, immature men are to be called Troiluses, all false women Cressidas, and all brokers-between Pandars. This sobering paradigm of human relationships seems bitterly to deny any hope for maturation in love and any hope for the values exhibited in the romantic comedies and in the Henriad.

Shakespeare's devastating portrayal of jealousy in *Othello* (1603–1604) seems a logical sequel to *Troilus and Cressida.* No Shakespearean tragedy more fully depicts both the beauty of married love and the violence of love's dissolution. Othello and Desdemona are well matched, despite the ugly insinuations with which the play commences. Her father suspects Desdemona of indulging in strange appetites or of being enchanted, but in fact she loves Othello for "his honors and his valiant parts"; she has seen "Othello's visage in his mind." Othello is attracted to one who pities his dangerous adventures. He is older than she and a foreigner in Venice, but he hails from a proud tradition and enters into the confines of marriage only because of his real love for Desdemona. When Othello and Desdemona justify their elopement before the Venetian Senate, they not only absolve themselves of wrongdoing but establish themselves as a truly self-knowing couple. Their love is fully spiritual and sexual, mutually responsive, ecstatic yet mature.

Why does Othello's belief in his wife's fidelity

fail? In part, Shakespeare externalizes the answer in the person of Iago, the villain of the play and its epitome of the jealous temperament. Iago has recently been passed over for promotion to lieutenant under Othello, and he has witnessed the marriage of Othello to Desdemona. Both events rankle; Iago has been doubly rejected. His vengeful response is to poison the marriage by implicating Desdemona as love partner with Cassio, the handsome officer who has won the position Iago desired. Iago's motive seems clear enough, yet his delight in evil and his own dark suspicions are wildly in excess of the occasion. In soliloquy, he confides to us that he feels threatened not only by Cassio but also by Othello, whom he suspects of having lain with Iago's wife, Emilia. These groundless fears are the workings of jealousy, an emotion that feeds on itself. As Emilia explains to Desdemona—and well Emilia might know—some men are jealous simply because they are jealous. Iago himself calls jealousy "the green-eyed monster, which doth mock / The meat it feeds on."

Iago's strategy with Othello is to implant the suggestion that a relationship between an older black man and a young Venetian woman is inherently "unnatural." Brabantio has already asserted as much, suggesting that the bias is common in Venetian society. Iago presses the idea with relentless logic: a young woman's appetite in such a relationship must change, and, once it has done so, who is a more plausible choice than Cassio? Iago bolsters his campaign of suggestion with brilliantly improvised circumstances: getting Cassio drunk on watch so that Othello will dismiss him; encouraging Cassio to seek the recovery of Othello's favor through Desdemona, placing Desdemona's handkerchief in Cassio's possession; and arranging a conversation with Cassio about his mistress Bianca, which Othello will overhear imperfectly and misinterpret as evidence of Cassio's guilt.

The essential objective of Iago's scheme is to get Othello to assent to the defamatory proposition that a young white woman cannot "naturally" love an older black man. Once Othello has formulated in his own words this monstrous lie, Iago has won, for the tragedy rests on Othello's deepest fear that he is unlovable. Believing himself rejected by the woman to whom he has turned for the nurturing once given him by his mother, Othello sees Desdemona as a monstrous threat. As with Troilus, his insecurity compels him to prove all such women whores. The very openness of Desdemona's love, her enjoyment of music and company, are now held against her as evidence of the voraciousness of her lustful appetite. Under Iago's baleful tutelage, Othello's mind becomes obsessed with bestial images of sexual coupling. No longer able to connect the sensual and idealized sides of his marriage, Othello falls into a vengeful longing to destroy the supposed betrayer of his trust—the same motivation that has driven Iago to destroy Othello's faith in Desdemona and to prove that all women are false. To the extent that Othello finally recognizes the ineffable goodness of the woman he has destroyed, Iago's plot fails; but Othello's realization affords him no comfort. His suicide is his acknowledgment that, whatever Iago's contribution, Othello's failure to thrive in Desdemona's great love is a failure for which he alone is responsible.

The fallen world of *King Lear* (ca. 1605) has no place for successful marriage or sexual fulfillment. Sexual attraction, such as that between Edmund and Goneril or Regan, is portrayed as monstrous. The seemingly innocent "good sport" through which Edmund was conceived is a pleasure for which his father, Gloucester, must ultimately pay dearly: "The dark and vicious place where thee he got," comments Edgar, "cost him his eyes." The Duke of Albany is jeered at for milky tenderness by his voracious, domineering wife, Goneril. In his visionary madness on the heath, King Lear associates women with centaurs and the feminine sexual anatomy with the inferno: "There's hell, there's darkness, there is the sulphurous pit; / Burning, scalding, stench, consumption. Fie, fie, fie!"

Other family relationships, especially those between the generations, prove equally fraught with conflict. Lear's intense bitterness toward womanhood is generated by the ingratitude of Goneril and Regan. Gloucester learns too late about the perfidy of his illegitimate son, Edmund. The fathers are also to blame. The aging Lear's willful intent to be the center of his daughters' lives elicits the calculated hypocrisy of Goneril and Regan and the truthful silence of Cordelia, which he interprets as rebellion. Knowing his sons only slenderly, Gloucester is gulled by Edmund into believing Edgar guilty of the same ingratitude that Lear fears in Cordelia.

Such failures contribute to a terrifying breakdown of love and justice in the world of *King Lear,* the most thorough portrayal of human evil that Shakespeare ever attempted. The evil is especially terrifying in the seeming absence of divine providence. When King Lear calls upon the gods for aid against his enemies, the apparent answer is a raging storm in which Lear himself is the victim because his enemies have taken all available shelter. Gloucester, too, is exposed to the storm by his well-meaning efforts to help Lear. Bereft of aid and comfort, the two old men find little to prevent a descent into madness, despair, and suicide.

One alternative to monstrous sexuality and generational conflict does present itself. When King Lear asks the disguised Earl of Kent, "What wouldst thou?" Kent's answer is "service." Kent has returned from the exile to which Lear sentenced him, and done so at considerable personal risk, because he sees in Lear the quality of "authority" that he would serve. Lear's Fool improvidently but loyally chooses to stay with his master, too, and through the Fool's conundrums we learn to associate "fool" with persons who serve those they love rather than seek worldly gain. Kent is a "fool," and so is Cordelia. Edgar, disguised as beggar and madman, anonymously assists his blind and despairing father to find some peace of mind, even though Gloucester had earlier turned against his true son and sought his life. The Fool labels such charity as folly and sardonically advises worldlings not to emulate such behavior. Still, the foolish choice is really the wise one according to any concept of moral human conduct. The actual fools in this inverted society are such worldly-wise characters as Cornwall, Regan, Goneril, and Edmund, characters who have lost their humanity. Folly and wisdom, injustice and justice, blindness and seeing, madness and sanity—all have gone topsy-turvy in the apocalyptic vision of this play. In this great stage of fools, true wisdom is a precious possession that can be achieved only through suffering.

The price of such wisdom is almost as fearful as the world in which it must be won. Cordelia must devote herself to the care of her aging and desperate father instead of to her marriage; she cannot persevere in the choice that Desdemona made, to leave her father and begin another generation, because Lear has been too cruelly treated. Lear's regressive wish to repossess his daughter is granted him by the hard necessities of the time, and he finds a brief moment of contentment in Cordelia's forgiveness. To die with her in prison becomes his fondest hope, a fateful wish that becomes fulfilled much sooner than he had intended. As he dies with the strangled Cordelia in his arms, Lear's very source of identity is gone. He is worse than mad.

The final vision of *Lear* is truly apocalyptic, reminding its beholders of the Last Judgment and offering little hope of renewed stability. The only consolation is that humanity has endured in such a tragic world and has at times found within itself the compassion to answer brutality and lust with self-sacrifice.

In *Timon of Athens* (1605–1608), Shakespeare pushes to its limit the misanthropic potential in *Lear.* For the most part, *Timon* denies even the redeeming note of compassion through which Lear's tragedy becomes bearable. Timon's servant Flavius is loyal and self-sacrificing, but Timon turns away in despair from the comfort Flavius offers. At the play's end, Alcibiades provides a path toward conciliation with Athens' citizens, but Alcibiades' is an accommodation that excludes Timon. Instead, Timon experiences unflinchingly the ingratitude of his onetime friends and dependents. He treats his sudden poverty, brought on by his own extravagant generosity, as a test of loyalty for those he has helped, and, to his disbelief and disgust, sees his friends all fail. As a consequence, Timon exiles himself from the world and broods on his ill treatment. Unexpectedly, he finds himself with unwanted, newfound wealth, which he uses only to prove once more how craven and self-serving are those who flatter for gain. *Timon of Athens* is not as suffused in terrifying evil as *Lear;* greed is an ignoble passion that invites bitter laughter rather than tears. Nevertheless, as in *Lear,* sexuality is used to symbolize man's carnal dissipation. For Timon, human society becomes nothing more than a polite disguise for prostitution and thievery. "To general filths / Convert o' th' instant, green virginity!" he exults. "Do't in your parents' eyes!" Shakespeare evidently did not finish writing *Timon,* and it may never have been acted during his lifetime. Even so, the play attests to the bleak vision of human depravity with which Shakespeare seems to have been absorbed at this point in his career.

Macbeth (1606–1607) centers its terrible crime in the family, in the relationship between husband and wife. Lady Macbeth's ambition for her husband may rationalize to some extent her involvement in the murder of King Duncan, but there is still something disturbingly masculine about her role. "Come, you spirits / That tend on mortal thoughts," she cries, "unsex me here, / And fill me from the crown to the toe top-full / Of direst cruelty!" When Macbeth's resolution wavers, Lady Macbeth taunts him with lack of masculinity and protests that, for such cowardice, she would dash out the brains of a babe to whom she had given suck. "Bring forth men-children only," marvels her husband, "For thy undaunted mettle should compose / Nothing but males." Lady Macbeth's power over her husband is often compared to that of the weird sisters, those bearded witches who tempt Macbeth with riddling half-truths only to betray him. The crime to which these dangerous women lead Macbeth is the murder of the fatherly Duncan, a generous king and patron from whom Macbeth can expect further benison. The monstrous perversity of killing such a goodly sire is apparent to Macbeth; he recognizes that it is a damnable act, one that will "return / To plague th' inventer." Lady Macbeth, on the other hand, considers it an easy thing to do: "A little water clears us of this deed." She says she would have undertaken it herself "had he not resembled / My father as he slept."

Macbeth knows all too well that the blood of Duncan will never be washed from his contaminated hands, and the deed does indeed return to plague him. He kills Banquo, both because Banquo knows too much and because of the promise of royal succession offered Banquo by the weird sisters. Later, his guilt takes the form of Banquo's ghost, returned to haunt the murderer. The slaughter of Macduff's family is yet another brutal consequence of Macbeth's first crime. Because he has killed and supplanted his fatherly king only to find a "barren sceptre" in his grip, Macbeth becomes an enemy to the very concepts of family and progeny. Tortured by the quibbling of the fiends who have led him into temptation, Macbeth returns to the weird sisters for more riddling prophecies that give him false hope and thus undo him. What makes Macbeth's tragedy so terrifying is its human plausibility. To prove manliness by slaying a beneficent fatherly figure is, in the vision of this play, man's tragic destiny. The sterile consequences of the deed seem incapable of deterring a man who is led to such a destiny by parricidal ambition and by the unnerving taunts of women.

Antony and Cleopatra (1606–1607) marks an important transition from the all-encompassing tragic vision of *King Lear* and *Macbeth* toward a vision that is more compensatory. To be sure, the play's protagonists end in death and even in worldly failure. Their great love affair is a tempestuous one, marked by separations, jealous quarrels, and suspicions of betrayal; even Antony's suicide is brought on by Cleopatra's sending him a false report of her death. Antony loathes himself for surrendering to Cleopatra's enervating way of life, and he realizes that he does so at the expense of his position as one of the rulers of the Roman Empire. When Antony attempts to end Cleopatra's sway over him by marrying Octavius' sister Octavia, the chaste opposite to Cleopatra in every respect, he proves incapable of steady commitment to the new union. In the end, Antony's shameful military defeat at Octavius' hands owes much, in his view, to having tied his fortunes to Cleopatra's apron strings. Enobarbus and Antony's other followers agree. Cleopatra is Antony's "Egyptian dish," his "serpent of old Nile"; but she also represents the "Egyptian fetters" to which he loses himself in "dotage," and she is "triple-turned whore." Antony is Mars surrendering to the arms of Venus instead of wielding the armor of war. Transvestite images convey to us a debauched Antony dressed in Cleopatra's attire while she wears his mighty sword.

Notwithstanding this unromantic view of their affair, we are attracted to Antony and Cleopatra. One reason is that the Roman alternative is so uninviting. Octavius' Rome is a place of shifting political allegiances, where Pompey is dispatched one day and Lepidus cashiered the next as expediency dictates. Octavius' devotion to this political world is obsessive. It leads him to marry his dear sister to the political rival he knows will desert her and thereby give Octavius a pretext for war. Octavius' coldness forbids him the enjoyment of wine or merriment, and therefore Cleopatra holds no fascination for him other than as a prize or object to be exploited. With unerring instinct, Cleopatra knows that Octavius intends to put her on display in Rome and that she cannot deal with him on her terms. Her answer is to "call great Caesar ass / Unpolicied!" and to deny him his triumph by a noble suicide. She joins her Antony in death, leaving Octavius behind to rule a "dull world" that is "no better than a sty."

Anthony and Cleopatra die believing that they will find immortality as lovers sporting in the Elysian fields. There, their "dolphin-like" delights will show their backs above the element they lived in, enabling the lovers to enjoy a fame exceeding that of Dido and Aeneas. And in truth, Shakespeare's play celebrates the immortality to which the lovers lay claim. Cleopatra's "infinite variety," her ability to make hungry "where most she satisfies," her paradoxical blend of transcendence and eroticism, transform Antony's tragedy into something visionary. In the vast chasm that separates Antony and Octavius, the play invites us to prefer the man who loves unstintingly and ruinously to the one who calculates his relationships in political terms. Cleopatra is unapologetically a hedonist, but hers is not the destructive whoring nature feared by men in Shakespeare's earlier tragedies. As Enobarbus says, "The holy priests / Bless her when she is riggish." Antony stands up to her (as Octavius will not) and is ruined, but the ruin has in it a greatness that makes Antony more fully human than his rival.

We must still account for the austere view of human failure in *Coriolanus* (ca. 1608), perhaps Shakespeare's last tragedy. For all his bravery and unsparing honesty, Coriolanus cannot provide the leadership that Rome needs. The people are in part to blame, with their wavering loyalties and their susceptibility to inflamed rhetoric. So are their spokesmen, the tribunes, who exploit division for short-term political ends. The primary focus of the play, nevertheless, remains on the failure of Coriolanus. He cannot be flexible, and he repeatedly insists on confirming the fears of those who regard him as autocratic.

His failure seems rooted in a dependent relation to his mother, Volumnia. To this fearsomely masculine matron, Coriolanus brings his military victories as love offerings. What Coriolanus has done for Rome, as everyone knows, he has done "to please his mother." She encourages this mingling of war and mother-love in him by speaking of his military feats as vicarious substitutes for "the embracements of his bed." Volumnia's ambition through her son, like Lady Macbeth's through her husband, leads the hero into a disastrous political career that ends in banishment. When he returns with an army, prepared to take vengeance against Rome, his mother once more stands in his way: he perceives that in destroying Rome, the mother city, he will be destroying her. Instead, he must allow her to destroy him. "O mother, mother! / What have you done?" he cries. ". . . You have won a happy victory to Rome; / But for your son . . . / Most dangerously you have with him prevailed." He is left no choice but to return to Aufidius, the dangerous rival and ally who undoes Coriolanus by calling him "thou boy of tears." This telling characterization of Coriolanus' failed manhood proves to be an epitaph, for Coriolanus is butchered as an enemy of the people. That such a noble person should come to such an

ironic and ignoble end bears testimony to the power of familial conflict.

The transition to romance is Shakespeare's final development in genre. In many ways, it represents a return to romantic comedy and to the restorative motif of young lovers happily reunited. Yet Shakespeare's late plays are markedly tragicomic and speak to anxieties raised by the tragedies. We find increased emphasis on separation, on error and conflict that seem destined to produce a tragic outcome, on bereavement and contrition eased only at long last by tearful reunion and a nearly magical sense of revived hope. The mood is often resigned and sad, though yielding to joy at a renewal that has seemed impossible.

In *Pericles* (1606–1608), for example, the hero's many tribulations separate him from his wife, Thaisa (supposed dead at sea), and a daughter, Marina. His early encounter with incest at the court of Antiochus stands as a grim warning against too intense an attachment between father and daughter, and his courtship of Thaisa at the court of King Simonides serves as an acting out of the generational rivalry through which the father learns to give his daughter to another man. Shakespeare here examines, in the genre of romance, a conflict to which he gave darker expression in *Othello* and *King Lear*. Characteristically, romance affords its protagonists a second chance. Thaisa is mysteriously restored to life; Marina is led through melodramatic perils to eventual reunion with her father. Pericles, all but dead with grief, can be revived only by this appearance of one so like the woman he married. The riddle of incest is unraveled when Pericles is able to find second happiness in his recovered daughter and yet, unlike Lear, bestow her willingly on another man. Once he has achieved this crucial rite of passage, Pericles is rewarded by the providential power (partly expressed in the figure of the Chorus) that has been looking after him, delaying his happiness and testing his resolve but eventually providing restitution. The full measure of Pericles' achieved self-knowledge is that he is finally restored to his wife. The motherly wife, so notably absent in *Lear*, so destructively ambitious in *Macbeth*, and so fearfully destroyed in *Othello*, is here the symbol of harmonious reintegration. The daughter, who must die as a consequence of her father's regressive wishes in *King Lear*, is here both recovered and released.

Jealousy, the tragic subject of *Othello*, becomes the tragicomic preoccupation of *Cymbeline* (1608–

1610). Like Othello, Posthumus Leonatus is persuaded by the villainous Iachimo that his chaste and devoted wife, Imogen, is untrue to him. Iachimo's motive, like that of Iago, is to destroy a marital happiness that challenges his own warped credo of human failing. Leonatus resembles Othello too in that his failure of trust is largely his own; some self-hatred in him provokes a conviction that he is unlovable, and his mind is tortured with gross physical images of Imogen's infidelity. In his diseased imagination, his chaste wife turns whore, and he orders his servant to slay her. Believing him to have succeeded, Leonatus lapses into deep penitence. It is much to Leonatus' credit that he hates himself for the deed and forgives Imogen even before her name has been publicly cleared. The restoration of Imogen's good name occurs when Leonatus returns with Iachimo from his Italian exile to the court of Imogen's angry and possessive father, King Cymbeline of England. When Leonatus and Iachimo are captured in a Roman campaign against the English army, a major scene of recognition restores Leonatus to the wife he has supposed dead. It also restores Cymbeline to his daughter, who had fled her father's court to find her husband, and to his long-lost sons, who have been brought up in a wilderness far from court (not unlike the forest in *As You Like It*). Tragicomic romance thus heals the wound caused by male insecurity toward womankind and by fatherly reluctance to part with a cherished daughter. Romance can harmonize those anxieties that prove destructive in tragedy.

The jealousy that has nearly destroyed Leonatus in *Cymbeline* is no less the affliction of King Leontes of Sicilia in *The Winter's Tale* (1610-1611). Leontes' chaste and gracious queen, Hermione, helps to persuade the King's childhood friend, King Polixenes of Bohemia, to extend a long visit at the Sicilian court, only to provoke in her husband an unreasoning fear that Polixenes is playing the role of seducer. Leontes' violent outbreak of jealousy appears to derive from his idealization of childhood, a time of boyhood innocence untroubled by the temptations of sex. Hermione's wholeness as a woman threatens Leontes. His fear of the sensual aspects of womanhood leads him to repudiate and disgrace his queen at a public trial despite oracles that assure her innocence. Leontes even goes so far as to condemn his infant child, Perdita, to be abandoned on a foreign seacoast. As a consequence of Leontes' fury and the gods' vengeance, the King's son dies and Hermione is struck down; even we as audience are allowed to believe her

dead. Under the tutelage of Hermione's lady-in-waiting, Paulina, the King, whose soliloquies have been as agonized as those of the great tragic protagonists, becomes penitent. He cannot be reminded too often of his unspeakable crime.

A long break in the action—some sixteen years—marks the transition from tragic error to tragicomic romance. Perdita does not die on the seacoast where she is abandoned, even though the persons who carry her there do pay the penalty of death; she is found by shepherds and raised in a pastoral atmosphere again reminiscent of that in *As You Like It*. Florizel, the princely son of Polixenes, is captivated by Perdita's simple grace and undertakes to court her in disguise as another shepherd. King Polixenes finds out about his son, and soon we are in the midst of a comic and romantic plot involving the wish of the young lovers to evade parental authority (as in *A Midsummer Night's Dream*). The lovers' attempt at escape brings them to Perdita's own land, where she is reunited with her father. Both fathers, Leontes and Polixenes, are now prepared to release their children and let them start their own, new lives. Once Leontes has achieved this necessary goal, like Pericles, he is rewarded by the return of his supposedly dead wife. Through her goodness, he is able to forgive himself and come to terms with what time has wrought in both their lives. As the person who unites Hermione with her husband, Paulina's role in this restoration resembles that of the dramatist, for she deals in the illusion of death and rebirth. It is she who opens the curtain on the "statue" of Hermione, setting the stage for a magical (but not black magical) second choice.

The artist in *The Tempest* (1610–1611) is Prospero, and the island is his world. One of the island's many benefits is that it enables Prospero to bestow his daughter on a younger man, freely and by his own volition. Prospero's strange anger and excitement indicate that it is a struggle for him to release his daughter, but the struggle is entirely inner. As Prospero conquers his anxieties, Shakespeare triumphantly resolves the generational conflict that led in *King Lear* to a regressive death wish and that is also to be found in all the late romances.

The island enables Prospero to stage illusory trials for his enemies who once banished him from mainland Italy. He induces Alonso, king of Naples, to believe that his son Ferdinand has drowned, and he leads Ferdinand to believe that his father is likewise lost. With the help of the spirit Ariel, Prospero lays before Sebastian and Antonio illusions of political gain through murder. The test proves them villains, but it also demonstrates that an invisible power protects those who are threatened. The same power, embodied in Ariel, exposes the plot of Caliban and his debauched companions against Prospero. Caliban is a native of the island, the son of a witch, gifted in perceptions of natural beauty but lacking in conscience; he is the "thing of darkness" that Prospero insists is to be found in all of us, even in Prospero himself. Ariel, conversely, represents a kind of inspiration that the artist can control for a time but that he must release to the elements as he prepares for death. In this mixed realm of Caliban and Ariel, Prospero comes to terms with himself as father, as man, and as artist. His surrender of his daughter and of his magical powers as artist coincides with his preparation for death. Having mastered his life and seen its temporal limitations, the artist resigns his power in a mood of exhilaration and deep humility.

The temptation to see *The Tempest* as Shakespeare's farewell to his art is irresistible, for he gave up his London lodgings in 1611 or 1612 to return to Stratford. Perhaps he came out of this retirement to write *Henry VIII* (1613), a history play in which elements of tragicomedy and romance are mixed. The sad events that open the play —the impeachment of Buckingham, the divorce and death of Queen Katharine, and the fall of Cardinal Wolsey—contribute to the "comic" action with which the play ends, the birth and baptism of the child who is to become Queen Elizabeth. Only through the sufferings of Katharine, the accession of Anne Bullen as queen, and the enigmatic behavior of the King himself is England's bright future assured. Great events transcend the stumblings of mortal men and women in a way that they cannot anticipate.

Shakespeare seems also to have had a hand in *The Two Noble Kinsmen* (1613–1616), though John Fletcher had a major share. The future of the King's Men lay now with Fletcher. Shakespeare had finished what he had to say.

BIBLIOGRAPHY

Peter Alexander, *Shakespeare's Life and Art* (1939; repr. 1961). Cesar L. Barber, *Shakespeare's Festive Comedy: A Study of Dramatic Form and Its Relation to Social Custom* (1959) and " 'Thou That Beget'st Him That Did Thee Beget': Transformation in *Pericles* and *The Winter's Tale*," in *Shakespeare Survey,* 22 (1969). Cesar L. Barber and Richard Wheeler, *The Whole Journey* (1985). Lynda E. Boose, "The Father and the Bride in Shakespeare," in *PMLA,* 97 (1982). Andrew Cecil Bradley, *Shakespearean Tragedy* (1904; repr. 1955). John Russell Brown and Bernard Harris, eds., *Early Shakespeare* (1961). Sigurd Burckhardt, *Shakespearean Meanings* (1968).

Edmund K. Chambers, *William Shakespeare: A Study of Facts and Problems,* 2 vols. (1930). Maurice Charney, *Shakespeare's Roman Plays* (1961). Wolfgang Clemen, *The Development of Shakespeare's Imagery* (1951). Rosalie L. Colie, *Shakespeare's Living Art* (1974). Reginald A. Foakes, *Shakespeare: The Dark Comedies to the Last Plays. From Satire to Celebration* (1971). Edgar I. Fripp, *Shakespeare, Man and Artist,* 2 vols. (1938). Northrop Frye, "The Argument of Comedy," in *English Institute Essays* (1948); *Anatomy of Criticism* (1957); and *A Natural Perspective: The Development of Shakespearean Comedy and Romance* (1965).

Marjorie Garber, *Coming of Age in Shakespeare* (1981). Harley Granville-Barker, *From Henry V to Hamlet* (1925). Robert Grams Hunter, *Shakespeare and the Comedy of Forgiveness* (1965). David Gwilym James, "The Failure of the Ballad-Makers," in *Scepticism and Poetry* (1937). Coppélia Kahn, *Man's Estate: Masculine Identity in Shakespeare* (1981). David Kastan, *Shakespeare and the Shapes of Time* (1982). Arthur C. Kirsch, *Shakespeare and the Experience of Love* (1981).

Alexander Leggatt, *Shakespeare's Comedy of Love* (1974). Maynard Mack, "The Jacobean Shakespeare: Some Observations on the Construction of the Tragedies," in John Russell Brown and Bernard Harris, eds. *Jacobean Theatre* (1973). Barbara A. Mowat, *The Dramaturgy of Shakespeare's Romances* (1976). Marianne L. Novy, *Love's Argument: Gender Relations in Shakespeare* (1984). Robert Ornstein, *A Kingdom for a Stage: The Achievement of Shakespeare's History Plays* (1972). Arthur P. Rossiter, *Angel with Horns and Other Shakespeare Lectures* (1961). Leo Salingar, *Shakespeare and the Traditions of Comedy* (1974). Bernard Spivack, *Shakespeare and the Allegory of Evil* (1958).

E. M. W. Tillyard, *Shakespeare's History Plays* (1944). Victor W. Turner, *The Ritual Process: Structure and Anti-Structure* (1969). Thomas F. Van Laan, *Role-Playing in Shakespeare* (1978). Robert N. Watson, *Shakespeare and the Hazards of Ambition* (1984). Theodore R. Weiss, *The Breath of Clowns and Kings: Shakespeare's Early Comedies and Histories* (1971). Richard P. Wheeler, *Shakespeare's Development and the Problem Comedies: Turn and Counter-Turn* (1981).

Shakespeare and His Contemporaries: Other Poets and Playwrights

M. C. BRADBROOK

Shakespeare's relations with contemporary poets and playwrights can be inferred only from his writing or from theirs, for no direct biographical or autobiographical records survive, such as those for John Donne or Ben Jonson. After Shakespeare's death, legends grew.

The wit combats described by Thomas Fuller in his *Worthies* (1662) cannot be firsthand: "Many were the wit-combats betwixt him and Ben Jonson, which two I behold like a Spanish great gallion and an English man of war." Fuller, eight years old at Shakespeare's death, beheld the combats in his mind's eye only. However, since wit combats were the usual form of education in grammar school, law school, and university, we can assume they took place. But the actual relationship between Shakespeare and Jonson was, of course, more complex.

Different centuries have taken different views of Shakespeare's relations with his contemporaries. Neoclassicists of the late seventeenth and early eighteenth centuries saw an untutored genius living, according to Richard Farmer (1767), in a general state of almost universal ignorance and license; yet Farmer stressed the significance of Shakespeare's contemporaries. In fully rediscovering the greatness of other Elizabethan poets, the Romantics initiated the process by which the nineteenth-century critics, while neglecting the living stage, with increasing professional pedantry discovered in other writers illumination of their own reading of Shakespeare and then attributed these as his sources. The ultimate fruits of their labors may be seen in Geoffrey Bullough's eight volumes of *Narrative and Dramatic Sources of Shakespeare* (1957–1975).

But this trend has now been reversed. Playwriting is now seen as part of an oral culture, including oratory and sermons. Working in a medium naturally collaborative, Shakespeare did not seek publication without special purpose. Yet he retained his integrity as a "maker"; when he alone, with the exception of Anthony Munday, survived the long closing of the theaters during the plague of 1592–1594 to emerge as a sharer in the lord chamberlain's company, his well-attested fluency made collaboration with outsiders unnecessary. The ability to dash off a play was greatly valued; Shakespeare seems to have combined the actor's natural gift of easy recall with an intuitive ability to select and order material. "All the images of nature were still present to him, and he drew them not laboriously, but luckily," observed John Dryden in his *Essay of Dramatic Poesy.* The well-trained memory of one educated in a largely oral culture, when combined with Shakespeare's power of preconscious selection and ordering, fused a great range of reference into organic form. Wisdom was traditional, gathered into commonplaces; this, after all, was a time when every schoolboy was encouraged to make his own commonplace book.

A play text, sold outright to the actors, was naturally withheld from publication, since publication would break a given company's monopoly on a play. The censor's signed copy protected a company of actors and might be inspected if disturbance arose or was even suspected. The limits of compliance are shown in the manuscript of *The Book of Sir Thomas More* (ca. 1592), in which an inserted speech, written by Shakespeare, seems designed to remove any incitement to anti-alien riots. Although its picture of London citizens differs from that given in the main text, it did not placate the censor. Such an unacted, popular play would hold no interest for London printers, though with the growth of playgoing their market also grew. At least 168 plays were published in Elizabeth's reign, of which no fewer than 103 appeared between 1590 and 1602. Under James, these numbers steadily increased.

Shakespeare's compliance with the interests of his fellows led them after his death to celebrate his poetic power by sponsoring publication of his plays in folio. Seven years earlier, Ben Jonson had excited some mirth by publishing in folio his dramatic works; the appearance of another folio would certainly help to consolidate the notion that they were rivals, in spite of Jonson's warm tribute to "My Beloved, the Author . . . and What He Hath Left Us!" Without Jonson's example, it is doubtful that the First Folio would have appeared; and only eighteen of the thirty-six plays had been printed in Shakespeare's lifetime.

In the second half of the twentieth century, a growing emphasis on performance has led to a stress on the nonverbal aspects of Shakespeare's dramatic art. Theories of the instability of the texts have been recently adopted by the general editors of the Oxford Shakespeare. Such assumptions are not yet fully established, but it may be that as the age of ignorance for literary historians was succeeded by the age of literary texts, the age of theatrical performance has now arrived. The consequence is a new sense of instability and possible collaboration in Shakespeare's text.

Like Caesar's Gaul, Shakespeare's interaction with his contemporaries may be divided into three parts. His early years show the great influence of Christopher Marlowe, his exact contemporary, and of Thomas Kyd. Spreading beyond Marlowe's death in May 1593, this influence culminated in the lyric tragedy of *Richard II* (ca. 1595). If Marlowe was the rival poet of the Sonnets, the wit combats referred to there may also be traced in Shakespeare's nondramatic poetry.

Next, the War of the Theaters, an obscure event of the years 1599–1602, by doubtful rumor set Shakespeare in opposition to Ben Jonson, who was then seeking opponents and who found one in John Marston, youthful survivor of a particularly ferocious wit combat with Joseph Hall, satirist and playwright for the boys of St. Paul's.

At the end of his career, Shakespeare collaborated with John Fletcher in *The Two Noble Kinsmen,* the lost *Cardenio,* and (some would add, though I should not) *Henry VIII. Pericles* is also considered collaborative by many. A short lyric, "The Phoenix and Turtle," appeared in 1601 in an anthology on a common theme, to which Jonson and Marston contributed, along with others. Shakespeare's relationship with Fletcher appears to be less important than his association with Marlowe or Jonson.

Shakespeare's continuing interaction with the Lord Chamberlain's (later, King's) Men, their repertory, and their rivals surpasses any purely literary influence. The rise of a more flexible and pragmatic genre criticism has implicitly relied on this view, with chronicle history, revenge tragedy, the comedy of humors, the romance, and the bitter tragicomedy of Jacobean times more frequently explored than Shakespeare's debts to individual writers. But it is well to remember that genres were shaped in the public theater by the acting potential of well-established companies and by popular demand. Perhaps the notion of Shakespeare among rival poets should be replaced by that of Shakespeare among rival play groups in theaters with reputations for special kinds of presentations: the Theatre versus the Rose, the Globe versus the Fortune and the Red Bull, and later the Blackfriars versus the Cockpit. Shakespeare's relations with his fellow poets, mediated through this context, may be traced as a series of ricochets or tensions. The more successful the plays of any one group, the stronger the impulse of others to steal its thunder. G. E. Bentley showed that in the cases of Shakespeare and Thomas Heywood, relations attested to have lasted for many years were probably contractual. Like Shakespeare, Heywood did not publish; but he revised, and he could succeed both at court and at the noisy Red Bull. It would seem that Alfred Harbage's *Shakespeare and the Rival Traditions,* a pioneer study in 1952, should now be extended to a wider field than the one he surveyed.

Since the capital necessary to mount a play came from the players or their management, it was the players who, with an eye to the box office, decided whether any drama should be extended by a second part. That Shakespeare designed a historical tetralogy implies an independence that no Elizabethan dramatist could assume. It was the play now known as *Henry VI, Part 3,* that in 1592 roused Robert Greene to the first public notice of Shakespeare. Addressing three fellow graduates—apparently Marlowe, Thomas Nash, and George Peele—he parodied "O tiger's heart wrapped in a woman's hide!" (I. iv. 137) when he wrote: "There is an upstart Crow beautified with our feathers, that with his *Tyger's hart wrapt in a Player's hide,* supposes he is as well able to bombast out a blanke verse as the best of you: and being an absolute *Johannes factotum,* is in his owne conceit the only Shake-scene in a countrey" *(A Groats-worth of Wit . . .).*

Greene was not renowned for history: a master of the revels was later to inscribe on a copy of his *Scottish History of James IV,* "The Scottish History or rather Fiction of English and Scottish Matters Historical." The English chronicle history was identified as Shakespeare's as late as 1638: in Richard Brome's *The Antipodes,* an aged play-loving lord boasts of his troupe,

These lads can act the Emperors' lives all over,
And Shakespeare's chronicled histories to boot.

(I. v. 66–67)

Greene's pamphlet was entered for printing three weeks after the author had died in wretchedness. Letters urging repentance on companions in former sins were familiar exercises for every schoolboy; but under cover of such piety, mudslinging easily passed as reproof.

Nash—later to repudiate angrily any link with this "scald lying pamphlet"—had already praised in *Pierce Pennilesse* (1592) not the author but the actors of *Henry VI, Part 1,* who had revived from his tomb "brave Talbot, the terror of the French." Such figures were frequently "revived" (represented by live figures) in civic pageantry, but here was action to draw tears from "ten thousand spectators."

The "upstart Crow" by writing plays had infringed the monopoly of those "gentlemen dramatists" to whom Greene made his appeal. The older view, that Greene accused Shakespeare of plagiarism, has been discarded. University men, even if discredited, might write themselves "gentle men," whereas common players ranked very low. In that hierarchical but mobile society, rank was imputed without much evidence; Nash, engaged in battle with Greene's archenemy, Gabriel Harvey, while claiming for himself no rank but that of jester, yet cast Harvey's lowly origin in his teeth.

Greene's printer, Henry Chettle, pamphleteer and minor playwright, added a handsome personal apology to his own next publication. In the preface to *Kind-Hart's Dreame* (1593), he says he has seen Shakespeare's "demeanour no less civil than he excellent in the quality he professes: besides, divers of worship have reported his uprightness of dealing, which argues his honesty, and his facetious grace in writing, that approves his art." Shakespeare did not respond with counter-accusations; instead, he found a worthy, perhaps his local vicar or an alderman in whose house he had performed, to vouch for him. But he had not ignored the insult, and years later Polonius was to observe that "beautified" is a vile phrase.

In its noblest form, the history play was composed by courtiers, such as Thomas Norton and Thomas Sackville, to counsel their sovereign, as was *Gorboduc* in 1561; at the other end of the scale, Richard Tarlton's (?) *Famous Victories of Henry V* (ca. 1594) and George Peele's *Edward I* (ca. 1593) were designed for a popular audience and were filled with national assertiveness. The first quarto of *Edward I* nevertheless carried an old-fashioned explicit: "Yours. By George Peele, Master of Arts in Oxenford. Finis." Print established a claim to dignity, as well as proof of popularity, though in these early years, many more plays of the witty and irreverent young clerks survive than of more popular dramatists, since the clerks had readier access to the press, and no such aversion from print as had the play troupes. Greene would describe himself as master of arts, even when the arts he displayed were the criminal skills of the confidence man.

Shakespeare's trilogy on King Henry VI excels in emblematic scenes, which were also a specialty of Peele. The quarrel scene in the Temple Gardens, a familiar London location, a scene that Shakespeare seems to have invented; the death of York; and the lament of Henry, seated between a father who has killed his son in battle and a son who has killed his father, are three "stills" building to a full dramatic storm. Rising tension reaches its climax with the emergence of Richard of Gloucester, murderer of the "faint Henry" and soon to be the protagonist of Shakespeare's first overwhelming success, *Richard III.*

The vitality and variety of moods in that protean hero fuse popular dramatic ingredients with the prize bogeyman of the Tudor historians, largely created by Sir Thomas More. The play thus has popular and noble origins. Richard's diabolic ancestry in early drama has been traced by Bernard Spivack in *Shakespeare and the Allegory of Evil* (1958); but Richard also owes much to Marlowe's Machiavellian and ironically witty aspirers. Kyd's tight structure and patterned speech are fused with the imagery of hell and night; yet the opening scene, Richard's wooing, strikes the note of macabre comedy. Until the final scenes, there is no more actual battle. The play, both more literary and more theatrically charged than anything that had yet been seen, established the reputations of both Shakespeare and Richard Burbage, who created the leading role.

In the extraordinary amalgam of disparate elements that went into Richard, there was also a personal one: Shakespeare was at this time in the company of Ferdinando Stanley, the heir to Lord Derby, whose ancestors are given full prominence in that final battle.

Titus Andronicus is not even nominally historic, but it was equally literary and popular. It was printed in 1594; one scene of madness was added in the First Folio. A performance was given by "London Players" on 1 January 1596 at the seat of Sir John Harington, father of the famous Lucy, Countess of Bedford, in Rutland. It was recorded by Jacques Petit, a servant of Anthony Bacon, who thought the spectacle better than the matter.

Ovid supplies part of the plot, and the play is closely linked with Shakespeare's *Rape of Lucrece* (1594). This poem dates to the time when, the theaters closed by plague, Shakespeare made a determined bid for aristocratic approval. Shortly after the deaths of Marlowe and Greene, Shakespeare published his two Ovidian poems, immediately following on Marlowe's unpublished but immensely influential *Hero and Leander* (1593). Shakespeare's *Venus and Adonis,* published in 1593, one month after Marlowe's death, became at once a model for other poets. In 1594, Thomas Heywood brought out his *Oenone and Paris,* the first of his many debts to Shakespeare. A year later, Michael Drayton published his vividly decorated *Endimion and Phoebe;* Thomas Middleton followed with *The Ghost of Lucrece* (1600). Chapman had in 1598 published Marlowe's "unfinished" poem with his own edifying and emblematic sequel. Francis Meres paid his compliment by suggesting metamorphosis—the sweet, witty soul of Ovid lived in mellifluous and honey-tongued Shakespeare. The mutilated Lavinia of *Titus* explicitly recalls Ovid (*Metamorphoses,* I, 154–170), though no doubt it was the love poetry that Meres meant; he praised Shakespeare for tragedy also.

Extremity of suffering and horror, presented in chillingly patterned speech and ritual displays, has today brought *Titus Andronicus* back to the stage. In 1955, the Peter Brook–Laurence Olivier production ensured its significance, especially in Poland and other countries under stress. Henslowe recorded it as "ne" (new) on 24 January 1594, when Sussex's men gave it at the Globe, and in his Induction to *Bartholomew Fair* (1614) Ben Jonson recorded its continuing popularity along with *The Spanish Tragedy* "as it was first acted." Kyd's Hieronymo is clearly behind Titus, as Marlowe's Jew of Malta is behind Aaron's death speech, although the Marlowe play was not to be printed until 1633. In the 1950s it was not unusual to place this play's composition in 1586: Peter Alexander thought it dated from around 1589 and termed it the offspring of youthful ambition.

Francis Meres's mention (in *Palladis Tamia,* 1598) of Shakespeare's "sugared sonnets among his private friends" put the playwright in a yet higher social bracket, among those too gentlemanly to seek print. The unauthorized publication by Nash of Sidney's *Astrophel and Stella* in 1591 had revived the sonnet sequence; Sidney's dramatic flexibility makes him the only rival to Shakespeare in this kind. If the rival poet of the Sonnets is Marlowe, the challenge to him in Ovidian romance becomes more explicable. General opinion now inclines to the years 1593–1596 for the composition of the Sonnets, which strengthens the case for the earl of Southampton as their central figure. Southampton was the center of admirers, and Shakespeare's acquaintance with such a circle is implied by the style of the early comedies of love. Few now take the Sonnets as mere literary exercises: the effect that they had upon the conventional sonneteer Michael Drayton is seen in his later verses, his best being written as late as 1619.

The reverse side of the medal appears in the courtly comedies of love, where wit combats form the very stuff of action. For these, Shakespeare turned to the third figure with whom, in his celebratory verses for the First Folio, Ben Jonson compared him—John Lyly, author of *Euphues.* Here the debt is altogether slighter than that owed to Marlowe or to Kyd. Lyly had begun publishing comedies a decade earlier, in 1582–1583. Witty mockery of love by the little choir boys of St. Paul's Cathedral derived from the cult of Elizabeth in all its variety. She is the one figure whose identity is clear: Sapho or Cynthia is unmistakable. Her admirers could be any members of the court, whether Oxford or Leicester matters little. Lyly invented a language for courtship that was almost as distinct as the language of thieves—a class language of artificial repartee aimed at "compliment" and combat, at flirtation. Cupid rather than Venus presided, and the witty pages who baited some dim, elderly blunderer brought in some elements of popular drama. Like Shakespeare, Lyly compounded many different elements and served them up in a light, unpretentious "dream."

While borrowing his style, however, Shakespeare aimed at a wider audience than Lyly; his plays are always more complex and "impure." Shakespeare used the wit combats of courtship in *Two Gentlemen of Verona*—though the range from the aubade for Sylvia to the misdeeds of Crab the dog is far beyond Lyly. The two courtly comedies of *Love's Labor's Lost* and *A Midsummer Night's Dream,* which mock love while indulging it, may have been written for specific occasions in a courtly household. They include an unusually large number of boys' parts. However, they soon came into public repertories. In 1598, *Love's Labor's Lost* appeared in print with Shakespeare's name on the title page—a new honor. Plays did not merit dedications, but it was advertised as having been played before the queen at Christmas. *A Midsummer Night's Dream* offered in the fairies a new type of being, an amalgam of folk legend and courtly poetry, which was copied by Michael Drayton (in *Nymphidia*) and by others.

Lyly's success was ephemeral; by his intervention in a more serious and ferocious wit combat, the Marprelate controversy, he brought about the closure of the choristers' theaters and thereafter stood shivering in the wings, waiting for favors that did not arrive. His style, which depended on strict conventions, was displaced by one more robust. The "stabbing simile" won the day over euphuistic erudition; before long, Falstaff was to parody *Euphues* in his fatherly exhortations to the recalcitrant Prince of Wales, as Pistol was to quote the resounding utterances of tragic villains like Peele's Muly Mahomet. Such parody had appeared in the "Pyramus and Thisbe" episode of *A Midsummer Night's Dream* and also in the Masque of the Nine Worthies in *Love's Labor's Lost.* In the courtly comedies,

Shakespeare was able to establish a perspective upon earlier popular styles. But as he moved forward, he did not discard these materials altogether, for in 1594 he threw in his lot with the common players once more and became a sharer in the Lord Chamberlain's (later, King's) Men, with whom he remained for the rest of his working life.

The lord chamberlain, Lord Hunsdon, was not a literary man but a deeply trusted and good soldier, who kept the Border, and a first cousin to the queen. In 1594 he was about seventy years old. That winter the common players presented *The Comedy of Errors* as part of the winter sports at Gray's Inn. If in returning to the common stages Shakespeare looked for a center of wit, it was to be found in the Inns of Court. The earl of Southampton was a member of Gray's Inn, largest and most play-loving of the four "colleges" that made up this "Third University of the Kingdom." In 1592, young John Donne had entered Lincoln's Inn from one of the minor Inns of Chancery. He became "a great frequenter of plays" and distributed his mocking verses among his friends; the vogue for these verses was to change the nature of the love lyric into a more dramatic, sparkling form that was also coarser and more direct. Nash had written for "Lord S" a "wanton elegy" of such obscenity that it survives only in manuscript but prefixed it with verses to "the loveliest bud the red rose ever bore!"

A more elegant form of this mood is found in Mercutio. *Romeo and Juliet* is built on a frame of love sonnets and wit combats; it proved one of Shakespeare's immediate successes in the public theater and among the young wits. The name *Montague* might have been taken to compliment the dowager countess of Southampton and had been already used as translation for the Italian *Montecchi* by George Gascoigne in a wedding masque. Perhaps Marlowe contributed by the memory of his tragic death in a brawl no less than by the literary example of *Hero and Leander.* But Shakespeare had found his own range. He lightly picked up an image from Samuel Daniel's "Complaint of Rosamond" for Romeo's lament over Juliet, but the more limited poetry of such as Daniel and Drayton was becoming as irrelevant to the stage as Lyly's.

Marlowe remained an influence: in Shakespeare's next success, *The Merchant of Venice,* Shylock was more closely modeled on Barabas than any previous figure in Shakespeare had been on

Marlovian heroes. This is a dramatic, not a merely literary, recall and is in every way an improvement. The statelier rhythms of *Tamburlaine* appear in Morocco's praise of Portia, again as a live theatrical impulse, heightening the ritualistic effect of the first casket scene. Tamburlaine's lament over his queen, soon to be lapped in a coffin of gold, reflects upon the tawny Moor's choice of a golden casket, which conceals a death's head. This reminiscence is not casual.

The most lyrical of the early tragedies, *Richard II,* generally ascribed to 1595, was printed by 1597 (in which year also a pirate, by his mangled version, witnessed to the great fame of *Romeo and Juliet*). *Richard II* follows the same kind of story as Marlowe's *Edward II* (ca. 1592), so that the two plays are often given in tandem in the modern theater. *Edward II* had itself been indebted to Shakespeare's earlier history plays; the relations between Mortimer and the boy prince are linked with *Richard III.* Shakespeare toned down the homosexuality of the king and raised the political issues of deposition in a more complex way. Thus, in the last act the hero's self-analysis and self-questioning turn this one man into a little kingdom filled with competing "selves," giving a foretaste of tragedies yet to come. Powerful emblematic scenes—the lists at Coventry, the garden scene, above all the deposition—are bound together poetically by "symphonic imagery"—recurrent poetic motifs, here deployed in several different modes. The play was not a popular success.

The play was out of favor by February 1601, when the Essex faction paid to have it staged on the eve of their fatal and futile rebellion. Clearly it was felt to be politically dangerous (the deposition scene was not printed until 1623), but it was possibly staged privately by Sir Edward Hoby in December 1595, and Sir Robert Cecil was invited to attend. There is still no agreement on the balance so delicately held between Richard and Henry of Lancaster, whose role depends on pregnant silences. Yet popular playwrights borrowed: Dekker used some images from Gaunt's dying speech for the triumphant entry of King James into London in March 1604.

Shakespeare had now reached his zenith and drew easily upon a multiplicity of dramatic levels. As G. K. Hunter (1971) has observed, the classical author was still an influence and an authority; but henceforth his power derived from his capacity to release Shakespeare's own faculties. And Shakespeare learned more about plays by living among plays and playwrights than he did from any classical sources. The assumption by older writers, such as Virgil K. Whitaker, that Shakespeare began by imitating the classics he had learned at school and then went on to learn from contemporaries does not gain decisive support from what fragmentary chronology we have. I see his beginnings in more popular plays, and his classical works—*Titus Andronicus, The Comedy of Errors*—as part of the period of trading upmarket in the years when he wrote and published his Ovidian poems. The speed of his forward leap in the years 1594–1596 meant that he himself became the object of imitation. He had raised the level of popular theatrical art.

In 1596, when Shakespeare gained the right to term himself a gentleman by the grant of arms, he showed how gentlemen could behave by the creation of one of his most famous characters, Falstaff. Encores were demanded. The confidence that presented an old jester who improvised plays in taverns and worked himself out of tight corners by fantasies, attended by a ranter of play scraps, marks Shakespeare's emancipation from noble patronage. Prince Hal cannot reject Falstaff until the "old player" has rejected youthful glamor. Soon after Shakespeare acquired New Place, his mansion in Stratford, Falstaff goes down to visit the Gloucestershire gentry; he dismisses "honor" as a "word" soon after the paradoxical epithet of "gentle Shakespeare" could be applied to a player. Of course, it did not mean that he was mild; it meant that he had moved upstairs from downstairs. Falstaff became a household word. A rival play, *Sir John Oldcastle, Part 1,* was written for Henslowe by a team consisting of Anthony Munday, Michael Drayton, Robert Wilson, and Richard Hathaway, who were paid £10 on 14 October 1599; this included an advance for a second part. Later, Thomas Dekker was paid for additions. To add to the injury, the second quarto edition of this play, printed in 1619 with a false date of 1600, bore Shakespeare's name upon the title page.

The multiple ancestry of Shakespeare's chronicle history included an old play of Tarlton and, as J. Dover Wilson thought, the tradition of the morality play, with Falstaff as Vice; yet the various layers of satire, like the various levels of parody, forbid any limitation by genre. Hotspur parodies Glendower and the popinjay lord; Hal parodies Hotspur; and Falstaff parodies Hal as well as Hal's father. Pistol parodies the common players; when he is in full flood no one can stop Pistol, and even Falstaff has to play his game.

Prince Hal's condemnation of "the unyoked humor of your idleness" (*1 Henry IV,* I. ii. 184) would appeal to the young lawyers whose own taste for printing satire is surveyed by Alvin Kernan in *The Cankered Muse* (1959). From the combative habits of this group and of Ben Jonson, the personal challenges known as the War of the Theaters emerged.

A well-intentioned but clumsy portrait of Jonson in John Marston's *Histriomastix,* probably staged at the Christmas Revels of the Middle Temple in 1598, provoked a caricature of Marston in Jonson's *Every Man Out of His Humour,* staged by Shakespeare's company in 1599. The literary aspects of the quarrel have been recently given by Cyrus Hoy in an introduction to *Satiromastix* (Fredson Bowers, ed., 1980). Dekker became a second object of Jonson's satire, probably because he joined Marston in writing for the company of choristers who appeared at St. Paul's Cathedral in November 1599. Marston wrote two more comedies, plainly criticizing Jonson, who in turn left Shakespeare's group to give the second company of choristers, opening at Blackfriars in 1600, his own comical satires. In its initial stage the war between two poets developed into a war between two new theaters.

Pamphlet wars such as those between Gabriel Harvey and the playwrights Greene and Nash had been familiar; Marston had already fought a poet's war with John Hall. Jonson throughout his life battled for the cause of a rationally structured classic form for drama, for "art." Years later he said to Drummond of Hawthornden that Shakespeare wanted art. In 1599, Marston's turgid exuberance disgusted Jonson, while Jonson's claims for art were taken for grossly inflated self-promotion thinly disguised as general doctrine.

Since both parties were interested in the publicity of print, the literary war records survived. Shakespeare was not given to such self-display; his concern sprang from the then current aspects of theatrical competition, which provide a larger context, less easy to recover. Recent investigations into structure of the theaters, involving records of litigation between actors, theater managers, and financiers, have illuminated the underlying causes and the course of the War of the Theaters.

When the financier Philip Henslowe opened the Rose theater in 1587, on the South Bank of the Thames, it proved popular, perhaps because of the relatively easy access by water. Henslowe's records of his daily takings kept between 1592 and 1597 furnish the leading evidence for theatrical economics in this period. In 1595–1596 another financier resident in the area, Francis Langley, prepared to build another house within his manor of Paris Garden; and in 1596, Shakespeare moved from the vicinity of the Theatre to lodge within the liberty of the Clink, the manor of the bishop of Winchester, where the Rose had been built, and which was largely exempt from civic control. Here, churchwardens exercised some of the duties of magistrates; Henslowe was a churchwarden of St. Saviour's. In November 1596, Shakespeare and Langley became connected implicitly by a writ swearing the peace against both, together with two unknown women. The real antagonist in this move was a local justice named Gardiner, and Leslie Hotson linked the whole affair with *Henry IV* in his *Shakespeare Versus Shallow* (1931), suggesting that Gardiner had been the original of Shallow. Langley may have hoped to entice Shakespeare's company to his house; it was named the Swan, and a flying swan was the lord chamberlain's badge and therefore that of his company.

Shakespeare may have been reconnoitering for his company's move to the South Bank, which occured within three years, when they built the Globe east of the Rose. Henslowe, like an animal in an invaded territory, moved off to the northwest of the City, where in 1600 he built the Fortune. The opening of the choristers' theaters had meanwhile added to the competition; these so-called private houses were also built in liberties exempt from civic supervision. In the final stages of the war, Shakespeare's company and the choristers of St. Paul's separately gave Dekker's *Satiromastix,* directed against the boys at Blackfriars and Jonson. The most recent historian of the choristers thinks it "may have been a purely contrived situation, a seventeenth-century version of a modern publicity campaign to control taste" (Reavley Gair, *The Children of Paul's* [1982], p. 134).

Henslowe, Langley, and the syndicates who ran the choristers' theaters tried to lure fashionable writers as well as actors into their control. Langley obtained some of Henslowe's men, but in early August 1597, Ben Jonson and the actors Gabriel Spencer and Robert Shaw were arrested for participating in a production of *The Isle of Dogs* by Pembroke's Men at the Swan. On 15 August the Privy Council described this play as "lewd . . . containing very seditious and slanderous matter." The three men were set free on 3 October, but Langley's Swan fell out of dramatic competition, and he turned his attentions toward yet another house, the Boar's Head in Whitechapel, and a third troupe of men actors forming there.

The considerations governing these frequent changes of plan were the convenience of location for whatever type of audience was sought and the reputations that different locations had acquired for specific types of drama; and the acquisition, and if possible the monopoly, of the services of good actors and of good dramatists, whose names began to be more prominent attractions. The real war was a trade war.

It was within this frame of movement and expansion that the War of the Theaters came about. The Boar's Head catered to foreigners and sailors, and to popular demand; their resident playwright became Thomas Heywood, with plays of adventure or popular histories. Henslowe and Edward Alleyn also played popular theater, with rapid changes of bill, plenty of spectacle, and a readiness to copy their chief rivals, the players at the Globe; among their regular dramatists were Munday and Dekker.

When in *The Poetaster* (1601) Jonson directly satirized dramatists, he chose to yoke Dekker and Marston together—that is, the bottom and the top of the scale. Dekker's plays *The Shoemaker's Holiday, Old Fortunatus,* and *Patient Grissel,* unpretentious but not primitive, pleased at all levels. *Old Fortunatus,* with its epilogue honoring the queen, was given at court in 1599, while Jonson's *Cynthia's Revels* (1601), with its one just man being made arbiter and its sharp Palinode, was not found amusing.

There is no evidence that Jonson was attacking Shakespeare; in the final Apology for *The Poetaster,* after defending himself against a charge of libel, Jonson writes:

> Now, for the players, it is true I taxed 'em,
> And yet, but some. . . .
> Only among them, I am sorry for
> Some better natures, by the rest so drawn,
> To run in that vile line.

Shakespeare was unique in his relation with the players of his company and, like any responsible member of a group, would accept a majority decision. He must have voted for *Satiromastix.*

The trilogy of Parnassus plays (1598–1602), at Robert Greene's college, St. John's, are in Greene's manner; the climax comes when two desperate, unemployed graduates reject the idea of working for these "glorious vagabonds," the play-

ers. The third Parnassus play is probably to be dated 1601; it shows Kempe and Burbage (both of whom acted in Jonson's plays) discussing a wit-combat, a familiar form at Cambridge. Kemp says, "Why here's our fellow Shakespeare, puts them all down: aye, and Ben Jonson, too. O that Ben Jonson is a pestilent fellow: he brought up Horace giving the poets a pill: but our fellow Shakespeare hath given him a purge that made him beray his credit." The "pill" is given in *The Poetaster;* as Kempe had left the company in 1599, the writer is not up to date on events in London. Shakespeare's one unequivocal reference to the conflicts of the theater, in the players' scenes in *Hamlet,* appears, like Jonson, to have targeted the clowns' theater, on the one hand, and the amateur satirists of the choristers' theater, on the other. The 1603 bad quarto of *Hamlet* objects to the clowns' monotonous catchphrases and limited range of jests, as well as to their ad-libbing. Since Kempe had forsaken the sharers at the Globe to join the group at the Boar's Head, this probably registers the company's resentment. Yet in the graveyard scene, the clown is permitted to hold his own against Prince Hamlet; this scene was to be closely imitated by the new clown who played it, Robert Armin, when years later, as I believe, he wrote *The Welsh Ambassador.*

When the good quarto of *Hamlet* appeared in 1604, the arrival of the players did not include any reference to the choirboys' theater. When this appeared finally in the First Folio, it was nineteen years out of date. Yet the bad quarto contains a brief reference about the principal public audience being turned to private plays and to "the humours of children." The suppression must have been for the printing only of the 1604 version, and the phrase "the humours of children" suggests that it could have been originally directed more against Jonson. The debate in *Hamlet,* as it stands between three witty young men, opens with the prince's sardonic questions, in reply to which the well-informed Rosencrantz tells Hamlet that "there was, for a while, no money bid for argument unless the poet and the player went to cuffs in the question" (II. ii. 347–349). The cooler Guildenstern adds, "O, there has been much throwing about of brains!" Hamlet's pointed inquiries are directed not to the dramatists but to the children who were being so exploited. In a ruthlessly financial reduction of the whole affair, the prince loftily brushes it aside, no doubt in the tone with which the court had dealt with *Cynthia's Revels.* "The tragedians of the city" could be shown driven out from the theater they had acquired, but only in the most successful production the company had ever mounted— and only after, in April 1600, they had been given permission to play at the Globe, which the boys are jestingly described as removing.

The outcome of the debate was a general increase in playhouses, and a great increase in the self-consious artistry of all the companies. Before long both sides were mocking the unsophisticated playgoer: Dekker in *The Gull's Hornbook* chided the young sprigs of gentry; Beaumont in *The Knight of the Burning Pestle* took aim at the citizens' taste for Shakespeare; and Webster in the Induction to Marston's *Malcontent* mocked the would-be judges. Jonson's impulse to define, to theorize or "anatomize," had set a fashion. Shakespeare refrained from putting forward any countertheory; instead, he sat down and wrote *Hamlet,* the most influential and original drama of the Renaissance, after which nothing could ever be the same again. And if Ben Jonson wrote the surviving "additions" to *The Spanish Tragedy*—he was paid for such work by Henslowe—he was himself deeply affected, perhaps in ways he did not recognize. On either side of *Hamlet,* two graceful and penetrating comedies displayed courtly manners in a positive way, with just enough acidity to give them bite. *As You Like It* and *Twelfth Night* proved Shakespeare still the Johannes Factotum of ten years earlier. To claim, however, that he drew a personal caricature of Jonson, either in Jaques in *As You Like It* or in Ajax in *Troilus and Cressida,* would be to attach too much significance to the rhetoric of the anonymous Cambridge author of the Parnassus plays.

Hamlet was rooted in the earlier revenge drama and specifically in Kyd's lost companion piece to *The Spanish Tragedy,* and its influence permeated the men's and choristers' theaters. A mourning Hamlet, renamed Hippolito by Dekker, appeared in Part 1 of *The Honest Whore* (1604) at the Fortune. The Boar's Head troupe may have taken *Hamlet* abroad, for *Der bestrafte Brudermord,* a degenerate version of *Hamlet* surviving in Germany, must derive from an early version, to judge by its dumb shows. Marston's *Antonio's Revenge,* for the choristers, cannot be dated with accuracy, but it incorporates Jonson's satiric humor with a more indefinite but powerful influence from Shakespeare. *The Revenger's Tragedy,* performed by Shakespeare's own company, is the kind of play that might have been written by Hamlet in one of his

black moments. Henslowe's concession to fashion, whether in Chettle's *The Tragedy of Hoffman* or the anonymous *Lust's Dominion,* includes some parody.

Chapman, Jonson, and Marston's *Eastward Ho!* (1605) at Blackfriars has the preposterous Gertrude, daughter of Touchstone, accompanied by a lackey named Hamlet, so that when she calls for her coach he can be admonished, "Sfoot, Hamlet, are you mad?" She sings a parody of Ophelia's dirge, ending it, "God be at your labor!" At the end of the decade, *Hamlet* was still being shadowed in Beaumont and Fletcher's *Philaster,* in the hero of the anonymous *Second Maiden's Tragedy* (both given by the King's Men), and in Heywood's Orestes in *The Iron Age* (1612–1613). Chapman wrote his anti–revenge play *The Revenge of Bussy D'Ambois* (1610) for the choristers. As late as 1630, in *The Fatal Contract,* William Heminge, son of Shakespeare's editor, shows a wicked queen rebuked by her son; in one scene "O, my prophetic soul!" occurs three times and "Hold, hold, my heart!" four times. D. J. McGinn has assembled over four hundred echoes of *Hamlet* in plays before 1642.

Shakespeare's work had become part of the common stock of any playwright or actor; but it had not been without stress that he had transmitted the best of older drama, including his own, and focused and shaped it to feed the new theater. G. K. Hunter has observed in "The Heroism of Hamlet" that the play represents an enormous and convulsive effort to move forward to the heroism of the individual without abandoning the older social and religious framework of external action. It appears that Shakespeare continued to reshape his drama, as Goethe was to reshape his *Faust;* it has become part of European mythology, especially in Germany and Russia. *Hamlet* has been refashioned by modern dramatists such as Tom Stoppard and Samuel Beckett, and it is the basis of a chapter of Joyce's *Ulysses.*

It was after the accession of James that Jonson's impulse to correct Shakespeare began to appear. Jonson more than once quoted (or, rather, misquoted) a line that he imputed to Julius Caesar: "Caesar did never wrong but with just cause." He parodied Mark Antony's "O judgment, thou art fled to brutish beasts," which he must have heard in the theater, since *Julius Caesar* was not printed before 1623. It may be that Shakespeare's invasion of Roman history seemed to Jonson improper, but if so, he himself soon set to work on *Sejanus,* to show how tragedy should be written in the high

Roman fashion. Shakespeare's company again generously put it on in 1603 only to be hissed off the stage. Jonson's chagrin would have been compounded by the great success of Shakespeare's *Julius Caesar.*

Shakespeare is listed by Jonson as acting in *Sejanus.* Jonson says he had a collaborator, whose part he rewrote. Chapman is often suggested, but he had no connection with the King's Men, and it would seem more likely that their own playwright helped. Jonson was well known for his backstage tantrums, and even made capital of them in the Induction to *Bartholomew Fair:* "He has, sir-reverence, kicked me three or four times about the Tiring-house, I thank him, for but offering to put in, with my experience," exclaims the Stage-Keeper. Someone was needed to stand between Jonson and the practical needs of the company; since, as a sharer, Shakespeare would have had to survey the script, the stage version would have had to meet his requirements.

However, Ben Jonson had publication as his true object. He had published his satiric comedies with additional pieces, although the Apology for *The Poetaster* did not appear until later editions, since it was "restrained" by the authorities. In 1605, Jonson published *Sejanus.* He provided a dedication (another claim for the high seriousness of his text), and he also provided a full list of sources—the best and most scholarly, not a mere gossipy Plutarch. He gave references to the original editions used; there are 318 marginal notes. Commendatory poems were provided by Chapman, Marston, and others. Jonson was cited before the Privy Council on the subject of this play, and he altered a line or two for his folio version. The dedication to Esmé Stuart, afterward duke of Lennox, the cousin and close friend of James I, was perhaps a proud political vindication: Jonson lived on Stuart's bounty for five years. But the publication of *Sejanus* and the four comedies initiated a change in the status of the text: it was no longer collaborative, it was supported by extra material. Indeed, *Sejanus* acquired a literary reputation among younger playwrights; Webster copied the Address to the Reader in his own piece prefixed to *The White Devil* (published 1612), which, like *Sejanus,* had failed on the boards. Yet the influence of *Hamlet* and *King Lear* is more obvious in Webster than the quotations from *Sejanus.*

The outcome and sequel to the War of the Theaters was to establish Shakespeare and Jonson as the two models for younger men. Jonson was consciously cited; he gave prestige and dignity to the claimants of poetic independence. Shakespeare's instinctive and pervasive influence was inescapable for anyone actually working with production in mind. Ben Jonson, Machiavellian in his visions of power and Marlovian in his blend of aspiring grandeur and deflating irony, was to Shakespeare's later years what Marlowe had been years before. He provided the stimulus to which Shakespeare could react.

The stress of these years is shown by the group of Shakespearean dramatic works isolated in the present century as "the problem plays." *All's Well That Ends Well,* a hybrid form, shows the effect of "deeds and language such as men do use" (Jonson's phrase) upon a traditional story: the exposure of Parolles is Jonsonian in tone. In *Measure for Measure,* an old play is condensed and reshaped in a darkly satirical form. *Troilus and Cressida,* an ambiguous work that came into its own only in the middle of the twentieth century, a play designed in the first case most probably for the Inns of Court, is built upon large public debates. The armed prologue inevitably suggests Jonson, while the strange, laboring vocabulary suggests Chapman; it stands in sharpest contrast to the mastery of *Julius Caesar.*

The first decade of King James's reign also saw the emergence of several new forms that Shakespeare did not adopt. He never tried a City comedy. He never wrote, or was never asked for, a court masque. The Italian form of tragicomedy, created by Giambattista Guarini in the 1580s, was taken up by Shakespeare's company when in 1604 they put on Marston's *Malcontent,* already in print and dedicated as a "bitter comedy" to Ben Jonson. The impulse to question and invert, to combine incompatibles, arose in the newly self-conscious public and private stages; actors parodied one another's styles or presented in multiple plots "a wilderness of mirrors," to use T. S. Eliot's apt image.

Dramatists still imitated earlier plays. For example, in *The Family of Love* (1602), the young Middleton inserted chunks from *Romeo and Juliet.* The quarrel scene of *Julius Caesar* was widely copied. Philip Massinger was especially given to imitations of *Othello. Coriolanus* offered a popular model of the plain soldier trapped by politicians. The magpies picked up famous lines: Heywood misquotes the dying Cleopatra's "There is no earth in me, I am all fire!" in his *Rape of Lucrece* and Othello's "I kissed thee ere I killed thee" in *The Golden Age.* It may have been Shakespeare's reversion to Roman tragedy in *Antony and Cleopatra* and *Coriolanus* that moved Jonson to his second, disastrously unsuccessful tragedy, *Catiline* (1611).

The deeper engagement of Jonson and Shakespeare in these later years came with the interplay of the court masque and Shakespeare's final romances. Like the problem plays, the subgenre of Shakespeare's last plays has been popular in recent decades. In the 1930s, these plays were interpreted in terms of anthropology, such as the myth and ritual of rebirth. Latterly, they have been linked with the Neoplatonism of Ficino and the Rosicrucians by Frances A. Yates, and tied in to court ceremonial by Glynne Wickham. Stephen Orgel has stressed the distinctive form of the Stuart masque. Earlier attempts to relate the romances to Fletcher's tragicomedy have fallen into disuse, but links with some of the romances of Shakespeare's youth have been detected by modern editors—for example, by J. M. Nosworthy in his New Arden edition of *Cymbeline.*

After 1604, Jonson secured a monopoly in the Christmas and Shrovetide court masques. His views were set out in printed texts, notably in *Hymenaei* (1606), with notes directed to the education of the Prince of Wales. The dynastic wedding of two children, the earl of Essex and Lady Frances Howard, arranged by James was used to reflect the union of the crowns of England and Scotland (the king did not succeed in unifying the two governments). The visionary sublimity of the masque, the epiphany of divine powers in royal forms, conferred a true sacramental grace; Jonson claimed that his verses gave it "soul." The royal masquers did not themselves speak, and when later players were introduced to give an antimasque, their parts, by contrast, were grotesque. In *The Masque of Queens* (1609) the King's Men appeared as witches. In this enchanted realm, Shakespeare, to contrast with the royal masquers, would find himself cast as the equivalent of his own Caliban or Trinculo.

Shakespeare's reaction was to assume the napless vesture of humility by concealing his art in the revival of simple, archaic forms. For *Pericles* (which may date from 1606) he revived ancient Gower. Northrop Frye termed it "the first opera," and C. L. Barber linked its transformations with those of the masque. It was lastingly successful, being given at court as an entertainment for the French ambassador in 1619 and chosen by the master of the revels for his benefit performance in 1631. Two years before, Ben Jonson, now old, sick, and out of

favor, had in the angry *Ode to Himself* termed it a "mouldy tale" that kept up "the Play Club." The artful artlessness of this "poetry of the gaps" builds up to the recognition scene, an epiphany that remains dazzling today. The editors did not include *Pericles* in the First Folio, which may imply a collaborator, but like its Shakespearean successors, while recalling earlier models, *Pericles* influenced younger dramatists: in 1624, Heywood borrowed extensively from it in *The Captives.*

Cymbeline, as well as *Hamlet,* is reflected in Fletcher's *Philaster* (ca. 1609)—though some would put Fletcher's play first. *The Winter's Tale* was based on a tale by Shakespeare's long-dead rival Greene, and perhaps his cony-catching pamphlets gave something to Autolycus. The revival of Hermione could be paralleled with both court masques and popular plays like *The Trial of Chivalry* (1605). A final problem play witnessed to the stress behind the achievement; *Timon of Athens* (1606–1608) was slipped into the First Folio at the last moment. It is masquelike in its cosmic implications, yet the humors of the City sharks are Jonsonian. In this play, the Poet and Painter discuss their arts, the Poet defining his work as spontaneous and self-generated. The broken and startling juxtapositions of this "show" witness to some convulsion that brought savagery into the masque form, and that blended old interludes and games from the Inns of Court revels. A grotesque, anonymous *Comedy of Timon* also survives, like an attendant Fool upon a battered King Lear.

Each of these last plays sets its own style. *The Tempest,* proudly placed at the head of the First Folio, was presented at the royal wedding festivities in February 1613. It challenges Jonson in its observance of the classic unities, and its brief span includes three masques. Jonson was to lump it with its predecessors when he made the Stage-keeper of *Bartholomew Fair* apologize in his Induction, "If there be never a servant-monster in the Fair; who can help it? he [that is, the author] says? nor a nest of antics? He is loath to make Nature afraid in his plays, like those that beget Tales, Tempests, and such like drolleries, to mix his head with other men's heels." This implies knowledge of a text not yet in print and introduces a play offered not to the king but to Shakespeare's old rivals and Jonson's first employer, Henslowe, for the new playhouse, the Hope on Bankside. The banter sounds good-natured. Jonson, who had given the King's Men both *Volpone* and *The Alchemist,* his greatest plays, was about to retire from the stage for a decade, after which he would return with a more Shakespearean brand of comedy. In 1616 he put the ancient English poets Chaucer, Gower, Lydgate, and Spenser into his masque *The Golden Age Restored,* and the supposedly primitive native poets gained a new esteem. At the end of his life, Jonson was to develop a nostalgia for Elizabethan romantic comedy, as Anne Barton shows.

Shakespeare, as he was no man's disciple, was no man's enemy. Prospero may represent a significant variation upon Jonson's wise and judging commentators, though he is more than that. *The Tempest* invokes two of the works that sustained Shakespeare's poetry, Arthur Golding's translation of Ovid and John Florio's translation of Montaigne's essays. Cranmer, a less obvious mentor, emerges from humility in *Henry VIII,* also presented for the season of the wedding of Princess Elizabeth, namesake of the great queen who appears as an infant in the final scene. The prophecy of Queen Elizabeth's greatness is given to a man whose writings had influenced Shakespeare throughout his life—Thomas Cranmer, compiler of the *Book of Common Prayer.* Yet the heavenly masque is presented to the dying Spanish Catholic Katharine. Some critics would assign a share in the composition of this play, at once archaic and celebratory, to John Fletcher. But Heminge and Condell printed the play as Shakespeare's when Fletcher had become their leading dramatist. The Fletcherian cadence here and there may represent no more than a favorite cadence for the King's Men. The effect of Fletcher upon the last plays may be compared with that of Lyly in earlier days; he supplied a fashionable accent for Shakespeare's retentive ear.

The Two Noble Kinsmen and the lost *Cardenio* were true collaborations. The return to Chaucer in the first may have been Shakespeare's choice as a vehicle for the masque of country people, from Beaumont's wedding masque. In *The Winter's Tale,* a dance from Jonson's *Masque of Oberon* (1611) had been incorporated.

Shakespeare, Jonson, and Fletcher were constantly compared, for these three alone attained the distinction of having collected works published in folio. Fletcher, like his fellows, borrowed from Shakespeare: *The Women's Prize* (1611) supplied a sequel to *The Taming of the Shrew;* comparison with the Roman plays was invited in *The False One* (1620); in 1622 both *The Prophetess* and *The Sea Voyage* recalled *The Tempest.* To Dryden, Fletcher was "a limb of Shakespeare."

Heminge and Condell, in their address "to the great variety of readers" (1616), praise Shakespeare's "easiness," which suggests that he would react to opposition not by antagonism but by transformation. Marlowe and Jonson were not only the greatest dramatists he met, but intellectually provocative and personally hot-tempered men as well. Both had stood trial for murder. It would appear that Shakespeare achieved the rare distinction of keeping out of London jails entirely.

Kyd, Lyly, and Fletcher stimulated him, and he regained lively feelings for the simple dramas of his youth, reshaping them in his later years. His fellow players collaborated in his art in ways yet to be explored. Although stimulating discussions in great households, in the fellowship of the lawyers, in the clubs at the Mermaid or the Devil Tavern had much to give, Shakespeare's club consisted primarily of his fellow actors. These were the friends he remembered in his last will.

BIBLIOGRAPHY

Peter Alexander, *Shakespeare's Life and Art* (1939). Anne Barton, *Ben Jonson, Dramatist* (1984). G. E. Bentley, *The Profession of Dramatist in Shakespeare's Time, 1590–1642* (1971). M. C. Bradbrook, "Shakespeare's Debt to Marlowe" and "Thomas Heywood, Shakespeare's Shadow," in *Collected Papers,* III (1983). David L. Frost, *The School of Shakespeare* (1968). Alfred Harbage, *Shakespeare and the Rival Traditions* (1952). E. A. J. Honigmann, *Shakespeare's Impact on His Contemporaries* (1982). G. K. Hunter, "Shakespeare's Reading," in K. Muir and S. Schoenbaum, eds., *A New Companion to Shakespeare Studies* (1971); "Lyly and Shakespeare," in *John Lyly* (1962); and "The Heroism of Hamlet," in *Dramatic Identities and Cultural Tradition* (1978). D. J. McGinn, *Shakespeare's Influence on the Drama of His Age Studied in "Hamlet"* (1938). D. M. McKeithan, *The Debt to Shakespeare in the Beaumont-and-Fletcher Plays* (1938). Kenneth Muir, *Shakespeare as Collaborator* (1960). Gary Taylor and Michael Warren, eds., *The Division of the Kingdoms: Shakespeare's Two Versions of "King Lear"* (1983). Peter Ure, "Shakespeare and the Drama of His Time," in *A New Companion to Shakespeare Studies* (see above). F. P. Wilson, *Marlowe and the Early Shakespeare* (1953). J. Dover Wilson, *The Fortunes of Falstaff* (1953).

Shakespeare's Language

MARVIN SPEVACK

Reading Shakespeare is, among other pleasures, an exercise in historical linguistics. It may not immediately seem so, because Shakespeare is normally known in modern packaging, the typographical appearance of his plays and poems resembling that of modern printed works. But even in its original form Shakespeare's text, despite the erratic spelling and odd punctuation, is in the main recognizable and graspable. Shakespeare wrote early modern English at the end of the sixteenth century, by which time most of the grammatical changes from Old and Middle English had taken place, such as the loss of inflections in nouns and adjectives. Changes in pronunciation were still in progress, although the main shift—the long vowels pronounced with a greater elevation of the tongue and closing of the mouth—is presumed to have been almost concluded. One interesting result was that the gap increased between English spelling—left behind, as it were, by phonological change—and English pronunciation. Another was that English spelling was overrun by semantic developments, among them a luxurious growth in vocabulary and an escalating pressure on the existing vocabulary, reflected most obviously in the burgeoning homography, polysemy, and other indications of the increased number of meanings a given orthographic unit might carry. But pronunciation aside, even a cursory glance at Shakespeare illustrates most of the similarities or differences between his English and ours.

But which sample is to be regarded as typical of Shakespeare, who wrote or had a hand in thirty-eight plays, two long narrative poems, a lengthy sonnet sequence, and a few shorter poems over a period of some twenty-five years, roughly from 1588 to 1613? Shakespeare's language was a response to both personal and professional pressures—to changes in his own psyche as well as to changes in literary modes and theatrical conditions—over the course of those twenty-five years. That is why it is possible to talk of early, middle, and late Shakespeare in terms that are not merely chronological, just as it is possible to talk of Shakespeare the poet or Shakespeare the man of the theater. Just as obviously, Shakespeare's language was the instrument of the genres and subgenres he was engaged in: drama (comedy, history, tragedy) and poetry (dramatic, narrative, lyric).

Further complicating Shakespeare's language was the influence of his association not merely with the theater but with his own theater and company. Since Shakespeare wrote plays for performance by that company, with individual actors in mind, for presentation in a particular theater, or for a special audience and for a specific occasion, it is not surprising that the plays should be as they are because they were so conceived and produced. And since Shakespeare evidently paid little heed to the printing of his plays, the printing house was more than a little involved in establishing texts of Shakespeare's works. If we assume that what we call Shakespearean was indeed by Shakespeare, then many of the puzzling aspects of the text, such as the varying styles of punctuation, can be solved only by a study of printing-house conditions, an identification of the compositors, and a reconstruction of the history of the transmission of the text—and for each work individually. Indeed, the major contribution to Shakespearean studies in this century may lie in the efforts to understand the stages through which a text passed from author to viewing public and then to reading public. Although most of what is revealed concerns such accidentals as spelling and punctuation variants or very circumscribed word substitutions that may derive from the style of a particular compositor or printing house, or from the requirements of a commemorative volume such as the First Folio (not to mention a supervisory agency such as the Master of the Revels), the task of determining the authority of a text—the decision as to which version is to be the basis of any modern edition—is based on an assessment of what the linguistic corpus of Shakespeare should contain and is, simultaneously, a fixing of that corpus.

The fact that each play, having its own history, must be approached individually tends to fragmentize Shakespeare. Given all the factors involved in the reading of Shakespeare, generalizations about the writer and his language are statistically precarious. Either the sample is too small or the assertion is made vague by a quasi-quantifier such as *generally* or *commonly.* A reading may be too myopic, a charge sometimes leveled against the New Criticism, or too hyperopic, a charge sometimes leveled against deconstructionism.

Finally, to the widening gyre of concerns involved in the reading of Shakespeare must be added the extremely dynamic state of the English language in the time of Shakespeare. However much Shakespeare contributed to its enrichment, English itself was almost explosively unrestrained. It was undergoing a surge that remains unsurpassed. Shakespeare's was the period of the most rapid growth in vocabulary in the recorded history of the language. English had about 44,000 words by 1623; fully 10,767 are recorded as having made their first appearance between 1580 and 1623 (Finkenstaedt et al.). The causes were many and so simultaneously reinforcing that it is difficult to say which were dominant. Among those most often mentioned are the abundance of talented writers in many fields, the high regard Elizabethans had for writing (and especially for writing in English), the increasing number and importance of printing houses, and the emergence of a modern society and of a middle class in need of education. If language

is like an endless ocean, constantly moving on and under the surface, if English at the time of Shakespeare was particularly fluid, then any attempt to read Shakespeare must take into account all the factors contributing to what may appear to have been a period of instability, if not incorrigibility. (Grammars existed in Shakespeare's time, as did spelling manuals and pronunciation guides, but these popular works uttered caveats, not injunctions.)

To read Shakespeare and Elizabethan English is to be introduced to the true nature of historical linguistics. If understanding Shakespeare is the goal, a coming to terms with change is essential. The modern reader must exercise knowledge and imagination to bridge the centuries and to gain access to Elizabethan nuances of intent and affect, realizing all the while that an analysis of Shakespeare or any writer is at best a series of crude snapshots of a swiftly moving object. It is no simple matter for readers four hundred years later to grasp and describe the language of a poet and dramatist of such remarkable talent as Shakespeare's, particularly when he was writing over a period of a quarter of a century, in a linguistic (not to mention personal, political, and sociological) context of remarkable vitality.

One reassuring thing about reading Shakespeare is that his work all seems to fall into place, to be settled, the achievement of a disciplined, controlling master. One of the most striking attributes of Shakespeare's genius is his ready employment of the natural agitation of language, his ceaseless utilization of its plasticity. He reflects not the chaos of a powerfully emerging early modern English but the opportunities that are inherent in it. As Albert C. Baugh has remarked, "This was in keeping with the spirit of his age. It was in language, as in many other respects, an age with the characteristics of youth—vigor, a willingness to venture, and a disposition to attempt the untried. The spirit that animated Hawkins, and Drake, and Raleigh was not foreign to the language of their time." Early modern English presented options to a degree perhaps unparalleled since. Options—which poets thrive on —constitute the constant that can best be cited in discussing Shakespeare's language. These options are to be found in varying degrees in the main types of linguistic organization—orthography, phonology, lexicology (including semantics), and grammar (including morphology and syntax).

The fundamental premise in dealing with Shakespeare's language is that whatever is, is right.

Acceptance of this premise, which includes Shakespeare's personal linguistic habits and even his idiosyncrasies (but excludes his obvious errors owing to carelessness), throws the burden of explanation on the reader. He must try to find out what Shakespeare's language is, why it is, and what it reflects. The effort is not as difficult as it may seem, for numerous differences between early modern English and modern English are obvious and self-evident. Furthermore, they have been assembled in the existing grammars of Shakespeare, such as E. A. Abbott's *Shakespearian Grammar,* whose rationale is explicit in the subtitle, *An Attempt to Illustrate Some of the Differences Between Elizabethan and Modern English.* To a certain extent, a scholastic enumeration of differences is superfluous, for they are apparent to any modern reader in command of current English grammar. That reader accepts Elizabethan usage as normal for that time and as different from usage today, but he must avoid the larger temptation to believe that if some of the differences are deleted, with some of the fossils replaced by modern forms, then early modern English will become modern English. What has been only partially attempted by modern grammars, however, is an investigation of the larger patterns that govern individual instances. An understanding of Shakespeare involves a wider perspective, which alone can counter the doubts about accepting whatever is as right. The particularities and alternatives are best known and understood when assembled and systematized. Thus practiced, the doctrine of accepting whatever is as right is in reality both analysis and synthesis.

Orthography

Elizabethan orthography, which is not immediately apparent in modern editions, is of more direct interest to the scholar than to the reader. Still, its consequences for a modern audience are considerable. Although there were admonitions from pedants, prelates, and princes, Elizabethan spelling was in the main not prescriptive. There was an interplay of standardization and individuation. On the one hand, as D. G. Scragg observes, "The period 1550–1650 saw the universal acceptance by printers of the stable spelling system that with very few modifications is in use today." Moreover, the pedagogical and social pressures promoting the growth of general literacy were conformistic and irresistible, as evidenced everywhere, from the plethora of manuals, dictionaries, and the like (*"gathered for the benefit & helpe of Ladies, Gentlewomen, or any other unskilfull persons,"* according to the title page of Robert Cawdrey's *Table Alphabeticall* of 1604) to the newly founded Royal Society's claim to "have exacted from all their members, a close, naked, natural way of speaking; positive expressions; clear senses; a native easiness: bringing all things as near the Mathematical plainness, as they can: and preferring the language of Artizans, Countrymen, and Merchants, before that, of Wits, or Scholars" (Sprat).

On the other hand, there were two major conflicting systems of reform. One, advocated by John Hart and Sir Thomas Smith, favored phonemic spelling: "to use as many letters in our writing, as we doe voyces or breathes in speaking, and no more." The other, advocated by Richard Mulcaster, rejected those who "appeall to *sound,* as the onelie soveran," favoring traditional forms, with an acceptance of etymological spelling. Edmund Coote's first attempt at an English dictionary ("wished for" by Mulcaster) is even organized along etymological lines: "al written with the Romain . . . taken from the Latine or other learned languages, these with the Italike letter . . . French words made English: those with the English letter . . . meerely English, or from some other vulgar tongue." Printing houses developed individual house styles, their preferences governed by practice rather than by pedagogical considerations. Until the process of standardization was completed, there was no full agreement as to what constituted standard usage; it was often conventional and occasional, not necessarily rational and predictable. Alfred W. Pollard was led to conclude, "The tragedy of Tudor spelling is not that it had no system, but that it had a bewildering number of rival systems."

There have been attempts to justify rhetorically the "extraordinary copiousness of presentation of one and the same word": M. H. Spielmann has fashioned a "rule of enrichment of orthography by variety" that he likens to the contribution of synonymity to the "richness of a language." And there were the great and influential figures to whom spelling was not simply an irregular or idiosyncratic tic, like Shakespeare's so-called old-fashioned forms, but a deeply rooted personal mode of expression—as much a reflection of a *Weltanschauung* as the "constant Resolution" of the Royal Society "to reject all the amplifications, digressions, and swellings of style: to return back to the primitive purity, and shortness, when men deliver'd so many *things,* almost in an equal number of *words"* (Sprat). John Milton was splendid in his spelling and was certainly not in isolation.

The free-enterprise mixture of liberties and restraints may seem chaotic, but its richness makes it all the more a treasure trove of information for linguistic scholars. The existence of personal and professional spelling styles has nurtured the study of orthography in the service of author identification, one notable example being the controversial efforts to identify Shakespeare's hand in certain quartos on the basis of what J. Dover Wilson (1923) considers "abnormal" spellings presumably used by him (as Hand D) in three pages of the play *Sir Thomas More.* Individual spelling practices have also been used as a key to compositor identification on the basis of personal habits and practical pressures. Spelling has been used in the determination of copy-text, the dating and transmission of texts, and the dependence of editions. In its relationship to book production and the book trade, Elizabethan spelling has even contributed to a larger discussion of the interaction of medium and message in the hermeneutical process, as well as to the general subject of graphostylistics. For linguists, orthography has long been a major source of information about pronunciation. The orthoepists of Shakespeare's time and after, no matter how pedantic, were not interested simply in correct spelling. Even more important, as the title page of Hart's *Orthographie* makes explicit, they were in search of *"the due* order and reason, howe to *write or paint thimage of mannes voice, most like to the life or nature."* The modern-spelling edition of Shakespeare presents perforce a different "voice," except perhaps for the few remnants to be found in rhymes that no longer rhyme except to the eye (forms like *prove/ love, mind/wind, sound/wound*), in puns, or in the various contractions and expansions due in the main to the requirements of the meter, of dialect, or of such extralinguistic pressures as line justification.

However conjectural the nature and application of orthographical evidence, there is no mistaking the playfulness of Shakespeare's spelling. If we omit deliberate wordplay and the ambiguity inherent in such forms as were at that time interchangeable orthographically (like *human/humane* or *travel/travail*), we are left with charming little scenes or insets. Though no schoolroom scenes appear in Shakespeare's plays, there are "lessons" given by schoolmasters to those ignorant of the "right writing of our English tung." Holofernes is an advo-

cate of etymological spelling: "I abhor such fanatical phantasimes, such insociable and point-devise companions; such rackers of orthography as to speak 'dout' fine when he should say 'doubt'; 'det' when he should pronounce 'debt'—d, e, b, t, not d, e, t. . . . This is abhominable, which he would call 'abominable' " (*Love's Labor's Lost,* V. i. 17–24). Here Shakespeare mocks the false etymology of *abominable,* as does Mercutio, another deflater, in his comic reference to Romeo "without his roe, like a dried herring" (*Romeo and Juliet,* II. iv. 37). But the poet is in turn indirectly mocked by the fact that the phenomenon is by no means infrequent in standard English spelling. Ironically, every instance of *abominable* and its derivatives in the Shakespeare corpus is spelled with *b* according to Holofernes' directions. It seems natural for Juliet's nurse to represent the reforms advocated by Hart and Smith, as in her orthoepic assertion that R is "the dog's name" (*Romeo and Juliet,* II. iv. 197). Also involved in Shakespearean word play are the foreign-language speeches, such as Katherine and Alice's Franglais *nailès* and *fingres* (*Henry V,* III. iv), as well as dialect, be it of the London streets, the English countryside, or the British realm. Indeed, word games in Shakespeare, in both serious and comic contexts, are often constructed as spelling lessons that enact and comment on the diverse theories and practices of the time.

Punctuation

Elizabethan punctuation appears even more individualistic, if not anarchistic, than Elizabethan spelling. Here, too, were advice, authority, and admonition; here, too, were indifference, irreverence, and irascibility, which can be attributed either to the absence of binding rules or to their confusing number. The Elizabethans were active, if not enthusiastic, punctuators. Authors' manuscripts, especially those intended for private circulation, were sparingly punctuated, which is understandable, given the relatively casual manner and circumstances of their production. They were nevertheless punctuated, and when they were reproduced, they were repunctuated without hesitation. Not all scholars today are convinced that there is enough evidence offered by Hand D's part in *Sir Thomas More* to prove Shakespeare's identity, much less his system of punctuation. But it cannot be doubted that the punctuation of the quartos printed in Shakespeare's lifetime differs from that of the copy upon which they were based; and in any event, the quartos differ in punctuation style. The punctuation in the First Folio differs from that of the quartos and, within the Folio, from play to play. The editors of the Second Folio (1632) made major alterations in punctuation and spelling. The editors of the Third (1663–1664) and Fourth (1685) Folios went further, introducing new errors in their attempts to adapt the text to the requirements of their times.

The eighteenth century imposed its own standards. Pope's high-handedness in rewriting Shakespeare and Dr. Johnson's all-powerfulness with regard to the punctuation were not merely manifestations of their own considerable egos: they were reactions to earlier punctuation systems held to have little worth. Edward Capell, the most important campaigner for the restoration of the "true text" of Shakespeare, avowed in his introduction to the *Comedies, Histories, and Tragedies* (1767–1768), "It becomes an editor's duty, (instead of being influenc'd by such a punctuation, or even casting his eyes upon it) to attend closely to the meaning of what is before him, and to new-point it accordingly." This was substantially the maxim of all editors of Shakespeare until the twentieth century. Despite their awareness of the "very different principles from those that guide the punctuation of this day," the editors of the monumental Cambridge edition of Shakespeare (1863–1866) decided in favor of a punctuation that is "very little dependent upon the Folios and Quartos, but generally follows the practice which has taken possession of the text of Shakespeare, under the arrangement of the best editors." In 1926, Hilary Jenkinson summed up the situation thus: "What we have to examine is a period in which there is practically no general standard of punctuation . . . and in which individuals may or may not have standards of their own."

The twentieth century has not been content to accept this view uncritically. It has shifted the emphasis from a passive acceptance of the lack of a system, with a concurrent application of the cumulative best punctuation, to an active attempt to explain sixteenth- and seventeenth-century systems of punctuation. This impulse led the earliest of the New Bibliographers to conclude that Shakespeare was not only an "old-fashioned" or "abnormal" speller but also an almost negligible punctuator. Whether or not this kind of assertion can be proven, the fact is that the study of punctuation has been applied broadly in author identification and intensively in Shakespeare studies to compositor identification. Compositors have been identified

and printing-house conventions described. As a consequence, the question of Shakespeare's punctuation has become somewhat academic, for Elizabethan punctuation, from this standpoint, "represents, in its entirety, although some of the stops may be the author's, the printer's interpretation of the text" (Howard). Although this view may not be totally acceptable, the implications for bibliographical theory and editorial policy are dramatic and have been used to justify every possible shading in the pointing of the text of Shakespeare. The editorial tradition of the twentieth century has largely succeeded in disencrusting the punctuation (as well as the emendations) that had either accumulated over the years (as was the case with the Cambridge edition) or that reflected standard English practice at the time a given edition appeared (as was the case with the Oxford edition of 1891, which "thoroughly revised" the punctuation to accord with "the recognized orthography of the present day").

Most modern editions, aimed at students and at a generally literate public, are obliged to follow modern rules of punctuation. In doing so, they are reflecting—consciously or not—a theoretical position regarding Shakespearean (and, by extension, Elizabethan) punctuation, a position that regards the punctuation as grammatical and logical, especially at the sentence level. As Vivian Salmon has stated, "Semantic punctuation was mandatory, though the exact choice of stop was largely subjective; structural punctuation . . . within the sentence was not obligatory, though desirable" ("Early Seventeenth-Century Punctuation"). The use of the colon in *Antony and Cleopatra* affords an excellent illustration. Of the 563 colons in the First Folio edition of the play—an astonishingly large number by modern standards—all but two have a logical-grammatical justification. At the other end of the spectrum is the view expounded by Percy Simpson: "Modern punctuation is uniform; the old punctuation was quite the reverse. . . . A flexible system of punctuation enabled [the poet] to express subtle differences of tone." J. Dover Wilson, writing in 1921, followed this up: "This punctuation is dramatic, that is to say it is a question of pause, emphasis and intonation; and is quite independent of syntax." Wilson anticipated the critical fashion of the 1980s: "The old texts were prompt-copy, more akin to operatic score than to modern literary drama. This explains the ungrammatical punctuation. . . . The stops, brackets, capital letters in the Folio and Quartos are in fact stage-directions, in shorthand. They tell the actor when to pause and for how long, they guide his intonation, they indicate the emphatic word, often enough they denote 'stage-business.'" The connection of punctuation with elocution, propounded by A. E. Thiselton and Simpson, has its roots in an earlier system outlined by Walter J. Ong, who observes, "The fact that man has to breathe had been a primary consideration at a time when all discourse . . . was conceived of as a thing spoken rather than written."

In point of fact, an exact division between the logical-grammatical and the rhetorical-dramatic is difficult to discern, as is shown in the by no means untypical description by Mulcaster of his system of punctuation:

Cõma, is a small crooked point, which in writing followeth som small branch of the sentence, & in reading warneth us to rest there, and to help our breth a litle, as *Who so shall spare the rod, shall spill the childe.* Colon is noted by two round points one above another, which in writing followeth som full branch, or half the sentence, as *Tho the daie be long: yet at the last commeth evensong.* Period is a small round point, which in writing followeth a perfit sentence, and in reading warneth us to rest there, and to help our breth at full, as *The fear of God is the beginning of wisdom.* Parenthesis is expressed by two half circles, which in writing enclose som perfit branch, as not mere impertinent, so not fullie concident to the sentence, which it breaketh, and in reading warneth us, that the words inclosed by them, ar to be pronounced with a lower & quikker voice, then the words either before or after them, as *Bycause we ar not able to withstand the might of temtation (such is the frailtie of our natur) therefor we praie God, that our infirmitie be not put to the hasard of that triall.* Interogation is expressed by two points one above another, wherof the upper is somtimes croked which both in writing & reading teacheth us, that a question is asked there, where it is set, as *Who taught the popiniaye to speak? the bellie:* These five characts, that I have allredie named, ar helps to our breathing, & the distinct utterance of our speche, not ruling within the word, as al those do which follow, but by the word, & therefor com here in note, bycause theie ar creatures to the pen, & distinctions to pronoŭce by, & therfor, as theie ar to be set down with iudgement in writing, so theie ar to be used with diligence in the right framing of the tẽder childes mouth.

There is obvious overlapping of function among the punctuation marks in Mulcaster's system. In practically all instances, the outer limits of application are recognizable, as is the particular application of the punctuation marks within the passage, so long as their contemporary definition is borne in mind. A comma as full stop, for example, was not the exception then that it is now. What is beyond debate, especially considering the attention given to compositorial and scribal practice, is that there were different styles and that they could appear, as in the First Folio, often within the same work.

The newest editions of Shakespeare adopt a flexible stance: they must punctuate "correctly," according to modern practice, but they also tend to respond sensitively to the pointing found in the copy-texts of the individual plays. The result may be something of a pastiche if all the plays of Shakespeare are taken together, but there is a discernible overall effort toward lighter pointing. The rigorous imposition of quarto or folio pointing on an otherwise modernized text—as practiced by G. B. Harrison in his Penguin Shakespeare (1937–1959) and M. R. Ridley in his Arden *Antony and Cleopatra* (1954)—has produced more confusion than conviction. Instead, the main tendency has been to translate, as it were, the original pointing to something valid today and yet indicative of what may have been originally intended. In this respect, bibliographical theory and editorial practice have mellowed since the early days of the New Bibliography. The inconclusiveness of only partial evidence has been recognized; extremities are no longer acceptable. Simpson's note on decorum in the use of capitals for emphasis, and "hence the implied courtesy in their use with proper names," is as questionable today as Spielmann's thesis that variations in spelling—he cites, among others, six ways of spelling the names of Herrick and five of Ben Jonson— were "due to the deliberate ingenuity of diversification and love of innovation . . . not so much the idiosyncracy of one man, but the custom of most of the printing-offices of the day."

In Shakespeare studies, punctuation has until now proved more revealing in connection with the printing house and the transmission of the text than with the reconstruction of Shakespeare's own system. Lamentably so, for it is the mortar of the text. Interpretation may be possible without it, as it has been despite it, but there is little doubt that once all the syntactic patterns are assembled, they will reveal the main options for punctuation. The study of punctuation has been largely fragmentary: we know of Ralph Crane's use of the parenthesis (Howard-Hill) and of the apostrophe with the genitive singular in the period (Brosnahan), but we have no modern systematically detailed study of the major punctuation marks in the Shakespeare corpus. Until we do, we will have to do with clues, of which there are bewilderingly many. Shakespeare himself was aware of the difficulties of the situation:

> *Theseus.* This fellow doth not stand upon points.
> *Lysander.* He hath rid his prologue like a rough colt; he knows not the stop. A good moral, my lord: it is not enough to speak, but to speak true.
> *Hippolyta.* Indeed he hath played on this prologue like a child on a recorder—a sound, but not in government.
> *Theseus.* His speech was like a tangled chain; nothing impaired, but all disordered.
>
> (*A Midsummer Night's Dream,* V. i. 118–125)

Phonology

Parallel to the study of orthography—and to a certain extent of punctuation—is phonology. It can be argued that orthography and phonology are indivisible in English; our alphabetic writing system employs symbols that attempt to reflect, in the main, the particular sounds of the language. "Orthographie," as defined by John Hart in the opening sentence of his epistle "To the doubtfull of the *English Orthographie,*" "is a Greeke woorde signifying true writing, which is when it is framed with reasõ to make us certayne wyth what letters every member of our speach ought to bee written." Despite some striking distortions, spelling and speech do mirror each other in English. And where speech has to be reconstructed, spelling is naturally the major source of information. This is especially true for Elizabethan and Shakespearean pronunciation, for, although the language as a whole was so dynamic that even a few years could make a considerable difference, its very dynamism tended to make it accessible in sections. Linguists could, with certain reservations, assign labels like "early" modern English (ca. 1500–1700) and "later" modern English (since 1700) based on theoretical constructs like the Great Vowel Shift. And they have done so, although aware that, as with the movement of glaciers, the fixing of dates is somewhat arbitrary. In this respect, too, Shakespeare, himself dynamic, appears in the midst of the dynamic movement and is difficult to pinpoint phonologically.

For the modern reader using a modernized text, phonological differences or patterns are not easily perceived, nor do they have immediate significance. With the exception of some "unusual" rhymes (such as *love/prove* and *sound/wound*) and allied homophonic puns (*dollar/dolour, coat/quote),* or an occasional difference of stress usually determinable from the meter (*Milan* stressed on the first syllable, *revenue* on the second), or the frequent stretching and compressing of syllables, also according to the requirements of the meter or the compositor (*-tion* as bisyllabic, *the* contracted with the initial vowel of the following word), Shakespearean English is easily read as if it were modern English. There are, however, pitfalls: *board* and *bawd,* for example, constitute neither a Shakespearean rhyme nor a pun, though they would seem to do so according to current British English pronunciation.

The Elizabethan interest in language was alive not only in its poets, politicians, and philosophers but in its pedants. As a means of self-assertion and self-improvement, of personal and social consequence, the mastery of language was a prime topic. R. C. Alston's *Bibliography of the English Language from the Invention of Printing to the Year 1800* is an impressive testament to the activity and devotion with which language was addressed. A number of the works Alston lists are characterized and commented upon by E. J. Dobson, the first volume of whose authoritative *English Pronunciation 1500–1700* is entitled *Survey of the Sources.* In one way or another, the sources were all concerned with the interaction of pronunciation and spelling. As Mulcaster puts it, "The matter of speche is a thing well thought of, whether ye waie the words and the forces which theie have, or the uttering thereof by p̃ & voyce." "Pen & voyce" was the province of these orthoepists. Their methods and achievements were uneven and limited, to be sure. Their attempts to construct an adequate system of phonetic description were crude, although not without moments of ingenuity. But the difficulties in tracing an emerging standard pronunciation must be borne in mind. Shakespeare may have employed bits of his Warwickshire dialect, but his words were spoken by actors from various regions on the stage in London. It is thus to the great credit of the orthoepists that they provided the main data we have: theoretical frameworks; specific descriptions of vowels, diphthongs, and consonants; lists of homophones and rhymes; letters and syllables. This information, rough and inconsistent though it may be, does help to circumscribe the possibilities for a reconstruction of the pronunciation of a language no longer spoken. In one way or another, such information has been used in this century by those phonologists whose work focuses on Shakespeare or his time, including Wilhelm Viëtor, R. E. Zachrisson, Helge Kökeritz, Dobson, and most recently Fausto Cercignani.

Viëtor bases his work mainly on "one of the internal sources . . . rime"; the second part of his book is a "rime-index" offered by the poems, serving as a "pronouncing vocabulary." Zachrisson, although avowing his "distrust in the sound-analysis of the early English orthoepists and [his] confidence in the importance of the testimony of occasional spellings," nevertheless chooses to base his phonetic description mainly on his modifications of the amended system of orthography of William Bullokar, external evidence that he felt came nearest to standard English pronunciation in the time of Shakespeare. Kökeritz uses both internal and external evidence, giving somewhat more weight to the former: "The First Folio of 1623 and all the Quarto texts, good and bad, preceding the Folio have been excerpted for rhymes, phonetic spellings, homonymic puns, and various metrical indications of contraction and elision. . . . They have been compared with the testimony of 16th- and 17th-century orthoepists and with occasional spellings in private documents from the same period." Dobson, aiming at a critical revision of earlier discussions, favors the data of the orthoepists, whose "evidence, though often discrepant, does not seem to be truly conflicting—it merely illustrates the variety of contemporary pronunciation." He is critical of the use of puns, preferring rhyme. And he attempts to give due attention to the fact that "the explanation of early Modern English pronunciation often depends on Middle English developments." Cercignani, strongly reacting against Kökeritz's overemphasis of questionable internal evidence and his conclusion that "Shakespeare's pronunciation strongly resembled modern English," applies the methodology of Dobson to the corpus of Shakespeare, with special attention to the development of early modern English from Middle English. The result is a new pronouncing vocabulary of Shakespeare.

About the pronunciation of the consonants at about the year 1600, there is relatively widespread agreement among phonologists. Notwithstanding normal fluctuation and variation, regional and personal, the consonants were by and large sounded as they are today. Some exceptions may be attributed to the fact that Kökeritz posits pronunciations of certain consonants that the others view as coming into general standard usage later in the seventeenth century. Shades of agreement and difference exist between individual phonologists. For example, there is lack of clarity about when the final cluster [-ŋg] was simplified to [-ŋ]. And there is some fuzziness about such statements as "/r/ could occur in pre-consonantal and final position" (Barber) and it "may still have been weakly sounded" (Kökeritz), whereas Cercignani is certain that the "loss . . . had not yet occurred." Kökeritz's conclusions apart, and the impossibility of a narrow phonetic description for an exact time or place accepted, the consonants present relatively few problems. The same supply, with much the same values, existed in Shakespeare's day as in Middle English and in modern English (Gimson).

The vowels and diphthongs are quite another story. If the consonants are approximated in today's English, the vowels and diphthongs are at best approximations of approximations—a situation that is not unusual. Even today phonetic descriptions are only approximate: in *wide* and *night,* for example, the diphthong is normally rendered with the same phonetic symbol [ai], although a narrower description would certainly be desirable. The following broad description, based on the work of Gimson, represents more or less the present consensus of conjectural opinion on the conservative pronunciation of vowels and diphthongs at about the year 1600. (An overview of the development of these sounds to the present day may be derived from the words whose italics indicate a change in pronunciation today.)

Although the exact pronunciation of Shakespeare's words remains elusive and may appear to be of interest only to scholars, the fact is that the very evidence used by both the older orthoepists and modern phonologists is intimately connected with the modern reader's immediate understanding and appreciation of Shakespeare, for to an even greater extent than its correlates spelling and punctuation, phonology illuminates those perspectives that have most occupied twentieth-century criticism. Externally, as has been seen, phonology contributes, in its attention to the relationship between spelling and sounding—between "pen & voyce"—to the recognition of compositorial and scribal habits and conventions, to author identification, and to the establishment and transmission of the text. And it merits consideration in the ongoing discussion of the proper procedure for modernizing older works. The spoken Shakespeare is of particular interest to those occupied with Shakespeare as a man of the theater. Internally, a century of close analysis

Vowels

[i:] seem, be
[ɪ] wit, give
[e:] *fear, beard*
[ɛ:] *pale, break*
[ɛ] *set, bed*
[æ] path (Brit. *path*), back
[u:] whose, move
[ʊ] wolf, pull
[o:] *over, ghost*
[ʏ] *world, murder*
[ɑ:] *walk, cause*
[ɑ] not, offer
[ə] unaccented (or weak), as the first syllable of *about* and the second of *over*

Diphthongs

[əi] *mine, like*
[əu] *house, now*
[iu] or [ju] *new, due*
[eu] *dew, shrew*
[ou] *grow, old*
[ɔi] joy, boy
[ui] *point, boil*
[ɛi] *day, they*

—from New Criticism to deconstructionism—has been posited on the belief that poetry is a voice, a mouth, an instrument of speech. Whether the voice is that of the author or the reader, the vocabulary of analysis is often the vocabulary of phonology and phonetics, however loosely used or disguised. Discussions of meter, rhyme, stress, pitch, contraction, and elision—indeed, of the patterns of speech in general—reflect the dynamics of phonology. The identification of visual and aural puns depends on a recognizable system of spelling and pronunciation. These are not merely literary, scholarly, or background concerns, for together they provide data for the most difficult area of the reconstruction of Shakespeare's language—that type of linguistic variety often called register.

Dialect characters are useful to phonologists for information about pronunciation, and even for considerations beyond the dialect itself. The spellings associated with a character like Mrs. Quickly are seen by Cercignani and Kökeritz as evidence for the presence or absence of a particular phoneme. Cercignani points to Mrs. Quickly's *tashan (tertian)* as evidence that in early modern English the pronunciation was [s] not [sj]; Kökeritz uses it as a clue that "her normal pronunciation of *er* was doubtless *ar*, i.e., [a:] . . . with loss of its preconsonantal *r.*" Register, however, is not an interest in the pronun-

ciation of particular phonemes but a defining of the discourse according to its psycholinguistic and sociolinguistic organization. Dialect is easy enough to spot; unfortunately, there is relatively little of it in Shakespeare. The same is true of foreign languages, like the French in *Henry V.* There is a deep dilemma in attempting to evaluate phonetic data when it is acknowledged that the actor was an English-speaker of unidentifiable dialect speaking French words to an audience of largely non-French-speakers (Shakespeare very often incorporates an English translation into the dialogue, in the manner of a school lesson) and not unusually with a slightly ironic attitude toward that foreign language. This is even more the case with dialect characters whose language is strongly parodied. But pronunciation and spelling and even punctuation are nevertheless important guides to the level of discourse being dramatized, and thus to the shape and intent of dramatic characterization and interaction. Dialect and foreign-language speakers appear in Shakespeare's plays, always as minor characters. Bits of Shakespeare's own Warwickshire dialect or deliberate archaisms in vocabulary or grammar are heard, albeit only rarely. Shakespeare's "old-fashioned" spelling is worthy of study, too, less for the identification of Shakespeare himself than as a clue to the pronunciation and consequently the register of the speaking characters.

Vocabulary

Shakespeare's vocabulary has received more attention than any other feature of his language. This is natural, since it is the most accessible and in some ways the least complicated feature. It seems easiest to deal with, bolstered as it is by abundant collateral information—contemporary spelling and pronunciation guides arranged alphabetically, as well as dictionaries and glossaries—that has been shaped and given a larger frame by the great *Oxford English Dictionary (OED).* In vocabulary studies, literary and linguistic interests—synchronic, diachronic, and achronic—overlap considerably. They are further reinforced by obvious and numerous utterances in Shakespeare's works on the nature and power of words; on their use and abuse; on the fascination evident in the frequent pausing over single words; and on the repeating, turning, examining, and commenting on their sound, construction, nature, implications, and potential.

Until recently, there was no precise information about the size, scope, and nature of Shakespeare's vocabulary. The lack was not merely of primitive tools like word-frequency and reverse-word indexes; there was not even a complete list of Shakespeare's words and their occurrences. Bartlett's *Concordance* provided most of the words, but not all, and only about one-third of the occurrences; Alfred Hart's vocabulary studies offered certain statistics but only rarely the words. These guides were known to be incomplete or inaccurate but it was impossible to say just how incomplete or inaccurate they were. Educated guesses or even statistical extrapolations put the total of different words anywhere from fifteen thousand to twenty-five thousand. Even Otto Jespersen's reconciliatory twenty thousand—which attempted to reduce the margin of error from catastrophic to only drastic proportions—did not overlook the fact that the estimates were often made without any indication of, and certainly without any agreement on, how they were arrived at or indeed how *word* was defined. The treatment of vocabulary has been quite limited. Works on Shakespeare's language have been, on the whole, literary in orientation. We learned all there was to know about "multitudinous seas incarnadine" without knowing very much about Shakespeare's Romance vocabulary. We learned all about *fool* or *nothing* in Shakespeare without knowing very much about nouns in Shakespeare (Abbott omits nouns entirely). We learned all about the complexity and ambiguity of Shakespeare's words but without a definitive grammar either of Shakespeare (despite the excellence of Franz) or of early modern English and without a definitive dictionary either of Shakespeare (despite the impressiveness of Schmidt) or of early modern English. Literary critics and linguists alike detailed Shakespeare's "delight in words" and his "mastery of language," his "boldness" and his "felicity," his "directness" and his "flexibility." There was consensus that "he had an instinct for the heart or centre of language" (Willcock) yet no agreement on the exact size, scope, and nature of his vocabulary.

It is now possible to place Shakespeare's vocabulary within the context of the English of his time (and within the context of modern English) and at least to trace the distributional contours of the two corpora. According to ongoing research, there are 20,138 lemmata in Shakespeare—44.87 percent of the total recorded for English up to the year 1623. (A lemma, to oversimplify somewhat, is the head-

word in a dictionary.) Roughly the same percentage (46.34 percent) is arrived at for the number of lemmata in Shakespeare first dated between 1580 and 1613 (there are 4,239) if set against the same group for English as a whole (there are 9,147). If we compare the length (in letters) of the lemmata, we find almost total overlapping. There is no difference at all of more than 2 percent; only lemmata consisting of four, five, seven, eight, and nine letters differ more than 1 percent. Similarly, the distribution of lemmata according to the initial letter reveals a striking similarity: none differs more than 2 percent; only *A, C, I, U,* and *W* differ more than 1 percent.

Distribution according to part of speech may also seem suggestive. Nouns account for 42.98 percent of the lemmata in the Shakespeare corpus, as contrasted with 55.70 percent in English to 1623; verbs in Shakespeare account for 21.86 percent as against 19.70 percent in English. The distribution according to etymologies is likewise intriguing. Of the main etymological sources, the two corpora contain practically identical percentages of lemmata of French (including Old French) origin; the Shakespeare corpus has 4.5 percent more lemmata of Germanic origin, but English to 1623 has twice as many words of Latin origin. There must be important and characterizing differences of vocabulary between Shakespeare and the English of his time. And they can obviously be best understood in relation to each other, certainly not in isolation.

Understanding Shakespeare's vocabulary involves first and foremost a precise semantic focus. In the main, interpreters of Shakespeare, although they freely acknowledge the semantic changes that occurred within the twenty-five years of Shakespeare's career and, even more, between his time and ours, have in practice tended to deal with "interesting" words only (a parallel to the attention paid to neologisms and other manifestations of the unusual). The approach would seem to have been diachronic: the orientation of Onions' *Shakespeare Glossary* is much the same as Abbott's. Semantics has been understood as word semantics only and has come to be practiced as defining, or glossing, words in terms of synonyms and paraphrase. Underlying this semantic attempt has been a belief in synonymy. Leaving aside the fact that synonymy is by no means a universally accepted notion, this method suffers from several deficiencies. One is that the defining words tend to be modern words.

Consequently, one set of semantic conditions is superimposed upon another.

Another deficiency of synonymy is that the semantic confusion increases as the attempt is made to define more precisely by giving not one but several synonyms, loosely arranged or often without a full consideration of the implications of such concerns as polysemy and hyponymy, or stylistic and affective meaning—as, for example, in an innocent explanation of *brawl* as "to wrangle, to squabble . . . perhaps simply to contend, to strive, quarrel." A particularly pernicious expansion of synonymy is paraphrase, in which sense and sensibility are often sacrificed to blague and banality. "I told him of myself" (*Antony and Cleopatra,* II. ii. 78) is rendered by Joseph Rann as "I intimated to him the state I was in at our former interview."

For a sense of Shakespeare's language it is useful to consult works of his period, such as Robert Cawdrey's *A Table Alphabeticall* (1604), John Bullokar's *An English Expositor* (1616), and Henry Cockeram's *The English Dictionarie* (1623). These "hardword" dictionaries are very derivative: Cawdry's so-called first dictionary, for example, appropriated the table already published in Coote's *English Schoole-Maister* (1596). They are also very inaccurate: Cawdrey even has trouble with the alphabetical order of the entries; and his omission of the letters *K, W, X,* and *Y* is rectified by Bullokar. The definitions in these dictionaries are in the main primitive synonyms, but they are works of Shakespeare's time and they provide an immediate Elizabethan context. Their selection of hard words, although not adequately explained, is in itself an important assortment of qualitative as well as quantitative information.

Together, lemmata and defining words provide not merely a core vocabulary but also a differentiated one. Cockeram, in fact, went so far as to include a kind of reverse dictionary: "The first Booke hath the choisest words themselves now in use. . . . The second Booke contains the vulgar words, which whensoever any desirous of a more curious explanation by a more refined and elegant speech shall looke into, he shall there receive the exact and ample word to expresse the same." Etymology, not always accurately practiced despite the parading pedantry, adds a further dimension. In his second edition (1626), Cockeram even labels twenty-five entries—he seems to have gotten only as far as the letter *I*—that he considers "now out of use, and only used of som ancient Writers." And

the synonyms themselves, crude as they are, are most valuable in being often close to the etymon: they may not yet have undergone the kind of semantic shift that causes difficulties for modern readers. Thus, among numerous examples from Coote (followed by Cawdrey): *casualitie* is defined as "chaunce," *decent* as "comlie," *edition* as "putting forth," *idiot* as "unlearned," *mortifie* as "kill," *sinister* as "unhappie," *translate* as "turne." For all their shortcomings, these works serve the essential purpose of rendering the "feel" of the Elizabethan vocabulary, of highlighting the phenomenon of semantic change, and of everywhere reminding the modern reader that he is dealing with a vocabulary not entirely his.

Although there is no substitute for a restrained and sensible use of dictionaries old and new, it is nevertheless possible to isolate certain areas of the Shakespearean vocabulary and, by introducing some new data, to offer suggestions for dealing with the vocabulary systematically. To begin with, the most difficult words are not the rare or structurally complicated ones per se, for they tend to stand out as lexical forms, and in their further development either drop out of usage very quickly or remain semantically more or less frozen. Nor are the heavy-duty words of the main word classes particularly problematic. The lemmata in the Shakespeare corpus for which the *Shorter Oxford English Dictionary (SOED)* records, say, forty or more meanings to this day—*set* (ninety-five meanings), *strike* (seventy-one), *take* (sixty-one), *run* (fifty-eight), *draw* (fifty-seven), *go* (fifty-six), *make* (fifty-five), *pass* (forty-seven), *turn* (forty-six), *serve* (forty-six), *will* (forty-four), *draught* (forty-three), *stand* (forty-three), *point* (forty-two), *stock* (forty-one)—cause little or no trouble. They are all obvious refinements of the basic meaning and are immediately apparent in context. The main problem is a failure to recognize polysemy, the various meanings of one lemma, especially (but not only) when one instance is no longer current, as *fact* ("thing done," and "thing known") or *atone* ("at one" and "make amends"). Or there may be a failure to recognize homography, two distinct lemmata, identically spelled but with different etymologies and meanings, as in *clip* ("to cut" and "to grip") or *let* ("to allow" and "to hinder"). This matter of word semantics may be illustrated in glossaries, function words, and affixation, for example.

A comparison of the glossaries of four one-volume editions (addressed to much the same audience of students) that have appeared over the past fifty years—Kittredge (1936), Alexander (1951), Evans (1974), Bevington (1980)—reveals that they have in common only ninety-three lemmata. This handy "basic" glossary of Shakespeare, on which there is essential semantic agreement, consists of the following:

addition	pack (be off)
advice	pack (conspire)
affect (*v*)	pain (*n*)
affection	passion (*n*)
atone	passion (*v*)
bate (abate)	practice (*n*)
bate (flutter)	practice (*v*)
character (*n*)	pregnant (fertile)
character (*v*)	pregnant (cogent)
clip (embrace)	present (*adj*)
cog	prevent
color (*n*)	proof (*n*)
complexion	purchase (*v*)
conceit (*n*)	quaint
cousin	quality
curious	quick
curst	quit (*v*)
discover	rank (*adj*)
ecstasy	rate (estimate)
engine	remorse
entertain (*v*)	resolve (*v*)
fact	respect (*n*)
fame (*n*)	respect (*v*)
fantasy	round (*adj*)
favor (*n*)	roundly
fine (*n*)	rub (*n*)
flaw (gust)	sad
flaw (fragment)	sensible
flesh (*v*)	several
habit	shrewd
head (*n*)	spleen
humor (*n*)	state (*n*)
inform	still
instance	stomach (*n*)
learn	success
let (hinder)	suggest
liberal	suggestion
list (boundary)	take
list (desire)	tall
list (catalogue)	train (*v*)
mean (*n*)	unkind
mere	use (*n*)
modern	virtue
modest	watch (*v*)
motion	weed (garment)
nice	wink (*v*)
owe	

One conclusion that might be drawn from the fact that the list is so short is that the overall selection is personal, a matter of individual judgment; a second might be that there are in reality few words that really need special attention.

The words themselves suggest further conclusions. Fifteen of them—*affect, complexion, fact, fame, habit, inform, modern, modest, nice, passion, pregnant, remorse, resolve, sensible, spleen*—are already in Cawdrey's hard-word dictionary in more or less the same sense. Others that appear in Cawdrey and that have undergone a semantic shift do not appear in all these glossaries: for example, *demerite* ("deserving, worthines"), *patheticall* ("vehement, full of passions, or moving affections"), *reduce* ("to bring back againe"). Of the fifteen words in common only one, *pregnant,* is a homograph in Cawdrey (he gives only one lemma but both senses, "wittie, substantiall, with child"). The remaining homographs —*bate, clip, flaw, let, list, owe (=own), pack, rate, weed* —are few and would seem to be listed because of an apparent alternative in interpretation, as in Hamlet's "I'll make a ghost of him that lets me" (*Hamlet,* I. iv. 85), or more often simply to alert the reader to the existence of the homograph even though a semantic alternative is unlikely, as in "weeds of Athens he doth wear" (*A Midsummer Night's Dream,* II. ii. 71). This latter impulse connects with the majority of words, which would seem to be listed because of polysemy, some special sense within the semantic range of a word. All the words (in more or less the senses glossed) appear in recorded English before 1550—except *atone* (1555), *modest* (1565), *rub* (1586), *character* as a verb (1591), *list* ("catalogue," 1602)—from which we may conclude that there does not seem to be anything inherently special about them. Further, the etymological distribution—sixty-six are Romance words, twenty-four are Germanic, and three are of unknown or unclear etymology—runs roughly parallel to that of the Shakespeare corpus, again suggesting that there is apparently nothing unusual about them. What may be genuinely striking, however, is the fact that all are classified by the *SOED* as *"common* to literature and everyday speech" except *pregnant* ("cogent"), which is labeled "obsolete." The conclusion cannot be that the Shakespearean vocabulary is simple. On the other hand, in context it is not as difficult as it may seem to be. If so, despite the brevity of the list, there is too much glossing. It may, in fact, be sufficient to call attention to homographs where genuine alternatives are possible (including pairs that the Elizabethans themselves interchanged or had not yet disambiguated, like *band/bond, fly/flee, ingenious/ingenuous, metal/mettle, naught/nought, travel/travail*). For the great majority of instances, no assistance would seem to be necessary.

Although prepositions and conjunctions—two parts of speech that are usually listed among the so-called function words—are relatively few in number (there are some eighty English prepositions and some fifty conjunctions in Shakespeare), they account in frequency for a considerable part of the corpus. As in modern English, they do heavy duty semantically and grammatically. Since their form remains the same even though their function may change—*for* serves as both preposition and conjunction—they resemble homographs and are normally treated as separate lemmata. In Shakespeare, the orthographically identical forms serving both functions are *afore, after, against, before, but, ere, except, for, notwithstanding, or (=ere), since, sith, till, until, while,* and *without.* Since within a particular function they may be subjected to a broad range of semantic senses—*for* as preposition is defined by Onions as, among other things, "in place of," "because of," "in the character or quality of," "in spite of," "for fear of"—they resemble the meanings accorded to one and the same lemma and are so formulated not simply to indicate function or usage but mainly to fit the grammatical requirements of the unit being explained.

Another easily isolated group—prefixes and suffixes—presents a similar situation. For one thing, homography is to be found among the morphemes; for another, the respective allomorphs seem to offer a range of interpretive possibilities. On the whole, homography among prefixes presents few problems: the lemmata are so well known that the meaning is obvious despite the ambiguity of the spellings of the morphemes and allomorphs. It is not necessary to recognize that the *a-* in *avoid* is an allomorph of *ex-* or that the *a-* in *alike* is an allomorph of *y-* in order to understand the construction, although one form, *in-* (and corresponding allomorphs), representing semantic opposites in Shakespeare's time, is to be found in *illustrious, incontinent(ly), inhabit(able),* and *incorporate/incorporal.*

Homography among suffixes is greater but even less problematic, as is evident in the homographs at the morpheme level: *-er* (as in *follower, mariner*); *-ess* (as in *princess, largess*); *-ing* (as in *meeting, Fleming*);

-le (as in *girdle, dazzle, cattle*); *-ling* (as in *changeling, groveling*); *-ly* (as in *lovely, briefly*); *-or* (as in *author, error, mirror, priority*); *-th* (as in *growth, fourth*); *-y* (as in *bloody, victory, remedy, county, baby*). All are unambiguous in structure and semantics, although the grammatical function of *-ly* can be unusual or ambiguous (*kindly, unkindly, verily, wearily, wrongfully* as adjectives or adverbs).

Morphology

Recognizing homographs and pointing out ambiguities are essentially passive and cautionary activities, useful but limited. Since they imply options and involve semantics and may thus hint at features of Shakespeare's vitality and creativity, a discussion of some aspects of morphology, or word-formation (mainly affixation and conversion), is indispensable to an understanding of Shakespeare's language in itself and in the context of the developmental possibilities of English. As Quirk has said, "Rules of word-formation are . . . at the intersection of the historical and contemporary (synchronic) study of the language, providing a constant set of 'models' from which new words, ephemeral or permanent, are created from day to day. Yet on a larger scale, the rules themselves (like grammatical rules) undergo change: affixes and compounding processes can become productive or lose their productivity; can increase or decrease their range of meaning or grammatical applicability."

For the schoolmasters of Shakespeare's time, word-formation was a standard topic. Mulcaster devotes consecutive chapters to the themes of compounding and derivation; Coote suggests that for the proper spelling of *public* "the best help is derivation, for we write *publike* because we say *publication*, (for *(c)* and *(k)* here be both one)." From the beginning, linguistic commentators on Shakespeare's art were aware of the main processes of word-formation—affixation, conversion, and compounding. Lewis Theobald remarked in 1726 that "it is a Licence in our Poet, of his own Authority, to coin new *Verbs* both out of *Substantives* and *Adjectives;* and it is, as we may call it, one of the *Quidlibet audendi's* very familiar with him."

John Upton in 1746 noted that the "rules" of Shakespeare's grammar, "which savour of peculiarity," "are not difficult to be traced from a more accurate consideration of [his] writings." Among the rules that he describes—"because when these are known, we shall be less liable to give a loose to fancy, in indulging the licentious spirit of criticism"—are further types of conversion. Rule IV—"He uses one part of speech for another"—includes "verbs of adjectives," "verbs for substantives," "verbs of substantives," "substantives adjectively," and "adjectives adverbially." Richard Hurd, in his "Notes on the Art of Poetry" (1749), also mentions these forms of conversion as examples of Shakespeare's "artful management" of language, and adds examples of "composition"—"compound epithets," of which he lists five of "a thousand instances more in this poet"— and "compound verbs," by which he means derivational affixation (as opposed to the "zero affixation" of conversion), giving instances of the addition of the prefix *dis-* to the bases *candy* and *limn.* Morphological behavior is one of the main criteria for Alfred Hart's analyses of the vocabulary of *Edward III* and of *The Two Noble Kinsmen.*

Of prime importance is not *that* Shakespeare practices word-formation; it is *how* he practices it. Of interest is whether the processes of word-formation are normal or abnormal in their structure and distribution, productive or unproductive, grammatically and semantically pertinent or not pertinent. Even a brief examination of aspects of affixation and conversion as practiced by Shakespeare within the concentric contexts of the Elizabethan and English corpora may help sharpen the focus of critical comment. Affixes—suffixes and prefixes—are interesting for a number of reasons: the recognition and identification of a word class by its structure (by adding a suffix to the base, as in *sing→singer* or by adding a prefix, as in *witch→ bewitch*) with the consequent possibilities for exploiting the flexibility of grammatical rules to create "new" words; the semantics of the affixes themselves and the structures that result (evident in the formulas of dictionary definitions: *-er,* "a person who, a thing that"; *-ion,* "act, action, or state"); the semantic (and stylistic) alternatives in a particular selection of affixes that appear to have the same meaning and function *(-ful/-ous, un-/in-/dis-).*

It is fairly safe to say that Shakespeare invented no suffixes, that he used them according to the regular rules, and that those he used (more than seventy-five morphemes) are to one degree or another still current.

Concerning the semantics of certain suffixes, Neuhaus has shown that Shakespeare's usage of the *-ish* formation "is quite proportional to the general productivity of the system in the sixteenth century. There is no bias for more recent or for older formations." Yet of the four semantic subsystems, Shakespeare "favours . . . the system accepting common and proper nouns denoting humans or animals and transforming them into adjectives with a distinctive addition to their semantics. In all, there are 50 lemmata of this subsystem. . . . Examples are *childish, swinish, goatish, boyish."* And, of significance for those who tend to overstress the value of coinages per se, the cited study finds that the thirteen "new" instances credited to Shakespeare are less interesting than his "nearly total disregard for one semantic subsystem of adjectival derivatives," the one with the formulaic "more or less," represented in Shakespeare only by *bluish.*

Another area is that of alternative suffixes attached to the same base, as in the rather frequent pairs as *beautiful/beauteous, bountiful/bounteous, (un-)dutiful/(un-)duteous, (dis-)graceful/(dis-)gracious, joyful/joyous, pitiful/piteous, plentiful/plenteous, rightful/righteous, wonderful/wondrous* (and perhaps also in such doublets as *forgetful/oblivious, hateful/ odious*), *childish/childlike, dragonish/dragonlike, mannish/manlike/manly, slavish/slavelike, womanish/ womanly, brother-like/brotherly, clerklike/clerkly, courtlike/courtly, cowardlike/cowardly, godlike/godly, priestlike/priestly, princelike/princely, rascal-like/rascally,* and *unkinglike/kingly,* as well as in the less frequent but related pairs *revengeful/revengive, spleenful/ splenative, sportful/sportive* (perhaps also *vengeful/ wreakful/vindicative*), *faultful/faulty, healthful/ healthy, mightful/mighty* (perhaps also *lustful/lusty, easeful/easy), advantageable/advantageous, contemptible/contemptuous, treasonable/treasonous, incomprehensible/uncomprehensive, plausible/(un-)plausive, manful/manly, sprightful/sprightly,* and in such rarer pairs as *deceivable/deceitful* (perhaps also *delectable/ delightful*), *healthful/healthsome, quarrelous/quarrelsome, troublous/troublesome, crescive/crescent, loathsome/ loathly, penetrative/penetrating* (not in Shakespeare; first appearance in 1598), and so on along the chain. And whether or not there is a reason— semantic, grammatical, metrical, phonological, or other—for the alternation, the grammatical situation of the suffix must be considered. In Shakespearean usage *-able (-ible),* for example, may be used in both an active and a passive sense, as in "contemptible [=contemptuous] spirit" (*Much Ado About Nothing,* II. iii. 168) and "contemptible [=miserable] estate" (*1 Henry VI,* I. ii. 75), whereas in modern English it is normally passive only. The active and passive senses, albeit often difficult to distinguish, are also found in suffixes that are today normally active: *-ful, -ive, -less,* and *-ous.*

Prefixes are fewer than suffixes in Shakespeare: there are some fifty at the morpheme level. They are somewhat more difficult to deal with, especially since there are numerous forms and homographs at the allomorphic levels. As with the suffixes, Shakespeare makes use of practically all the prefixes available to him, even those that were losing ground: for example, *a-* (as in *a-hungry*), *y-* (as in *yclad*), and *for-* (as in *fordo*). And he uses them in the same functions and with much the same semantics as today. Since statistics about Elizabethan English are incomplete, there is little point in attempting a comparison with the distribution in Shakespeare. It is enough to acknowledge that, although some prefixes are difficult to recognize—like the allomorph *tres-* (of the morpheme *trans-*) in *trespass* or the allomorph *pur-* (of the morpheme *pro-*) in *pursue*—the words themselves are on the whole semantically obvious. A few prefixes have undergone some semantic change, like *be-,* frequent (some 166 constructions) and mainly neutral in Shakespeare, but now "often . . . [with] pejorative or facetious overtones" (Quirk et al.). Others have undergone an expansion in usage, like *trans-,* used most often metaphorically in Shakespeare with Latin and neo-Latin verbs *(transgress, translate)* but now also applied to adjectives *(transatlantic, transcontinental).*

One example may serve to illustrate the ambiguities of form and semantics, the matter of alternatives, and, to an extent, the Shakespearean stylistic preferences or peculiarities: the cluster of negative prefixes *un-/in-/dis-.* First, the problem of homography must be clarified. The negative prefix *un-* (as in *untrue*) must be separated from the reversative or privative homograph (as in *unhorse*), the former seven times more frequent than the latter; the negative prefix *in-* (as in *intolerable*) must be separated from the homograph (as in *intend*); the negative prefix *dis-* (as in *displease*) must be separated from the reversative or privative homograph (as in *disrobe, discolor*). Second, certain morpheme homographs must be disambiguated from allomorphs: the allomorph *de-* (of the morpheme *dis-*), as in *deflower,* must be isolated from the homographic morpheme prefix with a different semantic or syntactic function (as in *descend, despoil*). Third, some forms are so complex semantically that they remain ambiguous. This is especially true for *un-* in the negative and reversative or privative functions, as in *untied* ("not tied," "loosened"), *unarmed, unmanned.*

In Shakespeare negative *un-* is mainly combined with adjectives and participles. Only in a few instances is it prefixed to a noun *(unrest, unthrift, untruth)* or an adverb *(unaware, unawares, unearth, unwares). In-* is normally added to adjectives only, although it is untypically used with a participle in *indigested, indistinguished, invised.* Where a noun is formed—as, for example, *infamy, iniquity,* and *insurrection*—a Romance or Latin formation is to be assumed, a situation that also holds for nouns about which it is difficult to say with certainty whether they are derived from *in-* and a noun or *in-* and an adjective, as in *impatience, imperfection,* and *incertainty* (to use examples showing the typical suffixation). *Dis-* is attached in the main to adjectives and verbs, but also—unlike modern English, which forms abstract nouns—with concrete nouns, as in *disbranch, disburden, discandy, disedge,* and *dishorn.*

The grammatical functions have semantic implications and also provide hints as to features of Shakespeare's style: they may be inferred from the fact that there are alternatives of various constellations of the prefixes *un-, in-, dis-.* Thus it is interesting to note that *dis-* and *un-* in the reversative or privative sense are attached in Shakespeare to the same bases: *arm, burden, candy, case, cover, furnish, heart(en), mask, root.* It is also important to note that *dis-* and *un-* are not roughly synonymous when attached, as they are in Shakespeare, to the same bases, as well as to *claim(ed), fame(d), joint(ed), possess(ed), possess(ing), taste(d),* and *value(d);* they are, however, in *quiet, quietly,* and perhaps in *gracious, please(d), pleas(ing),* and *proportion(ed). Dis-* and *in-* in the reversative or privative sense coexist only in the bases *piteous* and *temperance.* The coexistence of *un-* and *in-* in the negative sense, however, is widespread. They are attached in Shakespeare to *capable, certain, certainty, charitable(y), civil, constant, curable, dispose(d), distinguishable, distinguished, dividable, fallible, firm, fortunate, grateful, hospitable, justice, noble, partial, perfect, possible, proper, provident, reconcile(d), removable, satiate, separable, substantial, vulnerable,* and perhaps coexist also in the pairs *incomprehensible/uncomprehensive, indubitate/undoubted, inequality/unequal, innumerable/unnumbered, inhabitable/uninhabitable.*

The alternatives are spread over Shakespeare's career and may or may not be especially purposive.

Still, it is difficult to assume that they are simply interchangeable. One study has demonstrated, in fact, that "with just one word-class, adjectives, the absolute numbers of words attested in the 17th century show a general preference for negations with the *in-* prefix or one of its allomorphs. . . . In Shakespeare just the opposite is the case. Contemporary adjectives with *in-* prefixes found their way into the Shakespeare corpus in a quite proportional manner. But there are many more *un-* forms in Shakespeare. . . . In all, there are 35 forms from that period not even mentioned in the SOED" (Neuhaus). Obviously, a detailed analysis involving all instances of the pairing of roughly synonymous and, as the case may be, homographic prefixes and suffixes would help deal with a considerable part of the vocabulary, providing information about Shakespearean and Elizabethan morphology and the creative interplay of semantics and grammar.

The phenomenon of conversion is "the derivational process whereby an item is adapted or converted to a new word-class without the addition of an affix" (Quirk et al.). Despite the general caveats implicit in a discussion of conversion and in any attempt to establish the chronological precedence and direction of the conversion, an ongoing systematic study reveals that Shakespeare practiced the main forms of conversion, that he favored the most productive forms in English—that is, verb-to-noun and noun-to-verb conversion—and that he most preferred noun-to-verb conversions. If homograph pairs of nouns and verbs in Shakespeare (with at least one word class occurring for the first time between 1588 and 1623) are examined—there are some 230—about 67 percent of these pairs are verbs derived from nouns (that is, the noun is recorded before 1588, the verb between 1588 and 1623) and about 27 percent are nouns derived from verbs. (In about 6 percent of the cases both noun and verb are dated between 1588 and 1623.) It is tempting to draw conclusions. In Barber's admittedly inconclusive sample of the same conversions for early modern English, the ratio is quite different—noun formations outnumber verb formations by about five to four—but a preliminary systematic investigation of the phenomenon in English for the period 1588–1623 reveals a closer parallel to the situation in Shakespeare. Whether Shakespeare's practice reflects the normal pattern of English as a whole is also difficult to say, since comparative statistics are not yet available.

That conversions are so prominent despite the fact that the procedure is common, that they are so striking despite the fact that there are so few (when the entire corpus of more than twenty thousand lemmata is considered), is testimony to their vitality and power. Conversions may also provide another bit of statistical evidence that the individual instance carries more weight than the statistical sums. This is certainly true for the process of compounding, frequently celebrated but so complex as to almost defy generalization.

Taxonomy

A grouping or organizing of the vocabulary according to even a preliminary taxonomic system of words and things is one way to reveal how language expresses the objects and ideas that make up the total experience of an individual or society. A vocabulary as extensive as Shakespeare's is especially inviting. Studies of recurring or repeated words, images, clusters, and patterns make up a major portion of modern Shakespeare scholarship. These studies deal mainly with aspects of Shakespeare the dramatist and poet; only occasionally do they touch on Shakespeare the man, as in such classic examples as Spurgeon's book on the imagery and Armstrong's on the imagination.

The Shakespearean vocabulary is interesting both for what it contains and for what it does not contain. Leaving aside the important but too complicated question of frequency of occurrence, it is perhaps sufficient to deal with a few concrete nouns. There is a host of eye-catching groups. A family of expressions for the head comprises such words as *brain-pan, costard, crown, death's-head, head, mazard, noddle, noll, pash, pate, poll, scalp, sconce, skull,* and *top,* not to mention such metaphorical uses as *ass-head, blockhead, calf's-head, cittern-head, fool's-head, jolthead, loggerhead,* and *ox-head.* Head-coverings might include *beaver, biggin, blue-cap, bonnet, burgonet, cap, casque, chaplet, coif, copataine, corner-cap, coronet, coxcomb, crants, crest, crown, crownet, cucullus, diadem, fillet, frontlet, garland, hat, head-piece, helm, helmet, hood, kerchief, night-cap, periwig, sallet, sea-cap, ship-tire, statute-cap, tire, tire-valiant, turban, veil, wimple, wreath.* Among the substantives for *dog* in Shakespeare are *bandog, beagle, bitch, blood-hound, brach, canis, chien, cur, ditch-dog, dog, grey-hound, hound, lyam, mastiff, mongrel, night-dog, puppy, sheep-biter, shough, spaniel, tike, trundle-tail, watch-dog, water-rug, water-spaniel,* and *whelp.* Some dogs answer

Knowledge (1667). Caroline F. E. Spurgeon, *Shakespeare's Imagery and What It Tells Us* (1936). De Witt T. Starnes and Gertrude E. Noyes, *The English Dictionary from Cawdrey to Johnson, 1604–1755* (1946).

Lewis Theobald, *Shakespeare Restored* (1726; repr. 1971). A. E. Thiselton, *Some Textual Notes on "A Midsummer Night's Dream"* (1903). Mindele Treip, *Milton's Punctuation and Changing English Usage, 1582–1676* (1970). John Upton, *Critical Observations on Shakespeare* (1746; rev. ed., 1748). Wilhelm Viëtor, *A Shakespeare Phonology* (1906). Stanley Wells, *Modernizing Shakespeare's Spelling* (1979). G. D. Willcock, "Shakespeare and Elizabethan English," in Harley Granville-Barker and G. B. Harrison, eds., *A Companion to Shakespeare Studies* (1934). F. P. Wilson, *Shakespeare and the Diction of Common Life* (1941). J. Dover Wilson, "Bibliographical Links Between the Three Pages and the Good Quartos," in *Shakespeare's Hand in "The Play of Sir Thomas More,"* vol. 2 of A. W. Pollard and J. Dover Wilson, eds., *Shakespeare Problems* (1923), and, as ed., "Textual Introduction" and "A Note on Punctuation," in *The Tempest,* New [Cambridge] Shakespeare (1921). C. L. Wrenn, "The Value of Spelling as Evidence," in *Transactions of the Philological Society* (1943). Henry Cecil Wyld, *Studies in English Rhymes from Surrey to Pope* (1923; repr. 1965). R. E. Zachrisson, *The English Pronunciation at Shakespeare's Time as Taught by William Bullokar* (1927; repr. 1970).

Shakespeare's Poetic Techniques

GEORGE T. WRIGHT

Until this century, the prevailing critical view held that Shakespeare was an untutored genius, a gifted creator of characters, poetry, and dramatic situations, but a careless and not entirely conscious artist. The adverse part of that judgment has now been almost wholly reversed. Closer textual analysis and the development of a modernist literature scrupulously attentive to the patterning of images and the dramatic control of symbolic design and mythic reference have helped us to discern in Shakespeare's text a range of artistic patterns and effects that earlier readers often sensed but lacked the critical tools to trace. Readers, scholars, and performers continue to make new discoveries about his work, but we now have a clearer idea of the extraordinarily complex art that Shakespeare practiced and of the unparalleled skill with which he practiced it. That art, poetic drama, was a mixed art, whose visual and verbal elements can never be wholly disengaged from one another. But we can understand better how it worked if we can appraise accurately the technical poetic resources that Shakespeare drew on.

For many readers, the most immediately obvious feature of Shakespeare's language is its difference from the language of ordinary conversation—its unusual words, its sometimes intricate syntax, its highly metaphorical texture, the length of some sentences, and the fact that most of it is written in verse. Yet even the most bewildered student may also be touched by the directness, grace, and simplicity of many phrases and passages:

> The course of true love never did run smooth
> (*A Midsummer Night's Dream,* I. i. 134)
> I think it was to see my mother's wedding.
> (*Hamlet,* I. ii. 178)
> She gave me for my pains a world of sighs.
> She swore, i' faith, 'twas strange, 'twas passing strange;
> 'Twas pitiful, 'twas wondrous pitiful.
> (*Othello,* I. III. 159–161)

Shakespeare's poetic language is remarkable for the ease and strength with which it combines contrary qualities—simple and elaborate, patterned and natural. Although the characters often speak in what seems an elevated diction and style, they usually speak also in familiar tones—those we have heard ourselves or others adopt when angry, troubled, or amused. The tone also changes a great deal, as scenes and situations change, as a new character speaks, or as a character moves into a new mood. As the words fly by, we cannot analyze the principles on which the language works; but after several centuries of critical attention and scholarly study, it has become possible to attribute to Shakespeare's mastery of certain consciously exercised verbal techniques much of the power his words have over us.

Formal Verse Patterns

Iambic Pentameter. By Shakespeare's time, iambic pentameter (rhymed for narrative poems and sonnets, blank for plays) was the most elegant and expressive meter a poet or playwright could use. It was also closest to the normal cadence of speech, largely because it does not readily break, songlike, into two segments of equal or near-equal weight as lines of other lengths do, and because it is much more open than other meters to casual metrical variation. Although Shakespeare's plays include some passages of shorter or longer verse, they come to us mainly in three modes: song, iambic pentameter, and prose. The songs are often very free and the prose highly patterned, but the special strength of iambic pentameter is its combination of a speechlike flow of language with some degree of metrical obligation. As Shakespeare became more adept at his craft, his lines came to sound increasingly natural, often passionate, without compromising their metrical authenticity. Iambic pentameter, it turned out, did not have to be the language either of rant (as in the work of some of Shakespeare's dramatic predecessors and in parts of his own early plays) or of overrefined decoration; it could also express swift and deep feeling, intense and quiet meditation, and a wide range of stages and states of soul.

Despite brief experiments with doggerel verse in some early plays, Shakespeare used iambic pentameter not only for almost all his narrative and lyric poems but also as the basic verse system of his plays. The verse of the plays is nevertheless very different from the verse of the long poems and Sonnets, which are much more regular, much more "correct," and which rarely deviate from the norm: one sonnet is written in tetrameter (Sonnet 145); one consists of six couplets (Sonnet 126); one has fifteen lines (Sonnet 99); and two rhyming lines in *Venus and Adonis* (758 and 760) are not of a length. Otherwise, the only departures from strict regularity in the poems and Sonnets are those standard ones that provide melodic variety and expressive grace: variable location of a midline phrasal break; occasional mild enjambment; variation in strength of stress among the five stressed syllables and among the five unstressed ones; and the three metrical variations obtained by arranging the phrases in such a way as (1) to place a lightly stressed syllable where a strongly stressed one is expected (a pyrrhic foot),

(2) to place a strongly stressed syllable where a lightly stressed one is expected (a spondaic foot), and (3) to do both at once (a trochaic foot). All three metrical figures appear in order in the first line below, and in different order in the second:

Ŏf thĕ / wíde wórld, / dréamĭng / on things to come

(Sonnet 107, 2)

Whĕn tŏ / the ses / sĭons ŏf / swéet sĭ / lent thought

(Sonnet 30, 1)

A substantial majority of Shakespeare's lines use at least one of these three standard variations.

Shakespeare uses these metrical variations in combination with phonetic and rhetorical patterning (see below) to make his lines of verse sound natural, forceful, and expressive. In some passages the effect is notably melodious, as when Duke Orsino, at the beginning of *Twelfth Night,* rapturously listens to the music he has called for to nourish his love:

Ó, ĭt / came o'er / my ear / like thĕ / swĕet sóund
That breathes / upon / a bank of vi / olets

(I. i. 5–6)

Within the basic iambic frame, some syllables are slightly amplified or slightly muted to form spondees or pyrrhics, which have the effect of slightly delaying or hurrying the iambic pattern; and the initial trochee in the first line helps to convey the impetuous languor of the Duke. None of these devices in itself establishes the feeling of delicacy and grace, but they all contribute to it.

In a different mood, the same devices function very differently. Trembling with anger, Brabantio confronts Othello:

Ó thŏu / fóul thĭef, / whĕre hăst / thou stowed my
daughter?

(*Othello,* I. ii. 62)

The words he chooses require special emphasis, and the two trochaic variations and the spondee convey his strong feeling without deforming the basic meter. Hamlet's father's ghost, recounting his murder, uses pyrrhics to speed the tale:

Ănd ĭn / the por / chĕs ŏf / my ears did pour

(*Hamlet,* I. v. 63)

Timon's two pyrrhics direct the emphasis naturally to three other stressed syllables:

Ĭt ĭs / her há / bĭt ón / lў thăt / ĭs hónest

(*Timon of Athens,* IV. iii. 114)

The three standard metrical variations can help to establish a multitude of feelings and tones, and Shakespeare uses them with a keen ear to their appropriateness.

Verse Forms. In his three major nondramatic poems, Shakespeare learned to combine such lines skillfully into couplets, quatrains, and stanzas. He apparently saw that even in a rhymed and heavily end-stopped style, the iambic pentameter lines of a given rhymed stanza may be combined in a great variety of ways. That is, the sentence (the rhetorical unit) may or may not follow the arrangement of the quatrain and couplet (the stanzaic unit). All three poems combine quatrains and couplets, but the proportions are different in each. The stanza of *Venus and Adonis* comprises a quatrain and a couplet *(ababcc),* that of *The Rape of Lucrece* adds a third *b*-line between the quatrain and the couplet to form rime royal *(ababbcc),* and the sonnet form provides three quatrains and a couplet *(ababcdcdefefgg).*

In all three forms, the concluding couplet, with its immediate rhyme, may function to intensify, focus, or clinch (or sometimes to diverge from or answer) whatever perception has been advanced by the separated rhyming lines of the preceding quatrain (or quintain). In *Venus and Adonis,* for example, the opening quatrain often expands a theme with description and imagery; the narrowing couplet shepherds it toward its conclusion:

Hot, faint, and weary with her hard embracing,
Like a wild bird being tamed with too much handling,
Or as the fleet-foot roe that's tired with chasing,
Or like the froward infant stilled with dandling,
He now obeys and now no more resisteth,
While she takes all she can, not all she listeth.

(559–564)

But Shakespeare is bound by no strict formula. The actual arrangement of phrases, sentences, and clauses within the six-line stanza is extremely various. The quatrain may be broken into separate lines, separate pairs, or groups of three and one. The last two lines may recapitulate the first four or provide additional details; they may (as in the lines quoted) include the heart of the sentence (subjects and verbs), dependent phrases or clauses, new clauses, or new sentences. Shakespeare shows a similar versatility in fitting the slightly amplified stanza of *The Rape of Lucrece* to a great variety of clause and sentence lengths. As always in rime royal, the fifth line is the pivotal one and may be closely linked in sense or syntax either with the complete quatrain it follows or with the ensuing couplet.

If these similar stanzas offer impressive opportunities for varying the proportions between rhetorical and prosodic units, the longer sonnet form permits an almost infinite variety of arrangements. Despite the efforts of some scholars to find a systematic classification of the ways in which Shakespeare combines the quatrains and couplet of a sonnet, his actual procedures are inexhaustibly various. Sentences and clauses sometimes sit down easily within a rhymed quatrain, but they often carry over the boundaries or are disposed within them in ways that tease the neat proportions of the sonnet scheme. A Petrarchan octave-and-sestet argument may seem to be superimposed on the three-quatrains-and-couplet form. Rhetorical divisions within a quatrain may be of unexpected proportions, or the quatrains may relate to each other oddly. Indeed, in almost every sonnet the relationship between verse structure and rhetorical structure is both intricate and unique (Booth) and the couplet's relation to the quatrains varies from one sonnet to the next. The couplet's apparent task of completing or resolving the matter proposed in three earlier quatrains often seems more than it can manage, and this has led some critics to see in the Shakespearean sonnet structure either a basic flaw or a built-in irony, an undertone of inadequacy and vulnerability that belies the assurances presented in the first twelve lines or that inadequately counters their gloom. But the formal disproportion of twelve lines to two is not always what it seems. The turn the couplet provides (if it does) is often a turn only within a smaller unit (for example, the last six lines) that has already effected a turn, and its characteristically gentle tone usually makes only a modest claim to redress or redirect the poem's assertions. In any case, the structural tensions between stanzaic form and rhetorical divisions are often highly complex and problematical—qualities that help to make these graceful poems incomparably subtle and elusive.

The Meter of the Plays. Ultimately, the verse of the plays is equally problematical, but its surface is very different. Most of the lines are unrhymed (blank); many are short or long, or have missing or extra syllables. In part, this must be because the plays were meant to be performed and heard, unlike the poems, which were written to be printed or at least read. The plays, therefore, did not have to exhibit the standard of visible correctness to which the poems would be held. In preparing the text of the plays, the author, editor, printer, or compositor may have been careless, forgetful, or intrusive. But, the aims of verse drama being different from those of printed verse, the deviations from iambic pentameter in Shakespeare's plays may often be intentional, meaningful, and expressive. When Shakespeare writes a scene in prose or presents a song or a small poem in one of his plays, he does so deliberately, for specific dramatic purposes. Other deviations may be equally purposeful, and Shakespeare deviates often from regular iambic pentameter in two other ways: from the iambic and from the pentameter. He deviates from the iambic not only by introducing trochaic feet or trochaic phrasing into his lines, neither of which materially disturbs the iambic current of the verse, but also by choosing to omit syllables theoretically needed to complete the pattern and by adding extra ones. According to E. K. Chambers' metrical tables, in the plays from *Julius Caesar* on, Shakespeare uses one of the three major types of deviant lines (3, 10, and 11 in the list below) almost once in every eight lines.

Thus, the following deviations occur, with the indicated frequency: *Often* (1) An extra syllable or two at the end of the line (feminine or triple ending):

To be, or not to be—that is / the qués͡tion

(*Hamlet*, III. i. 56)

And tediousness the limbs and out / ward flóuris̆hĕs

(*Hamlet*, II. ii. 91)

Feminine endings are common enough in the iambic pentameter of most English poets and appear with some frequency in Shakespeare's Sonnets and narrative poems. All the deviations listed below, however, are rare in later English verse and probably do not occur even once in Shakespeare's poems. According to Paul Ramsey, even the anapest, which did not become an acceptable variation in an iambic line until the nineteenth century, makes not a single appearance in Shakespeare's Sonnets. *Rarely* (2) An extra syllable at the beginning of a line:

A̅nd Ĭ chál / lenge law. Attorneys are denied me

(*Richard II*, II. iii. 134)

Often (3) An extra syllable at midline, before a phrasal break (epic caesura):

His acts being se / vĕn ágĕs. / At first, the infant

(*As You Like It*, II. vii. 143)

Rarely (4) Two extra syllables at midline:

In rest / less e̅cst́ăs̆y. / Duncan is in his grave

(*Macbeth*, III. ii. 22)

Occasionally (5) An extra syllable elsewhere (anapest):

A poor physician's daugh / tĕr m̆y wífe? / Disdain

(*All's Well That Ends Well*, II. iii. 114)

But Shakespeare often *omits* syllables, too, sometimes with notable expressive effect: *Occasionally* (6) An omitted unstressed syllable at the line's beginning (headless line):

ᴧ Stáy! / The king hath thrown his warder down

(*Richard II*, I. iii. 118)

Occasionally (7) An omitted unstressed syllable after a phrasal break (broken-backed line). For example, to exhibit Northumberland's unctuous self-justification for calling King Richard II merely Richard:

Your grace / mistákes. / ᴧ Ón̆ly tŏ / be brief,
Left I his title out.

(*Richard II*, III. iii. 10–11)

Or to express Claudio's unenthusiastic gratitude for Isabella's irrelevantly generous offer:

Isabella. O, were it but my life,
   I'd throw it down for your deliverance
   Ăs fránk / ly̆ ăs / ă pín. ̆ ̆
Claudio. ᴧ Thanks, / dear Ísăbel.

(*Measure for Measure*, III. i. 104–106)

Infrequently (8) An omitted unstressed syllable else-where, to give special force to syllables spoken with particular emphasis:

> Stáy. / Spéak, / spéak. / I charge thee, speak.
>
> (*Hamlet*, I. i. 51)

> Deny to speak with me? They are sick, they are
> weary,
> They have travelled all / the night? / ∧ Mére / ∧ fétches
>
> (*King Lear*, II. iv. 84–85)

Infrequently (9) An omitted stressed syllable, so that the line may seem to require some gesture, groan, or other stage reaction to fill the gap, as when Worcester's impertinence to Henry IV excites a metrical gasp from the assembled court, before Northumberland tries unsuccessfully to bridge the awkwardness:

> *Worcester.* And that same greatness too which our own
> hands
>   Have holp to make / so pórt / ly. ∧
> *Northumberland.*   / My lord—
>
> (*1 Henry IV*, I. iii. 12–14)

Henry later pays back Worcester in kind. To Worcester's pious assurance that

> I have not sought the day of this dislike

he replies, in pique or outrage,

> You have / not sought / it! ∧ / How comes / it then?
>
> (*1 Henry IV*, V. i. 26–27)

Shakespeare also deviates from the pentameter: *Often* (10) Hexameter lines, sometimes to express some balanced antithesis:

> A thousand times more fair, ten thousand times more
> rich
>
> (*The Merchant of Venice*, III. ii. 154)

But some hexameter lines lack any distinctive symmetrical pattern:

> Fleeter than arrows, bullets, wind, thought, swifter
> things
>
> (*Love's Labor's Lost*, V. ii. 262)

Often (11) Short lines. These constitute about 5 percent of all the unrhymed lines. A short line may start a speech or end it, may appear in midspeech, may constitute the whole speech of a character (frequently a servant or inferior), or may be one in a series of comparable iambic short lines:

> *Iago.* What say'st thou, noble heart?
> *Roderigo.* What will I do, think'st thou?
> *Iago.* Why, go to bed and sleep.
>
> (*Othello*, I. iii. 302–304)

Short lines may also join with others to form whole lines; a regular line is frequently split between two (or more) characters:

> *Macduff.* Our royal master's murdered!
> *Lady Macbeth.*   Woe, alas!
>   What, in our house?
> *Banquo.*   Too cruel anywhere.
>
> (*Macbeth*, II. iii. 83–84)

Sometimes such shared or split lines involve a short (or squinting) line that could be linked either with one before or with one after. (Joseph B. Mayor calls the middle line a "common section"; E. A. Abbott, an "amphibious section.")

> *Portia.* Hark, boy! What noise is that?
> *Lucius.*   I hear none, madam.
> *Portia.*   Prithee, listen well.
>
> (*Julius Caesar*, II. iv. 16–17)

Editors have difficulty deciding, in such cases, how to arrange and number the lines (Bowers). Shakespeare evidently had no such concern; he wrote the words of his plays to be heard, not read. As we listen in the theater, we do not know when a short or long line will appear, and we may not notice it when it comes or be able to say exactly how it has fitted into, or violated, the iambic pattern. Some sentences of prose speeches sound like verse, and Shakespeare often shifts between prose and verse so unobtrusively that it would be hard, merely by listening, to say where the shift occurred. Similarly, short and long lines may throw off our conscious or subliminal count of the pentameter. Shakespeare presents some scenes in such a mixture of prose, verse, and short or split lines that we can hardly follow the verse as verse, though we do take in its shifting and often iambic currents somehow. Perhaps the most remarkable such scene is the one in *Troilus and Cressida* (V. ii. 1–61) in which Troilus and Ulysses eavesdrop on the conversation between Cressida and Diomedes and in turn are overheard by Thersites. We can identify four different registers in which the characters speak: prose, iambic pentameter, split lines of iambic pentameter, and short lines (most, but not all, iambic); but all four registers are composed mainly of short phrases, some of which combine into longer units (verse lines or prose sentences). Thersites always speaks prose here, but the other characters drift from one register to another, and the presence of three separate groups on the stage permits Shakespeare to mount a complex music reminiscent, for modern readers, of Verdian opera. How much of this complex music we hear, or anyone ever could hear, in a stage performance is debatable.

Rhyme. One effective means to help us hear verse as verse is end-rhyme, and Shakespeare, like his contemporaries, wrote all his poems in rhymed stanzas. In the plays the standard verse form is blank verse, but there are extended passages of couplet-verse (or even quatrains or sonnets), especially when the characters are engaged in formal argumentation or elevated lyrical discourse. *Love's Labor's Lost* and *Romeo and Juliet* include whole sonnets among their formal rhymed verse. In the early plays, Shakespeare frequently uses rhymed doggerel verse for sprightly comic exchanges:

> *Balthazar.* Good meat, sir, is common; that every
>   churl affords.
> *Antipholus E.* And welcome more common, for that's
>   nothing but words.
> *Balthazar.* Small cheer and great welcome makes a
>   merry feast.
> *Antipholus E.* Ay, to a niggardly host and more sparing
>   guest.
>
>   (*The Comedy of Errors,* III. i. 24–27)

Doggerel virtually disappears in Shakespeare's middle and later plays; and rhyme diminishes, according to Frederic W. Ness, because of "a distaste for rhyme in more complicated stanzaic forms, the development from a lyrical to a dramatic medium, the shift from doggerel to prose for lively comic dialogue, and the mastery of a flexible blank verse to convey complex emotional states."

Rhymed couplets, nevertheless, either alone or in extended series, are still used for special purposes even in the later plays, especially to signal the end of a scene or to achieve some special effect—for example, to produce an air of formality in the opening court scene in *King Lear* and in the play within the play in *Hamlet;* or, in *Macbeth,* to point

up the contrast between the Macbeths' outer cheer and inner evil:

> Away, and mock the time with fairest show;
> False face must hide what the false heart doth know.
>
>   (*Macbeth,* I. vii. 81–82)

Aphorisms and sententiae are frequently rhymed:

> How far your eyes may pierce I cannot tell;
> Striving to better, oft we mar what's well.
>
>   (*King Lear,* I. iv. 336–337)

A single couplet may stand out from a series of mainly blank-verse lines with striking premonitory effect, as when Brabantio, foiled in his effort to prevent his daughter's marriage, utters a warning to Othello that anticipates Iago's later plot:

> Look to her, Moor, if thou hast eyes to see:
> She has deceived her father, and may thee.
>
>   (*Othello,* I. iii. 292–293)

Some of Shakespeare's mature plays, such as *Troilus and Cressida, All's Well That Ends Well,* and *Timon of Athens,* still find uses for rhyme in passages of extended exposition. But as a rule, blank verse is much preferred for exposition and development, and rhyme is clearly auxiliary and ancillary. Without rhyme, the sense of a sentence can more easily run over the line-ending, and Shakespeare's increasing tendency to "enjamb" his lines (that is, to run his sentences from one line into the next), in an effort to reflect more accurately the rhythms of speech, makes rhyme less useful to him, except for the tightening or clinching effect with which it may close a speech or a scene:

>   Ever till now,
> When men were fond, I smiled and wondered how.
>
>   (*Measure for Measure,* II. ii. 186–187)

The Play of Phrase and Line. By the time Shakespeare began to write, the relation between the iambic pentameter line and the rhythm of English phrasing had passed through two crucial stages. In the first, earlier Elizabethan poets, apparently seeing the line as a compound measure consisting of a four-syllable iambic segment and a six-syllable iambic segment, searched for phrases of these dimensions. Later, poets realized that the phrasing in an iambic pentameter line did not have to break after the fourth syllable but might break anywhere. If we understand the caesura to be an obligatory structural break (whether or not marked by a pause) at a predictable place in the line, then it ceases to exist in later verse of this kind; what is often called a caesura is a break or pause in phrasing that may occur at different places in different lines —or not at all. In Shakespeare's verse, even if the line is usually composed of two phrases, the phrases in adjacent lines will usually be of different lengths and rhythmical contours, which means that the rhythmic unit we are constantly aware of as recurring again and again is the line, not (not ever again) a four-syllable phrase and a six-syllable phrase.

When the phrasal break occurs after an odd-numbered syllable (usually the fifth or the seventh), the inner rhythm of the line is likely to be trochaic. The unreserved exploitation of this option made it possible for poets to admit great numbers of trochaic English phrases into iambic poetry, a development of crucial importance to the making of convincing dramatic dialogue. In both his poems and his plays, Shakespeare seizes this opportunity to vary the phrasal patterning in successive lines, for the sake of both melody and expressive force:

> Then, in the blazon of sweet beauty's best,
> Of hand, of foot, of lip, of eye, of brow,
> I see their antique pen would have expressed
> Even such a beauty as you master now.
>
> (Sonnet 106, 5–8)

Another option Shakespeare exercises is to locate the phrasal break later in the line, as in line 7 of this sonnet. The effect is to make it more likely that the sense of the line will run over the line-ending, that the line will be enjambed (Oras). When this happens frequently, as it does in Shakespeare's later plays, the relation between the line and the phrase is radically altered. Where once the phrase had to be obedient to the line, to fit into its slots, the larger unit of the flowing sentence comes more and more to be felt as a competing force. Ultimately, a new creative rivalry between line and sentence makes possible the great dramatic verse of Shakespeare's mature plays.

Accordingly, as Shakespeare's career progressed the lines of his plays came less and less to be composed line by line or in strings of single lines, as earlier plays by Marlowe and others had been. Shakespeare, following the example of older poets,

had worked this way in the Sonnets, narrative poems, and earlier plays:

> O, turn thy edgèd sword another way;
> Strike those that hurt, and hurt not those that help!
> One drop of blood drawn from thy country's bosom
> Should grieve thee more than streams of foreign gore.
> Return thee therefore with a flood of tears
> And wash away thy country's stainèd spots.
>
> (*1 Henry VI,* III. iii. 52–57)

As George Saintsbury says of similar lines by Marlowe, "The lines are not merely stopped at the end, but they are constructed to stop at the end. They are moulded individually, not collectively. . . . [They are] separable into line-parts as Shakespeare's own greatest things are not." It is largely this characteristic of pre-Shakespearean dramatic verse—along with its rhetorical habits of bombast and fustian—that makes it so well suited to declamation. It may even have seemed a virtue in a playwright that his blank-verse line, without the advantage of rhyme, should make its metrical structure so evident to the ear. The audience needed to be trained, and this freestanding line perhaps did Shakespeare the service of preparing his audience for the more expressive rhythms he would later expect them to note.

If so, what Shakespeare developed, further than any poet before him or after, is a principle of metrical organization that connects the meter (with its standard or unusual variations), the sentence (with its constituent segments), and the dramatic and psychological situation of the speaking character. According to this principle, the interior organization of the metrical *line* is one thing: where the midline pause will come; how the phrasing is adjusted to the required sequence of iambic feet; how far the line strays from perfect regularity toward spondaic, pyrrhic, or trochaic variation. But we are also constrained to listen to the emerging *sentence,* which, even as its separate phrases take their places in individual lines and parts of lines, imposes a compelling interest of its own, distinct from that of the metrical line and following a different course. Furthermore, the extent to which the phrase unsettles the foot, and the sentence unsettles the line, gives some indication of the mental or emotional character or predicament of the person who speaks the lines, or of the depth of disturbance that the world of the play is registering or suffering.

In the middle and later plays, therefore, the

phrases and clauses more and more run from midline to midline:

> No! To be once in doubt
> Is once to be resolved.
>
> (*Othello,* III. iii. 179–180)

Or if they begin with a full line, they often stop in midline; or, beginning in midline, they may run over and stop at the end of a line:

> And then it started, like a guilty thing
> Upon a fearful summons.
>
> (*Hamlet,* I. i. 148–149)

> This earth that bears thee dead
> Bears not alive so stout a gentleman.
>
> (*1 Henry IV,* V. iv. 91–92)

And each of these patterns may be amplified by additional full lines between the first and the last:

> Let the great gods
> That keep this dreadful pudder o'er our heads
> Find out their enemies now.
>
> (*King Lear,* III. ii. 49–51)

Line and sentence run their independent courses, which are only occasionally congruent. The line often ends in midphrase, the sentence in midline; and we hear their rhythms mounted on one another, along with all the other rhythmic designs that contribute to the complexity of a dramatic utterance such as phonetic patterns, the repetitions or antitheses of wordplay, the emotional curve of an extended rhetorical period, and the rise and relief of intensity during a scene. Shakespeare's metrical designs begin at the level of the foot and the phrase, but his patterns of repetition and variation are themselves so diverse and of so many dimensions and scales that no description of any of his more impressive scenes can quite catch the full measure of his art. In some of his later plays, especially from *Coriolanus* to *Cymbeline,* Shakespeare breaks up the line even more and, apparently in reaction against facile rhetoric, virtually abandons the flowing sentence for brief and abrupt bursts of staccato phrases that seem almost, at times, in their jagged discourse, to mock both line and phrase:

> O Jove, I think
> Foundations fly the wretched—such, I mean,
> Where they should be relieved. Two beggars told me
> I could not miss my way. Will poor folks lie,

> That have afflictions on them, knowing 'tis
> A punishment or trial? Yes. No wonder,
> When rich ones scarce tell true.
>
> (*Cymbeline,* III. vi. 6–12)

But by the last two acts of *The Winter's Tale* and for all of *The Tempest,* the autonomy of the phrase is once again established; the sentence and line, like warp and woof, weave their double-stranded verse in a newly graceful pattern:

> Our revels now are ended. These our actors,
> As I foretold you, were all spirits and
> Are melted into air, into thin air.
>
> (*The Tempest,* IV. i. 148–150)

Lines with "light" endings, such as prepositions and conjunctions (the second line above is an example), or "weak" endings (auxiliaries and some pronouns) are common in the late plays and facilitate the passage of sense from one line to the next.

Such endings do not make it easier for us to hear the line as a line. Shakespeare's unusual variety of line types, his frequent use of metrical variations, trochaic phrasing, and feminine endings, and his willingness in the late plays to run the rhythm and contour of the sentence against the rhythm and contour of the line help to make his theatrical verse line harder to hear as a line. In modern theaters, or even in Shakespeare's own, audiences hear his verse most imperfectly, hear perhaps an iambic current rather than lines of verse, usually remaining uncertain of the stresses, willing to let some lines go by without measure, as some speeches go by without being understood, hardly knowing whether lengthy passages are prose or verse and not even wondering about it, and yet somehow absorbing the deep rhythmical currents of the verse that measure out the characters' utterances line by line (Wright, 1983).

Syllabic Value. With its deviant lines and its frequent counterpointing of line and sentence, Shakespeare's blank verse is radically different in character from that of any later poet; it is less predictable, and is varied in many more ways, than the comparable verse of Pope and Wordsworth and even of Milton and Browning. Even when we read the plays in the best editions available, our sense of the meter is likely to be continually disturbed by what seems an insufficiency or a superabundance of syllables. To make his lines still more problematical, Shakespeare sometimes elides contiguous vowels, even over an intervening *h* or a glide. Examples: *I am, hideous, mutual, Thou hast, th' hour, I would, merry as, being, knowing, power.* By 1600 his readiness to elide and syncopate syllables had become extreme. He frequently reduces the syllabic value of such phrases as *in the* to one syllable *(i' th').* In his earlier verse he permits the syncopation of syllables connected by an intervocalic *th, v, r, l,* or *n: either, heaven, general, easily, enemies.* In the later plays almost any polysyllabic word may be syncopated no matter what its consonant pattern, as in *vag'bond, Im'gen, count'feit, carc'sses,* and *rem'died* (Kökeritz).

By a different convention, usually implying the survival (in verse, at least) of archaic forms of pronunciation, Shakespeare sometimes adds syllables to words. He often treats the suffix *-tion* as dissyllabic, according to his metrical convenience, and he uses the *-ed* suffix of verbs and participial adjectives as an extra syllable when the meter requires it. He may expand words, too, especially when they involve diphthongs followed by an *r* or when they can sustain an extra vowel before a post-tonic *r* or *l: weird, more, fair, fierce, fourth, hair; world, angry, monstrous, entrance, children, fiddler, dazzled, wrastler, changeling, frailty,* and *bounty.* Perhaps the most famous example appears in Lady Macbeth's lines:

> The raven himself is hoarse
> That croaks the fatal *entrance* of Duncan
> Under my battlements.
>
> *(Macbeth,* I. v. 36–38)

With all these metrical variations, metrical deviations, and syllabic opportunities, Shakespeare's compositional options are so numerous that frequently the same or very similar syllabic combinations in the same lines will be treated in different metrical fashion even though the actual pronunciation is probably about the same:

>   What
> If *I* / *had* said / *I had* seen / him do you wrong?
>
> *(Othello,* IV. i. 23–24)

And here Shakespeare treats the last two syllables of Imogen's name in three metrically different ways:

> *Posthumus.* My queen, my life, my wife! / Ŏ
>   Im / ogen, Imo / gen, Im / ogen.
> *Imogen.*   Peace, / my lord. Hear, hear—
>
> *(Cymbeline,* V. v. 226–227)

To what extent these apparent condensations of syllabic value reflect actual pronunciation is hard to say. It may be that many elisions and syncopations required by the meter are metrical only, not phonetic. At least it is possible that Shakespeare's ear could tolerate, even enjoy, the extra little tail, the enclitic half-syllable, that makes the line sound fuller than usual, crammed with more morphemes than it technically has room for. To write ten-syllable lines that have, in a sense, eleven or twelve syllables (or eleven and a half) is to crowd the air with meanings only half-spoken, partly concealed.

Phonetic Patterns. The ambiguity as to the number of syllables in a line works in conjunction with linear ambiguity (ambiguity as to which set of words, as they pass, constitute a line) and with a high degree of phonetic patterning to compose a dramatic verse texture of great complexity. As David I. Masson and Stephen Booth have shown for the Sonnets, Shakespeare's patterning of phonetic recurrences is pervasive, and his evident understanding of their expressive functions (emphasizing connections or contrasts, intensifying mood or emotion), however deliberate or "instinctive," is awesome. The most obvious patterns, nevertheless, he employs with considerable restraint. Few lines in the sonnets alliterate so blatantly as

> *Bor*ne on the *bier* with white and *bristly beard*
>
> (Sonnet 12, 8)

In fact, ostentatious patterning often discredits a dramatic speaker. The pompousness of the Dauphin of France, for example, shows in his egregious assonance:

> What l*u*sty tr*u*mpet th*u*s doth s*u*mmon *us*?
>
> *(King John,* V. ii. 117)

And Quince's alliteration is ridiculous:

> Whereat, with *bl*ade, with *bl*oody *bl*ameful *bl*ade,
> He *br*avely *br*oached his *b*oiling *bl*oody *br*east.
>
> *(A Midsummer Night's Dream,* V. i. 145–146)

Still, at a tense moment, Macbeth can use the same, or nearly the same, vowel on five successive stressed syllables:

> Ere w*e* will *eat* our m*ea*l in f*ea*r, and sleep
>
> *(Macbeth,* III. ii. 17)

Shakespeare's usual technique is more concealed. Assonance, alliteration, and consonance (recurrence of consonant sounds regardless of where they appear in a word) are often carried on through an extended passage or at least for several lines. Patterns connecting one sound will be interwined or combined with patterns connecting others. In Claudio's passionate imagining of death, for example (see below), *r* is heard in all of the lines and *l* in most; plosives *(p, b)* burst through in lines 124–126 and again in lines 130–131; the long *i* is audible in lines 118–122 (as internal rhyme in *Ay, die,* and *lie*) and again in lines 123 and 125, the short *i* in lines 122–123; and one can pick out notable examples of intertwined alliteration (*th* and *r* in line 123, *w* and *l* in line 129). There is also an opening of the vowels at the alliterative climax of the passage (how*l*ing, ho*rr*ible), followed by more closed vowels as the passage lowers both its volume and its pitch.

> *Ay,* but to d*ie,* and g*o* we kn*o*w n*o*t where,
> To *lie* in c*o*ld obst*r*uction and to *r*ot,
> This sensib*l*e *w*ar*m* *mo*tion to beco*me*   120
> A knea*d*ed c*l*od; an*d* the *d*e*l*ighted spirit
> To bathe in *f*iery *fl*oods, or to *r*es*id*e
> In *thr*ill*i*ng region of *th*ick-ribbèd *i*ce,
> To be im*p*rison*ed* in the *viewless winds*
> And *bl*own with *r*est*l*ess *viol*en*c*e *r*ound about   125
> The *p*endent *worl*d; or to be *w*orse than *w*orst
> Of *th*ose *th*at *l*awless and incertain *th*ought
> Imagine *h*ow*l*ing, '*t*is *t*oo *h*orri*b*le.
> The *w*earie*s*t and m*o*st *l*oathèd *worl*d*l*y *l*ife
> *T*hat *a*ge, *a*che, *p*enury, and im*p*ri*s*on*m*ent   130
> Can *l*ay on *n*a*t*ure is a *p*ara*d*ise
> To *wh*at *w*e *f*ear of *d*eath.

> (*Measure for Measure,* III. i. 118–132)

All these devices intensify the expression of Claudio's feeling by making his words seem dense with pattern, hence significance, and by giving special emphasis to words and syllables especially crucial to the pattern. The metrical variations—not remarkable in this passage but representative—serve similar purposes: the pyrrhics and spondees (especially in lines 120, 123, 129, and 130) invite the speaking voice to treat the syllables of a line with those slight hurryings and delays, those withdrawals and augmentations of stress, that mark fervent speech.

Syntactical Patterning. A high degree of syntactical patterning, especially of "simultaneously emphasized parallelism and nonparallelism," which Booth finds in Shakespeare's Sonnets, is also evident in this passage. Most of Claudio's vision is built around a long series of parallel infinitive phrases, but they are almost all different in construction. Only the first and the fourth verbs *(die* and *rot),* which begin and end the first two lines, are absolute; between them, *go* is completed by a dependent clause, and *lie* by a prepositional phrase. The more elaborate verbal phrases that follow are developed with a wide variety of syntactical patterns, and they take different lengths of line to complete them. When the sentence finally breaks the infinitive pattern, it uses a different *too* to do so (line 128)—the figure *antanaclasis* (Booth), which uses the same word in another of its meanings. A *to* used in a third sense opens line 132, which completes the final sentence. The sentence itself includes parallel but differently formed superlatives *(weariest* and *most loathed)* and a list of parallel troubles that are both mono- and polysyllabic, Anglo-Saxon and Latin. Note also the diverse derivations of other pairs of closely connected words: *cold obstruction, warm motion, delighted spirit, thrilling region, viewless winds, restless violence, pendent world,* and *lawless and incertain.* Shakespeare frequently couples terms of contrasting derivation and length, joins an abstract word to a concrete one *(warm motion)* or a learned word *(pendent)* to a commonplace one *(world)* (Rylands; Frye). A notable mannerism of Shakespeare's middle and later plays especially is the linking of nouns or of adjectives to form doublets *(help and vantage, ponderous and marble, griefs and clamor, sound and fury).* The linked terms are sometimes synonymous, sometimes complementary, and sometimes related in the more complex pattern of *hendiadys,* in which the coordinate linkage masks a dependent relationship, as in *clamorous griefs, furious sound* (Wright, 1981).

Onomatopoeia. Throughout his work, Shakespeare's practice is to devise sounds that seem appropriate to the sense, but not to imitate natural or nonverbal sounds. In this sense of *onomatopoeia,* Shakespeare's poetry is probably almost never onomatopoeic except in its use of single words or short phrases that can sound like what they mean, as with *hiss, crack, jangled, whisper,* and *whip.* Actors can make the most of lines like the following:

> *Blow, winds,* and *crack* your *cheeks. Rage, blow.*

> (*King Lear,* III. ii. 1)

> But with the *whiff* and *wind* of his fell sword

> (*Hamlet,* II. ii. 461)

The king doth wake to-night and takes his rouse,
Keeps wassail, and the *swaggering upspring reels*

(Hamlet, I. iv. 8–9)

And kissed her lips with such a *clamorous smack*

(The Taming of the Shrew, III. ii. 174)

Dramatic Inflection

Along with a complex and problematical metrical style, Shakespeare gradually evolved a convincing dramatic language. He began with conventions already established by his predecessors—a style largely declamatory, figurative, balanced, sometimes melodious, often flat. Shakespeare never gave up declamation, figure, balance, and melody, but he learned how to mix them with their contraries, and in the course of his career the language of his characters became at once more concentrated and more natural.

From the beginning Shakespeare had written fluent and natural-sounding lines:

Tell her I am arrested in the street

(The Comedy of Errors, IV. i. 106)

I greatly fear my money is not safe.

(The Comedy of Errors, I. ii. 105)

But, whiles he thought to steal the single ten,
The king was slily fingered from the deck.

(3 Henry VI, V. i. 43–44)

Such easy English phrasing fits perfectly (perhaps too perfectly) the iambic pentameter line. But in longer speeches the line-by-line accumulation often loses the natural tone. Here is the way the Duke of Gloucester speaks to his wife in *Henry VI, Part 2:*

Nay, Eleanor, then must I chide outright.
Presumptuous dame, ill-nurtured Eleanor,
Art thou not second woman in the realm,
And the Protector's wife, beloved of him?
Hast thou not worldly pleasure at command
Above the reach or compass of thy thought?
And wilt thou still be hammering treachery
To tumble down thy husband and thyself
From top of honor to disgrace's feet?
Away from me, and let me hear no more.

(I. ii. 41–50)

No line here is absurdly unspeechlike, but for an angry man, Gloucester employs a rhetoric that is remarkably uninflected. He finds formal epithets for his wife, puts weighty rhetorical questions to her, calls her twice by name, refers to himself in the third person, banishes her grandly from his sight, all in a public, declamatory, linear style that seems wholly inappropriate to the private speech of a husband to a wife even in a courtly age.

Anger in later plays is expressed much more forcefully:

Duke. O thou dissembling cub, what wilt thou be
When time hath sowed a grizzle on thy case?

(Twelfth Night, V. i. 158–159)

Hotspur. I'll keep them *all.*
By God, he shall not have a *Scot* of them!
No, if a Scot would save his *soul,* he shall not.
I'll *keep* them, by this *hand!*

(1 Henry IV, I. iii. 213–216)

Leontes. Traitors!
Will you not push her out? Give her the bastard.
Thou dotard, thou art woman-tired, unroosted
By thy dame Partlet here. Take up the bastard.
Take't up, I say. Give't to thy crone.
Paulina. For ever
Unvenerable be thy hands, if thou
Tak'st up the princess by that forcèd baseness
Which he has put upon't!
Leontes. He dreads his wife.

(The Winter's Tale, II. iii. 72–79)

Even in these short outbursts, Shakespeare's later technique for showing anger is clear. None of them proceeds in the even, line-by-line rhetoric of Gloucester. Rather, they focus on key words and images, which instantaneously raise the emotional temperature. Duke Orsino's anger is relatively cool, but he finds an extremely effective image to focus his disgust. Hotspur's tantrum concentrates its force in a few words spoken with special vehemence (and here italicized). Leontes' passion is alternately shrill ("Traitors!"), peremptory, and contemptuous ("thy crone" and "He dreads his wife"); Paulina's is prophetic and priestly. Each angry speaker is characterized by a different sort of phrasing, for the principle on which the rhetoric is founded is that every moment of the play (not just its angry moments) must be marked by some significant change in form, emotional tension, point of view, or other stylistic or dramatic feature. The feet in a line must be varied; the lines themselves must be different from one another in syntactical structure, in force, in metrical patterning, in rhetorical character; scenes and parts of scenes must develop in different ways, whatever deep parallels may later make themselves felt. Among the many techniques Shakespeare uses to inflect his speeches, to help them rise and fall in intensity as animated speech naturally does, are the following:

Departures from Balance and Symmetry. One notable feature of Shakespeare's early verse is its balanced and symmetrical patterning. Contrasts are often arranged in neatly parallel lines or phrases:

> Was ever woman in this humor wooed?
> Was ever woman in this humor won?
>
> (*Richard III*, I. ii. 227–228)

The manner of the later work is utterly different. Antitheses are often developed in unbalanced lines:

> The serpent that did sting thy father's life
> Now wears his crown.
>
> (*Hamlet*, I. v. 39–40)

> I am afraid to think what I have done;
> Look on't again I dare not.
>
> (*Macbeth*, II. ii. 50–51)

Balanced categories are split up between lines and parallel phrases usually placed in different parts of corresponding lines:

> When you speak, sweet,
> I'ld have you do it ever. When you sing,
> I'ld have you buy and sell so, so give alms,
> Pray so, and for the ord'ring your affairs,
> To sing them too. When you do dance, I wish you
> A wave o' th' sea
>
> (*The Winter's Tale*, IV. iv. 136–141)

Such techniques, combined with Shakespeare's later metrical practices, produce a dramatic verse capable of combining an extremely high degree of recurrence of sounds, words, or phrasal forms with an equally high resistance to perfect parallelism or symmetry (Booth). The metrical pattern, with its basic formality but also with its openness to frequent metrical variation and even deviation, follows a similar procedure.

Focus on the Single Word. Even in his very early plays Shakespeare sometimes concentrates emotion in single words, which rise above the level intensity of the rest of the line:

> *York.* I will, my lord, so please his majesty.
> *Suffolk.* Why, *our* authority is his consent,
> And what *we* do establish *he* confirms.
>
> (*2 Henry VI*, III. i. 315–317)

Later flare-ups of anger or annoyance (like Hotspur's quoted above) are often focused on key words:

> Why, *yet* he doth deny his prisoners
>
> (*1 Henry IV*, I. iii. 77)

> *Love?* his affections do not *that* way tend
>
> (*Hamlet*, III. i. 162)

> What *beast* was't then
> That made you *break* this enterprise to me?
>
> (*Macbeth*, I. vii. 47–48)

The suddenness of Richard III's anger at Lord Hastings is a classic early case:

> *Hastings.* If they have done this deed, my noble
>   lord—
> *Richard.* If? Thou protector of this damnèd strumpet,
> Talk'st thou to me of *ifs?* Thou art a traitor.
> Off with his head!
>
> (*Richard III*, III. iv. 73–76)

The skill with which Shakespeare allows such focal words to rise out of the metrical line and shape the utterance shows how aware he is that in speech we single out, particularly at moments of emotion, the words and syllables that seem specially empowered to carry the force of our feeling, and that such singling out often gives a stretch of words its distinctive character. Even in longer speeches, where Shakespeare had learned to let the rhetorical rise and fall follow a clear emotional curve, as in some of Lear's majestic cries or curses, a crowning emphasis may fall on a single word. If Goneril cannot be sterile, at least her child may cause her such pain

> that *she* may feel
> How sharper than a serpent's tooth it is
> To have a thankless child.
>
> (*King Lear*, I. iv. 278–280)

And the storm may do its worst against the genuinely wicked, but

> *I* am a man
> More sinned *against* than sinning.
>
> (King Lear, III. ii. 59–60)

Pithy Phrasing. Another technique Shakespeare uses in his middle and later plays is the linguistic shortcut, the pithy phrase that says briefly what in earlier plays took a line or more to say:

> He that conceals him, death.
>
> (King Lear, II. i. 63)
>
> More matter, with less art.
>
> (Hamlet, II. ii. 95)
>
> Fewness and truth, 'tis thus
>
> (Measure for Measure, I. iv. 39)

This compression of speeches is apparently one sign of Shakespeare's awareness that human talk is made up of many different sorts of ingredients—short speeches and long, emotional and reasoned, expanded and compressed—and that a few choice words may count for more than much high-toned speech.

Parenthetical Phrases. Every phrase or line in an early speech (like that of Gloucester to his wife from *Henry VI, Part 2,* quoted above) is likely to be weighted equally. The later dramatic dialogue is full of parenthetical expressions, sometimes throwaway phrases that are often relative clauses or otherwise grammatically subordinate or merely transitional. Such phrases may, however, carry a startling image or confer a notable grace on the passage:

> And in his mantle muffling up his face,
> Even at the base of Pompey's statue
> *(Which all the while ran blood)* great Caesar fell.
>
> (Julius Caesar, III. ii. 187–189)
>
>   and withered murder,
> Alarumed by his sentinel, the wolf,
> *Whose howl's his watch,* thus with his stealthy pace
>
> (Macbeth, II. i. 52–54)
>
> Our revels now are ended. These our actors,
> *As I foretold you,* were all spirits and
>
> (The Tempest, IV. i. 148–149)

Such phrases, whether merely melodious or unexpectedly powerful, are part of a rhetoric much more curious than the early verse had been to regis-

ter different levels of strength or degrees of centrality in the successive segments that make up a sentence, and they make the verse speech much more dramatic.

Beginning and Ending Scenes in Midconversation. Another technique Shakespeare uses frequently in later plays is to end scenes in midconversation, so that the scene seems more authentically a fragment of life overheard by an audience as people overhear scraps of talk in the street. Several scenes in *Antony and Cleopatra* begin with lines that contain an as yet unidentified *he* or *him.* Another begins, "Nay, nay, Octavia, not only that—" (III. iv). And several end with language notably lacking in features appropriate to closure:

> Choose your own company, and command what cost
> Your heart has mind to.
>
> (III. iv. 37–38)
>
> With news the time's with labor and throws forth
> Each minute some.
>
> (III. vii. 80–81)

Figures and Images. Later sections of this essay will treat figures and imagery in some detail, but these devices, too, stir up emotion in Shakespeare's dramatic verse. The metaphorical force of a single word may radiate through a whole line:

> Now, lords, if God doth give successful end
> To this debate that *bleedeth* at our doors
>
> (2 Henry IV, IV. iv. 1–2)
>
>   Lord Angelo, a man whose blood
> Is very *snow-broth*
>
> (Measure for Measure, I. iv. 57–58)

Sometimes a running image is developed in more than one line, as when Sicinius predicts that Coriolanus' hatred of the people

>   will be his fire
> To kindle their dry stubble; and their blaze
> Shall darken him for ever.
>
> (Coriolanus, II. i. 246–248)

Elsewhere the current of the imagery may be subterranean and hardly noticed, but it nevertheless charges the lines with feelings, as in Sonnet 30 (quoted below).

Even when these six devices are used with inverted syntax, neologisms, or other unspeechlike features, they have the effect of giving the lines a more natural-sounding intonation pattern, of adjusting the formal metrical pattern in the direction of speechlike rhythm and emphasis.

The Longer Speech and the Eloquent Passage. But if Shakespeare is master of the single word or phrase that gives sudden force and intensity to a speech, he has also the gift of the flowing passage, the rounded, well-arranged series of lines and sentences that work their way through carefully adjusted syntactical segments toward heightened climaxes from which they then modulate down again. Claudio's speech on death or Florizel's on Perdita (both quoted above), or Edgar's on the beach seen from the cliff (quoted below), may serve as examples, and so might almost any of the famous set speeches—Gaunt on England, Hamlet on dying, Lear's curse on Goneril, Prospero's abjuration—for which Shakespeare's plays are justly celebrated. By his command of expressive syntax, which involves too many variables to be analyzed here in detail, Shakespeare fits his figurative and metaphorical language to an extended emotional curve—an aria of the spoken word—whose phrasal constituents and long, developing melody should be easily perceptible to the silent ear but which modern actors, better trained in the telling performance of the single phrase, too often disdain to "sing" from the stage. Indeed, the elocutionary skills required to give to each segment of a long Shakespearean speech its due prominence—no more, no less—and to regulate its delivery by attention to all the syntactical, metrical, and rhetorical pressures under which the whole passage achieves its intensity and grace are not skills with which actors today feel comfortable, although there are splendid exceptions. In such later plays as *Coriolanus, Timon of Athens,* and *Cymbeline,* Shakespeare appears to have declined, for reasons that are not entirely clear, to write long, flowing speeches of the kind that a reader might be moved to learn by heart. Perhaps he distrusted for a time the force of an eloquence that could so easily win sympathy for evil agents and enterprises—the Macbeths, for example. Nevertheless, even in these plays, and everywhere else in the later Shakespeare, there is evidence of his ability to contrive melodious and well-modulated speeches, brief or extended, for any psychological or formal occasion:

> Not poppy nor mandragora,
> Nor all the drowsy syrups of the world,
> Shall ever med'cine thee to that sweet sleep
> Which thou owedst yesterday.
>
> (*Othello,* III. iii. 330–333)

Distinctive Speech Mannerisms. One other means Shakespeare uses to give his dramatic verse the inflection of natural speech is to match the speech to the character. In the early plays, there is little to distinguish the speech of one personage from that of another, except for the comic characters like Holofernes, Launce, and Grumio, whose eccentric language is largely confined to comic interludes, often in prose, between the more dignified scenes. When the play turns serious, the characters speak the standard figurative or declamatory language. But some notable antic characters of the plays written from about 1594 on are of another breed. For one thing, these characters are not there just for laughs; they play crucial roles in the main actions, which could not carry on without them. Like Dickens, Shakespeare discovered early the almost hypnotic value of creating "characters" with distinctive speech mannerisms, personages whom an audience will remember when it has forgotten the rest of the play. Juliet's Nurse constantly loses the thread, Shylock repeats phrases obsessively ("I'll have my bond"), Pistol uses a bombastic high-style verse for low content, and such other characters as Richard III, Mercutio, Capulet, Falstaff, Shallow, and Polonius are all notable for the strategies or mannerisms that mark their speech and betray their character (Hibbard).

Although Shakespeare continued to present memorable clowns and eccentrics to the end of his career, he also learned to inflect the speeches of his central characters, especially his tragic heroes, with distinctive speech habits of their own. The huge terms in which Othello continually imagines events in which he is concerned betray a significant vulnerability in a man whose "broad simplicity of syntax suggests a simple nature" (Bethell). Lear's language is often characterized by its strongly parallel or antithetical structures, his temper by its frequent slow ascents to extreme passion. Hamlet, as Wolfgang Clemen (1977) rightly observes, is a character mercurially capable of speaking memorable words in a wide variety of styles; his command of so many registers and his ease in shifting from one of them into another is both a measure of his intelligence and a reason for the difficulty we have in appraising his character.

Personal Speech: The Sonnets

The Sonnets have properly been studied as poems in their own right and, since their dates are uncertain, not for their stylistic influence on the plays. There is widespread agreement that at least some and probably many sonnets were composed in the early 1590s, perhaps during the period when the theaters were closed by the plague. If so, it is not unreasonable to suggest that the writing of the Sonnets helped Shakespeare to develop a more powerful dramatic language for his plays, a language more fully expressive of inner thought and feeling (Ferry). Two features in particular mark the style of the Sonnets: the extraordinarily rich exploitation of figurative language and the deeply personal tone. In a large number of the Sonnets, the figures, however ingenious, take on the warm color of the speaker's feeling and even help to create that feeling. A gracefully developed conceit may provide a moving allegorical parallel that contributes poignancy and depth to the lover's situation, as with the judicial and financial metaphors (italicized here) of Sonnet 30:

> When to the *sessions* of sweet silent thought
> I *summon up* remembrance of things past,
> I sigh the lack of many a thing I sought,
> And with old woes now wail my *dear time's waste:*
> Then can I drown an eye, unused to flow,
> For *precious* friends hid in death's *dateless* night,
> And weep afresh love's long since *cancelled* woe,
> And moan th' *expense* of many a vanished sight.
> Then can I grieve at *grievances* foregone,
> And heavily from woe to woe *tell o'er*
> The sad *account* of fore-bemoanèd moan,
> Which I new *pay* as if not *paid* before.
> But if the while I think on thee, dear friend,
> All *losses* are *restored* and sorrows end.

The parallel of the bankruptcy court, though continuous, is never obtrusive; it always remains subordinate to the personal complaint.

The Sonnets use the figures to convey feelings more intimate, more private, and more problematical than Shakespeare had usually treated in his early plays. The complex turns of argument reveal a speaker who is often divided in his feelings, but

only some of the divisions appear to be explicitly recognized. Undertones of ambiguity haunt these poems, whose ingenious exploration of paradox and antithesis has seemed to almost all readers to betray more than mere ingenuity. Furthermore, the association of the speaker's feelings with imagery of the sea and of growing things, with natural cycles of day, season, and year, and with many other ranges of reference suggests that the intricate arguments and clever wordplay are being used to address affections and forebodings that are linked with a larger world.

The plays Shakespeare wrote in the mid-1590s and later show a greatly increased skill in involving the characters' complex inner feelings (and the softer tones of private reflection) in their public actions and conflicts. Instead of announcing decisions, characters from Richard II to Olivia, to Hamlet, to Othello often take us through the tergiversations by which they are reached. Their feelings take form on the stage or give signs of having been anxiously arrived at. The language in which they wrestle with divided loyalties or disturbing passions is the language of "silent thought," now for the first time conveyed from the sonnet to the stage, in dialogue as well as in soliloquy. The quiet voice of reminiscence or experience, the muted tones, the pyrrhic dips, the spondaic gravity, the metaphorical and figurative surface, all the stylistic regalia of troubled reflection familiar from the Sonnets make their presence deeply felt in the plays that follow.

The effect of these devices—varied, developed, and differently combined during the rest of Shakespeare's career—is greatly to increase the range of what is happening on stage, by giving even to a villainous character like Claudius a language and tone inaccessible to characters invented only a few years earlier. What Claudius says to Laertes as he draws him into his plot to kill Hamlet seems to spring from personal reflection on the dynamics of love and of resolutions:

> Not that I think you did not love your father,
> But that I know love is begun by time,
> And that I see, in passages of proof,
> Time qualifies the spark and fire of it.
> There lives within the very flame of love
> A kind of wick or snuff that will abate it,
> And nothing is at a like goodness still,
> For goodness, growing to a plurisy,

Dies in his own too-much. That we would do
We should do when we would, for this "would"
     changes,
And hath abatements and delays as many
As there are tongues, are hands, are accidents,
And then this "should" is like a spendthrift sigh,
That hurts by easing.

                              (*Hamlet*, IV. vii. 109–122)

This is not to suggest that Claudius is a more deeply meditative and therefore more sympathetic character than we have usually thought. The style he uses is a common resource of Shakespeare's characters in this period, not an indication of his particular sensibility. As one critic puts it, "We cannot judge the degree of a character's poetic imagination by the quality of his utterance" (Bethell). The style, nevertheless, suggests a reserve of private observation and insight on the part of any character who can use it and thus contributes to our sense of the character and of human beings generally as harboring unrevealed depths and contradictions.

Rhetorical Figures

Shakespeare and his contemporaries understood that the effective use of language was the result of training and practice, of learning to deploy rhetorical strategies and techniques that past writers had used with skill and that had been classified and described by ancient, medieval, and Elizabethan rhetoricians. These writers, some of whom Shakespeare had certainly studied in school (Baldwin), provided long lists of figurative devices appropriate for persuading or moving an audience on two principal kinds of occasions—the making of speeches and the writing of verse. In poetic drama these occasions come together: characters meet on a stage in various postures of conflict and perplexity and explain their situations, confide in others, persuade them, entrap them, revile them, mock them, give counsel or consolation, and impart their views and feelings. For all these purposes, the traditional schemes and tropes were indispensable instruments, and Shakespeare, like other writers, had to learn the tools of his trade.

Sister Miriam Joseph, in her classic study of these devices, has identified some two hundred schemes, figures, and tropes discussed by contemporary rhetoricians and turned to good use by Shakespeare. Some of these allow a writer to add or subtract a syllable from a word in any of several patterns—for example, 'twixt (for *betwixt*), *bretheren* (for *brethren*), *prosp'rous, is't, haught* (for *haughty*). Some permit an alteration of normal word order: to reverse the logical sequence ("fly and turn the rudder," *Antony and Cleopatra*, III. x. 3); to transfer an adjective to the wrong noun ("Tarquin's ravishing strides," *Macbeth*, II. i. 55); or to mismatch connected ideas (as in Bottom's "The eye of man hath not heard, the ear of man hath not seen," *A Midsummer Night's Dream*, IV. i. 208–209) or twist grammar to show agitation (as in Othello's "Thou hadst been better have been born a dog / Than answer my waked wrath!" *Othello*, III. iii. 362–363). Other figures of grammatical distortion permit a writer to use one part of speech for another (*anthimeria*: Cleopatra's "He words me, girls, he words me," *Antony and Cleopatra*, V. ii. 191), to omit the conjunction between words (*brachylogia*), and to use one for every new clause (*polysyndeton*), or to use one case, person, gender, number, tense, or mood for another (*enallage*). Zeugma (the use of one verb serving several clauses), *diazeugma* (one subject with several verbs), and *syllepsis* (zeugma except that the verb has the wrong form for one of its subjects) are among the schemes that involve the omission of some grammatical element.

Sister Miriam also identifies numerous figures of repetition (for examples, see the section below on wordplay): repetitions of letters, sounds, beginning elements in phrases or sentences *(anaphora)* or final elements *(epistrophe)* or both *(symploce);* repetition of words in reverse order *(antimetabole),* of the same word in different forms *(polyptoton),* of a final word in one clause or sentence or line as the first word in the next *(anadiplosis),* of a word after an interval *(ploce* or *diacope),* immediately *(epizeuxis),* or as the first and last word in a clause, sentence, or line *(epanalepsis).* Thus, "To-morrow, and to-morrow, and to-morrow" (*Macbeth*, V. iv. 19) is an example of ploce and epanalepsis; "Never, never, never, never, never" (*King Lear,* V. iii. 309), of epizeuxis. Sister Miriam lists as well "vices of language," such as mispronunciation, ambiguous grammar, affected speech, excessive alliteration, inane repetition, and bombast. More productive strategies of "invention" include definition, description, analysis, antithesis, ambiguity, appeals to authority, riddles, comparisons, similes, and metaphors; there are dozens of argumentative procedures, from syllogism, climax, and chains of reasoning to all the techniques for disputing a point (one may anticipate it, refute it, reject it, mock it, deplore it, evade it, or confuse the issue, among other options). Under *pathos,* Sister Miriam lists figures that help to put the listener in a receptive frame of mind; under *ethos,* the figures that show us how good and sincere a speaker is.

Shakespeare knew these devices and used them at will in his poems and plays. But he deployed them very differently early and late. From the beginning, he exhibits a mastery of the Elizabethan art of using figures to embellish a narrative or make discourse more forceful. As the similes quoted earlier in this essay from *Venus and Adonis* (559–564) suggest, the decorous use of figures might arouse pleasure in an audience able to appreciate not only the pictorial subject but the artistry with which it is rendered. On the whole, the early use of figures reveals nothing about a speaker's character except his wit or, if he uses them foolishly, his foolishness.

But as Shakespeare explored more deeply the problems of representing characters on the stage, his use of figurative language changed. The early character who consciously devises figures for the amusement of friends or himself or to make points in debate, such as Berowne, Richard II, or the pre-Juliet Romeo, gives way to the character whose figurative resources appear to be spontaneous, such as Juliet, Hamlet, Isabella, or Macbeth. The conscious use of figures may be a sign of folly or evil, but the speech in which figures seem to come to mind as naturally as leaves to the tree becomes the norm. In this new language, figures of grammatical omission or distortion, of repetition, ambiguity, or similitude, are now fluently employed by characters who have not chosen these figures in order to move others but who show by the figures they use how deeply they themselves have been moved. In Shakespeare's middle and later plays, the most forceful figures are usually a convincing sign of dramatic passion, not of rhetorical calculation. (On the intimate connection between the figures and emotion, see Vickers.)

Wordplay

What modern critics have called wordplay includes a variety of traditional figures and schemes. In its simplest form, wordplay involves the repetition of words and phrases: anaphora, epistrophe, symploce, epanalepsis, antimetabole, anadiplosis, polyptoton, ploce, diacope, and epizeuxis. Most of these figures are illustrated in the passages that follow. Shakespeare sometimes lets these repetitive patterns expose the inanity of characters like Egeus, who uses *homiologia* ("tedious and inane repetition"), diacope, epizeuxis, and epanalepsis in the first line; *perissologia* or *macrologia* ("the addition of a superfluous clause which adds nothing to the meaning") in the last; and a variety of figures in between (epizeuxis, diacope, ploce, antimetabole, and anadiplosis) (Joseph):

Egeus. Enough, enough, my lord! you have *enough.*
I beg *the law, the law,* upon his head.
They would have stol'n away; *they would,* Demetrius,
Thereby to have defeated *you and me—*
You of *your wife,* and *me of my consent,*
Of my consent that she should be *your wife.*

(*A Midsummer Night's Dream,* IV. i. 153–158)

But such wordplay is often far from trivial. Claudius repeats in ingeniously varied syntax a cluster of mainly simple words, whose schematic arrangement (involving ploce, antanaclasis, antimetabole, and polyptoton) mirrors the merciless circularity of his own thoughts:

What then? *What* rests?
Try *what repentance can. What can it not?*
Yet *what can it* when one *cannot repent?*

(*Hamlet,* III. iii. 64–66)

The impatience of Coriolanus focuses on one phrase, essentially on one word (ploce), but its arrangement of the key phrase involves anaphora, antimetabole, anadiplosis, and polyptoton:

Your voices! For your voices I have fought;
Watched *for your voices; for your voices* bear
Of wounds two dozen odd; battles thrice six
I have seen and heard of; *for your voices* have
Done many things, some less, some more. *Your voices!*
Indeed, I would be consul.

(*Coriolanus,* II. iii. 121–126)

Polixenes' repetition takes only one line, yet still involves such figures as double alliteration *(d, n)* and antimetabole:

Camillo. I dare not know, my lord.
Polixenes. How *dare not? do not? Do* you *kn*ow and *dare
    not*

(*The Winter's Tale,* I. ii. 374–375)

Such word-patterning, inexhaustibly subtle and
various, can be found in Shakespeare's plays right
to the end. But wordplay also takes the form of the
quibble, or pun, which some critics (including Dr.
Johnson) have found irritating, and others rich and
revealing. Wordplay of this kind takes advantage of
the fact that in English the same word may have
different senses or meanings, and different words
may be close in sound. In Elizabethan rhetoric, the
chief figures of ambiguity that yield this sort of
wordplay are *antanaclasis* (in which a repeated
word shifts from one meaning to another), a second
form of *syllepsis* (in which a word used only once
has two simultaneous meanings), *paronomasia* (in
which the pun is on two words not quite identical
in sound), and *asteismus* (in which one character
picks up an unintended sense of a word used by
another). Thus, Richard II uses antanaclasis when
he shifts the meaning of *face* in "Was this the face
that faced so many follies / And was at last outfaced
by Bolingbroke?" (*Richard II,* IV. i. 285–286). Angelo employs syllepsis when he tells Isabella,
"Your *sense* pursues not mine" (*Measure for Measure,* II. iv. 74). Lady Macbeth's paronomasia after
Duncan's murder is even more chilling:

> If he do bleed,
> I'll *gild* the faces of the grooms withal,
> For it must seem their *guilt.*

(*Macbeth,* II. ii. 54–56)

Hotspur's asteismus is whimsical:

> *Lady.* What is it *carries* you away?
> *Hotspur.* Why, my horse, my love—my horse!

(*1 Henry IV,* II. iii. 72–73)

Such figures may at first hearing seem merely
witty, but they often have a greater resonance. The
accidental incorporation in one sound pattern of
two different meanings is comparable to metaphor
in its bringing together widely different meanings
or spheres of reference. The mind is required to
leap from one to another, as it does when surprised
by a metaphor, and quibbling characters show "a
vitality, a supercharged mental energy, that makes

them pack as much meaning into a word as it can
be made to carry" (Mahood). When John of Gaunt
tortures his own name on his deathbed ("*Gaunt* am
I for the grave, *gaunt* as a grave," *Richard II,* II. i.
82), his pun is not merely frivolous but connects
with themes of self-definition that ring ominously
throughout the play. Such connections may be
made explicitly, as when the Fool treats Lear to a
series of puns on such words as *crown, pared, fool,*
and *dolors* that effectively sums up Lear's predicament (*King Lear,* I. iv, v; II, iii). The play on words
may more subtly reinforce a quiet network of associated metaphors that define and extend the
play's deepest meanings. Angelo's pun on *sense,* for
example, is consonant with the play's intercon-
nected themes of sensuality and order, and Lady
Macbeth's *gild* and *guilt* bring together in the virtual moment of the murder its motive and its
"deepest consequence."

Imagery

Shakespeare's "imagery" means at least two things:
what we see during the performance of a play and
the mental images that the language of the play
invites us to form. Together, these two kinds of
imagery advance and color the action, explore the
themes, and help to suggest and reinforce major
symbolic meanings. The characters often refer in
gestures to objects on the stage (such as mirrors,
letters, or corpses) or to each other, to the audience, or to the stage itself and its different dimensions (down, up, inner; right, left; above, below;
horizontal, vertical, as in "this brave o'erhanging
firmament" and "the great globe itself"). The stage
also provides a metaphor that Shakespeare eagerly
develops in some famous speeches. The plays themselves include many interior spectacles—dances,
songs, masques, plays, dumb shows, duels, ban-
quets, battles, murders, and moments of intense or
significant stage action. We see characters symbolically kneel, embrace, part, and wear black, armor,
or motley; they may assume disguises, leap into a
grave, drop a handkerchief, or be chased by a bear;
and they sometimes serve as icons or emblems of
tyranny, innocence, lovesickness, jealousy, or guilt.

All of these elements exploit a dimension of
imagistic presentation that nondramatic poetry
does not have, but this visible imagery interacts
with other kinds—with that which refers to or describes offstage matters and with the imagery of

metaphor and simile—to "reveal the relations between the world of the play and a wider surrounding world or universe" (Ellis-Fermor) or to universalize the events or predicaments presented on the stage (Foakes). By referring to matters of common knowledge offstage (such as Wittenburg, Milan, France, fifteenth-century England, biblical story or classical myth, or current events), the characters' words not only place the events in a larger context but bring that context to bear (and just such elements of it, and in such proportion, as the playwright judges relevant) on the action of the play. Descriptive imagery often treats matters immediately germane to the play's action: time of day, setting, or weather (all of which needed on Shakespeare's stage to be conveyed through words):

> Look, love, what envious streaks
> Do lace the severing clouds in yonder East.
> Night's candles are burnt out, and jocund day
> Stands tiptoe on the misty mountain tops.

> *(Romeo and Juliet, III. v. 7–10)*

> This castle hath a pleasant seat. The air
> Nimbly and sweetly recommends itself
> Unto our gentle senses.

> *(Macbeth, I. vi. 1–3)*

> Alack, the night comes on, and the high winds
> Do sorely ruffle.

> *(King Lear, II. iv. 295–296)*

Or Shakespeare's characters may need to describe events imagined, past, or unsuitable for presentation on the stage. Such narrative "insets" (Berry) are often vivid and memorable: Mercutio's Queen Mab speech; Queen Gertrude's report of Ophelia's death by drowning; Enobarbus' description of Cleopatra in her barge; and other reported encounters, courtships, quarrels, and reconciliations. Acknowledging the limitations of the stage, the Prologue to Act I of *Henry V* invites the audience to

> Piece out our imperfections with your thoughts:
> Into a thousand parts divide one man
> And make imaginary puissance.
> Think, when we talk of horses, that you see them
> Printing their proud hoofs i' th' receiving earth;
> For 'tis your thoughts that now must deck our kings,
> Carry them here and there, jumping o'er times,
> Turning th' accomplishment of many years
> Into an hourglass.

> *(23–31)*

Instigated by Shakespeare's words, the audience must use its imagination to re-create the entire reality of troops, ships, and battles. The words, however, must initiate the process. The most extraordinary conjuration of a visual scene is a literally false one: Edgar, in *King Lear,* like the playwright creating our illusion that Edgar and Gloucester are present on the stage, persuades his blind father that they are standing at the edge of a cliff:

> Come on, sir; here's the place. Stand still. How fearful
> And dizzy 'tis to cast one's eyes so low!
> The crows and choughs that wing the midway air
> Show scarce so gross as beetles. Halfway down
> Hangs one that gathers sampire—dreadful trade;
> Methinks he seems no bigger than his head.
> The fishermen that walk upon the beach
> Appear like mice; and yond tall anchoring bark,
> Diminished to her cock; her cock, a buoy
> Almost too small for sight. The murmuring surge
> That on th' unnumb'red idle pebble chafes
> Cannot be heard so high.

> *(IV. vi. 11–22)*

All such imagery both reminds us powerfully of "a world elsewhere" (*Coriolanus,* III. iii. 136) and draws us into the illusion that it has been transported here to contrast with what we can see (Ewbank).

The metaphorical imagery, too—that is, the images of things, conditions, and creatures not onstage that characters use for comparison, the rhetoricians' figures of similitude—give the language a significance and an intensity beyond the level of ordinary speech, not so much in the early plays, where the declamatory style and the ornamental figurative language slow the pace and seem at odds with dramatic development, but certainly later on, when the language is integrated much more fully and deeply with the whole dramatic action. The chief modes of poetic imagery—simile, conceit, metaphor, personification, and wordplay—show a development from the precocious and clever figures of the early plays toward greater complexity, concentration, and dramatic purposefulness. In the early plays, imagistic figures, like others, often appear to be used for their own sake; the young playwright takes pleasure in the achieved figure, however much it may retard the action. In later plays, as a rule, figurative language charges a speech or a situation with suddenly amplified meaning and, where the same imagery or word-patterns are recurrent throughout a play, enriches "the content and implications that lie within the play itself" (Ellis-Fermor). Or, as Clemen (1977) says, "With deep irony Shakespeare often lets the ambiguity of the world shine through the ambiguity of the metaphor."

Similes. Shakespeare's early similes are frequently conventional in both form and idea. The lines quoted earlier from *Venus and Adonis* (559–564) exhibit Shakespeare's mastery of the technique. The comparisons are apt and show a progressive quieting that is appropriate to the description of Adonis yielding to Venus. Animal imagery is frequent in other Elizabethan verse, dramatic and nondramatic, though Shakespeare's particular examples seem to derive from personal observation rather than books. Many early similes have an attractiveness that is in keeping both with the traditional taste for sweetness and harmony and with immediate experience:

> Like as the waves make towards the pebbled shore,
> So do our minutes hasten to their end
>
> (Sonnet 60, 1–2)

> How silver-sweet sound lovers' tongues by night,
> Like softest music to attending ears!
>
> (*Romeo and Juliet*, II. ii. 166–167)

Even from the beginning, many of Shakespeare's similes avoid or mock the conventional figures in favor of more homely ones:

> Fie, fie, how wayward is this foolish love
> That, like a testy babe, will scratch the nurse
>
> (*Two Gentlemen of Verona*, I. ii. 57–58)

> Am I so round with you as you with me,
> That like a football you do spurn me thus?
>
> (*The Comedy of Errors*, II. i. 82–83)

In later plays, similes drawn from common knowledge often find a concise and strikingly dramatic form. Hotspur says of "mincing poetry":

> 'Tis like the forced gait of a shuffling nag
>
> (*1 Henry IV*, III. i. 133)

> I see you stand like greyhounds in the slips
>
> (*Henry V*, III. i. 31)

> Our natures do pursue,
> Like rats that ravin down their proper bane,
> A thirsty evil, and when we drink we die.
>
> (*Measure for Measure*, I. ii. 124–126)

Similes may multiply:

> But were they false
> As o'er-dyed blacks, as wind, as waters, false
> As dice are to be wished by one that fixes
> No bourn 'twixt his and mine
>
> (*The Winter's Tale*, I. ii. 131–134)

Even those developed at length are anything but obvious or conventional:

> If you give way,
> Or hedge aside from the direct forthright,
> Like to an ent'red tide they all rush by
> And leave you hindmost;
> Or, like a gallant horse fall'n in first rank,
> Lie there for pavement to the abject rear,
> O'errun and trampled on.
>
> (*Troilus and Cressida*, III. iii. 157–163)

They may reflect the character of the speaker, as Othello's grandiose similes do:

> Like to the Pontic Sea,
> Whose icy current and compulsive course
> Ne'er feels retiring ebb, but keeps due on
> To the Propontic and the Hellespont,
> Even so my bloody thoughts, with violent pace,
> Shall ne'er look back, ne'er ebb to humble love,
> Till that a capable and wide revenge
> Swallow them up.
>
> (*Othello*, III. iii. 453–460)

The imagery, modulating from a formal simile to the metaphoric "swallow them up," powerfully conveys the uncompromising character of Othello himself and the epic scale of his revenge, and anticipates the course it will take in the play: violent, irreversible, and tragic.

Metaphors. In the early verse, lovers are apt to use the stock metaphors of courtship:

> Tranio, I saw her *coral* lips to move,
> And with her breath she did *perfume* the air.
>
> (*The Taming of the Shrew*, I. i. 171–172)

Setting, too, is rendered in predictable metaphors:

> The sun begins to *gild* the western sky
>
> (*Two Gentlemen of Verona*, V. i. 1)

But Shakespeare soon begins to make many of his metaphors, like his similes, less obvious and to draw his implied comparisons from commonplace objects and settings rather than from Petrarchan precedent. As Clemen shows (quotations in this section are from *The Development of Shakespeare's Imagery*), "the images adapt themselves more and more organically to the structural form of the drama . . . to the atmosphere of the play or to its theme . . . and the language . . . becomes more and more saturated with" metaphor:

> *Worcester.*   Peace, cousin, say no more;
> And now I will unclasp a secret book,
> And to your quick-conceiving discontents
> I'll read you matter deep and dangerous,
> As full of peril and adventurous spirit
> As to o'erwalk a current roaring loud
> On the unsteadfast footing of a spear.
> *Hotspur.* If he fall in, good night, or sink or swim!
> Send danger from the east unto the west,
> So honor cross it from the north to south,
> And let them grapple. O, the blood more stirs
> To rouse a lion than to start a hare!
>
> (*1 Henry IV*, I. iii. 187–198)

The effect of such speech is not only to give greater life and interest to ordinary talk but to compress and concentrate; to make meaning more ambiguous, character more problematical. Later, "premonitory imagery" will awaken "the presentiment of coming catastrophe," as in the Macbeths' sinister invocations of night. Thus, "the art of indirectly referring to coming events and of employing imagery with dramatic irony attains its height of perfection in the tragedies. In the tragedies, too, cosmic imagery constantly suggests the grand scale on which events are understood to be taking place. "The imagery gives the horizon of the individual occurrence a comprehensive perspective; it transforms human matters into mighty universal events." Imagery is everywhere, and "much of it belongs to the type of the merely suggested, implied and concealed imagery that has unobtrusively melted into the language." Frequently, it is conjured up by a single forceful word:

> 'Tis deepest *winter* in Lord Timon's purse
>
> (*Timon of Athens*, III. iv. 15)

> *Ripeness* is all.
>
> (*King Lear*, V. ii. 11)

At the other extreme it may be mixed and complex, especially at moments of great agitation and disorder:

> Was the hope *drunk*
> Wherein you *dressed* yourself? Hath it *slept* since?
>
> (*Macbeth*, I. vii. 35–36)

Or, in moments of anguish, the metaphors may come thick and fast:

> Life's but a walking shadow, a poor player
> That struts and frets his hour upon the stage
> And then is heard no more. It is a tale
> Told by an idiot, full of sound and fury,
> Signifying nothing.
>
> (*Macbeth*, V. v. 24–28)

And they may be hyperbolic:

> His legs bestrid the ocean: his reared arm
> Crested the world: his voice was propertied
> As all the tunèd spheres
>
> (*Antony and Cleopatra*, V. ii. 82–84)

Complex or simple, the metaphor is almost always "wholly adapted to the situation and the emotion of the speaker."

Perhaps what is most notable about Shakespeare's metaphorical language is its astonishing energy. Instead of retarding the action with well-worn comparisons, the images Shakespeare uses are drawn from the most lively and familiar frameworks of domestic life and natural experience, and the sudden mutation of a simple statement to a metaphorical one immediately raises the emotional level of a speech:

> The bow is bent and drawn; make from the shaft.
>
> (*King Lear*, I. i. 143)

> If I must die,
> I will encounter darkness as a bride,
> And hug it in mine arms.
>
> (*Measure for Measure*, III. i. 83–85)

No poetry in English comes near to Shakespeare's in combining this metaphorical power and passion with the intonation of natural speech.

Conceits. The term *conceit* may refer to any simile or metaphor but especially to one that is developed in some detail. Again, the early conceit is often a conventional comparison intended to make its subject more picturesque. Conceits appropriate to declarations of love (and frequently used in sonnets) often involve conventional images of Cupid or Eros, arrows, worship from afar, paleness and agitation in the lover, a catalog or blazon of attributes in the beloved (eyes like stars, cheeks like roses, teeth like pearls, breath like perfume, hair like golden wires) (Ruthven). Shakespeare's early lovers use some of this machinery, or like Romeo, they find new images that are wholly in keeping with its tone and spirit:

> If I profane with my unworthiest hand
> This holy shrine, the gentle sin is this;
> My lips, two blushing pilgrims, ready stand
> To smooth that rough touch with a tender kiss.
>
> (*Romeo and Juliet*, I. v. 93–96)

But Shakespeare is also capable of mocking this tradition:

> My mistress' eyes are nothing like the sun;
> Coral is far more red than her lips' red;
> If snow be white, why then her breasts are dun;
> If hairs be wires, black wires grow on her head.
>
> (Sonnet 130, 1–4)

The dangers—even the dramatic absurdity—of using elaborate conceits to make a subject more attractive are evident in *Titus Andronicus* when Marcus, finding his niece in the severest distress ("her hands cut off, and her tongue cut out, and ravished," according to the stage direction), is not deterred by compassion or common sense from developing several elaborate conceits and invoking mythological parallels:

> Speak, gentle niece, what stern ungentle hand
> Hath *lopped* and *hewed* and made thy body bare
> Of her two *branches*, those sweet ornaments
> Whose *circling shadows* kings have sought to sleep in,
> And might not gain so great a happiness
> As half thy love? Why dost not speak to me?
> Alas, *a crimson river of warm blood,*
> *Like to a bubbling fountain stirred with wind,*
> *Doth rise and fall between thy rosèd lips,*
> *Coming and going with thy honey breath.*
> But sure some *Tereus* hath deflow'rèd thee,
> And, lest thou shouldst detect him, cut thy tongue.
> Ah, now thou turn'st away thy face for shame,
> And, notwithstanding all this loss of blood,
> *As from a conduit with three issuing spouts,*
> Yet do thy cheeks look *red as Titan's face*
> *Blushing to be encount'red with a cloud.*
>
> (II. iv. 16–32)

Lavinia, at this moment, is a speaking picture of "ravished nature" (Mehl), and the language Mar-

cus finds is appropriate, in its way, to the experience of contemplating a picture. But it is a poetic response, not a dramatic one (Hibbard), and Shakespeare, early in his career, came to mock such figurative devices—"Taffeta phrases, silken terms precise, / Three-piled hyperboles, spruce affection / Figures pedantical"—and to prefer "russet yeas and honest kersey noes" (*Love's Labor's Lost*, V. ii. 407–409, 414).

In later plays, the extended comparison is likely to be drawn from a commoner, or even a harsher, frame of reference and to be conducted without sentimentality and often in an unconventional form. We can see the difference in these two conceits, the first fairly early and the second quite late:

> *Ursula.* The pleasant'st angling is to see the fish
> Cut with her golden oars the silver stream
> And greedily devour the treacherous bait.
> So angle we for Beatrice, who even now
> Is couchèd in the woodbine coverture.
>
> (*Much Ado About Nothing*, III. i. 26–30)

> *Leontes.* There may be in the cup
> A spider steeped, and one may drink, depart,
> And yet partake no venom, for his knowledge
> Is not infected; but if one present
> Th' abhorred ingredient to his eye, make known
> How he hath drunk, he cracks his gorge, his sides,
> With violent hefts. I have drunk, and seen the spider.
>
> (*The Winter's Tale*, II. i. 39–45)

Even though Ursula introduces her conceit in a refreshingly original way, the conventional epithets of "golden oars" and "silver stream" embellish her figure of Beatrice as a fish approaching the bait. But Leontes' harsher image is not at all set up as a formal comparison. The apparently gratuitous image of the spider in the cup is developed dramatically, with strong auxiliary metaphors ("cracks" and "infected"), and only at the last few words do we suddenly see the force of the conceit.

Personification. The attribution of human qualities to abstractions, natural forces, collective terms, or inanimate objects is a trope that Shakespeare uses extensively and dramatizes in two principal ways. Abstract powers or gods at times are actually represented on the stage (Rumor in *2 Henry IV*; Iris, Ceres, and Juno in *The Tempest*); much more frequently, the language refers to such powers. These references—essentially, images—take many forms:

384

Gods or supernatural beings are mentioned, described, or identified with the phenomena they control:

> The mailèd Mars shall on his altar sit
> Up to the ears in blood.
>
> *(1 Henry IV,* IV. i. 116–117)

> And ye that on the sands with printless foot
> Do chase the ebbing Neptune, and do fly him
> When he comes back.
>
> *(The Tempest,* V. i. 34–36)

Abstract forces or powers, such as Time, Nature, Truth, Peace, Sleep, Love, Death, or Fortune, act with human purposefulness in a human world. Often these forces are treated as quasi-allegorical figures, in the tradition of the morality plays or emblem books:

> Time doth transfix the flourish set on youth
> And delves the parallels in beauty's brow,
> Feeds on the rarities of nature's truth,
> And nothing stands but for his scythe to mow.
>
> (Sonnet 60, 9–12)

> Time hath, my lord, a wallet at his back,
> Wherein he puts alms for oblivion,
> A great-sized monster of ingratitudes.
>
> *(Troilus and Cressida,* III. iii. 145–147)

>   for within the hollow crown
> That rounds the mortal temples of a king
> Keeps Death his court; and there the antic sits,
> Scoffing his state and grinning at his pomp
>
> *(Richard II,* III. ii. 160–163)

Human feelings (patience, pride, jealousy, envy, grief) are detached from the self and personified:

> Grief fills the room up of my absent child,
> Lies in his bed, walks up and down with me
>
> *(King John,* III. iv. 93–94)

> O, beware, my lord, of jealousy!
> It is the green-eyed monster, which doth mock
> The meat it feeds on.
>
> *(Othello,* III. iii. 165–167)

Parts of a self (either faculties or organs) are said to act in their own right, as if they were persons:

>   Your constancy
> Hath left you unattended.
>
> *(Macbeth,* II. ii. 67–68)

> Not an eye
> But is aweary of thy common sight,
> Save mine, which hath desired to see thee more
>
> *(1 Henry IV,* III. ii. 87–89)

General terms are used to designate persons:

> Opinion, that did help me to the crown,
> Had still kept loyal to possession [its possessor]
>
> (Ibid., 42–43)

> The skipping king
>
> (Ibid., 60)

> Enfeoffed himself to popularity
>
> (Ibid., 69)

Here *popularity* is a contemptuous abstract term for the populace. In this passage, Henry IV achieves a majestic detachment, even remoteness, by using this device repeatedly. Henry also uses one form of the similar figure *hypallage,* the transferred epithet, when he says that the late King Richard II "grew a companion to the common streets" (Ibid., 68) rather than to the common people in the streets.

Individual characters are identified with specific qualities: "Farewell, fair cruelty" (*Twelfth Night,* I. v. 274); "Bravely, my diligence" (*The Tempest,* V. i. 241). Other characters in the plays are given such titles as Lady Wisdom, Signior Love, Monsieur Melancholy, and Sir Valour.

Individual characters become visual icons, representing particular virtues, vices, human types, or predicaments (Doebler; Mehl). Kings and tragic heroes can often be read as visual embodiments of pride, anger, jealousy, or other emblematic sins; other characters, especially in the comedies, represent various kinds of folly. Lavinia, in *Titus Andronicus,* becomes a speaking picture of ravished innocence; later, her ravishers consciously adopt the masks of Rapine and Murder, and their mother, representing herself as Revenge, unwittingly helps Titus wreak his own.

Finally, human feelings or powers are attributed to the sun, moon, morning, day, the winds, to the ground or land or a kingdom, to cities, castles, and other inanimate entities:

> Purple the sails, and so perfumèd that
> The winds were lovesick with them
>
> *(Antony and Cleopatra,* II. ii. 194–195)

Go to the rude ribs of that ancient castle;
Through brazen trumpet send the breath of parley
Into his ruined ears.

(*Richard II,* III. iii. 32–34)

Most of these devices help to make the moral force of some abstract power become visible on the stage or take vivid form in the audience's imagination.

Image Clusters and Complexes. Edward Armstrong has shown that sets of apparently unrelated images (kites and bedding; crows and beetles; goose, disease, music, bitterness, seasoning, and restraint) recur in Shakespeare's plays, apparently as the result of the poet's personal associations. Other critics have emphasized the multifarious ways in which related metaphors in any play connect with each other and set up symbolic networks of meaning. A play's metaphorical complex may even be our most accurate guide to its profoundest levels of significance. What Richard Altick calls "symphonic imagery in *Richard II*" links together many images (from earth, land, and soil to crown, words, and breath) to form a thematic chain of meanings. Clemen finds that Hamlet's extraordinary imagistic resourcefulness is the measure both of his own dazzling character and of the "surprisingly new possibilities of language" that we find in Shakespeare's plays from this point on. His imagery is often of everyday things (shoes, tears, meats, tables), as well as of a whole range of disagreeable matters that also interest other characters in the play; disease, ulcers, sickness, infection, weeds, corruption, and maggots. Caroline Spurgeon and other scholars have noted the extent to which the plays of Shakespeare, especially the tragedies, are dominated by controlling images and image clusters: images of light in *Romeo and Juliet;* of earth, land, and garden in *Richard II* (Altick); of food, cooking, and disease in *Troilus and Cressida;* in *Macbeth,* of ill-fitting clothes, echoing sound, light and dark, and disease, among others; and in *King Lear,* along with images of animals and violent weather, "a human body in anguished movement, tugged, wrenched, beaten, pierced, stung, scourged, dislocated, flayed, gashed, scalded, tortured and finally broken on the rack" (Spurgeon).

These image complexes relate directly to the fundamental meanings of the play. The food and sickness imagery of *Hamlet* and *Troilus and Cressida* provide objective correlatives for the intense alienation and disgust that pervade these plays. The cosmic imagery of *Hamlet, King Lear,* and *Macbeth* greatly enlarges the actions, characters, and issues of those plays, and the hyperbolic and "world" imagery give to *Antony and Cleopatra* its distinctive note of grandiose majesty (Charney). Charney's detailed analysis stresses and clinches the important point, made earlier by Foakes, that "imagery" must include what transpires, or is referred to, onstage as well as what is evoked by figures of similitude. Together, all the kinds of imagery, controlled and directed by Shakespeare's masterly art, may be the most effective stylistic feature in extending the symbolic range and dramatic power of Shakespeare's plays.

Conclusion

These generalizations, necessarily incomplete, about Shakespeare's poetic style and stylistic development need to be qualified by an understanding of two fundamental points. First, all the plays are different from one another, and Shakespeare's different purposes in each keep it from being merely one in a series of progressively changing works. Each comedy, history, and tragedy has a style of its own, which may or may not incorporate fully the large changes described here. Second, Shakespeare's verbal and dramatic resourcefulness is so variable in the way it proceeds from line to line and from speech to speech that no list of stylistic techniques or description of effects can adequately convey the diversity of his workmanship. Shakespeare's every line is not perfection, but in the literature of the world, nothing so rare, so huge, so "constant in a wondrous excellence" (Sonnet 105, 6) has ever appeared again.

BIBLIOGRAPHY

E. A. Abbott, *A Shakespearian Grammar* (1879). Richard D. Altick, "Symphonic Imagery in *Richard II,*" in *PMLA,* 62 (1947). Edward A. Armstrong, *Shakespeare's Imagination: A Study of the Psychology of Association and Inspiration* (1946). T. W. Baldwin, *William Shakspere's Small Latine and Lesse Greeke,* 2 vols. (1944). Francis Berry, *The Shakespeare Inset: Word and Picture* (1965). S. L. Bethell, "Shakespeare's Imagery: The Diabolic Images in *Othello,*" in *Shakespeare Survey,* 5 (1952). Stephen Booth, *An Essay on Shakespeare's Sonnets* (1969). Fredson

Bowers, "Establishing Shakespeare's Text: Notes on Short Lines and the Problem of Verse Division," in *Studies in Bibliography,* 33 (1980). M. C. Bradbrook, "Fifty Years of the Criticism of Shakespeare's Style: A Retrospect," in *Shakespeare Survey,* 7 (1954).

E. K. Chambers, *William Shakespeare: A Study of Facts and Problems,* 2 vols. (1930). Maurice Charney, *Shakespeare's Roman Plays: The Function of Imagery in the Drama* (1961). Wolfgang Clemen, *The Development of Shakespeare's Imagery* (2nd. ed., 1977) and *Shakespeare's Dramatic Art: Collected Essays* (1972). Richard David, *The Janus of Poets* (1935). John Doebler, *Shakespeare's Speaking Pictures: Studies in Iconic Imagery* (1974). Alan S. Downer, "The Life of Our Design: The Function of Imagery in the Poetic Drama," in *Shakespeare: Modern Essays in Criticism,* Leonard F. Dean, ed. (1957). Heather Dubrow, "Shakespeare's Undramatic Monologues: Toward a Reading of the *Sonnets,"* in *Shakespeare Quarterly,* 32 (1981).

Philip Edwards, Inga-Stina Ewbank, and G. K. Hunter, eds., *Shakespeare's Styles: Essays in Honour of Kenneth Muir* (1980). Una Ellis-Fermor, "The Functions of Imagery in Drama," in *The Frontiers of Drama* (1964). William Empson, *Seven Types of Ambiguity* (rev. ed., 1947). Ifor Evans, *The Language of Shakespeare's Plays* (3rd ed., 1964). Inga-Stina Ewbank, " 'More Pregnantly than Words': Some Uses and Limitations of Visual Symbolism," in *Shakespeare Survey,* 24 (1971).

Anne Ferry, *The "Inward" Language: Sonnets of Wyatt, Sidney, Shakespeare, Donne* (1983). Richard Flatter, *Shakespeare's Producing Hand* (1948). R. A. Foakes, "Suggestions for a New Approach to Shakespeare's Imagery," in *Shakespeare Survey,* 5 (1952). Roland Mushat Frye, *Shakespeare: The Art of the Dramatist* (1970). Ulrich K. Goldsmith, "Words Out of a Hat? Alliteration and Assonance in Shakespeare's Sonnets," in *Journal of English and Germanic Philology,* 50 (1950). Harley Granville-Barker, *Prefaces to Shakespeare,* 2 vols. (1946). Harley Granville-Barker and G. B. Harrison, eds., *A Companion to Shakespeare Studies* (1934).

F. E. Halliday, *The Poetry of Shakespeare's Plays* (1954). G. R. Hibbard, *The Making of Shakespeare's Dramatic Poetry* (1981). Sister Miriam Joseph, *Shakespeare's Use of the Arts of Language* (1947). G. Wilson Knight, *The Wheel of Fire: Interpretations of Shakespearian Tragedy, with Three New Essays* (1949). Helge Kökeritz, *Shakespeare's Pronunciation* (1953). Hilton Landry, ed., *New Essays on Shakespeare's Sonnets* (1976).

M. M. Mahood, *Shakespeare's Wordplay* (1957). David I. Masson, "Free Phonetic Patterns in Shakespeare's Sonnets," in *Neophilologus,* 38 (1954). Joseph B. Mayor, *Chapters on English Metre* (1901; repr. 1968). Dieter Mehl, "Visual and Rhetorical Imagery in Shakespeare's Plays," in *Essays and Studies,* 25 (1972). Kenneth Muir, *Shakespeare's Sonnets* (1979). Kenneth Muir and S. Schoenbaum, eds., *A New Companion to Shakespeare Studies* (1971). Frederic W. Ness, *The Use of Rhyme in Shakespeare's Plays* (1941).

Ants Oras, *Pause Patterns in Elizabethan and Jacobean Drama: An Experiment in Prosody* (1960). Robert Ornstein, "Character and Reality in Shakespeare," in *Shakespeare, 1564–1964: A Collection of Modern Essays by Various Hands,* Edward A. Bloom, ed. (1964). A. C. Partridge, *The Language of Renaissance Poetry: Spenser, Shakespeare, Donne, Milton* (1971). Anton M. Pirkhofer, " 'A Pretty Pleasing Pricket'—On the Use of Alliteration in Shakespeare's Sonnets," in *Shakespeare Quarterly,* 14 (1963).

Paul Ramsey, *The Fickle Glass: A Study of Shakespeare's Sonnets* (1979). K. K. Ruthven, *The Conceit* (1969). George H. W. Rylands, "Shakespeare the Poet," in Harley Granville-Barker and G. B. Harrison, eds., *A Companion to Shakespeare Studies* (1934), and *Words and Poetry* (1928). George Saintsbury, *A History of English Prosody from the Twelfth Century to the Present Day,* I–II (2nd ed., 1923). Jakob Schipper, *A History of English Versification* (1910). Carol M. Sicherman, "Meter and Meaning in Shakespeare," in *Language and Style,* 15 (1982). Hallett Smith, *The Tension of the Lyre: Poetry in Shakespeare's Sonnets* (1981). Caroline F. E. Spurgeon, *Shakespeare's Imagery and What It Tells Us* (1935).

Marina Tarlinskaja, "Evolution of Shakespeare's Metrical Style," in *Poetics,* 12 (1983). Brian Vickers, *Classical Rhetoric in English Poetry* (1970). George T. Wright, "Hendiadys and *Hamlet,"* in *PMLA,* 96 (1981), and "The Play of Phrase and Line in Shakespeare's Iambic Pentameter," in *Shakespeare Quarterly,* 34 (1983).

Shakespeare's Use of Prose

BRIAN VICKERS

In all but four of Shakespeare's plays *(Henry VI, Parts 1 and 3; King John; Richard II)* prose is used as an alternative and contrasting medium to verse. The proportion of prose to verse can range from less than one-tenth *(Titus Andronicus, Richard III, Julius Caesar, Antony and Cleopatra, Henry VIII)* to nine-tenths *(The Merry Wives of Windsor)*, but in every instance its use is carefully controlled for artistic effect. As for such plays as *Henry IV, Parts 1 and 2, Much Ado About Nothing, As You Like It, Hamlet, Twelfth Night, Troilus and Cressida, All's Well That Ends Well, Measure for Measure,* and *King Lear,* the scenes and speeches in prose contain so much of the vital experience of the drama as to make it the normal vehicle of some of Shakespeare's most memorable characters: Falstaff, Beatrice and Benedick, Rosalind and Touchstone, Hamlet, Pandarus and Thersites, Pompey and Mistress Overdone, Poor Tom and Lear's Fool.

For poets and writers of poetic drama, prose is inevitably the inferior medium. (Milton called his prose works the achievement of his left hand.) On this basis it is undeniable that prose is given the lesser role by Shakespeare. In terms of social divisions, prose is the medium of servants, clowns, sailors, and workingmen in general. When a member of the verse-speaking, ruling classes in Shakespeare comes into contact with these embodiments of a lower realm, he normally descends to their level. The entry of a clown will always reduce the medium to prose, even in a tragic context: *Titus Andronicus, Othello, Hamlet, Macbeth, Antony and Cleopa-*tra. This law of adaptation to a lower social level is a mark not of condescension but of sociable adjustment, putting off dignity, accepting the other on his terms. To address a clown or servant in verse can be the mark of a stranger. Thus, in *Twelfth Night,* where Viola has always gone down to prose to talk to Feste, the sudden arrival of her twin brother, Sebastian, ignorant of the customs of Olivia's household, is marked by his addressing Feste in verse (IV. i. 1–19). Verse can be used to scold servants, marking the speaker's authority over them, as in *The Merchant of Venice* (II. ii).

Prose is given a lesser role in terms of subject matter, too. In Shakespeare's plays no serious or dangerous conspiracies are plotted in prose. Hotspur, solus, can mock the letter of a fainthearted rebel in prose (*1 Henry IV,* II. iii), but he rises to verse for all his public doings. In *Coriolanus* it is significant that the rebellious citizens, whose grievances can be easily contained by the patrician class, are given prose among themselves; whereas the tribunes, that much more dangerous source of civil discord, conspire in verse (I. i; II. i, iii; III. i, iii). No important person in Shakespeare dies speaking prose—in fact, hardly anyone, except for despicable people such as the rebel Jack Cade (*2 Henry VI,* IV. x), is denied the higher medium for his last words. Even Enobarbus, so often a satirical or debunking speaker of prose, is given verse to express his remorse over abandoning Antony and for his subsequent suicide (*Antony and Cleopatra,* IV. vi, ix). For much the same reason, no serious love affairs are conducted or concluded in prose. (The wooing of Princess Katherine by Henry V is the nearest to an exception, but since she cannot speak English her few words of reply could hardly rise to the dignity of verse.)

The different resonances of the two media can be illustrated most graphically with two parallel passages. Othello, safely reunited with Desdemona in Cyprus, exclaims:

> O my soul's joy!
>
> . . .
>
> If it were now to die,
> 'Twere now to be most happy, for I fear
> My soul hath her content so absolute
> That not another comfort like to this
> Succeeds in unknown fate.
>
> (II. i. 182–191)

In *The Merry Wives of Windsor,* Falstaff, arriving for his first assignation with Mistress Ford, enters with a line stolen from Sidney's *Astrophil and Stella,* but then reverts to his true medium:

> "Have I caught thee, my heavenly jewel?"
> Why, now let me die, for I have lived long enough.
> This is the period of my ambition. O this blessed hour!
>
> (III. iii. 35–37)

Undoubtedly there is a vast difference between the two characters, but the fact that Shakespeare could exploit the incongruity of that kind of romantic assertion being made in prose confirms the conclusion that to limit people to prose is to deny them certain kinds of seriousness or dignity.

This inferiority of person and medium is beautifully shown by those cases in which a character from the lower depths aspires to verse but fails to sustain his ambitions. The tinker Christopher Sly, in the framing Induction to *The Taming of the Shrew*—a play outside the play, as it were—is picked up in a drunken sleep by the local lord, dressed as a gentleman, and made to believe that he belongs in the upper world. He begins with suitably coarse prose—"Y'are a baggage, the Slys are no rogues. Look in the chronicles: we came in with Richard Conqueror. Therefore pocas palabras, let the world slide. Sessa!" (Ind. i. 3–5)—and we are amused when, under the pressure of deception, he ascends to verse:

> Am I a lord, and have I such a lady?
>
> · · · · · · · · · · · · · ·
>
> I smell sweet savors and I feel soft things.
> Upon my life, I am a lord indeed.
>
> (Ind. ii. 66–70)

Yet he cannot sustain the pretense for very long; desires of "the flesh and the blood" make him revert to prose and bawdy (123–140).

A less innocent pretender to higher status is Jack Cade, ringleader of an uprising, who speaks prose with his fellow citizens (*2 Henry VI,* IV. ii. 29–109). To gain status Cade illegally and comically knights himself, suddenly speaking verse:

> As for these silken-coated slaves, I pass not.
> It is to you, good people, that I speak,
> Over whom (in time to come) I hope to reign.
>
> (116–118)

Despite his fellows' raucous comments, Cade continues in his pretender's verse. Yet when he is confronted by the forces of law and order, Buckingham and Clifford (IV. viii), Shakespeare returns Cade to prose and keeps him where he belongs for his meeting with Alexander Iden, a Kentish gentleman who speaks verse legitimately and defeats the rebel (IV. x), winning a victory for order but also for the superior mode. Another character deceived into speaking above his level—here intellectual rather than social—is Ajax. He is established as a prose character (*Troilus and Cressida,* II. i, iii), but when Ulysses and Agamemnon (who have mocked him earlier in prose asides) address Ajax in their plot to build him up as the rival to Achilles, they do so in verse. As he sees a heroic future beginning to unfold, Ajax moves up to verse, slowly, ponderously (II. iii. 196–200); yet he is able to sustain it only for a few lines, slipping back to his native depth.

If some prose characters are below a given social norm, others are conceived as being outside society or outside the resources of English blank verse. No foreigner in Shakespeare speaks verse: this is true for Dr. Caius in *Merry Wives,* for the Welshman Evans ("one that makes fritters of English": V. v. 140), for the "four nations" scenes in *Henry V* (III. i, vi), and for Princess Katherine's unwittingly bawdy French lesson (III. iv). Shakespeare's two Latin lessons, the one ignorantly commented on by Mistress Quickly in *Merry Wives* (IV. i), and the parsing of a verse from Ovid's *Heroides* used by Lucentio as a cover for wooing Bianca *(The Taming of the Shrew)*, are in prose.

Drunkards also cannot be expected to speak English verse: this is evident from the barge scene in *Antony and Cleopatra* (II. vii), from the Porter in *Macbeth* (II. iii), and from Cassio, made drunk by Iago. In his remorse Cassio exclaims that in his scuffle with Roderigo "the devil drunkenness" gave "place to the devil wrath" *(Othello,* II. iii. 283–284). Prose is the appropriate medium for all disturbances of the normal psychological balance, the norm being expressed in verse. The uncontrollable anger of Kate in *The Taming of the Shrew* is shown by the way in which she speaks verse to her father but, when left alone, releases an outburst of prose abuse (I. i. 102–104). For Thersites, railing and abuse have become a way of life, and only prose could accommodate his catalogs of curses *(Troilus and Cressida,* II. i, iii; V. i).

The most dramatic use of prose for marking psychological imbalance is for madness. It was a convention in Elizabethan drama that mad people spoke in prose. When Hamlet puts on his "antic disposition," he also adopts prose in the public scenes, when he is with Claudius or those whom he suspects of being Claudius' agents. When Polonius first accosts him, the deferential counselor descends to prose, as one would do with a servant or clown (II. ii. 171–216). Rosencrantz and Guildenstern do the same, as does the obedient Ophelia later (III. i, ii). Claudius also humors Hamlet in the play scene by talking to him in prose (III. ii), but after the murder of Polonius he treats Hamlet as a much more serious opponent and addresses him in verse (IV. iii). The contrast between the sane characters speaking verse, and the mad ones prose, recurs—this time for real—with the pathetic madness of Ophelia (IV. v) and with the momentary collapse of Othello into a fit, Iago standing over him in full control:

> *Othello.* . . . It is not words that shakes me thus.—Pish!
> Noses, ears, and lips? Is't possible?—Confess?—
> Handkerchief?—O devil!
> *Iago.* Work on,
> My medicine, work! Thus credulous fools are caught.
>
> (IV. i. 41–45)

This correlation between media and states of mind is repeated with Lady Macbeth's sleepwalking. Her confused prose, collapsing distinctions of time and action, is followed by the Doctor's verse, expressing medical and ethical authority:

> Foul whisp'rings are abroad. Unnatural deeds
> Do breed unnatural troubles. Infected minds
> To their deaf pillows will discharge their secrets.
>
> (V. i. 66–68)

Given the consistency with which the distinction between sanity and madness was observed in the linguistic medium, it may be significant that Leontes' mad jealousy never collapses into prose, as if to suggest that his mind is only temporarily "infected" and may soon clear *(The Winter's Tale,* I. i–III. ii).

In the cases so far examined the verse-prose distinction represents various distinctions existing in real life. The two media are being used mimetically to record divisions (between higher and lower social levels or between the sane and the mad) that exist outside the play. It is clear that the distinction between verse and prose was made systematically by the writers for the Elizabethan stage, was carried out in performance by the actors, and was immediately evident to the audience. In the extant promptbooks the pages are divided into four equal columns, the first containing speakers' names; the text would fill the middle two columns if in verse and would extend across all three if in prose. This distinction was observed by Shakespeare's own characters. When Malvolio reads the letter by which he is duped into thinking that Olivia loves him, he recites the verse, notes the change of the metrical form from short lines to octosyllabics ("The numbers altered!"), and observes the final change: "Soft, here follows prose" *(Twelfth Night,* II. v. 93–94, 129–130). When Longavile, one of the courtiers who has vowed a three-year abstention from the company of women, breaks his vow and writes poetry, he is dissatisfied with the result:

> I fear these stubborn lines lack power to move.
> O sweet Maria, empress of my love!
> These numbers will I tear, and write in prose.

Berowne, apostle of health and normality, thereupon comments from his hiding place, "O, rimes are guards on wanton Cupid's hose" *(Love's Labor's Lost,* IV. iii. 50–53)—that is, the necessary trimmings to love.

But although poetry is the medium for love, it has to have an authentic language. Hamlet concludes his verse and reverts to prose as an index of a feeling that cannot be bound in formal constraints:

> Doubt truth to be a liar;
> But never doubt I love.

O dear Ophelia, I am ill at these numbers. I have not art to reckon my groans, but that I love thee best, O most best, believe it.

(II. ii. 118–122)

There, real suffering and real sincerity could be expressed only in prose. In performance, actors must have spoken verse with much more emphasis on the rhythm, so that prose would have at once seemed, by contrast, relaxed or formless (a distinction that is seldom if ever audible in the modern theater). Conversely, where prose is the established norm in a scene, verse can be made to look affected. When Rosalind, Jaques, and Celia are speaking prose, Orlando enters with just one line of verse:

> Good day and happiness, dear Rosalind.

At this Jaques leaves in disgust, saying, "Nay then, God b' wi' you, an you talk in blank verse" (*As You Like It,* IV. i. 27–29).

The ability to appreciate swift changes from one form to the other was essential in the live theater. In the "external" or mimetic category that I have so far been discussing, the use of prose could be underlined by visual, theatrical means—servants dress as servants do in real life, foreigners are audibly such, mad people behave in a deranged way, drunkards stagger and hiccup. But this ability to spot the difference between the two media was even more vital to the successful working of what I shall call the "internal" distinction between verse and prose—that is, where it expresses a contrast internal to the play as an aesthetic system or represents the deliberate act of a character who is not bound to speak prose by the mimetic representation of everyday life. The dramatist can maintain the decorum of a scene or produce effects of local contrast by making some characters who would normally speak prose remain in verse, or vice versa. Thus, the servants in *The Taming of the Shrew* speak prose among themselves but ascend to verse when Petruchio arrives (IV. i). In *Love's Labor's Lost* two prose characters, Jaquenetta and Costard, enter a verse scene and speak verse (IV. iii), so preserving

the decorum of style. In *The Merry Wives of Windsor,* predominantly a prose comedy, verse is associated with the lovers Fenton and Anne Page: when they enter into the final scene, the medium moves up to verse to mark their newly married state.

The movement from verse to prose can reflect movement from public to private business or from tense to relaxed states. A striking instance occurs in *Measure for Measure,* in the scene in which Isabella's anguish at Angelo's corrupt proposal that she should yield him her virginity in order to keep Claudio alive is exacerbated by Claudio's wish to live even at the cost of her sin. When the confrontation has reached an impasse and Isabella has collapsed into hysterical abuse of her brother, the Duke, disguised as a friar, steps forward and calms the scene down with a long and fluent prose exposition of the plot by which he will trap Angelo (III. i).

The lesser medium often acts as a foil for inset song (as in *As You Like It,* II. v) or rhyme. So in *Pericles,* when Cerimon opens the chest containing the preserved corpse of Queen Thaisa and other mysterious relics, the medium drops from verse to prose, against which the octosyllabic couplets of the message on the scroll then stand out in sharper relief (III. ii). Verse after prose always has a greater resonance. The conjuring scene in *Henry VI, Part 2,* begins with characters who normally speak verse talking prose, so that when they move to verse the magic ceremonies seem even more awesome (I. iv). A most unusual shift to the lower medium occurs in *Henry V,* when the French king's message of defiance is communicated by the herald, uniquely, in prose, so that Henry's angry reply in verse will echo more strongly (III. vi. 114–167)— a patriotic gesture, too.

In the tragedies, we find examples of the media division being used for local effects, germane to the scene or dramatic impact rather than to the characters. When Desdemona, safely landed on Cyprus, is awaiting Othello's arrival, she persuades Iago to play the clown. He obliges, extemporizing couplets mocking women. Both Desdemona and Cassio are given prose, which may serve as a foil to Iago's rhymes but also makes the shift to verse at Othello's entry seem more resonant (II. i). In *Macbeth,* the prose scene between Lady Macduff and her son, in which the boy's naive remarks on liars and swearers add another level of comment on the perversions in the play (IV. ii. 36–63), gives way to verse for the messenger and for the murderers sent to kill them. Even more horrible is the contrast between the prose in which Cornwall, Regan, and Goneril discuss the punishment of Gloucester (III. vii. 1–12) and the verse in which they commit it: from theoretical evil to its practice. The irruption of violence into a domestic scene recurs in *Coriolanus* when the relaxed prose spoken by Volumnia and Virgilia while sewing is interrupted by the manic verse in which Coriolanus' mother fantasizes her son smashing his enemies (I. iii. 1–45). Here the move is from reality to fantasy, revealing the tensions of a militaristic society in the early days of Rome.

In *Antony and Cleopatra* the move from prose to verse, by a character we associate more with prose, takes us from present to past but also emphasizes a key element in the play. When Enobarbus is impressing Caesar's friends Maecenas and Agrippa with stories of wild revels in Egypt, the medium drops to prose (II. ii. 172–191), but it returns to verse to describe Antony's first view of Cleopatra:

> The barge she sat in, like a burnished throne,
> Burnt on the water: the poop was beaten gold.

The change from lower to higher register—like that from a minor to a major key in music or from black-and-white to color in film—is justified here by the subject matter (since serious love in Shakespeare is the province of verse) rather than by the psychology of the character. But in all these instances of dramatic contrast or structural effect, the audience, like the reader, must be alert to the shift of media.

The other internal category—where the choice of a medium is not governed by mimetic demands—results from a character's deliberate act, often involving dissimulation. This convention was not unique to Shakespeare: in Marston's *The Malcontent,* Malevole speaks verse in his own character and prose in his disguised persona, the move between the two being recorded in the stage direction "Malevole shifteth his speech." Those who disguise or dissimulate in Shakespeare often change to the lower medium. In *The Two Gentlemen of Verona,* Julia, disguised as a boy to overhear the infidelities of Proteus, also steps down to prose (IV. ii). Henry V, imitating the practice of other rulers by moving disguised among his soldiers on the eve of Agincourt, speaks a plain and functional prose (IV. i) very different from the lighthearted style he uses to court Kate (V. ii). In his nocturnal wandering the

king, who belongs to the verse-speaking world, meets a man speaking verse who has no right to do so, the ancient Pistol. His verse is a tissue of imitations of Kyd and Marlowe, the stiffest of iambics glued together, as if Bottom had extended his play verse into real life. This bizarre confrontation between two refugees from their real media points up the difference between Henry, who (like Shakespeare's other truly eloquent speakers) can move easily from prose to verse and back, and Pistol, who is stuck in his pretense. It is appropriate that the pretender Pistol is finally humiliated by Fluellen, a limited but honest representative of prose (V. i).

Dissimulation is forced on Hamlet yet embraced by him, and perhaps by Shakespeare, as a way of demonstrating his great resourcefulness. For Hamlet's resort to prose is not limited to his feigned madness. He uses it to welcome the players in a relaxed and affectionate mode, against which Aeneas' tale to Dido of the destruction of Troy stands out with all the more force (II. ii. 411–531). Prose is here not only a mode of disguise against Polonius but also the medium with which one addresses social inferiors politely, a polysemous application that becomes more frequent in the tragedies. On all counts it is fitting that Hamlet should rise to verse when he is left alone at the end of this scene, in the soliloquy "O, what a rogue and peasant slave am I," in which the seriousness of his dilemma is expressed in a way that could never be attempted in prose.

When we next see Hamlet he again shifts between media, but in the reverse order, moving from the "To be or not to be" soliloquy to the milieu of prose satire against women's vices when he is confronted by Ophelia (III. i. 56–149). When he leaves, Ophelia, who had descended to prose to humor his madness, returns to verse for her feeling soliloquy, a contrast between the media of sanity and of madness that foreshadows her own collapse. Hamlet uses prose to instruct the players in acting and to comment bitterly on their play and its moral (III. ii), to sport with the gravediggers (V. i. 62–199), and to mock Osric (V. ii. 83–176). Whereas all these instances establish Hamlet's chameleon wit, the fact that he continues to speak prose with Horatio after Osric has gone (V. ii. 176–213) is a sign of the decorum of the play as a whole and the working of local contrast. The relaxed tone of their dialogue—"There is special providence in the fall of a sparrow"—gives way, with the appearance of Claudius, Laertes, and the others, to verse and tragedy. Prose has no business with these "carnal, bloody, and unnatural acts."

Hamlet's brilliance in verse, prose, and rhyme is matched by only one other character in Shakespeare: Iago. The fact that the two plays were probably written in close proximity suggests that Shakespeare carried over to his villain the flexibility that he had developed for his favorite hero, a striking instance of artistic detachment. For Iago, verse is the norm for serious involvement with the public world, much of it embodying malice and trickery, but also for his soliloquies, where he reveals some, at least, of his true motives. Prose is primarily the medium for his private plots, manipulating Roderigo (I. iii; II. i; IV. ii) and subsequently Cassio (II. iii) by presenting himself as a confidential, sympathetic friend, assuring them satisfaction of their desires. Prose in Iago's hands is a flexible tool, especially good at disvaluing concepts or people. Virtue is "a fig! 'Tis in ourselves that we are thus or thus"; love "is merely a lust of the blood and a permission of the will" (I. iii. 319–320, 333–334). Desdemona's love for Othello—so sympathetically presented in verse before the Venetian council (I. iii. 76–170)—is travestied by Iago's prose: "Mark me with what violence she first loved the Moor, but for bragging and telling her fantastical lies; and will she love him still for prating?" (II. i. 220–222). Iago poisons everything he touches, and prose seems only too appropriate for his lewd announcement to Brabantio that "your daughter and the Moor are now making the beast with two backs" (I. i. 115–116), as for his aside of hatred against Cassio (II. i. 166–175). Iago reduces prose to its lowest level. Only Thersites equals him in foulness, and Thersites' foulness is limited to verbal abuse: he does not plot the destruction of others. Even more threatening is the ease with which Iago ascends to verse, especially in the soliloquies ending so many scenes. His control over language is a sign of his powers of transformation, a skill in manipulating the self and others in which he exults.

If Hamlet and Iago willingly embrace pretense and the consequent need to flick back and forth from verse to prose, other tragic characters have prose and pretense thrust upon them. In *King Lear* the loyal Kent, banished yet returning to serve Lear, has disguised his appearance and plans to borrow "other accents . . . That can my speech defuse" (I. iv. 1–2). He does so by speaking prose in his new role as Caius, the plainspoken type that Iago seems to be and Enobarbus is: "I do profess to be

no less than I seem, to serve him truly that will put me in trust, to love him that is honest" (I. iv. 12–13). Kent reverts to verse only on serious occasions, either when he is not heard by Lear—to denounce the compliant servant Oswald to Cornwall (II. ii. 67–103) and to negotiate Lear's safety with Gloucester and Cordelia's supporters (III. iv, vi; IV. iii)—or to express his love and care to his master directly (III. ii, iv). Similarly Edgar, betrayed and banished, feigns a madman's prose in his role as Poor Tom (III. iv, vi; IV. i) but comes up to verse when he speaks soliloquies or asides in his own person, especially to express his anguished feelings for Lear and Gloucester. Shakespeare would never express emotions of such intensity in prose. The dissimulation produced by the shift between prose and verse is not limited to the good characters in this play. At their first appearance, Goneril and Regan speak unctuously flattering verse to protest their love to Lear, but when left alone they descend to prose for the bleak revelation of their true feelings (I. i. 283–306). In the next scene, Edmund delivers a verse soliloquy justifying his bastardy but abruptly shifts to prose to begin manipulating Gloucester against Edgar. Left alone, Edmund (like Iago and Hamlet before him) returns to verse to give us his real self (I. ii; V. 1).

Another character who must assume prose and pretense, though both are foreign to his own nature, is Coriolanus. Forced by the patrician party to become their candidate for consul, to go and strip his wounds before the people and solicit their votes deeds that his patrician upbringing makes most abhorrent to him—he descends to prose, "a low transformation." But the patrician attitudes come through: contempt (" 'Twas never my desire yet to trouble the poor with begging") laced with a smooth irony ("I will, sir, flatter my sworn brother, the people, to earn a dearer estimation of them. . . . I will practice the insinuating nod and be off to them most counterfeitly"; II. iii. 67–68, 91–96). Coriolanus' "heavy descension" is temporary, for he is soon back in verse; but Cloten, son of the Queen in *Cymbeline,* seems to be permanently degraded to prose. His oafish wit is mocked by his own companions (an effect already used for Jack Cade and Ajax). To an Elizabethan audience, Cloten speaking prose was the sign of an inherent baseness unfitting a royal prince (I. ii; II. i, iii; III. v), and since people come down to prose to talk to him and revert to verse once he has left, he is more of a clown than a prince. The fact that Cloten speaks verse when attempting to woo Imogen is a sign that Shakespeare does not wish to humiliate her by his presence any more than necessary. A comparable inversion of expectations occurs in *The Tempest,* where Caliban, whom we might have imagined as speaking prose, is given verse in the company of Stephano and Trinculo, to indicate that, savage though he may be, he is still superior to these degenerate humans.

These are some of the ways in which Shakespeare applied his two media to delineate character, situation, and plot. As for the textures and styles of his prose, they range very widely, from the heavily accented epistolary style of Armado, full of stiff rhetorical balance, to the cut and thrust of Beatrice and Benedick, and the manic repetitions and illusory jealousies of Ford. Prose can contain the energy and bawdy of youth, as with Mercutio or, more coarsely, with Lucio in *Measure for Measure,* and the doddering ramblings of age, as with Justice Shallow. It can serve the romantic plots of Rosalind and the totally unromantic, matter-of-fact arrangements of Pandarus. The Duke's descent to prose in *Measure for Measure,* with his fluent, all-embracing periods, sets up a totally successful plot and saves the play. In *Julius Caesar,* Brutus' decision to make his funeral oration in prose, full of elaborate but unfeeling rhetoric, is a fatal mistake: he and the other conspirators are swept away by the tide of Antony's verse and the anger that it generates. For Falstaff prose is not an occasional medium but a way of life, a vehicle of endless resource: rich, full, life-enhancing, but also corrupt, evasive, deceitful. The individualization achieved by Shakespeare in prose —not even Verdi, in *Falstaff,* could equal his feat, in *The Merry Wives of Windsor,* of creating ten characters instantly recognizable by their styles—is such that those of his characters who never speak prose (Richard II and Leontes, for instance) may seem somewhat limited by contrast. Although overshadowed by verse, the lesser medium in Shakespeare's plays may be legitimately accorded Dryden's praise of "the other harmony of prose."

BIBLIOGRAPHY

Jonas A. Barish, "Continuities and Discontinuities in Shakespearian Prose," in Clifford Leech and J. M. R. Margeson, eds., *Shakespeare 1971* (1972) and "Pattern and Purpose in the Prose of *Much Ado About Nothing,*" in *Rice University Studies,* 60 (1974). Milton Crane, *Shakespeare's Prose* (1951). Richard David, *The Janus of Poets* (1935). Traudl Eichhorn, "Prosa und Vers in vorshakespeareschen Drama," in *Shakespeare Jahrbuch,* 84–86 (1950). Elisabeth Tschopp, *Zur Verteilung von Vers und Prosa in Shakespeares Dramen* (1956). Brian Vickers, *The Artistry of Shakespeare's Prose* (1968; repr. 1979). Henry W. Wells, "The Continuity of Shakesperian Prose," in *Shakespeare Association Bulletin,* 15 (1940).

Shakespeare's Dramatic Methods

BERNARD BECKERMAN

Shakespeare was so thoroughly a dramatist that it is virtually impossible to disengage what is dramatic in his work from what is not. This is true even of so lyric a form as the sonnet. His Sonnets bristle with suggestive confrontation, and though their story—if indeed there is one—eludes us, we cannot refrain from tracing in the sequence of verses the drama of a strange triangle.

What is true of Shakespeare the dramatist is true of Shakespeare the poet. A wholeness of sensibility infuses his writing. Theatrical and even melodramatic as his situations are, they are couched in words and sentences that invite detachment: detachment of speech from scene, of image from action, of sentiment from character. The readiness with which readers have lifted speeches from his plays and recited them as poems testifies to the seductive autonomy of Shakespeare's language. Ultimately, of course, isolated passages become distorted passages. Only reference to the scenic context reinvigorates the extract, reminding us that in Shakespeare, as in no other writer, the dramatist and the poet are indivisible.

Particularly in the playhouse and most particularly the Elizabethan playhouse, this indivisibility is absolute. There the poet cannot be independent of the dramatist. To begin with, the writer must surrender his script to the actors. In fact, as his words and forms take stage, they no longer seem to belong to him but appear to be the autonomous invention of the players.

To a considerable extent such a surrender inheres in all theatrical writing. The dramatist always yields his work to so-called interpreters. But in Shakespeare's day the surrender was much more thoroughgoing than in our own: players bought plays by the act; they sold them when in need; they shuffled the contents at convenience; and they preserved them by chance. In principle, the dramatic poet as descendant of the Greek and Roman tragedians occupied a noble place in the literary pantheon; in practice, he was at best an artificer of stories and at worst a botcher of lines.

For writers whose temperaments or talents did not accord with these practices and conditions, the act of surrender was continually painful. John Webster seems to have endured uncommon anguish. So did Robert Greene and, in a complex way, Ben Jonson. Webster chafed at how the actors misplayed his *White Devil,* and Greene saw the players as his rival mouthpieces. Jonson, in a less defensive manner, sought to assert autonomous stature as a dramatic poet and to protect the integrity of his scripts by supervising their printing.

By contrast, Shakespeare was the quintessential dramatist. Professionally and constitutionally, he seems seldom to have distinguished between the script and its performance. In the preface to the 1604 quarto of *Hamlet,* he seems to reflect a desire to put before the reader a text that goes beyond the play performed. And in the Sonnets he celebrates the poet's immortalizing power. Yet in *Hamlet* he also has the Prince insert a speech into an old play to achieve a special effect—the unmasking of

Claudius. Elsewhere, when Shakespeare shows a play-within-a-play, preparing a performance is a workmanlike business, the playing inseparable from the writing. Indeed, unlike Ben Jonson, who reveals himself through Horace in *The Poetaster,* Shakespeare never shows us a writer at work. Instead, he concentrates on the rehearsal of a script, as with the mechanicals in *A Midsummer Night's Dream,* or on the adaptation of traditional material, as with "The Mousetrap" in *Hamlet.*

This lack of discrimination between poet and player fits the peculiar conditions within which Shakespeare worked. Initially as player, but soon and for years thereafter as both player and writer, he had no need to separate one job from another. Each fed and supported the other. Further, within a few years of his start as a player, Shakespeare rose to the position of sharer in the Lord Chamberlain's Men, thus becoming one of the few Elizabethan dramatists to retain proprietary interest in his plays. Thus, even with the occasional printing of a script, whether with his consent or not, he did not become alienated from his works; and instead of being forced to surrender them to strangers, he could share them with his fellow players.

The Elizabethan Idea of Theater

What the theatrical conditions supplied seems to have agreed with how the man felt. Contemporaries speak of the sweetness of Shakespeare's temper. One or two anecdotes reveal a lusty sense of humor. Scattered documents suggest a capacity for business. There is no sign of overweening ego, as with Christopher Marlowe, or of domineering intellect, as with Ben Jonson. Neither are there any clues that allow us to see the writer figured in any of his creations. Whatever his nature may have been, it remains hidden from us, diffused throughout his scenes and characters, defying attempts to reconstitute and explicate it. We are thus left with his art itself, "an impersonal art," in Una Ellis-Fermor's words. It is a peculiar art because it seems to have two contradictory sides. One side we best know as the "literary," by which we usually mean the vision of the poet transmitted through imaginative language. This is taken frequently to be the "true" face of the dramatist. The other side is the "theatrical," the trappings of dress and gesture that necessarily—and, to some people, unfortunately—accompany the literary personality. But while drama may indeed incorporate and transform literature, the former does not exist as a schizoid off-shoot of the latter. Drama has its own distinct character arising from its own roots. Perhaps the most direct way of seeing the difference between the nondramatic and the dramatic is in a comparison of Shakespeare's poems and plays.

In the Sonnets we always hear the poet's voice. But what act does the voice perform? It addresses the poet's friend, it berates his lover, it muses on the poet's evil fortune. More than anything else, it reveals the mind of the poet. We seem to hear the mind speaking, and through this inner utterance we are in immediate touch with that mind. Though the poet speaks of public things, his utterance is entirely private, and it is entirely his own. It suffers no appropriation by actors, as does the sonnet in dialogue that Romeo and Juliet speak at their first meeting (I. v. 93–106).

Even the more impersonal tone of *The Rape of Lucrece* does not transcend the private arena of the lyric poem, where the circle of Lucrece's fate is bound within the circle of the narrator's judgment. Lucrece's anguish, it is true, assumes a rhetorical form not unlike stage speech; even so, the story remains under the control of the narrator. It is he who describes Tarquin as "lust-breathèd" (3). It is he who tells the reader that "by our ears our hearts oft tainted be" (38). Such observations lack the ambiguity and resonance that they might have if spoken by other characters. Rather, they act as wise counsel from the writer, addressed to us personally, untouched by the question of whether they embody the character's thought or the author's. At the end of the poem, when Brutus heartens Lucrece's aggrieved father and husband, the author puts into the narration and then repeats in Brutus' own words the information that Brutus, who hitherto was known for foolish comments, "throws that shallow habit by / Wherein deep policy did him disguise" (1814–1815). Here narration confirms character. The objective and subjective explanations of Brutus' behavior are identical, but so, too, are the authorial and narrational points of view. Interpretation thus moves under the hand of the author, and through his guidance we read his work.

No such guidance exists in the theater. Despite the occasional use of presenters such as the Chorus in *Henry V* or Gower in *Pericles,* once a scene begins, events and the characters caught within them escape the narrator's manipulations. Tarquin and Lucrece never elude the frame that literature places round them; dramatic characters, by contrast, lack a narrational context. That is the crucial distinction between literary and dramatic characters. No matter how autonomous the literary character may seem, the reader is repeatedly reminded that his actions stem from the narrator's intentions or recollections. Not so the dramatic character, who moves under his own power. His will and passion and plotting give impetus to his words, his acts, and what we learn of his thoughts.

The self-generative quality of drama arises from the public nature of the medium. The actor, not the poet, goes before the audience. He neither tells nor confides but presents. Everything he offers must be made public, not only what is formally public, such as ceremonies, trials, and processions, but also what is most private, including ruminations and even the deepest dreams. In short, the player is always "onstage"; he is always displaying himself and his passions and so expects from the dramatist the means to "publicize" a full range of experience.

The art of the dramatist, then, lies partly in how he manages this public medium to create the illusion of private events and partly in how he gives public events a personal intimacy. In this Shakespeare and his fellow writers had a distinct advantage. Their age was a flamboyantly public one, much in the way that classical Greece was public. It was public in the ceremony that played a large part in daily existence, in the overt signs of conformity that it extracted from private citizens, and in its taste—witness the frenzy for sumptuous dress by people in all walks of life. Homes of all but the meanest sort were filled with apprentices and servants, so that not even the recesses of one's rooms were entirely free from observation. The Elizabethan dramatists merely formalized and heightened the context that naturally surrounded the audience.

Shakespeare's dramatic practices were deeply embedded in the practices of his times. Although he was an innovator in important respects, notably in the development of the history play, he more usually refined the work of his predecessors rather than blazed a path for his successors. Arriving on the London scene sometime in the 1580s, he inherited the changes of that remarkable decade. Dramatic verse, which as late as 1584 was still an amalgam of fourteeners and ballad forms, soon shone in the dazzling shape that Christopher Marlowe and Thomas Kyd gave it. Theatrical narrative, evolving from its medieval origins and transformed by classical example, fused into a fairly stable but idiosyncratic pattern. Performing troupes, following the lead of the twelve-member Queen's Men of 1583, grew to a size able to sustain stories of extended romantic scope. All these elements converged to provide a foundation for Shakespeare's art.

But as a public art, theater had an anomalous position. Under constant attack as sinful and corrupting, it nevertheless flourished, proving to be the most representative art of the English Renaissance. How far Shakespeare's contemporaries recognized this is uncertain. Shakespeare himself attributes such recognition to Hamlet, who calls the actors "the brief abstracts and chronicles of the times." The fact that Shakespeare did not seek to escape the playhouse by writing masques for the court or pageants for London argues that he too thought of the public stage as the key art of his age.

The centrality of the stage was enhanced by its metaphoric importance. Theater was not only the reflection of the times but the very embodiment of eternity. Since the days of Plato and Democritus, poets and philosophers had likened life to acting out a play. "The world's a stage, life a play," cried Democritus. Every man makes his entrances and his exits in the great world theater, and God, the master spectator, judges how well or ill each person plays his or her assigned role.

Renaissance England shared this metaphor with the rest of Europe, but it differed in the degree to which it gave substance to the metaphor. Nowhere else did the performers' building—the public playhouse—concretize the image of the world theater so thoroughly. A visitor from the Continent, such as Johannes De Witt, might see the similarity between the Swan playhouse and the ancient Roman theater, but the Elizabethan playgoer would have been conscious of another association. The public playhouse, however much it might incorporate classical features or proportions, as some scholars have recently argued, was an embodiment of the traditional theatrical metaphor, a metaphor that could recede into obscure convention but that a dramatist could vitalize at any moment, as Anne Righter and others have shown. Each time Shakespeare introduces a theatrical analogy—whether in Macbeth's realization of life as "a poor player" or in York's description of Richard II as a poor actor coming onstage after the star, Bolingbroke, has left —he activates the latent metaphor that his playhouse embodies. It is a commonplace, of course, to note that the building in which Shakespeare worked was the Globe. And though it is probably farfetched, it is not entirely improbable that Shakespeare, just about to write Jaques's famous speech "All the world's a stage," suggested the name of the new playhouse to his company in 1599.

This metaphor of the theater-as-world imparted a valuable resonance to the player's performance. It suffused his words and gestures with the potential for poetry. When he assumed a role or when he played the game of a show, the player was not merely pretending to be someone else; rather, he was acting out the recurrent story of everyman, enlarging the specific act of a specific person into a universal commentary. In this light, nothing he did was existential; everything was symbolic.

By Shakespeare's day, overt displays of theatrical allegory no longer dominated the stage. Players represented particular persons rather than mere universalizing types. However circumscribed the traditional dramatic types might be, the Elizabethan impulse toward individualizing character was strong. In the work of most playwrights, including Shakespeare, certain familiar figures appear and reappear. Counselors, tyrants, fools, wantons, throbbing lovers, chaste heroines, scheming scamps march onstage and off again. Yet even as they share the common heritage of moral demonstration, they flash into moments of unpredictable individuality.

Shakespeare arrives on the scene just when the memory of the universalizing function is fading, though it has not disappeared entirely. He still has a lively tradition to draw upon. Against the normalizing metaphor of the "wide and universal theater . . . wherein [men] play in" (*As You Like It,* II. vii. 137–139), he sets the reality of particular action. The metaphor of world-as-theater contributes to the context of his writing. It lies dormant, ready at hand, easily aroused to give the specific circumstance of a historical action, such as Julius Caesar's assassination, a larger symbolic significance. But it no longer swamps human action. Where the metaphorical demonstration of life's journey to salvation once curtailed possibilities of idiosyncratic behavior, the drama that emerged when Shakespeare came to London thrust contradictory and unpredictable creatures before the public. No longer did a character need to move inevitably to occupy a place in the moral framework of the world. His final moments did not need to confirm social expectation; they could, rather, suggest the inexplicable and finally arrive at the puzzled particularity of Lear's pathetic request "Pray you undo this button" (*King Lear,* V. iii. 310).

Throughout Shakespeare's career, a tension persists between the earlier universalizing imperative of theater and the individualization of events. In brief scenes of choral commentary and in recurrent passages on time, harmony, and enactment, Shakespeare never lets us quite forget the macrocosmic frame, of which the scene before us is only an example. Yet he never lets the cosmic image overwhelm the momentary one so that it becomes mere illustration. Instead, he maintains an ever-shifting balance between two impulses, one of which we can recognize as essentially medieval, the other of which we see as essentially classical.

It was the medieval tradition that sustained and vitalized the theatrical metaphor, even though the metaphor had its origin in premedieval thought. Inherent in the medieval outlook, which so directly affected Elizabethan drama, was belief in a universe that was essentially ordered. Whether this belief was cast into a concept of the stage-as-universe or of life-as-journey, it affirmed a fundamental rhythm of existence; and so, it could tolerate loose and disjointed circumstances. Hence, it did not matter that stories sprawled or that sequences of events defied logical explanation. So long as episodes followed the irresistible line of the universe's movement toward the testing of the soul and the exercise of heavenly judgment, all else could be accommodated. It is no wonder that dramatic forms inherited from medieval examples could seem irregular, even formless, within the encompassing framework of the determination of human destiny.

The classical world provided quite a different inheritance. Known by the Elizabethans mainly through the Roman plays of Seneca and Plautus, ancient drama supplied a highly articulated theatrical form, articulated not only in its dramaturgic features but in its very premises. Its events had to be strictly limited. Its figures were reduced to a manageable few. Its progression was deliberately organized in measurable and, for the most part, equally spaced steps so that the action could move unwaveringly to its conclusion. Unlike the medieval play, the classical drama could not tolerate digression. It insisted that each event proceed from the one before and give rise to the next. So rigid a formulation was a desperate attempt to contain the chaos in which humans swirled.

For the Elizabethans, then, the dramatic forms they inherited were complex means not merely for reflecting their age but for interacting with it. To meet the willfulness, the unreasonableness, and indeed the ruthlessness of life, classical dramatists offered the model of an iron logic for human action. By contrast, medieval dramatists showed men how to play with the seeming pointlessness of events, with the rambling copiousness of life. As long as they accepted an overarching logic in the universe, they could be diverted by its digressions. Scrutinized in detail, scene by scene, this kind of drama seems arbitrary and irrational. Seen as a whole, it expresses existence as a comprehensive illumination of an eternal idea. For Shakespeare and others writing at this conjunction of influences, the possibilities of order and disorder, rationality and irrationality, offered unpredictable opportunities.

The kind of drama that evolved in response to these conflicting impulses was distinctly Elizabethan. It bore little or no resemblance to earlier dramatic styles, although it drew upon them. Neither the Italian nor the French theater ever quite produced dramatic works on a similar scale. So distinctive was the Elizabethan pattern of composition and so removed from conventional European design that only recently have critics acknowledged its artistic integrity. For over three centuries after Shakespeare wrote, the common wisdom was that the Elizabethans lacked dramatic art and that Shakespeare's mastery overcame his age's crudeness—a transcendence of the poet over the playwright. But however long that view may have prevailed, it no longer does so. The last generation has increasingly marveled at Shakespeare's dramatic skills and has even recognized that many of his contemporaries, Marlowe, Jonson, and Middleton among them, also possessed considerable dramaturgic art.

From Literary Source to Dramatic Expression

Shakespeare and his fellow writers possessed in common certain shared habits in writing drama. Although there is little evidence, aside from the *Sir Thomas More* manuscript, that Shakespeare collaborated frequently in writing plays, the profession was rife with collaboration. As the accounts in Henslowe's diary show, writers working on a script together divided their assignments by act. Even when a play contained several plots, assignments were distributed not by story but by sections, according to G. E. Bentley (1971). This tells us two things. First, writers shared a sufficiently uniform set of habits to permit such a division; that is, they could readily agree on the rough progression of a scenario. Second, they thought of a play as a sequence of incremental units, whether scenes or acts. The set number of units does not seem to have been fixed, for anywhere from two to several writers might collaborate on the same material. Evidence for collaboration is fullest in the 1590s. It may have been then that Shakespeare worked as a collaborator, if he did at all; it is also the period during which playwrights set the pattern for Elizabethan and Jacobean drama.

The prevalence of dramatic collaboration was one aspect of the pragmatic rationale that conditioned all writing for the stage. From the mid-1570s on, commercial theater expanded rapidly and stabilized socially. The construction of playhouses intended solely for dramatic performance testifies to the popularity of playgoing. Two things seem to have happened. After the 1570s, London was able to supply a large enough population to make continuous performance possible, yet not one so large that a single play could run indefinitely. On the one hand, more people, citizens and visitors alike, attended plays; on the other, many of the same people attended more plays. The result was a marked escalation in the demand for scripts. Unlike twentieth-century dramatic writing, which usually entails a lengthy period of gestation followed by an often lengthier period in search of production, Elizabethan playwriting led directly to, if it did not coincide with, production. Thus, the pattern that distinguishes Elizabethan drama evolved organically in the day-to-day climate of performance.

The volume of plays required—each acting company needed fifteen to twenty new plays a year—imposed enormous demands on the writers, especially on playwrights attached to a specific company, as with Shakespeare's attachment to the Lord Chamberlain's (later, King's) Men. No single imagination, however fecund, could invent all the adventures for which the stage hungered, nor, indeed, did the age expect the individual writer to invent his own material. Instead, writers freely drew from their common storehouse of literary, dramatic, and historical materials. Writing for the commercial stage only accelerated an already well established process—raiding literature to produce new literature. The rapid expansion of printing in England during the sixteenth century gave the would-be dramatist a host of materials: translations of Italian novellas, Spanish romances, and French tales; massive chronicles from English history, several key ones appearing in the 1570s; pamphlets on local catastrophes; and biographies of notable figures, especially those of Greece and Rome. So widespread was the practice of drawing material from such sources that there are only a few of Shakespeare's plays—*Titus Andronicus, Love's Labor's Lost,* and *The Tempest* most apparently—for which we cannot locate the source or sources upon which Shakespeare based his work.

For the most part, the literary sources, whether historical, fictional, or poetic, possessed good stories, and it was the story that was of most use to the dramatist. His source might suggest a character or supply a phrase or a line of dialogue, but principally it provided a plot, part of a plot, or, at the very least, a striking situation. In this respect the imitation of plots from a wide range of sources reinforced the narrative bias of medieval drama. Earlier the story of man's fall and redemption had been traced in mystery plays, in which different characters appeared in successive scenes even though the narrative thread was continuous. Later, the moral interlude traced the fortunes of a representative human being as he traveled through life, wrestling with vice and virtue. This type of narrative adventuring seems to have been transferred by the 1570s to chivalric romances, so that when the new drama emerged in the 1580s, it was rambling in manner, crammed with characters, and diverse in tone. Even when no more than five men and a boy made up a troupe, they did not stint on the complexity of their stories or the multiplicity of their roles, as David Bevington shows. By the time that Marlowe, Kyd, and Shakespeare began to write, these habits were deeply ingrained in theatrical practice.

Along with most Elizabethan dramatists, Shakespeare was an omnivorous reader. If the research of historians is correct, he worked not from one or two sources in composing a play but drew upon a wide variety of materials. Thus, while a chronicle or a romance might supply the main subject, a host of supplementary histories, essays, poems, and stories contributed sentences, ideas, and situations. How one person could have retained such abundant and diverse matter in his mind simultaneously is astonishing. Certainly, he had a powerful synthetic imagination that could absorb and correlate dissimilar stimuli into a coherent dramatic whole. Even if present source study exaggerates the extent of Shakespeare's gatherings, his demonstrated reliance on source material is impressive. Any discussion of Shakespeare's dramatic practice, therefore, must start with his tremendous ingestion of literature.

In handling sources, Shakespeare seems to have observed a pragmatic freedom. It is not hard to find passages in his plays in which he all but slavishly copied his source. Enobarbus' famed description of Cleopatra coming to meet Antony in her barge is such a case. Elsewhere, in contrast, he departed radically from his source, as in the meeting of Leontes and Perdita in *The Winter's Tale.* Throughout his plays the degree of faithfulness to the original varies; sometimes it is close, sometimes remote, often modulated. No one principle of adaptation seems to have existed for Shakespeare; he copied and altered stories and characters as he saw fit.

Along with this flexible habit of adaptation went Shakespeare's practice of "contaminating" his sources, as the Romans would say. He readily joined matter from one source with that from another. This practice is most clearly apparent in the multiple plot of *King Lear,* where he grafted the story of Gloucester onto the ancient tale of Lear and his three daughters. But it is also evident in such plays as *The Taming of the Shrew, Timon of Athens, As You Like It,* and *The Merchant of Venice.*

Parallel to this habit of joining diverse stories is Shakespeare's practice of liberally modifying established sources with the products of his own invention. The portrait of the social-climbing steward Malvolio is original and introduces into the romantic comedy of *Twelfth Night* a contrasting tonality that is not merely ludicrous but also abrasive. From the very beginning of his writing career, Shakespeare shared with other writers the inclination to link dissimilar, even conflicting, materials in order to achieve a comprehensive synthesis. Among his early plays, *The Two Gentlemen of Verona, Titus Andronicus,* and *Henry VI* sustain a uniformity of subject and tone. At almost the same time, however, *The Comedy of Errors* and *Richard III* play with strongly contrasting moods—in the first case, farce and romance, and in the second, parody and terror. *Love's Labor's Lost* perhaps offers the most striking instance of extreme contrast, when Shakespeare brings Marcade onstage to interrupt the absurd comedy of the Nine Worthies by announcing the death of the king of France. This violent shift exemplifies the boldness with which Shakespeare juxtaposes moods and circumstances, and it points to the more subtle kinds of contrast out of which Shakespeare molds his plays.

The relation that choice of subject has to dramatic contrast is best illustrated by Shakespeare's second historical tetralogy: the fall of Richard II and the triumph of the Lancasters. The historical material all comes from the same chronicles, supplemented though these may be by additional histories about Richard II. Yet each of the plays has a distinct and different tonality, only slightly influenced by the source. The idea for the Falstaff of *Henry IV, Part 1,* comes from the sketchy figure of Oldcastle in the anonymous *Famous Victories of Henry V.* In Shakespeare's imagination, however, that figure undergoes a transformation that completely alters the temper of the historical setting. So vivid has Falstaff become and so powerful is his contrast to the flamboyantly realized personality of Hotspur that Hal, the principal character thematically, all but disappears. Out of the same historical material that led to the tragedy of Richard II, Shakespeare extracts the comedy and satire of Falstaff and Hotspur, with Hal a lagging mediator between them. Not until *Henry V,* after the dramatist has killed off both Hotspur and Falstaff and changed the tonality of his work into heroical romance, does Shakespeare manage to make Hal the worthy protagonist of his own story.

For Shakespeare, then, choosing and combining source material was the first step in composing a play. The choice often set the tone of the work, whether comic, tragic, or historical, but then only in the most general way, for as we have seen, the tone might be modified by new invention or by adroit infusion of contrasting matter. Presumably the very shaping of this raw material into a dramatic sequence was already under way in his imagination, although, of course, we have no means of knowing how this occurred. What it is possible to say is that preexisting dramatic patterns served as schema upon which Shakespeare's imagination could work.

By *schema,* I do not mean *formulas.* Unquestionably, Shakespeare did not write to a formula. At the same time, Elizabethan drama had evolved conventions and narrative structures stable enough to provide a loose frame upon which an author could hang his plots. In simplest terms, these conventions and structures offered model sequences for arranging a story, as well as a sample of sequences and techniques that invited refinement.

A case in point is the finale of a play. Whatever the source of a work, its action moved toward a particular kind of concluding presentation. The exact form of this presentation depended on the genre of the play, but in the main all finales had certain features in common. First of all, the narrative itself moved toward firm closure. To whatever extent certain thematic motifs remained unsettled (as in *Lear* and possibly in *Measure for Measure*), the story itself ended conclusively. Second, it ended in a public accounting. That is why the finale is also an impressive "production number." Except for *Troilus and Cressida* (there are always exceptions where Shakespeare is concerned), the conclusion is communal, not personal, and so verified by witnesses, both active and mute. Third, the finale brings together and accounts for all the disparate elements in a story. Whether completely resolved in each instance (we are never explicitly told what happens to Lear's Fool), each play ties up all loose ends, thereby making the last scene a knot of peculiar intensity and activity. For that reason it takes not only literary artistry but also performing magic to invent a finale that unites all the diverse characters in a convincing and wondrous manner. Shakespeare does this either by dramatizing victory in battle, duels to the death, or fateful suicide in tragedy and history, or by staging discoveries and trials as preludes to marriage in comedy. Usually, though not always, these acts, by resolving the complications of the narrative, bring about the restoration of order. Where they do not, as in *Richard II* or *King Lear,* they serve to crystallize a moral and political dilemma.

So prevalent are these features of the finale that Shakespeare, we can assume, had templates of admissible conclusions in his mind while he was gathering material for a play. Within the general scheme of finales, he could vary the form, as he did, and indeed could exploit the possibilities of the form. *The Comedy of Errors,* for instance, ends with the double discovery of the confused identities of the double twins and of the identity of the Abbess as mother of the twins and long-lost wife of Egeon. In the dynamics of the conclusion, Solinus, the Duke of Ephesus, and Emilia, the Abbess, serve as agents in clearing up all confusion. The Duke, representing local authority, gives the finale the framework of a trial for Egeon's life. The Abbess, through sheer chance, is instrumental in bringing the two Antipholuses together. Yet neither the Duke nor the Abbess really exercises autonomous power. They are agents of the plot—or, one might say, conveniences to tie loose ends together. Rather than acting as self-motivating human beings, they act as surrogates of the author, who has set an obvious machine into motion and now must bring it to a stop.

In *As You Like It,* written in midcareer, Shakespeare also depends upon discovery as the substance of the finale. But in this instance he involves the agent of discovery, Rosalind, organically in the action and, at the same time, combines her with extrahuman authority, the god Hymen. The partnership of a human agent (who, through wisdom, orders the lives of disparate couples) and a connubial divinity (who sanctifies the union of lovers) endows the mechanism of discovery with a spiritual authority, parallel with, yet transcending, Shakespeare's use of the Abbess and the Duke in *The Comedy of Errors.*

At the last, near the end of his career, Shakespeare endowed Prospero with the twin qualities of discovery and authority. Possessed of godlike powers and judgment, he chastises the wicked, blesses the virtuous, and liberates the bound spirit of Ariel. Dramaturgically, then, the process of bringing all the characters together and sorting out their loves follows a fundamental scheme from the beginning of Shakespeare's career to the end. But, with time, Shakespeare finds ways to infuse his agents of closure with their own internal rationale so that their mortal and divine parts can exercise joint power.

In ordering other sections of his plays, Shakespeare follows similar schema, although these are not as easy to distinguish as those of the finales. He follows common Elizabethan practice in telling an extended story through many scenes. In only a few plays does he confine the action to a short period and a limited space *(The Comedy of Errors, The Tempest).* More commonly, he induces the illusion that the characters are traversing considerable space and acting over a long period of time. Seldom does he define space and time exactly, with the result that he can create the illusion of events speeding up or slowing down, and sometimes both simultaneously. His arrangement of contrasting scenes of Egypt and Rome, with Cleopatra languidly dreaming of Antony in the east while Antony rapidly comes to an understanding with Octavius in the west, is just such a manipulation of time.

This flexible approach to space and time parallels a flexible attitude toward the sequence of scenes. Events as they appeared in a source were subject to considerable modification. Shakespeare had an arsenal of techniques for dramatizing them. They could be reported, they could be conveyed in dumb show, they could be truncated, or they could be extended. Shakespeare collects the long series of promenades that the poet Arthur Brooke has Romeo make beneath Juliet's window in *The Tragi-*

call Historye of Romeus and Juliet (1562) and compresses them into one exquisite scene in the orchard. So perfectly does he do this that it seems to be the only way to portray Romeo's wooing of Juliet. But when the page was blank, Shakespeare could have chosen many other ways to convey Romeo's devotion.

Granted, then, the flexibility with which Shakespeare could, and did, treat his source material, his plays nevertheless follow some underlying performance patterns. These patterns are revealed in several ways. In many, though not all, plays, a distributive pattern of public and private scenes is apparent. Where this most clearly occurs, as in *Hamlet, Julius Caesar,* and *Macbeth,* the play has a major public action in either the first or the second scene, another long public scene at the center of the play, and at the end the public finale. In *Hamlet,* in which this sequence is most obvious, the first public action occurs in the second scene of the play. Whether considered a court scene or a council scene, it is one in which Claudius makes a public announcement, sends forth ambassadors to Norway, hears a petition from Laertes, and then considers Hamlet. "Let the world take note," he assures Hamlet, "You are the most immediate to our throne" (108–109). Centered in the play, at Act III, scene ii, is the second court scene, in which the court assembles to see a performance about the murder of Gonzago. At the end of the play comes the final court scene, in which Hamlet and Laertes play out a duel before the assembled lords. The only other public or quasi-public scene is the burial scene (V. i), though in this instance, the maimed rites of Ophelia's interment stress the private nature of what should be a more ceremonious event and therefore indicate that the scene is a negative sign of a public action. All other scenes in the play are either quasi-public (for example, the return of the ambassadors) or more frequently strictly private (Claudius at prayer, Gertrude in her closet).

This distributive pattern is widely though not invariably followed. Sometimes the central scene is not formally a public scene, as in *Lear* and *Twelfth Night.* But when it is not, the center of the play still contains a powerful nexus of action. At the center of *Twelfth Night* is Viola's duel with Sir Andrew, and the consequent exposure of Antonio in the streets of Illyria. This scene has a quasi-public aspect. Within the unfolding action of the play, it is the moment when Viola's disguise as the page Cesario comes under greatest challenge. Likewise,

King Lear sustains a series of contrasting scenes between Lear in the storm and his enemies in Gloucester's castle. Lear's pathetic courting of mad Tom and the violence done to Gloucester in his own home stress the absence of public accounting.

One of the significant variants in Shakespeare's tragedies is the gradual abandonment of the central public scene and its replacement by chaos. *Julius Caesar, Hamlet,* and *Macbeth* have formal public scenes at the heart of their action. In *Othello,* on the other hand, Shakespeare places an intensely private action, Iago's seduction of Othello, at the center of the play (III. iii). That privacy, coming at the point when the audience might well have expected a more ceremonial action, reinforces the disordering of social relationships. By the time Shakespeare wrote *Antony and Cleopatra* he had abandoned the convention of an intense central public scene, calling attention thereby to the void at the core of the play.

In *Shakespeare at the Globe,* I have argued that the center of a Shakespearean play, whether public or private, rises to a level of intensity that does not come to a climactic point so much as it expands through a series of sustained reactions, as in the three scenes of Lear on the heath or Macbeth's repeated responses to Banquo's ghost. It is toward this center of intensity or climactic plateau that Shakespeare fashions the first half of his play and away from it that he makes the succeeding action flow. Simultaneously, in tandem yet in contrast to this rise and fall of dramatic intensity, Shakespeare maintains a continuous narrative interest that proceeds to the public accounting at the end of the play. These two related patterns, by working with and against each other, contribute immensely to the impression of complexity that the action projects. It is probable that in Shakespeare's day both patterns evoked equal interest in the audience. For today's audiences, however, the dramatic line is more compelling than the narrative line.

Act and Scene Structure

Scholars differ in the ways in which they describe and explain the patterns I have indicated. T. W. Baldwin and, to a lesser extent, G. K. Hunter argue for the persistence of a classical method of dramatic writing. Baldwin especially has claimed that Shakespeare followed the Terentian model in composing his plays. In that model the center of the play is the catastrophe, and therefore Shakespeare's heightened action is merely a Renaissance version of a classical form.

Few critics have accepted Baldwin's views. They are not prepared to adopt his arguments for Shakespeare's learned craftsmanship. Furthermore, the function and effect of such a part of the play as the catastrophe is substantially different in Terence from what it is in Shakespeare. But if Baldwin's argument as a whole is unconvincing, one aspect of it remains controversial and unsettled. Baldwin claims that Shakespeare wrote to the classical five-act plan. In favor of the five-act division, Hunter cites the presence of act and scene divisions in some of the published plays as well as the use of the Choruses in *Henry V* and *Pericles* to divide these plays into five parts. Collaborators, as we saw, divided their assignments by acts, and Jonson, in supervising the printing of his plays, observed the five-act convention.

On the other hand, the evidence against the five-act division is formidable. None of Shakespeare's plays printed in his lifetime show such division, including the 1604 *Hamlet,* in the printing of which Shakespeare probably had a hand. Nor do the plays consistently lend themselves organically to subdivision along these lines. So far as we know, performance was continuous in the public playhouse. Moreover, although the running plots or scene summaries that come directly from the playhouse show scene markings and what may be act markings, nothing in the plots indicates that the action is interrupted at these points. Thus, whatever meager evidence exists of playhouse practice argues against such division.

Critics therefore are forced back upon internal evidence from the printed texts and from the few surviving manuscript plays of the period. On the basis of this evidence, it seems that the five-act convention did exist in the private playhouse, where music was introduced between the acts, but that it was not common in the public playhouse. So far as Shakespeare's plays are concerned, there is no indisputable evidence one way or the other. He was undoubtedly familiar with the convention and toyed with it in *Henry V* and several other plays. But in the one case in which he imitated a five-act classical play, *The Comedy of Errors,* he does not imitate its structural pattern.

In recent years other critics, Emrys Jones most fully, have put forth the theory that Shakespeare usually wrote a two-part play. This theory, based on analysis of written scripts, points out the widespread practice of developing the action to the center of a play and then changing direction. The most vivid examples of two-part plays are *Measure for Measure* and *The Winter's Tale,* in which the tone, the line of action, and even the setting change radically in the middle. In *Measure for Measure,* verse changes to prose; the Duke, hitherto passive, becomes the active shaper of events; and the potentially tragic action turns to comic intrigue. In *The Winter's Tale* the change is more violent. The story leaps sixteen years. It leaves one set of characters and turns to a new set. As with *Measure for Measure* the earlier tragedy gives way to pastoral intrigue and comedy.

Shifts, though less wrenching ones, occur in other plays such as *Julius Caesar, Macbeth,* and *King Lear.* In the first, one line of action leads to Caesar's assassination. Thereafter, Antony and Octavius come into prominence, lesser actors of the first part disappear, and the dramatic issue turns to the consequences of the assassination. Likewise, the first half of *Macbeth* moves through the murder of Duncan to Macbeth's assumption of power and his effort to purge his overheated imagination of the consequences of his action. The second half dramatizes the counteraction, and his doomed attempt to wipe out all opposition. The rhythm in *King Lear* follows Lear's discovery of his vulnerability, which drives him to madness and his consequent adjustment to his altered state. In the last two plays the shift from the first part to the second part is marked by the protagonist's disappearance from the stage for all or most of the fourth act.

The origins of the two-part play have not been so thoroughly explored as those of classical structure. Whereas Renaissance critics, following Aristotle, Horace, and Donatus, elaborated a standard of five-act progression, no one at the time proposed a theory of two parts. Yet this idea, well grounded in medieval and English Renaissance practice, has many analogues. Popular images of the goddess Fortune show man mounting a turning wheel only to fall after he reaches the top of circling destiny. This is a visualization of *de casibus* tragedy—of the fall from greatness. But whereas the classical version of *de casibus* concentrates on man's fall, the two-part play, a descendant from medieval influences, shows the rise and fall or the fall and rise of human fortune. It is this path that the heroes of the morality plays take. *Everyman* pictures the successive stripping away of Everyman's reliance on worldly goods and affections, and then his successive acquisition of the spiritual powers that lead him to salvation. This pattern is echoed in many of the later moralities, such as *Horestes* and *Susannah.* Even in those plays in which the figure of Humanum Genus (Everyman) is absent, the primary rhythm of rise and fall is embodied in the figure of Vice, who moves from success to success through the first half of the play until the opposing virtues gather head and begin to assert themselves in the second half *(Like Will to Like, Tide Tarrieth No Man).* While this pattern was never formalized, it existed in enough examples to provide later writers with one possible model for organizing dramatic material.

Altogether, then, Shakespeare experimented with several available models for building a play. He never settled on a single formula; instead, he restlessly tried a range of possible forms. Nevertheless, he does reveal the key tendencies of his dramatic practice in his major works. They show that he explored the two-part structure intensively between the writing of *Julius Caesar* and *Antony and Cleopatra* and that both early and late he tried variants of it. Yet even while playing with this arrangement, he was not unmindful of the five-act model and from time to time tried it out. In following these general patterns, he also developed various types of scenic order, the most important of which was the alternation of public and private action. With a few exceptions, he arranged his plays into sequences of many scenes (fifteen at least), the overall form of which consisted of major public scenes at the beginning, in the middle, and at the end of the play. Theatrically, these scenes, with their ceremonial action and large groups of actors, served as production numbers that set off the more intimate events.

Of equal importance with the use of source material and the broad sweep of the action are the types of scene Shakespeare wrote and the art with which he related them to each other. Ever since H. T. Price's trailblazing article "Construction in Shakespeare," Shakespeare's skill in juxtaposing scenes has stirred our admiration. We have become increasingly aware that Shakespeare works not only through five-act and two-part narrative patterns but through provocative associations that crisscross the action. Most often Shakespeare writes scenes that mirror each other. Just as Edgar, regarding the outcast Lear, sees that the old man is "childed as I fathered" (III. vi. 108), so do we readers and spectators discover how one part of a play reflects another. Reflection may be through events, as in the parallel sufferings of Lear and Edgar. Or it may be through character, as when Hamlet sees in Horatio "a man that Fortune's buffets and rewards hast ta'en with equal thanks" (III. ii. 64–65). Or it may be through language echoes, as when Macbeth's invocation "Come, seeling Night, scarf up the tender eye of pitiful day" (III. ii. 46–47) recalls his wife's earlier cry "Come, thick Night, and pall thee in the dunnest smoke of hell" (I. v. 48–49). Through such correspondences, Shakespeare imbues his plays with a profound resonance that repeatedly provokes fresh appreciation of the interpenetration of people and events.

To produce such evocative drama, however, Shakespeare had to be the master of the individual scene. Nor was he alone in this mastery. The scope of Elizabethan drama gave each scene of a play the potential for a semiautonomous existence. In fact, it is argued, Elizabethan dramatists organized their work by scenes, often sacrificing dramatic logic to realize striking moments. This view of Elizabethan dramaturgy may be exaggerated, but it does contain a germ of truth. The best Elizabethan dramatists, Shakespeare preeminent among them, strike a balance between the scene as a separate, sharply defined entity and the scene as a single step in a continuous story. In the past, Shakespeare's skill in connecting one scene to another received considerable attention; only now is his art in shaping each individual scene stirring the interest it merits.

Early in his career and again at the very end, Shakespeare wrote plays with relatively few scenes. *Titus Andronicus* and *The Comedy of Errors* have fewer than fifteen each. *The Tempest* has nine. The action in these plays is confined to a limited area; events flow seamlessly on and off stage. From the opening scene, the threads of the plot are compactly tied to one another. In *The Tempest* each scene flows from a previous one, so that there is none of the jolt that spectators experience when they have to shift their attention from one set of characters to another, as in the opening three scenes of *Twelfth Night.* But this seamless method of scene composition is unusual for Shakespeare. Normally, he arranged his action into a sequence of twenty to thirty scenes. Some scenes are very brief, others are relatively long; few, however, extend beyond three hundred lines (roughly fifteen minutes of playing time).

With few exceptions each scene is self-contained as a performing unit. To achieve this effect of autonomy, Shakespeare observes the so-called law of reentry. This is not so much a formal principle as a practical axiom that playwrights of the period seem to have followed. Characters who close one scene almost never appear at the opening of the next. As a result, movement from scene to scene involves one or more characters walking off the stage and another set of characters coming on. Occasionally Shakespeare reveals the new set of characters by drawing a curtain to show them already onstage. But this is unusual, and his prevailing practice produces a rhythm of coming and going as scene moves to scene.

As for the scenes themselves, there are a number of ways of examining them. First, there is the subject matter. Within the flow of a story, Shakespeare had to choose what he wished to include and exclude. Certain events demanded realization, others could be omitted or introduced obliquely. Should he, for instance, present the actual moment when Antony sees Cleopatra flee from the naval battle at Actium? Nothing in the theatrical technique of his stage hindered him from doing so. He chose, however, not to show this moment but, instead, to dramatize Antony's reaction to her flight. His decision about subject then leads to a second aspect of dramatization: how to stage material once it is selected. Since Shakespeare's principal theatrical medium was poetic language, he had to find a distinctive angle of approach for conveying narrative information as well as for creating a dramatic statement, mainly through speech.

Often scenes with minor characters illuminate the way Shakespeare fuses subject and approach. In those historical plays that include a series of battle scenes, Shakespeare first introduces illustrative fights between anonymous or minor persons. Most striking are the two mirror scenes in which a father discovers that he has killed his son and a son discovers that he has killed his father in *Henry VI, Part 3* (II. v). Together they emblematize a moral statement on the "piteous spectacle" of war. Later, Shakespeare forgoes this kind of obvious moralizing, instead raising more elusive questions by choosing what battle encounters to include. In *Macbeth* he shows only two encounters, the key one between Macbeth and Macduff and an illustrative one between Young Siward, untried in battle, and Macbeth. The exchange between them is brief, only thirteen lines, and it unfolds in three sections. First, Macbeth, alone onstage, admits he is at the end of his power but still believes he cannot be defeated by man born of woman. Next, Young Siward appears, demanding of Macbeth his name. On hearing it, young as he is, he challenges Macbeth and is slain. Lastly, Macbeth mocks the corpse, "Thou wast born of woman" (V. vii. 11). In choosing to dramatize this moment, Shakespeare achieves two things. He reinforces the already established delusion of Macbeth, setting the stage for his imminent discovery that Macduff was untimely ripped from his mother's womb. But the scene accomplishes something else. In it, Shakespeare opposes weary tyranny with youthful idealism. The climax of their meeting comes when Young Siward refuses to be frightened upon hearing Macbeth's name. Thus, the scene has the double purpose of contributing to the dramatic development and emblematizing innocence versus tyranny.

After the subject and approach to a scene are set, shaping follows. It is in this respect that Shakespeare's artistry shows itself most brilliantly. His remarkable ability to be simple in structuring events and yet profound in conveying effect stems from his extraordinary skill in building interchanges between characters. In each scene, particularly in his middle and later plays, he portrays events as the organic consequences of the give-and-take among people rather than as impositions of a poet. His early work betrays traces of these impositions, mainly in set speeches and rigid verbal duels. But in his more mature writing, especially of the middle period, expression is articulated thought and impassioned assertion. Power over language makes this expression possible, but the language is powerful precisely because it is rooted in carefully contrived scenes.

Two aspects of Shakespeare's scenes are worth noting. First is the pattern of ordering a scene; second is the use of characters within a scene. Whether short or long, a scene consists of a series of more or less well defined parts. The battle between Macbeth and Young Siward, short as it is, has three segments. This three-part arrangement, as Mark Rose has pointed out, is fairly common in Shakespeare's plays. Frequently, he arranges a scene so that it falls into short opening and closing sections and a longer midsection. Rose calls this arrangement a triptych.

In complex scenes Shakespeare puts parts within parts. Thus, the first scene of *King Lear* has an opening segment, Gloucester and Kent discussing Edmund, and a closing segment, Cordelia's farewell to her sisters and the sisters' consultation about how to check their father. These segments frame the central action: the division of the kingdom. That action, in turn, consists of three parts: the ceremony of the division, Lear's disinheritance of Cordelia, and France's acceptance of Cordelia. By giving definition to each segment, Shakespeare accentuates the rhythm of the action and sharpens the form of each segment.

Related to his arrangement of a scene as a series of segments is Shakespeare's deployment of characters on stage. He uses public scenes to give form to his entire play. Naturally these scenes require many actors, and as a matter of course, the last scene of a play usually requires the maximum number of players to appear simultaneously. In bringing so many characters onstage, however, Shakespeare faced the practical challenge of keeping his story moving and his performance effective.

Better than any other dramatist, he understood the conflicting needs of performance and representation. To represent the "natural" flow of life, the writer tends to produce the illusion of a spontaneous, unpremeditated sequence. Yet, to sustain the attention of an audience, he must maintain sharp focus on one thing at a time. The Greeks understood this dilemma too. They solved it by limiting the number of actors in tragedy to three, thus assuring that no more than those three would appear onstage at one time. In practice, however, the Greeks depended mainly on two-character scenes, relieved by interchanges with the Chorus. The Elizabethans faced a different set of challenges. Because of their preference for extensive narratives and their taste for multiple plots, they had to achieve concentration of effect while juggling many different characters and situations.

Shakespeare achieved such concentration by mastering the binary basis of dramatic presentation. Although he wrote scenes involving single individuals, small groups, and crowds, he relied principally on the duet. In some plays, such as *As You Like It,* the bulk of the action unfolds in scenes involving only two people. But what constitutes a duet in performing terms is deceptive. It is not merely a scene in which only two characters appear but a scene in which the action divides into two sides or issues. For example, in *Henry IV, Part 1,* in the scene in which the rebels argue over whether or not to fight King Henry (IV. iii), Hotspur and Douglas take one side, Worcester and Vernon the opposite. The result is that while numerically this scene is a quartet, dramaturgically it functions as a duet; that is, two characters on each side share a line of action, so that Shakespeare, instead of tracing four different motives, presents us with a sharply differentiated dialectical opposition. Throughout his plays, in fact, Shakespeare employs variations of this conflating method. Therefore, if we are to appreciate his structural skill, we need to distinguish the simple duet, which contains only two players, from the complex duet, which contains more than two yet functions as if there were only two sides to the action.

Shakespeare has several different devices at hand for creating the complex duet. Frequently he has two characters play out the action before attendants or onlookers, as in Richard's wooing of Anne in *Richard III.* In some cases, Shakespeare enforces muteness so insistently that he deliberately suppresses characters who otherwise might be expected to speak, doing so in order to preserve concentration of performance (Isabella at the end of *Measure for Measure,* Sylvia at the end of *Two Gentlemen of Verona*).

More artful than the duet with mutes is the duet with redundant figures, like the scene in *Henry IV, Part 1,* in which characters are aligned on two sides. In such scenes two or more characters, though they appear to exist as separate individuals, share a line of action. This effect is most obvious when two characters speak a single line of dialogue together as Cornelius and Voltemand do when Claudius sends them to Norway (*Hamlet,* I. ii. 40). But this technique is far more widespread. When Rosencrantz and Guildenstern meet Hamlet, they alternate lines as they address their old schoolfellow, so that Hamlet, while speaking to two people, really deals with one situation. Likewise, when Antony begins addressing the Roman populace over Caesar's body, the members of the crowd echo each other redundantly. Thus, that scene is fundamentally a duet composed of Antony on one side and redundant figures on the other. By this method Shakespeare achieves concentration of effect, so necessary to successful performance, as well as an impression of diverse thoughts and feelings.

The last of the techniques for building a play on duets is the sequencing of action in a series of short duets, both simple and complex. In *Othello* the long scene of Cassio's drunkenness and dismissal (II. iii) consists of such an arrangement. Even through Othello's interrogation of Cassio, Montano, and Iago after the fight, Shakespeare follows an orderly

binary sequence. Where extremely short sequences alternate with longer ones, an effect of lifelike waywardness emerges. In his finales particularly, Shakespeare uses this technique to preserve dramatic focus as he brings the various lines of the plot together. Here a combination of subject matter and structure works its power. In his mature comedy Shakespeare uses a magistrate (such as a duke or king) or a presenter (Paulina in *The Winter's Tale*) to direct the action and so preserve the binary sequence. In the tragedies it is the action itself, a duel or a suicide, that supplies the center to which others relate in binary order.

Shakespeare depends upon this structural foundation for arranging action, we can assume, because his experience as a player and his intimate connection with practical stagecraft taught him what Laurence Olivier recognized when he remarked that "the greatest heights in drama are always between two players." Shakespeare's plays are filled with the most exciting encounters of this sort: Hamlet and Gertrude, Hamlet and Ophelia, Iago and Othello, Coriolanus and Volumnia, Macbeth and Lady Macbeth, Antony and Cleopatra, Romeo and Juliet. In fact, in every play Shakespeare is certain to give the audience an exciting duet between his leading characters. Not only is such a scene often the high point of the play, but it also reverberates throughout the rest of the action.

The duet, however, is not the only type of scene. Shakespeare also wrote varieties of multipersoned scenes. But the problem he recognized and every playwright faces is how to increase the lines of action beyond two without diffusing the dramatic performance. To a large extent, the Elizabethans solved this problem through a variant of the Greek method but in a characteristically Renaissance fashion.

Greek tragedy focused on a series of encounters between two characters. These encounters unfold not only before the actual audience but also before the Chorus. In the majority of tragedies, this Chorus does not engage in the action proper, so that it is indeed an audience. Its leader may at times become an interlocutor in a scene, but for the most part he merges with his flock as an observing bystander. The Chorus thus serves as mediator between the actors and the actual audience, a mediation that is reinforced by the acoustics of the Greek amphitheater, where the onstage and offstage audiences enjoy a shared resonance.

The Elizabethan use of onstage audiences is far more complex. Through scenes of eavesdropping and plays-within-plays, the dramatists created successive planes of action and observation. Instead of a duet, such scenes are in effect trios. While two characters play a scene, a third observes them and may make comments. Othello watching Iago and Cassio joke about Desdemona (as he thinks); Rosalind and Celia peeping at Silvius and Phoebe; Puck and Oberon overseeing the frantic lovers—all are variants of the trio, that is, of a duet occurring in the sight of a third party. The most elaborate pattern of this kind is the one in *Troilus and Cressida* where Troilus and Ulysses watch Cressida flirt with Diomedes while Thersites watches their reactions as well as the flirting itself.

Whether through eavesdropping, a play-within-a-play, or a trial scene in which a judge mediates between disputants, Shakespeare often creates a schematic trio that enables three characters to interact effectively. This triangulation is so useful that even when a scene has no schematic structure, one character out of three will assume the role of audience in order to maintain dramatic clarity.

In addition to the sharply defined formal arrangements, Shakespeare creates scenes that at first do not appear to conform to a set structural arrangement. By interpolating lines here and there and by subtly modulating redundancies, Shakespeare creates scenes that seem to transcend binary or trinary patterns. Closer examination reveals that they do not depart far from the principles stated. For example, in *Richard III*, the first scene at court includes nine characters, each of whom speaks at one time or another. Among them they comprise at least five evident interest groups (Elizabeth and her family, Margaret, Richard, Stanley, Hastings, and possibly Buckingham). In the give-and-take of the scene, most of the interests are expressed at some point. Yet careful scrutiny shows that much of the action consists of a series of duets. In Margaret's conflict with the peers, and with Richard in particular, the peers function redundantly and in tandem with Richard. Thus, despite the apparent clash of diverse interests, the scene follows an orderly and largely binary progression.

From Script to Stage

The ordering of a story through scenes and of action within scenes is the primary way in which Shakespeare forms his plays. Complementary to this ordering is the way he physicalizes that action. This encompasses his use of the stage, stage properties, and costumes; his handling of theatrical conventions and devices; his introduction of song, dance, and effects; and most important, his integration of speech and gesture as expressive entities.

More than any dramatist of his time, Shakespeare was intimately involved with a specific playhouse. During his most fruitful period (1599–1609), he wrote exclusively for a single theater, the Globe. It was a building he must have known very well. He acted in it, perhaps daily. He owned a share of it. And he may have had a voice in determining its style and equipment. Even after 1609, when his company began to divide its time between the Globe and its indoor playhouse, at Blackfriars, he continued to play an influential role in all matters concerning the physical stage.

Shakespeare, we can assume, had the command of the playhouse and could use it in any way he saw fit. He could ask for special equipment if he so desired, or he could incorporate into his plays any sort of stage furniture he might fancy. In short, nothing but his imagination and the capacity of the playhouse limited his use of stage facilities. Yet so far as his plays can speak and assiduous theatrical research can discover, he made no unusual demands upon the stage. In the flow of movement from scene to scene, he seldom required more than the two entrances that the stage certainly had. At times he makes significant use of the large platform in conjunction with an entrance, as when Coriolanus speaks at length to Aufidius about Volumnia, who is gradually approaching him. In fact, throughout the period when Shakespeare was writing for the Globe alone, entrances and exits—the very foundations of dramatic continuity in the Elizabethan drama—never in themselves make extraordinary use of the physical stage.

Throughout this decade, Shakespeare never had a character enter from below, as a devil might. Even the Ghost of Hamlet's father is unlikely to have risen from the cellarage. In fact, the one time that the text specifically alludes to the manner of the Ghost's exit, Hamlet describes him as leaving through a portal. Nor does a character ever enter from the heavens. Shakespeare employed such spectacular entries only after the company began to work at Blackfriars. Both in *Cymbeline* and in *The Tempest*, avian figures—Jupiter on an eagle and Ariel as a harpy—descend. Shakespeare's resort to these effects may have been a response to the new playhouse as well as to the example of the court masques.

What is true of the stage facilities is equally true of stage furniture and properties. Most of Shakespeare's plays call for a few standard pieces of furniture and only occasionally for something more special. Stools are fairly common, as are tables. Otherwise, a play might require a grassy bank *(A Midsummer Night's Dream)*, a bed *(Othello)*, or a cauldron *(Macbeth)*. No play has very many pieces, and no play is dependent upon them for its staging style.

Costumes, on the other hand, played an important part in the mounting of productions. Henslowe's diary shows how important and expensive costuming was for Elizabethan stage companies. Along with the books of the plays, costumes were the players' most substantial investment. Shakespeare indicates, furthermore, that he was sensitive to the way dress reflected the temper of an individual. Rosalind in her role as Ganymede rejects Orlando scathingly as an unhappy lover because his dress lacks all signs of disorder. Olivia, in turn, according to the false letter Maria writes, asks her supposed lover, Malvolio, to wear yellow stockings and go cross-gartered to show his love. Through dress, lovers are known, and Shakespeare plays off this contemporary notion for comic purposes.

In a more serious vein, Shakespeare makes dress itself, and even more the donning and removal of dress, crucial at certain moments. Hamlet in black, obviously set off from the court, which has abandoned mourning, notes the inadequacy of dress to express his deepest feelings. Nevertheless, in introducing the character to us in this somber hue, Shakespeare indicates his temperament. Likewise, opening a doublet or removing a garment has strange poignancy in Shakespeare. At the trial in *The Merchant of Venice,* Antonio has to lay bare his breast to Shylock's knife. On the heath Lear tries to tear off his clothes to become one with Poor Tom; divestment of clothing is indeed an avenue to understanding for the old king. This theatrical use of clothing, moreover, parallels the rich imagery about clothing throughout the play. Elsewhere, Coriolanus' inability to open his robe to reveal his wounds to the populace is one of the issues that lead to his banishment.

Dress plays its most important role in the form of disguise, particularly in the disguise of girls as boys. Viola dresses like her brother Sebastian. Rosalind

dons the garments of a saucy page. Perdita in festive costume at the sheepshearing feels that she is committing a kind of hubris that will lead to her downfall. Florizel violates decorum by assuming more modest garments than his position warrants, only to be further degraded by changing into Autolycus' clothes. Whether to hide gender, rank, or person, disguise is a vital element in staging. Moreover, considering the high priority Elizabethans placed upon gorgeous clothing, the players must have felt impelled to make an impressive appearance. While much of what they wore in one play could also be worn in another, they were continually adding new costumes to their wardrobe, usually of a sumptuous kind. Onstage, therefore, the players must have appeared magnificent, a fair match for the appearance of their stage.

The Elizabethan playhouse, according to the diary of the Dutch university student Johannes De Witt, was a gorgeous playing place. In scale and color it presented an impressive face to the assembled crowd. When the stage was filled with handsomely garbed actors, it must have made a stunning sight, fully worthy of London, with its pageantry and bustling business. Add to this the variety of alternating scenes of different scale and fullness, and the distinctive richness of the Shakespearean theater becomes apparent.

Beyond appearance lies the question of how the actors enacted scenes on the Globe stage. Unfortunately, little direct evidence survives. To guess at the ways actors performed in the playhouse necessitates liberal and often dubious use of one's imagination. It is reasonable to suppose, for example, that in delivering a soliloquy the Shakespearean actor came to the forefront of the platform stage in order to establish intimacy with the audience. But that notion runs counter to some of the facts of the playhouse. By coming to the front of the stage, the player came closer to the groundlings. He also was in danger of reducing contact with the gentlemen who, it is thought, occupied the lords' rooms on either side of the stage. A good argument could be made that a position halfway out upon the platform —the position indicated for the actors in the drawing De Witt made of the Swan—would be the most effective point from which to command the entire playhouse.

Perhaps both the dramatist's and the players' work was most crucially affected by the scale of the playhouse and the number of spectators. The gallery arrangement made for a compact circle or near circle of listeners. According to John Orrell's latest calculations, the diameter of the playhouse was one hundred feet. Although this estimate supposes a larger playhouse than was previously assumed, such a size would still afford intimacy between players and the dense mass of the audience. The increased size argued by Orrell makes likely the hypothesis that a public playhouse such as the Globe held nearly three thousand people. To keep such a large number attentive as a company acted out an intricate plot employing complex poetry demanded an extraordinary amount of energy. No wonder Thomas Heywood recommended acting as a means of teaching audacity. To command so large a crowd and to convey the subtleties of scripts as rich as Shakespeare's must have entailed both boldness and immense control, clarity of dramatic design coupled with directness and simplicity of playing, and a vigor in maintaining the narrative flow. Thus, the scale of the playhouse, physically and decoratively, as well as the size of the audience, played the most influential role in determining the style and form of the drama. The physical details of the stage (doors, arras, furniture, and properties) played a relatively minor role in the final form of Shakespeare's plays. Only costumes seemed to blend with the scale and decoration to enhance the action.

In the public playhouse, music and dance did not occupy the same importance that they did among the boys' companies. The boys' training in singing made it profitable and virtually inevitable that their major skill would be exploited. An abortive attempt to recruit children who were not singers failed early in the seventeenth century, with the result that singing remained a major element in the private theaters. Nevertheless, singing and dancing appeared with some regularity in the public playhouses.

Shakespeare introduces song in the majority of his plays. Sometimes the songs serve as entertainment, both for characters onstage and for the audience; in these cases, the singer is usually someone who does not play a significant role. Among such entertainers are Amiens in *As You Like It,* the Boy in *Measure for Measure,* and Balthasar in *Much Ado About Nothing.* Whether their songs capture mood or provide a transition into critical action, they lend pleasure to the general entertainment. By and large, however, these songs are not closely integrated into the action.

Quite different from these entertaining songs are those that are elements of the dramatic action.

Ophelia's ribald songs and Desdemona's Willow Song express the mind or the mood of the characters. In these instances, Shakespeare enhances the expressive power of words by the use of music, especially traditional songs. Besides their psychological purposes, these songs, along with those that serve as entertainment, enhance the romantic aspects of the drama and supplement the variety that the Elizabethan playwright sought.

Dance, too, occupies a lively place in Shakespearean productions. It serves a regular theatrical function by sometimes supplying the conclusion to a play *(A Midsummer Night's Dream, Much Ado).* It is also a means for dramatizing encounters between lovers *(Romeo and Juliet, Much Ado, Love's Labor's Lost, Winter's Tale)* in a public setting. The fact that the "jigs," or light entertainments, that succeeded the main production in a public playhouse concluded with dances further emphasizes their general theatrical appeal. Song and dance together, integrated into the narrative though they often are, more importantly function as presentation or display, a showing-off that pleases audiences and that all strong theater finds a way of including. In other words, song and dance remind the audience that they are watching a show.

But of all the means for externalizing action, Shakespeare most depends on speech interacting kinetically with movement and gesture. One of the few things critics can agree on about Shakespeare's artistic development is that as he continued to write, his language became more and more responsive to the impulses of thought and passion reflected in implied gesture and movement. From reveling in rhetoric and set verse forms, Shakespeare moves through an irregular, pseudoconversational versification into complex syntax that nevertheless retains poetic clarity. Through all these changes he remains aware of the player's voice behind the written script and, behind that voice, of the urgency of thought and feeling. In the evolution of his writing, a certain circularity must have occurred. Shakespeare fed the actors his speeches and dialogues, and they in the course of acting must have suggested new possibilities. The scripts themselves bear the signs of this process, showing, as his career progressed, increasing subtlety in shifts of breath and leaps in intent.

To discuss, then, how language and gesture are concretized as the specific expression of an underlying dramatic action, it is convenient to speak of three streams of energy that flow through a play.

There is the narrative flow, which provides the continuity of events and, in its broad outlines, arises from the source material Shakespeare chose. There is a dramatic flow, which propels one scene after another, containing the shape of the action. The flow of language is the third stream; it is a particularized manifestation of the dramatic flow. How these three streams flow together may be seen by examining the type of scene that dominates Shakespeare's work—the duet.

Plutarch, through Thomas North's translation, supplied Shakespeare with the main lines for his drama of *Coriolanus*. Here and there Shakespeare makes changes in the biography, but inherent in the choice of the material is the intention to dramatize Coriolanus' banishment, his march against Rome, and his sacrifice of this objective at the behest of his mother. In short, the narrative already dictated a certain sequence and a certain vigorous flow of events. Shakespeare shapes this narrative flow into a series of separate scenes, one of which, following Plutarch, had to be his confrontation with his mother. The dramatic flow of that confrontation arises from the decisions Shakespeare made in locating and shaping the action. The fact that Shakespeare's decisions largely follow Plutarch's story sequence does not make it any the less his. For example, he heightens Plutarch's situation by putting immediately before it the failed embassy of Menenius to Coriolanus, reinforced by Coriolanus' remark to him, "Wife, mother, child, I know not" (V. ii. 78).

In setting forth the scene between mother and son, he makes other strategic decisions. He makes it a quasi-public scene, for he has Coriolanus insist that Aufidius and the Volscians witness the scene. In its essential structure he also makes it a complex duet, for the heart of the scene is Volumnia's exhortation to her son while all others stand mutely by. To heighten the appeal of the mutes, he brings on Coriolanus' wife, his son, and the chaste Valeria, emblem of Rome's purity. The narrative opportunity thus takes on dramatic definition. The actual shape of the action, however, is evident in the further strategy of arranging the confrontation.

The scene divides into opening and closing segments that frame a central action. A coda, wherein Coriolanus acknowledges the women's achievement, concludes the scene. The two framing segments show Coriolanus with Aufidius. In the opening frame, Coriolanus assures Aufidius of his loyalty to the Volscians and his rejection of the Romans. His mother, wife, son, and Valeria enter, and as he sees them approach, he reaffirms to Aufidius his determination to stand fast. Through it all, Aufidius says little, and then only to second what Coriolanus asserts. Thus, though a duet, the scene rises to a statement of Coriolanus' creed.

The closing segment is another duet between Coriolanus and Aufidius. This time Coriolanus apologizes for succumbing to his mother while asking for Aufidius' support. In response, Aufidius, outwardly noncommittal, ends the segment by muttering aside that he will use Coriolanus' mercy as a means against him.

Shakespeare forms the critical meeting between mother and son with incomparable mastery. It, too, falls into three fairly well defined subsegments. The first consists of greetings. The second contains Volumnia's first plea, and the last, the second and final plea. Opening the first subsegment, Virgilia greets her husband. In the very act of welcoming her warmly, Coriolanus forestalls her request to him. Next, Coriolanus greets his mother. They vie with each other by kneeling. Then Volumnia presents Valeria, and finally young Marcius, to Coriolanus. Neither says a word. Volumnia speaks for all of them in asking to be heard. Coriolanus denies their appeal before he hears it but nevertheless agrees to listen, insisting that the Volscians hear it too. The subsegment of greeting thus unfolds with a deliberateness that retards the crisis of Volumnia's appeal and highlights her dilemma. Volumnia's attempt to kneel to her son and Coriolanus' son kneeling to him give the action visual as well as oral force. The subsegment's formal quality is reinforced by Coriolanus bidding the invading soldiers to bear witness and then turning to his mother with the question "Your request?" In shaping this painful encounter, Shakespeare chose to introduce two appeals: the first one, cast in the form of entrance and welcome, is correctly read by Coriolanus as persuasion and rejected by him. In this way, before Volumnia starts her formal speech, Coriolanus has affirmed, once to Aufidius, once to himself, and once to his mother, that he will not be swayed. Thus, Shakespeare maximizes the opposition that Volumnia faces.

The next subsegment embodies the second, more urgent appeal. It starts with a formal unfolding. As it proceeds, Coriolanus remains virtually silent. In this Shakespeare follows Plutarch's lead. But whereas Plutarch's narrative text concentrates on Volumnia's words, Shakespeare's scene, by opposing the mute Coriolanus to the pleading mother, accentuates the tension between them. Given the situation, Shakespeare could have supplied words for Coriolanus' resistance to his mother, but he chose the far simpler and far more effective strategy of having him say nothing or nearly nothing. To heighten the intensity of the struggle further, Shakespeare has Virgilia and young Marcius echo Volumnia redundantly after she vows to slay herself if she cannot persuade Coriolanus to relent. This brings the subsegment to a climax. Coriolanus, revealing how deep his conflict is, attempts to leave lest he show a woman's tenderness. Volumnia prevents him, continuing to argue.

The third subsegment that follows is less formal. The pain of Coriolanus' silence becomes more evident, not through any line he says, but through Volumnia's reaction to him. As she bids her son speak, she gets no response. She and all her group kneel to him. He still does not answer. She accepts her defeat, and then, as she is about to depart, Coriolanus, "hold[ing] her by the hand, silent," yields.

Shakespeare's design can be partly appreciated by the fact that the second subsegment takes thirty-seven lines, and the third, more than fifty. Instead of accelerating as the scene approaches its climax, the scene decelerates, stretching out painfully. Through it all, Coriolanus' silence encourages the audience to project upon the character its sympathetic sense of what he is suffering. The player has little to do overtly but let us look for clues in his stony silence.

Shakespeare integrates action and language so tightly that it may be hard to distinguish the poetry from the drama. Indeed, there is no difference; one is the other. At first, in Coriolanus' address to his family and in Volumnia's pleas to him, Shakespeare maintains a regularity of rhythm and formality of expression. This is reinforced by the sober entrance of the embassy from Rome, so movingly described by Coriolanus, as well as by the proper acts of kneeling to show respect. Both oral and physical formality serve as violent contrasts to the desperation of the situation and the turmoil in the minds of the participants.

As the scene progresses, two things happen. Volumnia's examples become more homely: she speaks of herself as a "poor hen" who "clucked" her son to the wars and home again and of going back to Rome to "die among [her] neighbors." The formality of exhortation yields to a personal

awareness of family tragedy. Together with this change in language goes a change in rhythm. As the scene moves toward its conclusion, Volumnia bids Coriolanus or her daughter-in-law to speak. The lines indicate that silence intervenes, so that her speech loses its rolling persistence and disintegrates: "Speak to me, son," she says. "Daughter, speak you. . . . Speak thou, boy." No one does. Kneeling follows. "Down," she tells them all, and then, "An end! This is the last," waiting for a response after both commands. Thus, after so much speech, it is silence that builds in oppressiveness until the scene reaches that explicit moment when Coriolanus mutely takes his mother's hand—a gesture Shakespeare borrowed from Plutarch—and speaks so painfully and eloquently to her.

The persuasive mode, which is the root of the dramatic action and the foundation for the language of the scene, is also the specific means for concretizing the narrative of Coriolanus' fall. It belongs to a type of dramatic activity that Shakespeare uses with some frequency. Many of its features, including the presence of one character who makes demands and of another who rejects them, are common to scenes of this type. The way Shakespeare modulates that basic format for individual segments varies. The scene in which Lady Macbeth persuades Macbeth to kill Duncan shares a number of similarities with this scene from *Coriolanus.* Prior to the confrontation, Macbeth, like Coriolanus, is established in a position furthest removed from the one toward which he will be persuaded. Also like Coriolanus, Macbeth shows his opposition to his wife more in silence than in speech. But in the manner of expression, Lady Macbeth is not formal—perhaps because their scene is private. Instead, she is passionate and, as she intensifies the pressure upon her husband, becomes more extravagant in her claims. In both of these persuasion scenes, the basic action supplies a dynamic framework upon which the specific expressiveness of the scene is draped.

Persuasion scenes illustrate most clearly the dialectical dynamic that underlies much dramatic action. They embody a structure of tacit conflict wherein one character seeks to change the mind and thus the resistance of another. The two scenes I have already cited do this in a straightforward manner. But elsewhere in his plays, Shakespeare modulates this straightforward pattern in a subtle manner. In bringing Othello to distrust Desdemona, Iago appears to be persuading Othello not to leap to conclusions, although, of course, he is actually urging him to do so. In effect, Shakespeare separates the ostensible purpose from the true purpose in order to produce a terrifying, ironic seduction.

Complementary to persuasion scenes are scenes of castigation and contumely. The relation between the two is apparent in the closet scene in *Hamlet,* in which Hamlet castigates his mother for betraying his father and then seeks to persuade her to refrain from sexual contact with Claudius. Earlier in the play, persuasion and castigation combine in the nunnery scene. Like the persuasion scene, the castigation scene is inherently binary.

Shakespeare writes a wide variety of scene types, constantly modifying them, so that he never quite repeats himself but still builds his action on fundamental schemes. Besides persuasion and castigation, there are among many others, scenes of admonition (Polonius to Laertes), confession (Hamlet to Horatio), instruction (Polonius to Reynaldo), and intrigue (Claudius to Laertes). All of these have the form of an active scene; that is, the action is propelled by the efforts of one character working upon another—upon his emotions, will, and mind. In working upon another, the impellant figure has a specific objective in view and, in the course of the action, either gains it or fails to gain it. Lady Macbeth, for one, gains her objective. On the other hand, in his scene with his mother, Hamlet appears to gain his end with Gertrude, but after he leaves her and Claudius enters, Gertrude's response to the King suggests that Hamlet has failed. Yet in the last scene of the play Gertrude turns on Claudius, indicating that Hamlet did have some effect upon her after all. These mixed signals as to Hamlet's success show how dramatic action, though vivid and vigorous in its enactment, can produce ambivalent responses.

Shakespeare also writes scenes that are essentially reactive or reflective, in which the action does not contain a specific objective so much as a general reverberation. Scenes of lamentation offer the clearest examples. Lear bearing the dead Cordelia in his arms experiences a diminishing anguish as he vainly looks for signs of life. Intermixed are Kent's and Albany's ineffectual attempts to distract him. More purely reactive are the scenes of Constance's grief in *King John* (III. i, iv). King Philip begins the second of these scenes by lamenting his loss to John, but soon Constance enters. She begins by charging Philip to "see the issue of your peace," but when Philip bids her be patient, she goes

through a prolonged recital of her grief. A comparison of this scene with that from *King Lear* shows that in the years between the writing of the two plays, Shakespeare moved from expressing grief by anatomizing it rhetorically to contextual responses as evident at the end of *King Lear.* Lear's "Howl, howl, howl" is a raw but extremely brief outcry. The main of his reaction comes through his sight of the fluttering feather that he imagines carries Cordelia's breath (V. iii. 258–266). In reactive sequences, such as this one, where there is no specific objective to pursue, the impulse for the dramatic action comes from the effort to relieve pain or to share joy. The key character experiences the awful contrast between a terrible event and his or her capacity to absorb its effects. The cries and gestures are the reverberations of accommodation.

Shakespeare's soliloquies are often reactive or reflective; those in *Hamlet* are most notable. They usually start with an exclamation that reflects the accumulated tension within the Prince: "O that this too too sullied flesh would melt," "O, what a rogue and peasant slave am I," or "How all occasions do inform against me." Following these precipitating reactions, Hamlet reveals his anguish at his mother's wedding, his hesitant behavior, and his admiration for Fortinbras' aggressiveness, respectively. As the first soliloquy shows, the image of Gertrude's wedding builds an intense frustration within Hamlet, a frustration that subsides only as he realizes his helplessness. The other two soliloquies end with a decision to act: to catch the conscience of the king and to pursue bloody thoughts. Most reflective of all of Hamlet's soliloquies is "To be or not to be." It is also the most abstract, dealing with the general state of man rather than with the speaker's peculiar circumstances.

Obviously, the forward propulsion of a play is much easier to achieve through active rather than reactive scenes. But a play needs both forms of action to express the ebb and flow of existence. Most scenes contain both active and reactive elements, but some scenes are predominantly active, others mainly reactive. Shakespeare's skill in modulating these two kinds of action enables him to produce the rich array of fictional experience that makes him the foremost dramatist in the world.

Language and gesture, we have seen, convey and manifest the pulse of action. In their fullest realization, they express the mind and body of characters caught in the toils of events. Furthermore, they complement each other. Numerous critics, Nevill

Coghill, Maurice Charney, and Alan Dessen among them, have shown that Shakespeare frequently employs visual and nonverbal elements to convey his ideas. Coriolanus' mute holding of his mother's hand, as we have seen, is the most eloquent moment in the scene. But such use of silence and stage picture is intimately calibrated to the spoken lines. The eloquence of silence is possible only because of the preceding speech of Volumnia and its gradual disintegration as Coriolanus remains mute. With experience Shakespeare discovered how to create a lively pattern of verbal and nonverbal elements. The poetry of "Pray you undo this button" comes not from the intrinsic power of the sentence but from its context of dramatic action.

In this, Shakespeare's dramatic art is indivisible. Readers and spectators respond to it as a cohesive whole. Yet if actors, teachers, and critics wish to fathom its power, they must discern the diverse layers of story, dramatic action, and language. They also need to realize that Shakespeare does not formulate his plays out of elements foreign to other writers. Instead, he uses techniques and structures similar to those used by his fellow playwrights and indeed by playwrights of all periods. But he uses them more finely, more boldly, more variably, and, for the most part, more elegantly than others. He so perceptively penetrates his source and so artfully reshapes it into dramatic action that his plays pulsate with the essence of life.

BIBLIOGRAPHY

Thomas W. Baldwin, *Shakespeare's Five-Act Structure* (1947). Bernard Beckerman, *Shakespeare at the Globe* (1962) and "Shakespeare's Dramaturgy and Binary Form," in *Theatre Journal,* 33 (1981). Gerald E. Bentley, *The Profession of Dramatist in Shakespeare's Time* (1971) and *The Profession of Player in Shakespeare's Time* (1984). David Bevington, *From Mankind to Marlowe* (1962) and *Action Is Eloquence: Shakespeare's Language of Gesture* (1984). Max Bluestone, *From Story to Stage: The Dramatic Adaptation of Prose Fiction in the Period of Shakespeare and His Contemporaries* (1974). Muriel C. Bradbrook, *Elizabethan Stage Conditions* (1931; repr. 1968) and *Shakespeare the Craftsman* (1969). Alan Brissenden, *Shakespeare and the Dance* (1981).

James L. Calderwood, *Shakespearean Metadrama* (1971). Maurice Charney, *Style in "Hamlet"* (1969). Nevill Coghill, *Shakespeare's Professional Skills* (1964). Hardin Craig, "Shakespeare's Development as a Dramatist," in *Studies in Philology,* 39 (1942). Alan Dessen, *Elizabethan Drama and the Viewer's Eye* (1977) and *Elizabethan Stage Conventions and Modern Interpreters* (1984). Madeleine Doran, *Endeavours of Art* (1954). Una Ellis-Fermor, *Shakespeare the Dramatist, and Other Papers* (1961).

Michael Goldman, *Shakespeare and the Energies of Drama* (1972). Harley Granville-Barker, *Prefaces to Shakespeare,* 6 vols. (1927–1948; repr. in 4 vols., 1965). *Henslowe's Diary,* R. A. Foakes and R. T. Rickert, eds. (1961). James E. Hirsh, *The Structure of Shakespearean Scenes* (1981). G. K. Hunter, "Were There Act-Pauses on Shakespeare's Stage?" in Standish Henning, Robert Kimbrough, and Richard Knowles, eds., *English Renaissance Drama* (1976).

Wilfred T. Jewkes, *Act-Division in Elizabethan and Jacobean Plays* (1958). Emrys Jones, *Scenic Form in Shakespeare* (1971). Richard Louis Levin, *The Multiple Plot in English Renaissance Drama* (1971). Richard G. Moulton, *Shakespeare as a Dramatic Artist* (1885; rev. ed., 1906). John Orrell, *The Quest for Shakespeare's Globe* (1983).

Hereward T. Price, *Construction in Shakespeare* (1951). Anne Righter, *Shakespeare and the Idea of the Play* (1962). Mark Rose, *Shakespearean Design* (1972). Henry L. Snuggs, *Shakespeare and Five Acts: Studies in a Dramatic Convention* (1960). Thomas B. Stroup, *Microcosmos: The Shape of the Elizabethan Play* (1965). Thomas F. Van Laan, *Role-Playing in Shakespeare* (1978).

Music in Shakespeare's Work

F. W. STERNFELD
C. R. WILSON

It is hardly surprising that Shakespeare employed music in the majority of his plays, when we consider the precedents to be found in earlier and contemporary drama. The interludes of Thomas Heywood and William Cornish and of later Elizabethan comedy, beginning with Nicholas Udall's *Ralph Roister Doister* (ca. 1553), where song and dance are prominent; the court dramas of John Lyly, where songs are indicated or cued; the satires of Ben Jonson; Elizabethan entertainments and Jacobean court masques—these and many more use music as part of their theater. From the earliest days of English drama, it had been customary for actors and writers to intersperse music in spoken plays. Music served either as an entertainment-diversion, to alleviate possible restlessness among an audience otherwise subjected to an exclusive diet of speech, or to add another dimension to the drama, by conveying ideas and allusions that could not be as well set forth in verbal discourse. Shakespeare, therefore, did not create something new or even very different by having music in his plays. Nor, to judge by the lack of irrelevant musical diversion, would it seem that his audiences became bored too often.

In addition to an existing wealth of dramatic music in England, continental forms, notably the Italian *intermedio* and the French *ballet,* could have been known to Shakespeare. Whether they influenced him is highly questionable, but the way the Italians and French used music helps us to understand, by analogy, how Shakespeare incorpo-

rated it into his plays. Italian spoken comedies, performed at court especially in the second half of the sixteenth century, were sometimes punctuated by musical *intermedi* between the acts. As well as providing the audience with uninterrupted entertainment, the musical interludes allowed the actors to rest. Although Shakespeare does not employ music after this fashion—the few songs intended purely as entertainment appear in the middle of acts—there is some sense of the *intermedio* tradition in the musical conclusion, such as Feste's epilogue to *Twelfth Night* and perhaps in *Love's Labor's Lost.* Other precedents exist in Elizabethan jig finales, which in turn are related to the joyous choral-dancing finale of the *intermedio.*

As far as we know, music was performed between the acts of Shakespeare's plays, but only in their production rather than by authorial direction. According to the traditions of the day, acts were more obviously divided than scenes; music was most useful to this end. The custom of interact music was brought to the Globe Theatre, as Richard Hosley suggests, by Shakespeare's company only around 1609, after they had been performing in the private theater at Blackfriars. One example of interact music, Walter Greg suggests, is to be found in the interval between Acts III and IV of *A Midsummer Night's Dream.* The First Folio reproduces the stage direction "They sleepe all the Act." From this it appears that the enchanted lovers remain asleep onstage while music plays, awakening disenchanted in Act IV. The First Folio stage direction, however, comes from a prompt book that was most probably used in a 1609 or later revival of *A Midsummer Night's Dream,* with which Shakespeare almost certainly had little to do. Hypotheses apart, it is clear that interact music was not part of Shakespeare's original concept of either *A Midsummer Night's Dream* or any other play and therefore does not affect our discussion of his own use of music. It is worth noting here, in addition to the *intermedio,* that the other main form of Italian dramatic music, the newly born opera of Peri and Monteverdi, would not and did not interest Shakespeare, since his characters speak naturally and predominantly in verbal cadences, whereas in opera song and recitative are the natural and exclusive modes of utterance.

Neat divisions between the spoken play and music can be seen in Thomas Sackville and Thomas Norton's *Gorboduc,* a tragedy in blank verse acted before Queen Elizabeth in 1562, where each act is preceded by a pantomime to the accompaniment of instrumental music. But with the rapid development of dramatic art in the later sixteenth century and its growing independence of Seneca and other humanist models, no such division was again attempted, and music crept increasingly into the very body of the spoken play. The pantomime became integrated into the action of the play, as in Thomas Kyd's *Spanish Tragedy,* John Webster's *The Duchess of Malfi,* and Shakespeare's *Titus Andronicus* and *Hamlet.* As Shakespeare's dramatic art developed and intensified, his use of music became more sophisticated and increasingly integral, most noticeably in the comedies. This integration was brought about mainly by Shakespeare's use of dramatic characters singing or playing in their own character and in dramatic situations, rather than as walk-on musicians. And it was probably a result of the playwright's desire to explore the dramatic potential of his company of actors. Richard Burbage and Robert Armin were not cast as stereotypes, like the boy actors of Blackfriars; rather they were given scope to explore fully the "conceits" of their parts.

Deriving from the conventions of Elizabethan and Jacobean drama, the integration of music in Shakespeare's plays operates on differing levels of sophistication and meaning. The majority of musical cues can be readily divided into four main categories: stage music, magic music, character music, and atmospheric music. As we shall see, these categories inevitably overlap in some cases; the music for the banquet in *The Tempest* (III. iii) is both stage music and atmospheric; the music for the coming to life of the statue in *The Winter's Tale* (V. iii) is both atmospheric and magic music; Ariel's song "Where the bee sucks" *(The Tempest,* V. i) embodies both atmospheric and character music.

"Stage music" is the most straightforward category. It comprises functional or occasional music, prompted by or announcing an action on the stage, and usually eschewing allusion or hidden metaphor. It is used to accompany a banquet or procession, a duel or a battle; or it may herald the arrival or entry of kings and nobles. Trumpets and kettledrums announce the royal procession in *Hamlet* (III. ii). A flourish of trumpets conventionally ushers in Duke Frederick, lords, Orlando, Charles, and attendants in *As You Like It* (I. ii); and a flourish of cornetts announces the arrival of the Prince of Morocco *(The Merchant of Venice,* II. i) and his entry with Portia later in the same act. What else, then, could Shakespeare use but a flourish of trumpets for Quince's entry in *A Midsummer Night's Dream* (V. i)? Equally, stage music may also be employed simply and quietly for a serenade, as in *The Merchant of Venice* (V. i) and *The Two Gentlemen of Verona* (IV. ii).

The second category, "magic music," encompasses the age-old concept of the "ethos" of music, the Aristotelian philosophy of its power to affect. Music might induce sleep, make someone fall in love, or miraculously heal. When Lady Mortimer sings Mortimer to sleep in *Henry IV, Part 1* (III. i), her singing, accompanied by Hotspur's quizzical humor, involves and questions the extraordinary goings-on of Glendower, with his strange folklore and "skimble-skamble stuff." Or, when the fairies sing Titania to sleep in *A Midsummer Night's Dream* (II. ii), we know that theirs is no ordinary lullaby. Ariel entices Ferdinand "to these yellow sands" in *The Tempest* (I. ii. 375) with a magic song. Shakespeare does not rely on music alone to convey the magic effects. In addition to allusion and suggestion, stage effects help infuse the living world with the supernatural. Glendower's musicians who

Hang in the air a thousand leagues from hence,
And straight they shall be here.

(III. i. 223–224)

were hidden, most probably behind the curtain or arras at the back of the Globe stage, as were the spirits who accompany Ariel. Such effects are made plausible because the audience knows of the supernatural or magical powers of Glendower and Prospero. At other times, magic music is made effective when it rises from beneath the stage, as when the strange sound of "hautboys" presages the fall of the hero in *Antony and Cleopatra* (IV. iii). Here, magic music is also prophetic, and although there are no clear distinctions between magic, superstition, and prophecy, whenever the supernatural is implied, that music is concealed. In many cases, it is therefore neither heard nor felt, except by those to whom it is addressed, as in the music of the spheres in *Pericles* (V. i. 231).

To employ music as a means of revealing a person's character in a play, however, demands extraordinary skill and knowledge of the capabilities of music. A significant number of Shakespeare's songs have this dramatic function; indeed, all the songs in *The Winter's Tale,* following each other in fairly close succession, characterize Autolycus and his position in life. Without them, much of Shakespeare's dramatic "conceit" is lost. They rank among his most intense character songs, being psychological rather than philosophical. In *Troilus and Cressida,* the nature of Pandarus, the provider of soft luxuries, the diseased pander, is characterized by his sophisticated, lecherous song:

Love, love, nothing but love, still love still more!

(III. i. 107)

Pandarus' song also reflects upon the characters of Paris and Helen, for whom he sings, as well as upon the Elizabethan gentry, whom Shakespeare satirizes. Sometimes the personality generated through music is assumed rather than real. In *Othello,* Iago pretends to conviviality and pleasantness, while coldly plotting Cassio's downfall, when he sings

And let me the canakin clink, clink.

(II. iii. 65)

Bassanio in *The Merchant of Venice* is clearly marked as the preferred suitor by being the only one favored with a song before he chooses:

Tell me where is fancy bred,
Or in the heart, or in the head?

(III. ii. 63–64)

Music is the essential ingredient in the makeup of the professional entertainer, the clown. When Feste sings in *Twelfth Night:*

O mistress mine, where are you roaming?

(II. iii. 36)

such an easygoing belief in *joie de vivre* distinguishes both him and his audience, Toby and Andrew. When asked whether they want "a love song, or a song of good life" for their sixpence, they clearly demand the former, because they "care not for good life," the restrictions of the Puritan creed.

At times, Shakespeare does not employ song because his characters are better at declaiming than at singing, a device used with touching gentleness in *Cymbeline* to excuse the young actors' broken voices. Arviragus invites his brother:

And let us, Polydore, though now our voices
Have got the mannish crack, sing him to th'
ground . . .

but Guiderius replies:

Cadwal,
I cannot sing. I'll weep, and word it with thee,
For notes of sorrow out of tune are worse
Than priests and fanes that lie.

And they agree:

We'll speak it then.

(IV. ii. 235–243)

At other times, social status prevents Shakespeare's characters from singing and requires a servant to perform instead. Duke Orsino's excessive melancholy and lovesickness in *Twelfth Night* are wonderfully portrayed in Feste's performance of

Come away, come away, death,

(II. iv. 50)

a lyric that the Duke expressly commands to be performed for his gratification. A similar case of self-indulgence occurs in *Measure for Measure* when the unhappy and deserted Mariana asks a boy singer to recite the melancholy

Take, O take those lips away

(IV. i. 1)

to please her woe. Probably the supreme example of characterization, of revealing a protagonist's true mind, occurs in Ophelia's famous mad scene. When she sings songs and snatches of songs before the

King, the Queen, and Horatio, and when she breaks into song spontaneously without being urged to perform by others and without polite protestations on her own part, she betrays several crucial facts. First, she shows us that her mind is deranged, for the object of the devotion of the Prince of Denmark should not publicly break into song in a manner so unbecoming to her social station. Singing, as a private accomplishment, was one of the virtues of a well-educated and desirable woman, as Othello is not ashamed to confess of Desdemona:

> To say my wife is fair, feeds well, loves company,
> Is free of speech, sings, plays, and dances;
> Where virtue is, these are more virtuous.
>
> (III. iii. 184–186)

But contemporary etiquette forbade such public performances as Ophelia's, as is made plain in English and Italian manuals on the subject. Shakespeare was obviously aware of this, since he was careful to insert polite disclaimers in the surrounding dialogue when a member of the nobility did sing, as Balthasar does in *Much Ado About Nothing* and Pandarus in *Troilus and Cressida.*

Second, Ophelia's lyric unequivocally shows her profound grief for her father's death:

> White his shroud as the mountain snow—
>
> . . .
>
> Larded all with sweet flowers;
> Which bewept to the grave did not go
> With true-love showers.
>
> (IV. v. 36, 38–40)

The insertion of the monosyllable "not" in the third line, with its harsh disruption of the meter, illustrates how Shakespeare often departs from the original words of a popular song, well known to a contemporary audience, to heighten the dramatic effect; the clown's song in the gravedigger's scene (V. i) is another very obvious and notable example. In Ophelia's lyric, the superfluous "not" (often omitted in old editions), by its inclusion, indicates her sense of shock at the absence of proper decency and decorum at her father's burial. The three concerns of her deranged mind—Hamlet's love, Polonius' and Laertes' insinuations that it is dishonorable and false, and grief over the death of her father—are made manifest in the separate stanzas of her song. Whether she sings a mere snatch, such as

> For bonny sweet Robin is all my joy,
>
> (IV. v. 185)

or four entire stanzas of a not-wholly-proper St. Valentine's Day song (IV. v. 48–55), her concern with love—moreover, extramarital love—is perfectly apparent. Thus, both her singing and her songs themselves characterize her state of mind and preoccupations.

Perhaps better than any other technique or device, music is capable of indicating to an audience a change of tone within a drama; Shakespeare realized this more than any other dramatist of his day. "Atmospheric music" is the most subtle of the four categories, because it is concerned with such intangibles as mood, tone, and emotional feeling and because it may involve changes from suspicion to trust, from vengeance to forgiveness, or from hatred to love. The highly romantic denouement of *The Merchant of Venice,* after the harsh words and near tragedy of the trial scene, is prepared initially by increased lyricism in the poetry—with songlike stanzaic speaking and a setting of moonlight, stars, and candlelight—and finally by background music for Portia's arrival, with the martial interruption of a flourish of trumpets to bring on the men, adding to the romance their masculine swagger and impropriety. Music identifies the stages of Prospero's personal development in *The Tempest;* here we have both atmospheric and character music. Indeed, it is perfectly admissible to regard the music of *The Tempest* as the medium through which order emerges from chaos. As Theresa Coletti suggests, music "is the agent of suffering, learning, growth and freedom."

Music is probably the most effective and economical way to convey dramatic change; it obviates tedious verbal explanations and has performed such a role admirably in ritual and in drama. Nowhere did Shakespeare exploit this device more felicitously than in his last plays, where the miraculous element functions less as an object in itself than as a token of expiation and happiness. In *The Tempest,* the wedding masque in Act IV and Ariel's song in Act V certainly prefigure

> calm seas, auspicious gales,
> And sail so expeditious that shall catch
> Your royal fleet far off.
>
> (V. i. 314–316)

Other dramatic elements are also present in this music. The wedding masque is also stage music; Ariel's lyric is character music since, like Autolycus' "When daffodils begin to peer" *(The Winter's Tale,* IV. iii. 1), it indicates reflection on his future life. But those elements are subsidiary, and the larger aesthetic meaning is unmistakable.

The intervention of music in *The Winter's Tale* to prepare for the denouement is similarly timed. The masque (IV. iv) and the song and dance of the sheepshearing feast in Bohemia (IV. iv) emphasize the lightning change of tone from the dark, destructive world of the first three acts, which are devoid of music. This is followed by a more prominent musical interlude in Act V. When Paulina commands

> Music! Awake her, strike!
>
> (V. iii. 98)

and the statue comes to life, we know that the complete reconciliation within the older generation will soon follow that between Florizel and his father. The miracle of reconciliation is embodied in the magical powers of love. The music is also, therefore, and not surprisingly, magic. That Shakespeare did not place this music at the very end of the play meant that, although he denied himself a musical finale, he achieved a greater dramatic effect, unlike the conclusion of the early *Love's Labor's Lost,* where the placement of the two songs at the very end can in no way help to develop the drama. As it is, the instrumental music for Hermione's descent is only about fifty lines from the end, thereby emphasizing the important dramatic function of music in that play. Here we see how increasingly subtle and flexible Shakespeare's handling of music has become.

Shakespeare's development in the use of song is preeminently manifest in the comedies, for the tragedies and histories do not employ songs so frequently or consistently. In the first two comedies, *The Taming of the Shrew* and *The Comedy of Errors,* song is noticeably absent. In the last two, *The Winter's Tale* and *The Tempest,* song is integrated in the most masterly and flexible way. In the early comedies, song functions on a straightforward dramatic level, having more to do with immediate context than with the overall theme of the play. An anonymous singer is brought onstage solely to perform his song; having sung, he is quietly and quickly removed. As Shakespeare's song technique

advanced, his singers became actors, contributing to the action of the play and its development.

The songs in *Love's Labor's Lost* provide a useful link between the techniques of the early and later comedies. Here the final songs (of the 1597 revival) reflect on the very theme of the comedy, as well as providing resolution for conflicts and opposites left unresolved at the end. The music has an important unifying effect, even though that harmony is as yet only in the words of the songs. In *Much Ado About Nothing, As You Like It,* and *Twelfth Night* the technique advances rapidly. In *Much Ado,* there is a close connection between music and the theme of love. As Irene Naef points out, in drama "well-sung music can be artificial and bad, whereas a defective and unfinished song can be perfect music." Broken and imperfect songs are effectively used in *As You Like It,* and one can see in its five songs a miniature commentary on the two themes of the play, love and the life of retirement. Some of the songs are also character songs, helping to develop the person and attitudes of Jaques. In *Twelfth Night,* song is integrated still further into the thematic structure. A partly improvised song, such as "Farewell, dear heart" (II. iii. 93), even replaces spoken dialogue; "Hold thy peace, thou knave" (II. iii. 60) produces the subplot, a dramatic situation unique in the comedies. But above all, the play's songs augment the underlying notes of sadness that counterpoint the fun and lovemaking. They speak of death, reminding us that "what's to come is still unsure" (II. iii. 46), that "youth's a stuff will not endure" (49), and that despite the persuasion of comedy, the world is still a place where "it raineth every day." (381). The culmination of this technique is to be found in *The Tempest,* where the songs are most fully and perfectly integrated both in their immediate dramatic setting, as in the early comedies, and in the overall concept of the play.

Shakespeare's use of music was by no means shaped purely by aesthetic intention. He was also influenced by the musical resources available to him. When Robert Armin succeeded William Kemp, Shakespeare increasingly emphasized the importance of the adult actor-singer until, in the role of Autolycus, he created a figure who is both essential to the action and able to add another dimension through his singing. This dimension has a great deal to do with the turn from comedy to "romance," as the last plays are usually designated. Boy singer-actors were more numerous in Elizabethan times, as the rival companies at Blackfriars and St. Paul's attest. Shakespeare employed them effectively and variously, as when the thin, sexless tone of the anonymous boy actor endows the lyrics of Ophelia and Desdemona with pathos without evincing the sensuous aspects of the action. Boys not only performed the roles of tragic heroines; they also sang as fairies in *A Midsummer Night's Dream* and *The Merry Wives of Windsor* and rendered the music of Ariel and his troupe in *The Tempest.* The tone color of their voices, so different from that of adult actors, no doubt contributed to the illusion of the supernatural. Herein lies one advantage of Shakespeare's company over the boys of Blackfriars and St. Paul's: within one company he had available the possibility of contrast between the asexual sound of boys and the richer and more sonorous timbre of adults.

As for instrumental music, Shakespeare was usually specific because he wished to call upon the traditional symbolism or "ethos" attached to differing families of instruments. Certain instruments or consorts of instruments might be used to signify war or peace, to suggest divine or diabolical intervention, or to announce that a scene is domestic, courtly, or military. Such contextual music depended for its effect on the significance of opposites: loud and harsh music *(musique haute)* meant the opposite of soft and peaceful music *(musique basse);* trumpets, cornetts, and hautboys contrasted with strings and recorders. Thus it did not matter which particular composer's music was used but, rather, what kind of piece was played and for which instruments. When Othello bids farewell to war, he bids farewell to the "shrill trump, the spirit-stirring drum, th' ear-piercing fife" (III. iii). Squealing hautboys (much louder and harsher than the modern oboe) foretold doom, most notably in the banqueting scenes in *Titus Andronicus* and *Macbeth* and in their ominous music under the stage in *Antony and Cleopatra.* A flourish of trumpets or cornetts signified a military or royal presence; plucked instruments, such as the lute and cittern, represented domesticity. When the King in *Henry IV, Part 2,* on his deathbed, calls for music, he asks for soft music:

Let there be no noise made, my gentle friends,
Unless some dull and favorable hand
Will whisper music to my weary spirit.

(IV. v. 1–3)

In *King Lear,* music accompanies the restoration of "th' untuned and jarring senses" (IV. vii. 16) of the king. The references to "still" music and to the viol (a Renaissance stringed instrument, generally bowed but plucked on occasion) indicate soft music and its associations, such as when Cerimon revives Thaisa in *Pericles:*

The still and woefull music that we have,
Cause it to sound, beseech you.
The viol once more. How thou stirr'st, thou block!

(III. ii. 87–89)

Heavenly music, with its quasi-Pythagorean and Platonic associations of moral reward, healing, prophecy, and divine intervention, is generally represented by soft music, gentleness being as much an excellent virtue in musical tone as it is in a woman's voice.

An important antithesis was the contrast between the consonant, sweetly tuned silver strings (of Apollo and the muses), signifying the music of the spheres, and the discordant, harsh tuning (of the pipes of Pan or Marsyas), which reflected the unpropitious conjunctions of the planets. The peace and unity of the commonwealth were thereby set against the disruption of civil war so feared and denounced by Shakespeare and his contemporaries. The Renaissance ideals of harmony and perfection, of man in perfect harmony with himself, his world, and the universe, are represented in music by the perfect tuning of instruments and by man's response to those instruments, an idea most memorably expressed by Lorenzo in *The Merchant of Venice:*

The man that hath no music in himself,
Nor is not moved with concord of sweet sounds,
Is fit for treasons, stratagems, and spoils;
The motions of his spirit are dull as night,
And his affections dark as Erebus.

(V. i. 83–87)

It is with horror that the protagonists of Shakespeare's great tragedies contemplate man out of tune with himself. Ophelia, "that sucked the honey of his music vows" (III. i. 156), having been rejected by Hamlet, now sees his "noble and most sovereign reason,/Like sweet bells jangled, out of time and harsh" (157–158). Similarly out of tune are King Lear, "Who sometime, in his better tune, remembers/What we are come about" (IV. iii. 39–40), and Cleopatra, who worries that "saucy lictors/Will catch at us like strumpets, and scald rhymers/Ballad us out o' tune" (V. ii. 214–215).

Internal strife and the possible destruction of the commonwealth are alluded to in Ulysses' speech in *Troilus and Cressida:*

> Take but degree away, untune that string,
> And hark what discord follows.

(I. iii. 109–110)

Of the 100 or so songs, snatches, or quotations of songs scattered through the thirty-six plays in the First Folio, for more than half we have neither certain knowledge of, nor even a historically acceptable hypothesis for, the tune actually used by the King's Men in a first performance or early revival. Even when a melody has the appropriate title, incipit, or rubric in a commonplace book, manuscript miscellany, or printed source of the period, we cannot be certain that it was the tune used for an early production. On the other hand, modern scholarship and bibliographical methods have revealed so much about Elizabethan and Jacobean music since Edmund H. Fellowes began his major pioneering work in the 1920s that we may confidently fit most of Shakespeare's lyrics either to their proper tune or to a suitable one.

So little instrumental music for the stage has survived from the period that it is impossible to be at all sure what was played in a particular production. But, as we noted earlier, it is less important to know what was played than what was intended. What instrumental theater music has survived—notably BL Add. MS 10,444, which contains a large collection of music for the Stuart masque—shows that dances, marches, entries, and so on were short, simple, and mainly homophonic pieces. It is not difficult, therefore, to substitute a suitable piece. For lists of music and musical settings of songs, the reader is referred to Sternfeld and Seng, and, for additional hypotheses, to Long.

The music required for the songs ranges from simple, popular balladlike ditties, well known by contemporary audiences, to specially composed and more complex art songs. It is noteworthy that Shakespeare does not employ the madrigal, so much in vogue at the time. But this is hardly surprising, since its musical counterpoint would have obscured the text; this and other musical impositions would have detracted immensely from a song's dramatic or literary purpose.

The tunes of popular songs could easily be fitted or adapted to lyrics of three- or four-stress lines, and would be well known enough not to require the music to be written out but simply referred to in the usual way: "To the tune of. . . ." That Shakespeare could rely on this in both his actors and his audience is manifest, for example, when Mistress Ford exclaims, "They do no more adhere and keep place together than the Hundredth Psalm to the tune of 'Greensleeves' " (*Merry Wives,* II. i); or when Autolycus sells a merry ballad that "goes to the tune of 'Two maids wooing a man' " (*Winter's Tale,* IV. iv). Nearly all such popular tunes were unaccompanied. Anyone could hum or sing them at any time in any place without having an accompanying instrument, such as a lute, cittern, or viol, with him. Indeed, the presence of an instrument would have suggested that a musical performance was planned rather than spontaneous. Such are the balladlike ditties performed by the Fool in *King Lear,* by Silence in *Henry IV, Part 2,* and by Ophelia in *Hamlet.* Although the First Quarto of *Hamlet* has the stage direction "Enter Ophelia playing on a lute, and her hair down, singing," it is not repeated in the Second Quarto or the Folio. Nor is there any reference to a lute or other instrument in the surrounding dialogue. A simple accompaniment is unnecessary here; but on the other hand it would not be out of place. In *Othello,* however, Desdemona would have found it rather difficult to accompany herself on, say, a lute while Emilia undresses her. The song that she uses, having stanzas of two lines, each of four stresses, interspersed with the "willow" refrain, freely and incompletely recalls a preexistent song, extant today in several lute manuscripts, notably the Dallis lutebook (Dublin), a manuscript of lute music belonging to Thomas Dallis and bearing the date 1583, and the Giles Lodge book (Washington, D.C.), containing purely instrumental pieces from the early 1570s. Shakespeare sometimes adapted an existing composed song to an improvised ballad or folk song; one example is Peter's song in *Romeo and Juliet.* The words first appeared in a printed anthology of 1576, attributed to the musical poet and playwright Richard Edwards; the music survives in two manuscripts, unattributed but probably also by Edwards. At first sight it would seem that Shakespeare made a curious choice of lyric for his clown. But the song's four-stress line, its simple and fairly syllabic melody that is easily sung or hummed with or without accompaniment, the puns and jokes of its context—all combine to produce a ballad or popular song.

In contrast to these simple ditties are songs best termed "art music." These are distinguished in Shakespeare's text by their prosodical complexity or simply by their dramatic context. In other words, when the audience has been prepared, a song can allow the singer more textual sophistication and careful performance. The instrumental accompaniment that is generally required may well be referred to in the surrounding dialogue. In *Julius Caesar,* Brutus refers four times to the "instrument" with which Lucius is to accompany himself; in *Henry VIII,* Queen Katharine commands "Take thy lute, wench" (III. i. 1). In *Troilus and Cressida,* before beginning his song, Pandarus says, "Come, give me an instrument" (III. i. 89), and at another point, "I'll sing you a song now" (98). And when Helen commands "Let thy song be love" (102), Pandarus obliges with a lyric far removed in quality and sophistication from the metrically simple songs and ditties of Autolycus in *The Winter's Tale.* Ariel's songs in *The Tempest* also demand professional skill, especially "Full fathom five" (I. ii. 397) and "Where the bee sucks." Early-seventeenth-century settings for the latter two songs survive in John Wilson's *Cheerful Ayres or Ballads* (ca. 1659), attributed to the court lutenist Robert Johnson. Whether these settings were used in the first performance (1611) or for subsequent revivals is very difficult to know. But historical and stylistic reasons argue for connecting Johnson's settings with contemporary productions of Shakespeare, not only with regard to *The Tempest* but also for *Cymbeline* (ca. 1609) and *The Winter's Tale* (1611) Johnson also composed songs for Webster's *The Duchess of Malfi* (ca. 1613), for Middleton's *The Witch* (ca. 1616), and for five plays by Beaumont and Fletcher, not to mention music for several court masques. Thomas Morley, better known as a madrigal composer, may have been connected with two other art songs in Shakespeare, performed onstage by professional musicians. In *As You Like It,* two pages sing four stanzas of "It was a lover and his lass" (V. iii. 15). A setting for single voice and lute that appears in Morley's *First Booke of Ayres* (1600) can be easily adapted for two voices. And Morley's *The First Booke of Consort Lessons* (1599) includes an instrumental version of Feste's two-stanza song "O mistress mine." Morley is not known to have been connected with the theater, and his collaboration with Shakespeare is most unlikely—though by no means impossible. (For a Shakespeare-Morley bibliography, see Seng.)

In Shakespeare's hands music is never employed as a simple divertissement or idle distraction; its effect is carefully calculated in poetic and dramatic terms. "The words of Mercury," says Don Armado as he brings *Love's Labor's Lost* to a close, "are harsh after the songs of Apollo." It was Shakespeare's achievement to have broken down that opposition, to have fused the message of Mercury and the music of the sun god, so that the music of words, of instruments, and of melody coalesced to form a uniquely varied and sensitive dramatic medium.

BIBLIOGRAPHY

Mary Chan, *Music in the Theatre of Ben Jonson* (1980). Theresa Coletti, "Music and *The Tempest,*" in Richard C. Tobias and Paul G. Zolbrod, eds., *Shakespeare's Late Plays: Essays in Honor of Charles Crow* (1974). Catherine M. Dunn, "The Function of Music in Shakespeare's Romances," in *Shakespeare Quarterly,* 20 (1969). Walter W. Greg, *The Shakespeare First Folio* (1955). Phyllis Hartnoll, ed., *Shakespeare in Music* (1964). R. W. Ingram, "Music as Structural Element in Shakespeare," in *Proceedings of the World Shakespeare Congress, Vancouver, August 1971* (1972).

John H. Long, *Shakespeare's Use of Music,* 3 vols. (1955–1971). Kenneth Muir and Samuel Schoenbaum, eds., *A New Companion to Shakespeare Studies* (1971), esp. Richard Hosley, "The Playhouses and the Stage," and F. W. Sternfeld, "Shakespeare and Music." Irene Naef, *Die Lieder in Shakespeares Komödien* (1976), with summary in English. Edward W. Naylor, *Shakespeare and Music* (1896; rev. ed., 1931). Richmond Noble, *Shakespeare's Use of Song* (1923). Peter J. Seng, *The Vocal Songs in the Plays of Shakespeare* (1967). Frederick W. Sternfeld, *Music in Shakespearean Tragedy* (1963; rev. ed., 1967).

The Visual Arts
in Shakespeare's Work

JOHN DIXON HUNT

Of the dozens of references to the visual arts in Shakespeare's work, most are made in passing, and some are barely perceptible in the texture of the language, so that only an editor's annotation or a critic's commentary enables the reference to be appreciated. In a few, notable exceptions—the statue of Hermione in *The Winter's Tale* is a prime example—a work of visual art is specifically brought into focus, but these seem exceptions to a rule, which is that Shakespeare's usual tendency is to use references to the visual arts as an economical means of drawing commonplace assumptions and knowledge of all sorts, not only aesthetic, into his audience's understanding of what they see and hear.

Characters make references to painted cloths (a cheap form of tapestry), tomb sculpture, painted miniatures, and royal entries or progresses, which seem to reflect contemporary habits, vogues, and nuances of social life that by implication color both text and context; or by alluding simply to familiar visual items, they sharpen—fleetingly—a casual remark. Gratiano's grandfather "cut in alabaster" in *The Merchant of Venice* or Viola's reference in *Twelfth Night* to the figures of Patience smiling at Grief on some other funerary monument would have elicited from hearers wholly familiar with such a pervasive art form a ready appreciation of the speaker's imagery. And if elaborate funerary sculpture also implied the social status of a prosperous Venetian merchant or suggested Viola and Olivia's patrician world, allusions to "painted cloths" in *Troilus and Cressida* or to "fly-bitten tapestries" in *Henry IV, Part 2,* by contrast, would have suggested the seediness of Pandarus' end or Mistress Quickly's establishment.

Portraiture was a major art in Shakespeare's England, and long galleries came into fashion to accommodate portraits of family and friends; there is an allusion to this practice in *Henry VI, Part 1.* By far the largest number of references in the plays, however, concerns miniatures, which were both portable and, above all, intimate. This intimacy is signaled in *Hamlet,* where Hamlet carries a miniature of his father, and Gertrude one of Claudius; in *The Merchant of Venice,* where Bassanio's successful courtship of Portia is announced to him by her portrait in the casket; and in *Twelfth Night,* where Olivia presses upon Viola a "jewel" in which is incorporated "my picture." When Benedick, in *Much Ado About Nothing,* suddenly made aware of his love for Beatrice, rushes off to "get her picture," we may assume that he seeks a miniature, more prized for its intimacy than even a small easel painting. Similarly, Proteus' protestations to Silvia may be measured by his grandiloquent request for her "picture that is hanging in [her] chamber."

One of the major difficulties with Shakespeare's glances at the visual arts is precisely how to read them, how to penetrate the deep structures of contemporary culture that are briefly illuminated by their usually passing mention. Bassanio's praise of "fair Portia's counterfeit" certainly signals a sharp awareness of its lifelikeness ("Move those eyes?"), a quality much esteemed in Renaissance art. But when he specifically notes how the artist "plays the spider, and hath woven / A golden mesh t' entrap the hearts of men," is it justified to claim that Shakespeare alludes to "a prominent feature of many quattrocento portraits, executed by men who were trained as goldsmiths, as was the case with Antonio Pollaiolo"? Is Shakespeare more interested in displaying his or Bassanio's aesthetic knowledge or in promoting the themes of gold, silver, and lead caskets? And with a wealth of native artistry like Nicholas Hilliard's, why should the reference be to 100-year-old foreign artists whom it is doubtful that Shakespeare would have known?

The conclusion reached by M. F. Thorpe, that Shakespeare "had small knowledge and less taste," is not necessarily countered by arguing for Shakespeare's wide knowledge of the Renaissance arts. He refers to a variety of visual artifacts as and when his dramatic and poetic purposes are best served. Some allusions are more covert than others. The return of the Duke to Vienna in the last scene of *Measure for Measure* would have recalled vividly to the original audiences the state entry of James I into London (1603), but it is not conspicuously emphasized; today, we must work to recognize how the play utilizes this pervasive ceremonial of Renaissance princes and their cities. Similarly, the entertainment of newly wedded or betrothed couples is now a topic that modern scholarship has much illuminated; we are better placed by our knowledge of Medici *intermezzi,* Valois *ballets,* Elizabethan progresses, and Stuart masques to register the unassertive subtleties of *A Midsummer Night's Dream* (the play within a play, wedding guests onstage and in the original audience) and the more intricate relation of Prospero's masque to *The Tempest* as a whole.

Shakespeare's range of reference is eclectic, probably more so than our modern notions of the so-called fine arts would suggest. Court masque and civic ritual were both forms of *pictura* to be seen and "read." So were items of domestic decor like tapestries (Shakespeare's maternal grandfather specified eleven painted cloths in his will), which often incorporated moral sentences or emblems. Hence Pandarus' allusion to the moral platitudes associated with such artwork; while *The Rape of Lucrece* refers to "a sentence or an old man's saw" in relation to painted cloths and to their sententious wisdom. The simple moralistic message of popular imagery is frequently employed by Shakespeare's

characters: Macbeth is accused of fearing a "painted devil," and Coriolanus' honor is, unless exercised, considered "no better than picture-like to hang by th' wall." Popular visual arts are invoked in these instances for dramatic purposes of disparagement; so perhaps is Trinculo's "picture of Nobody," which Samuel C. Chew relates to a woodcut in a play, *Nobody and Somebody* (1606), or Costard's determination to scrape out Alexander the Great from a painted cloth of the Nine Worthies after the curate's disastrous performance.

Tapestries, like some that Cardinal Wolsey bought for Hampton Court, depicted more sophisticated but still familiar imagery, such as the Petrarchan Triumphs, where ideas and mythological creatures are represented symbolically. It is to such artwork that Troilus may allude when he claims that "in all Cupid's pageant there is presented no monster." These learned (often Ovidian) subjects were the topic of many Renaissance paintings. Though it is moot which, if any, Shakespeare may have seen, it seems clear that he could count upon his audience to acknowledge references to them in the Induction of *The Taming of the Shrew* and, since the point is that Christopher Sly is being tricked into thinking he is a nobleman, to recognize such pictures as apt for a patrician collection.

Yet a caveat needs to be entered here. Sly is certainly tempted with the offer of paintings, though the word "pictures" could equally have been used of verbal pictures. Fluellen admonishes Pistol that Fortune is painted blind and proceeds to instruct him in simple matters of iconology, but he ends with "the poet makes a most excellent description of it." Given the traditional maneuvers of *ut pictura poesis* (as in a painting, so in a poem), "painted" need not necessarily specify a visual reference; given, too, the traditions of *paragone,* or rivalry between the verbal and visual arts, to which the opening of *Timon of Athens* directly alludes, Shakespeare may often intend to propose his verbal descriptions as rivals to painted imagery. This is certainly part of his effort in *The Rape of Lucrece;* probably part of the effect of the servant who tempts Sly; and it is crucial to Enobarbus' image of Cleopatra in her barge that itself "o'er pictures" the painting of Venus that he invokes.

Shakespeare's references to the visual arts often insist—not surprisingly from a writer—upon their literary transcription or verbal accompaniment. The allusion to Talbot's monument in Rouen Cathedral in *Henry VI, Part 1,* involves our seeing the

39. Detail showing a masque in *Sir Henry Unton,* by an unknown artist (ca. 1596).

group of Talbot, dead, with the body of his son "inhearsèd in [his] arms" as some funerary monument, while we listen to Sir William Lucy recite the tomb's inscription of Talbot titles. But we are most aware of the verbal contribution to visual recognition in Shakespeare's extensive references to emblems and the related devices of the *impresa* and heraldry. The large number of these allusions is not unexpected, given the popularity, visibility, and ease of circulation that emblems especially enjoyed.

Much has been made of Shakespeare's debts to the emblem tradition since 1870, when Henry Green provided extensive parallels between Shakespeare's language and the verbal and visual languages of the emblem. Critics continue to find such parallels, but, as with the caveat already offered, it is not necessarily to the visual figure of the emblem that Shakespeare directs attention. Ulysses' "Time hath, my lord, a wallet at his back" in *Troilus and Cressida* may invoke emblematic woodcuts in popular broadsides, but it is equally possible that, besides or instead of visual imagery,

40. Woodcut illustration from the popular broadside "Poor Robin's Dream," from *The Bagford Ballads*.

Shakespeare wanted his audiences to hear in Ulysses' sententious words echoes of a trivializing popular morality. It is nonetheless clear that learned emblem books like Andrea Alciati's *Emblemata* (1536) or Geoffrey Whitney's *Choice of Emblems* (1586), as well as more popular equivalents, determined important elements in Shakespeare's work, where proverbial and pictorial aspects are inextricably mingled. Shakespeare exploits the full range of emblematic references to the sun and to fortune, both echoing their discursive and implying their figurative scope. Yet in Jaques's disquisition on the ages of man, where his "pictures" can be paralleled in engravings by Symeoni and Otto Vaenius, it is again the function of these references to satirize his sentimental mediocrity.

Closely connected to emblem, but distinct from it, was the *impresa.* The Belvoir Castle Household Book records a payment in 1613 to Shakespeare for inventing an *impresa* for the earl of Rutland; he was familiar with this form, in which image and cryptic aphorism combine to declare a character's particular identity. He uses it in *Pericles,* where six knights carry *imprese* on their shields, though their symbolic apparatus is directly indebted to Whitney's *Choice of Emblems,* which was based in turn upon Claude Paradin's *Devises heroiques* (1557). And in *Timon of Athens* the unresolved debate between Poet and Painter, together with the play's visual and verbal presentation of Timon's enigmatic character, has led Michael Leslie to see the whole drama as an adapted *impresa.*

Shakespeare's debts to popular imagery did not always come via the emblem or *impresa.* It has been argued that the graphic work of Albrecht Dürer in particular contributed to Shakespeare's apocalyptic imagery. Yet the availability of similar images makes the adjudication of specific debts extremely difficult. We can only assume that Shakespeare refers overtly or covertly to a whole range of Elizabethan and Jacobean visual arts—illustrated broadsides like those that Falstaff likes ("with mine own picture on the top on't"), masques, civic ceremony, portraits, mythological paintings, tomb sculpture, fountains, and even gardens. But what specifically he saw and invoked, and what visual knowledge he assumed audiences would bring to his work, are far more problematical. His contemporary, Ben Jonson, refers in *Underwoods* XCV to Romano, Tintoretto, Titian, Raphael, Michelangelo, Andrea del Sarto, and Sebastiano del Piombo; we have no such testimony from Shakespeare.

This lack of concrete evidence has authorized attempts to understand Shakespeare in terms of Renaissance art. John Doebler turns the traditions of *ut pictura poesis* to critical use in exploring the stage iconography of several plays, just as he examines *Venus and Adonis* in the light of Renaissance visual treatments of the subject. But inasmuch as these inquiries are based upon the matrixes of cultural history and not upon Shakespeare's own specific references, they fall outside the scope of this discussion, suggestive and locally illuminating though they may be.

More appropriate here are Shakespeare's references to works of art like Hermione's statue and to the Renaissance excitement regarding perspective. His interest in perspective seems to have been twofold: a fascination with point of view and a delight in lifelikeness. References to turning pictures, so-called because one image changes into another as the viewer moves across the face of the painting (they are painted upon sides of slatted wood facing in opposite directions), occur in *Antony and Cleopatra:* "though he be painted one way like a Gorgon, / The other way's a Mars." We find allusions to anamorphic devices, images that are meaningless unless viewed from one particular direction or with

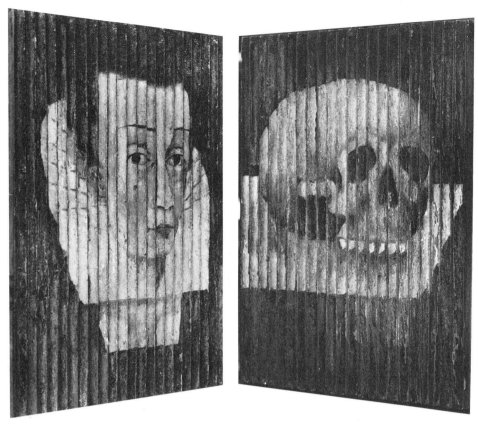

41. Anamorphic head of a woman, usually called Mary, Queen of Scots; by an unknown artist.

a cylindrical reflector, in *Richard II:* "perspectives, which rightly gazed upon, / Show nothing but confusion—eyed awry, / Distinguish form." And there is a memorable reference to the astonishingly lifelike appearance of a portrait on a two-dimensional surface in Sonnet 24: "perspective it is best painter's art." Shakespeare was as enthralled by the discovery of perspective as were many of his contemporaries, who produced innumerable treatises explaining its mathematical and technical aspects and who were equally fascinated by the games spawned by the new science. Anamorphic devices of all sorts—perspective boxes, trick pictures, mirrors, lenses, telescopes, prisms—all established the primacy of perspective in the visual arts. Shakespeare's few but strikingly direct allusions suggest, in turn, that the art of perspective permeated his thinking in ways that overt references will not declare. Ernest Gilman has even argued that the explicit reference to an anamorphic device in *Richard II* signals a concern with perspective that determines the staging of various crucial scenes in Shakespeare, a preoccupation that also becomes a metaphor for our viewing of historical event.

Shakespeare's interest in perspective enlarges our understanding and appreciation of his characteristically pluralistic mind. His generosity in accommodating alternative viewpoints, his tolerance of the contradictory or paradoxical, his increasing skill with language so that it becomes hospitable to density of allusion and to multiple claims upon our attention—these have always been recognized. But in the context of Renaissance perspective, his imaginative modes assume sharper definition and wider significance. Anamorphoses of various kinds, whether Cleopatra's turning picture or Bertram's "scornful perspective . . . Which warped the line of every other favor," speak directly of those difficult adjustments that an audience or reader is required to make to characters and situations that are either paradoxically both good and bad or that change from within. These verbal allusions and their implied resonances throughout the plays are of a piece with Shakespeare's delight in metamorphosis, though it is not usual to give this latter interest a specifically visual or optical dimension.

Another aspect of perspective that clearly conditions Shakespeare's dramaturgy is its way of favoring one spectator over another. The comic and tragic potential of right and wrong perspectives, or of viewpoints that augment clarity of perception according to their direction, is central to scenes in which characters watch each other. The lords eavesdropping on their fellows in *Love's Labor's Lost,* the

429

Host and Julia in men's clothes watching Proteus woo Silvia, and Thersites watching Ulysses and Troilus watching Diomedes and Cressida—these scenes would all be unthinkable in an age uninvolved with the amusing or disturbing effects of optical perspective.

The use of perspective gave painters the ability to achieve greater illusion in the depiction of the seen world: lifelikeness became highly prized. Shakespeare's invocations of portraits frequently insist upon this factor: Bassanio finds Portia's portrait in the casket an amazing "counterfeit"; Sonnet 24 plays elaborately with the painter's skill in picturing a "true image"; the Painter modestly confesses that his portrait of Timon "is a pretty mocking of the life," while his adversary Poet cannot but agree that the painting "tutors nature. Artificial strife / Lives in these touches, livelier than life." Sculpture, even painted sculpture, is considered lifeless in comparison to painting: "Fie, lifeless picture, cold and senseless stone, / Well-painted idol, image dull and dead" *(Venus and Adonis).* Shakespeare alludes to the legendary Greek painter Zeuxis in *Venus and Adonis* and to his painted representation of grapes that deceived birds into thinking them real. This, together with many other references to verisimilitude, suggest that Shakespeare was particularly fascinated by this painterly achievement. Yet the contexts also carry suggestions of his own verbal skills in bringing alive for us whatever is described: Venus compared to the birds deceived by Zeuxis is in fact deluded by her own amorousness, which Shakespeare's poetry has made real for us. And the servants who tempt Christopher Sly with erotic paintings speak of their astonishing lifelikeness ("that one shall swear she bleeds"), which, if it does move Sly or ourselves, is Shakespeare's artistic achievement.

In Richard Haydocke's translation (1598) of Giovanni Paolo Lomazzo's *A Tracte Containing the Artes of Curious Painting, Carving, and Building,* the reader's attention is specifically drawn to the "Arte of Painting, whereby the unskilfull eye is so often cozened and deluded, taking counterfeit creatures for true and naturall." It was clearly part of the visual excitement of the latest and most sophisticated pictures that they should "cozen" viewers. It is this fashionable effect of art that is invoked in Shakespeare's most prominent reference to a work of art, Hermione's statue in *The Winter's Tale.*

Shakespeare gives his own imaginary sculpture an authenticity by ascribing it to "that rare Italian master, Julio Romano." The statue of Hermione is of course doubly imaginary, being an invention both of Shakespeare's language and of Paulina's plot. Hence the striking effect of its verisimilitude: had Romano "himself eternity and could put breath into his work, [he] would beguile Nature of her custom, so perfectly he is her ape." Since there is no sculpture known to have been executed by Romano (who is perhaps best known for his illusionist frescoes in the Palazzo del Te, Mantua, dating from the 1530s), this allusion is sometimes considered Shakespeare's gaffe: obviously, it has been argued, his acquaintance with the fine arts was poor. But it may well be that his invocation of a famous name (it is also cited by Jonson) is merely a reference to an Italian artist who might be assumed to represent his sitters in exceptionally realistic poses. Or, since the statue is said to be "newly performed," Shakespeare may be invoking a modish name as the finisher of the sculpture. Polychromed terracotta work could well fit the description, and that the work must have been painted is deduced from Polixenes' insistence that "the very life seems warm upon her lip" and Leontes' that "the fixture of her eye has motion in't" and that "those veins / Did verily bear blood."

It has been suggested that Shakespeare was referring to another Romano, Gian Cristoforo Romano (ca. 1470–1512), a sculptor whose work fits the bill. But allusion to either Romano seems far less important than the insistence upon the sculpture's realism. Shakespeare's audience would have had opportunities to observe such work in and around London; a dramatic ascription to a famous Italian artist is of the same order of license as the infamous seacoast of Bohemia (III. iii) in the same play. What Hermione's "statue" contributes to *The Winter's Tale,* once its verisimilitude has been established, is, rather, a strikingly resonant scene that visually and thematically takes up and extends the play's debate on the rival potentialities of art and nature and on the quasi-magical process of recuperation in which nature is aided by art. Paulina's presentation of the "statue" plays subtly with these themes, so crucial to the drama that Shakespeare provides the doubly imagined work of art with circumstantial provenance.

It is, finally and not surprisingly, Shakespeare's verbal arts that contribute to and outdo his "painting." Once Hermione's statue comes alive, her speech is the ultimate miracle; into its marveling questions are gathered the play's final vision. Earlier in his career Shakespeare had implied that visual art was lacking in the essential dimension of speech (see *The Merchant of Venice:* "a proper man's picture, but, alas! who can converse with a dumb-show?"). And while he seems quick and skillful at defining visual reference even in passing, it is his own dramatic pictures, stage images in which word and *pictura* are melded, that seem his central concern.

BIBLIOGRAPHY

Anthony Blunt, "An Echo of the Paragone in Shakespeare," in *Journal of the Warburg and Courtauld Institutes,* 2 (1939). Samuel C. Chew, The *Virtues Reconciled* (1947) and *The Pilgrimage of Life* (1962). Sidney Colvin, "The Sack of Troy in Shakespeare's *Lucrece* and in Some Fifteenth-Century Drawings and Tapestries," in Israel Gollancz, ed., *A Book of Homage to Shakespeare* (1916). Arthur H. R. Fairchild, *Shakespeare and the Arts of Design* (1937).

Lucy Gent, *Picture and Poetry, 1560–1620* (1981). Ernest B. Gilman, *The Curious Perspective: Literary and Pictorial Wit in the Seventeenth Century* (1978). Henry Green, *Shakespeare and the Emblem Writers* (1870). C. H. Herford, "Shakespeare and the Arts," in *Bulletin of the John Rylands Library,* 11 (1927). Allan Shickman, "Turning Pictures in Shakespeare's England," in *The Art Bulletin,* 59 (1977). Margaret F. Thorp, "Shakespeare and the Fine Arts," in *Publication of the Modern Language Association,* 46 (1931).

Locating and Dislocating the "I" of Shakespeare's Sonnets

MARGRETA DE GRAZIA

Shakespeare's Sonnets are among the most highly valued poems in English. They are not only read but memorized; they are not only thought about but reflected on; they are not only admired but cherished. Even if they were not valued for their literary merit, they would still be of central importance, for there is one property that they alone possess: they are the only works of Shakespeare written in the first person. Only in the Sonnets does Shakespeare appear to be speaking in his own voice.

Shakespeare's two other major nondramatic works, *Venus and Adonis* and *The Rape of Lucrece,* are both long narratives. But in those poems, Shakespeare employs a knowing and distant narrator. Though the narratives are presented by another voice, the dedications prefacing each poem are written in Shakespeare's own. In these dedications, Shakespeare petitions for the favor of his patron, extolling the latter's graces and belittling his own merits. No particular importance has been attached to these dedications, although the one that prefaces *Lucrece* is often brought into the debates about the identity of the young man to whom most of the sonnets are thought to be addressed, because of its resemblance to Sonnet 26. They are generally viewed as conventional tributes rather than as words spoken in Shakespeare's own voice.

The only other Shakespearean poem that introduces the authorial first person is a long amorous narrative, *A Lover's Complaint,* the authenticity of which has been questioned even though it was first published with the Sonnets. The poem begins with descriptions given by a first-person narrator, but it quickly shifts to a plaintive account, delivered by a maiden, the lover named in the poem's title. The rare instances of Shakespeare's use of the first person in the nondramatic works other than the Sonnets are too formal or too fleeting to have commanded attention.

Readers of the plays have regularly attempted to identify Shakespeare's voice with that of certain of his characters who are thought to share qualities of mind with Shakespeare. Shakespeare's voice is believed to be heard in Hamlet's complex soliloquies or in Lear's profound diatribes because complexity and profundity are the presumed attributes of the author. The authorial voice is thought to be heard too in characters who share Shakespeare's dramatic powers: Iago in *Othello* and Prospero in *The Tempest* are sometimes seen as Shakespeare's counterparts because they plot out and cast scenes involving players, though often unwitting ones. Such identifications are based on finding resemblances between Shakespeare and his characters. Yet numerous other points of resemblance might also be posited. The reader probably would not care to identify Shakespeare with the doltish William of *As You Like It* or with the indocile William of *Merry Wives of Windsor,* yet they do have something in common with him. Nor would he be tempted to see Shakespeare in the loyal servant Adam of *As You Like It* or in the Ghost of *Hamlet,* even though according to tradition Shakespeare acted those very parts. It is probably wisest to assume that Shakespeare speaks through the words of every speaker in a play. If Shakespeare assumes an impersonal voice in the nondramatic narratives, he disperses his voice among a variety of different persons or characters in his dramatic works.

In the Sonnets there is good reason to identify Shakespeare with the first-person speaker. The "I" of the Sonnets is not like the "I" of Shakespeare's other works: there is no proper name to which it can be affixed except the poet's. The identification is encouraged by Sonnets 135 and 136, which play conspicuously on the poet's first name—especially 136, which concludes with "my name is Will." Because Will—like John and Jack—in Shakespeare's time was also a generic name for any man, such a phrase need not preclude the possibility of assigning to the first-person voice of the Sonnets the same status that we assign to the voice of any given character from the poems or plays. For, after all, why should the "I" of the Sonnets have a different relation to Shakespeare than the "I" of any of his other fictional creations—than that of Adonis or Hamlet, for example? But readers have been reluctant to consider the possibility that the speaker of the Sonnets is a fictional character, for it is difficult to dismiss the fact that the first-person pronoun is uniquely employed in the Sonnets and that it has no antecedent except Shakespeare himself, named on the title page. Why would Shakespeare not specify a proper name for the "I" of the Sonnets if the reader were meant to connect him with someone other than the author? Or why did he not write the Sonnets in the third person, perhaps setting the collection in an authorial frame, as he did partially in *A Lover's Complaint*? However sensitive the reader may be to the complicated relation between the author's real-life identity and the identity that he projects in a work of literature, it is unsatisfactory to try to convert the first person of the Sonnets to a third person, the Shakespearean "I" to an anonymous "he."

Even if the reader is cautious about assuming a direct relation between Shakespeare and the first person of the Sonnets, he listens with special attention to poems that begin "When I consider everything that grows" (Sonnet 15), or "So shall I live, supposing thou art true" (Sonnet 93), or "Two loves I have, of comfort and despair" (Sonnet 144). Expressing himself through that "I" is the Shakespeare about whom we so much desire to know. By attending to what that "I" says about himself, to

what he considers, supposes, and loves, we hope to learn more about the subject to which the "I" ostensibly refers. By pondering the claims of that "I", we hope to learn about what Shakespeare did, felt, thought, believed, and valued. In the Sonnets, there is no need to postulate or extrapolate a voice in order to hear Shakespeare. His use of the first person seems to offer direct access to him.

Preoccupation with the "I" of the Sonnets has been of major importance only since the late eighteenth century. It is commonly thought that aesthetic values remain constant over time and that editions simply make texts available without affecting the reader's understanding and appreciation. The extraordinary textual history of the Sonnets throws into question both of these assumptions. An examination of three powerful editions of the Sonnets—John Benson's of 1640, Edmond Malone's of 1780, and Stephen Booth's of 1977—will show how influential these editors have been in shaping how the Sonnets are to be read.

Shaping is necessary, for the Sonnets require a form, a structure in which they can be read. Without such a frame, they simply confront the reader with confusion as to how they are to be read. When Malone's edition presents the Sonnets as self-representation, as Shakespeare's writing about himself, we have a way of reading them: around the centered subject, the pieces can be comprehended and arranged. Yet that edition is not the only means of coming to terms with the confusion that the Sonnets can generate. In an edition much closer in time to Shakespeare, John Benson makes the Sonnets comprehensible by abstracting their content from Shakespeare. And in an edition much closer to our own time, Stephen Booth makes the Sonnets readable by activating rather than stilling the confusion latent in their vocabulary, syntax, and structure.

Malone's Edition of 1780

The Sonnets have not always been valued as the only work written by Shakespeare in the first person. In fact, there was a time when they apparently were not valued at all. Though the date of their composition is unknown, they are generally thought to have been written between 1592 and 1598. With the exception of versions of 138 and 144 published in a miscellany, *The Passionate Pilgrim* (1599), the Sonnets were published for the first time in 1609. They appear to have made no initial impact, perhaps due to their publication at the end of the Elizabethan sonnet vogue inaugurated by Philip Sidney's *Astrophel and Stella* in 1591. Not until the end of the eighteenth century did they begin to receive critical attention and acclaim. Until then, there is little evidence that the Sonnets were admired or even read. In the seventeenth century, they were not included in the volume that defined the canon, the First Folio of 1623, a collection of all the dramatic works (except two) that we now regard as Shakespeare's; nor were they included in any of the Folio's three subsequent reprintings (1632, 1663–1664, 1685). And unlike the major poetic narratives, they seem to have generated no demand for new quarto editions. If we except *The Phoenix and Turtle* and *A Lover's Complaint,* the latter of which appeared with the Sonnets in 1609, there are fewer allusions to the Sonnets in the seventeenth century than to any other work by Shakespeare. A spurious edition containing most of Shakespeare's Sonnets did appear in 1640—the Benson edition, on which we will shortly focus. While it was repeatedly published in the eighteenth century, the Sonnets were hardly recognizable in that edition. Scant as it is, the evidence we have indicates that the Sonnets were little valued either in their own right or in relation to the Shakespearean canon until the end of the eighteenth century.

In 1780, Edmond Malone published the first edition of the Sonnets that carried a commentary and notes as ample as those that the plays had been receiving throughout the century. In 1790, he included a reprint of this edition in the final volume of his collection of the complete works of Shakespeare, thereby raising them to canonical status. Shortly thereafter, studies of the Sonnets began steadily to emerge, with commentators attempting to elucidate their meaning and assess their literary merits. Thus only at the end of the eighteenth century—almost two centuries after their original publication—were the Sonnets as we know them authorized, admitted into the canon, and given critical attention.

It seems astonishing that it should have taken almost two centuries for the importance of the Sonnets to be recognized. The point seems to be that the feature that makes them uniquely important for us appears to have been of no special interest until around the time when Malone published his edition. The Sonnets' rise to prominence followed

hard upon the emergence of a preoccupation with first-person writing.

The eighteenth century abounded with diaries, journals, and letters. Written and marketed in unprecedented numbers, they attest to a special and widespread interest in what the author writes about himself. Attending this interest in first-person writing was a demand for biographies of men prominent in the world of literature as well as in politics and religion. These two concerns converged in the development of a form that was not named until the beginning of the nineteenth century: *autobiography,* biography written in the first person.

A preoccupation with self-representation also appeared in eighteenth-century Shakespeare studies. Interest in Shakespeare's life first became manifest at the opening of the century, when the earliest substantial life of Shakespeare was included in Nicholas Rowe's edition of his works. During the decades that followed, that biography was amplified with various historical documents (Shakespeare's baptismal record, marriage bond, and will, for example). This process culminated in a 700-page *Life of Shakespeare,* begun in the 1780s but not published until 1821, after the biographer's death. The author of the biography is Edmond Malone, the editor who in 1780 established the original text of the Sonnets and secured their importance. The Sonnets first won critical attention, in other words, at a time when self-representational writing had come to be newly prized. And they won it through an edition that discussed the Sonnets as poems in which Shakespeare writes about himself.

The state in which the Sonnets existed prior to Malone may be hard to imagine for those who have read them in one of the two substantive modern editions: Hyder Rollins' New Variorum Edition (1944), which requires two volumes to accommodate the notes it compiles from the past four centuries, or Stephen Booth's edition (1977), which includes an analytic commentary of over 400 pages. Prior to Malone's edition, the Sonnets had no critical apparatus whatsoever: no introduction, no notes, no commentary. They had remained in the stark state in which they were first published in the 1609 quarto volume. That volume contained nothing more than a title page, a cryptic dedication, 154 numbered sonnets, and the narrative poem *A Lover's Complaint.* There were no prefatory materials indicating how the Sonnets were to be read, no comments on connections with the rest of Shakespeare's work, no references to situations or experiences that the Sonnets might reflect, no guesses as to the names of the subjects the Sonnets identify only by often ambiguous pronouns.

Malone's 1780 edition fully supplied an interpretive context that repeatedly stressed Shakespeare's involvement in his Sonnets. The name that in the 1609 quarto appeared only on the title page was scattered throughout Malone's edition; so too were other individuating epithets ("our author," "our poet"). When Malone proposed emendations, his aim was not to correct or improve the text, but rather to retrieve the words that he thought Shakespeare had written. Often he suggested an emendation not because any problem was indicated in the text, but because he believed it did not represent the words that Shakespeare had put to paper. In the line "How with this rage shall beauty hold a plea" (Sonnet 65), Malone would substitute *his* for *this* because "Shakespeare, I believe, wrote—with *his* rage." In similar fashion, Malone thought that the phrase "moan th' expense of many a vanished sight" (Sonnet 30) should be changed because "I suspect the author wrote *sigh.*" Malone also offered glosses to disclose what Shakespeare meant. But it was not the meaning of given words or phrases that interested Malone so much as what he thought Shakespeare had in mind when he wrote them. In describing the rising of the sun (Sonnet 7), Shakespeare, Malone supposed, "perhaps . . . had the sacred writings in his thoughts." When he wrote "The earth can have but earth" (Sonnet 74), Malone suggested, "Shakespeare seems here to have had the burial service in his thoughts." Throughout his edition, Malone sought to determine and clarify not so much the words and meanings of the Sonnets as the words that Shakespeare wrote and the meanings that he intended in writing them.

Shakespeare's presence was rendered all the more conspicuous by Malone's central assumption: that Shakespeare and the "I" of the Sonnets were one and the same. Not only did the words and meanings of the Sonnets emphatically belong to Shakespeare; so too did the experiences they record. Having identified the first-person pronoun with Shakespeare, Malone moved on to other pronouns that had no antecedents. He greatly simplified his task by assuming that, though the majority of Sonnets do not specify gender, the first 126 were addressed to a man and the remaining twenty-eight were addressed to a woman, a distinction that has since rarely been questioned. In looking for candidates, Malone attempted to determine the

date during which the events registered in the Sonnets took place. On the basis of the first reference to sonnets by Shakespeare—the reference in Francis Meres's *Palladis Tamia* of 1598 to the circulation of "his sugred Sonnets among his private friends"—he assumed that they were written in that year. The date gave Malone grounds for rejecting certain candidates and considering others. He thus dismissed one candidate whose initials matched those in the dedication to the Sonnets because the young man would have been only twelve years old in 1598, and considered probable another W. H., W. Hughes, on the strength of a pun on his name: "A man in hue all hues in his controlling" (Sonnet 20). Though he ventured no nominations for the woman, Malone did identify the rival poet, the "better spirit" (Sonnet 80), by correlating a clue from the Sonnets, a reference to Shakespeare's envy for another poet, with historical fact: Edmund Spenser was "in the zenith of his reputation" when the Sonnets were written.

Malone looked to history not only for individuals but also for events corresponding with those in the Sonnets. Shakespeare's experience in the London theater was seen to be reflected in the stage simile in Sonnet 23:

> As an unperfect actor on the stage,
> Who with his fear is put besides his part.

And it was not only Shakespeare's external experience that Malone thought was recorded, but also his internal response to it: "He had perhaps himself experienced what he here describes." Though Malone was careful to qualify his comments on Shakespeare's internal states as conjectural, he directed the reader to such considerations. An inordinately long note, spanning five pages, dwelled on the question of whether jealousy could be imputed to Shakespeare on the basis of Sonnet 93, in which the poet compares himself to "a deceived husband." That Malone hesitated to commit himself on this and other matters made no difference; what was important was that he had formulated the questions and issues to be considered, on the basis of an assumption that Shakespeare himself was thoroughly involved in the events to which the Sonnets allude. Malone's notes persistently traced back to Shakespeare the words and meanings of the Sonnets.

Embedded in Malone's edition were assumptions that have affected if not dominated all subsequent readings of the Sonnets: (1) the Sonnets were addressed to two individuals; (2) those two individuals represented people Shakespeare knew; and (3) the situations they presented corresponded at some level with those in Shakespeare's own life. In short, Malone's explanatory notes prepared the foundation for future readings of the Sonnets as self-representation, as autobiography—and autobiography in an expansive sense: for it was not only Shakespeare's public life that Malone led the reader to contemplate, but his private, inner life as well.

It would be foolhardy to lump into a single category the vast and unruly body of criticism that the Sonnets have generated over the last two centuries. Yet the extent of Malone's influence would be hard to exaggerate. His 1780 edition not only established the text of the Sonnets but also provided the interpretive frame in which they would be read by future generations. Once Malone's textual apparatus had framed the Sonnets as self-representation, subsequent readers largely looked to them expecting to see the author as he portrayed himself. The facets of himself that Shakespeare chose to represent could be differently perceived: they might range from verifiable biographical facts to unfathomable psychic insights, from objective reality to subjective truth. And the mode of representation might be variously defined—as narrative, allegory, or satire. However subject and mode might be construed, virtually all readings retained their allegiance to the central assumption that informed Malone's edition: that Shakespeare in the Sonnets was representing himself.

Even readings that have questioned the Sonnets' autobiographical relevance have been shaped by Malone's edition. A desire to avoid the consequences of reading the poems as self-representation impels some commentators to dissociate Shakespeare from the contents of the Sonnets. Most readings can be described either in terms of self-representation or in terms opposed to self-representation. In either case, they concern themselves with self-representation as an issue.

The Shakespeare of the Sonnets

After Malone's edition was published, discussions of the Sonnets began extending the resemblances that Malone had suggested between Shakespeare and the first person of the Sonnets. Because the anecdotes and documents relating to Shakespeare's

own life were so unyielding, commentators looked to the histories of others for supplementary materials. Especially intriguing were the fuller lives of various socially and politically prominent noblemen who were Shakespeare's contemporaries. But, as time went on, the focus returned to the poet's life. At first, commentators sought the inward thoughts and feelings that attended outward events: the Sonnets were seen to "paint most unequivocally the actual situation and sentiments of the poet" (Schlegel). Eventually, however, the private overtook the public, so that historical correspondences became irrelevant to the poet's meaning; historical details, like the identity of the man, were therefore dispensable: "If the individual were known, it would not alter the feeling or meaning of a single verse" (Brown). For some commentators, the world of objective fact was seen to be so in conflict with that of subjective feeling that it was ignored altogether: "The particle of actual life of which verse is wrought may be, and almost always is, wholly incommensurate to the emotion depicted" (Bell). Whether the Sonnets are seen to depict the outer world of men and events or the inner world of ideas, feelings, and values, Shakespeare remained their subject.

Nineteenth-century readers were eager to read the Sonnets as the key with which, in Wordsworth's phrase, "Shakespeare unlocked his heart." Read as self-representation, however, the Sonnets presented a serious problem. They implicated Shakespeare in transgressive acts and desires. If Shakespeare were writing about himself in the Sonnets, then he would stand answerable to charges of adultery, perjury, and homosexuality. It would be his "own harmful deeds" (Sonnet 111) the Sonnets recorded, his "sportive blood" (Sonnet 121), his name that "receives a brand" (Sonnet 111), his brow stamped with "vulgar scandal" (Sonnet 112). Such possibilities were unacceptable; though little was known about Shakespeare, it could at least "be asserted with confidence, that at no time was the slightest imputation cast upon his moral character" (Boswell). But some readers did find the character that emerged from some of the sonnets objectionable; they complained that the inconstant, deferential, and self-pitying person the Sonnets disclosed was not compatible with the received image of the gentle Shakespeare. To spare Shakespeare's moral and ethical reputation, many of his readers labored to dissociate Shakespeare from the contents of the Sonnets.

In order to silence those who thought "they had caught the god kissing carrion," some commentators assigned the damaging sonnets to another voice, thereby insulating and preserving those sonnets which "afford us the most certain means to get at the man" (Massey). By allegorizing the subject matter, other readers devised ways not to "drag the name of the poet in the dirt" (Barnstorff): the Sonnets could be read as a dialogue between, say, genius and the drama. Others approached the Sonnets as fanciful effusions or literary exercises rather than as expressions of personal experience; by this means, too, the Sonnets could be depersonalized or impersonalized. Finally and perhaps most triumphantly, some readers evaded the indictment by converting it into commendation. In this approach, indiscretions and vices to which Shakespeare confessed in the Sonnets only attested further to their author's extraordinary capacities: "The errors of his heart originated in his sensitiveness, in his imagination . . . , in his quick consciousness of existence, and in the self-abandoning devotion of the heart" (Dowden).

Twentieth-century criticism may be described as a replaying of the same conflict. By supplying missing dates, names, relationships, and situations, literary historians have continued to try to fill out the picture that they assume Shakespeare has drawn of himself. For one, tenacious matching of topical references and verbal clues in the Sonnets to dates and names in history reveals both the time and the participants involved in the incidents that the Sonnets record (Rowse). For another, a possible allusion in Sonnet 108 to the British defeat of the Spanish Armada in 1588 provides a new time frame for the Sonnets and thereby introduces new historical individuals: an actor named Will and a court attendant whose name, Lucy, is the antithesis of the darkness attributed to her in the Sonnets (Hotson). For yet another, a rearrangement of the order of the Sonnets yields a situation that can be corroborated with historical materials: a narcissistic young nobleman needs to be instructed in the rules and graces of right patronage, just as the countess of Pembroke would have wanted her son William instructed (Padel). For some interpreters, the history of the 1609 quarto edition reveals peculiarities that contribute to our understanding of the content of the poems themselves (Giroux). For others, literary history illuminates Shakespeare's relationship with the young man, his patron, and discloses an intricate system of professional and personal relations among literary figures (Wait). The historical particulars may differ, but they are always introduced with the same intention as in nineteenth-century commentaries: to render Shakespeare's likeness in the Sonnets more distinct, more visible.

Most recent treatments of the Sonnets, even those that acknowledge the relevance of outward fact, have subordinated the outer to the inner, the historical to the imaginary. The Sonnets "may have some basis in fact," as one critic has put it, but their true concern is with mutability and mortality, the conflict between Agape and Eros, and the creation of immortal verse (Muir). Whatever their relation to the outside world, they are important as autobiography only in their representation of "happenings inside the much more extensive private world which is the field of [Shakespeare's] creative consciousness" (Winny). Whether Shakespeare intended to disclose this private world to the public remains a matter of dispute. Perhaps he wrote the Sonnets as a personal diary, a secret record of his most intimate desires and frustrations (Spender). Perhaps he intended them for public reading but not for public understanding: perhaps he hid their secrets in conundrums that only the privileged initiate could discover (Green). The question of what Shakespeare intended vanishes altogether when all poetry is seen to be radically self-revealing. Whether or not "Shakespeare deliberately engaged himself in a planned autobiographical project," the Sonnets are ultimately self-referential: "All poetry has its roots in subjective experience" (Seymour-Smith).

As in the nineteenth century, autobiographical readings in the twentieth century have met with resistance. In the twentieth century, however, the resistance has come from a different source: it emerges not from moral but from theoretical concerns, not from notions of what a poet should be or do but from theories about what a poem should be or do. Attention has accordingly been focused primarily on the poems, or on the tradition in which they participated, rather than on the poet and his sensibility. But, though in theory they deemphasize the importance of the author, in practice most twentieth-century critics have ended up once again by invoking Shakespeare as subject.

Focus on the formal and semantic properties of the Sonnets diverts attention from the author. As a consequence, it releases the poems from mimetic responsibility, from the necessity of reproducing the author's life or his perception of it. Thus abstracted from their author, the Sonnets become impersonal in content, ostensibly cut off from biographical and historical considerations. Interpreters can then apply themselves to establishing and elucidating the various modalities of the poems themselves. But almost inevitably, the modalities that are identified in the structure and diction of the Sonnets turn out to be correlatives for aspects of the author himself. Thus the verbal tensions and conflicts in the Sonnets are seen to reflect "factions in Shakespeare's mind and personal relationships" (Landry). Themes of selfless devotion, of fear and trust, are explored within the poems themselves, but these themes also project the vacillating states of mind that lie behind them (Mahood). Even lexical and syntactic ambiguity is seen as a function of the author's mind, a representation of his emotional and personal confusion and irresolution (Empson), so that, finally, the meaning or sense of the Sonnets is not properly theirs but his: it is Shakespeare's feelings and thoughts that they reflect when "expressing a variety of moods and psychological states" (Hubler). Even in readings that set out to make the poems independent of their author, critics end up attributing to the poems themselves the psychic qualities that formerly were reassigned to the author.

Some twentieth-century readings distance the Sonnets from Shakespeare by focusing on the reader's responses to the complex movement of the poems. As a reader moves through a sonnet, he experiences a series of shifting moods and verbal structures that duplicate rather than communicate the essence of experience: "The poem doesn't tell us anything; rather it gives us a sense of what experience is like" (Booth, 1969). The Sonnets' multiple and oscillating patterns reproduce in the reader the intractability of experience itself, experience as Shakespeare perceived it. When the Sonnets are read in sequence rather than individually, they draw the reader through the same experience as that undergone by their subject: the first 126 sonnets take the reader through a development from dependence to self-sufficiency, from insecure vacillation to bold self-assertion (Hammond). When the Sonnets are read thus, with the emphasis on the reader's perceptions and reactions, the author temporarily drops from sight. Yet those perceptions and reactions replicate those experienced by the author himself.

In some twentieth-century commentary, the Sonnets have also been removed from their author by discussions that consider them in the context of the Petrarchan and Elizabethan sonnet conventions. Such discussions show Shakespeare's involvement in techniques, structures, and themes that recur in the sonnets of his predecessors—in Petrarch, Spenser, and Sidney, for example. But these discussions of conventional sonnet treatments are usually intended to serve primarily as a way of setting Shakespeare's uniqueness into relief. Shakespeare is seen to define himself in opposition to the conventional medium he employs. Thus Shakespeare can be appreciated as a poet who deviates from, rather than conforms to, the norms he imitates and modifies: "When he is most Elizabethan he is least Shakespearean" (Leishman). By analyzing five representative sonnet sequences, one critic has sought to establish semantic and structural norms; Shakespeare's deviations from these norms are seen as providing a measure of the originality of his thought (Melchiori). While other poets participated in the sonnet tradition by imitating and adapting its conventions, Shakespeare set himself at a singular distance from which he alone parodied the characteristic tropes, modes, and stances of the sonneteers (Wilson). Attempts to place Shakespeare within a convention, in other words, do precisely the opposite: they contribute to establishing his unconventional originality, his uniqueness as subject.

The history of the criticism of Shakespeare's Sonnets has generally been described as an opposition between autobiographical and nonautobiographical readings. The two approaches have been seen to be in irreconcilable conflict: "Between such divergent positions there can be no common ground" (Schoenbaum). Yet there is common ground: an almost universally shared premise, first implanted in Malone's edition, that in the Sonnets Shakespeare represents himself. Moral and theoretical expectations have certainly complicated that assumption, yet it has remained constant and fundamental throughout two centuries of criticism. The subject of the representation has been variously defined in terms ranging from objective to subjective, from historical to psychological. And the representation has been variously located: in the work itself, in the reader's responses to the work, in the work's relation to tradition or to the work of other sonneteers. Yet, however defined and located, the subject has remained Shakespeare.

Benson's Edition of 1640

Given a basic continuity in the multitudinous readings of the Sonnets since Malone, it might be possible to conclude that there is no way to read them except as poems "about Shakespeare." For indeed, what is the alternative to interpreting them as autobiography? It would appear that Malone, by situating them in his editorial frame, simply made it possible for them to emerge as what they had always been: representations of the author. Yet one episode in the history of the Sonnets cautions against such a conclusion. In 1640, John Benson published a volume called *Poems: Written by Wil. Shake-speare, Gent.* Benson's text has already been mentioned as the only seventeenth-century edition to reprint the Sonnets in any form. What has not been mentioned is that this spurious edition supplanted the genuine one for almost 150 years. Throughout the eighteenth century until Malone, Shakespeare's Sonnets were known primarily in Benson's edition. When they were included several times in eighteenth-century editions of the works, they were reproduced from the 1640 rather than the 1609 text.

The content of Benson's edition makes it difficult to believe that his publication should have ever replaced the 1609 Sonnets; only with difficulty can the now familiar original Sonnets be recognized. The word *sonnet* does not appear in the collection, neither in the title nor elsewhere. Nor is the fourteen-line sonnet form predominant. All but eight of the original 134 Sonnets are included, but only one-fifth of them are printed as sonnets. The rest are combined into units ranging from two to five sonnets, so that the entire collection totals only seventy-two poems. Titles replace the numbers that identify the Sonnets in the 1609 text. Nor is the original sequence, as established by the numbering in that text, respected. The poems are rearranged so that the first sonnet in the 1640 edition is the sixty-seventh in the original, and the first in the original is the twelfth in Benson's text. Twenty-three poems of varying lengths—some by Shakespeare, most by other poets—are interspersed among the 1609 Sonnets. It was in this adulterated and shuffled form that the 1609 Sonnets circulated for almost a century and a half.

The overall effect of Benson's redaction was to destroy the apparent formal unity and continuity of the 1609 Sonnets. The uniform appearance of 154 Sonnets was lost when Benson combined the Sonnets to form poems of varying lengths and interspersed them among a miscellany of additional verse forms. The original succession of Sonnets, following one another with only a numeral between them, was broken by Benson's introduction of titles. Benson's interpolations corrupt and disrupt the original to such a degree that, until recently, it was assumed that his publication was fraudulent: "Nobody . . . can fail to see that it was an illegal publication" (Rollins). Scholars assumed that, by adding materials and altering the appearance of the Sonnets, Benson intended to deceive stationers and readers alike into believing that his edition was an authentic and previously unprinted collection of Shakespeare's verse.

Recent research into printing practices and copyrights has revealed that Benson was no literary pirate but rather a respectable printer who had the right to publish the contents of his edition. The anomalies and irregularities of his edition can no longer be dismissed as a consequence of his desire to disguise the Sonnets and delude the public. They must be explained another way. So too must the popularity of Benson's edition: how could it have replaced the original for almost 150 years? It cannot be that Benson's text was published in the absence of copies of the original, for there is evidence that such copies were not hard to come by in the eighteenth century. Two editions of the original version were in fact published, though they appear to have attracted little notice. It seems inescapable, in other words, that the 1640 edition was actually preferred over the 1609 version. Perhaps Benson's interpolations were seen as adding to rather than detracting from the appreciation of Shakespeare's Sonnets.

A reconsideration of the original format of the Sonnets may once again be helpful. When the introduction, notes, and textual commentary that accompany modern editions are removed, the Sonnets stand quite bare. The 1609 collection is given a generic title, *Shakespeare's Sonnets,* which reveals nothing but the author's name and that of the verse form he has employed. The individual Sonnets are not titled, but numbered in an order that may or may not be significant. The dedication preceding the collection is cryptic, as generations of speculation on its significance attest. No prefatory materials describe the author's intentions. A reader looking for signs about how to read the Sonnets will not find them; it may have been in response to this conspicuous lack that Benson supplemented the original text. What most modern critics have seen as a fraudulent supplanting of the genuine text by a spurious one may well have been regarded by seventeenth- and eighteenth-century readers as the superseding of an incomplete and incoherent edition with a complete and coherent one.

Seen in this light, Benson's edition would appear to present the first editorial and critical response to the need for a frame of reference for the Sonnets. By regrouping them, inserting titles, and anthologizing them among other love verses, Benson supplies the interpretive context that was absent from the 1609 text. After uniting the Sonnets that are linked by what he sees as a common subject or function, he assigns each one a title that reflects this subject or function. And once the rubric is assigned, the content of the sonnet is understood to conform to it, much as a painting will be viewed as corresponding to its title. When Benson entitles a poem "Constant Affection," "Loves Crueltie," or "False Belief," it takes on the identity of its designated substantive. A poem entitled "A Congratulation," "A Complaint," or "A Vow" assumes its specified function. The titles abstract the content of the poems, making them conceptual or even philosophical rather than simply accidental and experiential. By including additional verse, moreover, Benson expands the scope of the anthology: the general subject of love is further universalized by the addition of the metaphysical poem *The Phoenix and Turtle*, Ovidian verse translations, and bawdy and naive love songs.

Benson's contributions tell the reader a great deal about how the poems are to be received. The regrouping under rubrics, for example, determines that the poems will be read as self-contained units rather than as part of a continuing series. Each unit will be perceived in relation not to the Sonnets that precede or succeed it, but to the substantive or function announced by its title. And each poem will contribute to an expansive, generalized understanding of love. It is important to notice that in Benson's transformation the precise quality for which the Sonnets have been prized since Malone disappears entirely—or, rather, never appears. The subject of the poems, as the titles continually emphasize, is a representative lover, not an individuated one. The generalizing third-person titles—"Complaint for His Love's Absence," "Self-Flattery of Her Beauty," "An Intreatie for Her Acceptance"—prevent the poems from being read in relation to Shakespeare's experience or to

that of any other individual. They are universally applicable to states of mind, occasions, and experiences involving love. The editorial frame in which Benson situates the Sonnets ignores or obscures the very feature that, after Malone, secures the Sonnets' unique centrality.

In the preface to his edition, Benson promises that his reader will find the poems "serene, clear, and elegantly plain; such gentle strains as shall recreate and not perplex your brain, no intricate or cloudy stuff to puzzle intellect, but perfect eloquence." In the past, scholars have scoffed at the fatuous irony of the claim; Benson's interpolations were seen, if anything, as having intensified the confusion of poems that were already problematic. Yet a close and respectful look at Benson's insertions and additions reveals that his efforts were directed toward preventing or at least minimizing the reader's perplexity by mediating any confrontation with the inchoate original.

Now that Benson has been acquitted of literary piracy, it is possible to see his edition as the first attempt to do with the Sonnets what editors as well as literary critics have been doing ever since: to provide the interpretive markers necessary for reading them with comprehension. When Malone disposed of Benson's accretions, he hardly returned the Sonnets to their original state. As we have seen, he surrounded them with a textual apparatus that, no less than Benson's, indicates how to read them. Like Benson's insertions, Malone's annotations predetermine what the subject of the poems will be and how that subject should be interpreted. For the earlier editor, the universal abstraction *love* was the subject, and the poems were to be read philosophically—as definitions, occasions, and accidents of love. For the later editor, the unique author Shakespeare was the subject, and the poems were to be read as biographical and historical records of events and experiences.

A contrast of the original Sonnets with Benson's and Malone's editions reveals the urgent need for demarcations like those provided by the two later editions. The Sonnets cannot be read without some structuring principle, whether it be inscribed in the edition itself or taken for granted by readers. The Benson edition bears crucially on this recognition, for when freshly considered it suggests that the traditional, almost canonical approach to the Sonnets through the subject Shakespeare is neither necessary nor inalienable. The subject promoted by Malone and his successors is irrelevant to the edition closest in time to the writing of the Sonnets. If Benson's edition provided the first interpretive construct in which they could be read, and Malone the second, it may be that Stephen Booth's edition, published in 1977, will be of comparable moment to our own reading of them.

Booth's Edition of 1977

Booth's edition, like that of Benson and of Malone, is designed to make the Sonnets readable. Yet it does so not by providing an interpretive construct, but by claiming not to provide one. The 400 pages of notes and commentary are exhaustive rather than selective, admitting multiple possibilities rather than excluding any in favor of a single sense: they provide "an analysis that does not try to decide which of a poem's actions should be acknowledged but instead tries to explain the means by which all a poem's improbably sorted actions coexist and cohere within the poem." Because it does not dispense with any verbal feature of the poems, Booth's editorial practice describes itself as "conservative": "The notes to this edition are designed to admit that everything in a sonnet is there." By drawing attention to aspects of a sonnet that in no way enhance, support, or relate to what the poem seems to say or what we may presume that the poet wanted to say, Booth breaks radically with his predecessors.

Benson's generalizing rubrics and Malone's individuating glosses direct the reader's attention only to those features of the Sonnets that for the former established their generality and for the latter defined their individuality. Booth awakens the reader to a complex range of verbal activity that exists outside the pale of meaning and intention. He focuses on two distinct types of activity: the activity that delivers meaning and that which has no constitutive purpose. The two types occur, for Booth, simultaneously and compatibly: "the language of the Sonnets ordinarily limits its reader's mind to the terms of specific assertions while at the same time suggesting room and direction for vast multi-directional expansion." He repeatedly insists that the Sonnets' "specific assertions" remain untouched and unswayed by their concurrent "multi-directional expansion."

Booth's edition activates the text instead of stabilizing it, releases it from the constraints of logic and syntax, from the obligation or necessity to have univocal meaning. His edition makes it impossible to read the Sonnets—as Malone's edition urged— as representations of individuated experience. Or perhaps more accurately, his edition makes it impossible to read the Sonnets exclusively or even primarily as representations of individuated experience. For the reader who follows Booth's notes must acknowledge a full register of linguistic features independent of such a representational function. Alien intonations, resonances, insinuations, allusions, and ambiguities are shown to emanate from the text along with the meaning and intention of the speaking subject. The concentrated critical attention that Booth applies to these "marginal," "peripheral," or "incidental" effects invests them with an importance the reader must recognize, though Booth warns repeatedly that they have no importance. That is, Booth claims that they do not import, convey, or deliver content, or meaning— that they do not interfere with what the poem obviously is saying.

In the wake of Booth's edition, readers of the Sonnets can no longer ignore the nonsyntactic, nonlogical elements that were effectively absent for the readers of Benson's and Malone's editions. These elements radically complicate the search, inaugurated by Malone's edition, for the subject Shakespeare, outside and anterior to his Sonnets. Booth keeps these liminal linguistic effects at a safe distance from the subject and his representation by roping them off. Transgressive and unruly though they may be, they seem not to thicken, challenge, or disturb what the subject is saying through his poems: they are "actions of language that cannot be related to what the poem conveys about its subject or its author." Authorial meaning remains securely at the center of the poem, impervious to the linguistic incursions and infiltrations occurring in the margins.

Booth's edition, in short, fully activates the text of the Sonnets, asserting rather than denying its potential for plurality, illogicality, and contradiction—the potential for confusion that had been regulated and suppressed by Benson's and Malone's editorial edifices. A given sonnet's central and essential meaning, however, remains as firmly entrenched as before, unaffected by the often impertinent if not downright subversive activity at its borders. Whether this linguistic arrangement is viable, whether a linguistic sector can be at once energized and enervated, is not altogether certain. The only thing that is clear is that by energizing features of the Sonnets that previous editions had kept latent and dormant, Booth's edition has made it necessary for us to recognize a range of linguistic activity that works independently of the speaker's stated or implied intention and meaning. The Sonnets, which were once restricted by interpretive frames like Benson's and Malone's, have been enlarged by Booth's edition to comprehend the profusions and evasions of their language.

Approached through Booth's edition, the Sonnets cannot be read solely as factors of the subject's purpose, whether that purpose is to praise, to recriminate, to confess, to persuade, to assert, or to delude. They possess a semantic and syntactic freedom that complicates, dilates, even detracts from such ostensible purpose. To read them exclusively as projections of their subject's designs is, as Booth's edition displays, to curtail their activity and to underestimate their effect: in an important sense, it is to misread them. Yet if we are to recognize their transpersonal or impersonal activity, what happens to the personal, to the person, to the first person? What happens to the coveted Shakespearean subject, the "I" or self of the Sonnets?

The role of that subject shifted from Benson to Malone, from a universalized to an individuated subject. Can the subject, after Booth, retain the purposive identity that Malone attributed to him: choosing words, turning phrases, shaping sonnets that give expression to the inclinations that constituted his identity, the experiences that constitute his biography? Or does his identity disappear altogether amid the activity that is in excess of, indifferent to, and in conflict with his control and design? Or must a new type of self emerge, a self enmeshed in the linguistic surface that it only partially composes and perhaps in turn is at least partially composed by? It is to the Sonnets themselves that such questions must be posed.

The very form of the sonnet, in fact, invites questions, for it is perhaps the most highly contrived of poetic forms. Frequently termed a Procrustean bed, the sonnet form puts tight constraints on its content: rhyme and meter strictly regulate its fourteen lines of ten syllables each; patterns of phonetic and structural repetition frequently increase the formal pressures of the three quatrains and final couplet. Yet such constraints tend to accelerate and intensify the activity that they appear to hold in place. The form that proclaims the author's control at the same time exposes its limits; a sonnet's linguistic content at once submits to and resists its constraining form. If our reading admits only those elements which submit to the author's control, we have no difficulty presupposing a Shakespeare who suited the Sonnets to his purposes and made himself known through them. But if our reading also admits elements that resist that control, we may have to search for a different kind of self: not Benson's representative self or Malone's individuated one, but perhaps a linguistic self, one intricately wound into the language it fabricates.

E. K. Chambers has said that "more folly has been written about the *Sonnets* than about any other Shakespearean topic." Certainly inordinate degrees of ingenuity, persistence, and dedication have gone into reading and writing about them. But it might be fairer to say that these excesses are manifestations not of critical folly but of critical seriousness.

For at least two centuries, the Sonnets have been of central importance to our literary tradition. They have both reflected and emitted whatever has concerned readers most: moral expectations, metaphysical beliefs, literary values. Identifying the "I" of the Sonnets, therefore, has always involved more than identifying the historical individual William Shakespeare. The deepest preoccupations of generation after generation have informed that pronoun.

BIBLIOGRAPHY

A full bibliography for Shakespeare's Sonnets can be found in Herbert S. Donow, *The Sonnet in England and America: A Bibliography of Criticism* (1982).

The following works have been cited in the text: D. Barnstorff, *A Key to Shakespeare's Sonnets*, T. J. Graham, trans. (1862; repr. 1975). Robert Bell, ed., *Poems by William Shakespeare* (1861). John Benson, ed., *Poems: Written by Wil. Shake-speare, Gent.* (1640). Stephen Booth, *An Essay on Shakespeare's Sonnets* (1969) and, as ed., *Shakespeare's Sonnets* (1977). James Boswell, ed., *The Plays and Poems of William Shakespeare*, 20 (1821). Charles Armitage Brown, *Shakespeare's Autobiographical Poems* (1838; repr. 1972). Edward Dowden, *Shakspere: A Critical Study of His Mind and Art* (1875). William Empson, *Seven Types of Ambiguity* (1930; rev. 1947). Robert Giroux, *The Book Known as Q: A Reconsideration of Shakespeare's Sonnets* (1982). Martin B. Green, *The Labyrinth of Shakespeare's Sonnets: An Examination of Sexual Elements in Shakespeare's Language* (1974).

Gerald Hammond, *The Reader and Shakespeare's Young Man Sonnets* (1981). Leslie Hotson, *Shakespeare's Sonnets*

Dated, and Other Essays (1949). Edward Hubler, *The Sense of Shakespeare's Sonnets* (1952). Hilton Landry, *Interpretation in Shakespeare's Sonnets,* Perspectives in Criticism, 14 (1963). James B. Leishman, *Themes and Variations in Shakespeare's Sonnets* (1961). Molly M. Mahood, *Shakespeare's Wordplay* (1957). Edmond Malone, ed., *Supplement to the Edition of Shakespeare's Plays Published in 1778 by S. Johnson and G. Steevens . . . to Which Are Adjoined the Genuine Poems of the Same Author,* 2 vols. (1780). Gerald Massey, *Shakspeare's Sonnets Never Before Interpreted* (1866; repr. 1973). Giorgio Melchiori, *Shakespeare's Dramatic Meditations: An Experiment in Criticism* (1976). Kenneth Muir, *Shakespeare's Sonnets* (1979). John Padel, ed., *New Poems by Shakespeare: Order and Meaning Restored to the Sonnets* (1981). Hyder E. Rollins, ed., *The Sonnets,* 2 vols, in A New Variorum Edition of Shakespeare (1944). A. L. Rowse, *Shakespeare's Sonnets* (1964).

August Wilhelm von Schlegel, *A Course of Lectures on Dramatic Art and Literature,* John Black and A. J. W. Morrison, trans. (1846). Samuel Schoenbaum, *Shakespeare's Lives* (1970). Martin Seymour-Smith, ed., *Shakespeare's Sonnets* (1963). Stephen Spender, "The Alike and the Other," in Edward Hubler, ed., *The Riddle of Shakespeare's Sonnets* (1962). Reginald J. C. Wait, *The Background to Shakespeare's Sonnets* (1972). Katherine Wilson, *Shakespeare's Sugared Sonnets* (1974). James Winny, *The Master-Mistress: A Study of Shakespeare's Sonnets* (1968).

The Poems

HALLETT SMITH

Venus and Adonis

*V*enus and Adonis, which Shakespeare called "the first heir of my invention," was, during his lifetime, the most popular of his works. Printed by the poet's fellow Stratfordian Richard Field and dedicated to the young nobleman Henry Wriothesley, earl of Southampton, it went through ten editions by 1616 and six more by 1640. It is an erotic mythological poem, imitative of Ovid; the other important example of the type is Christopher Marlowe's *Hero and Leander,* which is nearly contemporary with it.

Shakespeare's poem was published in the spring of 1593; we have a record of the purchase of a copy on 21 June of that year. Marlowe had been killed in a tavern brawl the month before, and we cannot tell whether Marlowe's poem or Shakespeare's came first or whether either poem influenced the other. *Hero and Leander* is in a different verse form, and the subject does not come from Ovid, though the style is distinctly Ovidian. Shakespeare undoubtedly knew an earlier Ovidian poem by Thomas Lodge called *Scillaes Metamorphosis* (1589), from which he adopted the verse form of six-line stanzas rhyming *ababcc.* Three of Lodge's stanzas relate the end of the Venus and Adonis myth.

A novelty of Shakespeare's treatment of the story of the goddess of love and the young human hunter is that Adonis is reluctant and Venus is the wooer. In presenting the story this way, Shakespeare adapted from Ovid the myth of the nymph Salmacis and the god Hermaphroditus, in which the nymph is the pursuer. That this sort of treatment would appeal to the taste of a young courtly aristocrat like Southampton is made evident from a passage in the Induction to Shakespeare's early play *The Taming of the Shrew.* A lord and his servants are trying to persuade the drunken Christopher Sly that he is really a lord:

> Dost thou love pictures? We will fetch thee straight
> Adonis painted by a running brook
> And Cytherea all in sedges hid,
> Which seem to move and wanton with her breath
> Even as the waving sedges play with wind.
>
> (ii. 47–51)

The poem itself is highly decorated and pictorial. Its tone is a mixture of sensuous delight, humor, preciousness, and airy sophistication. There is rhetorical heightening, but the rhetoric is controlled and kept in place by the speed and verve of the narrative. In this sense, as J. C. Maxwell has said, "Shakespeare is the most Ovidian of all the Ovidians."

Examples of the speed of the action can be found at the beginning of the poem:

> Even as the sun with purple-colored face
> Had ta'en his last leave of the weeping morn,
> Rose-cheeked Adonis hied him to the chase.
> Hunting he loved, but love he laughed to scorn.
> Sick-thoughted Venus makes amain unto him
> And like a bold-faced suitor 'gins to woo him.

The urgency of the action is further emphasized by the use of the historical present tense, as in the last two lines of the quoted stanza. Sometimes the historical present is used in translator Arthur Golding's Ovid, Shakespeare's source for both the Venus-Adonis and the Salmacis-Hermaphroditus myths.

The poem is not primarily narrative, however. Of its 1,194 lines, 555 are speeches by Venus. Her arguments are sometimes rhetorical, like the catalog of the traits of "dissentious Jealousy" (655–660), and sometimes elaborately descriptive, as in the account of the pursuit of the hare, "poor Wat" (697–708), which has seemed to many readers to reflect not literary source material but actual experience in the field. Occasionally the descriptive passages foretell Shakespeare's lyrical tone in *Romeo and Juliet* and the songs in the plays:

> Lo, here the gentle lark, weary of rest,
> From his moist cabinet mounts up on high
> And wakes the morning, from whose silver breast
> The sun ariseth in his majesty;
> Who doth the world so gloriously behold
> That cedar tops and hills seem burnished gold.
>
> (853–858)

The tone is not consistently lyrical. It is punctuated by grave, sly, sometimes ironic observations (a trait shared with *Hero and Leander*). An example is Shakespeare's observation when Adonis' "pure shame and awed resistance" make him even more beautiful than he was before:

> Rain added to a river that is rank
> Perforce will force it overflow the bank.
>
> (71–72)

Some modern critics, noting that Ovid was moralized in the Middle Ages and that even Golding before Shakespeare and translator George Sandys after him saw allegorical meanings in the myths, interpret Shakespeare's poem allegorically. They are encouraged to do this because Adonis distinguishes love from lust and denounces the latter (769–810) and because Adonis' horse, escaping from his tether to pursue "a breeding jennet, lusty, young, and proud" (260), can be seen as a model of lust. But Shakespeare's treatment differs markedly from that of the allegorizers, and it is clear that contemporaries read the poem as straightforward Ovidian erotic verse.

Others, because of such details as Venus' ability to lift Adonis off his horse (30) though she is light enough to "dance on the sands, and yet no footing seen" (148), see the whole poem as fantastically comic. Again, this view is anachronistic. Contemporary renderings of Venus and Adonis, whether by Titian or by lesser artists, treat the figures seriously. There is no evidence that anyone laughed at Shakespeare's Ovidian characters before the twentieth century.

Many connections exist between *Venus and Adonis* and Shakespeare's Sonnets, particularly the first fifteen. Venus advocates to Adonis the same prodigality that the poet of the Sonnets urges upon the Fair Friend. She emphasizes, as does the poet, that beauty is temporary and can be lost, that self-love is fatal, that one who is begotten has a duty to beget, that the only way to immortality is to have offspring.

The earliest praise of Shakespeare that has come down to us is praise of *Venus and Adonis,* by Thomas Edwardes in 1593, William Covell in 1595, and Richard Barnfield in 1598. In 1598, Shakespeare was declared to be the reincarnation of Ovid by Francis Meres: "As the soule of *Euphorbus* was thought to live in *Pythagoras:* so the sweete wittie soule of *Ovid* lives in mellifluous & hony-tongued *Shakespeare,* witness his *Venus and Adonis,* his *Lucrece,* his sugred Sonnets among his private friends, &c." In 1599 an unscrupulous publisher, William Jaggard, attached Shakespeare's name to a miscellany of verse by various authors. Called *The Passionate Pilgrim,* it contained two unpublished sonnets by Shakespeare and three sonnets from the already published *Love's Labor's Lost.*

The same year John Weever published an epigram on Shakespeare that began with a tribute to *Venus and Adonis:*

> Honie-tong'd *Shakespeare* when I saw thine issue
> I swore *Apollo* got them and none other,
> Their rosie-tainted features cloth'd in tissue,
> Some heaven-born goddesse said to be their mother:
> Rose-cheekt *Adonis* with his amber tresses,
> Faire fire-hot *Venus* charming him to love her.

Weever was a Cambridge man, and about this time there seems to have been a vogue for Shakespeare at that university. In a play called *The Return from Parnassus* (performed ca. 1600) there appears a character named Gullio, a fop, a braggart, and, of course, a gull, who had been satirized by Weever

446

in an epigram. In the course of dialogue with Ingenioso, Gullio quotes passages from *Venus and Adonis* as if they were his own invention. Nevertheless, he says, "Let this duncified worlde esteeme of Spencer and Chaucer, I'le worshipp sweet Master Shakspeare, and to honoure him will lay his *Venus and Adonis* under my pillowe." It is not only a foolish character like Gullio who admires Shakespeare; in a sequel play, *The Second Part of the Return from Parnassus,* a character named Judicio says of Shakespeare:

> Who loves not *Adons* love, or *Lucrece* rape?
> His sweeter verse contaynes hart throbbing lines,
> Could but a graver subject him content,
> Without loves foolish lazy languishment.

Some time after its publication in 1598, Spenser's friend Gabriel Harvey bought a copy of Thomas Speght's edition of Chaucer's works and wrote in it comments on contemporary English poetry, including this: "The younger sort takes much delight in Shakespeare's *Venus and Adonis;* but his *Lucrece,* and his tragedy of *Hamlet, Prince of Denmark,* have it in them to please the wiser sort."

The Rape of Lucrece

In 1593, Shakespeare promised his patron Southampton that if *Venus and Adonis* pleased him, he would take advantage of all idle hours to honor him "with some graver labor." *Lucrece* (as it is called on the title page) accordingly appeared in 1594, again from the press of Richard Field. Its running title was *The Rape of Lucrece,* and that became the accepted title in editions of 1611 and later.

This "graver labor" belongs to a slightly different genre from that of its predecessor. *Lucrece* is a complaint poem, deriving from the long tradition of *The Mirror for Magistrates.* The poems collected under that title during the second half of the sixteenth century are complaints by the ghosts of the prominent dead, telling the causes of their downfalls. One of these was a poem called "Shore's Wife," by Thomas Churchyard. The complaint form was further popularized by Samuel Daniel, who appended to his sonnet cycle *Delia* (1592) a poem in rhyme royal, or Troilus stanza (*ababbcc*), called "The Complaint of Rosamond." Both wailing women were the mistresses of kings, Jane Shore of Edward IV and Rosamond of Henry II.

Shakespeare apparently started to write *Lucrece* in the six-line stanza form of *Venus and Adonis,* but, influenced by Daniel's popular poem, he shifted to the seven-line stanza. He had good critical backing for this, since the form had been judged by Gascoigne and others to be the one most suitable for complaints.

The subject of the poem—chastity, its violation and its value—was popular at the time. Soon after *Lucrece* was published, an anonymously authored poem called "Willobie His Avisa" (1594), celebrating the chastity of an innkeeper's wife, carried a commendatory stanza proclaiming that Collatine contrived

> To have a fair and constant wife,
> Yet Tarquin plucked his glistering grape,
> And Shakespeare paints poor Lucrece' rape.

Though *Lucrece* was less popular than the somewhat salacious *Venus and Adonis* if measured by the number of editions (six by 1616), contemporary anthologizers took more extracts from *Lucrece* than from *Venus and Adonis.* Robert Allot in his *England's Parnassus* (1600) chose thirty-nine passages from *Lucrece* (more than from all the plays then printed) against twenty-six from *Venus and Adonis.* John Bodenham's *Belvedere* (1600) favored *Lucrece* even more, with ninety-one selections compared to thirty-four from *Venus.*

Accounts of the rape of Collatinus' wife, Lucretia, by Tarquin and the subsequent expulsion of the Tarquins from Rome are given in Livy's history of Rome and in Ovid's *Fasti,* but it was the great story of the rape of Philomel by Tereus in Ovid's *Metamorphoses* that haunted Shakespeare's imagination. He had already made use of this legend in his early revenge tragedy *Titus Andronicus,* now thought to have been written in 1590, before the closing of the theaters gave him the opportunity to write his two long nondramatic poems. The relationship between *Titus* and *Lucrece* is very close; more than a dozen passages have similar imagery or phrasing. *Lucrece* is a much more dramatic poem than *Venus and Adonis.*

Shakespeare abandons the inherently undramatic wailing-ghost framework for his poem (a framework that Thomas Middleton later used in *The Ghost of Lucrece,* published in 1600 but probably written several years earlier). *Lucrece* is a highly rhetorical poem; the heroine's speeches often suggest the declamation that Christopher Marlowe and

Thomas Kyd had made popular on the stage. Lucrece's first denunciation is of Night, and it evokes an image of the English (not the Roman) theater:

> "O comfort-killing Night, image of hell,
> Dim register and notary of shame,
> Black stage for tragedies and murders fell,
> Vast sin-concealing chaos, nurse of blame,
> Blind muffled bawd, dark harbor for defame!
> Grim cave of death, whisp'ring conspirator
> With close-tongued treason and the ravisher!"
>
> (764–770)

She also utters ringing denunciations of Time and Opportunity, which rise to a climax with an extended curse on Tarquin. Finally Lucrece renounces words and decides to act (somewhat like Hamlet in his second soliloquy):

> "In vain I rail at Opportunity,
> At Time, at Tarquin, and uncheerful Night;
> In vain I cavil with mine infamy;
> In vain I spurn at my confirmed despite:
> This helpless smoke of words doth me no right.
> The remedy indeed to do me good
> Is to let forth my foul defilèd blood."
>
> (1023–1029)

Before her suicide, Lucrece has a touching dialogue with her maid, who is solicitous about her distress, and with the servant who is to take her message to Collatine at Ardea.

To fill the time between writing the message and the return of Collatine from Ardea, Shakespeare has Lucrece reflect on "a piece / Of skillful painting, made for Priam's Troy" (1366–1367). She moralizes at length on the disastrous consequences of rape, on the woes suffered by Priam and his family, and on the treacherous Sinon, who seems to her to be another Tarquin. She feels a special sympathy for Hecuba:

> In her the painter had anatomized
> Time's ruin, beauty's wrack, and grim care's reign;
> Her cheeks with chops and wrinkles were disguised;
> Of what she was no semblance did remain.
> Her blue blood, changed to black in every vein,
> Wanting the spring that those shrunk pipes had fed,
> Showed life imprisoned in a body dead.
>
> (1450–1456)

It was a description of Hecuba that a traveling player described so feelingly that it aroused Hamlet's wonder. Shakespeare may have included the description of a painting (some critics call it a tapestry) because Daniel had his Rosamond moralize on the pictures on a small casket.

The setting for the actual rape is established by Shakespeare in a stanza:

> Now stole upon the time the dead of night,
> When heavy sleep had closed up mortal eyes.
> No comfortable star did lend his light,
> No noise but owls' and wolves' death-boding cries.
> Now serves the season that they may surprise
> The silly lambs. Pure thoughts are dead and still,
> While lust and murder wakes to stain and kill.
>
> (162–168)

Lust and murder are akin in Shakespeare's mind; when he wrote the Scottish tragedy a decade later, he described a similar setting for the murder of King Duncan and recalled his own poem:

> Now o'er the one half-world
> Nature seems dead, and wicked dreams abuse
> The curtained sleep. Witchcraft celebrates
> Pale Hecate's offerings; and withered murder,
> Alarumed by his sentinel, the wolf,
> Whose howl's his watch, thus with his stealthy pace,
> With Tarquin's ravishing strides, towards his design
> Moves like a ghost.
>
> (*Macbeth*, II. i. 49–56)

The links between *Lucrece* and *Macbeth* are not confined to description; they even include characterization. The complex hero-villain of the tragedy has a long soliloquy while the King is at supper, in which he gives reasons why he should not proceed with the assassination: violence produces violence in return; Duncan is his king and his relative; the laws of hospitality require protection rather than harm; Duncan's virtues are so well known that they "will plead like angels, trumpet-tongued against / The deep damnation of his taking-off" (I. vii. 19–20). All this is developed from Tarquin's soliloquy after he lights his torch. In eight stanzas, Tarquin gives many reasons why he should not rape Lucrece, some of them similar to Macbeth's reasons for not murdering Duncan:

> "Had Collatinus killed my son or sire,
> Or lain in ambush to betray my life,
> Or were he not my dear friend, this desire
> Might have excuse to work upon his wife,
> As in revenge or quittal of such strife;

But as he is my kinsman, my dear friend,
The shame and fault finds no excuse nor end."

(232–238)

Some of Lady Macbeth's firm resolution immediately after the murder of Duncan seems to derive from Tarquin's comment when his will overcomes his reason:

Infirm of purpose!
Give me the daggers. The sleeping and the dead
Are but as pictures. 'Tis the eye of childhood
That fears a painted devil.

(II. ii. 51–54)

This recalls Tarquin's

"My will is strong, past reason's weak removing.
Who fears a sentence or an old man's saw
Shall by a painted cloth be kept in awe."

(243–245)

A couplet in the earliest of Shakespeare's romances, *Pericles,* describes the common theme of *Lucrece* and *Macbeth:*

One sin, I know, another doth provoke;
Murder's as near to lust as flame to smoke.

(I. i. 138–139)

If it is thought remarkable that *Lucrece* prefigured a play written a decade later, it may seem even more remarkable that its influence lasted yet another five years, until the writing of *Cymbeline.* In that play, no physical rape occurs, though the villainous Cloten plans one. There is instead the rape of an innocent wife's reputation. Lucrece took her own life because she would not permit the shame to herself and her husband; in *Cymbeline,* Iachimo gets access to Imogen's bedroom by hiding in a trunk. After Imogen prays and goes to sleep, he emerges from the trunk and describes his action:

The crickets sing, and man's o'erlabored sense
Repairs itself by rest. Our Tarquin thus
Did softly press the rushes ere he wakened
The chastity he wounded.

(II. ii. 11–14)

Iachimo observes enough details so that he can persuade Posthumus of his wife's failed chastity. The analogy of this scene with the classical rape in Ovid is made clear when Iachimo notices what Imogen had been reading before she fell asleep:

She hath been reading late
The tale of Tereus. Here the leaf's turned down
Where Philomel gave up.

(II. ii. 44–46)

Shakespeare's second nondramatic poem has important connections with his later, great achievements in tragedy. In Harold R. Walley's words, "Essentially, *Lucrece* is an examination of what constitutes tragedy and an explanation of how it operates. It is a rationale of tragedy which is both comprehensive and complete. What is more, it is also the very rationale which underlies the whole of Shakespearean tragedy."

The Phoenix and Turtle

Seven years after the publication of *Lucrece,* Shakespeare again appeared as a poet rather than a playwright, this time under unusual and still somewhat mysterious circumstances. In 1601, Robert Chester issued a volume called *Love's Martyr; or Rosalin's Complaint, Allegorically Shadowing the Truth of Love, in the Constant Fate of the Phoenix and Turtle.* Appended to Chester's effusion, with a separate title page, are "diverse poetical essays on the former subject . . . done by the best and chiefest of our modern writers, with their names subscribed to their particular works, never before extant." If Shakespeare's name had not been subscribed to the poem now called "The Phoenix and Turtle," it is doubtful that it would ever have been attributed to him, since it is quite unlike anything else he wrote.

Shakespeare refers to the phoenix several times in his plays, always as the unique bird that lives and dies on a tree in Arabia. The legend has it that the phoenix dies in flames and is resurrected from its own ashes, but this part of the legend Shakespeare ignores. The turtle (turtledove) was the feminine symbol of constancy in love. The poem is only sixty-seven lines long; the first fifty-two are in tetrameter quatrains, rhyming *abba,* the rest in three-line stanzas with only one rhyme. Shakespeare uses tetrameter verse elsewhere for somewhat formal songs in the plays, such as the fairies' song while they pinch Falstaff in *The Merry Wives* and Poor Tom's song when he says he will throw his head at Lear's dogs.

The first five stanzas of "The Phoenix and Turtle" are in the imperative mood and strongly order a mourning session of birds. "The bird of loudest lay" is to be the sad herald that leads the procession with a trumpet. The screech owl and tyrant birds, except the eagle, are excluded, but the swan and the crow are welcomed. The sixth stanza announces the second section of the poem:

> Here the anthem doth commence:
> Love and constancy is dead,
> Phoenix and the turtle fled
> In a mutual flame from hence.

The anthem is strongly declarative in mood. It consists of many propositions about the union of the two birds. Shakespeare's wording recalls the language the Schoolmen used in discussing the relationship of the Persons in the Trinity:

> So they loved as love in twain
> Had the essence but in one;
> Two distincts, division none:
> Number there in love was slain.

(It was proverbial in Shakespeare's time that "one is no number.") Each statement is a paradox, insisted upon by a compressed syntax that dazzles the understanding. Finally, Reason personified gives up:

> Reason, in itself confounded,
> Saw division grow together,
> To themselves yet either neither,
> Simple were so well compounded;
>
> That it cried, "How true a twain
> Seemeth this concordant one!
> Love hath reason, reason none,
> If what parts can so remain."

Reason composes a "threne" (Greek *threnos,* a dirge) "as chorus to their tragic scene." Its five three-line stanzas identify the cremated birds:

> Truth may seem, but cannot be;
> Beauty brag, but 'tis not she:
> Truth and Beauty buried be.

At the poem's end, all who are either true or fair are called to visit the urn containing the ashes and to "sigh a prayer" for the dead birds. It is a highly compressed poem, which some critics have called metaphysical.

A Lover's Complaint

If "The Phoenix and Turtle" looks ahead and shows that Shakespeare could write like Donne, his final nondramatic poem, "A Lover's Complaint," harks back to an older fashion, resembling in some ways John Lydgate's "Complaint of the Black Knight" (1432). It is the least well known of all of Shakespeare's works. Some critics have denied that the poem is by Shakespeare at all, partly because they think that it is of poor quality and partly because it contains a number of words that Shakespeare does not use elsewhere. Recent studies, however, have reasserted his authorship.

"A Lover's Complaint" was published in 1609 in the same volume with the Sonnets. Daniel's "Complaint of Rosamond," was followed in 1593 by Thomas Lodge's sonnet cycle *Phillis,* which concluded with "The Complaint of Elstred." "A Lover's Complaint" belongs to this popular genre, but it is in several ways peculiar. Shakespeare's heroine is not a historical character, and Daniel's and Lodge's are. The complaint is made not to the poet but to "a reverend man that grazed his cattle nigh" who makes no appearance at the end of the girl's complaint. But perhaps the poem is unfinished.

"A Lover's Complaint" is written in the seven-line stanza conventional for such poems, rhyme royal or the Troilus stanza, which Shakespeare had used for *Lucrece.* There are forty-seven stanzas, of which thirty-seven are the speech of the girl. She sits beside a stream, throwing into it gifts and letters from her faithless lover. Her speech is highly rhetorical, with lines like "To make the weeper laugh, the laugher weep" (124), "What with his art in youth and youth in art" (145), and "Religious love put out religion's eye" (250). Her lover was attractive to all women; even a nun fell in love with him; he was cold toward them, but not to the complainer. His pleas to her brought them both to tears:

> "O father, what a hell of witchcraft lies
> In the small orb of one particular tear!
> But with the inundation of the eyes
> What rocky heart to water will not wear!
> What breast so cold that is not warmèd here,
> O cleft effect! cold modesty, hot wrath,
> Both fire from hence and chill extincture hath.
>
> "For, lo, his passion, but an art of craft,
> Even there resolved my reason into tears;

There my white stole of chastity I daffed,
Shook off my sober guards and civil fears;
Appear to him as he to me appears,
All melting; though our drops this diff'rence bore:
His poisoned me, and mine did him restore."

(288–301)

How long before its publication "A Lover's Complaint" was written is not known with certainty. Its language links it with mature plays such as *Cymbeline, King Lear,* and *Timon of Athens,* and to some degree with the Sonnets. The language used in the third scene of *Hamlet,* for the warnings of seduction and the laments afterward, has something in common with the words of "A Lover's Complaint." Polonius says:

Do not believe his vows, for they are brokers,
Not of that dye which their investments show,
But mere implorators of unholy suits,
Breathing like sanctified and pious bawds,
The better to beguile.

(I. iii. 127–131)

The abandoned girl, sitting beside a stream in "A Lover's Complaint," describes her seducer's strategy:

"For further I could say this man's untrue,
And knew the patterns of his foul beguiling;
Heard where his plants in others' orchards grew;
Saw how deceits were gilded in his smiling;
Knew vows were ever brokers to defiling;
Thought characters and words merely but art,
And bastards of his foul adulterate heart.

And long upon these terms I held my city,
Till thus he 'gan besiege me: 'Gentle maid,

Have of my suffering youth some feeling pity
And be not of my holy vows afraid.' "

(169–179)

It would be a pretty paradox if Shakespeare's best-known work and his least-known work were written at about the same time. J. C. Maxwell sees a resemblance between "A Lover's Complaint" and *Troilus and Cressida;* of the period of its composition, he says, "If I had to choose a year, it would be 1601 or 1602." About that time, Shakespeare was also writing *Hamlet.*

BIBLIOGRAPHY

Douglas Bush, *Mythology and the Renaissance Tradition in English Poetry* (rev. ed., 1963). Ian Donaldson, *The Rapes of Lucretia* (1982). Roland Mushat Frye, "Shakespeare's Composition of *Lucrece:* New Evidence," in *Shakespeare Quarterly,* 16 (1965). Clark Hulse, *Metamorphic Verse* (1981). William Keach, *Elizabethan Erotic Narratives* (1977).

William H. Matchett, *"The Phoenix and Turtle": Shakespeare's Poem and Chester's "Loves Martyr"* (1965). J. C. Maxwell, ed., *The Poems,* The New Shakespeare (1966). Kenneth Muir, *Shakespeare the Professional, and Related Studies* (1973). Allardyce Nicoll, ed., *Shakespeare Survey 15* (1962). F. T. Prince, ed., *The Poems,* The Arden Shakespeare (1960).

Hyder Edward Rollins, ed., *The Poems,* The New Variorum Shakespeare (1938). Hallett Smith, *Elizabethan Poetry* (1952; repr. 1968) and "The Nondramatic Poems," in G. B. Evans, ed., *Shakespeare. Aspects of Influence* (1976). Richard Allan Underwood, *Shakespeare's "The Phoenix and Turtle": A Survey of Scholarship* (1974). Harold R. Walley, *"The Rape of Lucrece* and Shakespearean Tragedy," in *PMLA,* 76 (1961).

Shakespeare's Treatment of English History

PETER SACCIO

Shakespeare's ten plays named after medieval English kings appear in the First Folio as his "histories." By calling the volume *Mr. William Shakespeares Comedies, Histories, & Tragedies,* and by arranging its contents in three corresponding sections, Heminge and Condell indicated their conviction that the history constitutes a dramatic genre equal in status to the two major traditional kinds. There are some problems, however, about the term. Shakespeare's plays on ancient Roman subjects treat equally historical matter, sometimes with greater fidelity to the sources. His plays on pre-Conquest British themes *(King Lear, Cymbeline),* although handling legendary events, and sometimes handling them with great inventive freedom, display in places a strong historical concern. On title pages and elsewhere, Elizabethans applied the term *history* very loosely, to comedies, tragedies, and romantic tales, sometimes meaning no more than *story.* They omitted the term in cases where we would use it: the First Quarto of *Richard II* is entitled *The Tragedy of King Richard the Second.* And it is sometimes difficult to discern any formal principles that might distinguish the ten plays on English kings as examples of a single genre.

As used in the Folio, *history* appears to be a classification determined by subject matter. A history play is one that dramatizes major political events in the reign of an English king, a reign sufficiently recent so that the events could be known in detail. The playwright may, to some degree, rearrange these events, develop character, and even invent persons and incidents. He may, that is, take historical liberties out of artistic necessity, so long as the result is felt to reflect the received conception of the times in question. Hotspur's age may be altered for dramatic purposes, for example, but you cannot have him win the decisive battle of Shrewsbury. Shakespeare's histories are reasonably faithful to their two principal sources, Edward Hall's *Union of the Two Noble and Illustrious Families of Lancaster and York* (1550) and Raphael Holinshed's *Chronicles of England, Scotland, and Ireland* (rev. ed. 1587). This fidelity, the large range of history covered, and the great dramatic power of the plays have made them a lastingly popular account of English medieval history. It is Shakespeare who etched upon the common memory the graceful fecklessness of Richard II, the exuberant heroism of Henry V, and the dazzling villainy of Richard III.

Plays on historical subjects occur in all periods of theater from Aeschylus to the present, but in no other period do they provide so large a proportion of theatrical fare as in the Elizabethan. Some seventy titles of plays on post-Conquest English history are known, most of them written in the fifteen years between the defeat of the Spanish Armada (1588) and the death of Elizabeth I (1603). The actual texts of about half these seventy are lost, the titles being preserved only in the records of one theatrical entrepreneur, Philip Henslowe. Had similar accounts survived from other theatrical organizations, we would presumably know of many more. The popularity of the genre may be attributed to several causes. It appealed to the patriotic nationalism of Protestant Englishmen, a powerful feeling in the years immediately after the Armada. Elizabethans were also convinced that history was useful, that it provided models and lessons applicable to present problems. The profuse availability of historical materials, abundantly published in prose and verse chronicles, served as a stockpot for playwrights, under pressure to provide new scripts for theaters that ate them up very quickly. Shakespeare himself may be partly responsible: the success of his first history play, *Henry VI, Part 1,* is attested by Thomas Nash, and theatrical enterprises are deeply responsive to the fashions set by success.

Eight of Shakespeare's plays concern English politics from the deposition of Richard II in 1399 to the establishment of the Tudor dynasty in 1485. Collectively, they dramatize the decline and fall of a royal house, the reigns of the last seven Plantagenet kings of England. They were not composed, however, in the order of their events. Shakespeare started with the latter part of the story, writing *Henry VI, Parts 1–3,* and *Richard III* early in his career, probably completing the series by 1593. (For convenience, I shall refer to this set of four as the Yorkist tetralogy.) During the years 1595–1599, he moved back in historical time to compose the second set of four, the Lancastrian tetralogy: *Richard II, Henry IV, Parts 1 and 2,* and *Henry V.* At some point, probably between the two sets, he turned to earlier Plantagenet times to write *King John.* At the end of his career, in 1613, he composed his only play on a Tudor monarch, *Henry VIII.*

Shakespeare not only devoted himself extensively to the history play; he may also have invented it, insofar as any single artist can be said to invent a specific form. No predecessor paved his way with successful works in this genre, as Christopher Marlowe had done in tragedy and Robert Greene in comedy. The only Elizabethan play on English history that certainly dates before *Henry VI, Part 1,* is the anonymous, ramshackle *Famous Victories of Henry V.* A few plays, now sometimes called pseudohistories or romantic histories, make use of historical persons and may have suggested to Shakespeare the sort of romantic incident with which he diversified his political narrative. These plays, however, tell invented stories in comic form. They do not display the leading characteristic of Shakespeare's histories, the sustained exploration of political, dynastic, and military affairs.

Shakespeare's achievement in history stands out sharply if we compare it with the work of his distinguished contemporaries. Although the latter could compose comedies and tragedies that need not blush beside Shakespeare's, they could not rival his richness in handling history. They restricted their sights. Marlowe's *Edward II* (ca. 1592), although a fine play and something of a model for *Richard II,* is largely a tale of personal passions. We gain from it very little of what Shakespeare regularly gives us: a sense of general issues, of the commonwealth as a whole, of what it might have been like to live under the Plantagenets. Ben Jonson provides the other side of the coin. Eschewing English for Roman history, which came better digested and disciplined by the Roman historians, he produced in *Sejanus* (1603) a fine account of political intrigue and the decay of empire, but this account lacks the Shakespearean variety of character and human experience. Shakespeare's histories grasp both the personal and the public: individual people wrestling with the issues of power and caught in the web of time.

Henry VI

The events of the three plays named after Henry VI cover forty-nine years, from his accession at the age of nine months in 1422 to his murder at the hands of his Yorkist cousins in 1471. *Part 1* is largely concerned with foreign war, the long defeat of the English empire Henry V had established in France, concluding with the temporary truce of Tours in 1444. The chief figures are the English hero Lord Talbot and the French heroine Joan of Arc. *Part 2* dramatizes domestic broils from 1445 to 1455, power struggles involving the king's uncles and his energetic French wife, Margaret of Anjou. These quarrels climax in direct challenge of the crown by Richard, duke of York, and the latter's victory at St. Albans, the first battle of the Wars of the Roses. *Part 3* traces the Wars of the Roses through many battles, betrayals, and regroupings, and ends with the final defeat of the Lancastrians, the firm establishment of the first Yorkist king, Edward IV, and the ominous rise of Edward's youngest brother, Richard of Gloucester.

By and large, these plays lack the poetic variety and psychological richness of mature Shakespearean drama. Occasional effects prefigure the playwright's later mastery: the striking imagery of Joan's speech on glory as "a circle in the water" (*Part 1,* I. ii. 133), the grim humor of Jack Cade's rebellion in *Part 2*, the sardonic power of Richard of Gloucester's soliloquies in *Part 3*. Elsewhere, characters steadily vaunt and taunt, asserting their angers and ambitions in a fairly uniform heroical style. Many scholars from the mid-eighteenth to the early twentieth centuries found the plays sufficiently uncharacteristic of the genius they attributed to Shakespeare to doubt his authorship of them: Shakespeare was supposed to have contributed only the best bits while revamping scripts originally composed by others. Disapproval of the plays' aesthetic qualities was reinforced by uncertainty about the order of their composition and by bibliographical problems attending the surviving texts. (Although the Folio is our only authority for *Part 1*, the latter two parts had been published earlier in quarto texts differing extensively from the First Folio versions and bearing different titles.) The present scholarly consensus, however, dismisses earlier theories of multiple authorship and argues that the trilogy was entirely composed by Shakespeare in the natural chronological order of the events. Recent editors and critics have persuasively pointed out various aesthetic merits in the plays. Recent stage performances, especially a nearly uncut production of the entire trilogy by the Royal Shakespeare Company in 1977, offer powerful testimony to their theatrical vitality.

Modern readers approaching the plays for the first time may be daunted by the complexity and historical obscurity of the material. The chief sources, the chronicles of Hall and Holinshed, themselves compiled from diverse accounts, are vast, untidy attics of information, sometimes digressive, repetitive, and self-contradictory, minimally organized as year-by-year narration. The plays, however, demonstrate in the young Shakespeare an extraordinary skill in imposing thematic coherence on this multifarious matter. For *Part 1*, Shakespeare took a stretch of thirty-one years, chopped it to bits, jettisoned a large number of events, and rebuilt the remainder into a structure bearing little resemblance to the original historical sequence. That structure has a tense thematic unity. *Part 1* is a story of chivalric honor destroyed by French trickery and English quarrelsomeness. The French are characterized from a chauvinistic English point of view. Seldom allowed any heroism, they regularly engage in dishonorable stratagems and unchivalric mockery of their enemies. Even in the field, they rely on base, newfangled devices like gunpowder, whereas English victories are won through personal valor with traditional weapons.

The guile of the French is concentrated in Joan, who is presented first as a figure of powerful, ambiguous appeal, then as a successful rhetorician and tactician, and finally as a witch and a vixen of monstrous pretensions and ingratitude. Many of the English lords scheme only for personal advantage, frequently undermining the national effort by their refusal to cooperate with each other. In a brilliant variation on history, they finally cause the defeat and death of the outstanding English hero by their jealous refusal of reinforcement. In this hero, Talbot, the chivalric honor of the play is chiefly invested. Talbot captures French cities and evades French wiles; he avenges the deaths of noble Englishmen and rebukes the cowardice of base ones; he finally dies (together with his equally heroic son) at Bordeaux. After his death, the ambitious Suffolk arranges the dishonorable truce of Tours and the disadvantageous marriage of Henry VI to Margaret of Anjou.

The events of the ten years covered by *Part 2* receive a treatment equally sound with respect to theme and more richly various in social range and emotional impact. This play dramatizes the destruction of good government, embodied in the figure of the Protector Humphrey of Gloucester, and the consequent release of passions into open domestic violence. Shakespeare's sources had depicted the Protector as "good duke Humphrey," the single well-intentioned aristocrat near the throne, testy but fundamentally concerned for the welfare of the realm. Accordingly, the first half of the play displays his insight, his self-control, and his efforts to pursue a wise and patriotic policy. Since he blocks the ambitions of other peers, they contrive to undermine him, to strip him of office, and finally to murder him. Although his destruction is quickly avenged by the miserable deaths of the two chief conspirators against him, no one can fill his place as Protector.

The dam of domestic order is broken, and the country is overwhelmed by two waves of passion. The first emerges from the common people in Jack Cade's rebellion. The "rabblement" (Shakespeare ignores the participation of the gentry in this uprising, drawing his details instead from the Peasants' Revolt of 1381) are an ignorant mob who yearn to lynch those who can "write and read and cast account" and especially to "kill all the lawyers" (IV. ii. 70–78). The second wave is the overt civil war of Act V. In earlier scenes, antagonism had taken the form of conspiracy and random aggression. When men died, it was the result of plot, kangaroo courts, and mob violence. Act V gives us a full-scale battle sequence, one of the biggest in Shakespeare. This sequence climaxes physically in the victory of the Yorkists and verbally in one of Shakespeare's great speeches on chaos, a tremendous vow of revenge by Young Clifford, son of a slaughtered Lancastrian (V. ii. 31–65). The quarrels of the roses have become the Wars of the Roses.

Part 3 depicts very consistently an appalling degeneration of political life and political motive. Heroic chivalry and government having broken down, the only positive value left for the characters of *Part 3* is family loyalty—a desire to establish one's family's supposed rights and a particularly fierce desire to avenge their wrongs. Occasionally characters appeal to higher principle. Especially at the beginnings of scenes, they invoke the sanctity of an oath, the rules of royal succession, or the authority of a parliamentary act. But all such claims rapidly give way before the lust to avenge slain relatives. Young Clifford, slaughtering York's helpless child Rutland, utters the key line of the play: "Thy father slew my father. Therefore die" (I. iii. 47).

The degeneration is especially marked in the battles that occupy eleven of the play's twenty-eight scenes. Rarely do we see straightforward combat between equally matched principals; rather, we see butchery. Dying bodies are dragged about, helpless prisoners are murdered, corpses are verbally and physically abused. Rivalry between families gradually becomes destructiveness within families. This development is rendered with allegorical power and purity at the battle of Towton (II. v) when one anonymous soldier discovers that he has killed his father and another that he has killed his son. It becomes the leading motif of action when the terrible Richard of Gloucester starts his own drive to the throne, a drive entailing the extermination of most of the remaining Plantagenets.

The title character of the trilogy dominates none of the plays. Henry VI's inability to carry on the heroic leadership of his father, his pliability in the hands of his Lancastrian supporters, and his weakness in the face of Yorkist opposition constitute the political problem of the reign. Woe to the land when the king is a child, or when the king, albeit adult, is supremely innocent. Henry's inadequacy offers Shakespeare the opportunity for his first sustained exploration of kingship, which is both a real power supposedly ordained by God for the rule of his people and a fiction constructed by men as a stay against confusion. That is, it is both a genuinely

respected authority in itself and a role that can be played well or poorly by individual wearers of the crown. There is no doubt about Henry's personal sanctity or about the superior insight he develops into the turbulence of a kingdom bedeviled by the self-seeking of his lords. At the same time, he is unable to translate his perception into effective action against the superior energy of those lords. There is equally no doubt about the Duke of York's vigor, but aside from a tortuous dynastic claim, his only qualification for the crown appears to be his raw desire for it.

Each of the three plays begins with ceremony celebrating kingship, ceremony that is interrupted by unruly chance and the unrulier passions of insubordinate subjects. In *Part 1,* the splendid funeral of Henry V is disrupted by news of military losses in France, and the scene closes with Cardinal Beaufort's soliloquy expressing his overweening ambition. *Part 2* starts with an elaborate ritual welcoming the new queen to England, but the lords break into a rage when the terms of the marriage treaty are revealed, and the scene again closes with a soliloquy of destructive ambition, this time from York. In a slight variant, *Part 3* opens with the display of the bloody trophies of battle and a direct quarrel over the throne. The ceremony occurs when an accord is reached and is marked with a ritual embrace between Henry and York. Queen Margaret, however, vows the "utter ruin of the house of York" when the agreement is but minutes old (I. i. 254). Neither royal claimant has both the vigor and the moral authority to sustain the kingly condition. At the end of *Part 3,* a failed king and king-to-be confront each other in the Tower of London. They split between them the qualities desirable in rulers so absolutely that no health can be hoped for in the realm. Henry's insight has risen to prophetic heights, but he is quite helpless. The future Richard III is possessed of overwhelming energy and self-confidence, but his power lusts have led him to renounce all connection with the rest of the human race. The trilogy ends in the promise of further turbulence.

Richard III

The final act of each of the Henry VI plays is conspicuously open-ended: each demands a sequel. This, indeed, is a leading characteristic of history plays. Whereas tragedy finds a natural, full conclusion in death and comedy finds one in marriage, history is by nature continuous and does not usually admit of definitive closure. *Richard III,* however, constitutes a major exception to this principle. Although those who lived through the battle of Bosworth could not have known at the time that it had settled the late-medieval dynastic quarrels (and in fact the first Tudor kings at times had cause to fear surviving Yorkist heirs and pretenders), Elizabethans could look back on Bosworth as a major period in historical sequence. Richard's defeat by Henry Tudor, and Henry's marriage to a Yorkist princess, marked the end of an era. Shakespeare could construct from the events a theatrical conclusion more characteristic of providential romance than of history. The whole structure of *Richard III* manifests a firm symmetry that brings the Plantagenet saga to a clear conclusion under the hand of God.

The play begins in 1471 with the decisive victory of the first Yorkist king, Edward IV. Compressing selected events of the next dozen years into a half-dozen scenes, Shakespeare proceeds rapidly to Edward's death in 1483. He then dramatizes more closely the three-month nominal reign of the boy-king Edward V, during which Richard of Gloucester maneuvers for the crown. The last two acts cover Richard's own two-year reign, cut short at Bosworth.

The structural firmness of the play appears in two chief elements, the symmetrical balancing of scenes and a pattern of retribution whereby Richard's career is made to settle all the outstanding scores of late Plantagenet history. Both elements result from Shakespeare's own invention. His sources gave him two major scenes late in the play, Richard's courtship of Dowager Queen Elizabeth Woodville for the hand of her daughter and Richard's nightmare before the battle of Bosworth. To balance these scenes, Shakespeare devised two early episodes about which the Tudor chroniclers are mute: Richard's zestfully macabre wooing of Lady Anne and his brother Clarence's dream the night he is murdered in the Tower. These very obvious parallels prop the whole pattern of Richard's rise and fall. A series of remarkable successes (Anne succumbs to the man she has most reason to hate, Clarence perishes with no one but hired thugs knowing who is responsible) yields to a series of failures (Queen Elizabeth, apparently agreeing to Richard's suit, straightaway writes offering her daughter to Henry Tudor instead, and Richard's defeat is promised by

the dream phantoms of all his victims). The pattern of retribution is even clearer. In another carefully balanced pair of scenes, Shakespeare disregards history and brings old Queen Margaret back into the story, first using her to curse the triumphant Yorkists and then letting her gloat over their suffering. Queen Elizabeth and her Woodville relatives, Hastings, and Buckingham all carefully recall and acknowledge Margaret's witchlike prophecies when they come to grief.

So firm a structure, especially when coupled with fulfilled curses and the accurate predictions of ghosts, suggests that God directs Richard's story with an iron hand. Dramatically, a story so organized might appear to be a mere pageant of God's purposes. In fact, the play is diversified and animated by Shakespeare's first star part of lasting appeal. Second in length only to Hamlet, and the only title character to begin a play with a soliloquy, the role of Richard commands the stage throughout. Despite his villainy, he is the most attractive person in the piece, a creature of wit, intelligence, and, above all, histrionic skill. He is Shakespeare's first player-king. His self-conscious actorliness places him in special relation to the audience: he is often downstage, through his monologues bringing the audience into the position of silent co-conspirators. He plays a series of roles: loyal brother to Clarence, humble wooer of Anne, blunt and straightforward veteran who just cannot bear the upstart pretensions of the Woodvilles, pious churchman anxious not to be seduced from prayer by the worldly rhetoric of Buckingham. Often he warns the audience of the performance to come and comments on it afterward. The supporting characters are thereby flattened into upstage figures who function largely as the victims of this supreme stage Machiavel.

The heart of Richard's success lies in the playacting. Once crowned, he stupidly throws the technique away and thereby loses control of events in England. In bluntly asking Buckingham "Shall I be plain?" (IV. ii. 18) about the murder of the princes and forcing Buckingham's reluctance into an open quarrel, he loses control over his chief ally. In issuing incomplete and contradictory orders to meet Henry Tudor's invasion, he loses control over himself and thereby his administration. In letting Queen Elizabeth slip away from the second wooing scene to promise her daughter elsewhere, he allows others to control him. In shifting from the resourceful, witty villainy of seducing Anne and secretly murdering Clarence to the naked, clumsy tyranny of smothering the princes and drowning his mother's rebukes with drum rolls, he loses control over the audience, for his crimes have ceased to be amusing. After his rather unexpected seizure of conscience the night before Bosworth, however, Richard does recover his dazzling appeal. Shakespeare allows him to die with a full measure of his earlier sardonic zest, urging his troops to

> March on, join bravely, let us to it pell-mell,
> If not to heaven, then hand in hand to hell.
>
> (V. iii. 313–314)

Aside from the emphasis on the political usefulness of playacting, Richard is so thoroughly a bad king that the play contributes little to Shakespeare's exploration of the nature of kingship. Instead, it presents an exploration of characteristically Renaissance villainy within a medieval structure of providential history. The freedom of man to act, to try on roles, to "add colors to the chameleon" (*3 Henry VI,* III. ii. 191), stands in curious tension with the structural implication of the play—that God has ordained Richard to punish the remaining Plantagenets and pave the way for the Tudors. The play subsists not only on the irresistible opportunities afforded to star actors but also on a challenging philosophical ambiguity that imparts mystery even to so straightforward a tale of good and evil. In his opening speech, Richard announces that he is "determined to prove a villain" (I. i. 30). Subsequent passages support both possible readings of that line: that Richard chooses of his own free will to do evil and that a Calvinistic God has decreed he shall do so. *Richard III* leaves the realm of mundane history not only in offering us a romance ending where peace and plenty prevail without hint of any possible trouble to follow but also in raising unanswered questions about the origin of evil, questions that Shakespeare will pursue in later tragedies.

King John

King John has been nobody's favorite history play except for actresses playing the role of Constance in the nineteenth century, when theatergoers were especially moved by the lamentations of tragic mothers. Many critics have thought that the play lacks the unity and focus of the other histories. Unlike the two tetralogies, it has exerted no command over the popular conception of the historical persons represented. A modern reader who knows anything about King John knows that he reluctantly assented to Magna Charta, a document unmentioned in Shakespeare's play. (Magna Charta in fact gained its present nearly sacred character after Shakespeare's death, in the struggles between the Stuart kings and their Parliaments.) Moreover, since the events handled lie two centuries earlier than those of the two tetralogies, the play goes unsupported by any narrative connection with more popular works. It is not even clear at what point Shakespeare turned aside from his late-medieval saga to write *King John.* If, as can be plausibly argued, the composition falls about 1594, between the Yorkist and Lancastrian tetralogies, the pivotal position is appropriate. *King John* captures the anxiety of one stranded midstream in history:

> I am amazed, methinks, and lose my way
> Among the thorns and dangers of this world.
>
> (IV. iii. 140–141)

After the clear moral oppositions of *Richard III,* this is a fitting first step toward the sustained exploration of historical ambiguity in the Lancastrian tetralogy.

In history, John's reign was torn by three major conflicts. He fought with the partisans of his nephew Arthur over the succession to the throne of Richard Coeur de Lion. He struggled with Pope Innocent III over ecclesiastical appointments and was eventually forced to acknowledge that his crown stood in feudal obedience to Rome. He fought a civil war with his barons, who obliged him to seal Magna Charta and called in a French invasion, the latter not decisively repelled until after John's death. All three conflicts occur in Shakespeare's play, but the latter two are subordinated to the dynastic quarrel. The church difficulty crops up as a briefly complicating factor in the struggle between John and Arthur's champions. The baronial revolt and the French invasion arise largely as expressions of moral outrage when John is believed to have murdered Arthur. The hinge of the plot lies in the disputed dynastic succession: this element not only links the play with Shakespeare's other Plantagenet plays but also furnishes its compelling contribution to the dramatic exploration of history.

John is an adult, the only surviving brother of the

dead Richard I. Arthur is a child, the son of a deceased intermediate brother. Although the laws of primogeniture that existed in 1199 did not prescribe the proper lines of inheritance in such a case and although Shakespeare's sources presented the problem as capable of several acceptable solutions, Shakespeare makes John a clear usurper. As his own mother, Elinor, privately admits, he holds the throne by "strong possession much more than . . . right" (I. i. 40). He is an illegitimate king. Indeed, the notion of illegitimacy dominates the play. One of Arthur's partisans is a windbag of illegitimate pretensions: the buffoonish Duke of Austria claims to have killed Coeur de Lion and wears a lionskin to celebrate the deed, but he proves to be sheepish when confronted and is easily slaughtered in battle. The more serious pretensions of Rome are embodied in Cardinal Pandulph: he employs the scheming and choplogic believed by Reformation Englishmen to be characteristic of the papacy and is defied by John in language characteristic of the sixteenth-century Protestant reformers.

The play eventually finds its moral center in a literally illegitimate man, Faulconbridge, the bastard son of Coeur de Lion, who directs affairs when John falters and ensures the succession of John's son when the king dies. Yet the play is not built, as parts of the above summary may suggest, on a plain moral pattern of wicked usurpation appropriately punished, for clearly Arthur would make a poor king: he is not only a child but also a foreigner and a pawn of his ambitious mother, Constance, and of the French king. No satisfactory arrangement is available. The moral tangle extends to basic matters of life and death. John is no hero, but he is no straightforward villain in the mode of Richard III either. He orders the murder of his nephew, yet the order is not carried out. He regrets the murder before he learns that it has not been committed; yet Arthur soon dies by accident, and John incurs the odium of murder anyway. No divine power, in the manner of the ghosts and the battle at Bosworth, intervenes to declare judgment and set matters right. And these dilemmas extend from kings and noblemen to ordinary citizens. The bourgeois spokesman for the city of Angiers, which is caught between the armies of John and Arthur and may be demolished by both, desperately temporizes:

> Till you compound whose right is worthiest,
> We for the worthiest hold the right from both.
>
> (II. i. 281–282)

It was perhaps the pervasive nature of these moral dilemmas that attracted Shakespeare to the reign of John. Tudor historians had not molded the period to conform to current needs as heavily as they had the events and persons of the fifteenth century. Popular Elizabethan plays on Henry VI and Richard III had to make the former saintly and the latter wicked: John's times could be handled more inventively. Shakespeare could make John an interesting combination of energy and ineptitude, good intentions and evil impulses. He could also invent an almost wholly fictional character, the Bastard, to play a dominating role in events.

Amid these bemusing thorns and dangers, an extraordinary tension between the idea of kingship and concrete physical reality, a tension that will dominate subsequent histories, becomes a leading motif. The most shocking scene of the play depends on a physical atrocity: for some hundred lines, John's servant Hubert threatens to blind young Arthur with hot irons. A subsequent long scene centers on the corpse of Arthur, who has perished in a leap from his prison walls. The Bastard describes the broken body as "all England":

> From forth this morsel of dead royalty
> The life, the right and truth of all this realm
> Is fled to heaven.
>
> (IV. iii. 143–145)

To this "bare-picked bone" (148) the glory of the crown is reduced. Yet the Bastard closes this soliloquy by giving the royal title to John: "I'll to the king" (157). He attempts to re-create majesty from the most compromised materials by telling John to "be great in act" (V. i. 45). When John fails him by revealing his inglorious submission to Rome, the Bastard acts as royal surrogate. Although the king has collapsed, one can at least create rhetorically the idea of the commanding king and attempt to make it real by making it work in practice:

> Now hear our English king,
> For thus his royalty doth speak in me.
>
> (V. ii. 128–129)

When John dies wretchedly of poison, becoming a mere "clod . . . of confounded royalty" (V. vii. 57–58), the Bastard not only ensures the succession of John's son, but also creates with equally ringing rhetoric the idea of a country patriotically united, a country corresponding to the idea of the charismatic king:

Come the three corners of the world in arms,
And we shall shock them. Nought shall make us rue
If England to itself do rest but true.

(V. vii. 116–118)

King John depicts a world in which the received certainties are in flux (Kastan, 1983). Royal succession is unclear; loyalty to church conflicts with loyalty to state; crowned heads undertake noble aims and soon compromise them with shameful bargains. The very existence of kings and countries cannot be taken for granted: all are, at root, clods and morsels. In that context, it is left to the pragmatic and poetic efforts of a bastard, a man of inherently uncertain identity, to make a king and country, to make what we recognize as history.

Richard II

Of all Shakespeare's history plays, *Richard II* most sharply opposes the Elizabethan theory of kingship to practical facts about the man who happens to be king. As the last heir by undisputed blood succession of the Angevin line, Richard is supported by what is commonly called the divine right of kings, the doctrine preached in Tudor pulpits about the obedience owed to "the deputy elected by the Lord" (III. ii. 57) and the total wickedness of rebellion against him. Richard and his friends elaborate this doctrine so eloquently that the play has at times been taken as a straightforward essay in Tudor orthodoxy. Richard himself, however, although not an obvious villain like Richard III, is inadequate in fulfilling his high office. Morally undermined from the beginning of the play by his apparent collusion in the death of his uncle Woodstock, he wastes money, provides poorly for the defense of the realm, and responds to rebellion with self-pitying lamentation rather than resolute action. He attacks the very principle upon which his own crown depends, by seizing the inheritance of his cousin Henry Bolingbroke, duke of Lancaster.

Bolingbroke, by contrast, moves swiftly both in rebellion and in defense of the crown once he has won it, asserts control over the quarreling nobles, and judiciously mixes mercy with firm rule. By taking the throne, he rescues England from the "shame" (II. i. 63) of Richard's government. Yet by deposing and causing the murder of an anointed king and by taking a crown to which he has no clear lineal right, he creates a powerful source of future conflict. The play depicts a perfect political dilemma. Bolingbroke can rid the realm of a damaging king only by further damaging the realm. The play opens on a king whose hands are somehow stained with royal blood and who is perilously overindebted to some of his nobles. So also it closes.

Shakespeare dramatizes the fall of Richard II by a method unprecedented in his own practice and that of other Elizabethan playwrights. There are no battles. Aside from the penultimate scene of Richard's murder, there is very little stage action of any kind. Words are the significant tools, words used in persuasion or in the construction of ceremonial action. Most of the persuasions fail, and the ceremonies are aborted or ineffective. A rhythm of interruption dominates the play, appropriate for a play whose subject is the artificial termination of a reign. By description, exhortation, and accusation, various characters try to place their own interpretations on events—and rarely succeed. For example, in the climactic scene of deposition (cut from the early quartos, presumably because of its political sensitivity), three men attempt to cast a revolutionary act into a form satisfactory to themselves. The Duke of York hopes that he is merely assisting at a voluntary abdication: Richard is

To do that office of thine own good will
Which tired majesty did make thee offer—
The resignation of thy state and crown.

(IV. i. 177–179)

The Earl of Northumberland, acting as architect of the new Lancastrian regime, wants to establish its legitimacy by conducting an impeachment of its predecessor, a trial whose central deed will be Richard's public assent to a list of charges that will satisfy the "commons" (272). Richard enacts for himself a full deposition, a decoration reversing the traditional ceremonies of anointment and investiture in a way that will make clear his enemies' violation of sanctified political order. None of the three manages wholly to impose upon the situation the unambiguous clarity each desires. Since Richard leaves the stage still describing himself as a "true" king (318), no abdication, impeachment, or decoration has been accomplished. Instead, material has been provided for a flock of future inter-

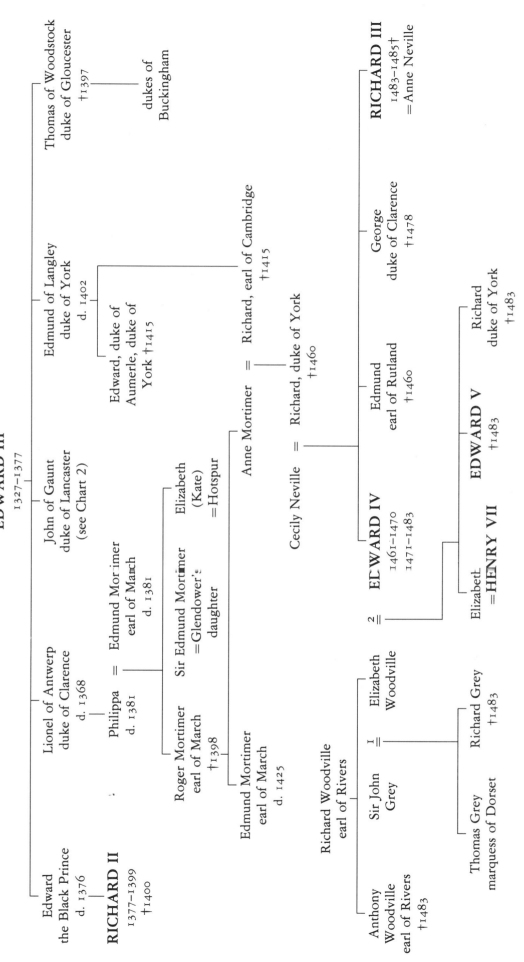

Chart 1: The Later Plantagenets: York and Mortimer lines with the Woodville connection

Chart 2: The Later Plantagenets: Lancaster and Beaufort lines

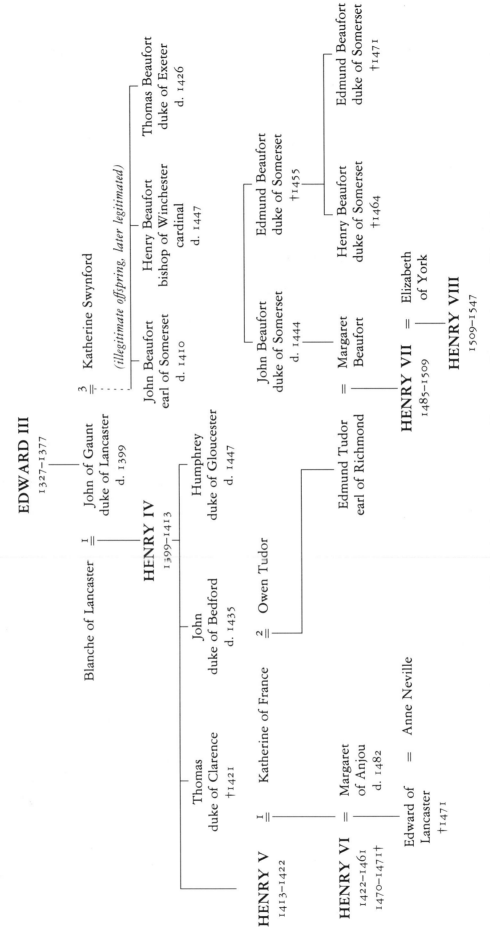

Notes to charts: Kings are in full capitals; others are in upper and lower case. Dates are the years of kings' reigns.
d. died of natural causes
† murdered, executed, or died in battle
= married

pretations that will rage through the subsequent plays of the Lancastrian tetralogy.

One of the few Shakespearean plays altogether eschewing prose in favor of verse, *Richard II* is striking for its lyrical mode. The style allows for allegorical elaborations, such as the scene in which two gardeners construct a painstaking analogy between their work and the government of the realm. It encourages patriotic effusions, most famously John of Gaunt's great aria on England as "this scept'red isle" (II. i. 40), which became firmly lodged in poetry anthologies within five years of the play's first performance. The chief product of this lyrical mode is the characterization of Richard himself. Shakespeare leaves his rival Bolingbroke a deliberately opaque person, by turns silent, vague, or ambiguous about his intentions. No soliloquy or conversation with his allies informs us of the mental process by which he decides to reach for the crown itself as well as his stolen patrimony. He attempts to impose no interpretation on the deposition, apparently caring only that the thing be done. As a result, the psychological interest of the play rests in Richard, and Shakespeare endows him with a voice that rewards that interest. Richard II is one of the great speakers in English drama, a fountain of metaphor, verbal music, and sensitive self-description. At the start, his verbal power derives partly from his position. As Bolingbroke observes when Richard shortens his sentence of exile,

> Four lagging winters and four wanton springs
> End in a word, such is the breath of kings.

> (I. iii. 214–215)

Even as political power slips from his grasp, Richard retains an intrinsic power of unforgettable expression, a power he uses largely to construct attractive images of himself. Like Richard III, he is a player-king. Unlike Richard III, whose roles are practical means to achieve specific political ends, Richard II turns metaphors into theatrical poses that glorify himself and his circumstances. Returning from Ireland, he caresses the soil of his kingdom as its guardian, "as a long-parted mother with her child" (III. ii. 8). The fine actor's gesture misrepresents Richard's actual behavior, for real guardianship would call for more sensible fiscal and military policies than Richard has sponsored. Likewise, his stirring comparison of himself to the sun "rising in our throne, the east" (III. ii. 50), exploits the glamour of a traditional analogy without doing

the work the analogy suggests, the practical labor of encouraging fertility and banishing the creatures of the night. Richard takes the metaphors of kingship as literalisms, holding that his divine right guarantees him divine support without corresponding personal effort.

Richard II's eloquence is exciting and touching by turns, and especially moving when he elegizes on "the death of kings" (III. ii. 156). Nonetheless, it can provoke in the audience, as it provokes in the supporting characters, a kind of impatience, an exasperation at the gorgeous verbal decor that substitutes for action. The fictions of kingship and the equally seductive fictions of graceful tragic fall distract Richard from the political and physical realities of his plight. Only in prison, stripped of both courtly trappings and courtly audience, does he try to break free of the self-glorifying images of his inherited position. Then he can arrive at some recognition of his own responsibility for his fall, accept purely for its own sake the love of a humble groom, and die in overt physical combat.

Henry IV

The two plays named after King Henry IV constitute the most diverse, entertaining, and profound accomplishment by Shakespeare or any other playwright in the dramatic rendition of history. The heart of the achievement lies in its richness. Several plot lines, numerous striking characters, and various sharply evoked modes of life thrive in a capacious dramatic structure that highlights both their virtues and their contrasts. *Henry IV* is a stunning example of what may be called positive irony. Its scenes throw into juxtaposition values that are in the long run incompatible but do so in a way that invites the audience to identify and sympathize with each one. As a minor character remarks, " 'Homo' is a common name to all men" (*Part 1,* II. i. 92). *Henry IV* dramatizes with both fullness and precision the great variety of common and uncommon men who are caught up in the web of history.

The political narrative enacts what Edward Hall had called the "unquiet time" of Henry IV. Having "snatched" the crown from his ineffective cousin Richard II (*Part 2,* IV. v. 191), Henry is a king with obvious liabilities: a questionable title, blood on his hands, and debts in his pocket. The Percy family (the earls of Worcester and Northumberland and the latter's son Hotspur), who had helped to crown Henry, becomes dissatisfied with his rule. One of the family's complaints originates in Henry's refusal to ransom Hotspur's brother-in-law, Edmund Mortimer, who has an arguably better claim to the English crown than Henry. Mortimer's captor and eventual father-in-law, the Welshman Owen Glendower, seeks Welsh independence from England. The Scots cause trouble in the north. Finally, a revered ecclesiastic, Richard Scroop, archbishop of York, kin both to the Percys and to a man Henry had executed during the deposition of Richard II, rises in arms to settle grievances he attributes to Henry's government. All these persons can claim Henry's dubious right to the crown and the murder of Richard II as justification for rebellion. Henry's struggle to hold the throne, rising to a climax in the battle with Hotspur at Shrewsbury in *Part 1,* and to a curious anticlimax when Prince John confronts the archbishop at Gaultree in *Part 2,* constitutes the chief historical narrative of the plays.

The leading role, however, belongs to Henry's eldest son, Prince Hal, who becomes Henry V in the last act of *Part 2.* By Shakespeare's time, a wealth of anecdotes had accumulated about the youth of this late-medieval hero, anecdotes best known to Elizabethan theatergoers from *The Famous Victories of Henry V.* These legends make Hal a prodigal son, a madcap who prefers highway robbery and drinking in taverns to the duties allotted him as Prince of Wales. In Shakespeare's rendering, his drinking buddies become the crew of the Boar's Head tavern, chief among them Shakespeare's most remarkable comic creation, the fat knight Sir John Falstaff. But an equally remarkable Shakespearean invention lies in the recasting of the prince. Shakespeare's Hal is a self-conscious prodigal, a political prince who designs (or thinks he designs) a wastrel career as appropriate training and as an effective manipulation of his public image, in order to gain maximum advantage when he does succeed to the crown. Accordingly, in many scenes Hal engages not in the military and administrative deeds recorded of him by history but in a series of private encounters with his Eastcheap cronies and his anxious father. In following Hal and Falstaff, the plays depict a panorama of English life not only in London taverns but also in rural locations populated by artisans, servants, and the lesser gentry.

In *Part 1,* this wealth of character and incident is organized on the structural principle of contrast. Three major groups—the king and his advisers at court, Falstaff and the tavern crew, and Hotspur and his allies in the rebel camp—are juxtaposed in similar activities that display their contrasting attitudes to life. Each, for example, has a different view of time. The king, burdened with the liabilities of his past and threatened with disloyalty from many quarters, has become a careful calculator, an administrator who squeezes every possibility out of each moment. For him, time is an extended linear chain crowded with dangers, and he responds with a practical series of contingency plans, meeting and manipulating every emergency.

Falstaff has nothing to do with such measured clock-time and the forethought it requires. For him, there are no appointments, no necessities. Time is a vast meadow in which to wallow, an unending cycle of repeatable pleasures: food, drink, jesting, sex, and sleep. Emergencies are not to be met but to be defused and evaded, largely by verbal improvisation. Worldly concerns like political order, social values like honor, simply do not matter for him except as topics he can wittily reduce to nonexistence.

For Hotspur, the northern border lord, time is opportunity. It consists of the immediate moment that will provide the chance for heroic exploit, the moment when one can "pluck bright honor from the pale-faced moon" (*Part 1,* I. iii. 202). Impulsive, loyal to family, enamored of military fame, free of guile or suspicion, Hotspur is the sort of young warlord upon whom a primitive civilization would depend, a fine example of old-fashioned chivalry. He is also anarchic and quite out of his depth in the tortuous politics of late Plantagenet England.

Each of these figures is admirable: Henry for his laborious responsibility, Falstaff for his jollity and his shrewdness in seeing through the pretenses and self-importances of the world, and Hotspur for his forthrightness and charismatic courage. Each provides a model (which also means a rival) for Hal. Hal in turn resembles each, proving himself as astute as the king, nearly as witty as Falstaff, and as chivalric as Hotspur. Each also badly underestimates Hal, seeing in him (with appropriate emotional responses) only the apparent wastrel. Each is ignorant of the farseeing calculation with which Hal prepares to "pay the debt [he] never promisèd" (*Part 1,* I. ii. 197)—that is, to assume the English crown with the astonished acclamation of the whole kingdom.

These contrasts continue (albeit mutedly, for Hotspur is dead) in *Part 2.* No other pair of Shakespearean plays exhibits such structural similarity. Each proceeds by juxtaposing scenes of grave political anxiety with scenes of comic irresponsibility. Act II of each play, for example, closes with a long tavern scene in which Hal plays a practical joke on Falstaff only to have Falstaff extricate himself with the skills of an extraordinary verbal escape artist, whereupon political necessities reassert themselves in a thunderous knocking on the tavern door. But despite the structural congruence of the plays, their essential lines of action differ. In *Part 1* a clear (if multiple) plot traces rebellion from inception to climactic battle. In the first three acts of *Part 2,* rebellion steadily simmers but little happens. A curious stasis affects these scenes. Most of the characters are aged. Falstaff, who had at least pretended to be young in *Part 1,* now laments, "I am old, I am old" (II. iv. 252). His whore, Doll Tearsheet, asks him, "When wilt thou leave fighting o' days and foining o' nights, and begin to patch up thine old body for heaven?" (II. iv. 214–216). The character most opposed to Falstaff, the Lord Chief Justice, is a grave and reverend figure. The rebels appear to be old as well—certainly their rebellion is. As they lengthily rehash the same old arguments about the deposition of Richard II, one wonders if the matter can ever be settled. The Gloucestershire gentry Shallow and Silence are elderly, given to rambling reminiscences about an ancient past, to talk of friends who are themselves aged or dead.

Disease, as well as age, pervades the kingdom. Northumberland is reintroduced clad in sickclothes; and Falstaff, by means of dialogue about the disorders apparent from his urine sample. Doll Tearsheet provokes talk of venereal infections. The illnesses spread to encompass the realm:

> Then you perceive the body of our kingdom
> How foul it is, what rank diseases grow,
> And with what danger, near the heart of it.
>
> (III. i. 38–40)

England itself seems a wasteland, infertile, disordered, suffering. The king sums up the national condition: he is old, ill, insomniac, and deeply weary.

Even the young characters—Hal, his brother John, his friend Poins—are cool, depressed, inactive.

This prevailing characterization of the times invites a major historiographic question. If history means an inquiry into the past as well as a narration of its events, *Henry IV, Part 2,* is the most thoroughgoing of the history plays, asking to what extent we shape history and to what extent history shapes us. Are men swept along by the current of the times, or can they to some extent direct that current? Many characters are trapped by their pasts: the king by his usurpation, Hal by his bad reputation, Falstaff by his age and disorderly life, Northumberland by a despair arising from the defeat of his son Hotspur and his own part in letting that defeat occur. Yet the two young princes, Hal and John, eventually do take charge of events. Given that the times' disorders include mental confusion—a maze of rumors, misunderstandings, mistaken hopes, unwarranted fears—they can assert control only through a kind of double- or triple-guessing calculation. John's version of this is ruthlessly Machiavellian. At Gaultree Forest he secures the dispersal of the rebel armies and the execution of the rebel leaders by a logic-chopping trick, a promise to settle grievances that the rebel lords reasonably but wrongly take to guarantee their own personal safety. Hal's version is the fulfillment of his longstanding promise (to himself and the audience) to "pay the debt [he] never promisèd"—to emerge as a just and stable king despite his father's fears and Falstaff's hopes. The revelation of his true intentions lets Henry die happy. It also leads to the public rejection and (in the next play) the unhappy death of Falstaff.

To what extent the two parts of *Henry IV* comprise a continuous narrative has been disputed. There is no evidence that Shakespeare's company made efforts to perform them in sequence. In Elizabethan times and now, *Part 1* has always been more popular. Only the special cultural reverence now accorded Shakespeare allows the seriatim production of the two parts. Such production, occasionally extending to the whole Lancastrian tetralogy and even to both tetralogies, has recently occurred on a lavish scale, and the plays are enriched by being rendered in this coherent way.

Obviously the political story of the two parts is sequential. In *Part 2* the royalists mop up the later phases of the Percy revolt, which had provided the major action of *Part 1.* Not until the end of *Part 2* does Hal carry out the rejection of Falstaff and the apparent personal reformation this act signals, although he announced this purpose early in *Part 1.* Yet the structural parallelism of the plays underscores the large extent of the repetition in the two plots. Hal seems to reform twice, rising to chivalry and military honor at the end of *Part 1,* to justice and good rule at the end of *Part 2.* No one in *Part 2* recalls that Hal had done well at Shrewsbury. Least of all does his father, whose life he had saved and whose praise he had earned, alter his gloomy expectations for England when it comes to be ruled by a rioter. Critics have offered useful observations supporting a naturalistic interpretation of this oddity: that conversion cannot be achieved all at once, that backsliding is natural when the pressure of circumstance relaxes, that a reputation for misconduct is likely to outlive deeds signifying reformation. Such interpretations provide convenient through-lines for actors playing Hal. These points notwithstanding, the two plays do not really give us a continuous treatment of Hal's growth in the manner of a nineteenth-century novel. Governed here principally by theme, *Henry IV* gives us two versions of the same reformation. The prince becomes king in ways that stress two separable virtues of kingship. *Part 1* places him between the honor-debunking Falstaff and the honor-mad Hotspur: in that context, Hal can rise to valor and effective military leadership. *Part 2* places him between the anarchic Falstaff and the Lord Chief Justice: in that context, Hal can reject the former, who wants "the laws of England . . . at [his] commandment" (V. iii. 133), and proclaim the latter his surrogate father, thereby embracing justice and good rule as his mode of dealing with advisers, officials, and subjects.

But the rejection of Falstaff involves more than the semiallegorical choice of virtue over vice. The final scene of *Henry IV, Part 2,* has polarized audiences in a debate that has flourished for nearly three hundred years. Moreover, response to the rejection has heavily influenced response to the whole of the two plays. Those who find Hal's treatment of Falstaff a needlessly public and preachy humiliation usually also find the whole Lancastrian family distasteful, a tribe of cold opportunists. Those who approve the rejection of Falstaff, holding that Hal must put a stop (and must be seen to put a stop) to the pretensions of a dangerous old rogue, usually also approve of the Lancasters in general, of their effort to preserve public order

under difficult circumstances, of their ability to sacrifice personal inclination to the common weal. Both groups of critics have written brilliantly on the matter; both have also descended to disparaging each other as moralistic or sentimental.

Any scene that so polarizes audiences for three centuries clearly evokes deep divisions in human nature, at least in human nature as it has existed in recent Western culture. If one of the functions of myth is to dramatize conflicts that lie at a culture's heart, then Shakespeare has created a most powerful myth in this last confrontation between the young king and his old companion. Values high in our culture here conflict. On one side lies the Protestant ethic: devotion to duty, hard work, sobriety, self-sacrifice for the public welfare. On the other lies the ethic of self-fulfillment: psychic integrity, personal warmth, loyalty in friendship, and an accompanying skepticism about the establishment, especially about the establishment's demands for personal sacrifice on behalf of a theoretical (and sometimes self-serving) definition of the general good. And this conflict does indeed govern the two plays. The body politic is supported by all the fictions it generates of kingship, honor, and the common weal. Yet Shakespeare ensures that we know they are fictions: the king himself was once a rebel, honor is possessed by him "that died a Wednesday" (*Part 1,* V. i. 135), and many in fact do not do very well in the common weal. Balancing the body politic is the human body itself, best summed up in Falstaff: fat, disorderly, appetitive, shrewd, and rich in the fullness of living. Hal, as king of the body politic, rejects Falstaff, the body impolitic; "but Shakespeare does not reject Falstaff nor does he reject Hal for rejecting Falstaff" (Hunter, 1978).

Henry V

Edward Hall memorably expressed the dominant Tudor view of Henry V when he closed his account of "this noble and puissant prince" by asserting that "neither fire, rust, nor frettying time shall amongst Englishmen either appall his honor or obliterate his glory, which in so few years and brief days achieved so high adventures and made so great a conquest." For many readers and audiences, Shakespeare's play has seemed to celebrate exactly such a hero-king. In modern times, the buoyant and exciting film version made by Laurence Olivier in 1944 has made this view of the king and the play widespread.

A countercurrent of response has undercut the glory both of the king and of his chief exploit, the conquest of France. Many have seen Henry as a Machiavellian hypocrite, exploitative in human relationships, effective only in bombast, responsible for the deaths of personal friends and of anonymous thousands in an ethically dubious military expedition. Some productions, especially those mounted in periods of especial revulsion from nationalism, have presented the play as a satiric exposure of war and the scheming politicians who wage it.

This double valence cannot easily be taken as the sort of positive irony manifest in *Henry IV,* where contrasting values are embodied in different characters. The two responses to *Henry V* both hinge on evaluation of the central character and his main enterprise, and they appear to be quite contradictory. One widely influential essay on *Henry V* compares it to an optical illusion: the play contains two designs, both perceptible but not simultaneously (Rabkin). The play can be intelligently read either as celebratory epic or as political satire, but the reader must choose, presumably on the basis of his own temperament, focus, and times.

The Chorus introducing each act celebrates the virtues of king and country. The play's gross structure—war declared in Act I, victory in Act IV, peace treaty and diplomatic marriage in Act V—provides the pattern of epic achievement. But the selection and placing of incidents within this structure invites a dry, ironic reading. The opening Chorus excites the audience with an imaginative vision of "two mighty monarchies, [with] high-upreared and abutting fronts" (20–21); the next scene deflates the excitement by presenting two political bishops scheming to save money. Although the Archbishop of Canterbury claims that Henry's right to the French crown is "as clear as is the summer's sun" (I. ii. 86), the legal-genealogical argument by which he supports the claim, though fundamentally sound, is so obscure and complex as to be laughable to listeners who cannot quite follow it, and may raise doubts about Henry's right to the English crown for those who can. The Chorus opening Act IV speaks warmly of Henry's raising the morale of his army the anxious night before Agincourt: he bestows "comfort" and "a largess universal, like the sun. . . . thawing cold fear" (42–45). The next morning, four hundred lines later,

Henry does provide this sort of inspiration with his magnificent Crispin Day speech, but most of his nocturnal conversation is in fact contentious, self-centered, and deeply discouraging. The Duke of Exeter gives two slain noblemen a brilliant epitaph:

> In this glorious and well-foughten field
> We kept together in our chivalry.
>
> (IV. vi. 18–19)

This visionary idealism must compete with a commoner's toughly realistic description of death in battle:

> All those legs and arms and heads, chopped off in a battle, shall join together at the latter day and cry all, "We died at such a place," some swearing, some crying for a surgeon, some upon their wives left poor behind them, some upon the debts they owe, some upon their children rawly left.
>
> (IV. i. 128–133)

Yet these complexities need not drive critics to theories of contradictory effects. The combination of inspired values and brute, empirical reality need not disconcert readers and playgoers who have followed the Lancastrian tetralogy through. Although the contrasts appear sharper in *Henry V,* we are seeing the same complexity in history that *Henry IV* afforded. Agincourt is a remarkable victory, and in Shakespeare's time, when patriotic nationalism was a powerful and relatively new force, it could be celebrated in a way that is unavailable to many people today. As for Henry, whatever may be true of private persons, a large measure of conspicuous success is demanded of kings and may entail the sacrifice of more personal fulfillments. *Henry V* studies kingship together with its costs. It depicts the only king in all Shakespeare's nine Plantagenet plays who was remembered as a resounding success and explores the conditions to which he must submit in order to be successful.

Henry is another royal role-player, the master player-king with a whole gallery of parts in his repertoire. He gains popularity with an appearance of boyish impulsiveness, suitably decked out with imagery drawn from sports. He courts the French princess as an engaging country bumpkin. He can play the stern judge with traitors and the bestower of mercy in releasing from prison a drunk who has slandered him. With his advisers and with foreign diplomats, he is a keen politician. He is a skillful warrior and an inspiring leader, capable of oratorical wizardry in rousing his followers. In this last capacity, the role-playing becomes imaginative projection into the situation of his men: he finds roles for them and shows them how to play them. In the Crispin Day speech, knowing that he must deal with his soldiers' fear of injury, he converts the wounds they may get into the cherished badges of old honor they will boast of years hence. The veteran of Agincourt will

> strip his sleeve and show his scars,
> And say, "These wounds I had on Crispin's day."
> Old men forget; yet all shall be forgot,
> But he'll remember, with advantages,
> What feats he did that day.

(IV. iii. 47–51)

In order to do all this, Henry must display an absolute confidence in the justice of his undertakings, a kind of moral simplicity that makes issues conveniently clearer than they are (Kastan, 1982). The recalcitrant city of Harfleur he describes as "guilty in defense" (III. iii. 43). He lets Canterbury take the responsibility for justification of the war and omits to inquire very closely into the causes of treason. He permits the execution of his old Eastcheap crony Bardolph (who has broken the decrees against pillage) without acknowledging that he ever knew the man. When charged with responsibility for the men who die badly in battle, he diverts the discussion from questions about the royal cause into an argument about the soldiers' personal merits. In this regard, Henry is the exact opposite of Hamlet, for whom awareness of moral complexity inhibits action. By this means, however, he can indeed act. He can exert tremendous energy to accomplish definite purposes. The play celebrates his resourcefulness, his readiness under challenge. The play is a paradigm of effort, effort exerted to master situations, to meet contingencies, to galvanize others. In a theatrically powerful series of parallel effects, the king's efforts are matched by those of the Chorus, who must inspire the audience to imaginative perception, and by those of the actor playing the king, who must exert constant and varied effort to carry one of the longest roles in Shakespeare through a series of rhetorically hazardous orations (Goldman).

For all the public appearance of moral certitude, Henry is not in fact unaware of the complexity of his situation. He knows that kingship is a fiction.

He also knows that it is a necessary fiction and that to be a more effective king than his predecessors he must embrace the fiction. In his one soliloquy, he simultaneously deconstructs the ceremony of kingship and asserts his own power within it:

> No, thou proud dream [ceremony],
> That play'st so subtilly with a king's repose.
> I am a king that find thee; and I know
> 'Tis not the balm, the sceptre, and the ball,
> The sword, the mace, the crown imperial,
> The intertissued robe of gold and pearl,
> The farcèd title running 'fore the king,
> The throne he sits on, nor the tide of pomp
> That beats upon the high shore of this world—
> No, not all these, thrice-gorgeous ceremony,
> Not all these, laid in bed majestical,
> Can sleep so soundly as the wretched slave.

(IV. i. 243–254)

Henry here reduces kingship to a set of stage props that make him miserable. Yet he not only sees through the props but uses them with mastery. This combination of perception and ability enables him to assert his identity as king not only in words but in the triumphantly cumulative rhythm of these lines. The Hal who grew up in *Henry IV* has arrived at command. Of all Shakespeare's Plantagenets, Henry V can most falsely and most truly say, "I am a king."

Henry VIII

For at least three major reasons, Shakespeare's only play on a Tudor king sits oddly in the canon. First, like *King John* but unlike the other eight histories, the play has exerted little influence upon the popular notion of the title character. People who know anything about the historical figure of Henry VIII know that he brought about the English Reformation, that he married six wives and executed two of them, and that he eventually proved to be one of the greediest and most egotistical personalities of whom written record survives. Shakespeare's play, which closes when Henry is only forty-two, handles the Reformation lightly, brings in only two wives and no royal executions, and generally treats the king with great respect.

Second, argument over the play's authorship has hindered critical appreciation. For more than a century, scholars have disputed whether Shakespeare shared its composition with John Fletcher, his successor as principal dramatist for the King's Men. The suggestion is not unreasonable, since the two writers did collaborate on *The Two Noble Kinsmen* and the lost *Cardenio.* There is, however, no positive external evidence for the collaboration and some against it. Heminge and Condell included the play in the First Folio, which they claimed to present Shakespeare's plays "absolute in their numbers," while excluding *The Two Noble Kinsmen, Cardenio,* and the probably collaborative *Pericles.*

Third, the play differs radically from Shakespeare's other nine on English history. It was written after *The Tempest,* some thirteen years after Shakespeare had finished his work on the Plantagenet kings. Unlike the latter, Henry VIII is not engaged in civil or foreign war and is not subjected to close psychological scrutiny. Instead, the play depicts history in the mode of romance. Materials from Holinshed are adapted to suggest the pattern of regeneration characteristic of *Cymbeline, The Winter's Tale,* and *The Tempest.* The characteristic plot of the other late plays—loss and separation of family, leading to redemption and reunion through steadfastness, forgiveness, and a vaguely defined but firmly held religious faith—here becomes the historical redemption of a particular Christian kingdom. *Henry VIII* is providential history.

Two unusual dramaturgic features assist in this union of history with romance: a ceremonial treatment of narrative and a suppressed handling of character. With a few historical rearrangements, the play covers events from 1520 to 1533: from a French treaty celebrated on the Field of the Cloth of Gold; through the execution of the Duke of Buckingham on treason charges, Henry's divorce from his first queen, Katherine of Aragon, and the accompanying fall of Cardinal Wolsey, his marriage to Anne Bullen (Boleyn) and the accompanying rise of Archbishop Cranmer; to the birth of the princess who was to rule as Elizabeth I. The story is not dramatized as a series of political conflicts among highly individualized characters. Instead, a large amount of stage time is devoted to ritual, ceremonies embodying the state of affairs at any given moment. The First Folio stage directions minutely describe Buckingham's procession from trial to execution, the assembly of an ecclesiastical court to hear the king's divorce suit, Anne's coronation, the dying Katherine's vision of celestial comfort, and the christening of Elizabeth. (The British stage history of the play is notable for elaborate productions, often timed to coincide with real coronations and other royal occasions.) The burden of the narrative falls upon the gossip of minor and anonymous persons who lurk in the corridors of power. They regularly fill the gaps between the public displays. Rarely is the audience allowed to witness the detailed development of political action, the process of history; rather, it sees the outcomes of actions and listens to report and speculation about what will happen next.

A selective handling of character accompanies this unusual stage action. The three major tragic personages (roles attractive to many star performers) are most developed only as they cease to influence the plot. Buckingham, Katherine, and Wolsey, briefly appearing in prosperity, are given their richest dialogue and soliloquy as they respond to adversity with personal dignity, spiritual insight, and exalted patience. The king himself is less developed psychologically. Although his part is occasionally diversified with idiosyncrasy (his impatient exclamation "Ha!") and although one short passage directly presents his decision to reject Rome, he is largely a distanced figure of authority. We usually see him in moments of intervention, not in preparation or conflict. Having left affairs largely in Wolsey's hands in the early scenes, he comes into his own, ruling as well as reigning, a numinous figure of majesty. He emerges as what Richard II thought he was, God's deputy, and therefore a person whose mental processes are not altogether accessible to us. Indeed, several speeches richly confuse him with the Deity.

Compared with the other histories, a treatment of specific political events in early-sixteenth-century England as if they were the will of heaven seems parochial. Shakespeare does hint at some of the more appalling costs of Henry's triumphs, inviting thought of the eventual fates of Cranmer, Cromwell, Thomas More, and Anne Boleyn; but the allusions are inexplicit, available only to historically knowledgeable members of the audience.

Despite the narrowness and the odd dramaturgy, the play has power, local power in particular moments and overall effect in one large-scale transformation. The crucial moment lies in Henry's aside at the end of the trial scene. The elaborately displayed ecclesiastical panoply of Rome, pillars of silver and cardinals in scarlet, is of no help to Henry in meeting England's need for a royal heir, and he resolves instead to rely upon the learning and fidelity of Cranmer. The transformation occurs in the contrasts among the ceremonies. The opening description of the Field of the Cloth of Gold suggests a false, vainglorious state of affairs. There is far too much gilt, everybody is highly competitive, the great ladies "sweat to bear the pride upon them" (I. i. 24–25), and the treaty being celebrated proves to have been violated already. This febrile vanity eventually yields to the paired exaltations of Queen Katherine and Queen Anne in Act IV. Katherine has a solemn vision of welcome into heaven by six angels; Anne is magnificently crowned while pregnant with the princess whose glorious earthly reign will be predicted at the close of the play. Spiritual patience and natural fertility triumph over normal political machinations. History, rendered with the ceremonials appropriate to masque, is converted into myth, the great early modern myth of England as a chosen people delivered from the Roman obedience into Protestant freedom.

Conclusion

For some twenty years after the publication of E. M. W. Tillyard's *Shakespeare's History Plays* (1944), most scholars held that Shakespeare's histories reflected an orthodox "Tudor myth." Shakespeare was thought to be a political conservative writing a coherent eight-play epic out of belief in the divine ordination of kingship. The sacrilegious crime of deposing Richard II produced nearly a century of turbulence that could be resolved only by the accession of the Tudor dynasty and the reunion of the rival royal lines in the person of Henry VIII. Such a view of late-medieval history is implied by the title and organization of one of Shakespeare's chief sources, Hall's *Union of the Two Noble and Illustrious Houses of Lancaster and York,* which covers precisely the period in question.

More recent critics have doubted that Shakespeare was much governed by any such myth. The plays themselves qualify the achievements they depict even as they depict them. Furthermore, recent critics have doubted that such a myth was ever widely accepted: many readings of the past flourish in the pages of Hall, Holinshed, and the other Tudor historians. The plays are now seen to reflect not the superficial organization of Hall's title and chapter headings but the extraordinary wealth of material within the chronicles upon which Shakespeare drew. There is a deep correspondence between the voluminous character of Tudor historiography, the vast variety of incident and judgment offered in the chronicles, and the capacious form of Elizabethan drama. The five-act, multiplotted Shakespearean play can reflect the prodigality of history, housing the many incidents in different scenes and voicing the various judgments through individual characters. The plenitude of the Shakespearean history play is all the greater because of its open-ended nature. Unless a providential close is arranged (as in *Richard III* and *Henry VIII*), history by definition does not end. Act V can never be more than a temporary halt in an endlessly changing continuity.

Plenitude and open-endedness might make a recipe for dramatic chaos. Many lesser playwrights, picnicking upon Hall and Holinshed, produced only formless plays. That Shakespeare's plays hold together coherently as individual works while faithfully reflecting the prodigality of history is the mark of their greatness. Nowhere else in drama can we see so vividly the effort of men and women to impose significant pattern on their personal and political lives. Shakespeare's historical characters attempt to bring the chances and changes of their private and public lives to the point of achieved ceremony, a moment of celebration by which they hope to set a permanent shape on history, to channel its development into purely beneficent paths. Twice in the ten plays, in the final scenes of *Richard III* and *Henry VIII,* Shakespeare endorses the achieved celebration in its full significance. Elsewhere, flux is the rule. Men attempt to declare a morally clear state of affairs, as does Henry V in his French war. Men attempt to impose upon a striking event a specific meaning, as do York and Northumberland and Richard II in connection with Richard's deposition. Men build ideas like kingship and organizations of feeling like patriotism, and they celebrate the resulting patterns in formal language and ritual. But no such pattern comprehends the whole of any current condition, and no such pattern lasts. Public life consists of the constant interaction between such patterns and the human impulses that both produce and destroy them.

BIBLIOGRAPHY

C. L. Barber, *Shakespeare's Festive Comedy* (1959). Jonas A. Barish, "The Turning Away of Prince Hal," in *Shakespeare Studies,* I (1965). Sally Beauman, ed., *The*

Royal Shakespearean Company's Production of "Henry V" (1976). Ronald Berman, *"King Henry VIII:* History and Romance," in *English Studies,* 48 (1967). Edward I. Berry, *"Henry VIII* and the Dynamics of Spectacle," in *Shakespeare Studies,* 12 (1979) and *Patterns of Decay: Shakespeare's Early Histories* (1975). David Bevington, *Tudor Drama and Politics* (1968). A. C. Bradley, *Oxford Lectures on Poetry* (1909). Geoffrey Bullough, *Narrative and Dramatic Sources of Shakespeare,* III, IV (1960, 1962). Sigurd Burckhardt, *Shakespearean Meanings* (1968).

A. S. Cairncross, ed., *1, 2, 3 Henry VI,* The Arden Shakespeare (1962, 1957, 1964). Lily B. Campbell, *Shakespeare's "Histories": Mirrors of Elizabethan Policy* (1947). Wolfgang H. Clemen, *A Commentary on Shakespeare's Richard III,* Jean Bonheim, trans. (1968). David Daniell, "Opening Up the Text: Shakespeare's *Henry VI* Plays in Performance," in *Themes in Drama,* 1 (1979). Lawrence Danson, *"Henry V:* King, Chorus, and Critics," in *Shakespeare Quarterly,* 34 (1983). Paul Dean, "Shakespeare's *Henry VI* Trilogy and Elizabethan 'Romance' Histories: The Origins of a Genre," in *Shakespeare Quarterly,* 33 (1982). Howard Felperin, "Shakespeare's *Henry VIII:* History as Myth," in *Studies in English Literature,* 6 (1966). R. A. Foakes, ed., *Henry VIII,* The Arden Shakespeare (1957).

Michael Goldman, *Shakespeare and the Energies of Drama* (1972). Edward Hall, *The Union of the Two Noble and Illustrious Families of Lancaster and York* (1550). Antony Hammond, ed., *King Richard III,* The Arden Shakespeare (1981). Sherman H. Hawkins, *"Henry IV:* The Structural Problem Revisited," in *Shakespeare Quarterly,* 33 (1982) and "Virtue and Kingship in Shakespeare's *Henry IV,*" in *English Literary Renaissance,* 5 (1975). Raphael Holinshed et al., *The Chronicles of England, Scotland, and Ireland* (rev. ed., 1587). E. A. J. Honigmann, ed., *King John,* The Arden Shakespeare (1954). A. R. Humphreys, ed., *1, 2 Henry IV,* The Arden Shakespeare (1960, 1966). R. G. Hunter,

"Shakespeare's Comic Sense as It Strikes Us Today: Falstaff and the Protestant Ethic," in David Bevington and Jay L. Halio, eds., *Shakespeare, Pattern of Excelling Nature,* (1978) and *Shakespeare and the Mystery of God's Judgments* (1976).

Harold Jenkins, *The Structural Problem in Shakespeare's "Henry the Fourth"* (1956). Emrys Jones, *The Origins of Shakespeare* (1977). Ernst H. Kantorowicz, *The King's Two Bodies: A Study in Medieval Political Theology* (1957). David Scott Kastan, *Shakespeare and the Shapes of Time* (1982) and " 'To Set a Form upon That Indigest': Shakespeare's Fictions of History," in *Comparative Drama,* 17 (1983). Henry A. Kelly, *Divine Providence in the England of Shakespeare's Histories* (1970). Alvin Kernan, "The Henriad: Shakespeare's Major History Plays," in *Yale Review,* 59 (1969). Herbert Lindenberger, *Historical Drama: The Relation of Literature and Reality* (1975).

Michael Manheim, *The Weak King Dilemma in the Shakespearean History Play* (1973). Robert Ornstein, *A Kingdom for a Stage* (1972). Moody E. Prior, *The Drama of Power: Studies in Shakespeare's History Plays* (1973). Norman Rabkin, *Shakespeare and the Problem of Meaning* (1981). Irving Ribner, *The English History Play in the Age of Shakespeare* (rev. ed., 1965). David Riggs, *Shakespeare's Heroical Histories* (1971). A. P. Rossiter, *Angel with Horns* (1961).

Peter Saccio, "Images of History in *3 Henry VI,*" in *Shakespeare Bulletin,* 2 (1984) and *Shakespeare's English Kings: History, Chronicle, and Drama* (1977). Arthur Colby Sprague, *Shakespeare's Histories: Plays for the Stage* (1964). Gary Taylor, ed., *Henry V,* The Oxford Shakespeare (1982). E. M. W. Tillyard, *Shakespeare's History Plays* (1944). Peter Ure, ed., *Richard II,* The Arden Shakespeare (1956). Eugene M. Waith, *"King John* and the Drama of History," in *Shakespeare Quarterly,* 29 (1978). John Wilders, *The Lost Garden: A View of Shakespeare's English and Roman History Plays* (1978). J. Dover Wilson, *The Fortunes of Falstaff* (1943).

Shakespeare's Treatment of Roman History

J. L. SIMMONS

One can generally gauge the quality of Shakespeare's learning by the setting of his first tragedy, *Titus Andronicus,* with its amalgamation of the most popular—one might say the most vulgar—and the most sophisticated apprehensions of the glory that was Rome. It is apparent at the outset of his career that for Shakespeare Roman history comprehended more than a succession of events and that his idea of *Romanitas* was formed as much by literature, drama, rhetoric, and philosophy as by the Roman historians. Unlike those playwrights who set their tragedies in Spain, Malta, and other foreign places, the young man from Stratford knew the locale befitting a tragedy. Just as certainly as Ben Jonson, who would later sneer at *Titus Andronicus,* Shakespeare associated the formal genre with Rome; and this association, though his range expanded, would remain with him. One may lament the historical accidents that linked tragedy to Rome rather than to Athens, but Shakespeare's surpassing genius was animated even by the dissatisfying aspects of Seneca's classical example. As a corresponding advantage, this initial tragic impulse committed a large part of Shakespeare's intellectual life to Roman history itself as tragedy. Form and subject matter were thus happily inextricable.

An eighteenth-century chapbook, "The History of Titus Andronicus," is now believed to be a bibliographical recapitulation of Shakespeare's source, probably the "book intituled a *Noble Roman History of Titus Andronicus*" entered in the Stationers' Register on 6 February 1594. The narrative is independent of Shakespeare's play and yet affords a more cohesive source for its elements than the farrago of Ovid, Seneca, and Plutarch hitherto suggested, though the ingredients nevertheless remain a hodgepodge. The prose work evokes Tacitus and Suetonius in its depiction of a corrupt imperial Rome in decline. The Goths clearly point to the fall and suggest that barbarism is fast overtaking civility. The emperor (cited in this source as Theodosius) marries the Gothic Queen Attava in an attempt to end the indecisive wars between their two countries, a political compromise that Titus opposes, thereby motivating the Queen's hatred of the Andronici. Shakespeare omits this initial material; and yet it might have suggested to him, on the one hand, the pessimistic view of an effete Rome in moral collapse and, on the other, the incoherent but optimistic alliance between Lucius and the Goths when these enemies inexplicably wish to avenge Titus for Rome's ingratitude and to restore justice. These alliances in the source and in the play, though differently caused, are echoes of Tacitus in his account of Claudius' admission of the Gauls into the Roman senate (*Annals* XI. 23–24). Tacitus advances this action as an example of the Roman genius for incorporating opposition, a reconciliation that perhaps underlies Shakespeare's affirmative restoration that at the denouement rises out of the tragic mangle.

Imposed upon the popular pseudohistory of the chapbook, the opening of Shakespeare's "most lamentable Romaine tragedie" exhibits an internal opposition as dire as the international one between Romans and Goths. Shakespeare synchronizes two Romes—one imperial, one republican—as his idea of a Rome continually at war with itself. Saturninus, the eldest son of the deceased emperor, speaks first:

> Noble patricians, patrons of my right,
> Defend the justice of my cause with arms.
> And, countrymen, my loving followers,
> Plead my successive title with your swords.
> I am his first-born son that was the last
> That ware the imperial diadem of Rome.
> Then let my father's honors live in me,
> Nor wrong mine age with this indignity.
>
> (I. i. 1–8)

With this unhistoric late emperor to whom Titus tragically gives the crown, the horrific Rome of Suetonius emerges, the godless Rome of Nero, to persecute sadistically all goodness, ignorantly reckless of consequence. Because of Saturninus' lust, the Gothic enemy is already within the gate: Tamora is "incorporate in Rome, / A Roman now adopted happily" (I. i. 465–466).

Bassianus, Saturninus' younger brother, speaks with an opposing and beneficent voice:

> Romans, friends, followers, favorers of my right,
> If ever Bassianus, Caesar's son,
> Were gracious in the eyes of royal Rome,
> Keep then this passage to the Capitol;
> And suffer not dishonor to approach
> The imperial seat, to virtue consecrate,
> To justice, continence, and nobility;
> But let desert in pure election shine;
> And, Romans, fight for freedom in your choice.
>
> (I. i. 9–17)

Here is the Rome idealized by Renaissance humanism, a Ciceronian voice against tyranny. Bassianus' proposal is loosely a republican image, suggesting the opposition of Junius Brutus and Tarquin from the fountainhead of Roman history. The alternatives in these first two speeches are crudely advanced, but they clearly project an imperial hereditary right, based on primogeniture, in opposition to an elected monarchy with republican institutions preserved. Bassianus' regard for the Tribunes and the voice of the populace defines a republican hope against the corrupt Rome of Saturninus. Even though Elizabethan and most European forms of government were closer to Saturninus than to Bassianus, we are not surprised that the younger brother is the proper choice and that Titus errs in rigidly promoting the elder brother in the face of his manifested villainy.

The Rome of the twelve Caesars, at least in the decline following the Augustan golden age, represented a degeneracy matched only by that of the Goths. The barbarians are finally and ironically Rome's worthy adversary. The idealization of Rome apart from the Vergilian hiatus and the Pax Romanum that epically terminated the city's providential greatness was based in the Renaissance upon the humanism of the Republic, with tragic ambivalences allowing for glorification both of the Republic and of the Augustan Empire that replaced it. After Augustus—that time in *Titus Andronicus*—degeneracy would be anticipated in accord with the historiography of Tacitus and Suetonius; and a moral foil could be found, unless the cross of Christ loomed in the offing, only by an evocation of the republican hopes.

Despite the lack of historical dignity in Shakespeare's source, the playwright infused *Titus Andronicus* with the positive images of *Romanitas* and with the literary allusions to support those appeals. Other than that of Titus, the name of Lavinia was the only one that Shakespeare retained from the source, and along with the Vergilian associations he gathered other ideals to generate significance for the most sensational horror in the play. Lavinia's rape and mutilation figure the Gothic assault as one upon the humanism of Rome. As a chastity figure, she is Lucrece against the imperial lust of Tarquin as well as the bestiality of Tamora and her brutish sons. The Ovidian mutilation destroys that which traditionally distinguishes man from beast: speech. In this highly rhetorical play, eloquence as the end of rhetoric and human excellence is grotesquely eliminated:

> O, that delightful engine of her thoughts
> That blabbed them with such pleasing eloquence
> Is torn from forth that pretty hollow cage,
> Where like a sweet melodious bird it sung
> Sweet varied notes, enchanting every ear!
>
> (III. i. 82–86)

Lavinia exemplifies Roman education at its best, evoking the arts of poetry and oratory:

> Ah, boy, Cornelia never with more care
> Read to her sons than she hath read to thee
> Sweet poetry and Tully's Orator.
>
> (IV. i. 12–14)

Lavinia becomes almost a Lady Rhetorica, the rape of whom clarifies the nature of the violating evil and the conniving Roman decline. The story itself, as Shakespeare shapes it, becomes a commentary on Ovid and Seneca, themselves poets in decline from the golden measure of Vergil and Cicero. Even Titus' marital *virtus,* accomplished by his sacrificial hand, turns into a trope for the literary gesture:

> Which of your hands hath not defended Rome
> And reared aloft the bloody battle-axe,
> *Writing* destruction on the enemy's castle?
>
> (III. i. 167–169, my emphasis)

A major addition to the plot concedes the literary as Shakespeare's inspiration: Lavinia reveals the nature of the crime against her by turning the pages to the story of Philomela in Ovid's *Metamorphoses.* With her stumps she writes the names of the perpetrators in a "sandy plot" (IV. i. 69) such as Elizabethan schoolchildren might use.

Among the manifold significations of the hand in the play—the means of service, prayer, friendship, sociability—the communicative gestures of rhetoric and drama finally are the most critical:

> Marcus, unknit that sorrow-wreathen knot:
> Thy niece and I, poor creatures, want our hands,
> And cannot passionate our tenfold grief
> With folded arms. This poor right hand of mine
> Is left to tyrannize upon my breast;
> Who, when my heart, all mad with misery,
> Beats in this hollow prison of my flesh,
> Then thus I thump it down.
>
> (III. ii. 4–11)

"No, not a word," Titus later tells Tamora, who, disguised as Revenge, wishes to talk with him: "How can I grace my talk, / Wanting a hand to give it that accord?" (V. ii. 17–18). The Folio version "give it action" is an interesting reading, but both variants insist that for proper rhetorical delivery the word must suit the action, the action the word. Thus the play as a dramatic exhibition is itself threatened by the violating evil, for action is of course not only the proper gestures to grace oratory, such as are schematized in Quintillian, but also the action to propel the verbal plot:

> let us that have our tongues
> Plot some device of further misery,
> To make us wond'red at in time to come.
>
> (III. i. 133–135)

The process of dehumanization in *Titus Andronicus* has been called Ovidian and oddly incompatible with the medium of drama. The process is also Senecan, and the Senecan is likewise nondramatic in that the words are not suited to action. Seneca, establishing the classical example although he was never intended for the stage, affords the central figure no active part except to seize the opportunity that fate presents. Hamlet could not advise the mutilated actors in *Titus Andronicus* about tripping tongues and gentle hands: they are overcome by dumb show and noise.

It is remarkable how in his first tragedy Shakespeare's Roman inspiration engages the problem of plotting a play for the Elizabethan playhouse in a Christian age. If *Titus Andronicus* contained only the Senecan oratory of passion and the final sensational catastrophe, one could not speak of conflicting impulses in the conception. But Shakespeare has given his noble hero the part of initiating the tragic confrontation in the historical terms of a flawed ethos—even though human sacrifice was never practiced in Rome: even the barbarians can accuse him of "irreligious piety" (I. i. 133). Shakespeare added Alarbus and Mutius to the image of pitilessness that from *Henry VI, Parts 2 and 3,* to *Macbeth* always marked his depiction of chaotic evil, the murder of children. But here the first murderer is Titus, and he orders Alarbus sacrificed in the name of Roman religion. Then for his Roman honor he kills his own son Mutius. Thus the Roman exemplar comes onstage only to reflect paradoxically the enemy at the gates. "Thou art a Roman, be not barbarous" (I. i. 381). This tragic complexity, however, could not be resolved with Titus' becoming midway through the play merely the victim maddened into Senecan passion and revenge. When the Senecan propulsion takes over, Shakespeare gets no assistance from the Roman examples of literary or dramatic art. In the Ovidian and Senecan process of dehumanization, no words or gestures allow for a contradictory movement to self-knowledge or *anagnorisis.* Titus cannot rise above his sufferings; the catharsis and expiation effected by the ritualized revenge are at best rudimentary.

Shakespeare's major additions to the prose history all humanize a divided Rome as a city at war with itself, its best and its worst nature inextricable from each other. The hostile fraternity of Saturninus and Bassianus echoes the brotherhood of Romulus and Remus and perhaps even that of Cain and Abel. Lucius, Titus' last son who survives the catastrophe, is also Shakespeare's invention, the name of the character to be chosen almost twenty years later for a special role in *Cymbeline,* that of the representative of Augustus Caesar who reconciles a happy Britain to the Roman peace. The positive aura of the name Lucius comes from the tradition that a soldier so called was the first Roman converted to Christianity. The Lucius in *Titus Andronicus* is the nemesis figure who with the help of the Goths restores justice to Rome. In the first scene he is also the one to remind Titus that the Roman religion requires his sacrificing the noblest prisoner of the Goths, thus initiating the lopping of limbs in the play. Perhaps Shakespeare has confused the coherence of these functions by employing the character as a factotum, first to initiate Titus' religiosity that will motivate Tamora's ire and then to conduct the denouement. More purposefully, perhaps Shakespeare is suggesting a Coriolanus figure indeed, the quintessential Roman who will, with the aid of Rome's enemies, both defeat Rome and restore it.

We can only assume that Shakespeare was drawn to the pseudohistory of *Titus Andronicus* because of the Senecan horrors it demanded. The play reveals that he certainly had a grasp on the real history. He demonstrated his knowledge of Livy during this same time in *The Rape of Lucrece* (1594), and it was probably in that historian that he encountered Coriolanus in the events after the expulsion of the Tarquins. The reference to the hero of his last tragedy is remarkable in his first, for Coriolanus was not a notable allusion either historically or rhetorically. With the aid of the Goths, Lucius "threats in course of this revenge to do / As much as ever Coriolanus did" (IV. iv. 66–67). The structure and themes of *Titus Andronicus* indeed are an embryo of *Coriolanus,* just as those conflicting Romes of Republic and Empire point to the dialectic of Brutus and Caesar in *Julius Caesar.* Even the thematic opposition of Rome and Egypt in *Antony and Cleopatra* is quizzically foreshadowed in those bestial Goths who on the level of the fable unaccountably offer wholeness to a Roman state dehumanized by its corrupt *Romanitas.* Aaron the blackamoor mutely commands the opening spectacle of the play; and the final scene visually presents to the audience, again tacitly, the black baby that Aaron has refused to kill. In one of the most daring Shakespearean touches in the play, the black villain is the only character with a natural instinct to protect his offspring. *Mutatis mutandis,* the natural world, despite

its moral culpability, stands opposed to Titus' unnatural slaughter of his son in a way that anticipates the natural images of Egypt as a foil to the limits of Roman humanity in *Antony and Cleopatra.*

After a decade devoted to romantic comedy and the comic history of England, Shakespeare returned in 1599 to the tragic history of Rome, with *Julius Caesar.* Pseudohistory was behind him, and his three major Roman plays would draw upon Sir Thomas North's translation of Plutarch's *Lives* (1579), probably in the 1595 edition. Rome was now filtered through the biographical perspectives of the noblest Romans, and the civil dissension implied in the opening of *Titus Andronicus* was focused upon the multiple perspectives of actuality surrounding one of the most momentous events in Western history. This complex of perspectives on the assassination of Julius Caesar reveals Shakespeare at a stage in his dramaturgical art that allowed his historical point of view to be comprehensive. In his first tragedy for the new Globe playhouse in September 1599, his theatrical medium fully incorporated his favorite and most vitalizing theatrical metaphor, the *locus classicus* of which is in *As You Like It,* his first comedy for the Globe: "All the world's a stage, / And all the men and women merely players" (II. vii. 139–140).

Shakespeare's representation of Caesar substantiates the two extremes in the medieval and Renaissance attitudes toward this worthy: Antony's magnanimous Caesar, who was "the noblest man / That ever lived in the tide of times" (III. i. 256–257), and Brutus' ambitious Caesar, who would destroy the remaining vestiges of the Republic. At the center of this ambivalence is the enigma of an actor struggling to play for Rome the part of the positively conceived Caesar, and our perspective on his performance unites the Roman and the actual audience in the essential theatrical experience. Casca gives us the clue in describing Caesar's offstage theatrical: "If the tag-rag people did not clap him and kiss him, according as he pleased and displeased them, as they use to do the players in the theatre, I am no true man" (I. ii. 256–259). The hint for Shakespeare's method of histrionic portrayal originated in history: the tradition that the actual Caesar loved genuine acting was a familiar *topos* to dignify the profession. Furthermore, the dramatists of the neoclassical movement in Senecan drama had typed the role as "thrasonical" and in the first rendering by Marc Antoine Muret (1544) established the irony in the subsequent etymology of Caesar's name as separable from the man himself:

> Let others count their triumph when they will
> And name themselves from conquered provinces.
> To be called Caesar's more. Whoever seeks
> Elsewhere new titles, takes something there away.
>
> (Bullough, V, 26)

A direct hint for this separability of role and man was in Plutarch: "This humor of his was no other but an emulation with him selfe as with an other man" (Bullough, V, 79). Given the power of the name, Plutarch saw the struggle for and against the title *king* in one perspective as a tragedy of semantics: in response to the people's fear at hearing him named *king,* Caesar angrily "said he was not called king, but Caesar" (Bullough, V, 80). When Shakespeare in the central scene of the play has an anonymous voice shout to Brutus, "Let him be Caesar" (III. ii. 50), the irony of Casca's reactionary semantics is confirmed: " 'Brutus,' and 'Caesar.' What should be in that 'Caesar'? Why should that name be sounded more than yours? . . . 'Brutus' will start a spirit as soon as 'Caesar' " (I. ii. 142–43, 147).

As Shakespeare dramatized it, the assassination scene has the effect of a play-within-the-play, staged by the conspirators and starring an actor who at his grandest moment is surprised by the ending. The actors envision their scene as inspiring not only future history but future drama as well:

> *Cassius.* Stoop then and wash. How many ages hence
> Shall this our lofty scene be acted over
> In states unborn and accents yet unknown!
> *Brutus.* How many times shall Caesar bleed in sport,
> That now on Pompey's basis lies along
> No worthier than the dust!
> *Cassius.*   So oft as that shall be,
> So often shall the knot of us be called
> The men that gave their country liberty.
>
> (III. i. 111–118)

The perspective shifts, however, even as one contemplates it: Caesar is not bleeding "in sport"; Brutus' idealism, already tainted by Cassius' envy and duplicity, cannot fully transubstantiate the ritualized "savage spectacle" (III. i. 223). But the assassination fails primarily because of the more successful performance that follows. Caesar's funeral too is a play-within-the-play, complete with a stage

upon the stage. Brutus speaks effectively enough from what the stage direction calls a pulpit, but he is a Senecan orator. Antony's oration is that of an actor: emotively attuned to his audience, his performance involves stage props (Caesar's will, mantle, body) and stage movement. Most of all, Antony has a perfect sense of timing. In this dramatic peripeteia he wins us over along with the mob, until in the aftermath we remember that the actor and the demagogue have much in common.

Shakespeare showed off the technical brilliance of the new Globe by employing the famous omens, like Caesar himself, in the multiple perspective. Scenes iii to v are orchestrated with the thunder and lightning that provoke Casca's fear, Cassius' defiance, and Caesar's interpretive wariness. Cicero in his sole appearance in the play wisely notes the solipsistic tendency of all, at the same time that he grants some objective significance:

> Indeed it is a strange-disposèd time.
> But men may construe things after their fashion,
> Clean from the purpose of the things themselves.
>
> (I. iii. 33–35)

In the midst of the theatrical fireworks, Brutus' interiority is symptomatic of his failure in perceiving:

> The exhalations, whizzing in the air,
> Give so much light that I may read by them.
>
> (II. i. 44–45)

What he reads is the letter forged by Cassius, purporting to be from Rome's oppressed populace. The fatal egoism that Cassius has tapped in Brutus eliminates Cicero and his wisdom from further participation in the play:

> O, name him not. Let us not break with him;
> For he will never follow anything
> That other men begin.
>
> (II. i. 150–152)

Plutarch offered Shakespeare ample evidence for the tragic pressure working against Brutus' flawed but undeniably heroic vision. Plutarch approved of Brutus' part in the assassination despite his recognition of the evidence that Rome required an absolute ruler. He first indicates this necessity regarding the civil wars between Caesar and Pompey:

. . . the citie remayn[ed] all that tyme without government of Magistrate, like a shippe left without a Pilote.
Insomuch, as men of deepe judgement and discression
seing such furie and madness of the people, thought
them selves happy if the common wealth were no
worse troubled, then with the absolut state of a Monarchy and soveraine Lord to governe them. Furthermore, there were many that were not affraid to speake
it openly, that there was no other help to remedy the
troubles of the common wealth, but by the authority
of one man only, that should commaund them all.

(Bullough, V, 69)

After the overthrow of Pompey's sons in Spain,
Rome reluctantly makes Caesar a perpetual dictator, but for a reason appealing both to Plutarch and
to Tudor sensibilities:

. . . the Romanes inclining to Caesars prosperity, and
taking the bit in the mouth, supposing that to be ruled
by one man alone, it would be a good meane for them
to take breth a litle, after so many troubles and miser-
ies as they had abidden in these civill warres: they
chose him perpetuall Dictator.

(Bullough, V, 77–78)

By the time of Philippi, Plutarch grants that more
than practical considerations are at work. Thus he
accounts for the coincidence leading to Brutus'
final defeat, his not hearing of the victory at sea:

Howbeit the state of Rome (in my opinion) being now
brought to that passe, that it could no more abide to
be governed by many Lordes, but required one only
absolute Governor: God, to prevent Brutus that it
should not come to his government, kept this victorie
from his knowledge, though in deeds it came but a
litle too late.

(Bullough, V, 127)

Plutarch does not try to reconcile his approval of
Brutus with Brutus' apparent blindness regarding
the nature and condition of the state. If "men of
deepe judgement" and even providential wisdom
see the necessity for an absolute ruler, how could
a man whose life is directed by philosophy (Bullough, V, 90) and whose main concern is for the
good of Rome kill the obvious and even the de
facto choice?

This incoherence in Plutarch's account led
Shakespeare to discover an ambiguity in Brutus
that Plutarch did not develop: his "great minde"
and "good nature" (Bullough, V, 94) become

tragically flawed. The choice of Brutus as protagonist is indeed the most adventurous aspect of
Shakespeare's new Roman play. Up to the point
when Cassius and Brutus are left alone onstage the
structural similarities with *Titus Andronicus* are
striking: after an opposing show of force between
imperial and republican urges, a grand procession
brings onstage the traditional tragic hero, the greatest Roman exhibiting the definitive Roman virtue
of martial excellence. But in the Roman play of
1599 the titular hero departs for theatrics that we
do not witness; and, while we hear the sounds of
offstage applause, Shakespeare retains onstage the
man of thought, a character equipped with intellectual consciousness far beyond that of Titus, or
Romeo, or the sad Plantagenet kings Henry VI and
Richard II. Plutarch had all but unqualified admiration for Brutus the philosopher; but Shakespeare
saw moral and philosophical contradictions that he
historically perceived as distinctively Roman.

Brutus faces defeat in Stoic confusion, though he
is not conscious of the muddle. Perhaps Shakespeare allows Brutus to demonstrate the Epicurean
charge that a Stoic is one who cannot see a contradiction when faced with it. "Let's reason with
the worst that may befall," Cassius tells Brutus at
Philippi:

> If we do lose this battle, then is this
> The very last time we shall speak together.
> What are you then determinèd to do?
> *Brutus.* Even by the rule of that philosophy
> By which I did blame Cato for the death
> Which he did give himself—I know not how,
> But I do find it cowardly and vile,
> For fear of what might fall, so to prevent
> The time of life—arming myself with patience
> To stay the providence of some high powers
> That govern us below.
> *Cassius.*   Then, if we lose this battle,
> You are contented to be led in triumph
> Thorough the streets of Rome?
> *Brutus.* No, Cassius, no. Think not, thou noble
>   Roman,
> That ever Brutus will go bound to Rome.
> He bears too great a mind.

(V. i. 96–112)

The playwright chooses this moment of contradiction to echo Plutarch's laudatory phrase "great
minde." Philosophy, even before leading Brutus
into suicidal confusion, has betrayed his best affections, as when he responds stoically to the news of

Portia's suicide, which he pretends not to have heard:

> Why, farewell, Portia. We must die, Messala.
> With meditating that she must die once,
> I have the patience to endure it now.
>
> (IV. iii. 190–192)

Earlier, leading Brutus to a private confession of grief over Portia's death, Cassius had given him counsel: "Of your philosophy you make no use / If you give place to accidental evils" (IV. iii. 145–146); and a sympathetic Brutus then strikes the Stoic pose that displeases us (and puzzles editors) not only because it is factitious but also because it is a denial of feeling. Feeling, however, disturbs the quality to which the noblest Romans aspire: constancy. Shakespeare's Roman actors strive vainly for this state. There is Portia:

> I have made strong proof of my constancy,
> Giving myself a voluntary wound
> Here, in the thigh. Can I bear that with patience,
> And not my husband's secrets?
>
> (II. i. 299–302)

And at the center of the play there is the titular hero:

> I could be well moved, if I were as you;
> If I could pray to move, prayers would move me:
> But I am constant as the Northern Star.
>
> (III. i. 58–60)

Ironically, Brutus murders Caesar on the fearful grounds that once he is crowned he might not be constant, and Caesar dies proclaiming that he could not be otherwise.

Just as in the spirit of historical authenticity Shakespeare demonstrated in the funeral oration the Senecan prose style that, according to Plutarch, Brutus emulated, so he made Brutus throughout an exemplar of Roman philosophy. Shakespeare's interest in Brutus' Stoic philosophy corresponds to simultaneous attempts on the Continent and in England to reconcile Seneca's philosophy wholly to the Christian world, with apologia typified by Justus Lipsius' *De constantia* (1584). Brutus strives vainly for philosophical perfection as if he was conceived after Shakespeare's skeptical reading of Sir John Stradling's *Two Bookes of Constancie* (1594),

a translation of Lipsius' ultimately impossible attempt.

Shakespeare charts the tragic progress of Cassius to show the failure of the second most prominent Roman philosophy. If, as Cicero once observed, the Stoic forgets that he has a body, the Epicurean forgets that he has a soul. Cassius bases his cynical egalitarianism upon principles entirely materialistic, and therefore he is no believer in fate: "The fault, dear Brutus, is not in our stars, / But in ourselves, that we are underlings" (I. ii. 140–141). Brutus stands up against "the spirit of Caesar" (II. i. 167), regretful that the spirit is imprisoned in flesh and blood. Cassius is content to let Brutus proceed idealistically if the flesh and blood are removed. By the time Cassius has reached Philippi, however, he has felt the spirit of Brutus as well as the spirit of Caesar. He recognizes signs that forces are at work beyond his understanding or control:

> You know that I held Epicurus strong
> And his opinion. Now I change my mind
> And partly credit things that do presage.
>
> (V. i. 76–78)

The scene of his death comments upon the limits of his perspective: "My sight was ever thick" (V. iii. 21), he says. In his nearsightedness he misinterprets victory as defeat and kills himself. Titinius laments: "Alas, thou hast misconstrued everything!" (V. iii. 84). Then Titinius' role also concludes with suicide: "By your leave, gods. This is a Roman's part" (V. iii. 89).

Both Brutus and Cassius are conscious that their deaths effectuate Caesar's revenge and thus acknowledge a fate of crime and punishment, blood for blood. They come, that is to say, to the level of Senecan illumination; but, because they are blind to primary causes of Rome's fate, they fail to perceive their own role in that destiny. For the hero as well as for bit players like Titinius, "a Roman's part" is severely restricted, ending in a defeat not fully understood, a defeat inevitably involving a misconstruction. Generically, Shakespeare's age required no more from tragedy than a Roman's part allows. But Shakespeare also wanted to center tragedy on the heroic part that does come to full consciousness with the world of the play, and for this kind of tragedy he would have to leave Rome. It was no doubt the burgeoning of *Hamlet* that diverted Shakespeare from the continuation of Roman history rather than, as with Fulke Greville, any feared censorship imposed by similarities between the relationship of Cleopatra with Antony and that of Queen Elizabeth with Essex.

Antony and Cleopatra (1607) is decidedly Jacobean in the complexity of its perspective art. Shakespeare manipulates the audience from point to point of view until in the final scene his Cleopatra, in a comically exalted Roman fashion, brings us to a common coign of vantage just at the turning point of Roman and, from the Elizabethan perspective, universal history. Cleopatra is the one great character in the Roman plays whose consciousness is not bound by Rome; indeed for her, unlike for Coriolanus, "There is a world elsewhere" (III. iii. 136). The final scene reveals a simultaneous triumph of the poetic imagination and flawed human love. The best insight that modern criticism has had into Shakespeare's tragic art has been in its appreciation of the optimism and affirmation in this play, *Antony and Cleopatra* properly coming near *King Lear* in our estimation. The failure of earlier criticism can be attributed in part to the loss of Shakespeare's theatrical perspective: perhaps no great Renaissance play was less conducive to performance on the eighteenth- and nineteenth-century stage. The faulty theatrical medium discouraged perception of the corresponding moral fluidity that moves against the fixities of the Senecan and Roman perspective. The play certainly incorporates the received standards of moral temperance that made the story an exemplum of lust—the classical law, as it were; but it also points spiritedly to a transcendence of that law with the art of Shakespeare's comedies and the late romances.

The Roman historians treated Cleopatra unsympathetically. Vergil allowed his triumphant Aeneas to suggest the defeated Antony, his unsuccessful Dido an unfortunately successful Cleopatra. Shakespeare's Antony urges the comparable relationships in his ironic vision of an apocalyptic house of fame:

Where souls do couch on flowers, we'll hand in hand,
And with our sprightly port make the ghosts gaze:
Dido and her Aeneas shall want troops,
And all the haunt be ours.

(IV. xiv. 51–54)

The irony is that of course Cleopatra is not dead and that Antony is to die deceived and misconstruing within the limitations of the suicidal Roman's part. Plutarch treated the alliance of Antony and Cleopatra with some sympathy (and North's translation lent it vibrancy), but Shakespeare's source nevertheless did not allow for Antony's infatuation as anything more than destructive passion. Plutarch's Antony, after a lifetime poised between his vices and virtues, is unbalanced and overthrown by the affair: "if any sparke of goodness or hope of rising were left him, Cleopatra quenched it straight, and made it worse then before" (Bullough, V, 273). Plutarch's Roman has an exuberant heartiness that, as in the play, accounts for the love and loyalty he inspires in his followers. But, although it is a common paradox that a great capacity for life can be self-destructive, Plutarch does not develop the moral implications of this paradox in Antony's love for Cleopatra, and Shakespeare does:

His faults, in him, seem as the spots of heaven,
More fiery by night's blackness.

(I. iv. 12–13)

The heroic in Shakespeare's Antony arises from an appreciation of love not found in any classical source.

In Plutarch's treatment of Cleopatra, the quality of love is not strained as an issue. This historical Cleopatra certainly has no paradoxical nature, certainly not one "whom every thing becomes" (I. i. 49). She is more queenlike than in Shakespeare, if we mean that Shakespeare does not render her Grecian intellectual accomplishments; but Plutarch insists that she sees Antony first and last as a key to political power, and "the pitie and compassion she tooke of him" (Bullough, V, 310) at his death do not redeem either her political or her sexual lust. The nature of Cleopatra's love for Antony is of no real matter; only the nobility of her death is. Plutarch approves of Cleopatra at the last because in the humiliation of defeat, as Cleopatra knows, honor demands suicide; and she rises to this pagan occasion.

How Cleopatra meets her death was thus a palliative for the lovers' pathetic tragedy, one that offered the Senecan dramatists of the Renaissance a perfect fable for their art. Here was a heroine neither wholly good nor bad, or rather one whose bad life could dramatically be purged by a satisfying suicide. As the crucial event must occur within the confines of a tomb, the situation also afforded the unities of time, place, and subject. C. B. Giraldi Cinthio in the Prologue to his *Cleopatra* (ca. 1542) noted the perfect opportunity for a catharsis morally rationalized: the effect of Cleopatra's noble death would affirm the Senecan morals sanctioned by Christian ethics, an affirmation showing neither the philosophy nor the religion at their best but at their most compatible. Passion and sinful pleasure overthrow reason and virtue, leaving the tragic lovers to be victims of fortune and to discover the vainglory of empire. The opportunity for Shakespeare's Antony to achieve tragic knowledge and recognition was limited by the history of his preceding Cleopatra in death. There could be little more than the consolation of his being "a Roman, by a Roman / Valiantly vanquished" (IV. xv. 57–58). Cleopatra, however, was free to move beyond this level. Shakespeare begins her final scene with the heroine in the static posture of a Senecan queen, her moral vision evoking the neoclassical dramatists:

> My desolation does begin to make
> A better life. 'Tis paltry to be Caesar:
> Not being Fortune, he's but Fortune's knave,
> A minister of her will. And it is great
> To do that thing that ends all other deeds,
> Which shackles accidents and bolts up change.
>
> (V. ii. 1–6)

Likewise, Shakespeare opens the play with the perspective of conventional didactic wisdom, Roman wisdom certainly not to be despised:

> Look where they come:
> Take but good note, and you shall see in him
> The triple pillar of the world transformed
> Into a strumpet's fool. Behold and see.
>
> (I. i. 10–13)

Shakespeare did not contradict this moral point of view but added a paradoxical dimension that still keeps criticism trying, in its admiration, to avoid the partial. The Renaissance ideal of love and its reflection in the literature and drama of the time may offer a sufficient source for this new dimension; but Shakespeare was challenged, as was his Cleopatra, by "the high Roman fashion" (IV. xv. 90) of the English Senecan dramatists, especially Samuel Daniel. His *Cleopatra* (1594) was written under the influence of the Countess of Pembroke's *Antonius* (1592), a translation of Robert Garnier's play and a practical part of this noble lady's effort to turn back the tide of "Grosse Barbarisme" on the English stage. *Antonius* seems not to have in-

fluenced Shakespeare directly, but in the opinion of most scholars Daniel's play is an important source. The two Senecan plays extended the discovery of Cleopatra's death as an exemplary occasion for "classical" tragedy and afforded the opportunity for Shakespeare's thorough reconciliation of opposites.

The Cleopatra of the Countess of Pembroke's *Antonius* is a sentimentalization of the figure in Plutarch. Upon her first appearance in Act II, with Antony defeated and suspecting her of duplicity with Caesar, she protests to her attendants with unqualified sincerity that she has always loved Antony and has always been faithful, though she passionately accepts all blame for his defeat. She is determined not to outlive him. Charmian insists that Cleopatra can "honor his memory" even while she lives "in *Caesars* grace." Cleopatra answers:

> What shame were that! ah Gods! what infemie!
> With *Antony* in his good haps to share,
> And overlive him dead: deeming enough
> To shed some teares upon a widdow tombe!
> The after-livers justly might report
> That I him only for his Empire lov'd,
> And high estate: and that in hard estate
> I for another did him lewdly leave.
>
> (Bullough, V, 374)

In desperation to "wrest out of [Antony's] conceit that harmefull doubt" of her love (Bullough, V, 375), she sends Diomede with the false news of her death—a sentimental motive ineptly imposed upon the historical act. Antony, already determined to end his life honorably, is urged on by her false example. Cleopatra, whose death does not occur within the play, remains behind only to give him "due rites" (Bullough, V, 405). Their relationship has been one of passionate love that blinds reason and leads to dishonor and ruin. Antony, like Cleopatra, blames himself for the destructiveness of the passion, but their repentant defeat is sufficient expiation and permits their continuing to express love in honorable suicide.

Daniel seizes the moral significance of Cleopatra's death that *Antonius* merely touches in Cleopatra's exchange with Charmian. Her death entirely qualifies the lovers' tragedy. Daniel's most important change is to bring back the Cleopatra of Plutarch's historical account: pride, ambition, vanity, and lust have determined her feelings for Antony until they destroy each other. Then, in her misery, she discovers the truth of tragedy as Shakespeare's age inherited it: "onely the afflicted are religious" (Bullough, V, 444). She comes to a new spiritual awareness and, for the first time, feels a true love for Antony. Consequently, instead of dying merely to share her lover's poor fortune and to join him in death, as in *Antonius,* Daniel's Cleopatra must die to pay a debt to Antony for not having loved him, to prove to him and to the world of fame that now she does love him, and to perform a rite that will be a marriage in death, thus consummating her own new "religious" feelings. She also has a horror of being a trophy in Octavius' Roman triumph, but that fear is a part of the heightened sense of honor that demands her settling the account with Antony.

Daniel's Cleopatra has to struggle to achieve her victory. In the allegorical account of her last-minute conflict "twixt Life and Honor" (Bullough, V, 445), protracted for forty lines, she is tempted by "that enemy Base life," a phrase Shakespeare echoes:

> I am fire, and air; my other elements
> I give to baser life.
>
> (V. ii. 288–289)

Because Shakespeare has dramatized his Cleopatra's waverings throughout the play as a part of the character's enigma, Daniel's allegory is magnificently transformed. But the similarities of dramatic and moral concern are as clear as the literal debt. The triumph of Shakespeare's heroine—

> Husband, I come:
> Now to that name my courage prove my title!
>
> (V. ii. 286–287)

—is the triumph of Daniel's:

> These rites may serve a life-desiring wife,
> Who doing them, t'have done enough doth deeme.
>
> (Bullough, V, 435)

Both plays dramatize a new Cleopatra rising from Antony's ruin, and both invest her suicide with a moral significance that clarifies and illuminates the tragic experience of both lovers. By linking the capacity to love with a virtuous sense of honor and integrity, Daniel defines love as a value totally missing in earlier versions, distinguishing it from the passion that has destroyed them. His Cleopatra brings about a new relationship of husband and wife. Her confrontation with death

> tride the gold of her love, pure,
> And hath confirm'd her honour to be such,
> As must a wonder to all worlds endure.
>
> (Bullough, V, 446)

Daniel's heroine thus gives moral justification to her place, and to Antony's, in the House of Fame.

Daniel's version is the precedent for Shakespeare's unique employment of the double catastrophe: the quality of Antony's tragedy from the opening of Shakespeare's play is contingent upon Cleopatra, her enigmatic representation becoming as crucial as that of Julius Caesar in the earlier play. The hopeful paradox whereby she can "make defect perfection" (II. ii. 232) is caught in Enobarbus' praise, a praise explaining the hopelessness of Antony's entanglement:

> Age cannot wither her, nor custom stale
> Her infinite variety: other women cloy
> The appetites they feed, but she makes hungry
> Where most she satisfies. For vilest things
> Become themselves in her, that the holy priests
> Bless her when she is riggish.
>
> (II. ii. 236–241)

Cleopatra's "becomings" are poised upon this vision of a whore full of grace. After beginning his play as if presenting the commonly received exemplum—that Cleopatra is a "strumpet" and Antony a "fool"—Shakespeare brings his Cleopatra into this Roman perspective with the conditional word upon which the catastrophe hangs:

> *Cleopatra.* If it be love indeed, tell me how much.
> *Antony.* There's beggary in the love that can be
>   reckoned.
> *Cleopatra.* I'll set a bourn how far to be beloved.
>
> (I. i. 14–16)

Perversely breaking through Antony's Petrarchan cliché, Cleopatra teases Antony about precisely the crucial point, that limitations upon the lover's aspiration depend upon her. Antony thereupon instructs her: "Then must thou needs find out new heaven, new earth" (I. i. 17). Antony's is the climactic assertion in this opening movement that is a paradigm of the tragedy. The grand echo of St. John's Revelation—"And I sawe a new heauen, & a new earth: for the first heauen, and the first earth were passed away" (Geneva Version [1560], xxi:1)—cannot of course refer to the transcendent dimension of Antony's apocalyptic source. The assertion nonetheless initiates the hero's quest for an absolute perfection of human love bounded by the enigmatic potentialities of Cleopatra.

As if to frame its significance for the play as a whole, the apocalyptic imagery returns when the guards discover a dying Antony, whose "torch is out" (IV. xiv. 46):

> *2 Guard.*   The star is fall'n.
> *1 Guard.* And time is at his period.
>
> (IV. xiv. 106–107)

. . . there fell a great starre from heauen burning like a torche. (Rev. viii:10)
. . . time shulde be no more. (x:6)
Therefore in those daies shal men seke death, and shal not finde it, and shal desire to dye, and death shal flee from them. (ix:6)

As Antony's bungled suicide is associated with the falling star and the end of the temporal realm, Cleopatra's regal death evokes Charmian's ecstatic "O Eastern star!" (V. ii. 307)—suggestive of "the morning starre" promised to the triumphant (ii:28), as well as of the guiding light leading Eastern wisdom in the fullness of time toward true revelation.

The use of religious imagery to heighten the romantic experience is characteristic of Renaissance love poetry, but its employment here is as exactingly integral to the vision of the play as is Donne's employment of Christian imagery in his secular love poetry. Shakespeare sets the lovers' experience precisely, albeit ironically, in its historical perspective. For Antony's quest, bounded by the conditional Cleopatra, is also bounded by history: Antony's echo of Revelation is historically anachronistic and in fact awaits Antony's defeat. That failure, with the death of Cleopatra, will bring about the Pax Romana that Octavius foretells:

The time of universal peace is near.
Prove this a prosp'rous day, the three-nooked world
Shall bear the olive freely.

(IV. vi. 5–7)

Shakespeare did not get this historical point of view from Plutarch. The observation is not only Augustan; it is Augustinian. That the perspective is more than Vergilian is clear from the less than honorific portrayal of Octavius himself as "but Fortune's knave" (V. ii. 3).

The Roman history in *Antony and Cleopatra* looks forward to the Augustan age, just as in *Julius Caesar* Octavius' ultimate triumph over Antony is implicitly assumed, an irony pointing beyond the boundaries of the play and giving the qualification of history to the failure of the tragic Romans:

Antony. Octavius, lead your battle softly on
Upon the left hand of the even field.
Octavius. Upon the right hand I. Keep thou the left.
Antony. Why do you cross me in this exigent?
Octavius. I do not cross you; but I will do so.

(V. i. 16–20)

In the later play Octavius is confirmed as favored of destiny by more than the Soothsayer's warning to Antony, a *topos* that Shakespeare had Macbeth employ in his fatal opposition to Banquo:

> There is none but he
> Whose being I do fear; and under him
> My genius is rebuked, as it is said
> Mark Antony's was by Caesar.
>
> (III. i. 54–57)

The context in *Macbeth* is of course that of the Christian era, and the historical propulsion against which Macbeth struggles is above Senecan fatalism and unmistakably providential. The validation of history in James I, "the seed of Banquo," is nevertheless incorporated from outside the play: historical play and history confirm each other within Shakespeare's audience. Similarly in *Antony and Cleopatra* the historiographical perspective establishes the pagan world against the only standard by which it becomes meaningfully pagan, by an appeal to events in "the time of universal peace" that will presage "new heaven, new earth." The comic fullness of time, in this purely historical sense, requires the tragedy of the lovers. The West wins out over the East, empire over love: but the prudential virtues of the Roman Empire, exhibited in the cold impersonality of Octavius' honor and ambition, will have to yield, in our apprehension of Shakespeare's irony, to the reconciliation of East and West, love and empire, that Cleopatra conceives in the happy vision of her ecstatic pagan death. With the spirit of Shakespearean comedy, reconciling the world of the holiday with the world of history, Cleopatra rises above the Roman inspiration of her suicide and affirms "Immortal longings" (V. ii. 280) with a consciousness that comprehends even her self-deception.

In *Coriolanus,* for the first time since *Titus Andronicus,* Shakespeare wrote a Roman play for which he knew no dramatic tradition, Senecan or otherwise, though Alexandre Hardy had probably written his *Coriolan* by 1600 (published in 1625), and the subject thereafter was a favored one in the French neoclassical drama. In the inspiration for his final tragedy, Shakespeare moved back from the culmination of Rome's imperial greatness to nearly the beginnings of the city—its youth, as Florus divided the ages of Rome in his *Epitome* of Livy. Shakespeare was thus turning simultaneously to his own earliest essays into Roman history, for the appearance of Marcius Coriolanus follows hard upon the history of those wars immediately after the expulsion of the Tarquins in *The Rape of Lucrece.* In Livy, his source for the poem, Shakespeare might well first have read of the subsequent external struggles against Italian tribes and the internal divisiveness between patricians and plebeians leading to the introduction of Coriolanus. Plutarch, in Cominius' tribute before the Senate, offered a link between the youthful Coriolanus and Tarquin, which Shakespeare vivifies by reporting the sixteen-year-old Roman in his first battle to have struck "Tarquin's self" (II. ii. 92). From the allusion to Coriolanus in *Titus Andronicus* we know that Shakespeare had from the earliest years of his work absorbed the history as well as the potential drama of the Roman who must attack Rome as a result of the city's internal dissension. *Coriolanus,* therefore, is a retrospective summation of Shakespeare's treatment of Rome that gives evidence of the centrality of the subject throughout his career and helps to account for the play's almost classical design and singleness of purpose.

By 1608 Shakespeare had discovered a hero whose fate is an abstract of the Roman tragedy as the playwright was shaping it from the beginning. In this relatively obscure protagonist who becomes Rome's antagonist Shakespeare figures the history of Rome, its move both to greatness and to destruction. Even in a setting of almost village-minded squabbles, the Idea of Rome emerges, as in Menenius' scorn of the plebians:

> you may as well
> Strike at the heaven with your staves as lift them
> Against the Roman state, whose course will on
> The way it takes, cracking ten thousand curbs
> Of more strong link assunder than can ever
> Appear in your impediment.
>
> (I. i. 63–68)

But Menenius' grand appeal to the inevitability of Rome's national destiny cannot extricate itself from the equally intimated irony of Rome's inevitable decline and fall. The tragedy for both Rome and Coriolanus lies in the struggle to make it the truly Eternal City. When he is exiled, cut off from Rome like Lucius, Brutus, and the later Antony, Coriolanus' parting words historically predict what Shakespeare's audience would recognize post facto, the general decay of Roman *virtus* and the particular invasion of the Goths:

> Let every feeble rumor shake your hearts!
> Your enemies, with nodding of their plumes,
> Fan you into despair! Have the power still
> To banish your defenders, till at length
> Your ignorance—which finds not till it feels,
> Making but reservation of yourselves,
> Still your own foes—deliver you as most
> Abated captives to some nation
> That won you without blows!
>
> (III. iii. 126–134)

Near the end of the play, Menenius again assumes the permanence of Rome, this time in comparison with Coriolanus:

> See you yond coign o' th' Capitol, yond cornerstone?
> . . . If it be possible for you to displace it with your little finger, there is some hope the ladies of Rome, especially his mother, may prevail with him.
>
> (V. iv. 1–2, 4–6)

But Coriolanus by this point has yielded to his mother, wife, and child and has failed in his attempted immutability; and the Roman capitol will also become archetypally the ruins of time.

Coriolanus embodies the glory that will become Rome, in accordance with the city's definition of virtue as expounded early in Plutarch's "Life": "Now in those dayes, valliantnes was honoured in Rome above all other vertues: which they call *Virtus,* by the name of vertue selfe, as including in that generall name, all other speciall vertues besides. So that *Virtus* in the Latin, was asmuche as valliantnes" (Bullough, V, 506). The linguistic irony of equating valiantness and *virtus* with "the name of vertue selfe" leads to the moral irony of Coriolanus' failure; for the all-inclusive virtue proves wholly exclusive, indeed life-denying. Nevertheless, Shakespeare accepts this *virtus,* as did the Renaissance, as the excellence that accounted in human terms for the providential emergence of Rome as conqueror and ruler of the world. The practical need to defend, expand, and maintain Rome is idealized into an ethos, as Cominius acknowledges to the Senate, echoing the passage in Plutarch:

> It is held
> That valor is the chiefest virtue, and
> Most dignifies the haver. If it be,
> The man I speak of cannot in the world
> Be singly counterpoised.
>
> (II. ii. 81–85)

As an absolute, the virtue that Coriolanus exemplifies cannot be questioned or judged by the mutable populace entirely empty of that virtue. The humanistic excellence is as beyond the subhuman beast of many heads as heavenly knowledge is beyond Rome's aristocratic apprehension, represented here by Volumnia:

> Cats, that can judge as fitly of his worth
> As I can of those mysteries which heaven
> Will not have earth to know!
>
> (IV. ii. 34–36)

For his mother as for Menenius, Coriolanus symbolizes the essential Rome rising above the base and vulgar:

> As far as doth the Capitol exceed
> The meanest house in Rome, so far my son,—
> This lady's husband here, this, do you see?—
> Whom you have banished, does exceed you all.
>
> (IV. ii. 39–42)

In order to bring about the identification of Coriolanus with "the fundamental part of state" (III. i. 151), Shakespeare rejects the evidence in Plutarch that the Roman's failure was the result of the early loss of his father and the resulting loss of educational discipline:

> For this Martius naturall wit and great harte dyd marvelously sturre up his corage, to doe and attempt noble actes. But on the other side for lacke of education, he was so chollericke and impacient, that he would yeld to no living creature: which made him churlishe, uncivill, and altogether unfit for any mans conversation. . . . And to say truely, the greatest benefit that learning bringeth men unto, is this: that it teacheth men that be rude and rough of nature, by compasse and rule of reason, to be civill and curteous, and to like better the meane state, then the higher.
>
> (Bullough, V, 506)

The humanistic values that Plutarch and Shakespeare both appreciated are nevertheless not subsumed by the Roman *virtus.* Not extending the implications of the Roman ethos literally and tragically, Plutarch deems Coriolanus deficient even though he fully develops in valiantness. Shakespeare, with cruel irony, exhibits Coriolanus not as a product of neglect but as the epitome of Roman cultivation. Volumnia is not, in Plutarch, the stern Roman matron; she merely takes passive pride in her son's heroism. Shakespeare creates a martial version of Cornelia, who has actively and purposefully educated her son according to Rome's best light:

> Thou art my warrior;
> I holp to frame thee.
>
> (V. iii. 62–63)

With those who share the Idea of Rome, Coriolanus is not "altogether unfit for any mans conversation." He is "uncivill" only to those who, not Roman by ideal definition, perversely and inhumanly exist in Rome, thwarting excellence:

> I would they were barbarians, as they are,
> Though in Rome littered; not Romans, as they are
>   not,
> Though calvèd i' th' porch o' th' Capitol.
>
> (III. i. 238–240)

Shakespeare might have accepted the "rule of reason" and "the meane state" to be the norms that Coriolanus violates. But although *Coriolanus* can be partially interpreted in that Plutarchan and Senecan perspective—as *Antony and Cleopatra* can be viewed as a tragedy of lust in action—Shakespeare has added the dimension whereby Rome and Volumnia must reject their avatar in order for Rome to survive. Because Shakespeare's Coriolanus epitomizes Roman virtue, patrician Rome cannot find the moral terms to condemn him except to suggest, as does Menenius, that "His nature is too noble for the world" (III. i. 255). The boy-man cannot learn a contradictory lesson from his mother:

> You are too absolute;
> Though therein you can never be too noble,
> But when extremities speak.
>
> (III. ii. 39–41)

Volumnia is oblivious of her moral incoherence. When she must face the "extremities" of her son's exile, Coriolanus comforts her with the very precepts that she has just urged him to compromise:

> Nay, mother,
> Where is your ancient courage? You were used
> To say extremities was the trier of spirits;
> That common chances common men could bear;
> That when the sea was calm all boats alike
> Showed mastership in floating; fortune's blows,
> When most struck home, being gentle wounded
> craves
> A noble cunning. You were used to load me
> With precepts that would make invincible
> The heart that conned them.
>
> (IV. i. 2–11)

The climactic scene between mother and son, with Coriolanus' fatal yielding, thus becomes in Shakespeare, as it is not in Plutarch, the quintessentially Roman tragedy. Both Romans, like Rome, have compromised their immutability; and history for Rome will prove to be a disastrous conflict of extremities.

The certainty that Rome is doomed is determined by more than the Elizabethan consciousness of mutability. The Christian view of classical history had been anti-Roman from the start. Nevertheless, although Augustine wrote his *City of God* to absolve Christianity from blame in the decline and fall of the flawed city of man, he began a tradition of admiration for those pagan heroes who were exemplary according to their lights and of sympathy for their ultimate failure, a tradition articulated in the dedication of North's translation of Plutarch to Queen Elizabeth. The fall was attributable only secondarily to God's judgment, for the primary cause came from within, not from their stars but from themselves. This most popular view was thus tragic in the way that the Greek dramatists and Aristotle had conceived the tragic vision: the context lacked only the possibility of recognition, of *anagnorisis*—a limitation of the Roman part seen finally in Coriolanus as in Brutus, in *Julius Caesar,* and in Antony, in *Antony and Cleopatra.*

Shakespeare's vision of the Roman ethos and political impasse clearly comes within the perspectives and presentiments of this popular historiography. For the Elizabethan the most immediate and influential source of Rome's moral and temporal limitations was not Augustine or Orosius, whose *Seven*

Books of History Against the Pagans followed Augustine in defining Rome's providentially pagan role. Both of these seminal works in their turn looked back to the biblical source at the hand of every Elizabethan, accentuated with the interpretive marginalia of the Geneva Version, in the Book of Daniel. In its mystical history of the four monarchies, Rome was identified as the last; this final temporal empire would be replaced only by the eternal kingdom of Christ that was to begin, at the zenith of Rome's greatness, with the Nativity.

As the marginalia to the second chapter of Daniel explain, the seed of Rome's destruction lay within the fourth empire itself, distinguishing its fall from the directly divine terminations of the previous three. The fantastic "great image," the legs of which represent Rome, has feet partly of iron and partly of clay (ii:33) in order to suggest a paradoxical weakness in strength and Rome's inability to be at one with itself. The Romans will destroy all previous kingdoms "as yron breaketh in pieces, & subdueth all things" (ii:40); but, the marginalia notes, "They shal haue ciuil warres and continual discordes among them selues": "as yron bruseth all these things, *so* shal it breake in pieces and bruse *all*" (ii:40). If the clay offers premonitions of Rome's civic discord, the iron implies the cruelty of Rome's martial superiority that is also ultimately self-destructive.

Of the four visionary beasts in the seventh chapter that symbolize the four monarchies, the Roman beast with its teeth of iron and nails of brass is truly "a monster," the Geneva Version notes, "& colde not be compared to anie beast, because the nature of none was able to express it." The emblematic dilemma suggests Shakespeare's own images of Coriolanus that grope with metallic and mechanic properties to seek something beyond simile—"a thing / Made by some other deity than nature" (IV. vi. 91–92)—not quite beast, man, or god, but shifting figuratively and morally among those likelihoods:

> he no more remembers his mother now than an eight-year-old horse. The tartness of his face sours ripe grapes. When he walks, he moves like an engine, and the ground shrinks before his treading. He is able to pierce a corslet with his eye; talks like a knell and his hum is a battery. He sits in his state, as a thing made for Alexander. What he bids be done is finished with his bidding. He wants nothing of a god but eternity, and a heaven to throne in.
>
> (V. iv. 16–24)

He is a mechanical robot, a "mailed" and grim reaper, a "thing" like the fourth beast, who "deuoured & brake in pieces and stamped the residue vnder his fete" (vii:7):

> From face to foot
> He was a thing of blood, whose every motion
> Was timed with dying cries.
>
> (II. ii. 106–108)

> His bloody brow
> With his mailed hand then wiping, forth he goes,
> Like to a harvest-man.
>
> (I. iii. 32–34)

> Death, that dark spirit, in's nervy arm doth lie;
> Which, being advanced, declines, and then men die.
>
> (II. i. 150–151)

In the eleventh chapter of Daniel a detail from the angel's apocalyptic tracing of universal history captures the unnatural quality of the Roman civilization. The king who figures the monarchy and its history will "regarde [neither] the God of his fathers, nor the desires of women, nor care for any God: for he shal magnifie him self aboue all" (xi:37). Corresponding to the religious deprivation, the exclusively masculine bias of the Roman ethos signifies, according to the Geneva marginalia, "that they shulde be without all humanitie: for the loue of women is taken for singular or great loue." Shakespeare was fully conscious from the beginning that Roman ideals precluded the sexual harmony celebrated in his romantic comedies. We see the signs in Titus' treatment of Lavinia in offering her to Saturninus, in Caesar's impersonal dealings with Calphurnia, and indeed in the more positive cases in which Brutus' acquiescence to Portia's desires and Antony's regard for Cleopatra's lead to greater humanity and simultaneously, from the Roman perspective, to an even more certain failure. Coriolanus' inability to "[forge] himself a name o' th' fire / Of burning Rome" (V. i. 14–15) also comes when he accedes to the desires of his mother. And his wife, Virgilia, his "gracious silence" (II. i. 165), suggests throughout the play a tender humanity for Coriolanus that Rome cannot voice, let alone realize.

The humanity voiced in *Coriolanus* is not tender. As sounded by the mob, it proceeds from fear, insecurity, hostility, and hunger. As controlled by the ambitious Tribunes, it demands political power. The voice extorts not only free corn but also the innovation of pronouncing value quite independent of Rome's definition. By connecting all the political events leading to Coriolanus' banishment with the question of free corn for the populace, Shakespeare made the incidental issue in Plutarch central to the mouth-breath-voice imagery that can finally "whoop" the noblest Roman "out of Rome" (IV. v. 79). Shakespeare's treatment of the impasse is fully political, never partisan, even as the two elements in the city are helplessly at odds and require either political deceit or compromise with Rome's ethics for survival. The possible atonement is ironically suggested in the scene rendering an event that Plutarch merely reported as having successfully occurred without anyone's demurral— Coriolanus' appearance before the mob in the gown of humility. By dramatizing this play-within-the-play to initiate the turning point, Shakespeare was perhaps prompting, with the antique pagan custom, the audience's knowledge of the single other instance of such an action, when Christ, unlike Coriolanus, did not refuse to show his wounds.

For his last Roman play as for his first, Shakespeare went outside of Plutarch for his historical material, this time to Holinshed. Like *Titus Andronicus*, *Cymbeline* is a hodgepodge of ingredients, only the range of selection now is determined by the mixed genre of tragicomic romance. Four distinct worlds are conjoined: the Rome of Augustus, the Renaissance Italy of Machiavellian degeneracy, the pagan Britain of Cymbeline, and the pastoral mountains of Belarius. Each world lends its particular action to an intricate plot that culminates in the much admired construction of the final scene. For a Shakespeare play of such undeniable grandeur, the success and even the focus of *Cymbeline* are questions that require further investigation; but unquestionably the historical nexus of Rome and Britain is fundamental to Shakespeare's inspiration. That nexus emerges from the one unequivocal fact of the chroniclers:

> that during his reigne, the Sauiour of the world our Lord Jesus Christ the onelie sonne of God was borne of a virgine, about the 23 yeare of the reigne of this Kymbeline, and in the 42 yeare of the emperour Octauius Augustus, that is to wit, in the yeare of the world 3966, in the second yeare of the 195 Olympiad, after the building of the citie of Rome 750 nigh at an end.
>
> (Holinshed [1587], I, 32)

In that single final phrase anticipating the fall of Rome, Shakespeare is confirmed in his view of the place of pagan Rome in Christian historiography. Having anticipated the time of universal peace in *Antony and Cleopatra,* he brings that moment home to Britain, thwarting the providential Roman peace with the uncertain data that Holinshed presents of a possible conflict between Augustus and Cymbeline. Although most of the chronicler's sources report an uneventful reign—"all nations content to obeie the Romane emperors and consequentlie Britaine" (I, 32)—Holinshed offers Tacitus' account of the British refusal to pay the tribute established with Rome by Cassibellane:

> But whether this controuersie which appeareth to fall forth betwixt the Britans and Augustus, was occasioned by Kymbeline, or some other prince of the Britaines, I haue not to auouch: for that by our writers it is reported, that Kymbeline being brought up in Rome, & knighted in the court of Augustus, euer shewed himselfe a friend to the Romans, & chieflie was loth to breake with them, because the youth of the Britaine nation should not be depriued of the benefit to be trained and brought vp among the Romans, whereby they might learne both to behaue themselues like ciuill men, and to atteine to the knowledge of feats of warre. But whether for this respect, or for that it pleased the almightie God so to dispose the minds of men at that present, not onlie the Britains, but in manner all other nations were contented to be obedient to the Romaine empire.
>
> (I, 33)

Thus the timeless world of romance is pinpointed just at the fullness of time, at the watershed in human history. Given this movement from darkness to light and the providential necessity for universal peace, a war between Rome and Britain is charged with significance. Patriotic sentiments of the earlier English history plays are now voiced by the evil queen and her gross son Cloten, as the insular world of English history must yield. Only with this cosmic consideration can we understand why Shakespeare joyfully ends the play with Britain's agreeing to pay tribute:

> Never was a war did cease,
> Ere bloody hands were washed, with such a peace.
>
> (V. v. 483–484)

War and British pride would now deprive the world of the benefits both of the Vergilian golden age and of divine revelation. Concluding with this climactic consideration, Shakespeare affirms his treatment of Roman history throughout his intellectual life as clearly that of a Christian humanist.

BIBLIOGRAPHY

Harry Morgan Ayres, "Shakespeare's *Julius Caesar* in the Light of Some Other Versions," in *PMLA,* 25 (1910). Thomas W. Baldwin, *William Shakspere's Small Latine and Lesse Greeke,* 2 vols. (1944). J. Leeds Barroll, "Shakespeare and Roman History," in *Modern Language Review,* 53 (1958). John Philip Brockbank, "History and Histrionics in *Cymbeline,*" in *Shakespeare Survey,* 11 (1958). Geoffrey Bullough, ed., *Narrative and Dramatic Sources of Shakespeare,* I, V, VI, VIII (1957–1975). D. J. Gordon, "Name and Fame: Shakespeare's *Coriolanus,*" in George I. Duthie, ed., *Papers Mainly Shakespearian* (1964). Bernard Harris, " 'What's Past Is Prologue': *Cymbeline* and *Henry VIII,*" in John Russell Brown, ed., *Later Shakespeare,* Stratford-upon-Avon Studies, 8 (1966). George K. Hunter, "A Roman Thought: Renaissance Attitudes to History Exemplified in Shakespeare and Jonson," in Brian S. Lee, ed., *An English Miscellany* (1977).

George Wilson Knight, *The Imperial Theme* (1931). Mungo W. MacCallum, *Shakespeare's Roman Plays and Their Background* (1910). J. C. Maxwell, "Shakespeare's Roman Plays: 1900–1956," in *Shakespeare Survey,* 10 (1957). Robert S. Miola, *Shakespeare's Rome* (1983). Robin Moffet, "*Cymbeline* and the Nativity," in *Shakespeare Quarterly,* 13 (1962). Hugh M. Richmond, "Shakespeare's Roman Trilogy: The Climax in *Cymbeline,*" in *Studies in the Literary Imagination,* 5 (1972). Ernest Schanzer, *The Problem Plays of Shakespeare* (1963) and, as ed., *Shakespeare's Appian* (1956). Ethel Seaton, "*Antony and Cleopatra* and the *Book of Revelation,*" in *Review of English Studies,* 22 (1946). J. L. Simmons, *Shakespeare's Pagan World: The Roman Tragedies* (1973) and "Shakespeare and the Antique Romans," in P. A. Ramsey, ed., *Rome in the Renaissance: The City and the Myth* (1982). Alan Sommers, " 'Wilderness of Tigers': Structure and Symbolism in *Titus Andronicus,*" in *Essays in Criticism,* 10 (1960). Terence J. B. Spencer, "Shakespeare and the Elizabethan Romans," in *Shakespeare Survey,* 10 (1957).

John W. Velz, *Shakespeare and the Classical Tradition: A Critical Guide to Commentary, 1660–1960* (1968); "The Ancient World in Shakespeare: Authenticity or Anachronism? A Retrospect," in *Shakespeare Survey,* 31 (1978); and "Cracking Strong Curbs Asunder: Roman Destiny and the Roman Hero in *Coriolanus,*" in *English Literary Renaissance,* 13 (1983). Eugene M. Waith, "The Metamorphosis of Violence in *Titus Andronicus,*" in *Shakespeare Survey,* 10 (1957).

Shakespeare as a Writer of Comedy

DAVID YOUNG

Shakespeare's interest in comedy—in its conventions, characters, traditions, and forms—was both searching and lifelong. Even if we except the late romances as a separate but closely allied genre, we can count thirteen plays, one-third of Shakespeare's canon, as full-fledged experiments with dramatic comedy. When we add to that the recognition that some of Shakespeare's best comic characters and situations lie in other genres—witness Falstaff in the history plays, Mercutio and the Nurse in *Romeo and Juliet,* and the Clown-Gravedigger in *Hamlet*—we can say with assurance that a very substantial portion of Shakespeare's genius was expressed through his achievement as a writer of comedy. While this essay will concentrate on the plays that can be formally designated as comedies, genre was never a significant barrier for Shakespeare; and just as his comedies are sometimes invaded by elements that threaten their generic and tonal consistency, so his comic spirit could and did go a-visiting among his tragedies, histories, and romances.

This essay will trace the development of Shakespearean comedy through a chronological survey of the thirteen plays and then glance briefly at their history of performance and the body of commentary upon them. The chronology is necessarily conjectural at some points, but it seldom departs from that accepted by most modern editors, and when it does, that departure is acknowledged. The comedies fall into three categories: five "early" plays, five "middle" comedies, and three "problem" comedies. The chronological survey will close with

a look toward the late group of four romances, which represent an attempt on Shakespeare's part to subsume comedy (as well as tragedy) in a curious and extravagant new genre that was, in part, a revival of an old one.

The Early Comedies

While Shakespeare's earliest comedy, *The Comedy of Errors* (1592), scarcely matches his mature work in achievement, it tells us a great deal about the comic writer he was to become: for one thing, it mixes a sophisticated, intellectual interest in the genre with a powerful instinct for popular entertainment; in addition, it introduces romance elements that persist as a special interest throughout Shakespeare's career.

Literary theory and educational practice in Shakespeare's time held that writers should imitate classical models. In drama, that meant Roman writers: Seneca in tragedy and Plautus and Terence in comedy. The models are rather dubious in both cases, but Shakespeare dutifully began with them. Just as his first tragedy, *Titus Andronicus,* out-Senecas Seneca, so *The Comedy of Errors* out-Plautuses Plautus. To a typical Plautine plot of mistaken identity based on a set of twins, Shakespeare added a second pair, thus doubling the ensuing complications. He recognized that Plautus' plays were largely farces, fast-paced and physical, and he shaped *The Comedy of Errors* accordingly, with minimal characterization or verbal humor and maximum comedy of situation and action, including the comic beatings time-honored by the term *slapstick*. The result was a play that still holds the stage as robust and agile entertainment; the playwright gets good marks for theory—he even observes the "classical" unities of time, place, and action—and manages to succeed in practice, though in a narrow vein. Apparently, one exercise in strict Plautine comedy proved to Shakespeare that he could imitate the ancients closely and that he did not particularly care to observe such boundaries in future.

Other models, as it happened, were at hand. Earlier playwrights like John Lyly, Robert Greene, and George Peele had already gone beyond the limited recipe of Roman comedy in their use of myth, folklore, and romance elements. And the Italians—both in their popular theater, the commedia dell' arte, and in their literary efforts at comedy—had modified the classical comedy of intrigue with some success. Shakespeare's next comedies, *The Two Gentlemen of Verona* (1593) and *The Taming of the Shrew* (1593), reflect a clear-cut desire to expand the scope and scale of his comedy, again with a watchful eye on precedents. Whichever came first, *Two Gentlemen* is clearly the less successful. It uses the fashionable conflict between love and friendship to set out the story of two pairs of lovers. Its Italian setting, its use of disguise and intrigue, and its emphasis on romantic love, courtship, and marriage all suggest that Shakespeare was working from more recent models, though with mixed results. There are some successful scenes for the lovers (Julia, Valentine, Proteus, and Sylvia), one lovely song, and attractive set pieces for the clown Launce and his dog, but a sense that the playwright is finding his way and is not fully in control of his material is inescapable. The conclusion is rushed and confusing, and the sense of missed opportunities in the characterizations comes not so much from the greater success of Shakespeare's immediate predecessors as from his own later improvements with similar sets of characters and comparable plots. *The Comedy of Errors* may be more successful onstage, but *The Two Gentlemen of Verona* is the truer prototype, however crude, of Shakespearean comedy to come.

A word about the terms *romantic* and *romance elements* might be useful at this point. When we say that Shakespeare began writing romantic comedy after *The Comedy of Errors*, we refer to the fact that love, courtship, and marriage form the primary emphasis of his plots. However, to say that these plots have romance elements is to point to their use of conventions from the romance, the typical narrative form of the period. The romance features fantastic events and extravagant adventures leading to a happy ending. It has many branches: when it deals with the doings of knights-errant, for instance, it is called chivalric romance, while stories that involve shepherds and other rural characters are called pastoral romance. Shakespeare's interest in this strain of literature is evident in *The Comedy of Errors*, which he frames with the story of a family separated for many years by shipwreck and miraculously reunited, and in *The Two Gentlemen of Verona*, in which the hero lives in the woods as head of a band of outlaws until the intrigues and complications of the plot have been sorted out. Both plot features are typical of literary romance as Shakespeare and his audience knew it, on the stage and, more particularly, in prose and poetic narratives.

The Taming of the Shrew is as self-conscious a hybrid as anyone could wish for. To a farcical plot about wife-taming in a hearty native tradition, Shakespeare adds an Italianate plot about courtship and marriage engineered by intrigue. The story of Kate and Petruchio is English and, one might argue, rather medieval. It reminds us of folktales and of the little Tudor farces called interludes. The story of how Lucentio outsmarts his rival wooers and wins the hand of Bianca is Italianate and, by extension, neoclassical. The mixture works—the success of this play can be partly measured by the fact that it still performs well and is revived frequently to some extent because Shakespeare is not content to let his sources define their own limitations: the two plots complement each other more effectively than anyone might expect, and the more primitive one, the wife-taming story with its misogynist and slapstick tendencies, turns out to be the source of the most interesting characterizations. Kate and Petruchio learn to form a partnership of inspired foolery, which makes them superior sensibilities in a world that is largely ignorant of its own absurdity and folly.

If we had any doubts about this play's self-conscious experimentation with sources and conventions, they would be erased by its Induction, in which a drunkard, who has no idea what a comedy is (nor any other kind of play but the crudest kind of holiday entertainment—"a Christmas gambol or a tumbling-trick"), is hoaxed into thinking himself a lord and shown the subsequent mix of sophistication and broad fooling for his entertainment. The lordly peasant or peasantly lord, as the emblematic audience, makes the point nicely: *The Taming of the Shrew* is a play that spans the tastes of society and that subsumes a wide variety of possibilities for stage comedy.

Love's Labor's Lost (1594) could not have been predicted from its predecessors. While it continues in the vein of romantic subject matter (that is, the doings of lovers), it deemphasizes temporal plot interest in favor of a spatial structure—rather like a large picture with a complex and pleasing composition—that affords pleasurable relationships and a variety of verbal humor, heightened through our sense of the design. John Lyly's comedies form a sort of precedent, but there really had been nothing like this play, with its complex mirrorings and exuberant wordplay, in English or any other literature. Its notion that human folly can be identified and expressed through the use and misuse of language is familiar to comedy, but it is pursued with a delight and gusto that remind us that Shakespeare is not only our greatest playwright but our greatest poet. Some of the verbal humor is rather youthful (puns, learned allusions, in-jokes), and the fashions that are satirized are often so dated as to mystify modern readers, but our sense of the author's flowering genius, of his hitting his stride, is unmistakable. Modern scholarship has explored this play's richness and depth, and while good modern productions have been rare, the best of them have demonstrated that *Love's Labor's Lost* can be both hugely funny and oddly touching.

For the student of Shakespearean dramaturgy, this play's ending must afford exceptional interest, since it poses the question of comedy's adequacy as a genre at a remarkably early stage of Shakespeare's career. The lovers, four couples, are paired off and entertained by a ridiculous pageant staged by the clowns, but the harmonious closure is disrupted by the news of the death of the King and by the women's sensible imposition of a time period (one year) to test the men's newfound maturity. Full comic closure is thus deflected, and the play ends with two beautiful songs that remind us of a reality rather different from the semiutopian one of privilege and festivity we have been seeing. The conclusion would seem to be that Shakespeare had found the kind of comedy that most pleased him and at the same time was willing to point to its inevitable limitations—a remarkable conjunction in most authors but not, in fact, untypical of this one.

The movement away from temporal plot and to-ward a comic design based more on relationships and rebounding reflections, spatially perceived, is fully realized by the last play in this early group, *A Midsummer Night's Dream* (1595), a favorite for production and a perfect example, in its own way, of the author's comic genius. It integrates an enormous variety of materials, many of them thought to be incompatible, into a remarkably harmonious whole. Myth and folklore are brought together in a way that forces our recognition of their kinship, a concept now widely understood but new to Elizabethans. For them, the idea that the Celtic fairies and figures from popular lore like Robin Goodfellow should have anything in common with characters named Theseus and Titania must have been strange and wonderful. Shakespeare sets the play in a mythic Athens and a nearby wood, but he makes this world emphatically English by invoking two well-known holidays—May Day and Midsummer Eve—and by peopling his group of clowns with familiar figures from the workaday world of carpenters, weavers, tinkers, tailors, and bellows-menders. The play's deliberate mixing of homely and exotic is nowhere better illustrated than in the hilarious one-night love affair of Bottom the Weaver, one of Shakespeare's best comic creations, and Titania, queen of the fairies and victim of a love potion. Their unlikely relationship is representative of the marriages of disparate elements that abound throughout the play.

Shakespeare keeps this potentially chaotic mixture coherent by dividing the characters into four distinct groups—the Greek court of Theseus and Hippolyta; the four lovers who spend a night of confusion in the woods; the fairy court where another king and queen are engaged in a squabble over a changeling boy; and the group of workingmen who are rehearsing a play in honor of Theseus' wedding. All the groups interact at some point, but by keeping a clear sense of their separate adventures, we are able to take in the majesty and symmetry of the play's grand design. Once again, as in *Love's Labor's Lost*, temporal plot is minimized in favor of a vast, complicated, and balanced design. Meaning is clarified and laughter is provoked by the careful echoing of situations and relationships as each group's experience reflects the others', often in surprising ways.

Many of these reflections converge near the play's end, in the hilarious play-within-a-play that the clowns perform before the three newly married couples. The fairies reenter to perform a ritual blessing, after everyone has gone to bed, and Puck, the prankster who has played court jester to Oberon, the fairy king, speaks an epilogue in which he invites us, if we have disliked the play, to dismiss it as a dream. Serious issues, we begin to realize, have lain barely hidden beneath the play's enchanting surface: they have to do with the value of art and the nature of the imagination, with myth and ritual, and with the human relation to nature. Shakespeare's confidence in the power and meaning of his art, in its ability to synthesize diverse materials and to reflect many aspects of reality simultaneously, is evident in the spirit of the play at every turn, as well as in the implicit defense of poetry and imagination provided by the characters' attempts to define imagination and produce art. The perspectives we enjoy, which are denied to them, suggest a beauty and continuity in human life that is hard to perceive without the Olympian perspectives that great comedy can afford. A relatively youthful masterpiece—Shakespeare was just over thirty when he wrote it—*A Midsummer Night's Dream* is a play that readers and spectators can return to again and again without exhausting its potential or unraveling its mysteries completely. It is clearly a culmination of Shakespeare's interest in inventing a form of dramatic comedy that could be capacious, lyrical, and pleasingly complex. That it has no single source helps qualify the trite observation that Shakespeare always took his plots from other writers: the point is more that he was teaching himself what he could do by borrowing from and successfully integrating as wide a variety of potentially comic devices and materials as he could discover. His audience was mixed, his period and his medium encouraged eclecticism, and he himself enjoyed diversity to a remarkable extent. Two lines from one of his sonnets characterize his distinctive artistic sensibility:

> What is your substance, whereof are you made,
> That millions of strange shadows on you tend?

> (Sonnet 53, 1–2)

The Middle Comedies

The next group of comedies is so diverse that it is difficult to generalize about them. They clearly represent a series of considered experiments in comedy, some risky, some astonishingly successful.

What seems to separate them from the early group is a greater interest in the possibilities of dramatic characterization. Delightful as characters like Bottom and Puck and the four lovers may be, *A Midsummer Night's Dream,* while perfect as a play of its kind, cannot be said to have characterizations of depth or complexity: the demands of its manifold design and orchestrated harmonies simply do not allow for them. Shakespeare may or may not have considered that a limitation; what is clear from the next group of comedies is that he set himself the task of more complex characterizations, with results that are both problematic and exhilarating.

The Merchant of Venice (1596), while it follows *Dream* by only a year or so, has a very different feel and tone, if only because of Shylock. Set in Europe's most cosmopolitan city, it centers on a plot with values that seem clear enough: we are to sympathize with the love-and-friendship conflict, root for the lovers (Bassanio and Portia, Lorenzo and Jessica, Gratiano and Nerissa), admire Portia's cleverness at resolving the plot, and despise the comic villain and scapegoat Shylock. Yet there is something unsettling about this apparently clear-cut design: the casket story, in which three suitors vie to win Portia in an extremely predictable pattern, coexists rather uneasily with the sophisticated characters and cosmopolitan world of the play. The same may be said for the tale of the usurer demanding his pound of flesh and being tricked in court by a fine legal point that also illustrates the Christian value of forgiveness. We may decide, as many readers and commentators have, that Shakespeare simply chose (or had presented to him in a play he was to revise) plot situations that failed to do justice to the interest and complexity of the characters, but it is also worth considering that the discrepancies are deliberate, intended to provoke thought and even discomfort. The issue of anti-Semitism so clouds this play for many readers that they make it an overwhelming problem, but anti-Semitism in Shakespeare's England was such a different phenomenon from what it is in the modern world that it is manifestly unfair to impose our feelings about that particular prejudice on Shakespeare's play. The fact remains that Shylock is an unsettling figure and that he refuses to fit neatly, with his vengeful ways and his ability to feel deeply, into the category of comic scapegoat. The threat to design that is posed by complex characterization may or may not be adequately answered in *Merchant*—many ingenious interpretations have been offered to make us feel that the play's parts fit together in a whole that is a successful comic undertaking of a high order—but its presence is undeniable, and it is not just Shylock who threatens to grow beyond the configurations of plot, but Portia, Bassanio, Antonio, and Jessica as well. Despite its controversial status, the play is frequently produced, usually with a sentimentalized Shylock, and much discussed by critical interpreters. If not altogether successful as a "middle" comedy, it certainly ushers in the new phase with a sense of dramatic risk and an unmistakable change of direction and emphasis.

One other character in *Merchant* deserves special notice: Portia. She is the first of a series of Shakespearean comic heroines notable for intelligence, courage, and ability to control the action. Julia and Sylvia in *Two Gentlemen* were more admirable than the men who loved them, and we have noted that it is the women who impose a commonsense solution in *Love's Labor's Lost.* From these prefigurings, Portia emerges as a high-spirited and attractive heroine, the only character capable of outwitting Shylock and engineering a happy ending. Moreover, her house at Belmont becomes, especially in the lyrical last act, an alternative to the Venetian world of commerce and litigation. In her values, her wit, and her successful transition from passive object to active disguiser and rescuer, Portia would seem to be the true center of the play.

The comedy that probably comes next in chronology is *The Merry Wives of Windsor,* written around 1597 and revised about 1600. It is a hearty, often hilarious play, built along the lines of Italian comedy of intrigue but thoroughly naturalized to its English setting, Windsor and its environs. It is, in fact, the only play by Shakespeare that can be claimed to have the England of his own time as its setting. Theoretically set in the fifteenth century, since Falstaff is supposed to be a contemporary of Henry V, the England of *Merry Wives* was, in fact, extremely contemporary to its audience; it has a higher degree of social realism than anything else Shakespeare wrote. We have a particularly strong sense of the rising middle class of Elizabeth's time, its vigor, its values, and its problems.

The contemporaneity of *Merry Wives* is somewhat anomalous in Shakespearean comedy. His talented fellow dramatists who wrote comedy—Jonson, Middleton, Dekker, Marston—were increasingly drawn to realistic portrayals of life in the England of their audience, particularly London life in the so-called city comedies. But Shakespeare, after this single foray in that direction, returned to more fanciful and foreign settings, in regard to both time and place, a preference that the late romances would make emphatic.

The Merry Wives of Windsor has been somewhat neglected, on two counts: it seems mainly farcical and slapdash in a period when Shakespeare's drama was generally deepening and growing more subtle; and its main character, Falstaff, has been considered a disappointment, a shadow of his attractive self in the history plays. Tradition has held—and there seems no great reason to discount it—that Queen Elizabeth had expressed a desire to see Falstaff in love, and that Shakespeare had adapted a play about a rascal who gets his comeuppance from some women he is trying to seduce, with Falstaff forced, willy-nilly, into the part.

The truth of the matter, though, is rather more complex. Falstaff shares with Shylock the status of comic scapegoat, a role he had already undertaken in the *Henry IV* plays, particularly the second one, where he is emphatically rejected by his old friend, Prince Hal, now Henry V. In a real sense, his comic and dramatic disadvantages in *Merry Wives* are less costly than either Shylock's in *Merchant* or his own in the history cycle, where his rejection leads ultimately to his death. In *Merry Wives* the old rapscallion proves remarkably resilient: he is hidden in a basket of dirty laundry, thrown into the Thames, disguised as an old woman and beaten, and then, in the last act in Windsor Forest, dressed up in antlers and pinched, singed, and beaten by a group of children disguised as fairies. He rises from that final humiliation to regain his good humor and to be invited to a feast with the other characters. An emphatic comic conclusion seems to be made possible by all the practical joking and intrigue that have preceded it. The test of this play, as of all Shakespearean texts, lies in performance, and recent revivals have shown it to be very successful theater. If it lacks some of the poetry that Shakespearean comedy acquired in this period, it remains a fascinating portrait of life and manners in Shakespeare's time, a wonderful gallery of comic characters (at least a dozen of them), and an expertly plotted farce that rises to moments of poignancy and, more often, sheer hilarity. As for the trend to attractive comic heroines, while no one to match Portia is found here, the female characters, particularly Mistress Page and Mistress Ford, who conspire to hoax Falstaff in revenge for his amorous presumption and who manage to cure Mistress Ford's husband of his obsessive jealousy in the bargain, are the most sensible and capable people in the play. The men squabble and suffer from various forms of irrationality and pretension; the women seem to embody the comic spirit.

The next three plays, *Much Ado About Nothing, As You Like It,* and *Twelfth Night,* are (along with, perhaps, *A Midsummer Night's Dream*) Shakespeare's most universally admired comedies. That does not mean, however, that they have not posed problems of interpretation to commentators and performers. The structure of *Much Ado* (1598), for example, was long thought to be a weakness, a joining of a near-tragic and highly conventional "main plot" involving a marriage prevented by slander with a highly original "subplot" in which two attractive characters, Beatrice and Benedick, engage in wit-combats and arguments until they are tricked into falling in love. We have come more recently to understand that the design of the play is as integrated and successful as anything Shakespeare wrote, so that critical understanding has finally verified what performance had already testified to: that the play is wonderfully put together.

Much Ado is set in Messina, in a world of glamorous Italians and Spaniards, and the "nothing" of the title also refers, by a pun more evident in Elizabethan pronunciation, to "noting," the practice of overhearing and eavesdropping. Indeed, it is a world of appearances and mistakes, some of them serious, some hilarious; deception is used both for good ends, as in the matchmaking contrived for Beatrice and Benedick, and for bad ends, in the trick that slanders Hero, which is set up by the villain Don John (a comic scapegoat we have no trouble dismissing or disliking). All the denizens of this world are capable of folly through misjudging appearances, and it is indicative of the universality of their limitations that the slanderous plot is uncovered by accident through the clowns. Dogberry, one of Shakespeare's funniest creations, is the chief law-enforcement officer in Messina, and he has no more notion of how he is detecting wrongdoing and bringing the play to a happy conclusion than he does of his own consummate vanity and stupidity.

Like *Merchant,* and perhaps more deliberately so, *Much Ado* risks its own generic consistency by swinging close to irreparable loss and thus to tragedy, a swing that the play requires a good deal of ingenuity and momentum to recover from. The effect, especially in a strong production, is to make us cherish more fully the comic closure and sense of harmony at the end: the precariousness of such reassuring feelings has been demonstrated along the way. Some commentators have found it intolerable that Claudio should be reunited with Hero after believing a flimsy slander and rejecting her in public on their wedding day, but this is to ask more of these characters than we are meant to; their very conventionality and superficiality have been part of the point. And the limitations of Claudio and Hero have in turn, and by design, taught us how to value Beatrice and Benedick.

Beatrice is another especially attractive Shakespearean comic heroine, a complex and quick-witted woman in danger of remaining unmarried because there are no men who can hold a candle to her, except Benedick, her apparent enemy and a determined bachelor, "a professed tyrant" to the female sex. We sense almost immediately that this fascinating couple should, by the laws of comedy and of human nature, be brought together, but in its own way that proves as precarious as the reuniting of Hero and Claudio on a more mundane level. The point about Beatrice and Benedick is that their happiness is blocked not by the villainy and folly of others but by elements in their own makeup that prevent them from assenting to their own happiness. The psychological truth that lies at the heart of this deeply funny and strangely moving story is one that we can recognize and refer to our own experience. But the impulse to isolate Beatrice and Benedick was and is mistaken; they take their meaning from the less complex characters and more conventional situations that surround them.

If ideas like "main plot" and "subplot" are not especially adequate for describing the world and design of *Much Ado,* we can certainly admit that the play moves forward by virtue of complicated intrigue and a certain degree of dramatic suspense. The same cannot be said of *As You Like It* (1599), for its deemphasis on plot in no way detracts from our sense of the comedy's success. Like *Love's Labor's Lost, As You Like It* moves at a leisurely pace, exhibiting a dazzling array of verbal styles, and characters to go with them, without depending on the unraveling of intricacies and intrigues or suspense about the outcome. It takes place mostly within a sequestered world, where characters who supposedly suffer social alienation and exile are in fact released from social roles and responsibilities to a sense of festivity that encourages love and courtship, along with other forms of pleasure: singing, hunting, feasting, foolery, and friendly debates. All this is made possible, or is at least facilitated, by Shakespeare's use of pastoral romance. (The play adapts a contemporary pastoral novel by Thomas Lodge.) In such a genre, rural settings and situations are the backdrop for love games and leisurely courtship. A typical plot structure moves a group of characters to temporary exile in a rural setting while the society they have left behind sorts out its injustices. The song in the second act reflects the pastoral mood:

> Who doth ambition shun
>   And loves to live i' th' sun,
> Seeking the food he eats,
>   And pleased with what he gets,
> Come hither, come hither, come hither.
>   Here shall he see no enemy
> But winter and rough weather.

(II. v. 33–39)

A Midsummer Night's Dream and *The Two Gentlemen of Verona* both glanced at this pattern, but the Forest of Arden in *As You Like It* is Shakespeare's first full-blown pastoral setting, just as the "plot" of the play is his first full use of the conventions and preoccupations of pastoral romance.

Rosalind and Orlando fall in love early in the play. The obstacles to their happiness are of the most transparent and artificial sort, but the combination of Arden, where social barriers are relaxed, and Rosalind's disguise as a boy allows her to test Orlando's love and her own by staging a practice courtship in which the conventions of love are explored and teased in an enchanting fashion. Masquerading as a young shepherd, she suggests to Orlando that his passion for Rosalind is a sickness she can cure, if he will pretend she is Rosalind and will practice wooing her. The results are touching and hilarious, as Rosalind argues against her own feelings, lapsing in and out of lovesickness as she takes off and puts on her persona.

Rosalind may be the greatest and most fully realized of Shakespeare's extraordinary comic heroines. This is partly because her disguise allows her to explore both male and female viewpoints and, often, quite contrary feelings, and partly because the play's characters act as foils to her (and each other): Orlando, the naive, eager lover; her friend Celia, the amused witness of her courtship; Jaques, the professional melancholic and satirist, who wanders around the forest moralizing; her father,

the exiled Duke, who finds "tongues in trees, books in the running brooks, / Sermons in stones, and good in everything"; and most of all, the fool Touchstone, mock courtier, mock lover, mirror of every folly he encounters, a character who, like the forest, seems to be everything and nothing. Just as the design of *Much Ado* affords maximum interest in and appreciation of Beatrice and Benedick, so the design of *As You Like It* is for Rosalind like the setting for a jewel in which we cannot tell what we admire most—the jewel itself or the setting that surrounds it. Or, to make the metaphor more organic (and to borrow from Yeats), we cannot tell the dancer from the dance.

As You Like It is crowned by one of Shakespeare's fullest and most satisfactory comic resolutions. The two villains are converted to goodness, the exiles are restored to power and position, and a group of marriages is performed and celebrated in the forest, engineered by Rosalind, and all made possible by her transformation from "Ganymede" back to Rosalind. The actress who plays Rosalind speaks an epilogue that made full sense only in Shakespeare's theater, where boys played the women's parts: this woman, who was disguised as a boy, was a boy actor playing a woman. The epilogue—"If I were a woman, I would kiss as many of you as had beards that pleased me, complexions that liked me, and breaths that I defied not"— reminds us of the remarkable illusion by which we have been enchanted. We are listening to an artist at the height of his powers, speaking in the full confidence of his art. Shakespeare's restlessness would prevent him from writing another pastoral comedy as such (though not from further experiments with pastoral), but *As You Like It* shows how fully and satisfyingly his comic genius could be displayed while adapting a favorite Renaissance mode to the genre of stage comedy. The play's delight in language and in design links it firmly with *Love's Labor's Lost* and *A Midsummer Night's Dream* as comedy of a distinctive sort, short on plot but long on wit, dazzling with rebounding reflections, and, in the case of this play especially, delightful in the range and depth of its characterizations.

With *Twelfth Night* (1601), the final member of this group, we have a play that in many ways seems to recapitulate what Shakespeare had accomplished in comedy thus far. The twins and their shipwreck take us all the way back to *The Comedy of Errors* (as well as providing a glance forward to the romances). Its special setting, a dukedom called Illyria, recalls the festive and sequestered locales of the group mentioned above, as does its gallery of comic characters and its witty stylistic turns. The disguised heroine continues an experiment begun in *Two Gentlemen* and furthered in *The Merchant of Venice* and *As You Like It*. The plot against the comic scapegoat Malvolio represents a possibility explored in *Merchant* and *Merry Wives,* among others. *Twelfth Night* can also be said to foreshadow later developments: its somewhat more somber tone suggests the dark hues of the problem comedies to come.

Twelfth Night presents a world of opulence, eloquence, and folly. Duke Orsino is in love with Olivia, but passively so, more enchanted with the style of his passion than with its requital. Olivia is in turn cocooned in extravagant mourning for her dead brother. Their elegant follies, forms of self-love and self-indulgence, are comically mirrored in the helpless egotism of Sir Andrew Aguecheek, the drunkenness of Sir Toby Belch, and, most of all, the vanity and selfishness of Malvolio, Olivia's steward and would-be husband. The traits and behaviors of foolish characters are directly reflected, as in *As You Like It,* by the fool, Feste, who wanders back and forth between Orsino's and Olivia's households, entertaining the inhabitants with jokes and songs and mirroring their follies in ways they fail to understand.

The self-absorption of this world is resolved by Viola, who arrives as the result of a shipwreck. She disguises herself as a man in order to serve Orsino, falls in love with him, and in turn arouses the love of Olivia, whom she visits on Orsino's behalf. The hopeless triangle is rearranged by the arrival of Viola's twin brother, Sebastian, who is paired with Olivia in the comic finale, and whose resemblance to the disguised Viola causes some comic and pathetic moments of mistaken identity.

One marvelous aspect of the mature Shakespeare is the sheer amount of material he is able to include without destroying the unity and coherence of his comedies. While all the above is going on, an elaborate comic intrigue is being conducted against Malvolio, who is persuaded by a forged letter that Olivia is in love with him. This line of action moves from one of the funniest scenes Shakespeare ever wrote, to one that mixes humor and pathos, to one that is fairly distressing, so that the comedy modulates before our eyes from delight at a practical joke to second thoughts about its painful consequences. We worry, finally, about Malvolio's health and well being, and we take his side. His refusal to join in the harmonious conclusion—he exits vowing revenge—is as emphatic as Shylock's punishment, without the opportunity that *Merchant* affords of a fifth act in which we put the unpleasantness behind us.

The strange tone that Malvolio's story gives to *Twelfth Night* has been seen as a miscalculation on Shakespeare's part. But when we are given full details of a character's inner life—Malvolio recounts his daydreams to us with embarrassing intimacy—we cannot simply dismiss him from our sympathies. It seems more likely that Shakespeare wished to produce a disquieting ending, an implicit critique of the genre he was exploiting so fully, as he had done, in quite different ways, in several of the earlier comedies. This intention is confirmed by the beautiful song with which Feste closes the play, especially its refrain, "For the rain it raineth every day," reminding us that the world beyond the theater does not afford the protection against weather, time, and circumstance that we have seen in the play. Drawing a clear line between art and reality may constitute an implicit critique of either or both, but it also tends to enhance our appreciation of the privileges we have enjoyed for the duration of the performance. Such graceful farewells are often among the most exquisite touches in Shakespeare's dramatic writing.

And what about Viola? Does she rival Rosalind in our affections? Certainly she is the sane and sympathetic center of this whirligig, a character whom we can wholly like and admire. But *Twelfth Night* cultivates a remarkable distribution of interest— and sympathy—among its characters, rather in the manner of a Chekhov play. Sometimes Viola has been the star in a production, sometimes Malvolio, sometimes even Aguecheek, but the play is best served when played as an ensemble piece, where Viola suffers no detraction because so many other characters interest and attract us, too. Mellow, rich, full of fun and food for thought, *Twelfth Night* is, many would argue, Shakespeare's finest comedy.

The Problem Comedies

The differences between this group of comedies and the ones that precede it have probably been exaggerated. Shakespeare did not drastically alter his view of comedy between 1601 and 1602, and, as earlier remarks have suggested, his treatment of comic form and comic convention was seldom without its problematic aspects in the earlier plays. Nevertheless, the "problem" plays have a sophistication, a willingness to unsettle and challenge us, that appears to mark a new phase in Shakespeare's development as a writer of comedy. They may also help us understand his ultimate decision to abandon comedy in favor of dramatic romance. The order of discussion will differ slightly from the accepted chronology, which usually dates the three problem comedies as follows: *Troilus and Cressida*, 1602; *All's Well That Ends Well*, 1603; *Measure for Measure*, 1604. This order will be reversed in discussing *All's Well* and *Measure for Measure*.

Troilus and Cressida must surely be one of the strangest plays in the Shakespeare canon. Its title suggests a love story with a tragic ending (compare *Romeo and Juliet*, *Antony and Cleopatra*), and it has sometimes been taken and played on those terms. Yet it also seems clear that we must use terms like "satiric" and "mock-heroic" to describe its events and atmosphere. It was written during a vogue for harsh satire in verse and in drama, and it appears to be Shakespeare's one excursion into this realm. It also bears marks of being a coterie play, that is, one written for a smaller and more educated audience than that of the public playhouse, an audience with rarefied and somewhat decadent tastes. Other Shakespearean plays have been seen in these terms: *Love's Labor's Lost* has seemed to many readers to be full of private jokes for a select group, and *A Midsummer Night's Dream* is widely thought to have been written as a commission for aristocratic wedding festivities. But these plays were probably fully accessible to the larger public audience at the Globe, whereas *Troilus and Cressida* feels as though it carries some of the limitations of coterie tastes and interests in the form in which it has come to us. Its first "problem," then, might be said to be its distinctiveness, in tone and focus, from the rest of Shakespeare's comedies, which ceases to be a problem as soon as we accept the play on its own terms.

Because the love story of *Troilus and Cressida* had grown up in the Middle Ages and was attached to the events of *The Iliad*, it provides opportunities to satirize both the Homeric world and the medieval traditions of chivalric virtue and courtly love. To both these time-honored literary predecessors, Shakespeare, in his sardonic treatment of the story, is fairly merciless. The courtly lovers are mismatched and, for quite different reasons, unable to represent the ideals that supposedly define them.

The Homeric heroes are variously pompous, stupid, scheming, and disoriented. Strength is reduced to bullying, love to sensual indulgence, intelligence to manipulative cunning, generosity to self-interest in disguise, friendship and kinship to prurience and deceit. Images of venereal disease and bodily disorders riddle the language. The play begins with a florid and belligerent prologue ("Like or find fault; / do as your pleasures are: / Now good or bad, 'tis but the chance of war") and closes with Pandarus, the voyeuristic go-between, promising to bequeath his diseases to the audience.

For all its harsh and reductive images of human heroism and idealism, *Troilus and Cressida* must also be credited with a high intellectual content and an ambitious dramatic design. The war councils in the Greek and Trojan camps deal in lofty theoretical issues (though they come to nothing in practice), and while Ulysses is the play's primary philosopher, everyone has analytical tendencies, even the passionate Troilus, the loutish Achilles, and the "deformed and scurrilous" fool Thersites. The plot covers crucial events in the Trojan war—the death of Patroclus, Achilles' return to battle, and the killing of Hector—as well as the courtship, consummation, and dissolution of the love of Troilus and Cressida. The double setting, the shifts of tone, the complicated plot and interplay of philosophical concepts make the play extremely challenging to read or watch, and though it has tended to inspire respect rather than affection, it remains one of Shakespeare's most curious and revealing experiments.

The generic dubiousness of *Troilus and Cressida* —the editors of the First Folio placed it between the tragedies and the histories—stems from its lack of merriment, its failure to produce a harmonious closure or a restored society, and its use of tragic plot materials. As Northrop Frye (1949) has suggested, we expect a comic world to show itself capable of renewal, usually through love and marriage with their implicit promise of new generations, and the replenishment of the social microcosm. Many commentators see *Troilus and Cressida* as a comedy only by default: its characters and situations lack tragic stature and its harsh satiric tone allies it to the comic vision rather than the tragic. Perhaps it can be thought of as comic without being a full-fledged comedy, though we need to remember that the satiric vision of love and heroism, the insistence on what is problematic in human nature, is never wholly absent from the

Shakespearean comedies. The man who created Shylock and Malvolio, who set loose the satirist Jaques and the biting clown Touchstone in the forest of Arden, who invented the seamy, realistic world of Falstaff, was perfectly capable of pursuing such possibilities as far and as fully as they are pursued in *Troilus and Cressida.*

With *Measure for Measure* (1603–1604), we come to a play that has attracted much attention and a number of productions in recent years. If the play has seemed beset by problems in structure, tone, and characterization, it has also been recognized as rich, powerful, and compelling. Its urban setting is our first hint of its departure from Shakespeare's comic norm. There had, of course, been city settings (Venice, Padua, Messina) in previous plays, but the Vienna of *Measure for Measure* is an extremely problematic world for a comedy, with its brothels, prisons, convents, taverns, and law courts; it is a social microcosm struggling with issues of justice and order, without a great deal of success. The story that Shakespeare tells, against the background of this unsettled and unsettling society, is the familiar one (in his time and earlier) of the ruler who disappears and returns in disguise to walk in the streets and reestablish contact with ordinary people. The motives of the ruler and the beneficent results of such a plot are usually unquestioned in such stories, but Shakespeare manages things so that, even while we watch Duke Vincentio, disguised as a friar, guide the action to a harmonious conclusion, his own motives seem questionable, his skill intermittent, and the grand conclusion he arranges a piece of stage-managing we have difficulty assenting to, at least in its entirety. The resulting play seems to come even closer to a deliberate mixture of tragic and comic than do *Merchant* or *Much Ado;* without the intervention of the disguised Duke, irrevocable acts, including an unjust execution, would certainly destroy the comic potential. But it is not just a tension pitting the corrupt world of Vienna against the beneficent plotting of the Duke. The Duke's plot itself contains contrary possibilities, and we view him with a scrutiny we seldom give to comic heroes and their situations.

The potential tragedy centers on the behavior of Angelo, the apparently saintly but rather puritanical judge whom the Duke leaves in charge of the city, ostensibly with orders to conduct a cleanup that will also serve, apparently, as a test of character. When Angelo condemns Claudio to death because his fiancée is pregnant, Claudio's sister Isabella emerges from a convent she is about to join in order to plead for clemency. Her pleas fire Angelo's lust, and he proposes an exchange of her virginity for her brother's life. Her refusal leads to a scene in which Claudio breaks down and begs her for his life while she berates him harshly. At this point, Angelo's villainy, Isabella's priggishness ("More than our brother is our chastity"), Claudio's cowardice, and Duke Vincentio's evasion of his responsibilities as ruler all threaten to pull the play into chaos or tragedy, and we are relieved to see the Duke, still in disguise, take matters in hand. What he arranges, however, if it guarantees a comic ending, is equivocal as a moral solution: Mariana, whom Angelo jilted years before, is to sleep with him in Isabella's place, and this "bed-trick" will presumably save Claudio's life and right the wrong done to Mariana by forcing Angelo into marriage. The scheme threatens to backfire when Angelo, fearing revenge, orders Claudio's death anyway; hasty improvisation, aided by coincidence, is required to save the situation. The play then moves to a grand scene of revelation and comeuppance that is unsettling partly because it is overdone. Vincentio manages to right most of the wrongs, but since he never takes responsibility for anything and startles us by suddenly proposing marriage to Isabella, the questions about his motivation and goodness remain. Some Shakespearean comedies swing toward a tragic potential before achieving comic closure, and others remind us that harmonious resolutions are costly to plausibility and artificial when compared with life. But *Measure for Measure* goes further in posing questions and problems than any previous Shakespearean comedy, excepting *Troilus and Cressida* as a special case. We are pleased when the play turns toward a resolution of the dire consequences toward which it has drifted, and we are moved by the resolutions at the close—Angelo's forgiveness, Isabella's reunion with the brother she thought dead—but we are also unsettled and puzzled by our mixed response, and the trend of productions and commentaries has been to see the raising of questions as a strength of the play rather than a flaw.

Certainly *Measure for Measure* allows for strong and interesting characterizations. Comic characters usually do not change, but this plot can be seen as a journey to self-discovery for most of the major characters. Angelo finds that he harbors much more potential for evil than he thought possible. Isabella, at the beginning an atypical Shakespearean comic heroine in her relative naiveté and selfishness, learns to face the world and use her considerable powers for the good of others, while the Duke, we would like to infer, learns more about the relation between power and responsibility and emerges from an isolation and desire for unsullied perfection that are as unsuitable for him as they were for Angelo and Isabella. If *Measure for Measure* strains against the limitations of comic form, it does so productively, to the enhancement of characterizations and the enriching of the play's dark, mysterious, and manifold world. Because its view of human nature is uncompromisingly realistic—"They say best men are moulded out of faults," Mariana argues as she pleads for Angelo's life and Isabella's forgiveness of him—it cannot provide full reassurance through comic form. The recognition that comedy is relative to our chosen emphasis is in fact directly alluded to by Isabella in the very plea that arouses Angelo's lust for her:

> But man, proud man,
> Dressed in a little brief authority,
> Most ignorant of what he's most assured—
> His glassy essence—like an angry ape
> Plays such fantastic tricks before high heaven
> As makes the angels weep; who, with our spleens,
> Would all themselves laugh mortal.
>
> (II. ii. 117–123)

It is our difference from the angels that allows us to laugh at human folly. This is not a total repudiation of comedy, but it is a far cry from the Olympian comfort ("Lord, what fools these mortals be") of *A Midsummer Night's Dream,* and a rather grimly realistic view of comedy's limited place in the total scheme of human experience and understanding.

An employment of comic form that calls attention to its relativity and limitation is also characteristic of *All's Well That Ends Well* (1603–1604). That play has been placed last in this discussion because its greater use of magic and fantasy points the direction that Shakespeare's work was to take in the romances. As are those later plays, *All's Well* is an extremely sophisticated telling of a fairly primitive tale. Helena loves Bertram, who is far above her socially. Through a medicine inherited from her father, an uncannily skillful physician, she is able to cure the hopelessly ailing King of France. Her virginity and the power of her goodness seem somehow bound up with the efficacy of the cure. Her reward is to choose any husband she wishes,

but Bertram, when she chooses him, first refuses and then, after being forced into marriage, runs away to war, leaving her with a seemingly impossible charge: to get a ring from his finger and to prove that she is with child by him. As the folktale conventions lead us to expect, she does just that, using another "bed-trick" to substitute herself for a woman whom Bertram is trying to seduce. When the charge is fulfilled and the riddles solved, Bertram accepts her and everyone prepares to live happily ever after.

This simple story, clearly a kind of folk tale or fairy tale, heavily involved with wish fulfillment and idealized characters and situations, is presented with exquisite sophistication. Instead of being projections of fantasy, the people are extraordinarily real to us. The world of the play is elegant and autumnal. The older generation, whose wishes and views are often belittled and swept aside in comedy, are more sensible and attractive than the young people. The clown Lavatch is bitter and often broods on the essential sinfulness of humankind; the elaborate practical joke that exposes the braggart soldier and comic scapegoat Parolles is too disturbing to provoke much hilarity. If we look for typical comic patterns in this play, we find it apparently working against itself. Atmosphere and characterization are used to qualify and undermine the assumptions of the plot, and the result is a bittersweet flavor uncharacteristic of comedy.

With adjusted expectations, however, we can grow to love this play. Helena wins her Bertram, but he has been so callow and selfish that we wonder whether he deserves her and if she isn't wrongheaded to pursue him so determinedly. What is extraordinary is that these sentiments do not prevent our being moved at the conclusion: Helena's reappearance at the end has a remarkable power. To the people assembled on the stage, she has come back from the dead, and while we know that the miracle is stage-managed and a bit shopworn, with many questionable elements, something of the enchantment the characters feel sweeps over us, too, surprising us with its somber beauty. The result is somewhere between the effect of *Twelfth Night* and that of *The Winter's Tale.*

All's Well, along with the other problem comedies, may mark the end of the line for comic form in Shakespeare, but with its self-conscious use of primitive materials, its enchanted and tragicomic vision, and its sense of the worth of fantasy and the miraculous, it provides a clear line of continuity to

Pericles, Cymbeline, The Winter's Tale, and *The Tempest,* those late masterpieces with which we are still in the process of coming to terms. The romances achieve happy and harmonious endings, sometimes resoundingly, sometimes equivocally, but they do it by resorting to a genre more clearly distinct from real life. Some of the leading characteristics of romance—broken and reunited families, manifestations of the supernatural, providential disasters and miracles, an interest in folklore and magic—had been present in Shakespearean comedy from the beginning. It is as though, in his last phase, Shakespeare found it intriguing to distill them and to found a new dramatic genre on them—or revive an old one, since there were plays that had attempted stage romance when he was growing up, though they had come to seem outmoded and clumsy by the time he turned his full interest to the genre. We can say with some assurance that his interest in dramatic comedy, as demonstrated by his practice and his chronology, ceased in the early years of the seventeenth century, while his experiments with comic form and comic values continued in the group of plays we now call the romances.

History of Performance and Commentary

We do not know as much as we would like about the performance of Shakespeare's comedies in his own time, although we can infer a great deal. We know that as an actor and shareholder in the company, he could keep a close eye on how his work was performed. We know that he must have had great confidence in the boys who played the women's roles, since he created for them such parts as Rosalind, Beatrice, and Portia. We know that one clown, Will Kempe, for whom Shakespeare had written broad comic parts like Bottom and Dogberry, left the company in 1599 and was replaced by Robert Armin, a more subtle comedian for whom Shakespeare wrote parts like Touchstone, Feste, and Lavatch in *All's Well.* We would like to know more about costumes, makeup, and acting styles. Did Shylock, for example, wear the large false nose, red wig, and yellow gabardine of the traditional stage Jew, or did Shakespeare decide to represent him against the type? Many such questions will remain unanswered, but Shakespeare's popularity as a writer of comedy in his own time is well documented, and his confident handling of the

genre, even when he subjected it to radical experiments and sought such remarkable variety, does not seem to have distressed his audience. They seem to have found the speed, complexity, wit, and relative unpredictability of the comedies an invigorating challenge.

When the theaters reopened in the latter part of the seventeenth century, after the restoration of Charles II to the throne, Shakespeare's comedies were revived, but their producers and sponsors felt quite free to adapt and "improve" them. *A Midsummer Night's Dream,* for example, made one reappearance as *The Fairy Queen* (1692), with music by Henry Purcell, but with its Enchanted Lake, Chinese Garden, and appearance of the goddess Juno in a triumphal car, it may well have been unrecognizable as anything resembling Shakespeare's play. Another favorite assumption was that the comedies were assembled from interchangeable parts, so that under one title an adaptor could assemble an anthology of favorite passages and characters. Charles Johnson's *Love in a Forest* (1723) was a version of *As You Like It* that contained borrowings from *A Midsummer Night's Dream, Much Ado About Nothing, Twelfth Night,* and even *Richard III.*

During the Restoration, the histories and tragedies were more likely to be revived, the period having evolved its own special and popular brand of comedy. Whatever its virtues, Restoration comedy is a far cry from Shakespeare's, and the neoclassical Augustan period lacked an aesthetic that would have explained or justified Shakespeare's practice as a writer of comedy. In the second half of the eighteenth century, though, this mixture of condescension and ignorance began to modulate toward admiration. A fashion for "breeches parts," women dressed as men, helped lead to revivals of *The Merchant of Venice, Twelfth Night,* and *As You Like It,* all successful. David Garrick, the great actor of his era, brought a natural acting style to the stage and a new level of respectability to his profession, and his performances of Shakespeare's plays, though adapted to the taste of the time, did much to increase interest in, and respect for, Shakespearean drama. Garrick was best known for parts like Richard III and Macbeth, but he revived and performed a number of the comedies and romances as well. By the time he retired from the stage in 1776, his performances and his association with the leading literary men of the age had helped encourage the sense that Shakespeare was a writer of genius and distinction. Carefully edited texts of the plays, the beginnings of a thoughtful body of commentary, and productions that had greater fidelity to the Shakespearean originals were the result.

The Romantics, who felt that they had discovered Shakespeare, brought a new level of interest and respect to both texts and performances. Once again, regard for the comedies tended to lag behind the more obviously weighty plays. The Kemble family—John Phillip Kemble, his younger brother Charles, their sister Sarah Siddons, and Charles' daughter Fanny—presented reasonably accurate, if not especially inspired, versions of a number of the comedies, among them *All's Well, Much Ado,* and *Merry Wives.* The nineteenth century continued, without greatly modifying, this trend: the plays came more and more fully into view, but proscenium staging and the limitations of Victorian taste kept them from being fully realized in performance. The actor Edmund Kean was famous for his Shylock, but Kean's strength lay in his depiction of elemental passions, and the result did not reflect any particular fidelity to Shakespeare's original *Merchant of Venice.*

Nineteenth-century actor-managers discovered particular affinities with particular comedies. Charles Macready, who restored Lear to the stage in Shakespeare's version, was known for his playing of Benedick, Jaques, and the Duke in *Measure for Measure.* Samuel Phelps, whose productions of Shakespeare at Sadler's Wells had a high standard of quality and intelligence, was much praised as Bottom. Henry Irving, the first actor to be knighted, was famous as Benedick and Shylock, but his Shakespeare productions suffered from overelaborate effects. Something of the same problem haunted the work of Herbert Beerbohm Tree, but his Falstaff in *Merry Wives* (1889) was apparently a triumph. The attempt to restore the playing of Shakespeare's plays to something approximating Elizabethan stage conditions was initiated by William Poel in 1895, with a production of *Twelfth Night.* Poel's work was controversial and much criticized, but there is no doubt that it ushered in a new era, in which Shakespearean texts were vividly restored to theatergoers by virtue of a recognition of how they were meant to be presented.

The trend described above, toward greater fidelity and fuller admiration, has continued. The more popular comedies, like *Much Ado, Twelfth Night,* and *A Midsummer Night's Dream,* have benefited most, while plays like *All's Well* and *Love's Labor's Lost* have had to wait until very recently for

successful productions and wide regard. Modern staging of the comedies, at its best, has combined a healthy willingness to experiment—with period, dress, tone, and characterization—with an increasing respect for the language and plot as Shakespeare conceived them. Trusting the Shakespearean text has often proved that so-called problems of interpretation—for example, distress about the closures of the problem comedies—simply are not problems in performance. In this respect, contemporary directors like John Barton, known for accurate and low-key productions, and Peter Brook, famous as an experimenter and innovator, have much in common. Brook's famous production of *A Midsummer Night's Dream* (1970) was noticed for its unorthodox handling of setting, movement, and costume, but its effect was to clear away the cobwebs and clichés of previous productions and to bring us the Shakespearean text, sharply and clearly, as if for the first time. When the actors spoke the play's great set pieces, all movement stopped so that attention could be trained on the magic of language, which acted on the audience's imaginations in much the same way that it must have done in Shakespeare's theater. Barton's production of *Love's Labor's Lost* (1978), while less notorious, had a comparable effect. Accepting Shakespeare's verbal pyrotechnics and presenting them without apology or self-consciousness showed how funny the play can be and how full and delightful the characterizations are. Barton especially deserves mention among recent directors of Shakespearean comedy because he has managed, in an unobtrusive way, to give us straightforward and moving versions of *All's Well, Merchant,* and a number of other comedies.

Both Brook's *Dream* and Barton's *Love's Labor's Lost* came from England's Royal Shakespeare Company, a repertory company that currently manages to balance tradition and innovation very effectively. Strong productions of Shakespearean comedy have not been limited to England in recent years, however; they have been found at the Shakespeare Festival in Stratford, Canada, in the New York City productions of Joseph Papp, and in Minneapolis, San Diego, and Ashland, Oregon. Nor is good Shakespeare limited to the English-speaking world. Imaginative versions of his comedies are performed all over the world, in every language; and while we will never have, nor should we want, a standardized Shakespeare, it seems a safe observation that his comedies are now performed with more fidelity, imagination, and success than at any time in the past.

Something comparable can be claimed for the current state of criticism of the comedies. While there are undoubtedly biases and shortcomings in our view of Shakespeare, we have a fuller and firmer understanding of his plays than we have had before. That might seem a shortsighted claim were it not for the simple fact that what is useful in criticism tends to be preserved and to enter the general understanding, while what is wrongheaded or mistaken tends to be discarded. Past critics of Shakespeare, even the best ones like Dr. Johnson, Samuel Coleridge, and A. C. Bradley, have said wonderful things and they have said foolish things. Time has winnowed the wheat from the chaff, with the result that current criticism is greatly enriched by its reliance on a heritage of thoughtful commentary.

There are exceptions to this rule, of course. Good writings have been forgotten, and there is still a great deal of nonsense written and published. Richard Levin's book, *New Readings vs. Old Plays* (1979), is a useful survey of recent critical foolishness and a reminder that criticism's opportunity to draw on cumulative insights is not always exploited. Indeed, the greatest problem in both production and criticism of Shakespeare may well be the desire for novelty. A director may give a play a different setting or an unusual emphasis simply from the desire to seem original and creative, while a critic may distort a play, emphasizing some previously unnoticed passage or motif, in order to seem the first commentator who has truly understood it. Shakespeare is not well served by such mishandling, but he seems remarkably capable of surviving it.

Modern criticism of Shakespearean comedy also seems to have benefited especially from a willingness to take the plays on their own terms, without prejudice or presupposition. This approach has brought a clearer understanding of the principles of structure and design of the plays, deemphasizing the concepts of plot and subplot (since those do not greatly seem to interest the playwright) and finding spatial and musical formulations and analogies that give us a clearer sense of what is actually going on. Similar gains have been made in our understanding of how Shakespeare used his sources, and why, and of his handling of comic characterization and convention. Bardolatry is of no use at all in understanding Shakespeare, but the assumptions that he knew what he was up to and that the plays reflect his considered interest in his medium, his genres, and his available traditions seem to have produced more insights than earlier opinions that supposed him at the mercy of his ignorance, of popular fashions, of emotional traumas—or as simply unable to control his materials.

The two commentators in our own time whose work has most substantially enhanced our understanding of the comedies are Northrop Frye and C. L. Barber. In a 1948 essay, "The Argument of Comedy," Frye set out some basic laws of comic form, a "poetics" of comedy, more clearly and persuasively than they had ever been presented before. He began to apply them to Shakespeare's comedies, demonstrating how fully Shakespeare understood the fundamental meanings and principles of comedy, even when he elected to depart from them. Frye's subsequent writings, *A Natural Perspective* (1965) and *The Myth of Deliverance* (1983), have elaborated his view of Shakespeare in exhilarating ways. Frye has probably done more for our understanding of Shakespearean comedy (and of dramatic comedy in general) than any other critic.

Barber's work is related to Frye's and is mainly to be found in his important study *Shakespeare's Festive Comedy* (1959). As the title suggests, Barber is interested in the way that Shakespeare achieves an atmosphere of "festive release" in his comedies (as well as in history plays like *Henry IV, Part 1*) by invoking customs and meanings familiar to Elizabethans from their holidays. These holidays were linked to events in the Christian calendar, but they also had ties to older ceremonies in which the relation between human life and the natural cycle of the seasons was acted out in rituals that could be translated into dramatic action. During such times, social norms were often suspended in favor of a deeper sense of life, one that involved sexuality, death, and regeneration. Frye had pointed out that Shakespearean characters often retreat to a "green world," away from social problems, a place that holds potential for self-discovery and healing. By making it clear that this green world was elaborated and made real through reference to customs and rituals associated with seasonal holidays, Barber was able to ground the idea of the green world quite firmly in Elizabethan, and indeed European, culture, and to show how the design of plays like *Love's Labor's Lost, A Midsummer Night's Dream,* and *As You Like It* linked the idea of retreating to nature with familiar holiday customs and their meanings. Barber introduced for consideration less obvious examples, like the tavern in *Henry IV* and Illyria in *Twelfth Night* (a play that takes its name from a holiday), and he set forth a line of interest particularly useful in accounting for the development of Shakespeare's comedies from the early to the middle phase. Barber's criticism is notable for its wit and verve, its way with detail, and its appreciation of Shakespeare's language. His book remains a model of sound criticism.

Other studies of the comedies have added greatly to our understanding in recent years: Muriel Bradbrook, John Russell Brown, Bertrand Evans, Alexander Leggatt, and Leo Salinger come readily to mind. Work on the problem comedies has brought us a considerable distance, thanks to such critics as W. W. Lawrence, Ernest Schanzer, and Robert G. Hunter. And fine studies of individual plays have been produced by William Carroll and Jeanne Addison Roberts. Many things said here will probably provoke disagreement or qualification: generalization is tricky, and unanimity on the meaning and development of Shakespearean comedy is not to be expected. The leading points, however, are ones on which wide agreement can be secured: that Shakespeare was a highly original and remarkably experimental writer of dramatic comedy; that his development was intricate and fascinating; and that, while we do not deserve to be complacent about the excellence of modern productions and modern criticism, we can take some pride in our sense that we have gradually come to new levels of understanding and appreciation of the comedies and of the remarkable achievement they represent.

BIBLIOGRAPHY

C. L. Barber, *Shakespeare's Festive Comedy* (1959). S. L. Bethell, *Shakespeare and the Popular Dramatic Tradition* (1944). M. C. Bradbrook, *The Growth and Structure of Elizabethan Comedy* (1955). John Russell Brown, *Shakespeare and His Comedies* (1957). John Russell Brown and Bernard Harris, eds., *Early Shakespeare,* Stratford-Upon-Avon Studies 3 (1961). Geoffrey Bullough, *Narrative and Dramatic Sources of Shakespeare,* 8 vols. (1957–1975). Sigurd Burckhardt, *Shakespearean Meanings* (1968). William C. Carroll, *The Great Feast of Language in "Love's Labour's Lost"* (1976). Maurice Charney, ed., *Shakespearean Comedy* (1980).

Lawrence Danson, *The Harmonies of "The Merchant of Venice"* (1978). Una Ellis-Fermor, *Shakespeare the Dramatist* (1961). Bertrand Evans, *Shakespeare's Comedies* (1960). Northrop Frye, "The Argument of Comedy," in *English Institute Essays 1948* (1949); *A Natural Perspective: The Development of Shakespearean Comedy and Romance* (1965); and *The Myth of Deliverance: Reflections on Shakespeare's Problem Comedies* (1983). Leslie Hotson, *The First Night of "Twelfth Night"* (1954). G. K. Hunter, *William Shakespeare: The Late Comedies* (1962). Robert G. Hunter, *Shakespeare and the Comedy of Forgiveness* (1965). Frank Kermode, "The Mature Comedies," in *Early Shakespeare,* Stratford-Upon-Avon Studies 3 (1961). Alvin Kernan, "The Plays and the Playwrights," in Clifford Leech and T. W. Craik, eds., *The Revels History of Drama in English,* vol. 3 (1975) and *The Playwright as Magician* (1979). Robert Kimbrough, *Shakespeare's "Troilus and Cressida" and Its Setting* (1964).

W. W. Lawrence, *Shakespeare's Problem Comedies* (1931; 2nd ed., 1960). Alexander Leggatt, *Shakespeare's Comedy of Love* (1974). Richard Levin, *New Readings vs. Old Plays* (1979). M. M. Mahood, *Shakespeare's Wordplay* (1957). David Palmer and Malcolm Bradbury, eds., *Shakespearian Comedy,* Stratford-Upon-Avon Studies 14 (1972). Eric Partridge, *Shakespeare's Bawdy* (1947; rev. ed., 1955). Joseph G. Price, *The Unfortunate Comedy: A Study of "All's Well That Ends Well" and Its Critics* (1968). J. B. Priestley, *The English Comic Characters* (1925). Jeanne Addison Roberts, *Shakespeare's English Comedy: "The Merry Wives of Windsor" in Context* (1979). A. P. Rossiter, *Angel With Horns* (1961). Leo Salinger, *Shakespeare and the Traditions of Comedy* (1974). Ernest Schanzer, *The Problem Plays of Shakespeare* (1963). David L. Stevenson, *The Love-Game Comedy* (1946) and *The Achievement of Shakespeare's "Measure for Measure"* (1966).

Derek Traversi, *William Shakespeare: The Early Comedies* (1960). Peter Ure, *William Shakespeare: The Problem Plays* (1961). Enid Welsford, *The Fool* (1935). Richard P. Wheeler, *Shakespeare's Development and the Problem Comedies: Turn and Counter-Turn* (1981). David Young, *Something of Great Constancy: The Art of "A Midsummer Night's Dream"* (1966) and *The Heart's Forest: A Study of Shakespeare's Pastoral Plays* (1972).

Shakespeare's Tragedies

ARTHUR KIRSCH

Midway through his tragedy, Hamlet tells Horatio, "Thou hast been / As one in suff'ring all that suffers nothing." He then says longingly to him:

> Give me that man
> That is not passion's slave, and I will wear him
> In my heart's core, ay, in my heart of heart,
> As I do thee.
>
> (III. ii. 62–63, 68–71)

Only Hamlet can speak in this way, but he nonetheless indicates the predicament of all of Shakespeare's great tragic heroes. As A. P. Rossiter points out, "Shakespeare's conception of tragedy plainly and constantly concerns the man who *is* 'passion's slave'—in the extended, Senecan sense of 'passion.'" Renaissance writers were suspicious of acute states of emotion. They understood them as perturbations of the mind and ultimately as symptoms of man's fallen nature. And Hamlet himself, as we can see, considers them unwelcome. But however much Horatio may be a Renaissance model, as well as Hamlet's, he is also demonstrably not the hero of the play. His temperance makes him invulnerable to suffering and pain; but it is precisely that vulnerability, whatever its moral or psychoanalytic status, that distinguishes Hamlet as a tragic hero and that compels our own deepest imaginative sympathies. All the heroes of Shakespeare's tragedies—and especially those of the four titanic plays *Hamlet, Othello, Macbeth,* and *King Lear*—

suffer to the heart's core and suffer everything in suffering all. "Suffering," as Rossiter says, "beyond solace, beyond any moral palliation, and suffering because of a human greatness which is great because great in passion: that, above everything else, is central to Shakespeare's tragic conception."

T. S. Eliot contends that the passions of Shakespeare's tragic heroes, which he relates to their habits of self-dramatization and self-consciousness, are derived from the model of the Senecan tragic hero, a judgment that important recent scholarship tends to confirm, and Eliot argues in addition that in Seneca the favored theatrical theme is "the posture of dying." This is the governing theme of Shakespeare's great tragedies as well, though in them there is little of the sense of factitiousness that the word *posture* implies. For Shakespeare develops the whole emotional and spiritual landscape of death and dying. He characteristically transforms the formal requirement that a tragedy end in death, as well as the Senecan exploitation of it, into an understanding of human experience. There is indeed in all four tragedies an ironic base note—to which modern ears are often either not attuned or, like Eliot's, too much attuned—that represents the vanity and emptiness of all human passion and self-definition in the face of death. It is the note sounded in the Christian understanding of pride and presumption. It is expressed as well in the existential recognition, voiced in the lament of the Preacher in Ecclesiastes, that "all *is* vanitie" (1:2), that man's identity in this life is as "a shadow"

(7:2), and that "As he came forthe of his mothers belly, he shal returne naked to go as he came, & shal beare away nothing of his labour, which he hathe caused to passe by his hand" (5:14). It is this sense of death (to which the word *posture* is germane), as not only the absolute end of life but immanent within it, that animates Macbeth's speech comparing life to "a walking shadow, a poor player / That struts and frets his hour upon the stage / And then is heard no more" (V. v. 24–26) and that gives a sense of grotesqueness to the greatest efforts and largest passions of the heroes of all the tragedies, all of whom would be depicted on the stage by poor players. But Shakespeare's theatrical self-consciousness, like his irony, can be too much emphasized; and what is finally most important about the pressure of death in the tragedies is that it carves out, as much as it questions, the heroic identities of the heroes and that it increases rather than devalues the depth and scope of their passions. The sense of grotesqueness itself intensifies our own responses to those passions; it does not diminish them. "In tragedy," as Northrop Frye observes in *Fools of Time,* "the ironic vision survives the heroic one, but the heroic vision is the one we remember, and the tragedy is for its sake."

The relationship between these two visions, and specifically between the passions of the heart and death, is central to an understanding of Shakespeare's four great tragedies, and it is the theme with which this essay is mainly concerned. But each of these plays has its own particular heartbeat, and the purpose of the following separate discussions of the tragedies is less to prove a point about them as a group than to find a way of feeling their individual pulses.

Hamlet

Hamlet is a revenge play, a genre that enjoyed an extraordinary popularity on the Elizabethan stage. Part of the reason for that popularity was the theatrical power of the revenge motif itself. The quest for vengeance satisfies an audience's most primitive wishes for intrigue and violence, and, equally important, it gives significant shape to the plot and sustained energy to the action. But if vengeance composes the plot of the revenge play, grief composes its essential emotional content, its substance. There is a character in Marlowe's *Jew of Malta* who, finding the body of his son killed in a duel, cries out

in his loss that he wishes his son had been murdered so that he could avenge his death. It is a casual line, but it suggests a deep connection between anger and sorrow in the revenge-play genre that Shakespeare draws upon profoundly.

The note of grief is sounded by Hamlet in his first words in the play, before he sees the ghost, in his opening dialogue with the King and his mother. The Queen tells him to cast off his "nighted color" and not "for ever" to seek for his "noble father in the dust": "Thou know'st 'tis common. All that lives must die, / Passing through nature to eternity" (I. ii. 68, 70–74). Hamlet answers, "Ay, madam, it is common." "If it be, / Why seems it so particular with thee?" she asks; and he responds,

> Seems, madam? Nay, it is. I know not 'seems.'
> 'Tis not alone my inky cloak, good mother,
> Nor customary suits of solemn black,
> Nor windy suspiration of forced breath,
> No, nor the fruitful river in the eye,
> Nor the dejected havior of the visage,
> Together with all forms, moods, shapes of grief,
> That can denote me truly. These indeed seem,
> For they are actions that a man might play,
> But I have that within which passeth show—
> These but the trappings and the suits of woe.
>
> (I. ii. 74–86)

Though Hamlet's use of the conventional Elizabethan forms of mourning expresses his hostility to an unfeeling court, he is at the same time speaking deeply of an experience that everyone who has lost someone close to him must recognize. He is speaking of the early stages of grief, of its shock, of its inner and still hidden sense of loss, and trying to describe what is not fully describable—the literally inexpressible wound whose immediate consequence is the dislocation, if not transvaluation, of our customary perceptions and feelings and attachments to life. It is no accident that this speech sets in motion Hamlet's preoccupation with seeming and being, including the whole train of images of acting that is crystallized in the play within the play. The peculiar centripetal pull of anger and sorrow that the speech depicts remains as the central undercurrent of that preoccupation, most notably in Hamlet's later soliloquy about the player's capacity, "but in a fiction, in a dream of passion," to imitate Hecuba's grief (II. ii. 536).

After Hamlet answers his mother, the King offers his own homily on the "common theme" of "death of fathers" and, like the Queen, questions why Hamlet should in "peevish opposition / Take it to heart" (I. ii. 100–104). There is in fact much in Claudius' consolation of philosophy that is spiritually sound and to which every human being must eventually accommodate himself, but it comes at the wrong time, from the wrong person, and in its essential belittlement of the heartache of grief, it comes with the wrong inflection. It is a dispiriting irony of scholarship on this play that so many psychoanalytic and theological critics should essentially take such words, from such a king, as a text for their own indictments of Hamlet's behavior. What a grieving person needs, of course, is not the consolation of words, even words that are true, but sympathy—and this Hamlet does not receive, not from the court, not from his uncle, and more important, not from his own mother, to whom his grief over his father's death is alien and unwelcome.

After the King and Queen leave the stage, it is to his mother's lack of sympathy not only for him but for her dead husband that Hamlet turns in particular pain:

O that this too too sullied flesh would melt,
Thaw, and resolve itself into a dew,
Or that the Everlasting had not fixed
His canon 'gainst self-slaughter. O God, God,
How weary, stale, flat, and unprofitable
Seem to me all the uses of this world!
Fie on't, ah, fie, 'tis an unweeded garden
That grows to seed, Things rank and gross in nature
Possess it merely. That it should come to this,
But two months dead, nay, not so much, not two,
So excellent a king, that was to this
Hyperion to a satyr, so loving to my mother
That he might not beteem the winds of heaven
Visit her face too roughly. Heaven and earth,
Must I remember? Why, she would hang on him
As if increase of appetite had grown
By what it fed on, and yet within a month—
Let me not think on't; frailty, thy name is woman—
A little month, or ere those shoes were old
With which she followed my poor father's body
Like Niobe, all tears, why she, even she—
O God, a beast that wants discourse of reason
Would have mourned longer—married with my uncle,
My father's brother, but no more like my father
Than I to Hercules. Within a month,
Ere yet the salt of most unrighteous tears
Had left the flushing in her gallèd eyes,
She married. O, most wicked speed, to post
With such dexterity to incestuous sheets!

It is not nor it cannot come to good.
But break my heart, for I must hold my tongue.

(I. ii. 129–59)

This is an exceptionally suggestive speech and the first of many that seem to invite oedipal interpretations of the play. The source of Hamlet's so-called oedipal anxiety, however, is real and present; it is not an archaic and repressed fantasy. Hamlet does perhaps protest too much, in this soliloquy and elsewhere, about his father's superiority to his uncle (and to himself), and throughout the play he is clearly preoccupied with his mother's sexual appetite; but these ambivalences and preoccupations, whatever their unconscious roots, are elicited by a situation, palpable and external to him, in which they are acted out. The oedipal configurations of Hamlet's predicament, in other words, inhabit the whole world of the play; they are not simply a function of his characterization, even though they resonate with it profoundly. There is every reason, in reality, for a son to be deeply troubled by the appetite of a mother who betrays his father's memory by her incestuous marriage, within a month, to his brother (and murderer), and there is surely more than reason for a son to be obsessed for a time with a father who literally returns from the grave to haunt him. In any case, at least early in the play, if not also later, such oedipal echoes cannot be disentangled from Hamlet's grief; and Shakespeare's purpose in arousing them is not to call Hamlet's character to judgment but to expand our understanding of the nature and intensity of his suffering. For all these events come upon Hamlet before he has even begun to assimilate the loss of a living father, while he is still mourning, seemingly alone in Denmark, for the death of a king—and their major psychic impact and importance is that they protract and vastly dilate the process of his grief.

Freud called this process the work of mourning and described it in "Mourning and Melancholia" (*Collected Papers,* 6) in a way that is exceptionally pertinent to this play. The major preoccupation of the essay is the pathology of melancholy, or what is now more commonly called depression, but in the course of his discussion Freud finds unusually suggestive analogies and distinctions between mourning and melancholy. He points out, to begin with, that except in one respect, the characteristics of normal grief and of pathological depression are the same and that the two states can easily be confused—as they are endemically in interpretations of Hamlet's character. The characteristics of depression, Freud observes, are deep and painful dejection, a loss of interest in the outside world, an inability to act, and self-disgust as well as self-reproach. Except for the loss of faith in oneself, Freud continues, "the same traits are met with in grief":

> Profound mourning, the reaction to the loss of a loved person, contains the same feeling of pain, loss of interest in the outside world—in so far as it does not recall the dead one—loss of capacity to adopt any new object of love, which would mean a replacing of the one mourned, the same turning from every active effort that is not connected with thoughts of the dead.

Freud remarks that "although grief involves grave departures from the normal attitude to life, it never occurs to us to regard it as a morbid condition," and "we rest assured that after a lapse of time it will be overcome."

The process by which grief is overcome, the work of mourning, Freud describes as a struggle—the struggle between the instinctive human disposition to remain libidinally bound to the dead person and the necessity to acknowledge the clear reality of his loss. "The task," Freud writes, is "carried through bit by bit," at enormous expense of time and energy, "while all the time the existence of the lost object is continued in the mind. Each single one of the memories and hopes which bound the libido to the object" must be "brought up" and relinquished. "Why this process" Freud adds, "of carrying out the behest of reality bit by bit, which is in the nature of a compromise, should be so extraordinarily painful is not at all easy to explain in terms of mental economics. It is worth noting that this pain seems natural to us."

Freud's wonderment at the pain of grief seems odd, and it may be a function of his general incapacity, throughout his writing, to deal adequately with death itself. The issue is important because it is related to an astonishing lapse in the argument of "Mourning and Melancholia" that is critical to an understanding of *Hamlet* and that might have helped Freud account for the extraordinary pain of grief in his own conception of mental economics. For what Freud leaves out in his consideration of mourning are its normal but enormously disturbing components of protest and anger—initially anger at being wounded and abandoned, but fundamentally a protest, both conscious and unconscious, against the inescapably mortal condition of human life.

Freud finds such anger and protest in depression, and with his analysis of that state few would wish to quarrel. The salient points of his argument are that in depression there is "an unconscious loss of a love-object, in contradistinction to mourning, in which there is nothing unconscious about the loss," and that there is a fall of self-esteem and a consistent cadence of self-reproach that are also not found in mourning. The key to an understanding of this condition, Freud continues, is the perception that the self-criticism of depression is really anger turned inward, "that the self-reproaches are reproaches against a loved object which have been shifted on to the patient's own ego." The "complaints" of depressed people, he remarks, "are really 'plaints' in the legal sense of the word . . . because everything derogatory that they say of themselves at bottom relates to someone else." All the actions of a depressed person, Freud concludes, "proceed from an attitude of revolt, a mental constellation which by a certain process has become transformed into melancholic contrition." Freud's explanation of the dynamics of this process is involved and technical, but there are two major points that emerge clearly and that are highly relevant to *Hamlet*. The first is that there is, in a depressed person, "an *identification* of the ego with the abandoned object. Thus the shadow of the object [falls] upon the ego," so that the ego can "henceforth be criticized by a special mental faculty like an object, like the forsaken object. In this way the loss of the object [becomes] transformed into a loss in the ego." The second point that Freud stresses is that because there is an ambivalent relation to the lost object, the regressive movement toward identification is accompanied by a regressive movement toward sadism, a movement whose logical culmination is suicide, the killing in the self of the lost object with whom the depressed person has so thoroughly identified. Freud adds that in only one other situation in human life is the ego so overwhelmed by the object, and that is in the state of intense love.

With these analogies and distinctions in mind, let us now return to the opening scene at court. In his first speech to his mother, Hamlet speaks from the very heart of grief about the supervening reality of his loss and of its inward wound, and the accent of normal, if intense, grief remains dominant in his subsequent soliloquy. It is true that in that soliloquy his mind turns to thoughts of "self-slaughter," but those thoughts notwithstanding, the emphasis of the speech is not one of self-reproach. It is not himself, but the uses of the world that Hamlet finds "weary, stale, flat, and unprofitable," and his mother's frailty suggests a rankness and grossness in nature itself. The "plaints" against his mother that occupy the majority of his speech are conscious, and both his anger and his ambivalence toward her are fully justified. Even on the face of it, her hasty remarriage makes a mockery of his father's memory that intensifies the real pain and loneliness of Hamlet's loss; and if he also feels his own ego threatened, and if there is a deeper cadence of grief in his words, it is because he is already beginning to sense that the shadow of a crime with "the primal eldest curse upon't" (III. iii. 37) has fallen upon him, a crime that is not delusional and not his, and that eventually inflicts a punishment upon him that tries his spirit and destroys his life. The last lines of Hamlet's soliloquy are: "It is not nor it cannot come to good. / But break my heart, for I must hold my tongue." These lines show Hamlet's prescience, not his disease, and the instant he completes them Horatio, Marcellus, and Bernardo enter to tell him of the apparition of his dead father, the ghost that is haunting the kingdom and that has been a part of our own consciousness from the very outset of the play.

Hamlet's subsequent meeting with the ghost of his father is both the structural and psychic nexus of the play. The scene is so familiar to us that the extraordinary nature of its impact on Hamlet can be overlooked, even in the theater. It begins with Hamlet expressing pity for the ghost and the ghost insisting that he attend to a more "serious" purpose:

> *Ghost.*   List, list, O, list!
> If thou didst ever thy dear father love—
> *Hamlet.* O God!
> *Ghost.* Revenge his foul and most unnatural murder.
>
> (I. v. 22–25)

The ghost then confirms to Hamlet's prophetic soul that "the serpent that did sting thy father's life / Now wears his crown," and he describes his murder in his orchard and Gertrude's remarriage in terms that seem deliberately to evoke echoes of the serpent in the garden of Eden. The ghost ends his recital saying, "O, horrible! O, horrible! most horrible! If thou hast nature in thee, bear it not," and his parting words are "Adieu, adieu, adieu. Re-

member me" (I. v. 39–40, 80–81, 91). Hamlet's answering speech, as the ghost exits, is profound and predicates the state of his mind and feeling until the beginning of the last act of the play:

> O all you host of heaven! O earth! What else?
> And shall I couple hell? O fie! Hold, hold, my heart,
> And you, my sinews, grow not instant old,
> But bear me stiffly up. Remember thee?
> Ay, thou poor ghost, while memory holds a seat
> In this distracted globe. Remember thee?
> Yea, from the table of my memory
> I'll wipe away all trivial fond records,
> All saws of books, all forms, all pressures past
> That youth and observation copied there,
> And thy commandment all alone shall live
> Within the book and volume of my brain,
> Unmixed with baser matter. Yes, by heaven!
> O most pernicious woman!
> O villain, villain, smiling, damnèd villain!
> My tables—meet it is I set it down
> That one may smile, and smile, and be a villain.
> At least I am sure it may be so in Denmark.
> [*Writes.*]
> So, uncle, there you are. Now to my word:
> It is 'Adieu, adieu, remember me.'
> I have sworn't.
>
> (I. v. 92–112)

This is a crucial and dreadful vow for many reasons, but the most important, as Freud places us in a position to understand, is that the ghost's injunction to remember him—an injunction that Shakespeare's commitment to the whole force of the revenge genre never permits either us or Hamlet to question—brutally intensifies Hamlet's mourning and makes him incorporate in its work what we would normally regard as the pathology of depression. For the essence of the work of mourning is the internal process by which the ego heals its wound, differentiates itself from the object, and slowly, bit by bit, cuts its libidinal ties with the one who has died. Yet this is precisely what the ghost forbids— and forbids, moreover, with a lack of sympathy for Hamlet's grief that is even more pronounced than the Queen's. He instead tells Hamlet that if ever he loved his father, he should remember him; he tells Hamlet of Gertrude's incestuous remarriage in a way that makes his mother's desire, if not the libido itself, seem inseparable from murder and death; and finally he tells Hamlet to kill. Drawing upon and crystallizing the deepest energies of the revenge-play genre, the ghost thus enjoins Hamlet to identify with him in his sorrow and to give murderous purpose to his anger. He consciously compels in Hamlet, in other words, the regressive movement toward identification and sadism, which together usually constitute the unconscious dynamics of depression. It is only after this scene that Hamlet feels punished with what he later calls "a sore distraction" (V. ii. 218) and that he begins to reproach himself for his own nature and to meditate on suicide. The ghost, moreover, not only compels this process in Hamlet; like much of the world of the play, he incarnates it. The effect of his appearance and behest to Hamlet is to literalize Hamlet's subsequent movement toward the realm of death that he inhabits, and away from all of the bonds that nourish life and make it desirable, away from "all trivial fond records, / All saws of books, all forms, all pressures past." As C. S. Lewis insisted long ago, the ghost leads Hamlet into a spiritual and psychic region that seems poised between the living and the dead. It is significant that Hamlet is subsequently described in images that suggest the ghost's countenance, and it is significant too that Hamlet's own appearance and state of mind change, at the beginning of Act V, at the moment when it is possible to say that he has finally come to terms with the ghost and with his father's death and has completed the work of mourning.

Shakespeare intends for us always to retain a sense of intensified mourning rather than of disease in Hamlet, partly because Hamlet is always conscious of the manic roles he plays and is always lucid with Horatio, but also because his thoughts and feelings turn outward as well as inward and his behavior is finally a symbiotic response to the actually diseased world of the play. And though that diseased world, poisoned at the root by a truly guilty king, eventually represents an overwhelming tangle of guilt, its main emphasis, both for Hamlet and for us, is the experience of grief. The essential focus of the action as well as the source of its consistent pulsations of feeling, the pulsations that continuously charge both Hamlet's sorrow and his anger (and in which the whole issue of delay is subsumed), is the actuality of conscious, not unconscious, loss. For in addition to the death of his father in this play, Hamlet suffers the loss amounting to death of all those persons, except Horatio, whom he has most loved and who have most animated and given meaning to his life. He loses his mother, he loses Ophelia, and he loses his friends;

and we can have no question that these losses are real and inescapable.

The loss of his mother is the most intense and the hardest to discuss. One should perhaps leave her to heaven as the ghost says, but even he cannot follow that advice. Hamlet is genuinely betrayed by her, most directly by her lack of sympathy for him. She is said to live almost by his looks, but she is essentially inert, oblivious to the whole realm of experience through which her son travels. She seems not to care and seems particularly not to care about his grief. Early in the play, when Claudius and others are in hectic search of the reason for Hamlet's melancholy, she says with bovine imperturbability, "I doubt it is no other but the main, / His father's death and our o'erhasty marriage" (II. ii. 56–57). That o'erhasty and incestuous marriage creates a reservoir of literally grievous anger in Hamlet. It suggests to him the impermanence upon which the Player King later insists (III. ii. 186–195), the impermanence of human affection as well as of life; and it also, less obviously, compels him to think of the violation of the union that gave him his own life and being. It is very difficult, under any circumstances, to think precisely upon our parents and their relationship without causing deep tremors in our selves, and for Hamlet the circumstances are extraordinary.

Hamlet's loss of Ophelia spills over, in part, from his rage against his mother, but Ophelia herself gives him cause for anger. There is no reason to doubt her word, at the beginning of the play, that Hamlet has importuned her "with love / In honorable fashion. . . . And hath given countenance to his speech . . . / With almost all the holy vows of heaven" (I. iii. 110–111, 113–114); and there is certainly no reason to question his own passionate declaration at the end of the play, over her grave, that he loved her deeply:

> I loved Ophelia. Forty thousand brothers
> Could not with all their quantity of love
> Make up my sum.
>
> (V. i. 256–258)

Both Hamlet's grief and his task constrain him from realizing this love, but Ophelia's behavior clearly intensifies his frustration and anguish. By keeping the worldly and disbelieving advice of her brother and father as "watchman" to her "heart" (I. iii. 46), she denies the heart's affection not only in Hamlet but in herself; both denials add immeasurably to Hamlet's sense of loneliness and loss—and anger.

Rosencrantz and Guildenstern are less close to Hamlet's heart, and because they are such unequivocal sponges of the King, Hamlet can release his anger against them without ambivalence. But, at least initially, they too amplify both his and our sense of the increasing emptiness of his world. We are so accustomed to treating Rosencrantz and Guildenstern as vaguely comic twins that we can forget the great warmth with which Hamlet first welcomes them to Denmark and the urgency and openness of his pleas for the continuation of their friendship. "I will not sort you with the rest of my servants," he says to them, and he implores them repeatedly to "deal justly" with him and to tell him honestly why they have come to Denmark:

> let me conjure you by the rights of our fellowship, by the consonancy of our youth, by the obligation of our ever-preserved love, and by what more dear a better proposer can charge you withal, be even and direct with me whether you were sent for or no.
>
> (II. ii. 264–265, 280–285)

Rosencrantz and Guildenstern cannot be direct with him, and Hamlet cuts his losses with them quite quickly and eventually quite savagely. But it is perhaps no accident that immediately following this exchange, when he must be fully realizing the extent to which, except for Horatio, he is now utterly alone in Denmark with his grief and his task, he gives that grief a voice that includes in its deep sadness and its sympathetic imagination a conspectus of Renaissance thought about the human condition. "I have of late," he tells his former friends,

> —but wherefore I know not—lost all my mirth, forgone all custom of exercises; and indeed, it goes so heavily with my disposition that this goodly frame the earth seems to me a sterile promontory; this most excellent canopy, the air, look you, this brave o'er-hanging firmament, this majestical roof fretted with golden fire—why, it appeareth nothing to me but a foul and pestilent congregation of vapors. What a piece of work is a man, how noble in reason, how infinite in faculties; in form and moving how express and admirable, in action how like an angel, in apprehension how like a god: the beauty of the world, the paragon of animals! And yet to me what is this quintessence of dust?
>
> (II. ii. 292–305)

"In grief," Freud remarks in "Mourning and Melancholia," "the world becomes poor and empty; in melancholia it is the ego itself." During most of the action of *Hamlet* we cannot make this distinction. For the first four acts of the play, the world in which Hamlet must exist and act is characterized in all its parts not merely as diseased but, specifically for Hamlet, as one that is being emptied of all the human relationships that nourish the ego and give it purpose and vitality. It is a world that is essentially defined—generically, psychically, spiritually—by a ghost whose very countenance, "more in sorrow than in anger" (I. ii. 232), binds Hamlet to a course of grief that is deeper and wider than any in our literature. It is a world of mourning.

At the beginning of Act V, when Hamlet returns from England, that world seems to change, and Hamlet with it. Neither the countenance of the ghost nor his tormented and tormenting spirit seems any longer to be present in the play, and Hamlet begins to alter in state of mind as he already has in his dress. As he stands in the graveyard that visually epitomizes the play's preoccupation with death, there is no longer the sense that he and his world are conflated in the convulsive activity of grief. That activity seems to be drawing to a close, and his own sense of differentiation is decisively crystallized when, in a scene reminiscent of the one in which he reacts to the imitation of Hecuba's grief, he responds to Laertes' enactment of a grief that seems a parody of his own:

> What is he whose grief
> Bears such an emphasis? whose phrase of sorrow
> Conjures the wand'ring stars, and makes them stand
> Like wonder-wounded hearers? This is I,
> Hamlet the Dane.
>
> (V. i. 241–245)

It is an especially painful but inescapable paradox of Hamlet's tragedy that the final ending of his grief and the liberation of his self should be coextensive with his apprehension of his own death. After agreeing to the duel with Laertes that he is confident of winning, he nevertheless tells Horatio, "But thou wouldst not think how ill all's here about my heart. But it is no matter" (V. ii. 201–202). When Horatio urges him to postpone the duel, he says, in the famous speech that signifies, if it does not explain, the decisive change of his spirit:

Not a whit, we defy augury. There is special providence in the fall of a sparrow. If it be now, 'tis not to come; if it be not to come, it will be now; if it be not now, yet it will come. The readiness is all. Since no man of aught he leaves knows, what is't to leave betimes? Let be.

(V. ii. 208–213)

The theological import of these lines, with their luminous reference to Matthew, has long been recognized, but the particular emphasis upon death suggests a psychological coordinate. For what makes Hamlet's acceptance of Providence finally intelligible and credible emotionally, what confirms the truth of it to our own experience, is our sense, as well as his, that the great anguish and struggle of his grief is over and that he has completed the work of mourning. He speaks to Horatio quietly, almost serenely, with the unexultant calm that characterizes the end of the long, inner struggle of grief. He has looked at the face of death in his father's ghost, he has endured death and loss in all the human beings he has loved, and he now accepts those losses as an inevitable part of his own condition. "The readiness is all" suggests the crystallization of Hamlet's awareness of the larger dimension of time that has enveloped his tragedy from the start, including the revenge drama of Fortinbras' grievances on the outskirts of the action and the appalling griefs of Polonius' family deep inside it, but the line also defines what is perhaps the last and most difficult task of mourning, his own readiness to die.

Hamlet is an immensely complicated tragedy, and anything one says about it leaves one haunted by what has not been said. But precisely in a play whose suggestiveness has no end, it is especially important to remember what actually happens. Hamlet himself is sometimes most preoccupied with delay and with the whole attendant metaphysical issue of the relation between thought and action. But as his own experience shows, in the last analysis no action can be commensurate with grief, not even the killing of a guilty king, and it is Hamlet's experience of grief, and his recovery from it, to which we respond most deeply. He is a young man who comes home from his university to find his father dead and his mother remarried to his father's murderer. The woman he loves subsequently rejects him, he is betrayed by his friends, and, finally and most painfully, he is betrayed by a mother whose mutability seems to strike at the heart of human affection. In the midst of these waves of losses, which seem themselves to correspond to the spasms of grief, he is visited by the ghost of his father, who places upon him a proof of love and a task of vengeance that he cannot refuse without denying his own being. The ghost draws upon the emotional taproot of the revenge-play genre and dilates the natural sorrow and anger of Hamlet's multiple griefs until they include all human frailty in their protest and sympathy and touch upon the deepest synapses of grief in our own lives, not only for those who have died, but for those, like ourselves, who are still alive.

Othello

Othello is composed of an extraordinary mixture of antithetical states of feeling and being. The extremes are literally and emblematically represented in Desdemona and Iago, but they are most deeply incarnated in Othello himself, who moves from one to the other, from the transcendence and love celebrated in the first half of the play to the nearly utter disintegration and destructiveness that are dramatized in the second half. The contrast is so drastic that most critics find it insupportable. *Othello* is not the only Shakespearean tragedy to dramatize such oppositions—*King Lear* especially does—but *Othello* poses a peculiar difficulty for critics because its preoccupations are so unremittingly sexual.

At the core of *Othello* is an uncomfortably intense focus upon the sexual relationship between a man and a woman in marriage, a relationship that was as inherently paradoxical and mysterious to Elizabethans as it is to us. Its essential paradox is most explicitly and profoundly described in the words of St. Paul that are cited in the marriage liturgy from the Book of Common Prayer:

So men are bound to love their own wives as their own bodies. He that loveth his own wife, loveth himself. For never did any man hate his own flesh, but nourisheth it and cherisheth it, even as the Lord doth the Congregation: for we are members of his body, of his flesh and of his bones. For this cause shall a man leave father and mother, and shall be joined unto his wife, and they two shall be one flesh. This mystery is great, but I speak of Christ and of the congregation.

Referring to the Bible in an essay entitled "The Most Prevalent Form of Degradation in Erotic

Life" (*Collected Papers,* 8), Freud describes the same mystery in approximately analogous terms: "A man shall leave father and mother—according to the Biblical precept—and cleave to his wife; then are tenderness and sensuality united." He explains that "to ensure a fully normal attitude in love," the union of both "currents" of feeling is necessary. And he goes on to observe that this union is ultimately derived from a child's early symbiotic relationship with his mother, in which his love for her and for himself are identical. Both St. Paul and Freud are pertinent to an understanding of *Othello.*

The two most salient features of Othello's characterization are his blackness and his age, and both have enormous symbolic and literal significance in his marriage. The overtones of his blackness, as G. K. Hunter has shown, are primarily, though by no means exclusively, theological. The resonances of his age are more psychological. The marriage of an older man and a young girl was traditional material for comedy or farce, but Shakespeare invokes the stereotype in part to invert his audience's expectations and thereby to intensify its response. Desdemona is obviously no May. She loves Othello body and soul, unreservedly, and neither at the beginning nor at the tragic end of the marriage is she ever untrue to the ideal of one flesh to which she has consecrated herself. Othello, similarly, in the beginning is no January. He is a general replete with power and respect; and unlike his comic prototypes, as Shakespeare takes pains to establish, he is neither lascivious nor impotent.

The evocation of January and May, however, has a purpose deeper than simple inversion, for Shakespeare uses Othello's age, as he does his blackness, to dramatize the elemental composition of his marriage. January figures were commonly depicted in the second childhood of senility. Shakespeare, in his genius, appropriates the convention to give Othello much of the primal character of a child. A professional soldier, a stranger to Venetian culture and sophistication, and a man coming to marriage late in life, Othello seems innocent as well as vulnerable. And, without in the least depriving him of his actual manhood, Shakespeare endows him with many of the emotional responses and much of the peculiar vision of a very young boy. What Northrop Frye has described in *Fools of Time* as the "curious quality in Othello's imagination that can only be called cosmological," and what G. Wilson Knight has discriminated in a different way as "the *Othello* music," are both functions of that vision.

They both spring from the primal world of a child's feelings and fantasies, and Othello's habitation in that world is a potent source of his heroic energy throughout the play. In the early acts the accent is on a child's primitive capacity for wonder and worship, and it is demonstrated in Othello's "rude" speech as well as in the life history he runs through for Brabantio, even from his "boyish days," in which he speaks of "moving accidents by flood and field," of "hills whose heads touch heaven," of "the Cannibals that each other eat, the Anthropophagi," and of "men whose heads / Do grow beneath their shoulders" (I. iii. 132–145).

Othello's capacity to generate wonder is ultimately an expression of his capacity to feel it, and it is his own childlike wonder and reverence that make his love for Desdemona in the early acts so remarkable. A human being's first erotic relationship is with his mother, toward whom he develops intense feelings of affection and desire. Freud argues in "On Narcissism" (*Works,* 14) that a child initially experiences his mother and her nourishment as a virtual extension of himself: "We say that a human being has originally two sexual objects—himself and the woman who nurses him—and in doing so we are postulating a primary narcissism in everyone." In infancy both the mother and the child experience a sense of symbiotic union, and that sense continues in a child's early development, as his "possession" of his mother and her love become an objectification of his most idealized vision of himself. Eventually, with his father both an obstacle and a support, a boy surrenders much of his narcissism and learns to transfer his erotic feelings from himself and his mother to other women. But a man's image of his mother is never lost, and in his deepest and most complete sexual relationships, his early sense of union with his mother, "the primal condition in which object-libido and ego-libido cannot be distinguished," remains the model of sexual ecstasy and the source of his most passionate as well as most exalted romantic feelings.

Desdemona from first to last expresses these primal ideals in her love for Othello, a love that like a mother's is literally unconditional, though at the same time it is freely sexual, and at the beginning Othello responds to it with corresponding primal force. He invests his whole being in his love for her, and in the early acts he always speaks of and to her with that sense of symbiotic exaltation that is the remembrance of childhood—a sense that reaches its apogee in Cyprus, when they are reunited after their journey over "the enchafèd flood":

[*Enter Othello and Attendants.*]
Othello. O my fair warrior!
Desdemona.   My dear Othello!
Othello. It gives me wonder great as my content
To see you here before me. O my soul's joy!
If after every tempest come such calms,
May the winds blow till they have wakened death!
And let the laboring bark climb hills of seas
Olympus-high, and duck again as low
As hell's from heaven! If it were now to die,
'Twere now to be most happy; for I fear
My soul hath her content so absolute
That not another comfort like to this
Succeeds in unknown fate.
Desdemona.   The heavens forbid
But that our loves and comforts should increase
Even as our days do grow.
Othello.   Amen to that, sweet powers!
I cannot speak enough of this content;
It stops me here; it is too much of joy.
And this, and this, the greatest discords be
[*They kiss.*]
That e'er our hearts shall make!

(II. i. 180–197)

Freud observes, in discussing the love for which a man leaves father and mother to cleave to his wife, that the greatest intensity of sensual passion in men brings with it an overestimation of the object. In "On Narcissism" he writes that "this sexual overvaluation is the origin of the peculiar state of being in love" and that its deepest impulse is to recapture the early feelings of childhood: "To be their own ideal once more, in regard to sexual no less than other trends, as they were in childhood—this is what people strive to attain as their happiness." Freud's discussion of narcissism is closely analogous to the biblical theme of the regaining of Eden, "a world of original identity." In art, as Northrop Frye points out in *A Natural Perspective,* the theme frequently takes the form of a "return . . . not to childhood but to a state of innocence symbolized by childhood." Frye remarks elsewhere that in romance literature "the traditional symbolic basis of the sexual quest, which goes back to the Song of Songs in the Bible, is the identification of the mistress' body with the paradisal garden" (*Secular Scripture,* 1976).

The association of Desdemona with such symbolism is particularly strong in *Othello* (and accounts in part for Shakespeare's great insistence on her innocence), and Othello's reunion with her on Cyprus, the most ecstatic moment of the play, draws deeply on the primal psychological and religious sources of all erotic yearning. The movement of desire and feeling in Othello expresses precisely the state of being in love that Freud describes, and the scene is infused with visual and verbal hyperboles of erotic exaltation. It is true that there is a premonitory suggestion of the tragedy of Othello's primal quest. Freud argues that, in human development, the state of primary narcissism is the crossroads of the life and death instincts, as well as of love and hate. Although it provides the original model of the ego's movement toward others, it is also the model of the state in which the ego destructively incorporates others into itself; and the dissolution of the boundary between the self and the outside world represents the movement toward the "absolute content" of death itself. Macbeth represents this destructive and suicidal movement quite directly; and there is no question that Othello touches upon it when he speaks of wakening death and says, "If it were now to die, / 'Twere now to be most happy." But the comparison with Macbeth shows the crucial difference as well, for there is also no question that Othello is reaching out to another human being, as Macbeth never does and never can, and the intimation of death and the dark side of narcissism only increases our sympathy for the absoluteness of Othello's commitment to Desdemona. As he speaks, with Iago as witness, we recognize his profound vulnerability, and we may also find tremors of anxiety in what he says. But, given that very vulnerability, Othello's anxiety is justified and functions in this scene as a measure of the extraordinary intensity of his hope and of his love. Iago does not mistake the beauty of what he sees:

            O, you are well tuned now!
But I'll set down the pegs that make this music,
As honest as I am.

(II. i. 197–199)

Iago succeeds in his malevolent quest, and there is no doubt that he does so in part because he represents something that is within Othello himself. Shakespeare suggests in the simplest mechanics of the opening dialogue of the temptation scene (III. iii. 93–116), through Iago's insistent echoing of Othello's own words, that the process we are to witness is fundamentally an internal one, and Iago's psychomachic role would have been unmistakable to Elizabethans. The psychoanalytic ramifications of Iago's aggression against Othello—which is to say, Othello's aggression against himself—are deep. Iago is Desdemona's sexual as well as spiritual antagonist. Where she luminously represents a union of affection and desire, Iago wishes to reduce love to "merely a lust of the blood and a permission of the will" (I. iii. 333–334). He repeatedly assures Roderigo that the love of Desdemona and Othello cannot last, that she can have no delight in looking "on the devil," and that "very nature will instruct her in it and compel her to some second choice" (II. i. 224, 231–232). Considering the number of critics who end up agreeing with Iago's assumptions, it should be noted that Iago is speaking to Roderigo, the simplest of gulls (and even he objects), and speaking disingenuously. As Iago's soliloquies show, his deepest animus against Othello and Desdemona stems precisely from his belief that their "free" and generous natures make them capable of proving him wrong. The basic motive of his malignancy, like Satan's, is envy.

Iago nevertheless prevails with Othello because Othello eventually internalizes Iago's maleficent sexual vision and sees himself with Iago's eyes rather than Desdemona's. Again, at the nexus of Othello's vulnerability, as of his romantic disposition, are his age and color. At a critical turn in the argument of the temptation scene, Othello wonders that "nature" should be "erring from itself" in Desdemona (III. iii. 227). It is a line that could be construed and meant as a protest against Iago's insinuations, but Iago quickly transforms it into a deeply subversive sexual indictment:

> Ay, there's the point! as (to be bold with you)
> Not to affect many proposèd matches
> Of her own clime, complexion, and degree,
> Whereto we see in all things nature tends—
> Foh! one may smell in such a will most rank,
> Foul disproportions, thoughts unnatural.
>
> (III. iii. 228–233)

Shortly afterward, Othello adopts those thoughts as his own and explicitly associates them with his color and his age:

> Haply, for I am black
> And have not those soft parts of conversation
> That chamberers have, or for I am declined

> Into the vale of years—yet that's not much—
> She's gone. I am abused, and my relief
> Must be to loathe her. O curse of marriage,
> That we can call these delicate creatures ours,
> And not their appetites!
>
> (III. iii. 263–270)

This is the crux of Othello's fall, and his union with Iago's world of blood lust follows immediately. He believes that Desdemona cannot be true because he becomes convinced that he himself is unlovable and, believing that, he also becomes convinced that Desdemona's manifest attraction to him is itself perverse, a "proof" of her corruption.

Just before he strangles her, Othello and Desdemona have the following acutely painful dialogue:

> *Othello.* Think on thy sins.
> *Desdemona.*   They are loves I bear to you.
> *Othello.* Ay, and for that thou diest.
> *Desdemona.* That death's unnatural that kills for loving.
>
> (V. ii. 40–42)

Desdemona may be referring to the sin of disobeying her father. Othello may be condemning Desdemona for her very desire for him, or he may be projecting upon her his incapacity to accept his own desires, probably both. Hovering over the lines may be the sense of guilt of the original sin, which was at once physical and spiritual, and which first introduced death into the world. But whatever their precise meaning, the lines convey the ultimate horror of the play, which is Othello's tragic transmutation of the precept upon which his, or any, marriage is founded: "So men are bound to love their own wives as their own bodies. He that loveth his own wife, loveth himself." The tragedy of Othello is that finally he fails to love his own body, to love himself; and it is this despairing self-hatred that spawns the enormous violence, as well as the self-destructiveness, of his jealousy. For the killing of Desdemona anticipates his own actual suicide. He has loved her as his own flesh, and when he destroys her he destroys himself. And he knows it.

The awesome energy of Othello's jealousy, its primitive and superstitious murderousness, is a function of the same primal forces that animated his earlier exaltation and love. As a child matures, he must inevitably be separated from his mother. He must confront the reality, first, that he cannot incorporate her, that she is not a part of him, and, then, that she has a sexual love for his father from which he is obviously and necessarily excluded. In the Freudian cosmology this conflict is inescapable, and the child, before he experiences his inevitable oedipal defeat and learns to reconstitute himself, experiences profound feelings of betrayal and rivalry and threats of the loss of identity and of nurture. It is this constellation of feelings that is the primal source of sexual jealousy and that is tapped directly in the second half of *Othello:*

>   . . . alas, to make me
> A fixèd figure for the time of scorn
> To point his slow unmoving finger at!
> Yet could I bear that too; well, very well.
> But there where I have garnered up my heart,
> Where either I must live or bear no life,
> The fountain from the which my current runs
> Or else dries up—to be discarded thence,
> Or keep it as a cistern for foul toads
> To knot and gender in—turn thy complexion there,
> Patience, thou young and rose-lipped cherubin!
> Ay, there look grim as hell!

(IV. ii. 53–64)

This is not a pleasant passage to contemplate, but it is very important to an understanding of the play, for its conflation of images of the breast and of the womb expresses the precise etiology of Othello's jealous anguish and suggests the tragic presumption, as well as the vulnerability, of a love so absolutely rooted in, and dependent upon, the exaltation of symbiotic union.

In the broadest sense, Othello's behavior in the second half of the play is a dramatization of guilt. In Christian terms the temptation scene recollects the fall of man, which St. Augustine interpreted as an allegorical representation of an essentially psychomachic process, the disorder of the soul by which reason becomes subjected to passion, and particularly the self-destroying as well as self-exalting passion of pride. In analogous psychoanalytic terms, Othello's guilt is the aggression of the unconscious, again an internal process, in which Iago represents one part of Othello and Desdemona another and in which Othello's destruction of Desdemona is a literal enactment of his ultimately self-destructive aggression against himself. But it does not follow, as most theological and psychological critics seem to believe, that the play is therefore throughout or essentially a pathological study of either an idolator or a narcissist, however many

attributes of both Othello may in fact demonstrate. On the contrary, for a number of reasons, such approaches profoundly misconstrue—when they do not utterly ignore—the play's actual experience.

To begin with, and one cannot overemphasize the point, Desdemona is as much a part of Othello's soul, whether spiritually or psychically conceived, as is Iago. She is not a fantasy, or rather she is a fantasy made flesh: the life, not only the imago, of that union of tenderness and desire, that unconditional love, toward which all men aspire. And Othello marries her; the whole first half of the play celebrates his incandescent erotic feelings for her; and in the second half his torment and decomposition can be measured, as they always are in his own consciousness, by his loss of her. It is deeply fitting in his final speech, and cheering to us if not to him, that his dying recognition that she was true should enable him genuinely to recover a sense of his former being—just as his earlier delusion that she was faithless had caused him to lose it.

Correspondingly, Iago does not constitute the whole of Othello's spiritual state or of his unconscious. He is not simply a projection of Othello's own disposition to vice, though he plays upon it. He is not a vice but, as he himself repeatedly announces and everyone else in the play eventually realizes, a "hellish villain" (V. ii. 368). He is the eternal tempter, who succeeds because he attacks in Othello not just his frailty but the frailty of all men. W. H. Auden suggests, astutely, that Iago "treats Othello as an analyst treats a patient except that, of course, his intention is to kill not to cure." Auden goes on to observe that everything Iago says "is designed to bring to Othello's consciousness what he has already guessed is there." But a further and crucial point should be made, which is that what is "there" exists as part of the unconscious life of all men. It is not peculiar to Othello, though it is tragically heightened in him. The issue in *Othello* is not an abstract one, because within the world that Shakespeare creates, honest Iago is a spokesman for what everyone else, save Desdemona, feels or believes or represents. Othello's guilt, in fact, pervades his society; and Iago has only to return to Othello the image of himself that he can see reflected, not in fantasy but in reality, in the world about him. Brabantio, who was formerly his friend, who "loved" and "oft invited" him to his house, vilifies him and believes that Desdemona is bewitched and that the marriage is obscene; and the opening scene of the play implicates the audience as well as Venetian society in this deep racial prejudice. Cassio idolizes Desdemona but at the same time is capable of a sexual relationship only with a whore of whom he is essentially contemptuous. In a proleptic version of Othello's fall, he gets drunk and violent on Othello's wedding night. The only other marriage in the play is Iago's and Emilia's, and although Emilia's portrayal is very complex, it is nevertheless obvious that Iago has little affection for her and that at least the premises of her own worldly realism are not far from his. Only at the end, in a response to Desdemona's fidelity that neither she nor certainly Iago would ever have anticipated, does she move into another realm of feeling and value, and even then she finds Desdemona's marriage incomprehensible, if not repellent: "She was too fond of her most filthy bargain" (V. ii. 158). It is no wonder that Othello, literally an alien by his profession, his background, his color, and his age, should in such a world find it tragically impossible to hold to the scriptural belief, which is also Desdemona's, that he is "black, but beautiful." Freud remarks in *Civilization and Its Discontents* (*Works,* 21) that "in an individual neurosis we take as our starting-point the contrast that distinguishes the patient from his environment, which is assumed to be 'normal.'" No such assumption can be made about the environment of *Othello,* in either Venice or Cyprus. It is not normal, it is itself guilt-ridden, and Othello is at once its victim and its heroic sacrifice.

In a tragic universe, it is worth stressing, guilt and death are inescapable, and the hero commands our minds and hearts not because he is sick or healthy, saved or damned, but because he most deeply incarnates and experiences the inexorable tragic conditions that we recognize in our own existence. In *Othello* those conditions are primarily and explicitly sexual, whether they are understood in religious or psychological terms, or from an Elizabethan or a modern perspective. Freud's own view, expressed consistently in his writing, is that the oedipal drama that forms the basis of human development is fundamentally tragic. In "The Most Prevalent Form of Degradation in Erotic Life" he argues that the dissociation of affection and sensuality that characterizes cases of actual psychical impotence is in the last analysis a condition of all human beings, that the two currents of erotic feeling, "the same two that are personified in art as heavenly and earthly (or animal) love," are almost never completely fused in civilized man. He remarks:

It has an ugly sound and a paradoxical as well, but nevertheless it must be said that whoever is to be really free and happy in love must have overcome his deference for women and come to terms with the idea of incest with mother or sister. Anyone who in the face of this test subjects himself to serious self-examination will indubitably find that at the bottom of his heart he too regards the sexual act as something degrading, which soils and contaminates not only the body.

Freud concludes that "however strange it may sound, I think the possibility must be considered that something in the nature of the sexual instinct itself is unfavourable to the achievement of absolute gratification." The whole of this essay is the nucleus of Freud's later, more celebrated, discussion of aggression and guilt in *Civilization and Its Discontents.*

Freud did not originate these ideas. Similar concepts are inherent and often developed in a considerable body of medieval and Renaissance literature that combines erotic and theological themes. In his own time Shakespeare would have found them stated with Freudian explicitness in Montaigne's "Upon Some Verses of *Virgil,*" the essay from which he almost certainly drew directly in *All's Well That Ends Well.* Since Montaigne himself actually tended to degrade women, he demonstrates as well as parallels Freud's thought. His essay deals with sexuality, and a large part of it constitutes an argument against the possibility of uniting the affection that belongs to marriage and the "insatiate thirst of enjoying a greedily desired subject" that belongs to sensual love:

> *Love disdaineth a man should hold of other then himselfe,* and dealeth but faintly with acquaintances begun and entertained under another title; as mariage is. . . . Nor is it other then a kinde of incest, in this reverent alliance and sacred bond, to employ the efforts and extravagant humor of an amorous licentiousnes.

Like Freud, Montaigne finds something paradoxically degrading about the very "acte of generation":

> In al other things you may observe decorum and maintaine some decency: all other operations admit some rules of honesty: this cannot onely be imagined, but vicious or ridiculous. . . . Surely it is an argument not onely of our original corruption, but a badge of our vanity and deformity. On the one side nature urgeth us unto it: having thereunto combined, yea fastned, the most noble, the most profitable, and the most sen-

517

sually-pleasing, of all her functions: and on the other suffereth us to accuse, to condemne and to shunne it, as insolent, as dishonest, and as lewder to blush at it, and allow, yea and to commend abstinence. *Are not we most brutish, to terme that worke beastly which begets, and which maketh us?*

Montaigne, like Freud, observes the ultimate incapacity of erotic instincts to be fully satisfied or harmonized: "But withall *it is against the nature of love, not to be violent, and against the condition of violence, to be constant"*; and he says of marriage that "It is a match wherto may well be applied the common saying, *Homo homini aut Deus, aut Lupus. . . . Man unto man is either a God or a Wolfe."*

It is within this polarized erotic universe that Othello moves, and he traverses its extremes not only in the larger parabolic action of the creation and death of his marriage, but in the very constitution of his being. At the hinge of the play's action, just after Desdemona leaves him with her pleas for Cassio, and the instant before Iago begins his attack, Othello says:

> Excellent wretch! Perdition catch my soul
> But I do love thee! and when I love thee not,
> Chaos is come again.
>
> (III. iii. 90–92)

These well-known lines spring from the heart of Othello's existence and describe the essence of the paradox that at once animates and destroys him. At the end, in his last words, Othello speaks the truth, both of his experience and of our response to it, when he says that he is "one that loved not wisely, but too well" (V. ii. 344). The play has deep affiliations with romance. It is a full and moving tragic anatomy of love, not a clinical diagnosis or demonstration; and Othello is its hero not because he achieves triumph or suffers defeat, though he does both, nor because he learns or does not learn a theological or psychological lesson, but because he is indeed, as Cassio says, "great of heart," and because he enacts for us, with beautiful and terrifying nakedness, the primitive energies that are the substance of our own erotic lives.

Macbeth

In *The City of God,* St. Augustine calls the pride from which man's and Satan's rebellion resulted "a perverse desire of height," and his discussion both of the nature of this desire and of its consequences is extremely relevant to an understanding of Macbeth's aspirations. "What is pride," Augustine writes, "but a perverse desire of height, in forsaking Him to whom the soul ought to cleave, as the beginning thereof, to make itself seem its own beginning. This is when it likes itself too well, or when it so loves itself that it will abandon that unchangeable Good which ought to be more delightful to it than itself." Since man was created of nothing, Augustine continues, he was "lessened in excellence" at the fall: by "leaving Him to adhere to and delight in himself, he grew not to be nothing, but towards nothing." " 'Ye shall be as gods,' " the devil said to Adam and Eve, "which they might sooner have been," Augustine adds, "by obedience and coherence with their Creator . . . but man desiring more became less, and choosing to be sufficient in himself fell from that all-sufficient God." The just reward that Adam and Eve received for "desiring more" was the perpetuation of the paradox of that desire:

> What is man's misery other than his own disobedience to himself: that seeing he would not what he might, now he cannot what he would? For although in paradise all was not in his power during his obedience, yet then he desired nothing but what was in his power, and so did what he would. But now, as the scripture says, and we see by experience, "Man is like to vanity." For who can recount his innumerable desires of impossibilities.

Augustine's understanding of the "innumerable desires of impossibilities" that caused the fall, and that constituted man's state forever after it, subsumes the treatment by Renaissance moral philosophers of the human passions in general as well as ambition in particular. In *The French Academie,* for example, a vast and influential treatise of moral psychology first translated into English in 1586, Pierre de La Primaudaye writes that because the achievement of what men seek "doth not bring with it sufficient cause of contentation, they perceive themselves alwaies deprived of the end of their desires, and are constrained to wander all their life time beyond all bounds and measure, according to the rashness and inconstancie of their lusts." Ambition, for La Primaudaye, is not merely a species of this general predicament of human desire but, in some respects, its epitome. "Ambition never suffreth those that have once received hir as a guest, to enjoy their present estate quietly,'' he remarks,

> but maketh them always emptie of goods, and full of hope. . . . And the more they growe and increase in power and authoritie, the rather are they induced and caried headlong by their affections to commit all kind of injustice, and flatter themselves in furious and frantike actions, that they may come to the end of their infinite platformes.

In addition to providing suggestive glosses on the peculiar emptiness and insatiability of Macbeth's aspirations, these passages indicate the exceptional resonance of ambition in the Renaissance. The "infinite platformes" of Macbeth, moreover, comprehend an appalling measure of destructive as well as insatiable aspiration, and beyond his general observations, La Primaudaye has a number of particular reflections on ambition that illuminate the sources of this combination in human experience. He remarks, citing Plutarch, that "the desire of having more . . . bringeth foorth" in ambitious and great lords "oftentimes an unsociable, cruell, and beastly nature," and he adds:

> Further, if (as histories teach us) some have been so wretched & miserable, as to give themselves to the Art of Necromancie, and to contract with the devill, that they might come to soveraigne power and authoritie, what other thing, how strange soever it be, will not they undertake that suffer themselves to be wholly caried away with this vice of ambition? It is ambitio[n] that setteth the sonne against the father, and imboldeneth him to seeke his destruction of whom he holdeth his life.

If this remarkable passage was not actually in Shakespeare's mind when he wrote *Macbeth*, it nonetheless contains striking analogies with the play and discriminates some of its deepest currents of experience. Macbeth makes a pact with witches, if not the devil; Scotland, as the Porter as well as many others makes clear, becomes an express similitude of hell as a result; and the murder of Duncan, as Freud remarks, "is little else than parricide" (*Works,* 14). It is Lady Macbeth who explicitly says that the King resembled "my father as he slept" (II. ii. 13). But she speaks for Macbeth's soul as well, and the association of father and king was in any case inescapable in the Renaissance. It animates as well as haunts Macbeth from the first.

What is ultimately most interesting about the motifs of necromancy and parricide in *Macbeth,* however, is not their presence but their collocation, for Shakespeare suggests that the two are deeply connected, if not actually functions of each other. This connection, which La Primaudaye states explicitly, is at the center of the play. It is directly related to the dynamics of original sin, the desire for omnipotence, that Augustine describes, and at the same time it has precise and illuminating analogues in modern psychological thought. Freud argues that the fantasy of killing and replacing the father is the fulcrum of human psychological development. Less familiar and certainly less actively appreciated is his contention that oedipal guilt can have such potency in human development because for a small child a murderous thought is indistinguishable from a murderous deed. Clinical research has tended to confirm the presence of this form of magical thinking in infants, and even psychologists who distrust Freud's concentration upon oedipal rivalry do not generally question his outline of the earlier realm of thought and feeling upon which he argues it depends. In this infantile realm of narcissism the self is all-encompassing and its platforms do indeed seem infinite, for in an infant's mind distinctions between the self and the outer world tend to dissolve, nature seems animistic, and above all, thoughts seem omnipotent.

Because the theme of usurpation is so insistent in *Macbeth,* parricidal resonances are not hard to find. The real issue is to understand them in the proportions and with the particular inflections that the play gives to them. In the most directly voluptuous of her ambitious fantasies, Lady Macbeth tells Macbeth that the "great business" of murdering the King "shall to all our nights and days to come / Give solely sovereign sway and masterdom" (I. v. 67–68). The aspiration to be the only one, to have sole sovereignty, sole masterdom and possession, is the aspect of childhood thinking that has the deepest roots in the psyche and that forms the clearest analogue to Augustine's theology of the fall. In a child's imagination, the wish to be the one and only is absolute—it is so by definition—and the result is a particularly deep representation of the Augustinian dialectic of more and less. Very young children, in the unlovely exclusiveness of their egoism, feel that they are impaired by someone else's gain, that in any competition what one wins the other must inevitably lose, and that loss is self-diminishment. Such thinking is not confined to children. Montaigne remarks on its persistence in adults in a brief and unsettling essay entitled "The Profit of One Man is the Dammage of Another." He says, "Let every man sound his owne conscience, hee shall finde, that our inward desires are for the most part nourished and bred in us by the losse and hurt of others," and he associates this condition with the "generall policie" of "Nature": "for Physitians hold, that *The birth, increase, and augmentation of every thing, is the alteration and corruption of another.*" Freud contends, in his own domestication of these natural laws, that in a very young boy's fantasies of competition with his father this general policy can take on a murderous inflection.

Precisely such an inflection is given to competitive thinking by Duncan at the very outset of *Macbeth,* when he tells Ross to "pronounce" the "present death" of the Thane of Cawdor, "And with his former title greet Macbeth. . . . What he hath lost noble Macbeth hath won" (I. ii. 64–67). The inverse and murderous relationship between winning and losing that Duncan reveals in these lines suggests the dialectic that both Montaigne and Freud comment upon, and it describes the condition of the whole world of *Macbeth* in its early scenes, for the play suggests the anatomy of a parricidal nightmare long before the Macbeths enact one. The witches initiate the absolute opposition between winning and losing at the outset of the play—"When the battle's lost and won" (I. i. 4)—and their prophecies are often couched in the language of inverse functions and equivocal contest. But the rhetoric of their supernatural solicitations, at least at the start, is quite tangibly anchored in the natural world of the play, a world that invites, in Banquo's phrase, "the cursèd thoughts that nature / Gives way to in repose" (II. i. 8–9).

The diffusion of such thoughts in the early part of the play suggests not that Shakespeare is apportioning them for praise or blame, still less that he is exculpating Macbeth, but rather that he is presenting them as heightened, tragic conditions of the economy of nature that Montaigne discriminates and that Macbeth himself eventually incarnates. The "cursèd thoughts" of which Banquo speaks are in Macbeth's own mind from the very beginning. Freud suggests that a man sometimes will commit murder in order to rationalize his sense of guilt, that guilt may be the cause of the crime rather than its result (*Works,* 13). There is more than a suggestion of this condition in Macbeth (as opposed to Lady Macbeth, in whom guilt is a distinct aftereffect), both in his rapt reaction to his first meeting

with the witches and in the "thought, whose murder yet is but fantastical" that surfaces in his first soliloquy (I. iii. 139). But the lines that give the sharpest expression to the parricidal thoughts that both surround Macbeth and are within him occur when Duncan proclaims Malcolm Prince of Cumberland and heir to the throne. Macbeth says in an aside:

> The Prince of Cumberland—that is a step
> On which I must fall down or else o'erleap,
> For in my way it lies. Stars, hide your fires;
> Let not light see my black and deep desires.

> (I. iv. 48–51)

This speech depicts the crucial moment of Macbeth's commitment to the deed, long before Lady Macbeth enters the scene. Macbeth has ostensive reason to envy Malcolm, if he is to believe the logic of the witches' prophecy, but that logic is itself an expression of the murderous economy of competition that the rebellion has encouraged in the kingdom. The heart of the speech is its categorical and inverse reasoning: "I must fall down or else o'erleap" (an image that anticipates Macbeth's subsequent reference to "vaulting ambition, which o'erleaps itself" [I. vii. 27]); and this reasoning in turn is an expression of the dark and aspiring desires that both Augustine and Freud find to be at the source of human infirmity and guilt, and that Montaigne, less homiletically, sees as a natural basis of human conduct. As Coleridge suggests, Milton seems to be evoking this moment in the play (and an Augustinian interpretation of it) when he describes how Satan,

> fraught
> With envy against the Son of God, that day
> Honor'd by his great Father, and proclaim'd
> Messiah King anointed, could not bear
> Through pride that sight, and thought himself
> impaired.

> (*Paradise Lost,* V, 661–665)

Macbeth's sense of impairment is profound throughout the play, and some of its psychological resonances are so obvious as to be overlooked. The most basic is that the act of parricide (and to some extent the fantasies of it as well) is, like the denial of God, a negation of the source of one's being. As La Primaudaye suggests, it is self-destructive for a man "to seeke his destruction of whom he holdeth his life," and that precise insight is explicitly stated on two occasions in *Macbeth,* both times in seeming reference to Duncan's sons, but really in reference to Macbeth (II. iii. 93–95; II. iv. 27–29).

An equally profound psychological resonance of Macbeth's impairment, and one that reaches even deeper to the roots of his tragedy because it precedes the realm of parricidal contention itself, is both his and our constant sense that his usurpation, his quest—his ambition—is, and by its nature must be, entirely unattainable, a fantasy grotesquely out of reach in reality. A very young boy may wish in his imagination to take his father's place, but he obviously cannot do so in fact. He literally cannot perform his father's role, either sexually or in other ways, and in this respect such childhood fantasies are like the drunken lust that the Porter describes, only far more frightening. Macbeth always knows this. Lady Macbeth, at first, does not. She is most explicit in recognizing the parricidal impetus of the murder of Duncan, but though that recognition both deters and eventually destroys her, its most immediate effect seems to be to excite her.

Macbeth never experiences such excitement and is at first tenuous and doubtful and later savagely frustrated and enraged, because in him is represented that part of a childhood sensibility which always knows that the enterprise is physically impossible. The play's celebrated clothing images make this part of Macbeth's predicament unusually clear, for the garments to which he aspires do not ever fit him. Early in the play he calls them "borrowed robes" (I. iii. 109); later they are called the dress of his drunken hopes (I. vii. 35–36); and at the last they "hang loose about him, like a giant's robe / Upon a dwarfish thief" (V. ii. 21–22). That final description has many reverberations, but its purely physical impact is important. Macbeth is simply not big enough for the role and title to which he aspires. He is called a dwarf rather than a child because he has in fact had terrifying adult powers, but what the image nonetheless suggests is the radical disproportion between a small child and the grown-up man he wishes all at once to replace and become.

This sense of disproportion, if not disjunction, is central to the play. It is not confined to clothing images, and it is represented in ways that suggest even more fundamental sources of human experience. The Porter points to the obvious sexual manifestation of disjunction in discriminating the gap between drunken desire and performance, but his

speech is itself only a part of the prevailing concern in the play with the larger and deeper relationship of thought and action. That relationship is Macbeth's single most constant and important preoccupation, and its roots can be traced to the condition of primary narcissism. Freud argues in *Totem and Taboo* that external reality for an infant is composed of his own sensations and the projection, often hallucinatory, of his own wishes and fears—of his "thoughts"; and because these thoughts can ignore the coordinates of time and space in what we perceive as external reality, "since what lies furthest apart both in time and space can without difficulty be comprehended in a single act of consciousness," they seem magical and omnipotent. Freud suggests that this infantile narcissism is the source of animism and that it actually characterized primitive man, who practiced magic and peopled the universe with spirits, who "knew what things were like in the world, namely just as he felt himself to be," who "transposed the structural conditions of his own mind into the external world." Freud also argues that such animistic thinking is still present in more civilized and adult experience, in the very nature of dreaming as well as in more conscious life. Its more beneficent or paradisal residues he finds in the state of being in love, when, against the normal evidence of external reality, the lovers feel the "I" and "thou" to be one. And its more malign and hellish traces he finds in the behavior of neurotics (and psychotics), in whom the formation of symptoms is determined by "the reality not of experience but of thought," who "live in a world apart," who "are only affected by what is thought with intensity and pictured with emotion" (*Works,* 13).

A. P. Rossiter writes that in *Macbeth* Shakespeare represents "the passionate will-to-self-assertion, to unlimited self-hood, and especially the impulsion to force the world (and everything in it) to *my* pattern, in *my* time, and with *my* own hand." Behind this "will" and "impulsion" is the universal experience of infancy that Freud and others have discriminated. There is certainly no tragedy in Shakespeare's canon in which children figure so importantly and in which, particularly, there is such a profusion of images of infants and of infancy. These children and images have many functions, not least to serve as reminders of Macbeth's childlessness and of the future in which he cannot participate and tries to destroy. But their profoundest effect is to evoke the whole realm of primitive narcissism in which Macbeth is "cabined, cribbed, confined" (III. iv. 24) and with which the entire action of the play resonates, a realm in which there is no future except that which is pictured as being fulfilled in the present, in the moment of thought. Lady Macbeth suggests the character of such magical thought and its childhood origins quite precisely when she rebukes Macbeth for his unwillingness to face Duncan's dead body:

> The sleeping and the dead
> Are but as pictures. 'Tis the eye of childhood
> That fears a painted devil.

> (II. ii. 52–54)

Though Lady Macbeth correctly locates this "eye" in Macbeth's consciousness, the primitive world of magical and animistic thinking, like the filament of parricidal competition, pervades the whole play. Metaphorical analogies between the macrocosm and the microcosm are constant and have unusual power in *Macbeth,* and as A. C. Bradley and all subsequent critics have recognized, the state of mind within Macbeth and the state of Scotland outside of him seem often indistinguishable. Equally important, nature itself is literally animated in the play—most conspicuously when Birnam Wood moves to Dunsinane—and the play is filled with suggestions of magic. There is white magic in the "good" English King, who has "a heavenly gift of prophecy" and whose hand and "healing benediction" can cure "the disease. . . . called the evil" (IV. iii. 146, 156 157). Black magic is represented in the witches. Macbeth does not create the witches, and we see them before he does. They open the play and establish its environment before Macbeth appears, and when he sees them, so does Banquo; and though Banquo does not, like Macbeth, become obsessed with them, he does nonetheless respond to the magical potency of the realm of thought they represent.

It is nonetheless within Macbeth's consciousness that this realm has its most profound and compelling representation in the play. All Shakespearean tragic heroes "live in a world apart," but none so clearly and completely in "the reality not of experience but of thought." The Renaissance phrase "passions of the mind" is peculiarly apposite to Macbeth. His characteristic posture, virtually a physical posture on stage, is self-absorption, in manifold senses of that term. He is at first "rapt" (I. iii. 57) and then quickly literally "lost" in his

"thoughts" (II. ii. 70–71), not only in soliloquies, in which such preoccupation is conventional, but in the midst of communal occasions, the most memorable being the banquet, where the apparition that causes his withdrawal seems more purely the creation of his mind. The thoughts in which he is lost, the "sorriest fancies" he makes his "companions" (III. ii. 9), are usually not only about his state of mind; they are also about the very pressure of thought in his consciousness and most specifically about his urgent need to make the thoughts deeds and thereby to terminate them—in his own repeated words, to make the hand and heart one. This need is a recollection of the primitive, infantile fear of disintegration, and it reverberates complexly in Macbeth's persistent anxiety that the parts of his body are becoming separated and in the urgency and dread of his quest to bring them absolutely together in his mind.

Lady Macbeth touches directly upon these issues in her attack on Macbeth's manhood. She says, when he hesitates to kill Duncan,

> Art thou afeard
> To be the same in thine own act and valor
> As thou art in desire? . . .
> . . .
> When you durst do it, then you were a man;
> And to be more than what you were, you would
> Be so much more the man.

> (I. vii. 39–41, 49–51)

These lines, which anticipate the Porter's, reflect the parricidal motifs of the play, but they also suggest the more primal realm both of Macbeth's fear and of his ambition; most of his characterization, and much of the action of the play, are concerned with his efforts absolutely to unite desire and act and to transpose "the structural conditions of his own mind into the external world."

Macbeth's murder of Duncan is his first attempt to bring about such a transposition: in parricidal terms by making himself sole sovereign of his world, the one and only; and on the more primal level of narcissism by making himself and his kingdom coextensive, by literalizing the medieval and Elizabethan metaphor of the king's two bodies. Lady Macbeth, appropriately, plays a major part in the parricidal aspiration, but the conscious pursuit of the more primal quest is Macbeth's alone; and it intensifies after the murder of Duncan, as he successively plans the destruction of Banquo and Fleance and of Macduff's family without Lady Macbeth's knowledge.

In contemplating the first of these family murders, Macbeth says:

> For mine own good
> All causes shall give way. I am in blood
> Stepped in so far that, should I wade no more,
> Returning were as tedious as go o'er.
> Strange things I have in head, that will to hand,
> Which must be acted ere they may be scanned.
>
> (III. iv. 135–140)

The distance—in time if not in space—between head and hand is nearly gone by the time Macbeth conceives the murder of Macduff's family. Informed that Macduff has gone to England, he says:

> Time, thou anticipat'st my dread exploits.
> The flighty purpose never is o'ertook
> Unless the deed go with it. From this moment
> The very firstlings of my heart shall be
> The firstlings of my hand. And even now,
> To crown my thoughts with acts, be it thought and
>   done.
>
> (IV. i. 144–149)

This is the crown to which Macbeth has aspired all along—to be, in Lady Macbeth's words, "transported . . . beyond / This ignorant present" and "feel . . . / The future in the instant" (I. v. 54–56), to have the omnipotent power to contain the whole world within his own mind and to make it entirely in his own image—to be, as Augustine said man wished to be at the fall, and as he is in his mind in infancy, like a god. This moment is the apogee of Macbeth's ambition. It is also the turning point in the action. Unburdened of the gap between the heart and the hand, between thought and act, present and future, Macbeth loses the energy of his fear—"Direness, familiar to my slaughterous thoughts / Cannot once start me" (V. v. 14–15). But without the distinction between himself and the outside world, and without the future, he also begins to lose the energy and definition of life itself. "To-morrow" becomes a meaningless prolongation of today (V. v. 19–21), and he becomes "aweary of the sun" (V. v. 49). And as he begins to lose life, the outside world begins to regain it. Macbeth's crowning of his thoughts is followed by the slaughter of Lady Macduff and her child, but

also, immediately after that, by the scene in which Malcolm successfully tests Macduff: Malcolm states that his "thoughts cannot transpose" Macduff's inner nature (IV. iii. 21), but he nonetheless comes to "know" Macduff through an imitation of Macbeth that is also an exorcism of Macbeth's world of transposing thoughts.

Montaigne makes an extremely interesting comment about the nature of such a world of thought in his essay "Of Judging of Others Death." He remarks that "we make too much account of our selves" and presumptuously believe that the universe has the "same motion" we do:

> Forsomuch as our sight being altered, represents unto it selfe things alike; and we imagine, that things faile it, as it doth to them: As they who travell by Sea, to whom mountaines, fields, townes, heaven and earth, seeme to goe the same motion, and keepe the same course, they doe.

He associates this way of thinking most particularly with the fear of death:

> We entertaine and carry all with us: Whence it followeth, that we deeme our death to be some great matter, and which passeth not so easily, nor without a solemne consultation of the Starres; *Tot circa unum caput tumultuantes Deos.* 'So many Gods keeping a stirre about one mans life.' . . . No one of us thinkes it sufficient, to be but one.

All of Shakespeare's tragic heroes have the infantile presumption that Montaigne describes—none of them can be said to think it sufficient to be but one. Macbeth's presumptuous thinking, however, is more radical than and different from that of other Shakespearean heroes in a way that is profound and instructive. Lear's need, for example, to imagine that heaven and earth move as he does is indeed an infantile denial of his mortal limits, as he himself intermittently realizes—"They told me I was everything. 'Tis a lie—I am not ague-proof" (IV. vi. 103–104). But Lear regresses into infancy because old people naturally do so and because he is afraid of dying. He protests against death, in the last analysis, because he wants to hold on to life and its real human relationships—particularly, at the end, to the love of his child Cordelia. In *Macbeth,* "all is the fear and nothing is the love" (IV. ii. 12), and Macbeth's attempt to make the world keep to his motion is essentially a flight from human relationships and a denial not of death but of life. For his fear of the distance between his thoughts and the world outside them is finally a fear of consciousness itself; and his regression to the inordinate self-love of infancy is a return to the "perfect" safety and "perfect" integrity of a womb which, as Ross says of Macbeth's kingdom, "cannot / Be called our mother but our grave" (IV. iii. 165–166).

It is common to say that Macbeth's ambition is suicidal. It may be more exact and revealing to recognize that nonbeing is his ambition, that he commits himself from the first to the suicide that Lady Macbeth acts out at the end, that his deepest wish is to annihilate the very self he asserts. This paradox can be explained in complementary Augustinian and Freudian terms. For Augustine, inordinate self-love, the soul's desire to be its own begetter, to be everything, both results in and is born of emptiness, of nothingness. The Freudian analogue is the self-love of primary narcissism. The echoes of such narcissism exist in all human beings, and in an infant this state is natural. To regress to such a condition in adulthood, however, is truly to confound hell in Elysium, for except in the state of intense love in which the self is paradoxically at once lost and aggrandized, the godlike presumption of primary narcissism results in a sense only of the loss of the self, because a self that encompasses everything ultimately cannot be defined by anything and is indeed defined by nothing. The premise common to both the Augustinian and the Freudian conceptions of the self is that human beings must exist in relation to a reality outside themselves. As Wallace Stevens observes in *Opus Posthumous* (1957), "Nothing is itself taken alone. Things are because of interrelations or interactions."

The spiritual and psychological dimensions of Macbeth's loss are represented everywhere in the play: in the Porter's apparently inconsequential discussion of the emptiness of sexual desire; in the explicit acknowledgment by both Macbeth and Lady Macbeth immediately following Duncan's murder that "To be thus is nothing" (III. i. 48), that "Naught's had, all's spent, / Where our desire is got without content" (III. ii. 4–5); and in the very constitution of their marriage—its inversions, its hollow antinomies, its sterility, its increasing loneliness and exhaustion. The loss is also crystallized in the scenes and speeches that emphasize human relationships and human community. It is shown in the peculiar horror of Macbeth's isolation during the banquet scene. It is stated explicitly

when Macbeth laments that "that which should accompany old age, / As honor, love, obedience, troops of friends, / I must not look to have" (V. iii. 24–26). And it is asserted most profoundly in Macduff's grief over the loss of his wife and children. Macduff is not a hero, but he is Macbeth's proper nemesis; and it is fitting that it is he who announces at the end of the play, in words that echo with the depths of Macbeth's tragedy, that "the time is free" (V. viii. 55). When Malcolm tells Macduff to "dispute" his grief "like a man," Macduff answers:

> I shall do so;
> But I must also feel it as a man.
> I cannot but remember such things were
> That were most precious to me.
>
> (IV. iii. 220–223)

It is no accident that these piercingly moving lines should bring into focus what it really means to be a man. And a comparison with Macbeth's atrophied response when he hears of the death of his own wife is inescapable: "She should have died hereafter: / There would have been a time for such a word" (V. v. 17–18).

There is never any doubt in this play about how much is lost and what is lost in Macbeth's primitive quest of his "own good." The preciousness of life is lost.

King Lear

King Lear raises large metaphysical questions; but, as in *Hamlet,* it is the human anguish that gives rise to such questions upon which Shakespeare focuses. Hamlet, in his most famous soliloquy, speaks of the "heartache" of human existence (III. i. 62). In *King Lear* we hear of and see the breaking of the heart. Edgar tells us that when he died his father Gloucester's "flawed heart . . . / 'Twixt two extremes of passion, joy and grief, / Burst smilingly" (V. iii. 197–199). And at the moment of Lear's death, Kent says, "Break, heart, I prithee break!" (V. iii. 313)—a line that confirms the truth of what we have just witnessed, whether it refers to Lear's heart or to Kent's own.

The metaphor of a breaking heart, and its association with the extremity of dying itself, is critical to *King Lear.* For though, again like *Hamlet,* Lear's essential preoccupation is with the anguish of living in the face of death, it does not, like the earlier play, look beyond the grave. It focuses relentlessly upon actual human decomposition—the physical "eyes' anguish" (IV. vi. 6) of Gloucester's maiming, the mental "eye of anguish" (IV. iv. 15) of Lear's madness. And the fifth act brings no change, as it does in *Hamlet.* There is no recovery from grief at the end of *Lear,* nor is there even a glimpse of Providence. Lear's question over Cordelia's lifeless body, "Why should a dog, a horse, a rat, have life, / And thou no breath at all?" (V. iii. 307–308), is not answered in the play, certainly not by Lear's few succeeding words; and among those words the ones that are most unequivocal and most memorable are "Thou'lt come no more, / Never, never, never, never, never" (V. iii. 308–309). These lines express a universal human experience —the immediate response we all bring to the death of those we love. But they have an intensified and governing power in *King Lear.* They occur at the very end, they occur after protracted suffering, they violate the hopes that appear to have been raised by Lear and Cordelia's reunion, and they occur over the dead body of a character whose love has seemed imperishable. There is no scene in Shakespeare that represents the finality of death more absolutely or more harshly; and the scene is not merely the conclusion of the action, it is its recapitulation, the moment toward which the whole of it has been directed.

In this respect, *King Lear* is reminiscent of Ecclesiastes. The play has often been compared to the Book of Job, but there is no Satan at the beginning of *Lear* nor a whirlwind from which God speaks at the end to make the play's sense of human suffering even intellectually explicable. In conception as well as texture, Lear is closer to Ecclesiastes, the book of the Old Testament that is most nearly pagan in its outlook and that treats human life almost exclusively, and despairingly, in terms of the immanence of its ending.

There are many verses in Ecclesiastes that suggest motifs and even the specific language of *King Lear.* The Preacher's announced and repeated theme is "vanity," a word whose primary connotation (and whose translation in the New English Bible) is "emptiness." He speaks of man's identity in this life as "a shadow" (7:2) and his achievements as "nothing" (5:14; 7:16). He compares men to beasts:

> For the condition of the children of men, and the condition of beasts *are* even *as* one condition unto

them. As the one dyeth, so dyeth the other: for they have all one breath, and there is no excellencie of man above the beast: for all *is* vanitie.

(3:19)

He speaks of man's nakedness: "As he came forthe of his mothers belly, he shal returne naked to go as he came, & shal beare away nothing of his labour, which he hathe caused to passe by his hand" (5:14). He talks constantly of the paradoxes of wisdom and folly, and madness:

> And I gave mine heart to knowe wisdome & knowledge, madnes & foolishnes: I knewe also that this is a vexacion of the spirit.
> For in the multitude of wisdome *is* muche grief: & he that encreaseth knowledge, encreaseth sorowe.

(1:17–18)

He associates such paradoxes with kingship: "Better is a poore and wise childe, then an olde and foolish King, which wil no more be admonished" (4:13), and he associates them as well with eyesight (2:14). He also associates "the sight of the eye" with "lustes" (6:9), and he speaks of how men are killed like fishes in a net and birds in a snare (9:12). And he meditates upon the paradoxes of justice and injustice (7:17; 8:14). The premise, as well as the conclusion, of all these meditations is that

> All things *come* alike to all: and the same condition *is* to the juste and to the wicked, to the good and to the pure, & to the polluted, & to him that sacrificeth, & to him that sacrificeth not: as *is* the good, so *is* the sinner, he that sweareth, as he that feareth an othe.

(9:2)

These verses suggest many analogues to *King Lear:* the old and foolish king; the paradoxes of folly and wisdom that occupy the Fool's speeches and songs; the dramatization of the metaphors of sight in Gloucester's characterization; the nakedness of birth and death and of man's whole condition that is lamented by Lear and palpably represented in Edgar; the random wantonness of death of which Gloucester complains; the comparisons of men and beasts that suffuse the language of the play and that are especially prominent in Lear's speeches, including his last; the vision of the confluence of the just and the wicked that consumes Lear on the heath and that leads him to conclude, not unlike the Preacher, that "None does offend, none —I say none!" (IV. vi. 165). Shakespeare could have absorbed, and no doubt did absorb, each of these preoccupations from sources other than Ecclesiastes—in the Bible itself as well as elsewhere, most especially from Montaigne's "Apologie of Raymond Sebond." But the number of evocations of Ecclesiastes (and more could be cited), as well as their tone and configuration, make their correspondences with *Lear* particularly suggestive. The Preacher's lament that "he that encreaseth knowledge, encreaseth sorowe" is a line the Fool could sing: it has the cadence as well as the substance of his whole characterization. The Preacher's references to the heart—and he refers again and again to the anguish of his own heart—suggest the pain of protest as well as of resignation, a combination of feelings that *Lear* also elicits. And perhaps most important, if most obvious, *vanitas,* the theme that echoes endlessly in Ecclesiastes and that *Lear* catches up in its preoccupation with the word *nothing,* suggests not just the idea of emptiness in the play but its feeling, the feeling to which Edgar refers at the end when he says that we should "speak what we feel, not what we ought to say" (V. iii. 325).

What underlies all of these motifs is the focus upon death as the event that not only ends life but calls its whole meaning into question. At one point in Ecclesiastes the Preacher asks, "Who is as the wise man? and who knoweth the interpretacion of a thing?" (8:1), and the burden of the question is who *can* know. As in *Lear,* which also asks this question insistently, there is no satisfying answer, and certainly no consoling one. But again like *Lear,* Ecclesiastes offers a characteristic perception of human existence in the face of death, if not an interpretation of it. For the Preacher's haunting sense of the dissolution of all things in time almost necessarily impels him to think of those things in terms of polarities—the polarities of beginnings and endings especially, but also of their cognates in creativeness and destructiveness—and to think of life itself as a composition of extremes that are defined morally, but not necessarily, as a whole, morally intelligible. He suggests this understanding in the passage already quoted in which he says that "All things *come* alike to all," to the just and the wicked, the good and the pure, and that "as *is* the good, so *is* the sinner." And he does so strikingly in the passage for which Ecclesiastes is now best known and which is regularly cited in liturgies for the dead, the passage that speaks of a time to be born and a time to die, a time to slay and to heal, to weep and to laugh, to seek and

to lose, to keep and to cast away, to be silent and to speak, to love and to hate (3:1–8).

This landscape of antinomies suggests the deepest of the affinities between Ecclesiastes and *King Lear,* for the kingdom of *Lear* too is defined by the antinomy of "coming hither" and "going thence" (V. ii. 10) and by corresponding polarizations of human states of feeling and being. The play is composed of oppositions between weeping and laughing, seeking and losing, being silent and speaking, loving and hating. The characters embody such antinomies: the spirituality of Cordelia is opposed to the concupiscence of Goneril and Regan, the piety of Edgar to the rapaciousness of Edmund, the selfless service of Kent to the self-serving of Oswald, the kindness of Albany to the sadism of Cornwall. Some of these oppositions are combined in the Fool (certainly laughter and tears) and some profoundly in Cordelia; but the most manifest combinations occur in Lear and Gloucester, the two aged and dying protagonists who participate in, and must acknowledge the being of, all their children, the loving and the hateful, the legitimate and the illegitimate. Indeed, a large part of the action consists of Lear's and Gloucester's oscillations between extremities that are never ameliorated, that tear at them, and that ultimately break their hearts.

The contrasts that compose Lear's condition are particularly stark. In the second childhood of age, he is at the same time "every inch a king" (IV. vi. 106), and though he sometimes enacts these roles simultaneously, he cannot mediate between them: they remain in apposition until the play's end. His sense of humility grows, but it alternates with his wrath; it never replaces it. He howls at his last appearance in the play, as he did at his first. His increasing apprehension of the wrong he did Cordelia is balanced by his excoriations of his other daughters and by the fury of his madness, just as the joy of his recovery of Cordelia is balanced by the desolation of her loss. He imagines kneeling and humbling himself as a child before Cordelia in prison, but he presumes at the same time to be one of "God's spies," taking upon himself "the mystery of things" (V. iii. 16–17). The yoking of such disparities continues until his death and informs the very moment of it. Lear's last words express the hope—or delusion—that Cordelia is alive. They join with, but they do not transform, the knowledge that she will never return.

The schematized world of *King Lear* has often been compared to that of the morality plays, which seem similarly composed of radically opposing states of mind and being—virtue and vice, despair and hope, the good and the bad, angels and devils. In the moralities, however, the summons of death is not ultimately an end but a beginning that retrospectively gives meaning to the large contrasts of human existence. In *King Lear*, on the other hand, as in Ecclesiastes, the summons is to an absolute ending whose retrospect of existence is not morally comprehensible. Edgar tries to make it so for his father's death, and life, and there is perhaps a rough, if barbaric, moral economy in Gloucester's destruction by his bastard son; but the Gloucester plot, in any case, is only the secondary plot of *King Lear*. The primary plot is Lear's, and even Edgar cannot moralize Lear's story. He says of the spectacle of Lear's meeting with Gloucester on the heath, "I would not take this from report—it is, / And my heart breaks at it" (IV. vi. 139–140)—a response that, in this play, is identified eventually with death. The verb *is* in Edgar's comment suggests that the suffering of Lear presents us with a world of unmediated existential extremes such as we find in Ecclesiastes, a world where "as *is* the good, so *is* the sinner." The growth in Lear's understanding suggests this world. He changes on the heath, he accepts more of his own human limitations, and he learns to sympathize with others, but that knowledge increases his sorrow to the point of madness. Critics are sometimes fond of talking of the "privilege" of Lear's madness, but if we consult our own experience of mentally infirm human beings, we will, like Edgar, know better. It is a horror, and an anticipation of "the promised end / Or image of that horror" (V. iii. 264–265) that we witness in Cordelia's death.

Cordelia's death is, characteristically, preceded by her reunion with Lear after he awakens from his madness, a scene that has frequently been treated as if it were the climax of the action and that has often been compared with the reunion of Pericles and Marina in *Pericles,* Shakespeare's later romance. The two recognition scenes do have much in common, but the critical difference is that Pericles essentially experiences a rebirth, and Lear does not. At the outset of the play, Lear says of Cordelia, "I loved her most, and thought to set my rest / On her kind nursery" (I. i. 123–124); and it is the peculiar nursing, rather than rebirth, of Lear that we witness in the bedside scene, attended by a doctor, in which he is reunited with her. For Cordelia ministers not only to an aged father but to a man transformed by age into a child again. The metaphor of age as second childhood, which is pervasive in Shakespeare's sources for the play, is literalized in this scene very disturbingly. Lear kneels to Cordelia when he recognizes her and says:

I am a very foolish fond old man,
Fourscore and upward, not an hour more nor less;
And, to deal plainly,
I fear I am not in my perfect mind.

(IV. vii. 60–63)

As Barbara Everett has suggested, that Lear should have to kneel and confess the infirmity of age to his evil daughters is "terrible," but that he should do so to Cordelia as well "has also something of the terrible in it." The Fool repeatedly rebukes Lear for giving away his power and turning his paternal relationships upside down, but the saddest irony is that human beings of "fourscore and upward" usually cannot do otherwise. We often have no choice but to become the parents of our parents in their old age and to treat them as children. And it is hard because, whether our motives verge toward Goneril and Regan's or toward Cordelia's (and they may do both), the nursing of parents is not a form of nourishment for future life but a preparation for death. It is directly so for Lear. The music he hears in his reunion with Cordelia suggests no larger life into which he can be incorporated, as the music of the spheres does for Pericles, and his recovery of her is the immediate prelude to his wrenching loss of her as well as to his own death. In the manner of this play, it is a joy that heightens sorrow, that makes it more heartbreaking.

Dr. Johnson found Cordelia's death intolerable and, like many later critics, wished to avoid it. He wrote that "I was many years ago so shocked by Cordelia's death, that I know not whether I ever endured to read again the last scenes of the play till I undertook to revise them as an editor" (*Johnson on Shakespeare,* 2). Revisions such as Nahum Tate's, which left Cordelia and Lear alive and united at the end of the play, in fact held the English stage for over a century and a half; and there is an inner logic to them, for they are really re-revisions of Shakespeare's revision of the Lear story and are inherent within it. All of Shakespeare's sources—the old play of *King Leir,* Holinshed, Spenser, and others —end by giving life and victory to Cordelia and Lear. Only Shakespeare does not, and his insistence on Cordelia's death and Lear's final agony, as Frye remarks in *Fools of Time,* is "too deliberate even to be explained as inexplicable." Lear's and Cordelia's union in death is at the heart of Shakespeare's rendition of the Lear story. It is prepared for by every scene in which they appear together, including their earlier reunion, and it is the event that not only concludes the tragedy but wholly informs it. We cannot deny it, however much we wish to and however much the play itself makes us wish to.

Freud suggested in "The Theme of the Three Caskets" (*Works,* 12) that the choice among three daughters with which *King Lear* begins is the choice of death. He argues that Cordelia, in her muteness, is the representation of death and that, as in the depiction of such choices in the myths and fairy tales that *Lear* resembles, her portrayal as the most beautiful and desirable of the three women expresses the inherent, often unconscious, human wish to deny death. He points out that "Lear is not only an old man: he is a dying man," and that this reality subsumes both "the extraordinary premiss of the division of his inheritance" in the opening scene and the overpowering effect of the final scene:

> Lear carries Cordelia's dead body on to the stage. Cordelia is Death. If we reverse the situation it becomes intelligible and familiar to us. She is the Death-goddess who, like the Valkyrie in German mythology, carries away the dead hero from the battlefield. Eternal wisdom, clothed in primaeval myth, bids the old man renounce love, choose death and make friends with the necessity of dying.

Much of Freud's general emphasis upon the irremediable facts of age and dying in *King Lear* has been illuminatingly elaborated in recent criticism of the play, especially Susan Snyder's, but his focus upon Cordelia and his particular identification of her with death deserve more emphasis. The identification suggests the kind of allegorization in Freud that makes many critics uncomfortable, but understood in the full context of his argument it amplifies the resonances of Cordelia's characterization, and of the play; it does not reduce them.

To begin with, a primary focus on Cordelia is true to our actual experience of the play. She is the character who always counts most to Lear, and in the extraordinarily crowded action of the play it is Lear's relation to her that we most attend to and that most organizes our responses. Their relationship is the spine of the play. Cordelia is the absolute

focus of Lear's attention, and ours, in the opening scene; it is Lear's rejection of her that initiates the tragic action; and during that ensuing, often diffuse action neither he nor we can ever forget her. The Fool, who is Cordelia's surrogate, does not allow us to, both because he keeps her constantly in Lear's mind on the heath and because the combination of love and sorrow that he brings to Lear prepares us for a similar combination in Cordelia's final role. The collocation of her reunion with Lear and her death is of a piece with all the words of the Fool that weep for joy and sing for sorrow; and the paradox that these lines describe is eventually associated in the play with the moment of death itself—Gloucester's as well as Lear's.

An association between Cordelia and death in the opening scene of the play is comprehensible even on a literal level. Freud contends that her silence directly connotes death, as muteness does in dreams. But Cordelia also speaks in the scene, and what she says indicates clearly enough that Lear's rejection of her is precisely his denial of the impending death that he ostensively acknowledges in the very act of dividing the kingdom and in his explicit statement that he wishes "to shake all cares and business from our age" and "unburdened crawl toward death" (I. i. 39, 41). Cordelia tells her father that she loves him "According to my bond, no more nor less." She goes on to say:

> Good my lord,
> You have begot me, bred me, loved me. I
> Return those duties back as are right fit,
> Obey you, love you, and most honor you.
> Why have my sisters husbands if they say
> They love you all? Haply, when I shall wed,
> That lord whose hand must take my plight shall carry
> Half my love with him, half my care and duty.
> Sure I shall never marry like my sisters,
> [To love my father all.]
>
> (I. i. 93, 95–104)

What Cordelia declares in these lines is not only that she must live her own life but that Lear cannot be "everything," that he is not "ague-proof," that it is in the nature of things for her to have a future that is beyond his control. The curious spareness and sternness of her insistence on the word *bond,* as well as her reiteration of the word *nothing,* perhaps also suggests, even this early in the play, the particular sense of the nature of things that is evoked in Ecclesiastes—the sense of human vanity that comes with the awareness of our ultimate bond with death. At any rate, it is to the natural realities given expression in Cordelia's speech that Lear responds. His rage against her, like his colossal rage throughout the play, is his attempt to hold on to life, to deny death.

It is often difficult in our experience of *King Lear* to understand that Lear's denial of death is represented as much in his love for Cordelia as in his rage against her. It is even more difficult, but crucial, to understand that Cordelia's loveliness and love are themselves functions of this denial, that the expressive eloquence of her love at the end of the play is as much a signification of Lear's death as is the muteness of that love at the start. This is the paradox that is at the heart of Cordelia's characterization and at the center of most of the play's other paradoxes. Its full force is illuminated by the part of Freud's discussion of the identification of Cordelia with death that deals with the phenomenon of denial.

Freud points out that in all the myths of the choice among three sisters that are analogous to *Lear* (and he includes the choice among three caskets in *The Merchant of Venice*) the woman representing the power of death is transformed into a woman representing the power of love. He remarks that contradictions and contraries of this kind —when one thing is replaced by a precise opposite —are characteristic of the process of condensation in dreams. But he relates such contradictions in *Lear* primarily to the human disposition to deny what cannot be tolerated and to make use of the imagination "in order to satisfy the wishes that reality does not satisfy." Freud argues that in the myths of choice among three sisters the profound human wish to deny "the immutable law of death" is represented both in the identification of the most beautiful sister with death and in the presence of choice itself:

Choice stands in the place of necessity, of destiny. In this way man overcomes death, which he has recognized intellectually. No greater triumph of wish-fulfilment is conceivable. A choice is made where in reality there is obedience to a compulsion; and what is chosen is not a figure of terror, but the fairest and most desirable of women.

In the old play of *King Leir* the king has an explicit political motive both for his testing of his daughters' love as well as for the division of the kingdom, and the two wicked daughters are forewarned of it while the good one is not. All three daughters, moreover, are unmarried, and the issue of their marriages is related to the love test and to politics. Shakespeare entirely shears away such surface motives and rationalizations for Lear's action, thereby rendering its underlying motive of denial all the more stark and compelling. The whole scene echoes with negations and contradictions. Its sense of high order and ceremony is prefaced by Gloucester's casual talk of ungoverned instinct. The ceremony itself is a decoration, reminiscent of Richard II's undecking of "the pompous body of a king" as well as of his ambivalence: "Ay, no; no, ay; for I must nothing be" (*Richard II,* IV. i. 250, 201). Lear himself does not acknowledge that ambivalence, but he acts it out. The contradiction that governs Goneril and Regan is obvious. They flatter Lear as he flatters himself and tell him he is everything while eventually seeking to reduce him to nothing. The contraries that compose Cordelia are more profound and more moving. What is compelling about her from the outset is that she continuously represents both sides of the process of denial. She represents not only the vanity of denial but its animating power, the love of life as well as the reality of death, the mother who nurtures us, as Freud suggests, as well as the Mother Earth that finally receives us. She tells Lear the truth of his dying in the opening scene: "Nothing, my lord" (I. i. 87). She stands in mute rebuke to the folly of his attempt to deny it. And she eventually becomes that truth when she lies lifeless in his arms. But at the same time the very telling of that truth is replete with love: "What shall Cordelia speak? Love, and be silent" (I. i. 62). It is what makes Lear's rejection of her seem unnatural on the literal as well as symbolic level. As the play progresses she comes to stand more and more for everything that binds Lear most nobly to life and that makes his protest against death most heroic. Freud speaks of resistance to death as essentially a reflex of the ego's self-centered wish to be immortal. But another reason that we do not wish to die and see those close to us die, even the very old, is that we are capable of cherishing and loving others. Cordelia is an incarnation of this capacity.

Cordelia's representation of such love in *King Lear* is given religious, and specifically Christian, overtones, and perhaps the greatest pain of her death, and of her tragic embodiment of the futility of the denial of death, is that the promise of these overtones also proves empty. Cordelia's counterpart in the old chronicle play of *King Leir* is an explicitly homiletic Christian figure. When Cordelia is rejected by her father, she says:

> Now whither, poor forsaken, shall I go,
> When mine own sisters triumph in my woe?
> But unto Him which doth protect the just,
> In Him will poor Cordella put her trust.
>
> (I. iii. 129–132)

That trust is fully vindicated at the end of the play when she and her father are happily reunited. Shakespeare deliberately keeps, at the same time that he transmutes, the old play's association of Cordella with Christianity. There are unmistakable New Testament echoes in *King Lear,* and most of them cluster around Cordelia. They begin in the opening scene, when France uses the language of miracle and faith to question Lear's judgment of Cordelia (I. i. 222) and when he takes her as his wife:

> Fairest Cordelia, that art most rich being poor,
> Most choice forsaken, and most loved despised.
>
> (I. i. 250–251)

The allusion to 2 Corinthians 6:10, is clear—"as poore, and *yet* [making] mannie riche: as having nothing, and *yet* possessing all things"—and it resonates with the deepest preoccupations of the whole scene. The allusions and associations intensify at the end of the play. When Cordelia returns from France she says, "O dear father, it is thy business that I go about" (IV. iv. 23–24; cf. Luke 2:49). And Lear, when he awakens from his madness, associates his own deathly condition with hell and hers with bliss:

> You do me wrong to take me out o' th' grave.
> Thou art a soul in bliss; but I am bound
> Upon a wheel of fire, that mine own tears
> Do scald like molten lead.
>
> (IV. vii. 45–48)

At the very end, her death is associated with the Last Judgment (V. iii. 264–265), and Lear himself wishes for her revival in language that seems to echo the deepest of Christian beliefs:

> This feather stirs; she lives! If it be so,
> It is a chance which does redeem all sorrows
> That ever I have felt.
>
> (V. iii. 266–268)

But she does not live, and Lear, whether he dies thinking she does or not, is not redeemed by her. For in the pagan world of *King Lear* the New Testament's conception of death, and life, is the denial; the reality is that of Ecclesiastes, the book of the Old Testament that insists above all else that death cannot be denied, that it is utter loss, and that human existence itself is full of emptiness. Shakespeare draws upon the energies of the comic and romantic impulses of *King Leir* (and his other sources), particularly the association of Cordelia's role with the Christian hope of redemption, and makes them a part of our own hopes and thus of the process of denial within ourselves. There is no deeper a simultaneous use and generic transformation of a source in the canon, and it is the wellspring of the sense of grotesqueness as well as of desolation that is so peculiar to this tragedy.

Such an understanding of the use to which Shakespeare puts Christian evocations in the pagan world of *King Lear* can help clarify the religious issues that continue to vex criticism of the play, but it should not be interpreted to suggest that *Lear* is a homily on the inadequacy of pagan virtue or that the play's conception of death is unique among Shakespeare's tragedies. The sense that death defines human life and that after it, in Hamlet's last words, "the rest is silence" (V. ii. 347) is as germane to *Hamlet, Othello,* and *Macbeth,* which have manifest Christian settings, as it is to *King Lear.* Christian belief does give a providential perspective to death in those plays, most strongly in *Hamlet,* where the intimations of another world of being become a part of the hero's thought; but such a perspective, even in the case of *Hamlet,* cannot absorb or fully explain the hero's actual suffering. Nor can it fundamentally mitigate the effect of that suffering on us. One can spend much time gauging the level of irony in the endings of the tragedies, but when we see or read these great plays we do not construe the endings. We feel them, and what we feel is a paramount sense of loss. The distinction of *King Lear* is that the death of Cordelia compounds that sense of loss and focuses it. All of us are pagan in our immediate response to the death of those we love. The final scene of *King Lear* is a representation—among the most moving in all drama—of the universality of this experience and of its immeasurable pain.

BIBLIOGRAPHY

General: Gordon Braden, *Anger's Privilege: Renaissance Tragedy and the Senecan Tradition* (1985). Andrew C. Bradley, *Shakespearean Tragedy* (1904). James Vincent Cunningham, "Woe or Wonder," in *Tradition and Poetic Structure* (1960). T. S. Eliot, *Selected Essays* (1951). Sigmund Freud, *Collected Papers,* 6, 8, Philip Rieff, ed. (1963), and *The Standard Edition of the Complete Psychological Works of Sigmund Freud,* 12, 13, 14, 21, James Strachey, ed. (1953–1974). Northrop Frye, *Fools of Time* (1967). *The Geneva Bible: A Facsimile of the 1560 Edition,* Lloyd E. Berry, ed. (1969). Harley Granville-Barker, *Prefaces to Shakespeare,* 2 vols. (1951). John Holloway, *The Story of the Night* (1961). G. Wilson Knight, *The Wheel of Fire* (1930). Arthur P. Rossiter, *Angel with Horns* (1961).

Hamlet: Fredson Bowers, *Elizabethan Revenge Tragedy, 1587–1642* (1940). Helen Gardner, *The Business of Criticism* (1959). Arthur Kirsch, "Hamlet's Grief," in *Journal of English Literary History,* 48 (1981). C. S. Lewis, "Hamlet: The Prince or the Poem?" in *Proceedings of the British Academy,* 28 (1942). Bridget Gellert Lyons, *Voices of Melancholy* (1971). Maynard Mack, "The World of Hamlet," in *Yale Review,* 41 (1952). Alexander Welsh, "The Task of Hamlet," *ibid.,* 69 (1980).

Othello: W. H. Auden, "The Joker in the Pack," in *The Dyer's Hand* (1962). *The Book of Common Prayer; 1559,* John E. Booty, ed. (1976). Northrop Frye, *A Natural Perspective* (1965). G. K. Hunter, "Othello and Colour Prejudice," in *Proceedings of the British Academy,* 53 (1967). Arthur Kirsch, *Shakespeare and the Experience of Love* (1981). Michel de Montaigne, *Essayes of Montaigne,* John Florio, trans. (1933). Bernard Spivack, *Shakespeare and the Allegory of Evil* (1958).

Macbeth: St. Augustine, *The City of God,* 2 vols., John Healey, trans. (1945). Cleanth Brooks, "The Naked Babe and the Cloak of Manliness," in *The Well Wrought Urn* (1947). Helen Gardner, "Milton's 'Satan' and the Theme of Damnation in Elizabethan Tragedy," in *Essays and Studies,* 1 (1948). Arthur Kirsch, "Macbeth's Suicide," in *Journal of English Literary History,* 51 (1984). Pierre de La Primaudaye, *The French Academie* (1586). Norman Rabkin, *Shakespeare and the Problem of Meaning* (1981).

King Lear: *The Chronicle History of King Leir,* Sidney Lee, ed. (1909). Rosalie L. Colie, "The Energies of Endurance: Biblical Echo in *King Lear,*" in Rosalie L. Colie and Frederick T. Flahiff, eds., *Some Facets of King Lear* (1974). Barbara Everett, "The New *King Lear,*" in Frank Kermode, ed., *Shakespeare, King Lear, A Casebook* (1969). Samuel Johnson, *Johnson on Shakespeare,* 2 vols., Arthur Sherbo, ed. (1968). Leo Salingar, "Romance in *King Lear,*" in *English,* 27 (1978). Susan Snyder, "*King Lear* and the Psychology of Dying," in *Shakespeare Quarterly,* 33 (1982).

Shakespeare's Tragicomedies and Romances

JOHN RUSSELL BROWN

The Tragicomedies

After the close of the sixteenth century, Shakespeare wrote no more comedies that dally "with the innocence of love," like the songs in *Twelfth Night* (1600), and he created no more characters who would "fleet the time carelessly" as in the "golden world" of *As You Like It* (1598). For eight or nine years after 1600, much of Shakespeare's attention must have been given to the great tragedies *Hamlet, Othello, King Lear, Macbeth, Timon of Athens, Coriolanus,* and *Antony and Cleopatra.* During this time he completed only four plays that are usually categorized as comedies, and three of them date from the first few years of this new phase in his career.

The three comedies—*Troilus and Cressida, All's Well That Ends Well,* and *Measure for Measure*—written in the period 1602 to 1604 (they cannot be precisely dated) are strange and unsettling. They are among the few plays that modern critics have been willing to count as Shakespeare's failures, yet even their detractors admit that the texts bristle with invention and energy of thought and feeling. Whenever these three comedies are given the attention appropriate to innovatory works, they establish a distinctive hold over readers and playgoers. Throughout the centuries they have attracted the interest of poets and other artists, and in the twentieth century they have been staged with great success.

Each play contains some relaxed and traditional scenes that might have found a place in earlier comedies, but these scenes are cut across by passionate and sometimes lengthy argument, or by horrifying brutality or morally offensive behavior. Each play unfolds an amazing tale, and yet each occasionally stalls and shudders with psychological tensions derived from apparently unresolvable conflicts. These plays question the nature of psychological, political, and social reality and the basis of moral judgment. Even jokes are used to odd and challenging purposes, exposing scorn, morbidity, lubricity, or timidity in those who have caused the laughter. Nor are comic effects always assured: expressions of moral fervor or of painful uncertainty can seem absurd in performance, while vigorous merriment may come across as pitiful self-deception.

Modern critics have invented special categories to distinguish these three plays from other comedies by Shakespeare. These works have been called problem plays or problem comedies, as well as dark, tragical, or satirical comedies. Tragicomedy—meaning plays containing danger and even death, but ending with some happiness—is probably the most readily understood term.

Troilus and Cressida was evidently the first to be completed, following soon after *Hamlet* in 1601. The play has always been recognized as an unusual work. While a quarto edition of 1609 called it a history, the editors of the First Folio (1623) initially planned to place it among the tragedies, after *Romeo and Juliet.* For an unknown reason, this printing was abandoned after three pages; at the last moment, *Troilus* was printed on unnumbered pages and placed between the histories and the tragedies. A second issue of the quarto, which called it "The Famous History," carried an introduction telling readers that "you have here a new play, never staled with the stage, never clapper-clawed with the palms of the vulgar, and yet passing full of the palm comical." This preface considers the play alongside Shakespeare's other comedies, as though it were simply one of the same kind, only "amongst all there is none more witty than this."

Some modern scholars have argued that *Troilus and Cressida* was written for private performance at one of the Inns of Court in London (law schools for the fashionable, rich, and clever, as we might say today) and have so accounted for the slighting reference to vulgar applause in the quarto's preface, as well as for the brilliance of many of the play's speeches. The words of the Prologue set a highly cultivated tone, with a strong hint of dispassionate, even scornful, amusement:

> In Troy there lies the scene. From isles of Greece
> The princes orgulous, their high blood chafed,
> Have to the port of Athens sent their ships,
> Fraught with the ministers and instruments
> Of cruel war.

Like Shakespeare's history plays, *Troilus and Cressida* shows two sides of a political conflict and intersperses scenes of argument and battle with others that treat domestic and personal issues. But in *Troilus* victory crowns neither side: at the close, the war continues, and Troilus, having lost Cressida, who has been sent to follow her father to the Grecian camp, stands onstage asking the gods to "linger not our sure destructions on" (V. x. 9). Then he vows vengeance for the death of Hector, thus finding some comfort: "Hope of revenge shall hide our inward woe" (31). It is typical of this play that Troilus' exit line, despite an assured rhythm and a clinching rhyme, has a double qualification: he trusts only the hope of revenge, and he seeks only to hide, not even to mitigate, his deeper suffering. It is typical, too, that this is a false ending. Without warning, Pandarus appears on the battlefield: this go-between, who had led Troilus to Cressida's bed, now asks for attention and is dismissed, curtly and moralistically, by Troilus, who then leaves the stage. The tragicomedy ends with a complaining

and dispirited Pandarus asking not for applause but for tears, as if his "fall" were a tragedy and the chief business of the play. Yet he speaks with his usual self-deprecating wit and cheers up a little before he exits, accompanied by the laughter and applause of those whom he had asked to weep.

Predominantly comic scenes take place on both sides of the conflict. Within the walls of Troy the lovers are absurd and obsessed—not least Helen, whose abduction from Menelaus' kingdom in Greece was the occasion for an old rivalry to turn into the seven-year siege. The comedy is often strained, as if every lover is determined to be thought more witty than the others, or as if each seeks some exquisite consummation that eludes them all.

In the Greek camp, the most absurd scenes concern the rivalry between Ajax and Achilles for glory in war. But comedy is everywhere, because throughout the army:

> The general's disdained
> By him one step below, he by the next,
> That next by him beneath; so every step,
> Exampled by the first pace that is sick
> Of his superior, grows to an envious fever
> Of pale and bloodless emulation.
>
> (I. iii. 129–134)

This judgment is from Ulysses, who seems at first to be the one rational and sound mind among an army of fools and impotents; but he spurs his leaders forward by mere craft that is often humorous. At the end of the play, Ulysses has a marginal position in the story; he is more able to condemn corruption than to deal with it.

The need to win the war is the one issue common to both sides. In the Greek camp, this cause is argued pragmatically, in a way that highlights confusions and political double-talk. Within the walls of Troy, the debate is idealistic, with much definition of right and wrong; but Hector decides to fight only because that is the way to maintain "our joint and several dignities" (II. ii. 193). The extended debates tend to belittle rational argument and make all attempts to justify the war seem hypocritical.

Heroism on the field of battle is also revealed as shallow and ineffective. Hector is not killed by Achilles in open fight, which both warriors have said they seek, but after Hector has disarmed himself after chasing a nameless Greek to gain a suit of golden armor—and then he is killed not by Achilles but at the hands of his Myrmidons, the unquestioning and ruthless soldiers who attend the Greek hero. As Hector's dead body is hauled offstage, to be tied to a horse's tail and paraded to the army, the boastful lie goes up: "Achilles hath the mighty Hector slain!" (V. viii. 14). It is tempting to agree with Thersites, the cowardly commentator:

> Here is such patchery, such juggling, and such knavery. All the argument is a whore and a cuckold, a good quarrel to draw emulous factions and bleed to death upon.
>
> (II. iii. 67–70)

But Shakespeare's presentation is more complex than this. He has ensured that the pain of war and its appalling logic are also spelled out when Diomedes says that since Helen was able to speak:

> She hath not given so many good words breath
> As for her Greeks and Troyans suff'red death.
>
> (IV. i. 73–74)

Shakespeare is equally ambivalent in portraying Helen with Paris, Achilles with his "masculine whore" Patroclus, and, above all, the relationship of Cressida with Troilus and with his Greek successor, Diomedes. Pandarus is as ready to comment on coupling as Thersites has been to unmask political corruption; his mocking and salacious song reduces all loving to triviality:

> These lovers cry, O ho! they die!
> Yet that which seems the wound to kill
> Doth turn O ho! to Ha, ha, he!
> So dying love lives still.
> O ho! a while, but Ha, ha, ha!
> O ho! groans out for Ha, ha, ha!—Heigh ho!
>
> (III. 1. 111–116)

Yet in aspiration at least, the lovers do exhibit some tenderness and capacity to relate to others. When Cressida is told that Troilus "will weep you, an 'twere a man born in April," she grasps the image with both delicacy and foreboding: "And I'll spring up in his tears, an 'twere a nettle against May" (I. ii. 164–167).

In *Troilus and Cressida,* Shakespeare gave his most sensitive attention to the lovers, not to the warriors. Their words are impulsive, responsive, sensuous, and sometimes terse with bitterness, pain, and suspicion:

> Do to this body what extremes you can;
> But the strong base and building of my love
> Is as the very centre of the earth,
> Drawing all things to it. I'll go in and weep.
>
> (IV. ii. 101–104)

The lovers dominate the play, even though their happiness is insecure, perhaps illusory, and certainly short-lived. Sexuality is presented onstage in words and actions, as if Shakespeare forgot or disregarded the limitations of boy actors that had led him in earlier plays to make this element of love a matter of suggestion and allusion only. The excitement of these lovers does not exist only in the mind.

At first glance, *All's Well That Ends Well,* which probably was written a year or so after *Troilus,* seems to represent a turning back from experiment. It opens on familiar lines: Bertram, a healthy, handsome count, is loved by Helena, a beautiful and intelligent girl; and these young people are watched over by the boy's mother, the Countess of Rossillion, and then by the King of France and an "old lord," Lafew. Love does not prosper, however, because Bertram thinks of another girl (as we are told later) and is set on proving himself as a soldier in battle. So Helena takes a disguise, like Viola in *Twelfth Night* and Julia in *The Two Gentlemen of Verona*—but by this time the originality of *All's Well* has become obvious. Helena hides herself behind the appearance of a pilgrim, not of a "saucy" or "masterly" boy:

> Ambitious love hath so in me offended
> That barefoot plod I the cold ground upon,
> With sainted vow my faults to have amended.
>
> (III. iv. 5–7)

She tells no one—not even the audience—that she will follow Bertram to Florence but says that she will make a pilgrimage to the shrine of St. Jaques.

Helena is no ordinary romantic heroine but a subtle and unprecedented development of the Clever Wench of numerous folk tales. She is not of noble lineage, like Viola or Rosalind, but rather, as Bertram declares, "a poor physician's daughter" who "had her breeding at my father's charge" (II. iii. 113–114). Helena acts in defiance of social and theatrical custom. Before taking a disguise, she has already married Bertram, against his will. Having cured the King of a deadly fistula by means of a secret remedy that her father had bequeathed, she had won the right to choose her husband from among the young lords who were wards of the King. She had pledged to lose her own life if her cure failed.

The main narrative derives from Shakespeare's source, the story of Giletta in William Painter's *Palace of Pleasure* (1566–1567), but the nervous and lyrical intimacy of Helena's speeches, which draws an audience's sympathy toward her while underscoring the social and moral presumption of her actions, is wholly original:

> 'Twere all one
> That I should love a bright particular star
> And think to wed it, he is so above me.
>   . . .
>   'Tis pity
>   . . .
> That wishing well had not a body in't,
> Which might be felt; that we, the poorer born,
> Whose baser stars do shut us up in wishes,
> Might with effects of them follow our friends,
> And show what we alone must think, which never
> Returns us thanks.
>
>   (I. i. 81–83, 173–180)

In contrast, Bertram, in abrupt and assertive words, declares that he will never consummate his enforced marriage.

Other innovations take *All's Well* beyond the established forms of romantic comedy. Subplots illustrate and extend the main plot's themes, but in unexpected ways. Parolles, the foppish braggart, attains a winning honesty after being unmasked—"Simply the thing I am shall make me live" (IV. iii. 310–311)—and then becomes Lafew's dependent as "a fool and a knave" (V. ii. 51). At his most cowardly, he slanders Bertram with words that are among the shrewdest judgments in the play: while Bertram is honored as a young hero, Parolles declares him to be a "dangerous and lascivious boy" (IV. iii. 206). Lavatch, the licensed fool who seeks to marry Isbel for the plain reason that his "poor body . . . requires it" (I. iii. 28), learns very quickly that he begins to love "as an old man loves money, with no stomach" (III. ii. 16): he is, in Lafew's words, "a shrewd knave and an unhappy" (IV. v. 59). These subsidiary characters serve as exempla or analogues, in the manner of didactic histories and sermons based on biblical narratives; characters like these were used as structural devices in Shakespeare's earlier comedies. But these analogues lead an audience to question the needs of Helena and Bertram rather than to understand them and to wonder what reliance can be placed on their words and deeds, rather than to recognize their wider relevance.

Both hero and heroine often find themselves incapable of adequate response, and in those moments their attempts to show resolution and make correct judgments become ridiculous and the comedy reaches the brink of absurdity. The main story is concluded, as in Shakespeare's source, by Bertram's attempt to seduce Diana, a young Florentine, and by Helena's arranging to take Diana's place in bed so that Bertram fathers a child on his wife without knowing that he is doing so. Helena at last confronts Bertram, placing him in another situation from which he cannot escape—and this time he submits without complaining. Bertram had been "wondrous kind" (V. iii. 307) to Helena when he believed her to be someone else, so—despite the skepticism that the play has encouraged—some little credit may be given now to his assertion that he will love her as his wife in word and fact, even though it is still a conditional promise.

All's Well That Ends Well does not bring its characters so close to death as do Shakespeare's other seventeenth-century comedies—in all the others at least one death is crucial for the story—but, one after another, the characters are all forced into extreme positions to which they make inadequate responses. These crises are often handled lightly, but together they ensure that an audience reexamine many of its assumptions about inheritance, sexual drive, individual choice, social conditioning, and the usefulness of giving advice. There is no dance, as in *As You Like It* or *Much Ado About Nothing,* to round matters off. A conditional statement that pointedly qualifies the play's title serves for the King's conclusion:

> All yet seems well, and if it end so meet,
> The bitter past, more welcome is the sweet.

Twists in the plot, hesitations in the action, and verbal wit all keep the tone light—sometimes the author teases or tantalizes his audience—but the form of many scenes is uncompromisingly judicial. Parolles starts by interrogating Helena, and then she turns on him; the Countess questions her servants and then Helena; the King inquires about Helena; Lafew quizzes Parolles; Helena considers a number of husbands—and so on, until the widow,

Diana's mother, pins down the anonymous pilgrim and discovers her purposes. The long concluding scene puts Bertram through a searching inquisition during which he is forced three times to lie about his relationship with Diana. Shakespeare could have written this judgment scene so that it was intense and painful, but he chose instead to make Bertram look comically inept: "You boggle shrewdly; every feather starts you," comments the King (V. iii. 232). He thus reserves the crisis until very near the end, when Bertram becomes almost speechless, but still ambiguous, as he kneels to the victorious but serious, tender, and reserved Helena. Lafew confesses that he is on the point of tears, but he does so in a way that makes us laugh.

"Fortune brings in some boats that are not steered," says Pisanio as the plot thickens in *Cymbeline* (IV. iii. 46), and that seems almost true of *All's Well.* The characters have all done their shares of steering—Helena and Bertram, especially—and the older folk have always known what would happen—"My mother told me just how he would woo," says Diana (IV. ii. 69)—but at the close Shakespeare makes a fortunate outcome depend on calculated, judicial responses that an audience may or may not believe to be also heartfelt or instinctive.

Measure for Measure, which probably followed one year after *All's Well,* is more forthright in provoking an audience to judge. Its title points to moral and legal issues, and during its action numerous characters are sentenced to punishment. The very first moments are concerned with "government . . . speech . . . discourse . . . science . . . advice" and with "institutions . . . common justice . . . practice . . . commission." The Duke empowers Angelo to be his deputy, with the older Escalus to help him, and decrees that he must "enforce or qualify the laws" so that

> Mortality and mercy in Vienna
> Live in thy tongue and heart.
>
> (I. i. 65, 44–45)

But the clarity of this exposition is complicated at once, because the law that Angelo enforces awards death as the invariable punishment for fornication. Angelo uses his new authority in an attempt to seduce Isabella, a novice who has left a convent to plead for her brother's life, which has become forfeit under the law, notwithstanding mitigating circumstances. The strangest feature of this story is

that no character questions the wisdom of this law; the strongest comment is that leniency in enforcement would be humane or convenient. The Duke contents himself with taking the disguise of a friar to observe what happens in his absence.

Despite the barbarity, or absurdity, of the basic situation, some critics have interpreted the play as a Christian allegory. They have remarked upon the professed omniscience and good intentions of the Duke, the moral confidence of Isabella, and a host of biblical echoes in addition to that in the play's title. For them, the play shows men and women living in sin and watched over by a providential power; Angelo's life is saved by Isabella's redemptive plea for mercy.

But text and action are more complicated than this view suggests. Although Angelo exclaims in the last scene that "your grace, like power divine, hath looked upon my passes" (V. i. 365–366), the Duke has overreached himself on too many occasions for this assessment to hold. (If the Duke is a figure for God, as some critics have argued, Shakespeare had a poor opinion of the Almighty's operations.) The Duke's attempt to apply "craft against vice" (III. ii. 260) leads to hasty improvisations, glaring misjudgments, and comic overconfidence; and it is responsible for a good deal of unnecessary mental suffering. The Duke moralizes about human frailty with less sensitivity than do other spokesmen in the play who are notably less ambitious to be considered wise. Lucio, who is punished eventually with a whipping and an enforced marriage to a whore, has some "measure" of right on his side when he calls the absent ruler a "fantastical Duke of dark corners" (IV. iii. 154–155).

"Measure for measure" is a harsh precept, and when Shakespeare devised a play with this title, he wrote so that its validity is tested in a wide range of issues, personal and political. In a series of highly charged encounters, power and purpose, desire and conviction, connivance and rectitude, certainty and ignorance, eloquence and silence are all brought into conditions of stress, and the validity of each is exposed to scrutiny. Characters speak with passion and penetrating intelligence. Some scenes are so agonizing and some arguments so tense that they seem more suitable to tragedy than to comedy. But an underlying contrivance in the action ensures that the audience is not surprised by the final comic conclusion. Moreover, some of the characters stubbornly or wittily refuse to stand trial: Barnardine, the drunken prisoner, refuses to "rise and be put to death" (IV. iii. 26); while Master Froth, Kate Keepdown, Pompey the Bawd, and Lucio awaken a more relaxed enjoyment than the main plot ever suggests. The quiet Provost, in charge of the prison, is another counterweight to the main characters; he does not hold center stage, but he can be seen as a witness for the kind of careful, patient concern for others that neither seeks power nor avoids responsibility. These elements accentuate the daring with which the play was written and help to explain its success with modern audiences who view its certainties—"I'll pray a thousand prayers for thy death, / No word to save thee" (III. i. 146–147)—with some skepticism and its theatricality with some detachment. (*Measure for Measure* was never popular in the theater until the 1930s and 1940s.)

As the Fool and Poor Tom conduct King Lear toward the moment when he knows "how yond justice rails upon yond simple thief" and questions the "great image of authority," so there are comic and quiet elements in *Measure for Measure* that lead an audience toward an understanding that is not to be found easily in the more strident, passionate, and disputatious scenes. Escalus always takes second place to Angelo, but it is he who sees, when his superior cannot, that "some rise by sin, and some by virtue fall" and who asks, "Which is the wiser here, Justice or Iniquity?" (II. i. 38, 163). He prepares for Isabella's more eloquent question:

> How would you be,
> If He, which is the top of judgment, should
> But judge you as you are?
>
> (II. ii. 75–77)

and so helps to slue her question around, out of its narrow dramatic context, so that it reaches all aspects of the play's action and argument.

Isabella's challenge is grounded on a long-recognized Christian concept of God's mercy, but she does not voice it at once. As a novice of the order of St. Clare—a strict sisterhood that she has embraced as a "restraint" upon her life—she pleads at first for Claudio's life with little enthusiasm and little grace. Only after the impudent Lucio has instructed her to kneel and hang upon Angelo's gown does she press her case. Yet she is still terse and elicits only brisk refusals until Lucio has intervened yet again:

> *Angelo.* He's sentenced; 'tis too late.
> *Lucio.* [*aside to Isabella*]   You are too cold.

> *Isabella.* Too late? Why, no: I that do speak a word
> May call it back again. Well believe this,
> No ceremony that to great ones 'longs,
> Not the king's crown, nor the deputed sword,
> The marshal's truncheon, nor the judge's robe,
> Become them with one half so good a grace
> As mercy does;
> If he had been as you, and you as he,
> You would have slipped like him; but he, like you,
> Would not have been so stern.
> *Angelo.*   Pray you, be gone.
> *Isabella.* I would to heaven I had your potency,
> And you were Isabel; should it then be thus?
> No, I would tell what 'twere to be a judge,
> And what a prisoner.
>
> (II. ii. 56–70)

This passionate argument, sometimes slow and sometimes devastatingly simple, sustained by rhetorical structure yet sharp in counterstatement and accusation, is more than an affirmation of God's love of mercy. *Measure for Measure* may well be a play in which Shakespeare predicated a society founded on brotherly equality rather than authority, and on liberty of speech rather than on obedience to officers of the state.

The common factors in these three tragicomedies are experiment and investigation. The dramatist altered his accustomed practices and overturned theatrical conventions in order to question basic beliefs about the nature of man and of society. In *Troilus and Cressida,* warfare is shown to be wasteful, absurd, and dehumanizing; in all three plays, authoritative judgment, class distinction, and self-assurance are revealed as insufficient and dangerous. Everywhere there is a sense of risk and daring, as Shakespeare changed his former strategies and voiced new attitudes. In the twentieth century, theatrical directors who control every detail of a production have shaped performances that have held audiences completely; and academic criticism, intent on identifying the central meaning in a text, has begun to place these plays in the forefront of Shakespeare's achievement. Yet critics have not agreed with each other and directors are forever presenting the plays in new guises. The originality of Shakespeare's work is not easy to comprehend, and he may not have successfully subdued every element of the dramas to his purposes. If these are revolutionary as well as exploratory plays, we will respond best to them if we do not hurry to reach precipitously for explanations. They are plays that yield immediate excitements, but they also repay patient reappraisal.

The Romances

After *Measure for Measure,* Shakespeare proceeded to his most ambitious and most thoroughly achieved plays, sustaining his imagination through the passionate struggles of Othello and Lear, the deep anguish of Macbeth, and the destructiveness of Timon. These tragedies seem to have taken the whole of his attention through 1604, 1605, and 1606. Around 1607, before or after writing *Antony and Cleopatra,* Shakespeare turned aside and, with *Pericles Prince of Tyre,* began a series of four comedies that are now usually known as the romances. Written within four or five years, these plays have many elements and themes in common: a long story, full of marvels and coincidences; a suffering father or king as a central character; a distinctly younger generation, most of whom find themselves in love for the first and seemingly only time; and a series of journeys that end with the reunion of broken families. They all contain a judicial testing or a trial scene that carries forward the use of debates, investigations, and judgments from the tragicomedies, but these elements are offset in the romances with a new emphasis on what happens when suffering and injustice are replaced, not by reward or punishment, but by reconciliation and new hope. As in the early comedies, the natural world of the open countryside is the setting for crucial scenes—as if cities, palaces, battlegrounds, law courts, and prisons are not the sole or most significant arenas for human drama, as they had been in the tragicomedies.

These new plays contain few fanciful, funny, or lyrical scenes of any length, like those that served earlier to reveal deep and sustained feelings; nor do they follow ardent and intelligent lovers through long mazes and vicissitudes. Their canvasses are much wider, and laughter and single-minded love are relegated to subsidiary positions. Perhaps their most surprising quality, compared with Shakespeare's other plays, is the manner in which the dilemmas of individual characters or the issues of a single moment yield in importance to what happens within a family as a whole over a long passage of years.

The romances are also united in featuring marvels, supernatural events, majestic shows, and dreamlike visions: the goddess Diana and Cerimon the magician-king in *Pericles;* Jupiter and potent drugs in *Cymbeline;* an oracle, a convenient storm, and a seeming statue that comes alive in *The Winter's Tale;* and, in *The Tempest,* a sequence of masquelike displays of quaint creatures, goddesses, dancers, and angry, bloodthirsty hounds, together with enchantment that stops people still in their tracks and can render its master invisible. In this last romance, Shakespeare used music more extensively than in any other play and provided its central father-king with two contrasted attendants, Caliban and Ariel, almost as if they represented Brute Beast and Spiritual Intelligence in an allegorical manner.

Many critics have written about the "vision" of these plays. In notes for an 1818 lecture on *The Tempest,* Coleridge calls it "almost miraculous," an "ideal" play, a kind of waking dream "the interests of which are independent of all historical facts and associations, and arise from their fitness to that faculty of our nature, the imagination I mean, which owns no allegiance to time and place." Later critics have argued that Shakespeare has stepped back from closeup studies of individual crises and historical events in order to provide an optimistic or escapist account of how love, forgiveness, wisdom, and patience can resolve almost all ills. E. M. W. Tillyard's *Shakespeare's Last Plays,* an elaboration of a lecture given at the Sorbonne, argued that

> it is almost as if [Shakespeare] aimed at rendering the complete theme of *The Divine Comedy.* Indeed, it is not fantastic to see in *The Winter's Tale* Shakespeare's attempt to compress that whole theme into a single play . . . and it was with this notion in mind that I spoke of the country scenes as an earthly paradise. The motives of hell and purgatory in Leontes are obvious enough, while the statue scene is conducted in a rarefied atmosphere of contemplation that suggests the motive of paradise.

For G. Wilson Knight, the final plays, as he called the romances, released a "yet more indestructible and sublime music" than the tragedies, a "dynamic and universal drama of the Christian Trinity."

Such rhapsodic criticism was answered by D. G. James, who drew attention to a "sense of inexpressiveness and failure" recurrent in the romances; by J. M. Nosworthy in his New Arden edition of *Cymbeline* (1955), who stressed the artistic experiment of this play as an end in itself; by Frank Kermode in his New Arden *Tempest* (1954), who showed Shakespeare wrestling with, but by no means resolving, the philosophical challenges of a newly discovered world; and by R. A. Foakes, who saw an attempt

> to create a dramatic world in which human intentions, the will, the act of choice, play a very subdued role,

and actions by characters are referable to a psychological condition or compulsion, or to chance, or the influence of an uncertain heaven.

By the 1980s, Shakespeare's romances were seldom seen as a group of delightful and reassuring dream-plays; a new point of view held that each reveals distinctive concerns and stylistic innovations. The surface characteristics that they share so obviously were considered to be the playwright's means of reaching out to satisfy his restless mind and perhaps to reflect the changing world at a time when men of all classes were apprehensive and increasingly embattled.

In *Pericles,* the first of the romances, a long narrative is presented almost consistently in a primitive mode, as if Shakespeare were copying a play dating from the 1580s or, as some scholars have argued, using extensive quotations from it. Rapidly and with two-dimensional simplicity, the "inflamed desire" of Pericles for the "celestial" beauties of King Antiochus' daughter starts the action moving. To win her as his bride, he must solve a riddle that carries a penalty of immediate death to all who fail to probe its secret. A Chorus (in the person of the English poet John Gower, who had told the same story in his *Confessio Amantis* at the close of the fourteenth century) has informed the audience that Antiochus is his daughter's lover and that Pericles is only the latest of "many princes" who have taken the risk—"As yon grim looks do testify," he adds, pointing to a row of severed heads. Pericles reads the riddle correctly, whereupon he flees Antioch in justified expectation of treachery. The narrative moves from one demonstrative tableau to another, introduced by "ancient Gower"; it is enlivened occasionally by ironic comments such as Antiochus' reference to the disappointed suitors as "martyrs slain in Cupid's wars."

Political debate, fearful exile, attempted assassination, disastrous famine, shows of gratitude, and a shipwreck follow in quick succession. A second courtship begins, this time of Thaisa, daughter of King Simonides, for whose love Pericles and competing knights give an exhibition dance dressed in full armor. Pericles and Thaisa marry, and in a frightening storm at sea their daughter, Marina, is born. Thaisa is thought to be dead, and orders are issued to place her in a coffin and throw her overboard. Only forty-seven lines into the next scene, the coffin has been washed ashore and soon Thaisa is restored to life by Cerimon, a magician-king.

Meanwhile, political necessity separates father and daughter. Years pass and an attempt to murder the Princess is foiled at the last moment by the unexpected arrival of pirates who carry her off and sell her to a foreign brothel keeper.

This procession of scenes displays a great variety of human depravity, helplessness, and bad luck, as well as occasional wisdom, faithfulness, shrewd judgment, and cunning. In the end, the "good" qualities triumph, but it is dramatic coincidence, good luck, or the intervention of gods that is chiefly instrumental in effecting this conclusion. Marina takes the most significant human role: she is advertised as the latest and choicest offering of the brothel but is able to convert to virtue the young lechers who rise to the bait. In a brief and hilarious episode, two of these gentlemen hurry off to "hear the Vestals sing" (IV. v). More prosaically, Marina's good education enables her to start a school for practical arts such as singing, weaving, dancing, and embroidery; she survives, active and admired. Pericles, convinced by the false story of Marina's death, has meanwhile become misanthropic and totally incapable of action. He keeps himself alone and unshaven, and remains on board a ship that is "driven before the winds" until it arrives, on Neptune's Feast Day, at the city where Marina lives, respected and loved by all and not least by Lysimachus, the young governor who had been her first would-be client in the brothel. By this fortunate chance, father and daughter are reunited, and Pericles regains that purposeful life which had set him off on his "painful adventures."

As the reunion takes place, the style of the play changes decisively. Pericles and Marina are left alone on shipboard, and she sings to comfort him. He does not respond, and she then tries to speak, only to be pushed away roughly. But she continues:

> I am a maid,
> My lord, that ne'er before invited eyes,
> But have been gazed on like a comet. She speaks,
> My lord, that, may be, hath endured a grief
> Might equal yours, if both were justly weighed.
>
> (V. i. 85–89)

Slowly and painfully, stiffly even, but then with tears of joy, father and daughter recognize one another. Depicted with a delicacy unmatched in Shakespeare's plays, their encounter is solemn, gentle, and intimate. Yet, as Marina gives her name, this mood is cut across by Pericles' fear of some deception:

> O, I am mocked,
> And thou by some incensèd god sent hither
> To make the world to laugh at me.
>
> (143–145)

Marina bids him be patient, as the Chorus has already enjoined the audience. But Pericles now tries to delay the revelation:

> O, stop there a little!
> [Aside]
> This is the rarest dream that e'er dull sleep
> Did mock sad fools withal.
>
> (162–164)

A "great sea of joys" is about to rush upon him, and he is again afraid lest they should

> O'erbear the shores of my mortality
> And drown me with their sweetness.
>
> (195–196)

When he calls Marina to him, his words become biblical and ceremonial, characterizing the whole action of the play as a riddle, legend, myth, or awesome reincarnation:

> O, come hither,
> Thou that beget'st him that did thee beget;
> Thou that wast born at sea, buried at Tharsus,
> And found at sea again! O Helicanus,
> Down on thy knees, thank the holy gods as loud
> As thunder threatens us. This is Marina.
>
> (196–201)

Pericles now hears the "music of the spheres"— although no one else can hear it—and the goddess Diana appears to him in a vision, directing him to her temple at Ephesus, where he will be reunited with Thaisa.

Under the twin influence of Neptune and Diana, the "play has ending" (Epilogue, 18): father and daughter have become, in the last act, sensitive and subtle in their relationship; this evolution makes a far stronger and more lasting impression than all the pageants that have been seen earlier in the play. But it is not their efforts that have created the miracle. In its powerful and affecting climax, this romance-comedy has a double focus: it seems both actual and improbable, particular and representative, grounded in human responses and yet contrived by superhuman intervention. It is easy to be of two minds about Shakespeare's achievement. Ben Jonson had reason to call his great rival's play a "mouldy tale," yet its last scenes display his most mature and humane artistry.

In another way Pericles is problematical: it was not included in the 1623 First Folio, and it has survived only in the manifestly "bad" version of a quarto edition of 1609, printed from a copy made by inefficient reporters. Over the years, many theories have been advanced to account for the shoddy state of much of the text: Shakespeare was revising, incompletely, an old play; he had a collaborator; it was not Shakespeare's at all but ascribed to him in the quarto and added to the Second Folio (1632) without authority. More recently, along with greater knowledge of other "bad" quartos and of printing-house practices, scholars have discovered that two reporters provided the manuscript copy for the printing house, one for Acts I and II, and the other for the remainder; the former tried to patch up the meter and thereby provided a smoother but less comprehensible text. But many problems remain, and no one is quite sure that the whole play is by Shakespeare. Changes in the verse form used for the Chorus, which can be observed very easily in a first reading of the text, illustrate these problems. The presence of two reporters or even of two writers is insufficient to account for all the variations. Nonsense, repetitions, confusions, lacunae, and clumsy, trite, and feeble phrasing are plentiful throughout the play, so much so that it is amazing that enough has survived to bring the play alive. Three features have ensured that this should be so: the plan of the play seems complete and balanced; many themes from earlier plays, and others that were to be developed in later plays, are here given embodiment; and sections of the text, more sustained in the last three acts and most notable in the recognition scene, could have been written only by Shakespeare at the height of his powers.

Shakespeare seems to have left the text of Pericles, like the coffin of Thaisa, to survive or perish as chance and fortune decreed. That may well have been appropriate to his state of mind when he wrote or rewrote it. One idea that runs throughout Pericles is that man is at the mercy of forces outside himself, some explicable only in supernatural terms, some merely accidental, and others deriving from social and political decisions made by others.

The hero's words in the first scene announce that "the earth is thronged by man's oppression, and the poor worm doth die for't" (102–103). When a Fisherman marvels how fishes live in the sea he is told:

> Why, as men do a-land—the great ones eat up the little ones. . . . Such whales have I heard on o' th' land, who never leave gaping till they swallowed the whole parish—church, steeple, bells, and all.
>
> (II. i. 28–34)

The schematic presentation of much of the action, the multiple twists of the narrative ("This world to me is a lasting storm, / Whirring me from my friends": IV. i. 20–21), and the passivity of Pericles in the latter half combine to place conscious reactions and individual decisions in a new perspective. The resonant conclusion, as trust slowly banishes disbelief, shows an acceptance of danger, brutality, and helplessness quite as much as an achievement of will, intelligence, and romantic longing.

The other three romances can be viewed as developments or comments upon what was achieved in *Pericles*. *Cymbeline* was first performed in 1609 or 1610. Its last act has stage directions calling for military processions, hand-to-hand fighting, headlong flight, and cries of victory. These elements may account for the decision of the editors of the First Folio to entitle this romance *The Tragedie of Cymbeline*. But while prowess, courage, and honor are important issues, warfare and violent death do not bring about its conclusion. Shortly after the beginning of Act V, scene iv, "as in an apparition," Posthumus' dead ancestors circle the stage to solemn music and then Jupiter "descends in thunder and lightning, sitting upon an eagle." The god leaves a message inscribed on a tablet, but it is not deciphered until the end of the next long scene, which is more obviously in a comic mode. That final scene presents a sequence of twenty-five denouements (most computations agree on this number, but there is scope for miscounting among the lesser ramifications). The stage is now as full as it was in the battle scenes, but the mood is quite different and "pardon's the word to all" (422). At last everyone moves off under new orders:

> Our peace we'll ratify, seal it with feasts.
> Set on there! Never was a war did cease,
> Ere bloody hands were washed, with such a peace.
>
> (482–484)

The dominant mood is now clearly that of comic celebration, but at its conclusion *Cymbeline* shares with *Pericles* a sense of loss and needless suffering. It also adds a specific recognition of the limitations of human willpower and purposeful activity. A Soothsayer, named Philarmonus, is at hand to explicate:

> The fingers of the pow'rs above do tune
> The harmony of this peace.
>
> (465–466)

And this is echoed by Cymbeline himself:

> Laud we the gods,
> And let our crooked smokes climb to their nostrils
> From our blest altars.
>
> (475–477)

Throughout the greater part of this romance, the King takes a back seat. The main focus is on his court, and he does not travel away from it, as Pericles had from Tyre; Cymbeline reacts rather than acts, and most of the time he seems unable to judge effectively. His Queen, the stepmother to his children, is the more dominant figure, busy with intrigue and the manufacture of poisons. The foreground of the play is a complicated mesh of several plots, all concerned with deceit and trust, loyalty and self-concern. An anonymous gentleman opens with words that seem intended to alert the audience to division and dissension:

> You do not meet a man but frowns. Our bloods
> No more obey the heavens than our courtiers
> Still seem as does the King's.

A sustained complexity of style matches that of the action. The imagery is sometimes surprising; metaphor and descriptive detail intrude upon the narration; the syntax is frequently involved and at other times taut and challenging. By line count, *Cymbeline* is one of the longest of Shakespeare's plays, but it seems even longer in reading or performance because each scene has speeches that demand careful and often subtle consideration. Many effects are fragmentary and idiosyncratic. Almost all the named characters have asides or soliloquies to make their sentiments clear in isolation.

Whereas *Pericles* moved easily from one location to another, following the fortunes of its hero and his family, *Cymbeline* withdraws its King and titular hero from the audience's attention for much of the time, right up to the last scene, in which he has to try to superintend the unraveling of all the plots. This last scene has something of a comic, deflating effect, particularly because the King is not convincingly in charge even here.

The action starts when Cymbeline's daughter, Imogen, is separated from her husband, Posthumus, because he is not of royal blood and because her stepmother, the Queen, wants her own son, Cloten, to marry the Princess and so secure succession of the throne. Cymbeline has two sons, but they are believed dead until Shakespeare reveals them halfway through the play, living in rustic isolation with Belarius, who had earlier fled from court. Posthumus goes to Rome, where he meets a group of friends who belong to the Renaissance Italy of Shakespeare's source for this part of the play, Boccaccio's *Decameron,* rather than the Britain of Holinshed's *Chronicles,* which provided the substance of the main narrative. Having instigated a wager with Posthumus on Imogen's chastity, Iachimo travels to Britain and, taken into the Princess' bedchamber hidden in a trunk, he emerges to steal a bracelet and to note intimate details that will make Posthumus believe he has seduced his wife. Lucius, the Roman ambassador of Augustus Caesar, demands British tribute and, as general of the Roman forces, fights a battle to exact it; although the British are victorious, Cymbeline releases Lucius and agrees to pay the tribute. In the course of these events, Shakespeare contrived opportunity for Cloten to woo Imogen and, when she flees the court, to follow her, disguised in Posthumus' clothes. A little later Imogen disguises herself as a boy and, so dressed, finds her long-lost brothers; she subsequently becomes page to Lucius. Meanwhile Pisanio, Posthumus' servant, has to refuse his master's orders to kill Imogen, and Cloten is killed when he arouses the anger of one of Cymbeline's sons. When the two boys again find Imogen, still disguised as Fidele, they believe that she is dead—she has taken a sleeping potion prepared by the Queen; together they speak a dirge for her. They leave her beside Cloten's headless body, and when she wakens she mistakes it for Posthumus', since he wears her husband's clothes. It is in this predicament that Lucius with his army marches onto the stage and takes care of her. The battle sequences follow.

No summary can catch all the twists and turns of these extraordinary events, nor can it give a fair impression of the deliberately shocking way in which some of them are presented. An example of the latter is Imogen's impulsive reply to Pisanio's expression of concern when he is ordered to kill her:

> *Pisanio.*   O gracious lady,
> Since I received command to do this business
> I have not slept one wink.
> *Imogen.*   Do't, and to bed then.
>
> (III. iv. 99–101)

This registers like a shudder of intense feeling or of frustrated mockery, or, perhaps, as a momentary flash of cynical insouciance—such ambiguity is also common in this romance and is one of its most distinctive features. Acute feeling or minutely observed fantasy can undermine or transcend a prevailing mood: so Iachimo notes on the sleeping body of Imogen:

> A mole cinque-spotted, like the crimson drops
> I' th' bottom of a cowslip.

A moment later he hides with:

> Swift, swift, you dragons of the night, that dawning
> May bare the raven's eye. I lodge in fear.
>
> (II. ii. 38–39, 48–49)

The sensational techniques employed in *Cymbeline* have led some critics to see a debt to the tragicomedies written by Francis Beaumont and John Fletcher for the King's Men at about the same time that Shakespeare was turning to romance plays for the same company of actors. But the earliest plays by the younger writers—*Philaster, The Woman's Prize,* and *The Maid's Tragedy*—are so close in date to Shakespeare's experiments and so distinct in their well-ordered form that no one can show in which direction any influence might have prevailed. As G. E. Bentley argued, all three dramatists may well have been reacting to changes when the King's Men took possession of the smaller Blackfriars theater; unusual events and fashionable wit suited a wealthier audience, and sensational, fast-moving, and intimate dramatic action looked well on the artificially lit stage.

Emrys Jones, in another important article, has suggested that James I and his fondness for eulogies were another influence on the creation of *Cymbeline.* James was proud of being the first king to unify Scotland and England and of striving in his foreign policy to establish peace abroad. The bewildered and deceived Cymbeline could be no flattering image of James, but the absent and famous Augustus Caesar was a monarch with whom James was pleased to be compared because he had been responsible for the era of peace that had preceded the birth of Christ. The many references to Milford Haven, where Lucius lands (according to Shakespeare but not according to Holinshed), are allusions, Jones has also argued, to the port where Richmond, later Henry VII, had landed to bring peace and to unite the houses of York and Lancaster after the long Wars of the Roses.

But this dramatic romance does not yield all its secrets to a simple key. Flattery of James cannot go far to explain the jangling, deceptive world that is portrayed, in which love, kinship, loyalty, and self-preservation are likely to be treacherous and in which luck plays such a large part in the outcome of every effort. In the middle of the last battle, Posthumus tells an inquirer:

> Nay, do not wonder at it. You are made
> Rather to wonder at the things you hear
> Than to work any. Will you rhyme upon't
> And vent it for a mock'ry?
>
> (V. iii. 53–56)

Few critics rate *Cymbeline* high among Shakespeare's plays, but after several recent studies most would acknowledge its interest as an innovative and ambitious work. Some, like the present writer, believe that the innovations show Shakespeare alert to the tensions of changing and dangerous times; he created the dramatic means of presenting both the realities of unsettled political life and the uncertainties of rebellious and isolated minds. Perhaps Shakespeare wished to show that men and women live together in peace only by collusion, willing or unwilling, with forces that are outside and more powerful than themselves. Such efforts can provide the dearest joys in life:

> See,
> Posthumus anchors upon Imogen,
> And she like harmless lightning throws her eye
> On him, her brothers, me, her master, hitting
> Each object with a joy; the counterchange
> Is severally in all.
>
> (V. v. 392–397)

Critical opinion about Shakespeare's last two romances, *The Winter's Tale* and *The Tempest*, which

followed shortly after (between 1610 and 1612), has been largely positive, especially since the 1930s, when critics began to value Shakespeare's plays for meanings implicit in their texts rather than for characterization or explicit wisdom.

The Winter's Tale, especially, retains enough of the fabulous freedom of the first two romances to exempt its critics from seeking a recognizable reflection of ordinary life, but it is much easier than its predecessors to grasp in familiar terms. The progress of its narrative is regular and straightforward, and most of its sentiments are unambiguous. The first act establishes the character of Leontes, King of Sicilia, in much the same way as a leading character in one of Shakespeare's tragedies might be established. His words express irrational jealousy when he suspects that his guest Polixenes has seduced his queen, Hermione, and that she is nearly nine months pregnant with his friend's child. Until Act III, scene iii, the setting is in or near Leontes' court, and each action is consequent upon what the audience has witnessed: Leontes tries to have Polixenes murdered, but Camillo chooses rather to warn his victim and they escape together; Hermione is imprisoned and gives birth to a daughter whom Leontes tries to have killed but then decides to abandon in a remote, desert place; Hermione is put on trial and vindicated by Apollo's oracle, which Leontes has invoked; five lines after Leontes cries, "There is no truth at all i' th' oracle" (III. ii. 138), his son, Mamillius, is reported dead; Leontes repents, Hermione swoons, and the King is told by Paulina, the Queen's friend, to "see what death is doing." When Hermione has been carried from the stage, she also is reported to have died, and Leontes vows to spend the rest of his life acknowledging his fault and shame.

But as this first half of the play establishes characters and motives with absolute clarity, the audience is also encouraged to see larger issues. The Queen's words at her trial invoke supernatural powers and three simple words—"as they do"—express her belief in a way that makes contact with an equally fervent belief among the members of the audience:

> But thus: if powers divine
> Behold our human actions, as they do,
> I doubt not then but innocence shall make
> False accusation blush and tyranny
> Tremble at patience.
>
> (III. ii. 27–31)

At this point, the audience is engaged not only with the characters but also with Innocence, False Accusation, Tyranny, Patience, and the Powers Above. *The Winter's Tale* has been cited as proof that Shakespeare turned, at the end of his career, to an allegorical and symbolic dramaturgy.

The oracle supplies a riddle as well as a judgment: "The king shall live without an heir if that which is lost be not found" (III. ii. 133–134). The rest of the play shows how this prophecy is borne out by events. The next scene is on the seacoast of Bohemia, where Antigonus, Paulina's husband, who has seen Hermione in a dream and is following her instructions, leaves the babe, now named Perdita, to cry without succor in this remote place while a horrifying tempest rages. That the play has shifted decisively into the world of romance is established by a stage direction that calls for the ancient courtier to be chased out of sight by a bear. The next moment an old Shepherd enters, soon followed by Clown, his son; they exchange simple incredulity and simple wisdom in garrulous confidence. The ship that had brought Antigonus is reported sunk with all hands, and the bear "half dined on the gentleman" (III. iii. 101); yet they themselves are alive and fortunate. At this point Time, as Chorus, announces that sixteen years have passed and introduces the name of Polixenes' son, Florizel. Soon this prince enters dressed as a shepherd; he is courting Perdita, dressed as queen of a May Day feast. Before that Polixenes and Camillo have been shown preparing to disguise themselves to find out what business is keeping Florizel from court.

Instead of a quick succession of varied scenes, as in the earlier romances, the action stays among the shepherds in Bohemia. A single scene (IV. iv) of over 800 lines—the longest Shakespeare ever wrote—elaborates the shepherd's feast with decorous and wild dances, songs, flowers, courtship, and the King's unmasking, plus a great deal of intimidation and plotting that sends almost all the characters off to Sicilia. Autolycus, a pickpocket, peddler, and former courtier, is at hand as a perpetual entertainer. This is all hugely enjoyable, but it also establishes the young lovers as almost fearless in their love: Perdita knows that the "selfsame sun" that shines upon the King's court "hides not his visage from our cottage but looks on alike" (IV. iv. 437–439). Florizel prizes his "affection" before duty to his father and his royal responsibilities. He dares to be guided by his "fancy":

> If my reason
> Will thereto be obedient, I have reason;
> If not, my senses, better pleased with madness,
> Do bid it welcome.
>
> (IV. iv. 475–478)

His commitment to Perdita has the reckless practicality of Imogen's to Posthumus.

By this time the end of the play has been all but announced. In Sicilia, the families are reunited in terms that transcend ordinary values: Leontes welcomes the loving couple "as is the spring to th' earth" (V. i. 151), and an anonymous gentleman, recounting Leontes' offstage recognition of Perdita as his daughter, says that "they looked as they had heard of a world ransomed, or one destroyed" (V. ii. 14–15). The final scene is both a surprise and an innovation. Shakespeare has given no hint before that Hermione did not die after her trial. But now Paulina brings the other characters to her "gallery," where she shows the Queen as a statue that comes alive; she has kept her secretly while Leontes has languished in his penitence. She manages the reunion like a stage show, drawing a curtain, calling for music, and requesting silence; she then announces, "It is required you do awake your faith" (V. iii. 94–95). The audience's awareness of improbability may well be surrendered in wonder and pleasure. Hermione descends from her dais in silence, whereupon Leontes takes her by the hand and cries out:

> O, she's warm!
> If this be magic, let it be an art
> Lawful as eating.
>
> (V. iii. 109–111)

The onlookers direct attention to the now silent center of the tableau: "She embraces him. . . . She hangs about his neck" (111–112). So the last moment of the fabulous romance is perceived in the most everyday and physical terms.

Full recognitions follow and, with a certain lightness of spirit, Leontes calls on Camillo to become Paulina's new husband. Few comedies end so confidently assured that the heavens and well-intentioned human aid direct lives to long-delayed happiness: only a reluctance to speak and a quickening of pace suggest contrary reactions on the stage. However, the obvious artifice of the last scene— nowhere else does Shakespeare so deceive his audience in order to spring a surprise—is an unspoken reminder that this is a romance and that reasonable expectations are being mysteriously or perhaps mockingly overturned.

The story of *The Winter's Tale* is told clearly and with delightful elaboration, its characters are fully presented, and its dialogue is delicately responsive to situation and resonant of both the natural world and metaphysical speculation. It has the aura of complete mastery, and in performance—especially in sophisticated modern productions that exploit all elements, sensational and realistic—a matching confidence in an audience's response can light up every scene. It seems grudging to suggest that the off-key prominence of Autolycus (who reduces all issues to his own convenience and sings happily of the simplest pleasures), the officiousness of Paulina, and the surface shine of expert dialogue that is evident in the more devious passages of the play's action betray an unease in Shakespeare's mind. Shakespeare is indulging his artifice, not expressing an underlying disbelief or despair. But the last romance, *The Tempest,* does have at its heart an unmistakable asperity that may be a sign that toward the end of his career Shakespeare refused to accept in absolute terms his own magisterial ability "to make these doubts all even" (*As You Like It,* V. iv. 25).

Prospero, as ruler, father, and worker of wonders, dominates *The Tempest.* A storm at sea—which must have stretched the resources of a Jacobean stage manager to the utmost—threatens a ship's company and a king's court with imminent death. Afterward, Prospero is revealed as the author of the storm. Unmoved by his daughter Miranda's sorrow for the suffering of others, he tells her, with careful emphasis, how he was evicted as the duke of Milan by his brother, Antonio, and exiled on the island that the stage represents. He announces that "accident most strange" (I. ii. 178) and the storm he has raised have now brought his enemies into his power. Prospero introduces Ariel, a spirit whom he has freed and then mastered, and Caliban, a witch's son who had been in possession of the island before Prospero's arrival and who had once tried to rape Miranda. After demonstrating his power over these servants, Prospero stands by to watch Ferdinand, son of Alonso, King of Naples, being led by Ariel in disguise as a "nymph o' th' sea," so that he meets Miranda. Prospero must control the Prince, as he has controlled his servants, and must deceive his daughter so that the two young people fall in love. Subsequently he provides a betrothal masque in which he insists on the importance of premarital continence and then arranges, in the play's last scene, that they are shown to all the other characters, while they are absorbed in a game of chess. He introduces them as a "wonder," and it might appear at this point that Prospero has achieved a perfectly happy conclusion were it not that Miranda's first words are: "Sweet lord, you play me false" (V. i. 172).

The main action is concerned with bringing Antonio and Alonso, who had once been allies against Prospero, to a recognition of their crime in usurping the dukedom of Milan:

> They being penitent,
> The sole drift of my purpose doth extend
> Not a frown further.
>
> (V. i. 28–30)

But at the same time, Prospero has to prevent and punish a new attempt on his life to which Caliban incites a drunken butler and a fool from Alonso's court. Ariel is sent in the figure of a harpy to denounce the noblemen as "men of sin," and a vision of a banquet that precedes this confrontation turns suddenly into a chaotic image of mockery and horror so that his victims become desperate and mad. Prospero defeats the "foul conspiracy" of the "beast Caliban and his confederates" (IV. i. 139–140) by a booby trap of "glistering apparel" and then a chase through stinking water, where they are pursued by spirits in the shapes of hounds.

With his enemies vanquished and his daughter betrothed, Prospero might seem set to conclude the play in the affirmative mode of *The Winter's Tale,* but the last scene is overcast by his sense of inadequacy and loss. When Miranda sees the courtiers assembled, she, who had grown up knowing only her father and Caliban, exclaims in pleasure at this "brave new world," to which her father remonstrates with a terseness that is equally affecting, " 'Tis new to thee" (V. i. 184). Antonio, his brother, shows no sign of penitence, but he is forgiven even his "rankest fault." Caliban is kept in service, although he seeks for "grace." Ariel is freed and then—although Prospero calls him "My Ariel, chick," a phrase implying intimate affection —he disappears without a word. Prospero expects to "retire me to my Milan, where every third thought shall be my grave" (V. i. 310–311).

This last romance, set in an island full of music and magic, shows how forgiveness and reconciliation are necessary if men are to live at peace and the world's pleasures are to be enjoyed. It is a symbolic and visionary play, like the Jacobean court masques, whose dances, gods, grotesques, and transformations Shakespeare borrowed to express his own fancies. But in the rebellion of Caliban, who is fired by a sense of possession and a love of natural beauty, and in the resistance of Ariel, who seeks only to fly away to live with summer merrily, "under the blossom that hangs on the bough" (V. i. 94)—and who sings of it so that his master will assuredly miss him—an audience is shown opposing views and is drawn in sympathy to those who resist Prospero's intentions. The visionary who holds center stage almost throughout the play has to learn the limits of his own powers, even though they are above ordinary human might. As he asserts his authority a passion of anger "works him strongly" (IV. i. 144); when he is faced with obduracy, he decides to "tell no tales" (V. i. 129) but to forgive without conditions. When Prospero renounces his magic, he does so with an obvious yearning for its beauty and compulsion.

Gonzalo, the faithful and idealistic councillor, weeps for sorrow and for joy as the story draws to a close. Then he claims that everyone has found a true self, "when no man was his own" (V. i. 213). Thereafter he is silent, and the last judgment of the play is provided when Prospero steps forward to speak an Epilogue, still in his stage character:

> Now I want
> Spirits to enforce, art to enchant;
> And my ending is despair
> Unless I be relieved by prayer,
> Which pierces so that it assaults
> Mercy itself and frees all faults.
> As you from crimes would pardoned be,
> Let your indulgence set me free.

The Tempest is Shakespeare's most splendid and enchanting play, with each scene bringing fresh inventions and new marvels. But it is not an indulgent extravaganza. Action is confined to a single time period and, with the exception of the opening storm, to one small island; the plot is Shakespeare's own invention; reactions are expressed with great economy, and ideas are carefully defined; moreover, the most sustained focus is on a visionary, wise, and experienced man, who remains isolated, unsatisfied, insecure, and helpless, even as his "high charms work" and he brings remission or delight to others. For Shakespeare *The Tempest* was a reassessment as well as an opulent masterpiece and innovating experiment. Despite the strong central focus, it is a mysterious play and rewards repeated reading and performance.

BIBLIOGRAPHY

General. Reginald A. Foakes, *Shakespeare: The Dark Comedies to the Last Plays: From Satire to Celebration* (1971). Northrop Frye, *A Natural Perspective: The Development of Shakespearean Comedy and Romance* (1965). David J. Palmer, ed., *Shakespeare's Later Comedies: An Anthology of Modern Criticism* (1971).

Tragicomedies. Oscar James Campbell, *Comicall Satyre and Shakespeare's "Troilus and Cressida"* (1938; repr. 1970). Michael Jamieson, "The Problem Plays, 1920–1970: A Retrospect," in *Shakespeare Survey,* 25 (1972). Robert Kimbrough, *Shakespeare's "Troilus and Cressida" and Its Setting* (1964). Mary Lascelles, *Shakespeare's "Measure for Measure"* (1953). William W. Lawrence, *Shakespeare's Problem Comedies* (1931). Robert Ornstein, ed., *Discussions of Shakespeare's Problem Comedies* (1961). Joseph G. Price, *The Unfortunate Comedy: A Study of "All's Well That Ends Well" and Its Critics* (1968). Ernest Schanzer, *The Problem Plays of Shakespeare* (1963).

Romances. G. E. Bentley, "Shakespeare and the Blackfriars Theatre," in *Shakespeare Survey,* 1 (1948). John Russell Brown and Bernard Harris, eds., *Later Shakespeare,* Stratford-upon-Avon Studies 8 (1966). F. David Hoeniger, "Shakespeare's Romances Since 1958: A Retrospect," in *Shakespeare Survey,* 29 (1976). David Gwilym James, *The Dream of Prospero* (1967). Emrys Jones, "Stuart *Cymbeline,*" in *Essays in Criticism,* 11 (1961). G. Wilson Knight, *The Shakespearian Tempest* (1932). Anthony D. Nuttall, *Two Concepts of Allegory: A Study of Shakespeare's "The Tempest" and the Logic of Allegorical Expression* (1967). Gary Schmidgall, *Shakespeare and the Courtly Aesthetic* (1981). E. M. W. Tillyard, *Shakespeare's Last Plays* (1938).

Shakespeare and His Audiences

ANN JENNALIE COOK

Who goes to see Shakespeare? Answering such a question taxes the strengths of any researcher or thinker. Everyone knows a farmer, taxi driver, or butcher who attends productions in Ashland, Oregon, New York City, or Stratford-upon-Avon. Students and tourists by the busload dutifully pay homage to Shakespeare, especially as part of a predetermined itinerary or class assignment. But though drawing a mass audience numerically, Shakespeare tends to attract playgoers rather more sophisticated than those of hit movies or Broadway musicals. To go beyond such rough generalizations would require surveys on a global scale over a period of several years. To date, no one seems sufficiently interested to undertake such an impossible task. Thus, four hundred years from now, those curious about Shakespeare's twentieth-century audience will have to rely upon such newspaper accounts, scraps of statistics, records of individual attendance, and other references as may survive.

And so it was with the audiences of Shakespeare's day. The same shards of information from the past tantalize the historian but offer no definitive portrait of the playgoers who were fortunate enough to see Richard Burbage as Hamlet or Robert Armin as Feste. Any hypothesis about those vanished spectators must rest upon inference, fragmentary information, and a good deal of imagination, all refracted through a world view varying radically from that of the Renaissance.

In fact, the spectrum of opinion in the first half of the twentieth century regarding Shakespeare's audience reveals distinct and changing cultural biases. In 1907, his Victorian morality affronted, Robert Bridges castigated the "vulgar" playgoers for that "grossness" in Shakespeare "which we must swallow." He cautioned his readers against "degrading ourselves to the level of his audience, and learning contamination from those wretched beings who can never be forgiven their share in preventing the greatest poet and dramatist in the world from being the best artist." By 1941 many intellectuals perceived the common man not as a vulgar boor but as the very measure of decency and good sense. Reflecting this shift in perspective, Alfred Harbage regarded an audience dominated by ordinary folk as responsible for Shakespeare's glories rather than his "grossness":

> We may say in the present case, quite apart from Beaumont's satirical use of them as the spectators in *The Knight of the Burning Pestle,* that a grocer, his wife, and their young apprentice form as acceptable an epitome of Shakespeare's audience as any the facts will warrant us to choose. If Shakespeare did not write to please such a little cockney family as this, he did not write to please his audience. But if he did so write, then there must be some correspondence in quality between the plays and our sample three—the grocer, his wife, and their young apprentice.

According to Harbage, when the players began catering to the decadent tastes of the elite, the caliber of dramatic art declined.

Clearly, Bridges and Harbage see in the nature of Elizabethan audiences a ready explanation for what they find objectionable or admirable in the plays, together with reinforcement for their social preconceptions. Even modern playwrights and critics find it all too easy to blame failure on an unappreciative audience, to chide the bad taste of those masses who make some mindless play a hit, or to applaud the discernment of those who patronize serious drama. Shakespeare himself had similar attitudes. *Troilus and Cressida* was "never staled with the stage, never clapper-clawed with the palms of the vulgar," never "sullied with the smoky breath of the multitude" (Preface, 1–3, 31–32). Hamlet speaks of the play that "pleased not the million; 'twas caviary to the general, but it was (as I received it, and others, whose judgments in such matters cried in the top of mine) an excellent play" (II. ii. 425–428). The Prince condemned "the groundlings, who for the most part are capable of nothing but inexplicable dumb shows and noise" (III. ii. 10–12). Yet in other plays the audience is flattered for its intelligent approval, and excuses are offered for the plays' imperfections: "Gentles, do not reprehend. / If you pardon, we will mend" (*A Midsummer Night's Dream,* V. i. 418–419) and "Piece out our imperfections with your thoughts" (*Henry V,* Prologue, 23) and "Gentle breath of yours my sails / Must fill, or else my project fails, / Which was to please" (*The Tempest,* Epilogue, 11–13). Other playwrights, such as Ben Jonson and John Webster, exhibit the same alternation between praise and contempt for their spectators—depending, of course, upon the reception that their works received.

From the outset one must divorce the issue of audience taste from that of audience identity. Otherwise, critical responses reveal a good deal about their authors' attitudes but very little about the actual composition or behavior of the audience. For that information one must look to more complex evidence drawn from economics, demography, social history, theater history, public documents, and private records. And even then the picture emerges blurred because of inadequate data from which only probable conclusions can be drawn.

As an initial step toward identifying Shakespeare's audience, one can consider the various places where his plays were presented. The Globe comes to mind immediately and, for many, almost exclusively. However, Shakespeare and his company (the Lord Chamberlain's Men under Eliza-

beth, the King's Men under James) performed in many different locations, each of which suggests a particular kind of playgoer. For example, the records show more than a hundred appearances at court during Shakespeare's career. Though most plays at such presentations are simply listed without title, eighteen are clearly identified as Shakespeare's. For the company's performances in several royal palaces, the audiences included members of royalty and the nobility, often visiting dignitaries or ambassadors, together with lesser courtiers. The spectators at private performances in the homes of aristocrats like Lords Cobham and Southampton, Sir Walter Cope, and Sir Walter Raleigh were scarcely less impressive. On some of these occasions, Shakespeare was called for: *A Midsummer Night's Dream* almost certainly commissioned for a noble wedding, *Richard II* at Sir Edward Hoby's supper in 1595, and *Sir John Oldcastle (Henry IV, Part 1)* at a feast of the lord chamberlain in 1600. The Inns of Court, which accommodated "the sonnes of the best or better sort of Gentlemen of all the Shires of England," according to John Stow, frequently hired Shakespeare's company to perform at their festivities. *The Comedy of Errors* graced the Gray's Inn Christmas revels in 1594, and *Twelfth Night* was presented for the Middle Temple eight years later.

Yet most people saw Shakespeare's plays in a theater. While a few of his earliest plays may have been presented at Philip Henslowe's Rose or the Newington Butts, both on the south side of the Thames, most of his work up to 1600 was performed at the Theatre or the Curtain in Finsbury Fields, north of the City. From 1599 onward, the Globe housed Shakespeare's troupe, and from 1609 until the Puritans shut down the playhouses in 1642, the King's Men also operated out of the enclosed, or "private," Blackfriars theater during the winter, shifting to the open-air Globe in summer. Thus, even during his lifetime, Shakespeare saw his dramas staged at several different playhouses, as well as in more exclusive settings.

The structure and policies of these theaters provide further information about their audiences. The great public playhouses, like the Theatre and the Globe, were open to anyone with the money, the leisure, and the inclination to attend. On those afternoons when the house was full, up to three thousand people crowded their way through the narrow doors. Once inside, a spectator could choose to be a "groundling," standing for two or three hours in the open space around the stage and paying no more than a penny or two for his place. However, to enter the roofed galleries, which surrounded the house to a depth of ten or twelve feet, required another payment. A seat on a bench, a cushion, a private room, or the exclusive lords' room directly over the stage were increasingly expensive, while a stool onstage with the actors was the costliest place of all. Shrewd businessmen like Philip Henslowe and the Burbages constructed the playhouses so that two or three times as much space was devoted to the galleries as to the standees' pit, for "penny stinkards" alone could hardly finance the expenses of a dramatic company. In the smaller Blackfriars, which accommodated somewhere between five hundred and nine hundred, prices were scaled a good deal higher, starting at sixpence. Besides the costs of admission, playgoers spent money on food and drink, books and pamphlets, and hiring a boat to the Bankside or a carriage to Blackfriars. In addition, the pickpockets and prostitutes who frequented the theaters could make an afternoon's entertainment still more expensive.

Quite clearly, the theaters catered to a moneyed clientele. The hordes of destitute outcasts who thronged into London were far more likely to spend a spare penny on a loaf of bread than a play, while those fortunate enough to find work had to labor two or three hours to earn even a penny. The law required workers to be at their tasks from daylight to sunset six days a week, with a fine for every hour missed. In addition, rampant inflation meant that wages, also fixed by law, bought less than they had for three centuries. Time spent in getting to the suburbs, where most theaters were located, to while away the entire afternoon represented a luxury that ordinary folk could enjoy only on an occasional holiday. When Sunday brought a day of rest, the playhouses were closed. On weekdays a truant schoolboy or apprentice with a rare penny in hand, a threadbare schoolmaster or clerk, perhaps a law student on a strict allowance might endure the rigors of the weather and journey to stand looking up at the six-foot-high stage. But most patrons of Shakespeare spent considerably more money to sit or stand in comfort in the roofed galleries and, after 1609, to sit indoors at the Blackfriars during the winter. With weather so bitter that this period has been termed "the Little Ice Age," there may have been many times when no groundlings braved the elements.

Who, then, did fill the galleries at the Theatre and Globe, the benches and boxes at Blackfriars? Those with sufficient money and leisure to support a thriving theatrical enterprise were a varied group, even though they represented a small minority of the society at large. They were the privileged—the wellborn, the wealthy, the educated, the successful. Comprising less than 10 percent of the total population, they made up a much higher percentage of the London population during the reigns of Elizabeth and the Stuarts. The government, the court, the legal system, business affairs, the lure of profits in trade, sophisticated schooling, the hope of preferment, and a dazzling array of extravagant pleasures drew the privileged to London on either a permanent or a temporary basis. Shakespeare himself was part of this influx. Where else could an intelligent, ambitious, talented man achieve great success? Certainly not in Stratford-upon-Avon.

"All the people which be in our country be either gentlemen or of the commonality," Richard Mulcaster wrote in 1581. And gentlemen, even those aspirants like the Shakespeares (who had yet to be granted a coat of arms), stood firmly apart from the commonality, their difference marked in countless subtle ways. One of those distinctions lay in the association of the privileged with the drama. Classical plays, as well as composition and performance of new works, constituted part of the formal training in grammar school and at university. The first English tragedy in blank verse, *Gorboduc* (1562), was written by two aristocrats at the Inns of Court, Thomas Norton and Thomas Sackville. Ben Jonson, educated at London's Westminster School, became tutor to the Raleighs and received preferment at court. Playwrights like Christopher Marlowe and Robert Greene were university men, while Thomas Lodge and John Marston had attended the Inns of Court. And all the acting troupes enjoyed the prestige and protection of noble or royal patrons. In fact, the very rationale for public performances averred that these were rehearsals to perfect appearances before the sovereign. Yet both the court and private performances could never have accommodated all those who had developed a taste for the theater, especially after the privileged began to pour into London in such great numbers. To satisfy an audience of thousands required regular productions in large, permanent locations.

In *The Gulls Handbook,* Dekker wrote that "your Gallant, your Courtier, and your Capten had wont to be the soundest paymaisters" for the players.

And indeed, paymasters were necessary to maintain all the acting companies, including Shakespeare's. Command performances and occasional gifts from patrons to tide the troupes over during rough times —when the plague forced the theaters to close, for example—were never refused. But, like all commercial ventures, the theaters also required plenty of paying customers in order to stay in business. Magnificent playhouses, costumes, scripts, salaries for the gatherers at the doors and the hired men onstage—all took their toll before any profits could be divided among the company's sharers, or owners. Yet apparently there were enough playgoers to finance several companies and several theaters, accommodating perhaps ten thousand people by 1610. As the world traveler Fynes Moryson described the situation, "The Citty of London alone hath foure or fiue Companyes of players with their peculiar Theaters Capable of many thousands, wherein they all play euery day in the weeke but Sunday . . . as there be, in my opinion, more Playes in London then in all the partes of the worlde I haue seene."

The patterns of attendance and repertory provide further clues to the identity and behavior of the audience. According to Henslowe's diary, plays were not presented in consecutive runs, as at modern theaters, but in a repertory that changed daily. After its initial performance, a play continued to be offered every two weeks or so until receipts dropped below a certain level; it was then removed from the stage. Except for holidays, profits were highest for new plays, even though admission charges were doubled for first performances. Apparently novelty was more important to audiences than money. Curiously, premieres were not offered on holidays, perhaps because the common folk enjoying a rare day of leisure could not afford the doubled prices and did not know (or care) whether the play was new or old, as long as it provided entertainment. Plenty of others patronized the dozens of fresh efforts each year, regardless of cost, rather than wait two weeks to see the newest presentation.

However, without the special attraction of a holiday or a new play, companies could not expect a full house. Thomas Platter's report (1599) that "those which play best obtain most spectators" suggests considerable competition among the troupes for a rather limited audience. Though Henslowe's company rivaled Shakespeare's in importance, his receipts show the galleries only half full on an aver-

age afternoon, and he dropped most plays after a dozen showings. If everyone who cared to see a production could do so in such a short time, then the number of spectators must have been relatively small, especially since many of them came to see the same plays over and over again. Some of Shakespeare's greatest dramas, like *Hamlet,* either remained in the repertory or were frequently revived. Then as now, their subtlety could even satisfy spectators accustomed "to arraigne Playes dailie," as the First Folio has it.

Yet, even with such actors as Richard Burbage and playwrights like William Shakespeare, London's foremost company sometimes suffered from competition. When troupes of boys reappeared on the private stages about 1599 after a decade's absence, the novelty and notoriety of their performances hurt the adult actors. Ben Jonson complained in *The Poetaster* that "this winter ha's made vs all poorer, then so many staru'd snakes: No bodie comes at vs; not a gentleman." But the inroads of the "little eyases" into the audiences of the public theaters proved to be temporary, with the King's Men's takeover of the Blackfriars in 1609 marking the triumph of the adults. However, they still had to contend with the day-to-day competition of other troupes. Unlike lesser groups, many of which folded, Shakespeare's company retained its supremacy, in part no doubt because his plays retained their attraction for the playgoers.

The records are replete with references to those who attended the theater, though many such references are biased in various ways. According to disgruntled Puritans, who deemed the "sumptuous Theatre houses, a continuall monument of Londons prodigalitie and folly," playgoers were no more than an "assemblie of Tailers, Tinkers, Cordwayners, Saylers, olde Men, yong Men, Women, Boyes, Girles, and such like" (Stephen Gosson, *Playes Confuted*). The governing officials of London, who had long since forbidden performances within their jurisdiction, kept up a steady protest to the royal Privy Council about the dangers of playgoing to public health and safety. In 1592 the lord mayor complained to the Archbishop of Canterbury that in their view, the theaters attracted "prentizes and Seruants withdrawen from their woorks," as well as "great numbers of light & lewd disposed persons, as harlotts, cutpurses" and "vagrant persons, Maisterles men, thieves, horse stealers, whoremongers, Coozeners, Conycatchers, contrivers of treason, and other idele and daungerous persons" (*Malone*

Society Collections, I, 68, 78). However, except in time of plague or Lent, when all public entertainments were closed, the civic authorities had remarkably little success in shutting down the playhouses.

Unquestionably some dissolute commoners did attend the theater. Though it was illegal, apprentices and other young servants occasionally slipped in to escape from work. "These are the youths," said Shakespeare, "that thunder at a playhouse and fight for bitten apples" (*Henry VIII,* V. iv. 57–58). And from time to time idle or irresponsible adults found the money to see a play, though most of the criminals came because the theatergoers offered enticing targets. Prostitutes and pickpockets did not have to pay admission and tie up an entire afternoon when they could solicit or steal on the streets for free—unless, of course, the other spectators were affluent enough to make the investment of time and money worthwhile. Despite the claims of politicians and preachers, common folk formed the principal audience only on holidays like Shrove Tuesday and May Day. Then, they occasionally made a shambles of the performance or even assaulted players and playhouses. In 1584, shortly before Shakespeare's career began, a disturbance between apprentices and gentlemen at the Theatre resulted in James Burbage's being summoned by the lord mayor, but no such incidents marred the later record of this company. The commoners at the Globe or "your sinfull six-penny Mechanicks" (as Ben Jonson called them) at Blackfriars seem to have behaved reasonably well.

While there is no doubt that ordinary folk with the price of admission patronized the theaters, the direct evidence, as well as the general economic and social patterns, points to preponderantly more privileged audiences. They were accustomed not only to plays but to indulging in pleasure during the long London afternoons. As Thomas Nashe described the situation in 1592, "For whereas the after-noone being the idlest time of the day . . . men that are their owne masters (as Gentlemen of the Court, the Innes of the Courte, and the number of Captains and Souldiers about *London*) do wholy bestow themselues vpon pleasure, and that pleasure they deuide (howe vertuously it skils not) either into gameing, following of harlots, drinking, or seeing a Playe." Some slept until the noon meal, and those with legitimate business took care of it in the morning. Performances beginning about two o'clock therefore fitted conveniently into what

Thomas Overbury called "the best leasure of our life, that is between meales, the most vnfit time, either for study or bodily exercise." With several plays available each weekday afternoon, gentlemen became inveterate theatergoers.

And the list of specific individuals who attended is impressive indeed: Edmund Spenser, John Donne, Sir Dudley Carlton's correspondent John Chamberlain, Sir Humphrey Mildmay, Simon Forman, and Inns of Court students John Greene and Edward Heath, as well as noblemen like the earl of Rutland, who went by boat "to the play house sondry times" in a single year. Wealthy foreign travelers always included the curious English theaters on their itinerary. Such figures as Samuel Kiechel of Ulm, Johan DeWitt of Amsterdam and Utrecht, and Thomas Platter of Basel all recorded visits, as did Prince Lewis of Anhalt-Cöthen and Duke Philip Julius of Stettin-Pomerania. Prince Lewis Frederick of Wurtemburg saw *Othello* at the Globe in 1610, and a few years earlier the Venetian ambassador Giorgio Giustinian spent more than twenty crowns when he took the secretary of Florence and the French ambassador to a Globe performance of *Pericles.* Just before his assassination in 1628, the duke of Buckingham requested a performance of *Henry VIII* at the Globe, where the spectators also included the Savoyan ambassador and the earl of Holland.

Other, more general references, without specifying particular individuals, confirm the presence of large numbers of gentlemen in Shakespeare's audience. In 1602, at the height of competition from the boys' troupes at the private theaters, an impressment order for "idle loose dissolute and suspected persons . . . notwithstandinge they goe apparelled like gentlemen" (*Malone Society Collections,* II, Part 3, 318) went badly awry at the playhouses. There, "they did not only presse Gentlemen, and sarvingmen, but Lawyers, Clarkes, country men that had law cawses, aye the Quens men, knightes, and as it was credibly reported one Earle," according to Philip Gawdy. When the Globe burned in 1613, knights and lords were in the audience. But the continuing patronage of such spectators should come as no surprise. By the 1590s, playgoing had become so entrenched in the lives of many gentlemen that they formed the targets for satirists like Sir John Davies, who wrote of Fuscus:

He's like a horse, which turning round a mill,
Doth always in the self-same circle tread:

First, he doth rise at ten; and at eleven
He goes to Gyls, where he doth eate till one;
Then sees a Play till sixe, and sups at seuen;
And after supper, straight to bed is gone;
And there till ten next day he doth remaine,
And then he dines, and sees a Comedy
And then he suppes, and goes to bed againe
Thus round he runs without variety.
Save that sometimes he comes not to the Play,
But falls into a whore-house by the way.

With less venom, Shakespeare simply addressed his hearers as "gentlemen" and "gentlewomen."

The attractions of an afternoon at the playhouse were obvious. For those gentlemen short of money, a modest admission bought access to three hours of poetry and pageantry. For those with fatter purses, the theater offered a place to display one's taste, wealth, and clothes. Either the lords' room directly above the actors or, better still, a stool on the stage especially appealed to gallants. If the satirists are to be believed, the gentlemen onstage amused themselves by playing cards, saluting acquaintances in the audience, smoking pipes of tobacco, laughing, talking, whewing, whistling, walking out on the performance, and otherwise attracting attention.

Even offstage, the audience could distract from the presentation. There were objections to the noise of nutcracking and conversation, as well as the snores of the sleeping. Beaumont and Fletcher, among other playwrights, especially disliked anyone who stole their best lines, using "table-books" "To write down, what again he may repeat / At some great table to deserve his meat." Rarely, but more seriously, violence disturbed the playhouses. However, the only disorders on record for Shakespeare's company occurred either before he joined the Lord Chamberlain's Men or after his retirement and death. His plays, unlike Jonson's, are remarkably free of rancor about the behavior of the audience.

Yet one favored activity occurred at every playhouse. In a society where the behavior of women was somewhat circumscribed, their presence in the theaters inevitably attracted attention. Disapproving Puritans claimed that young men deliberately went to playhouses to press "as nere to ye fairest as they," seducing the credulous with "talke upon al occasions." If successful, the unscrupulous gentlemen "eyther bring them home to theire houses on small acquaintance, or slip into tauerns when ye plaies are done." To some extent, the theaters deserved their reputation as haunts for prostitutes, scenes of seduction, or places for casual dalliance. However, many respectable women came to see Shakespeare's plays, as the records clearly show, and he often took the trouble to acknowledge their presence. In the Epilogue to *As You Like It,* Rosalind says, "I charge you, O women, for the love you bear to men, to like as much of this play as please you; and I charge you, O men, for the love you bear to women (as I perceive by your simp'ring none of you hates them), that between you and the women the play may please" (11–16).

For Shakespeare, as for all playwrights of the era, the drama that pleased a demanding, volatile, and easily distracted audience was no easy thing to create. Tastes varied wildly, and not every spectator focused his attention on the performance, as the Epilogue to *Henry VIII* acknowledges. Applause, then, depended upon factors beyond the company's control—the spectators' mood, interests, intelligence, and social biases; offstage distractions; the whims of fashion; and the influence of critical opinion. And it still does. *Pericles* was wildly popular in its own day but is seldom performed now. The frank sexuality of *Measure for Measure* offended Victorian sensibilities but intrigues those of the late twentieth century. By 1681, Nahum Tate had rewritten the bleak ending of *King Lear,* an alteration that seems a travesty today. As long as audiences see Shakespeare, the list of plays that please will need continual revision. And this ever-shifting pattern of taste will always inform our view of the audience itself. Were Shakespeare's original spectators ignorant groundlings or capricious gallants, sturdy commoners or wellborn connoisseurs? Is he now the playwright for the masses or for the discerning few? Whatever the answers, Shakespeare's audiences will continue to be privileged.

BIBLIOGRAPHY

William A. Armstrong, "The Audience of the Elizabethan Private Theatres," in *Review of English Studies,* n.s. 10 (1959). Henry Stanley Bennett, *Shakespeare's Audience* (1944). A. C. Bradley, "Shakespeare's Theatre and Audience," in *Oxford Lectures on Poetry* (1909). Robert Bridges, "The Influence of the Audience on Shakespeare's Drama," in *Collected Essays,* I (1927). Muriel St. Clare Byrne, "Shakespeare's Audience," in Shakespeare Association, *A Series of Papers on Shakespeare and the Theatre* (1927).

Ann Jennalie Cook, "The Audience of Shakespeare's Plays: A Reconsideration," *Shakespeare Studies,* 7 (1974); " 'Bargaines of Incontinencie': Bawdy Behavior at the Playhouses," *ibid.,* 10 (1977); and *The Privileged Playgoers of Shakespeare's London, 1576–1642* (1981). Alfred Harbage, *Shakespeare's Audience* (1941). Clifford Leech, "The Caroline Audience," in *Modern Language Review,* 36 (1941). Michael Neill, " 'Wits Most Accomplished Senate': The Audience of the Caroline Private Theaters," in *Studies in English Literature,* 18 (1978). Moody E. Prior, "The Elizabethan Audience and the Plays of Shakespeare," in *Modern Philology,* 49 (1951). Robert Weimann, *Shakespeare and the Popular Tradition in the Theater,* Robert Schwartz, ed. (1978).

time some necessary question of the play be then to be considered. That's villainous and shows a most pitiful ambition in the fool that uses it.

(III. ii. 1–42)

Implicit in Hamlet's discourse are three major components of the dramatic enterprise: (1) the script used as the basis for performance; (2) the company that produces a given performance; and (3) the audience for whom the performance is produced.

The first component, the script, is the most important of the three, the irreducible essence of the enterprise—so much so that in Hamlet's opinion it is almost, as it were, a Platonic idea, unmediated by (and therefore unsullied by commerce with) the other two components. In Act II Hamlet reminds the lead Player of a speech he once heard him deliver, a passage from a play that "was never acted, or if it was, not above once," for it "pleased not the million; 'twas caviary to the general." The script Hamlet describes implies a playwright uncompromisingly committed to the integrity of his artistic creation. This author's sole concern has been to compose "an excellent play, well digested in the scenes" (its parts coherently related), unified in its "matter" (with neither extraneous "sallets in the lines to make the matter savory" to lowbrows nor "affectation" in the phrasing to curry the favor of would-be highbrows), "handsome" in its perfectly articulated form, and "wholesome" in its effect upon the taste and digestion of the audience. By refusing to condescend to "cunning" devices that would appeal to "the million," Hamlet tells us, this playwright has forfeited their support at the box office, choosing instead to adhere to his own aesthetic standards with the "modesty" of an artist confident that his work would eventually be understood and appreciated by the only audience ultimately of any importance to him: those with "judgments in such matters."

What Hamlet seems to be saying here is that once a conscientious playwright has completed a worthy script, the result *is* "an excellent play," whatever its fortunes in the theater. Under ideal conditions, an excellent play will fare well in performance; but those ideal conditions can obtain only when the audience is intelligent and receptive, and even then only when the company producing the play performs it properly. In Act III, Hamlet insists that a troupe's primary obligation is to render every detail of the script with fidelity to the playwright's intention. "Suit the action to the word, the word to the action," he says, thereby emphasizing not only the interdependence of dialogue and gesture but also the more general interdependence of script and performance. A role should neither be "overdone, [n]or come tardy off," he notes; the actor's responsibility is to "acquire and beget a temperance that may give . . . smoothness" even to a speech depicting "passion." Nor should the actor "speak . . . more than is set down for him"; the "villainous" clown who wantonly introduces words or gestures not specified in the script "shows a most pitiful ambition" in his inordinate disregard for the playwright's overarching design. The script, in short, is to be regarded as both normative and limiting, a set of signals that must be obeyed with unerring accuracy if the performance is to be a true enactment of the playwright's "matter."

But if the actor must attend to the "word" and "action" called for in the playwright's script, he must at the same time be mindful of "nature," imitating the "accent" and "gait" of "humanity" convincingly. Decorum requires that he represent personality without distortion or exaggeration, that he "o'erstep not the modesty of nature." And then, finally, the actor must address his enactment of the script not to the "groundlings," the "barren spectators" who laugh at inappropriate moments and "who for the most part are capable of nothing but inexplicable dumb shows and noise," but rather to that fit audience though few, the "judicious, . . . the censure of the which one must in [the actor's] allowance o'erweigh a whole theatre of others." To do all this, the actor must possess and exercise "discretion," that combination of innate good judgment and nurtured technique by means of which he may both understand and render the role defined by the script, thereby imitating humanity convincingly and mediating faithfully between the playwright and the audience.

Taken together, Hamlet's comments provide a framework within which each component of the dramatic enterprise may be logically related both to the other components and to the more general principle underlying the whole: "the purpose of playing," which is "to hold, as 'twere, the mirror up to nature, to show virtue her own feature, scorn her own image, and the very age and body of the time his form and pressure." In sum, the purpose of dramatic art is to "imitate" nature in some way that will not distort reality—as perceived by the playwright of "honest method," by the actor with "discretion," and by spectators with "judgments in such matters"—and to do so in such a way as to reveal to the "age" some sense of its own ethical and spiritual qualities.

Let us now assume a properly executed production based on a meritorious script and performed before a cultivated audience. What will be its effect? Or, to state the query in more classic terms, what will be the nature of the dramatic catharsis it induces? Will every member of the audience respond in the same way, or will different people respond differently? The answers may depend to some degree on the occasion and nature of the play, but at least three general principles can be inferred from Shakespeare's remarks in *Hamlet.*

The most fundamental effect of any well-produced play, even a tragedy, should be pleasure or, in the more familiar Renaissance critical terminology, "delight": the satisfaction generated by any art form that derives its success from the audience's perception of properly executed imitation. In Act II, after Hamlet has recited a dozen lines from the speech he wants the Player to enact, Polonius ejaculates: "Fore God, my lord, well spoken, with good accent and good discretion." The point is neatly made: good accent and discretion are enjoyable to perceive, just as bad accent and lack of discretion "cannot but make the judicious grieve."

A second effect of a properly performed play (and one that should be an aspect of the first) is enhanced awareness—or, in the more usual Renaissance terminology, "instruction." If a dramatic work is analogous to a mirror, one of its primary functions is to reflect, to show or teach in such a way as to illuminate the relationships between one thing and another. Hamlet alludes to this when he says that players are "the abstract and brief chronicles of the time"; if they perform well, they show "the very age and body of the time his form and pressure."

A third effect of any well-produced play (and one that should derive readily from the first two) is heightened ethical and spiritual insight—what Renaissance critics often called profit. If ethical and spiritual qualities are an aspect of the humanity that a play imitates—if a play does in some way "show virtue her own feature, scorn her own image"—it follows that a play can serve as the agent of moral and spiritual edification in members of the audience.

I

That Shakespeare's plays do have ethical and even theological dimensions has long been assumed: his familiarity with the Bible, with the Book of Common Prayer, with the rituals and observances of the Church of England, and with the writings of theologians, commentators, preachers, and moral philosophers is well documented. And many a scholar has attempted to explain the playwright's works in the light of such philosophical and religious backgrounds. But to acknowledge the existence and pertinence of such contexts is of limited value unless one recognizes that it is frequently an undertaking of considerable complexity to relate them to the experience of seeing or reading a particular play. One might assume, from Hamlet's remarks, that "virtue" and "scorn" are readily identified, that the process of extracting a "moral" from a Shakespearean play is relatively straightforward. Sometimes it may seem that way, particularly when one hears characters like Polonius utter such high-sounding imperatives as "to thine own self be true." But more often than not, the most prudent strategy for an interpreter who would be "judicious" is to heed another piece of advice from Polonius and "by indirections find directions out."

Let us now return to *Hamlet* and, by way of illustration, ask what we should make of the protagonist's preoccupation with "the purpose of playing." How do the kinds of dramatic effect that concern Hamlet relate to the dramatic effects that Shakespeare's play, considered as a whole, seems calculated to have on us as audience?

Given his situation in the action, of course, it is the third kind of dramatic effect (ethical and spiritual) that interests Hamlet. Desiring "grounds more relative" than the Ghost's testimony before he proceeds against Claudius, Hamlet has the visiting troupe "Play something like the murder of my father / Before mine uncle" (II. ii. 581–582). There is no question in Hamlet's mind that such a performance will function like the exemplum of a homily and have a diagnostic effect: discriminating between those who are "free" of the evils depicted and are therefore "touched not" (III. ii. 233) and those whose "occulted guilt" (III. ii. 77) causes them to "wince" (III. ii. 233). Claudius may not be "struck so to the soul" that he will proclaim his "malefactions" (II. ii. 577–578) in public confession, but Hamlet assumes that if he does "blench" (II. ii. 583) involuntarily, he will thereby reveal himself as a murderer in the eyes of the Prince and his judicious fellow observer Horatio. For Hamlet in this particular instance, then, "the purpose of playing" will be to determine what role Claudius has been playing in real life. If the visiting players are successful in executing the kind of "seeming" that is the basis of dramatic art, Claudius will be unsuccessful in maintaining the kind of "seeming" (III. ii. 84) that has been the basis of his political art. Stagecraft will discover statecraft.

Having been so well prepared for the staging of "The Murder of Gonzago" as adapted by Hamlet, we are not surprised to see it function almost precisely as the Prince has expected. The King rises, calls for light, and departs "marvellous distempered." If that abrupt response is not as unambiguous as Hamlet seems to think, there can be no doubt in our minds about the play's effect when we later see Claudius alone. The guilty King has unwillingly experienced emotional, intellectual, ethical, and spiritual clarification: his conscience is "caught," and he is suddenly forced to perceive his "offense" as "heaven" perceives it. Brought face to face with his "action" in its "true nature," he realizes that his "wretched state" will prove damnable unless he repents. He therefore makes an earnest effort to do so, even bowing down on his "stubborn knees" in a desperate attempt to pray (III. iii. 36–70).

Up to this point, many members of the audience will probably have identified completely or almost completely with Hamlet's perspective on the action. After all, from the beginning, his intuitions into the corruption of the Danish court have been *our* intuitions, corroborated one after another by the testimony of others, by our own observations of the action, and now by a lie-detector test that has worked to perfection. Ever since his introduction to us in the opening act, Hamlet has continually taken us into his confidence, so to speak, by means of his soliloquies, asides, and ironic sallies. Unless we are unusual members of the audience, then, the all-but-inevitable consequence is that we will have come increasingly to view the court of Denmark through Hamlet's eyes.

But now we find ourselves confronted with a situation for which our identification with Hamlet may not have prepared us. Kneeling on the stage is a man who has hitherto seemed worthy of only scorn, a man who (if we accept the point of view of Hamlet and of the Ghost) is little better than a beast. Unexpectedly, Claudius is presented as a helpless fellow human who, like us all, must be forgiven if he is to escape damnation. In exemplary orthodox language, he acknowledges his need of grace and makes a sincere effort to bring his will to that point where grace may minister to it. How are we to feel about him at this moment? Are we to hope that the ethical and spiritual enlightenment induced as a result of the play-within-the-play will stop short of catharsis in its fullest, original sense: purgation or purification? If we accept the premises of the scene—that there *is* a heaven as well as a hell, and that there is joy in heaven "over one sinner that repenteth" (to cite a passage, Luke 15:7, that would have been familiar to Shakespeare's audience)—we are obliged to view Claudius as a lost sheep seeking its way back to the fold. We will not have *wanted* to see him in that light, of course. But there he is, and we cannot avoid taking some attitude toward him.

At this moment Hamlet enters. Will he too be surprised to find Claudius at prayer? Will *he* be moved to sympathy, pleased to think that the "sermon" exemplified in the play-within-the-play may effect the King's redemption? Will he see this as the ideal outcome of his plot to "catch the conscience of the King"? If the King confesses, repents, and surrenders the crown, will this provide the perfect solution to Hamlet's "cursèd" problem of somehow setting the kingdom "right"? Let us attend the Prince's words:

Now might I do it pat, now 'a is a-praying,
And now I'll do't. And so 'a goes to heaven,
And so am I revenged. That would be scanned.
A villain kills my father, and for that
I, his sole son, do this same villain send
To heaven.
Why, this is hire and salary, not revenge.
'A took my father grossly, full of bread,
With all his crimes broad blown, as flush as May;
And how his audit stands, who knows save heaven?
But in our circumstance and course of thought,
'Tis heavy with him; and am I then revenged,
To take him in the purging of his soul,
When he is fit and seasoned for his passage?
No.
Up, sword, and know thou a more horrid hent.

When he is drunk asleep, or in his rage,
Or in th' incestuous pleasure of his bed,
At game a-swearing, or about some act
That has no relish of salvation in't—
Then trip him, that his heels may kick at heaven,
And that his soul may be as damned and black
As hell, whereto it goes.

(III. iii. 73–95)

We should observe, to begin with, that Hamlet shares the King's eschatological assumptions: there *is* an afterlife, and it would be possible for even so egregious a criminal as Claudius to be "purged" of his sins and receive "salvation." But that, from Hamlet's perspective, would be a consummation devoutly *not* to be wished. Hamlet does not know where his father's soul is now—only that the elder Hamlet was not "fit and seasoned for his passage" —but he feels that he cannot be a true "father's son" if he allows Claudius to die at a time when there is any chance that his soul will receive a better destiny than the soul of his victim. For that reason, then, Hamlet delays taking his revenge at this moment, opportune though it may seem in other respects, because he says he wants to be certain of dispatching Claudius when he is "about some act / That has no relish of salvation in't."

One unexpected situation has led to another. No sooner have we been surprised into feeling sympathy for Claudius than we find ourselves stepping back to examine what may have been almost unquestioned sympathy for Hamlet. Are we really to identify with a cause, however just, that requires us to desire the eternal damnation of a soul that sues for "grace to help in time of need" (Hebrews 4:16)? If we are to take Hamlet's sentiments at face value here—and I see no reason to infer otherwise —it would seem to follow that the proper response is a shocked recognition that it is not as simple as we might have thought to identify the images of "virtue" and "scorn" in this enigmatic tragedy. We do not doubt that Hamlet, whatever his faults, is ethically and spiritually to be preferred to Claudius. But at this crucial moment it seems appropriate to ask whose soul is nearer heaven.

So what do we make of the Prayer Scene, and how does it affect our view of Hamlet and of *Hamlet* in general? We fail to respond properly, I think, unless we see that the scene reveals Hamlet as a man who believes, in Claudius' words, that "revenge should have no bounds" (IV. vii. 127). Neither here nor elsewhere does Hamlet (or anyone

else) explicitly recall the familiar Christian injunction against personal vengeance (Romans 12:19 ff), even though many of Hamlet's ethical and theological premises are explicitly Christian. How do we account for such a curious omission? Do we assume, as some modern commentators have argued, that Shakespeare expected his audience to do as Hamlet does after his encounter with the Ghost, and "wipe away" all consciousness of Christian doctrines that do not sanction the "commandment" (I. v. 99, 102) that Hamlet regards as a sacred duty? Do we accept the scene's Christian eschatological premises, while disregarding the Christian ethical premises that they call to mind? Or do we conclude that Shakespeare was assuming that the judicious members of his audience would bring to bear upon the action a perspective that enabled them to perceive contradictions lost upon even so intelligent and sensitive a protagonist as Hamlet?

If, on the basis of the Prayer Scene, we are prompted to become more cautious about accepting Hamlet's point of view uncritically, we may then begin looking more closely at other aspects of the play. And this may prompt a whole series of questions that might otherwise not have occurred to us. What if revenge as Hamlet conceives of it, instead of being a sacred duty, is a reprehensible— even potentially damnable—course of action? What if the play-within-the-play, which proves the Ghost "honest" in one sense, fails to prove that it is to be accepted as the spirit of Hamlet's father, rather than distrusted as "a devil" assuming "a pleasing shape" to "damn" Hamlet? What if examination of the scenes involving Rosencrantz and Guildenstern reveals them to be relatively guileless, well-meaning dupes rather than the "adders fanged" that Hamlet judges them to be when he sends them to their sudden deaths, "not shriving time allowed"? What if Hamlet's references to "divinity," "heaven," and "providence" near the end of the play, which many commentators view as signs of a new-found serenity and Christian faith, can be shown to occur in context with (and thus to be undercut by) the same emotional, intellectual, ethical, and spiritual confusion some critics are now finding in his earlier utterances? What if the *memento mori* meditation in the graveyard, in which many interpreters find a basis for Hamlet's presumed conversion to trust in Providence, is proven to be ineffectual by the "tow'ring passion" he exhibits soon thereafter in his confrontation with Laertes at Ophelia's grave? What if Hamlet's "readiness is all" speech, disregarding and rationalizing away a "gaingiving" that "would perhaps trouble a woman" and should make Hamlet less prone to be "remiss," reminds us of Julius Caesar's defective mental processes when, despite similar well-founded misgivings, he decides to make his fatal repair to the Capitol?

To pose such questions is neither to turn *Hamlet* on its head nor to suggest that nothing in this tragedy is as it appears. It is merely to pay attention to the play's implicit hermeneutics, which seem designed to alert us to the possibility of matter that goes unnoticed and unappreciated by all except the most judicious members of an audience. A corollary of this exegetical premise is the possibility that much of what we understand about a Shakespearean play may be based on misapprehensions.

It is not unusual for readers and viewers to assume, for example, that when Horatio bids "Good night, sweet prince, / And flights of angels sing thee to thy rest!" (V. ii. 348–349), he is serving a choric function and assuring us that Hamlet's soul is on its way to heaven. Perhaps. But if so, it seems odd that a moment earlier this same Horatio describes himself as "more an antique Roman than a Dane" and speaks of committing suicide. Can a character who forgets that "the Everlasting" has "fixed / His canon 'gainst self-slaughter" (I. ii. 131–132) become an authoritative Christian spokesman for Hamlet's beatific destiny in his very next utterance? Only if Shakespeare was so inattentive as an artist that he failed to notice—or expected judicious spectators to fail to notice—the blatant contradiction between two incompatible frames of reference: a Stoic view of suicide in Horatio's first remark and a Christian conception of "the last things" in his second. If we are disinclined to attribute such carelessness to the playwright, our only alternative is to regard Horatio's second speech as a noble sentiment but one with no more theological authority or authorial endorsement than the protagonist's own dying words: "the rest is silence."

Undoubtedly, the play prompts us to ask whether Hamlet finally discovers the way "rightly to be great," because it is replete with references to the rewards and punishments envisaged in Christian conceptions of the afterlife. But whether the play answers such a question in the affirmative is anything but self-evident. We can confidently assert only that Hamlet's ethical and theological statements are by no means self-consistent. In the fa-

mous "To be, or not to be" soliloquy (III. i. 56–90), for example, Hamlet draws on such incompatible systems as Renaissance Aristotelianism with its code of honor, late Roman Stoicism with its predilection to suicide, and orthodox Christianity with its rejection of both the code duello and the attractiveness of suicide. Taken as a whole, then, the play is an illustration of what T. S. Eliot once described as "an immense panorama of futility and anarchy." Whatever else it is, the "action" of *Hamlet* is a display, in Horatio's words,

> Of carnal, bloody, and unnatural acts,
> Of accidental judgments, casual slaughters,
> Of deaths put on by cunning and forced cause,
> And, in this upshot, purposes mistook
> Fall'n on th' inventors' heads.

(V. ii. 370–374)

II

To speak thus about a Shakespearean tragedy might seem tantamount to denying that it can have been informed by a Christian ethical and theological perspective. For surely a Christian playwright, writing for a Christian audience, would have taken pains to indicate that a noble prince such as Hamlet does the right thing in the end and is rewarded with life everlasting. It might be "pretty to think so," as Jake Barnes says in *The Sun Also Rises;* but in fact there was nothing either in the Christian doctrine of most Elizabethans or in the Renaissance conception of tragedy as a genre to require such a conclusion. On the contrary, it would probably have seemed peculiar in Shakespeare's time if a tragedy did provide positive assurances about its protagonist's eternal destiny.

For after all, it was universally assumed that the essential difference between tragedy and comedy was that a comedy ended happily and a tragedy unhappily. A play in which the protagonist's soul was clearly saved would be more like a comedy—specifically, a Divine Comedy—than a tragedy. A playwright might indicate that a character who suffered the consequences of his errors had learned something from the experience—as does Lear, for example. But to insist too emphatically on the protagonist's redemption, and to offer unambiguous signals that the protagonist died only to go to heaven, would have been inconsistent with the conventions of tragedy.

What do we make, then, of the tragedies in which there seem to be hints of uplift at the end? Granted that such protagonists as Richard III and Macbeth die in despair, how do we interpret the endings of such problematic "love tragedies" as *Romeo and Juliet* and *Othello* or of two "Roman tragedies" like *Julius Caesar* and *Antony and Cleopatra,* both of which might seem exempt from a Christian framework? And what about *King Lear?* If it is not clear that Lear's soul is bound for heavenly bliss when he dies, is it any more clear that "all's cheerless, dark, and deadly" (V. iii. 291) in the closing moments of the play? And finally, what can we infer from the comedies, tragicomedies, and romances that may have a bearing on the ethical and theological assumptions that pertain to Shakespeare's tragedies?

III

Looking first at *Romeo and Juliet,* we face the problem that, on the one hand, two young people have committed suicide and thus, in the words of Friar Laurence, have done "damnèd hate" upon themselves. On the other hand, we are told that through their deaths the lovers have reconciled their feuding families, so that, in the words of old Capulet, they will be memorialized as "poor sacrifices of our enmity." If we conclude that Romeo and Juliet are victims of mortal sin, can we then sanctify them as martyrs whom John Donne might have invoked as saints "canoniz'd for love"? Surely we cannot have it both ways. So the question once again is whether Shakespeare is being artistically careless (setting aside the possibility that he was simply theologically confused) or deliberately complex, relying upon the judicious members of his audience to sort out what appear to be contradictions in a complicated tragic action.

If we embrace the hypothesis that the playwright knew what he was doing (and with a literary genius like Shakespeare it is always better method to eliminate that hypothesis before leaping to the conclusion that difficulties for the interpreter can only be explained as the consequence of failures by the artist), our initial problem is to determine how we are expected to respond to the lovers' relationship. The play offers at least three perspectives. One, the idealistic, is that of Romeo and Juliet themselves, who regard their devotion as something pure and holy, and ultimately as something too precious and

fragile to survive the inhospitable environment in which it is placed: "Beauty too rich for use, for earth too dear" (I. v. 47). Another, the skeptical point of view, is that of such characters as Mercutio and the Nurse, for whom all talk of love is but a sublimation of sexual desire, a "humour" inflamed by "wanton blood" that can be satisfied as readily by a Paris as by a Romeo, by a Rosaline as by a Juliet. A third, the pragmatic outlook, is that of the Capulets, on the one hand (who precipitate the tragedy by insisting that Juliet marry Paris and thereby advance the family's fortunes), and the Friar, on the other (who inadvertently sets the stage for the tragic outcome when he marries the lovers in the misguided hope that their secret union will end the long-standing feud). Interestingly, the perspective of Shakespeare's principal source for the story, and the one that an Elizabethan audience would probably have expected the play to reinforce, seems irrelevant to *Romeo and Juliet*—namely, the view that the youthful lovers are wayward children who deserve to be punished for disobeying their parents. Given his unappealing portrayals of the parents—the Capulets seem insensitive and tyrannical in their effort to reduce Juliet to an instrument of their social aspirations—it seems inconceivable that Shakespeare intended us to experience any qualms about identifying with the children against their elders.

Even though it clearly has its sensual aspects, then, and even though it may seem too hasty in its consummation, the love that Romeo and Juliet pledge to each other is too absolute to be regarded as mere appetite, too tenacious to be dismissed as puppy love, and too noble to be condemned as disobedience. These, after all, are youths who "give and hazard all" for each other (to borrow a criterion of true love from the prize-winning motto in *The Merchant of Venice*); and their ardent courage impresses us as the most beautiful—and indeed the most worthy—element in a world that seems at best cynical and indifferent, at worst hostile and malevolent. Ultimately, it becomes clear that no one really understands Romeo and Juliet—not even such allies as the Nurse and the Friar. Their loyalty is severely tested by the circumstances in which it must forge its survival, and it never falters.

But if their relationship is the thing of greatest value in their world, does it follow that it is without its tragic flaws? Are our admiration and pity meant to prevent our observing the many indications that, for all the external forces arrayed against them,

Romeo and Juliet are parties to their own destruction? Are we to be so enraptured by the poetry of their first meeting and the starlight of their famous balcony scene that we feel no apprehension about the "idolatry" that transforms their love into a surrogate religion, drawing its imagery from, but setting itself up in opposition to, Christian faith? Are we to accept without demur the lovers' view that the heavens are conspiring against them, that there is "no pity sitting in the clouds"? Are we to feel no concern about the degree to which Romeo acts on the promptings of passion rather than reason? Are we, for instance, to approve of his reaction to Mercutio's dying words, a reaction which initiates the falling action of the play and leads Romeo, upon the return of Tybalt, to cry "Away to heaven, respective lenity, / And fire-eyed fury be my conduct now!" (III. i. 128–129)? And finally, are we to hear in Romeo's suicidal soliloquy anything other than the voice of despair?

> Come, bitter conduct; come, unsavory guide!
> Thou desperate pilot, now at once run on
> The dashing rocks thy seasick, weary bark!
>
> (V. iii. 116–118)

For an audience accustomed to distrust such all-consuming passions as those of Troilus and Cressida or of Antony and Cleopatra, an audience many of whose members would have been familiar with Boethius' *Consolation of Philosophy* and its caution against making any sublunary object one's *summum bonum*, it seems more than likely that the principal matter of *Romeo and Juliet* would have been apprehended as something other than a lyrical celebration of true love's triumph over hate and fate. For this audience, in all likelihood, Romeo would have been perceived as even more tragically "star-crossed" than he realized when he poisoned himself to gain

> . . . everlasting rest,
> And shake the yoke of inauspicious stars
> From this world-wearied flesh. . . .
>
> (V. iii. 110–112)

Such an audience would probably have found its perceptions echoed in the Prince's conclusion that in the end "all are punished" in *Romeo and Juliet.*

The lovers' deaths do bring about a cessation of civic strife in Verona. But the price for this reconciliation has been very high—and for the lovers themselves inestimable. How, then, should we respond? For some it will be difficult to derive much consolation from Montague's promise to raise Juliet's "statue in pure gold." For these members of the audience the proper reaction to a story of such woe will be the humility expressed in the traditional prayer of compassion, "There, but for the grace of God, go I."

IV

Let us now glance more briefly at some other plays with similar ethical and theological patterns. If our essential business as interpreters of a Shakespearean tragedy is to understand its matter as judicious members of the original audience would have understood it, we should now recognize that one of our most important tasks is to bring our judgments to bear upon the action in all its complexity. More often than not, that means that we must perceive error-prone characters with a clearer and broader perspective than that which they bring to bear upon their own situations and actions. Because we see even the worst of them as fellow human beings, we fear that we might err as they have, and we pity the suffering they must endure in consequence of their errors. But, lest we fail to register what brought them to their present pass—and thereby fail to develop the kind of ethical and theological sensitivity that may prevent our falling into similar errors—we must balance our pity and fear with judgment. This does not mean that we should be judgmental or try to play God with Shakespeare's characters. It means only that we should be alert to every clue in the text, including those that reflect unfavorably upon a character whom we are generally disposed to like, and that when all is said and done we should be able to draw some inferences about where each character went right or wrong.

It is in the nature of tragedy that its primary focus is upon characters who either fail to live up to their full potential or pervert that potential by inordinate lust or ambition. And much of our pity and fear results from our awareness of the discrepancy between what a character was before his fall (Macbeth or Othello are both presented, for instance, as magnificent warriors) or what he might have been but for some fatal flaw (Coriolanus' arrogance, for example, or Lear's habitual self-indulgence) and what he becomes in the circumstances in which we see him placed. Unless there is something to admire in the protagonist, there is a limit to the range of emotions we can experience when witnessing his downfall; thus we are little moved by the downfall of a reprobate like Iago. At the same time, however, to the degree that we do admire a protagonist, we may also find it difficult to bring enough objectivity to the action to develop an alternative perspective; we are constantly in danger of identifying with a character so completely that we become oblivious to his faults or blind spots. It may therefore give us a salutary shock to recognize, quite often through some kind of reversal in the action (as with the Prayer Scene), that a character who seems so much like us is prone to serious miscalculations or misdeeds.

As Aristotle pointed out long ago, those shocks of recognition are what the experience of tragedy is largely about. At times, reversals in the action bring about such recognitions in the characters themselves—as, for example, when Antony's magnanimity to the trusted soldier who has deserted him causes Enobarbus to condemn himself as a traitor, or when, in an earlier play, Cassius' realization that Caesar's spirit has triumphed over the armies of his assassins leads him to self-destruction by the same sword that slew Caesar. But only rarely do those tragic recognitions carry Shakespearean characters to a degree of self-awareness that equals the insight available to judicious members of the audience. In his perceptive essay " 'Twere Best not Know Myself': Othello, Lear, Macbeth," Robert B. Heilman observes that, more often than not, the protagonists of Shakespeare's tragedies "have the talent for self-knowledge" but are "unable or unwilling to use it." If so, and if a protagonist's resistance to, or failure to act on, self-knowledge is a part of the playwright's matter, it is crucial that the audience experience the recognition that the erring character finally misses or evades.

In *Macbeth,* for example, a proper response to the action will include the audience's recognition that much of what happens before the murder of Duncan derives from the protagonists' willful disregard of "conscience," both in the older sense of "consciousness" and in the more modern sense of an inner voice to be denied only at the peril of one's soul. The eventual price for such wanton unreason is either madness (Lady Macbeth in her sleepwalking scene) or the nihilistic desperation of a tyrant who becomes so "supped full with horrors" that his heart is impervious to all human feeling. In such a state Macbeth concludes that "Life's but a walking shadow, . . . a tale / Told by an idiot, full of sound and fury, / Signifying nothing" (V. v. 24–28). Here, in our eagerness to claim Shakespeare as our contemporary, we may find it tempting to infer that the protagonist is anticipating the sentiments of a modern existentialist. But that would be to remove the lines from their context in a play whose catharsis depends upon our exorcising the Macbeth who resides *in potentia* in all of us. A cultivated Elizabethan audience would probably have found Macbeth's cosmic bravado pitiable and frightening rather than persuasive.

So also, I suspect, with the grandiloquence of Othello's last words: though "great of heart," the noble Moor is finally incapable of realizing the irony of his defense of himself as "an honorable murderer." Had he been able to question the code of honor that Iago invoked to manipulate him into an instrument of "justice," Othello might have heeded his native impulse to act instead on "the pity of it" and show compassion for his bride. But regrettably, Iago's deification of "good name," "honor," and "reputation" has blinded Othello to every consideration other than the "black vengeance" that, he assumes, Desdemona's "dishonor" demands of him. As he dies, Othello recognizes that he has been deceived about his wife's supposed infidelity; but there is no indication that it ever occurs to him that another course of action would have been available to him even if Desdemona had been guilty as charged.

V

Othello's ethical obtuseness has its parallel in another "honorable" murderer. Mark Antony's eulogy for "the noblest Roman of them all" portrays Brutus as the protagonist would have liked to be remembered, and that appraisal has been widely accepted. To do so, however, is to forget not only what Mark Antony has himself said about Brutus on earlier occasions—as in his funeral remarks about the "honorable man" who delivered "the most unkindest cut of all" in the slaying of Caesar—but also what we have ourselves observed if we have been attentive.

For all his much-vaunted virtue, Brutus comes across as a man so preoccupied with his own integrity that he is blind to deficiencies in judgment and feeling that are apparent to others. A close reading of Brutus' soliloquy at the beginning of Act II, for example, will show that his rationale for the assassination is seriously lacking in rationality—just as in the session that follows his naive insistence that the conspirators think of themselves as "sacrificers, but not butchers" will prove tragically self-deluded in the face of what the audience, both Roman and Elizabethan, can only be horrified to witness as a bloody and "savage spectacle." Events prove Brutus wrong on several occasions in which he persuades his companions to disregard Cassius' counsel—most disastrously, of course, in Brutus' decisions to spare Mark Antony and, later, to allow Antony to address the Roman citizens who have assembled around Caesar's corpse. But Brutus never seems capable of learning from or even acknowledging his errors, any more than it ever crosses so "great a mind" that the faults he finds in others, such as Cassius in the quarrel scene (IV. iii), are but motes compared to the beams in his own eyes. By the time we see Brutus stage his display of Stoic "patience" for the messenger who comes with news of Portia's death (a fact that Brutus has reported to Cassius only moments before as a way of excusing his overbearing intemperance and keeping Cassius on the defensive), we have ample basis for inferring that in Brutus Shakespeare was offering his audience a devastating critique of what it really meant to be "the noblest Roman of them all."

For in Brutus, as several recent critics have observed, Shakespeare was drawing on sources as diverse as Cicero, St. Augustine, and Erasmus to portray a Roman Stoic in all his pharisaical self-righteousness and emotional sterility. By the end of the play there should be no doubt in our minds that Brutus is deceiving himself when he proclaims that he will "have glory by this losing day / More than Octavius and Mark Antony / By this vile conquest shall attain unto" (V. v. 36–38). Which is another way of saying that Strato—whom Brutus condescends to praise as one whose life "hath had some smatch of honor in it"—speaks more than he knows when he reports that "Brutus only overcame himself."

In writing *Julius Caesar* Shakespeare was engaging in an exercise of historical imagination that called upon him, above all, to portray Roman civilization in its own terms. It would have been unhistoric for a character in this play to refer consciously to anything related to the Judeo-Christian tradition, just as it would have been anachronistic for Cassius to ponder the role of providence in Christian terms

rather than in the idiom of his own Epicurean philosophy (V. i. 76) or of Brutus' Stoicism (V. i. 100). But does it follow that Christian ethical and theological precepts are irrelevant? Not if one notices the subtle (and, for the characters, unwitting) echoes of biblical paradigms—as, for example, in Caesar's invitation to his "good friends" to "taste some wine with me." This would surely have reminded Shakespeare's audience of another last supper in which a conspirator shared communion with an intended victim. And certainly not if one heeds the many signals that Shakespeare is, in effect, inviting the audience to participate in a Christian assessment of a pagan civilization that—precisely because it *was* pre-Christian—was incapable of seeing itself from the perspective of a later era blessed with the golden hindsight of divine revelation. J. L. Simmons has explored this subject elsewhere in these pages, so it will be sufficient here to reiterate that, especially in *Julius Caesar,* a proper response to the action presupposes an audience capable of insights lost on the characters themselves. It would not be going too far to say that the key to *Julius Caesar* reposes in our awareness of why it would have been difficult, if not impossible, for a Stoic like Brutus to experience a full recognition before his death: because a philosophy that made a man feel secure in his own virtue precluded the kind of humility, in Christian terms, that would enable him to acknowledge or repent of error.

Shakespeare's next Roman tragedy presents somewhat different problems. From the "Roman" perspective, represented by Octavius Caesar and his sister Octavia, Antony's relationship with Cleopatra is ethical and military truancy: a "dotage" that amounts to an abdication of manhood, self-control, and civic discipline. To the extent that Antony continues to evaluate himself as a Roman, he shares this appraisal of his own slothful indulgence. But from the "Egyptian" perspective of Cleopatra and her admirers, and of Antony when he is in his Egyptian mode, the world is well sacrificed for love and luxury. Why should Mars remain armed for battle when the charms of Venus are so much more inviting? And why should his Venus stay behind for a lesser man, when the one whose "legs bestrid the ocean" has taken himself away? The majority of interpreters have answered such questions in such a way as to place this "great solemnity" in its own, transcendent category. Finding the Roman characters bloodless and calculating, they have tended to accept Antony and Cleopatra at their own estimate and to canonize them in a shrine adjacent to that of Romeo and Juliet.

The difficulty with this interpretation is that it requires us to ignore repeated indications that both lovers are weak-willed, irrational, and irresponsible. It is easy enough to be stirred by the magic of Enobarbus' descriptions of Cleopatra's "infinite variety" and to admire the exotic poetry with which Antony and Cleopatra invest their death scenes. But before we allow ourselves to be seduced by the eloquence with which the lovers try to ward off or deny the inevitable, we should remember that it is easy to count the world well lost when it has already been conceded by default to one's adversaries. An apt Elizabethan gloss on the "new heaven, new earth" that Antony and Cleopatra seek to appropriate through suicide might well be borrowed from Shakespeare's Sonnet 129:

Th' expense of spirit in a waste of shame
Is lust in action; . . .

. . . . . .

All this the world well knows; yet none knows well
To shun the heaven that leads men to this hell.

VI

But if we search in vain for uplift in *Antony and Cleopatra,* what about *King Lear?* Is there a sounder basis for optimism about the destiny of Lear's soul than for that of Shakespeare's other protagonists? The answer is anything but unambiguous, but it seems to me that here we have a tragedy whose curve is unique in the Shakespearean canon. In all the others, notwithstanding the eloquence of the benedictions and eulogies that accompany the protagonists to their burials, we are left with a consciousness of "purposes mistook" that might have been set right. The basic pattern of the action has been a descent of one kind or another, and we come away feeling aware of something that the protagonists themselves have not been able or willing to perceive. In those tragedies in which the protagonists have taken their own lives, we are given signs that in doing so they are acknowledging failure or surrendering to despair, despite the brave words they utter to cheer themselves up or to put the best face on the tragic circumstances to which their choices and actions have brought them.

But in *King Lear* the spiritual curve, as distinguished from the curve of the protagonist's out-

ward fortunes, is essentially upward. To be sure, there have been tragic errors and terrifying consequences, but in this play we are encouraged to believe that at least some of the pain has been purgative. Both Lear and Gloucester are in some sense wiser and "better" at the end. And if a performance of *King Lear* emphasizes the protagonist's learning and growth through tragic suffering, the audience is more likely to emerge with what Milton in *Samson Agonistes* called "calm of mind" than with unmitigated pity and fear.

This is not to deny that there is tragic waste in *King Lear.* If Lear eventually realizes that he has been "a very foolish fond old man," and the blinded Gloucester recognizes that he "stumbled when [he] saw," both fathers have to acknowledge that their follies have caused unmerited pain and loss. Lear has turned over the kingdom to his two "pelican daughters," and, aided by Gloucester's bastard son Edmund, they have done their best to devour it. Meanwhile, the Fool has wasted away, Kent and Edgar have become "wretches," and Cordelia has died by hanging. The most troublesome of these injustices, of course, is the death of Cordelia, and for Lear it constitutes the final, insupportable consequence of his initial demand that his three daughters earn their divisions of the kingdom through public proclamations of their love.

In most productions, Lear's entry with the dead Cordelia in his arms (V. iii) is agonizing. But this concluding pietà can become "a chance which does redeem all sorrows" (V. iii. 267) if it is staged with sensitivity to the psychological and spiritual ups and downs of Lear's dying moments. Just before he says "Pray you undo this button" (V. iii. 310), Lear is convinced that Cordelia will never return, "Never, never, never, never, never." But after he says "Thank you, sir," Lear utters what many interpreters read as an expression of belief that Cordelia yet lives: "Do you see this? Look on her! Look, her lips, / Look there, look there—." Although some directors, actors, and critics have taken this final cry as an expression of despair rather than of faith or of merciful hallucination, many critics find most consistent with other evidence the interpretation that, like Gloucester's, Lear's "flawed heart / Alack, too weak the conflict to support, / 'Twixt two extremes of passion, joy and grief, / Burst[s] smilingly" (V. iii. 197–200). *We* realize that Cordelia is "dead as earth," as Lear has acknowledged a few moments earlier. But it seems altogether appropriate that as he dies Lear should see her as alive. Perhaps, like the protagonist of Sophocles' *Oedipus at Colonus,* Lear's agony is mitigated by the granting of one last wish, a sign of life that takes him out of "this tough world" to a vision of something better beyond.

In the end, as we "speak what we feel, not what we ought to say" (V. iii. 325), we may be unable to affirm so much as this. We may find ourselves praying that the dying Lear does not need Edgar's exhortation to "Look up, my lord." We may hope that by the end of his long journey, in the words of T. S. Eliot's poem "Little Gidding," the King has at last attained "a condition of complete simplicity (Costing not less than everything)." And we may be drawn to believe that in this tragedy the disparity between what the protagonist knows and feels and what the audience knows and feels is a signal that the protagonist's ultimate perspective is superior to that of the perceptive observer—that in this unique instance anagnorisis is swallowed up in epiphany. But in the last analysis we realize that we cannot *know* what really happens at the conclusion of this magnificent work of art. In accordance with the decorum of tragedy, Shakespeare has brought us to the frontier of Divine Comedy—but finally left the mystery intact.

VII

Let me now conclude these remarks with a brief glance at those parts of the Shakespearean canon that are generally regarded as less problematical. If it is in the nature of Shakespearean tragedy to explore ethical and theological questions in such a way as to leave some issues only incompletely resolved, the comedies offer at least the impression of interpretative closure. Both genres exhibit enough complexity and ambiguity to require an audience's complete attention and engagement with the action. And such plays as *The Merchant of Venice* and *Measure for Measure* offer almost as many cruxes as the tragedies that we have been considering. But the essential nature of Shakespearean comedy— and not only the "romantic" and "festive" comedies but also the "problem" comedies or tragicomedies and the romances—is to suggest that there are answers to the questions we raise and solutions to the problems we find ourselves confronting as we contemplate the human condition. By one means or another, the comedies achieve what we are clearly meant to respond to as happy

endings: mistaken identity leads to disclosure and recognition, doubt yields to certainty, and discord proves merely the prelude to concord.

The typical pattern of a Shakespearean comedy is to begin with strife and to end with reconciliation. In *As You Like It,* for example, a usurping younger brother, Duke Frederick, has banished Duke Senior and his followers to the Forest of Arden. In Act I a tyrannical older brother, Oliver, drives his virtuous younger brother Orlando to seek refuge in the same sylvan setting. Shortly thereafter, Orlando and his old servant Adam are joined in the forest by Duke Senior's daughter Rosalind and her cousin Celia. And eventually, Oliver and Duke Frederick enter the forest themselves in pursuit of their intended victims. In a play like *King Lear,* the pursuers would eventually inflict harm upon the pursued. But the Forest of Arden is not a stormy heath. Here, as Duke Senior reminds us, we have entered what Northrop Frye calls a "green world," where "sweet are the uses of adversity." The forest is a dangerous place, however, for men with wicked intentions; once they arrive in Arden, both Oliver and Duke Frederick experience miraculous conversions. Through a sacrificial act of compassion by a younger brother who has every justification for killing him, Oliver becomes a new man (and one whose description of his transformation [IV. iii] echoes Galatians 2:20). His reward is to win the hand of Celia and to marry her in a joint ceremony that includes the nuptials of Orlando and Rosalind. Meanwhile, Duke Frederick encounters "an old religious man" and, being "converted / Both from his enterprise and from the world" (V. iv. 154–156), restores the crown to his banished elder brother. As the play draws to a close, Hymen, the god of marriage, enters to "make conclusion / Of these most strange events" and the comedy is consummated with a feast that symbolizes both earthly revelry and cosmic harmony.

If "strange events" would seem indecorous in Shakespeare's tragedies (where probability is the rule), they are of the essence in his comedies. In the world of the tragedies, a victim of insult or injury will contemplate and eventually commit revenge. In the world of the comedies, revenge may be plotted, but its execution will be impeded, either because of some kind of external intervention (such as Portia's role in the Trial Scene of *The Merchant of Venice,* where Shylock's quest for "justice" is frustrated by a legal technicality) or because of some change of heart (such as Prospero's decision, once he has all his enemies at his command in *The Tempest,* to forswear vengeance in favor of the "rarer action" of forgiveness). In the world of the tragedies, every significant action has its consequences, and an error in judgment almost inevitably proves fatal. In the world of the comedies, characters are rescued by unseen forces that come between a motive or action and its seemingly inevitable consequences. In *Measure for Measure* the providential Duke forestalls the crimes that his deputy Angelo would commit (forcing Isabella to surrender her virginity to him and condemning Claudio to die for a much less serious offense); and at the end of the play, Isabella's willingness to plead for Angelo's life (when, in the words of the Duke, for all she knows "Her brother's ghost his pavèd bed would break, / And take her hence in horror") turns what might still have been a capital offense into a fortunate fall that molds a better man out of his "faults" (V. i. 431–432, 435).

The resolution of a Shakespearean comedy normally results from some kind of atonement or "at-one-ment"—to recall a pun from *As You Like It* (V. iv. 104)—some suspension of ordinary probability for the advent of a reconciling force that is openly acknowledged to be extraordinary and improbable. Its usual product is "clearer reason" (*The Tempest,* V. i. 68) and "a clear life ensuing" (III. iii. 82), free of lust, ambition, envy, vengeance, and pride. Such a resolution is frequently initiated by a sense of wonder in the presence of occurrences that can be attributed only to divine grace; and it is characteristically accompanied by humility, patience, forgiveness, and contentment. Quite often the arrival of a new order is symbolized by restored relationships, long-delayed reunions, and a recovery of faith, hope, and love. And in its suggestion that all these strange events have come about through help from above, a Shakespearean comedy frequently invokes the apocalyptic "new heaven, new earth" in a way quite different from the ironic use of that paradigm in *Antony and Cleopatra* (I. i. 17).

In his experiments with comic genres, then, Shakespeare provides another perspective, another way of imitating humanity. In some ways it is a less "serious" mirror than that of the tragedies, and it is manifestly less probable, at least in Aristotelian terms. And yet, despite its improbability, Shakespearean comedy may bring us even closer than Shakespearean tragedy to "the real thing." Among its many other valuable functions, it provides a norm by which we can measure mankind in its full

potential. By showing, through examples of forgiveness, what can happen when we choose not to act on vengeful impulses, it presents us with a positive alternative to revenge tragedy. By showing us Duke Senior's contentment with the mean estate of the pastoral life, it offers a counter to Macbeth's inordinate ambition. Shakespearean comedy gives us an image of what we can become when our minds are clear and our motives free of the drives that lead to discord and suffering. In doing so, it affords us a means, in Christian terms, of moving toward a fuller comprehension of the matter of Shakespearean tragedy.

BIBLIOGRAPHY

John F. Andrews, " 'Dearly Bought Revenge': *Samson Agonistes, Hamlet,* and Elizabethan Revenge Tragedy," in *Milton Studies,* 13 (1979). John S. Anson, "Julius Caesar: The Politics of the Hardened Heart," in *Shakespeare Studies,* 2 (1966). J. Leeds Barroll, "Shakespeare and Roman History," in *Modern Language Review,* 53 (1958). Roy W. Battenhouse, *Shakespearean Tragedy: Its Art and Its Christian Premises* (1969). Stephen Booth, *"King Lear," "Macbeth," Indefinition, and Tragedy* (1983). Fredson T. Bowers, *Elizabethan Revenge Tragedy, 1587–1642* (1940).

Lily B. Campbell, *Shakespeare's Tragic Heroes: Slaves of Passion* (1930). Neville Coghill, "The Basis of Shakespearian Comedy: A Study in Medieval Affinities," in *English Association, Essays and Studies,* n.s. 3 (1950). Dolora G. Cunningham, *"Macbeth:* The Tragedy of the Hardened Heart," in *Shakespeare Quarterly,* 14 (1963). James Vincent Cunningham, *Woe or Wonder: The Emotional Effect of Shakespearean Tragedy* (1951). Franklin M. Dickey, *Not Wisely But Too Well: Shakespeare's Love Tragedies* (1957). William R. Elton, *"King Lear" and the Gods* (1966). Northrop Frye, "The Argument of Comedy," in *English Institute Essays 1948* (1949). Roland M. Frye, *Shakespeare and Christian Doctrine* (1963).

Leon Golden and O.B. Hardison, Jr., *Aristotle's Poetics: A Translation and Commentary for Students of Literature* (1968). Sherman Hawkins, "The Two Worlds of Shakespearean Comedy," in *Shakespeare Studies,* 3 (1967). Robert B. Heilman, " 'Twere Best not Know Myself': Othello, Lear, Macbeth," in *Shakespeare Quarterly,* 15 (1964). Robert G. Hunter, *Shakespeare and the Comedy of Forgiveness* (1965) and *Shakespeare and the Mystery of God's Judgments* (1976). David L. Jeffrey and J. Patrick Grant, "Reputation in *Othello,*" in *Shakespeare Studies,* 6 (1970). Paul A. Jorgensen, *Lear's Self-Discovery* (1967). George Wilson Knight, *The Wheel of Fire* (1930). Ruth M. Levitsky, "Rightly to be Great," in *Shakespeare Studies,* 1 (1965). Barbara K. Lewalski, "Biblical Allusion and Allegory in *The Merchant of Venice,*" in *Shakespeare Quarterly,* 13 (1962).

Maynard Mack, *"King Lear" in Our Time* (1965). Richmond Noble, *Shakespeare's Biblical Knowledge and Use of the Book of Common Prayer* (1935). Eleanor Prosser, *Hamlet and Revenge,* 2nd ed. (1971). Norman Rabkin, *Shakespeare and the Problem of Meaning* (1981). William Rosen, *Shakespeare and the Craft of Tragedy* (1960). Susan Snyder, *The Comic Matrix of Shakespeare's Tragedies* (1979). Marvin L. Vawter, " 'Division 'tween Our Souls': Shakespeare's Stoic Brutus," in *Shakespeare Studies,* 7 (1974). Robert H. West, *Shakespeare and the Outer Mystery* (1968). Virgil K. Whitaker, *The Mirror Up To Nature: The Technique of Shakespeare's Tragedies* (1965).

Shakespeare's Psychology: Characterization in Shakespeare

MEREDITH SKURA

The central issue in a study of Shakespeare's dramatic characters is the relation between character and the total structure of action, whether that structure is seen as shaped from within, by the character's society, or from without, by the poetic logic of the play. The problem first became clear in the New Critics' attack on character criticism, an attack that defined the terms of the ensuing critical debate and that thus provides a good introduction to the topic. The following sections will examine the New Critics' argument before going on to discuss specific recent interpretations of Shakespearean characters that have profited not only from the New Critics' theories about poetic structure but also from contemporary feminist and psychoanalytic theories about character.

Character or Design

Shakespeare's first critics praised the "realism" of his characters and discussed them as if they were alive, speculating on their past, future, and inner lives beyond the action of the play. An early critic like William Hazlitt could claim that Shakespeare's characters "breathe, move and live" because they "think and speak and act just as they might do, if left entirely to themselves" (Salingar)—that is, because they seemed independent of any overall symbolic structure. As Hazlitt was among the first to point out, we often learn more about Shakespeare's

characters than we need to know. The heroes of the great tragedies are presented in the fullest human context: not only in relation to the moral and intellectual issues that critics isolate in discussing a given play's thematic structure, but also in relation to society, politics, and class structure, to the past, to their families, and to their own emotional and physical realities. But Shakespeare gives even minor characters extended contexts: Shylock meets his friend Tubal; Bottom sings himself back into confidence in the forest.

Such onstage fullness is supplemented, as Maurice Morgann noted in his famous study of Falstaff, by an unseen life offstage. Some of this unseen life is described in detail: Falstaff's capon snacks and his robbery; some of it is merely hinted at. Ophelia describes Hamlet's offstage visit to her closet, and we are made to wonder about the letters he gave her: How many letters? In what mood were they written? When were they delivered? Even more important in a discussion of Shakespeare's character psychology, these early critics suggested that Shakespeare also provides clues about his characters' unseen inner lives. What does Hamlet feel about Ophelia that makes him so vicious to her? Is it true, as A. C. Bradley speculates, that even before the witches appear, Macbeth and his wife have "no love of country, and no interest in the welfare of anyone outside their family"? There may be no answers to such questions. What matters is that audiences want to ask them, whereas almost no one is curious about Tamburlaine's life as a shepherd or about Volpone's career before he begins to outfox his would-be heirs.

It was just such speculation that twentieth-century critics objected to, on both aesthetic and historical grounds. L. C. Knights attacked uncritical reconstructions that tried to decide "How Many Children Had Lady Macbeth?" as one might in the case of a real woman. Characters are not people, he insisted. They are just words on a page or, rather, parts of a thematic design. "Apart from what we see and hear of Hamlet," as J. Dover Wilson put it, "there is no Hamlet." And what we do see of him is what is required for the play's total vision. Characters, G. Wilson Knight says, "are not human at all; but purely symbols of a poetic vision," and to focus on them is to distract attention from "the burning central core" of vision in the play. As L. C. Knights stated in a reconsideration (1959) of the topic, "Shakespeare was doing more than merely holding a mirror up to nature, more even than representing conflict in the souls of mighty characters: he was exploring the world and defining the values by which men live."

Levin Schücking, Samuel Bethell, and (most notoriously) Elmer Edgar Stoll added support to this argument with their investigations of the narrative and dramatic conventions governing Shakespeare's construction of character. Neither a Falstaff nor a Shylock is an imitation of life, Stoll said, but an imitation of other literary and dramatic figures, functioning as part of a given plot. It makes no sense to ask whether Falstaff is really a coward; Falstaff runs away on Gad's Hill because he is a braggart soldier, and braggart soldiers are supposed to run away. Hamlet has no inner reasons for his delay; he delays because the play would end too soon if he did not.

Critics like Stoll also reminded us, by calling attention to them, that many of Shakespeare's characters are not "realistic" at all. They assured us that the Duke in *Measure for Measure,* for example, is embarrassingly awkward unless you see that his actions are shaped by the Disguised Ruler convention and by his allegorical role as Providence (Lawrence). "In a real person [the Duke's] inconsistency might suggest mental aberration," but in the play it shows only that he is part of a conventional pattern (Powell). Maynard Mack suggested that Edgar's behavior in *King Lear* makes little sense—why does he wait until it is too late to tell his blinded father who he is?—unless we see him as shaped by an old morality-play tradition. These crit-

ics stressed Shakespeare's frequent preference for unsophisticated plots taken from folk tales and popular drama, in which the explanations for action lay not in any character's psychology but in the overall design of the action. Though these critics lacked the evangelical tone and moral fervor of Knights, who held that Shakespeare achieved his greatness by "defining the values by which men live," they too were concerned with the plays' moral and philosophical content rather than with the psychology of the characters depicted in them. And they ignored embarrassing questions about the Duke's cruelty, or Edgar's selfishness, interpreting these as aesthetic *felices culpae,* momentary lapses in the service of a unified and ultimately meaningful and satisfying view of human nature.

After a period during which the New Critics' fastidious concern for detail and structure made the old-fashioned kind of character criticism seem naive, critics have again begun to talk about Shakespeare's characters and the astonishing—and problematic—complexity they display, despite their existence as part of the plays' formal and symbolic structures. The questions that embarrassed the New Critics have again become starting points for character analysis. More sophisticated than the earlier, undisciplined character appreciations, the character studies of recent years have profited from the New Critics' lessons about the need for textual evidence and contextual analysis. Unlike earlier critics, more recent commentators pay attention to Hamlet's exact words and take into account the overall design that links him to the other sons in his play, a design that connects Hamlet's inner conflict to the larger ambiguities that hinder not only his revenge but also any early closure in his world. As a consequence, it no longer seems necessary to choose between character and design.

Critics now recognize that depth of character is often what is needed to fill out a play's design. Macduff must be a complex and not a simple person in order to play his role in Shakespeare's exploration of what it means to be a man. Even more important, while earlier critics tended to look only for moral or philosophical content in a play's design, recent critics find psychological content. Far from being irrelevant to the characters, the total action of the play can now be seen as a projection or externalization of the characters' inner lives. Whereas Cleanth Brooks saw the "naked babe" images in *Macbeth* as symbols of the future, critics now see them also as references to babies, about whom both Macbeth and Lady Macbeth have strong feelings, and with whom Macbeth perhaps identifies, surrounded as he is by witches and a wife who refuse to take care of him. While New Critics found *A Midsummer Night's Dream* to be about a conflict between reason and passion, and *Othello* to be about a conflict between good and evil, recent critics emphasize the degree to which both plays are about the relations between men and women in love.

The fact that Shakespeare draws on well-established conventions and primitive materials, rather than being seen as a sign of his indifference to psychology, is now viewed as a sign of his interest in psychologically reverberating materials (Stewart). Stoll had assumed that folktale plots were merely vehicles for generating good stories and that the older a tale was the less it had to do with the realities of any human situation. But as J. I. M. Stewart notes, these stories are often symbolic expressions of psychological realities. Psychological complexity is conveyed not only through a character's own actions and words, as in the tragic heroes, but also indirectly, through imagery, symbolism, and the overall design of the tale. The same is true of the plays. No one, for example, would mistake for a real person either twin in the Plautine farce *The Comedy of Errors.* Together, however, their collisions and near misses dramatize aspects of a psychologically complex personality. Stoll had shifted the issue of cowardice away from Falstaff by invoking the type character of braggart soldier and had called on the bed-trick convention to explain Isabella's willingness to send Mariana to Angelo's bed when she herself would rather die than go. But the braggart and the bed trick have endured as conventions precisely because they embody a psychological reality to which generations of audiences have responded as they have watched Falstaff and Isabella.

Recent character studies have been influenced by new views of this psychological reality as well as by new views of convention and the role it plays. Commentary on the Duke in *Measure for Measure* provides a good example, for he is one of those awkward characters whose "unnatural" behavior has been used as evidence that conventions in the plays distort the characters. Insofar as the Duke is odd, it has been claimed, the influence of the design is evident. But with the development of depth psychology and the growing recognition of how unnatural and odd even normal people can be, critics

have now begun to suspect that the Duke's oddness and inconsistency reveal something about the Duke as well as about the design (Skura; Richard P. Wheeler). Though hunger for the well-made icon—and for a morally simpler world—may lead us to assume that the "ghostly father" of *Measure for Measure* can do no wrong, we are now beginning to recognize that Shakespeare seldom satisfies such hungers. Those who would require more consistency of Shakespeare's characters make the same demands of a dramatic character that society does when it demands that individuals conform to certain proprieties (Stewart). Both demands are based on superficial rather than essential images of human nature.

The Duke's inconsistencies may not suggest "mental aberration," as Powell claimed they would in a real person, so much as they suggest the normal tensions and contradictions to be found in all our civilized lives. Wheeler has described the Duke as working out his own conflicts about authority and sexuality—not always rationally or altruistically—as he manipulates the other, more obviously conflicted characters.

Elsewhere we may detect this Shakespearean technique by observing how a relatively flat character like the Duke in the frame story of a play is rounded out by the inner action, both in itself and as he reacts to it. In *A Midsummer Night's Dream,* the mentality of Theseus on the eve of his wedding is suggestively dramatized in the context of the lesser lovers who wander in the woods that night—as if they constitute a cinematic flashback to Theseus' wanton youth and an explanation of how he got to be the way he is now. In a somewhat different way, the internal conflicts of Duke Orsino and Olivia in *Twelfth Night* are projected onto and worked out in the servants' world framed by the aristocratic love affair. It is simply more unsettling, not more unlikely, to see Duke Vincentio stage his own projections in *Measure* as Prospero stages his in *The Tempest.*

Though not all of Shakespeare's characters are equally rounded or equally implicated in and by the whole design, even relatively minor characters like Edgar in *King Lear* can be as illuminated by the design as it is by them. Conventional expectations may lead us to balk at the idea of the good son's being faulty, especially since Shakespeare provides such a terrible son to balance Edgar. Mack blames the exigencies of plot and not Edgar for his strained, aloof disguisings and for his failure to reveal himself to his father until the latter has learned his lesson. But Stanley Cavell has suggested that Edgar holds back for reasons of his own. And Janet Adelman has shown that Edgar creates in his disguise as Poor Tom "a creature through whom he can safely express his sense of helpless victimization" while disclaiming his threatening and unpleasant emotions. Adelman suggests that Edgar needs to see himself as more sinned against than sinning. In his own person, she notes, Edgar never expresses anger against the father who has thrown him out—instead he directs his anger more masochistically but more safely at himself. As he changes from mad beggar to poor man and from peasant to armed noble, Edgar's roles express, one by one, his newly reclaimed emotions and ideas: "Only when he has fully reclaimed himself can he fully reclaim his father."

Once more, then, Shakespeare dramatizes the psychological depth symbolized by conventional roles; he shows what it feels like to be a Disguised Ruler or one of the morality-play figures. One of the most recognizable traits of Shakespearean drama, in fact, is the playwright's way of bringing to life characters who derive from conventional sources. It is as if Shakespeare asked about John Lyly's stylized and witty courtiers, "Why would someone talk and act like this?" and came up with the charming but self-deluding aristocrats of *Love's Labor's Lost.* Or asked how it would feel to be caught in the plot of a revenge play and came up with Hamlet's very mixed reactions. Or asked what it was like to be cast in a Plautine farce and created the twins who are as astonished by it as we would be. Being part of a design enriches rather than impoverishes the minds of Shakespeare's characters, both because the design illuminates them and because they react—just as real-life audiences do—to the design.

Character and the Unconscious

Even if critics are now willing to see Shakespeare's characters as something more than part of a design, there is still a question about how deeply we can probe their motives. All we know is what they say and do. While Bradley based his 1904 study of the tragedies on an attempt to reconstruct "the inner movements which produced these words and no other, these deeds and no others," many twentieth-century critics have warned against trying to draw

inferences from seen to inner and unseen characteristics without more information (Nuttall). But as Barry Weller argues, it is unrealistic and unnecessary to expect total information about anyone, even in real life. Such expectations derive from novels, not real life, and they are an inappropriate prerequisite for speculations about "the mind's construction behind the face" (Goldman, 1981)—onstage or off. Sociologists like Erving Goffman have rejected the novelistic model for a theatrical model in analyzing offstage life, assuming that what we see of other people in life is analogous to what we see of characters on a stage: what they say and do. We have learned to read other people's characters even though we are often limited to external signs of unexpressed thought and feeling, the bare traces of past and inner experience. This is what the Duke does in *Measure for Measure* when he judges Angelo as a potential deputy. "There is a kind of character in thy life, / That to th' observer doth thy history / Fully unfold," he says, and he goes on to warn Angelo that it is not enough merely to be virtuous. One must also act virtuously, so that the signs of virtue may be seen: "For if our virtues / Did not go forth of us, 'twere all alike / As if we had them not" (I. i. 27–29, 33–35). "Character" here refers not to inner qualities but to the visible signs of personality.

Not only is it hard to observe the purely inner personality; it may make no sense even to conceive of a purely inner personality, to attempt to isolate the self from the society that shaped it and that provided the terms in which it must now express itself. Dramatic technique (showing who a character is by showing what he does) may coincide with social reality. Like real people, Shakespeare's characters are defined by their social roles—as king, father, shrew—as well as by their private selves (Weimann). But they are also defined by their theatrical roles—Richard III's as Clarence's dedicated brother, Rosalind's as Ganymede. Disguises in Shakespeare, whether sartorial or merely psychological, are often a means of self-revelation as well as a means of concealment. Role-playing, whether social or theatrical, not only presents a character but also makes him who he is. Goffman's theatrical model comes close to Shakespeare's own continued portrayal of role-playing as an essential means of realizing inner experience.

Even those psychoanalysts who deal with the deepest layers of the personality examine not the isolated inner self but the external self acting in the world. Indeed, it would be difficult if not impossible to speak about an unconscious buried deep and unavailable inside Shakespeare's characters, an unconscious that only psychoanalysts could know about. The unconscious mind is available and in the same way that the conscious mind is: through its expression in words and gestures. Unconscious attitudes manifest themselves in trivial details of action, gesture, dress, and speech, all of which are available to us in Shakespeare's characters. In *Julius Caesar,* for example, when Caesar offers his throat to be cut, and when Cassius bares his bosom to the thunder and then his naked breast to Brutus' dagger, their postures evoke Portia's when she wounds herself in the thigh, thereby suggesting the ambiguous sexual identity of the men in Shakespeare's Rome (Ebel). Shylock's locked house similarly implies his own image of himself. And, according to W. H. Auden, Falstaff's great belly is a symptom of his identification with a pudgy baby and a rounded mother rather than with a muscular adult male. Even supposedly given physical details can be symptoms of psychic realities, so that Richard III's crippled arm withers and recovers according to his mood. Most telling of all is the characters' language. "There is no surer indicator of . . . a person's inner experience," David Cole reminds us, "than the metaphors he is drawn to use to describe it." Thus Edward A. Snow detects "postcoital male disgust" with sexuality in Othello's talk of "the slime that sticks on filthy deeds" (V. ii. 149–150); and Troilus' immaturity—and distaste for sex—is suggested by his frequent use of repellent food imagery to talk about lovemaking.

A full-scale psychoanalysis of Shakespeare's characters is neither possible nor appropriate. A full analysis must be carried out over a long time and under special conditions that eliminate all external distractions in order to bring to the foreground internal fantasies. But as Ella Sharpe has said, what we lack in quantity in analyzing a Lear we partly make up in quality—in the intensity, condensation, and relevance of what we do find out. Just as we learn more about Lear's conscious life during the play than we would learn by watching a real king during two or three random hours of his life, even so we learn a great deal about his unconscious life, as long as we look to the text for evidence of unconscious attitudes and do not go outside the text for theories about the unconscious.

Recent critics have cited evidence to indicate that the plays not only allow but also encourage such

"deep probing into the spring of action" (Leech). In other words, the characters demand analysis. In some cases the deeper motives erupt in a kind of madness, like Lear's delusional hysteria on the heath or the young lovers' nightmarish instability in *A Midsummer Night's Dream.* During events like these, a character experiences another side of himself, though he may not analyze it. "In Shakespeare," as J. W. Lever has said, "self-knowledge comes not from reason but from madness and excess."

But most of Shakespeare's characters are not mad or even neurotic. They invite analysis because they display the contradictions common in all human lives. Shakespeare dramatizes the pressure points in life, the moments of transition from one stage to another when previously achieved balances of rational and irrational impulses are disturbed. The plays show characters in passage from childhood to sexual maturity, or from childhood to political and familial responsibility—or, at the other end of the spectrum, from a climax of power and authority to an acceptance of age, impotence, and death. These radical changes generate conflict among the roles that a character is expected to play and among his images of himself. Juliet's conflict is between being a dutiful child and daughter and becoming an independent and fully sexual adult wife; Hamlet's, between being a dutiful son and a bloody revenger; Othello's, between being an independent warrior and a circumscribed husband. Several critics have defined Shakespeare's typical tragic action as a hero's response to such conflicting roles (Bayley; Salingar; Ure). The hero's consciousness of being pulled apart by conflict is an important part of his experience, which we can examine philosophically, as the characters themselves do. How should Angelo behave? What is the relation between potential and actual virtue? What justification does Hamlet have for shirking responsibility?

But the play's crises call up other conflicts, of which the hero may not be aware, conflicts between conscious and unconscious roles: between Hamlet's role as his father's revenger and his role as his father's rival. The hero's crisis consists of more than a philosophical debate; it calls up old and powerful emotions and evokes his most intimate feelings. Thus Shakespeare examines Hamlet's dilemma as a psychological conflict as well as a philosophical one. The most common sign of such conflict throughout Shakespeare's plays is not madness but a certain strangeness. The characters are odd, if only in small details; they are inconsistent. The oddness most frequently noted is Hamlet's, because he himself worries about it: why does he delay his revenge so long? But we might ask, with even more cause, why Lear decides to hold his love test. He may feel no need to explain, but both his evil daughters and the critics have found it necessary to look for a reason: Goneril and Regan think that Lear is becoming senile, and Adelman and Boose suggest that Lear is on the verge of losing his last daughter to another man and wants to assert his priority in her affections. Or, again, why is Othello so gullible and Iago so malignant?

The formalists' answer had always been that such behavior cannot be explained. According to them, it is a given, an assumption needed by the plot and inherited by Shakespeare when he decided to reuse the old stories on which so many of the plays are based. But, as Stewart says, we cannot blame the old stories. Shakespeare's characters are almost always odder than their models in the sources. Shakespeare habitually makes his characters' motives more obscure. He leaves out explanations: Lear had a rational basis for his test in the source —just as the source Claudio had more reason to suspect Hero and the source Brutus had a reason to suspect Caesar. Shakespeare also adds material that obscures motive: Isabella in the source of *Measure for Measure,* for example, delivers no vicious tirade against her brother and bears no unsanctified anger to cast doubt on the religious origin of her chastity.

Such confusions about motive contribute to what we now think of as a particularly Shakespearean trait—the way the plays make problematic what we previously took for granted as unproblematic. Shakespeare's villains provide good examples of the way he explores motivation. Twentieth-century critics have for the most part resisted romantic efforts to sympathize with Shakespeare's villains and to understand why they are bad. We have been told to accept each of them, along with Iago, as a motiveless malignity, perhaps not as the literal devil that Othello thinks Iago may be, but at least in terms of the deadly sins: Iago's evil "must be taken like lust or pride as simply a given part of human nature" (Kernan), and Shylock is greed personified. To look for psychological complexity in symbolic characters like these would be to risk distorting the intellectual design that the New Critics had revealed.

Yet recent critics have suggested that these villains are neither motiveless nor one-dimensional

monsters but conflicted beings who invite analysis. Rational nihilist though Iago may be—and villainy in Shakespeare is often associated with Machiavellianism—his fantasies and obsessions belie his cool veneer. On the one hand, he teaches Roderigo that "we have reason to cool our raging motions, our carnal stings" (*Othello,* I. i. 329–330), and he never shows any open interest in sex himself; on the other, passion erupts in his images of rams and ewes or goats and monkeys, as well as in his fantasies of other men in bed with his wife and in his description of Cassio in bed with him. Iago's anger and jealousy also escape rational control, goading him to risk his life for a revenge that he would once have mocked just as he mocked Roderigo's passion. Iago's malice has origins, whether in his own sexual self-hatred or in the only partly repressed passions that belie his chosen self-image.

Certainly when a villain is at the center of a play Shakespeare explores the origins of his villainy, not only in adult passions and logical goals but also in the past and the unconscious, in unseen connections between the villain's current crime and the rest of his life. Richard III was not only deformed; he was also rejected at birth by his mother and was taught to think of himself as a monster (Neill). His current ruthlessness in getting the crown is inseparable from his infantile wishes about and hatred of women, who haunt his play like a chorus of furies (Fiedler) and whom he obsessively wooes.

The psychological complexity of Shakespeare's heroes, unlike that of his villains, is familiar, but the consistency with which Shakespeare questions heroism as well as villainy, by examining its psychological sources, has not been fully recognized. For as curious as Shakespeare may be about the motives of self-acknowledged butchers like Richard III and Iago, he is even more fascinated by the would-be sacrificers who become butchers. Critics like Sewell may deny this, claiming that if we are concerned with a hero's self at all, "we are concerned with that self at the very point where psychology breaks down," that is, at a point where he displays "moral responsibility, not psychological determination." But in Shakespeare moral judgments often derive from or rationalize psychological urges, so that as Wheeler suggests, for example, "the exposure of Bertram [in *All's Well*] releases a righteous feeling of moral outrage, and with it a kind of vindictive pleasure that corresponds to . . . sadistic attack." As William Empson has shown, Shakespeare explores "complex words" to reveal the surprising implications of a term like *honest;* he also explores the surprising ramifications of complex behavior like honesty and frequently explodes pious platitudes that blind us to the strangeness in good and noble behavior.

Perhaps the most obvious example of this kind of exploration is Shakespeare's treatment of the Roman heroes. Rome's association with the ideals of honor and piety may have been one source of Shakespeare's fascination with it, for the Roman plays enact the dark side of idealism. The early hero Titus Andronicus is an honorable, pious man who sacrifices his disobedient son as readily as he had sacrificed his enemy, both in the name of service to Rome. But the barbarism inherent in Titus' high-minded idealism is as destructive as the cruelty of the Goths or the Moors. When Shakespeare returned to Roman tragedy in *Julius Caesar,* he created a Tituslike Brutus willing to sacrifice his friend (and, as Shakespeare knew, his father) in the name of the state. In Brutus' case it has become clear that the suppression of feeling is in the service not only of idealism but also of other unacknowledged feelings. Brutus denies his love for Caesar in the name of patriotism, but his patriotism provides a cover for his ambition, vanity, jealousy, and need to be Caesar. By the time Shakespeare created Coriolanus, the ideal had become too thin a veneer to cover private fears and fantasies, and neither the citizens nor Coriolanus really believe in it.

Shakespeare's scrutiny is not reserved for the Romans. Nor is it focused only on the tragedies and on the "tragic flaws" that are bound so inextricably with a hero's greatness that we must come to reassess the greatness itself. Antonio in *The Merchant of Venice* displays something of the "ancient Roman honor" (III. ii. 295), for example, and has been much admired by critics who see him as a moral exemplar in the play because he is willing to lend money gratis in a world of Shylocks and to risk his life so that Bassanio can marry Portia. But Novy has noted a number of selfish and aggressive impulses in Antonio, impulses that he has only partly repressed in order to maintain his self-image. She points out the inconsistency of a noble hero who can rage at Shylock with a canine fury matching that of the Jew, a hero who can use his dramatically martyred pose to make a claim on Bassanio that Novy sees as echoing the poet's sexual claims in the Sonnets. The price that Antonio pays for maintaining his posture (and Gratiano in the first scene sees it as just that—a pose) is the inexplicable sadness

that he suffers in all the scenes in which he is not venting his spleen at Shylock. He is willing to pay the price because his noble selflessness is in its own way as self-serving as Shylock's greed—and it can be cured at the end only when Portia teaches him to take, for once, instead of giving, "life and living" (Novy, 1984).

Before leaving these examples of goodness exposed, we should mention the ideal of celibacy in *Love's Labor's Lost* and *Measure for Measure.* Destruction of the ideal provides the very structure of these plays. The young heroes in *Love's Labor's Lost* renounce sexual pleasure in the name of a higher "heavenly knowledge." But these youthful aristocrats betray their vain, self-aggrandizing motives in establishing their academe, and their scholarship functions not only as a defense against but also as a displacement of libidinal energies, which break out easily when the first woman tempts them. All this is good fun in *Love's Labor's Lost,* but the issue of chastity becomes more unsettling in the later play. In *Measure for Measure,* Angelo and Isabella are chaste exemplars, devoted to their strict regimes of government and religion. For these two characters, chastity serves to ease inner conflict fully as much as it expresses a rational, noble ideal. Angelo has repressed sexual impulses that he cannot bear to admit in himself and has taken on the role of obedient servant because it suits needs of his own (Wheeler). His superficial chastity and obedience fall apart the moment his Duke and "ghostly father" leaves him alone, and their collapse reveals the lust and hostility he had been trying not to see. Isabella's chastity is equally suspect. The convent and its vows provide a convenient way of running from what she does not want anyway. She is uneasy about sex, perhaps because she is devoted to the idealized images of her father and brother (Wheeler), perhaps because of some more directly physical fear. In any event, as with Angelo, her superficial posture of goodness breaks down under pressure. Isabella's imagery betrays a sensuality that Lucio also sees in her unwittingly provocative behavior with men. Her nun's vows scarcely cover her sexual fears and her tangled feelings toward her brother; when he asks her to save his life by sleeping with Angelo, she recoils as if from "incest."

Bad or good, characters may be aware of the contradictions and conflicts in their motives— Hamlet nags himself about his and Angelo is horrified by his. But such awareness is not necessary and is seldom complete. What makes the characters subject to analysis is precisely their misunderstanding of themselves. Their rational explanations and appropriate emotions are in conflict with only partly understood internal pressures—of emotion, of fantasy, and of physical existence.

Character and Infantile Experience

Even more than their conflicts, what finally makes Shakespeare's characters susceptible to analysis is the pressure of the past on their lives. Not only are they subject to unacknowledged sexual and aggressive impulses, plus a range of subtler emotions like Orlando's momentary fear when Rosalind playfully predicts that she will cuckold him (Montrose). Their perceptions of themselves and their worlds are also influenced by childhood attitudes and concerns.

Earlier critics had attempted to discover *The Girlhood of Shakespeare's Heroines,* like Mary Cowden Clarke, or Hamlet's early relation to his mother. But while the plays resist such reconstructions of the past, they do provide ample evidence that infantile experience makes itself felt in the present, in current remnants of childhood outlooks and experiences: in Angelo's filial deference to Duke Vincentio in *Measure for Measure,* or in Isabella's invocation in the same play of her father's image as talisman for her chastity. Shakespeare seems to be aware of the way people continue to see themselves on some level as children—seeking nurturance and protection and fearing powerful parents or the body and its yet-to-be-controlled needs and forces. Traces of oedipal love and jealousy in the family triangle, and of the infant's even earlier experiences as he emerges from union with his mother, affect the way the characters act and speak in their current lives. Their irrationality, contradictions, and conflicts arise from conflicts not only between contemporary feelings but also between current and infantile feelings. Jaques' "seven ages" are played simultaneously, and the "lover, / Sighing . . . a woeful ballad / Made to his mistress' eyebrow" is undone by the "infant" he once was, "mewling and puking in the nurse's arms" (*As You Like It,* II. vii. 143–149).

One indication of the temporally layered existence of Shakespeare's characters is the importance of their family backgrounds—more noticeable than in any other plays of the period. From the lovers in the early comedies and in *Romeo and Juliet* who defy onstage parents, through the childish Bertram who will not marry the girl he grew up with, to the orphaned Posthumus who cannot begin life on his own until he finds his father's armor to put on, to the double generations of each family in the other romances—the main characters are almost all defined as members of families. Even more important, whether or not a character's parents actually appear onstage, nearly every character shows traces of once having been defined as a child in his family. Hamlet has attracted so much psychoanalytic attention partly because he is so obviously struggling with his onstage parents that he seems to provide a textbook case of oedipal conflicts. But what makes Hamlet subject to analysis is not so much the presence of his actual parents as the fact that his current relations with them are heavily influenced by earlier childhood attitudes and feelings. Despite Sir Laurence Olivier's attempt to portray an openly and maturely amorous Hamlet, the play resists being cast as an adult sexual triangle, with Claudius and Hamlet competing to the death for sexual possession of Gertrude. Hamlet's oedipal wishes consist not simply of an adult's wish to murder his rival and marry his mother, but rather of a whole range of childish rivalries, attractions, wishes, and fears about both parents, and of childish ways of coping with these.

It is true that Hamlet is unduly interested in his mother's sexual life and is oddly intent on keeping the bloat king from tempting her to bed. But more telling is his own adolescent recoil from all sexuality—not only because he may fear Claudius' retaliation but because an awareness of his mother's sexuality destroys Hamlet's infantile image of his parents as parents and his image of himself as an innocent child. And he copes with the disgust as an oedipal child would, by splitting his image of Gertrude (his mother as his first sexual love and the continuing epitome of sexuality) into an idealized and a sexual version: the fair Gertrude with a rose on her forehead in "celestial" union with Hamlet's godlike father—and the blistered Gertrude, preying on "garbage" in the rank sweat of Claudius' "enseamèd" bed. (Hamlet's sense of her vaguely timed adultery may on some level simply be his recognition that there is no celestially pure marriage and that Gertrude actually sleeps with Claudius.) Hamlet is not so open about the source of his own self-disgust (inasmuch as for the oedipal child, all sexuality is "hers" or "theirs," not "mine"). But it flares out most openly when Ophelia tempts him into tender feelings that his image of his mother has contaminated. When she approaches, he pushes her away, invoking the "relish" of old Adam and turning on himself: "I could accuse me of such things that it were better my mother had not borne me" (III. i. 123–124).

Hamlet's is a tragedy of coming to age in an imperfect world and of feeling "the thousand natural shocks that flesh is heir to." But the recognition includes, along with Hamlet's current discoveries, the remnants of childhood fantasies and disillusionments as well. The oedipal family dynamics, though not always so central as in *Hamlet,* are important throughout the canon. The story of the Danish succession was preceded by two sets of history plays about the English succession in which conflict between fathers and brothers over possession of the crown is worked out in the larger-than-life scale of royal families. Both the idealized chivalric relations between Talbot and his son in *Henry VI, Part I,* and the snarling rivalries culminating in *Richard III* reflect aspects of every boy's experience as he vies for position with his father and brothers (Berman; Kahn). Norman Rabkin has even suggested that no ambition for the crown is pure and that beneath all attempts to be king, as Shakespeare portrays them, are motives that derive from the original family rivalries. In *Henry IV, Part 2* (IV. iv. 42), when he prematurely lifts the crown from his sick, sleeping, but still living father, Hal finds it difficult to separate his feelings about kingship from his feelings about his father (Hawkins; Kahn; Kris).

Other plays about political succession, although not literally about family rivalries, present heroes whose actions suggest that family rivalry is indeed the central issue. Duncan looks like Lady Macbeth's father and is actually Macbeth's kinsman. Duncan's fatherly praise for Macbeth—no less than the witches' prophecy—might be understood as a promise that Macbeth will be made his heir; so Macbeth seems to hope, until he watches Duncan make Malcolm crown prince, whereupon Macbeth promptly makes his murderous plans. Brutus in *Julius Caesar* was Caesar's "bastard," as Shakespeare called him in *Henry VI, Part II;* Caesar is treated with filial deference by both Brutus and Antony in the play's second scene (Ebel), and Cassius scorns him because he is a weak old man like Anchises. Like Hamlet, Brutus seems on some level to be coming to terms with an imperfect father, and he works out in his symmetrically balanced rhetoric ("I love [Caesar] well" [I. ii. 82] yet "I love / The

name of honor" [88–89]) what is acted out in the contrast between Hamlet's father's ghost and Claudius: the clash between the ideal of a father and what a father really is.

Although oedipal conflicts like these were the ones emphasized by the earliest psychoanalytic studies, recent critics have begun to examine the remnants of preoedipal attitudes toward mothers in the characters' current lives. They argue that even more important than oedipal masculine rivalries and ambitions is a primitive ambivalence about women. Murray M. Schwartz (1977) sees "a common theme: Shakespeare's mistrust of femininity within and without," which leads his heroes to disdain all intimacy and all emotion, even though they long for it. Shakespeare's heroes waver between seeking frighteningly intense unions with people and violently rejecting all dependency on others. Wheeler argues that Shakespeare's heroes display what psychoanalyst Margaret S. Mahler has described in *The Psychological Birth of the Human Infant* (1975) as "man's eternal struggle against fusion on the one hand and isolation on the other."

Mahler located the source of this struggle in the infant's first effort to separate himself from the symbiotic tie with his mother. The child, beginning to sense his separateness from his mother, is torn between his need for independence—which exhilarates but leaves him lonely and vulnerable—and his longing for reunion—which comforts, but now threatens to engulf his fragile new identity. While no one ever fully resolves what is to be a lifelong process of balancing identity and intimacy, for boys "the task of separating and individuation carries an added peril," as Kahn puts it. Not only the boy's sense of independence but his very identity as a male depends on his rejecting the mother with whom he has so long intimately identified. This is a difficult process and one that often goes wrong. As a result, "a man whose separation from the mother was problematic . . . has not fully secured his masculine identity. No matter how much status or power his sex *per se* allows him, he is likely to feel anxious when he is called upon to 'be a man' as husband or father. Once again, he finds himself dependent upon a woman to confirm his identity" (Kahn).

Feminist critics have traced a persistent theme of male ambivalence toward women in the plays (Lenz; Greene; Neely). They have argued that, throughout the canon, admiration of men for women is undermined by their fear of women—

and, similarly, that a condescending attitude toward women is in part a reaction against that fear. They suggest that, in the patriarchal societies in the plays, "structures of male dominance grow out of and mask fears of female power and of male feminization and powerlessness" (Greene, 1980).

In their closely related exploration of male psychology in the plays, psychoanalytic critics suggest that fears of female power grow out of an infant's fears of its engulfing mother and that such fears remain tinged with infantile imagery and expectations. The importance of literal mothers is most obvious in the early plays, where important mothers appear onstage, a terrible one in *Titus Andronicus* (Willbern), a number of other frightening ones in the early histories (Fiedler), and a wonderful one in *The Comedy of Errors* (MacCary). In the latter play particularly, Shakespeare's double focus on present and past experience is evident. The hero's attempt to leave home and to find himself in the person of his twin—and incidentally to find a wife—brings him emphatically back home to his lost parents and re-creates a family that had been broken since his birth. Antipholus is not aware of the way his present search for his brother re-creates his earliest search for identity apart from his mother. But his language conveys the connection:

> I to the world am like a drop of water
> That in the ocean seeks another drop,
> Who falling there to find his fellow forth,
> Unseen, inquisitive, confounds himself.
> So I, to find a mother and a brother,
> In quest of them, unhappy, lose myself.
>
> (I. ii. 35–40)

"Water itself," MacCary argues, "is the most frequent dream symbol for birth, and with the mention of the mother and brother, we are set firmly in the child's world. . . . The water here . . . is the overwhelming aspect of the mother, the mother from whom the child cannot differentiate himself. She projects to us the image of what we shall become; but it is a fragile image, and if we lose it we risk reintegration with her, reabsorption." When we meet the two sisters we see them largely through Antipholus' eyes as opposites comprising the split image of the mother: the good mother (benevolent, yielding Luciana) and the bad mother (domineering, shrewish Adriana). Bad Adriana, mistaking Antipholus for her husband, reminds him that he and she should be as close as two drops

of water mingled in the gulf—and terrifies him with this version of his own oceanic imagery. But even the good union he imagines with Luciana is one that drowns him (though this time blissfully): "Spread o'er the silver waves thy golden hairs, / And as a bed I'll take them and there lie; / . . . He gains by death that hath such means to die" (III. ii. 48–51). The action is finally resolved—and so is Antipholus' ambivalence about women—when his real mother appears at the end to correct Adriana, to show what a benevolent, protective mother ought to be, and to save everyone.

There are no mothers to speak of in the middle comedies, but critics have suggested that the heroes do identify their young mistresses to varying degrees with seductive and threatening mothers, and that "the comic hero's love for the heroine includes aspects of . . . a boy's relation to his mother" (Wheeler). Norman N. Holland remarks that the playboy Bassanio in *The Merchant of Venice,* for example, seems as much enticed by the Portia who is a bounteous maternal provider as he is by her potential as a wife. She is not only infinitely rich but also promises nourishing "drops" of mercy: she drops manna in the way of starving people, and after having played a role that is as strong and saving as the mother's in *The Comedy of Errors,* she gives "life and living" to Bassanio's friend. Just as Bassanio sees her attractions, he also, if only glancingly, feels the threat of such a powerful woman. He is alert to potential traps even before he chooses his casket, and after he has won Portia's portrait he sees there a "spider" to "entrap" his heart. By the end of the play he says, albeit jokingly, that he would rather cut off his arm than face Portia's wrath. Despite all this, in the comedies such infantile fantasies only barely color the love, and the hero's ambivalence is overcome, often through play—as in *Merchant*'s ring episode, in which Portia only pretends to be a possessive mother, or in *As You Like It* when Rosalind, dressed safely as a boy, only pretends that she will be a fickle and demanding wife.

In the tragedies the hero's ambivalence is catastrophic, and real mothers like Gertrude and Volumnia reappear. But even where there is no mother, the hero's betrayal by fortune is associated with his betrayal by a woman or by the womanliness in himself; and the betrayals invariably echo the infant's fear of maternal betrayal. The mother's role is clearest in *Coriolanus,* where even the citizens comment on Coriolanus' devotion to his mother. As Adelman has shown, Coriolanus' devotion is more far-reaching than in a healthy adult relationship. It derives from infantile conflicts about being fed—or not fed, in Coriolanus' case. The mother, who herself refuses food and claims, "Anger's my meat. I sup upon myself, / And so shall starve with feeding" (IV. ii. 50–51), has produced a son who also hates food and dependence. But Coriolanus' self-denying, martial posture, Adelman suggests, began as a fragile defense against the hungry neediness that once made him dependent on a frustrating mother like Volumnia. His lonely heroic stance against the world is inseparable from a boy's defiance of his mother. Coriolanus' current battles act out old conflicts. If he cannot bring himself to appease the plebeians, it is because he associates their hunger with the hunger he still fears in himself. And what he fears in Rome is what he fears in his mother: "an unnatural dam [who] / Should now eat up her own" (III. i. 292–293). In Adelman's interpretation, "the cannibalistic mother who denies food and yet feeds on the victories of her sweet son stands at the darkest center of the play, where Coriolanus' oral vulnerability is fully defined. Here, the talion law reigns: the feeding infant himself will be devoured." The fantasy that Adelman sees in Coriolanus' political action is very close to the fantasies surrounding Tamora in Shakespeare's first Roman play, *Titus Andronicus,* where the Queen literally does devour her sons.

Hamlet is as much troubled by his mother's betrayal as by Claudius' crime. The other heroes have no mothers, but the fantasy of maternal danger still affects them. Lady Macbeth is not Macbeth's mother, but she describes herself (it seems gratuitous) as an even more terrifying mother than Volumnia, one who would, while her baby "was smiling in my face, / Have plucked my nipple from his boneless gums / And dashed the brains out" (*Macbeth,* I. vii. 56–58)—just as the witches dash Macbeth's hopes. Even with no literal mother present, Macbeth lives in a world controlled by seemingly female forces: not only his wife but also the three sisters, aspects of the bitch goddess Fortune, who nurtures or betrays at whim. In response, Macbeth's rebellion echoes a much earlier struggle with the mother. In an article in Carolyn Lenz, ed., *The Woman's Part,* Madelon Gohlke writes: "The world constructed by Macbeth attempts to deny not only the values of trust and hospitality, perceived as essentially feminine, but to eradicate femininity itself. . . . [He] has no room for maternal values, as if the conscious exclusion of these values would eliminate all . . . dependence, making him in effect invulnerable. To be born of woman, as he reads the witches' prophecy, is to be mortal. Macbeth's . . . violence, involving murder and pillage in his kingdom and the repression of anything resembling compassion or remorse within, is designed, like Coriolanus' desperate militarism, to make him author of himself."

The maternal threat that is avoided in the early comedies and that helps destroy the tragic heroes, is, several critics have suggested, finally confronted and to some degree overcome in the romances, at least in *The Winter's Tale.* In that play, Shakespeare "recast[s] the problem" of maternal threat by showing it to be a "product of male fantasy and betrayal" (Erickson). Lady Macbeth really does threaten to kill the babe that milks her, but in *The Winter's Tale* it is Leontes who tears his newborn daughter from Hermione's breast and has her "haled out to murder" with "the innocent milk in it most innocent mouth" (III. ii. 99–100). Far from being betrayers or smotherers, the women in *The Winter's Tale* are associated with the "process of great nature" (II. ii. 60) that "free[s] and enfranchise[s]" the child in the womb and brings about the play's central birth and many rebirths (Neely).

From early to late plays and from comic to tragic to romantic modes, the plays record the changes in Shakespeare's portrayal of the ways in which the ambivalent derivatives of powerful childhood experiences help shape the heroes' adult lives.

An Example: Othello

Though historically there has been an opposition between the New Criticism's concern with detail and structure on one hand and a more impressionistic character analysis on the other, the strength of recent psychological criticism lies in its attention to textual details and to the patterns that New Critics have taught us to recognize. Psychological critics may hypothesize any number of external analogies between Hamlet's experience and that of an oedipal-stage boy; but the best evidence for Hamlet's unconscious fantasies lies in the character's actions and particularly in his language—in the details of the text that reveal analogies that Hamlet himself sees between ongoing and childhood events.

This kind of character analysis can best be understood by focusing on a single text. *Othello* belongs to the curious and important group of Shakespearean "jealousy" plays (including *Much Ado, Cymbeline,* and *The Winter's Tale*), all of which have received close attention from psychoanalytic and feminist critics. All of these plays examine the depths of misogynist male psychology, and all suggest not only the current operation of that psychology but also the infantile origins of the irrational hatred that the plays portray. The development of *Othello* criticism provides a good example of contemporary character analysis. The best New Critical studies of *Othello* had already revealed Shakespeare's careful presentation of something irrational at work in Othello's action: "The vision of human nature which the play offers is one of ancient terrors and primal drives—fear of the unknown, pride, greed, lust—underlying smooth, civilized surfaces" (Kernan). The action, Kernan suggests, presents an allegory of Othello's internal conflicts as he moves from the enlightened Desdemona in himself—the loving, generous self who makes civilization possible—to the dark Iago in himself—the anarchic, self-centered, hostile self who destroys civilization.

But in this traditional account, although "evil is somehow inextricably woven with good," it remains essentially different from "good" in nature. Othello may feel both love and hate, but the two have little to do with one another. The Iagolike hatred that overcomes the hero remains essentially as mysterious as an external or cosmic force, "a diabolism so intense as to defy rational explanation" (Kernan). Recent critics, instead of taking love and hate in the play as opposites that are givens and that cannot be explained, have studied Othello's jealousy as an inevitable accompaniment to his idealistic love—perhaps even as a precondition for it (Kirsch; Snow), and they have offered several explanations of its origins. In examining the nature of motive and belief in Othello, critics call attention to the complex interaction of social and internal pressures on him, to the close relation between seemingly opposite aspects of his psychic life, and to the infantile forces that have helped shape his adult experience. Analyses of Othello's unconscious attitudes are not intended to replace his obvious feelings by "truer" ones but rather to show how much is tacitly implied by what is explicitly manifested—to show how Othello's current feelings depend on invisible internal and external

pressures both past and present, and to show, finally, how what is actually said or done—even what is actually felt—is only the last stage of a conflicted process incorporating many earlier acts, feelings, and fantasies. What makes Othello, like other Shakespearean characters, seem so real is not only his richness and spontaneity but also the way in which his speech and actions reveal a variety of pressures and influences on his life and mind. He is overdetermined just the way real people are.

Where then does Othello's jealousy come from? One recent answer is provided by feminist critics who focus on the patriarchal structure of Othello's world. In this view, Venice, though an enlightened civilization in the way Kernan describes, where the senators treat even violence with rational understanding rather than immediate punishment, is less rational and enlightened in its treatment of women. If Brabantio is a model, fathers in Venice assume that a daughter remains a devoted child until bestowed as the father wishes—and when she disobeys, she is disowned. Brabantio's hysteria about Othello may seem justified by circumstance, but his dreams and fantasies suggest that he would have considered nearly any successful suitor an "extravagant . . . stranger," a black ram, a thief stealing his daughter. He had nightmares about losing Desdemona before she married Othello ("This accident is not unlike my dream": I. i. 141); and his image of Desdemona's immature, asexual shyness is more fantasy than fact. In this world, fathers control not only their daughters' acts but their desires as well—while secretly fantasizing the inevitable betrayal.

Not only fathers but husbands too fear betrayal: "She has deceived her father, and may thee" (I. iii. 293), Brabantio tells Othello as he relinquishes Desdemona. So long as Desdemona "subdues" herself totally to Othello's way of life, he loves her extravagantly. But at the first suspicion of her independent sexual existence, he explodes. Othello reacts so strongly, Kahn says, not so much because he is sorry to lose her but because he has become "a fixèd figure for the time of scorn / To point his slow unmoving finger at" (IV. ii. 54–55). He has accepted "Iago's vision of society as a network of cuckoldries, man against man, with women merely incidental to their contests" (Kahn). His jealousy is not so much a sexual as a political concern in a society of other men.

But it is not just that other concerns are more important than sexual love. Some critics go even further and find at the core of Othello's passion not only a frustrated and helpless loss of something desired but also a displaced hatred of something feared: "In *Othello,* language condemning adultery both masks and draws authority from an underlying guilt and disgust about sexuality itself" (Snow). For Othello, as well as for Iago, sex is simply loathsome. Othello's initial image of himself depended on his not being sexual, on his superiority to the flesh ("the young affects [are] in me defunct": I. iii. 263–264). His obsession with images of Cassio and Desdemona in bed, Snow argues, is in part a displacement of his own self-loathing at having had his sexuality awakened—and of his loathing for Desdemona, whose sexuality shatters his idealized image of her. That she did the deed at all offends him. When Iago suggests strangling Desdemona "even [in] the bed she hath contaminated," consciously he means that the bed was contaminated by adultery, but unconsciously, Snow argues, he is suggesting that the bed was contaminated by what took place there between Othello and Desdemona on their "much-delayed wedding night." As a result, no proof of Desdemona's innocence with Cassio will do, because it is not the supposed crime with Cassio that causes Othello's passion, but the crime with Othello.

Stephen Greenblatt has located this self-loathing in the inevitable discontents that civilizing Christianity brings with it. "Christianity is the alienating yet constitutive force in Othello's identity," he argues, for it finally teaches that even married sexuality is abhorrent—as in St. James's definition of an adulterer as "he who is too ardent a lover of his wife." Not only is Christianity fundamentally in conflict with the anarchic, appetitive physical self; it also demands that sexual pleasure be repressed in the name of another acceptably sexless but false self.

Others see Othello's disgust as something even deeper and more fundamental than anything Christianity could impose. His disgust at Cassio, Arthur Kirsch suggests, is ultimately a rage against himself that reaches back to the "elemental and destructive triadic fantasies" of oedipal boys and is thus inseparable from sexuality itself. Othello's current sexual feelings evoke the original triangle in which as a child his first sexual feelings were experienced. Oedipal fantasies are ready in each new potential husband to reinforce the father's patriarchal fears (Othello is all too willing to see himself through Brabantio's eyes as a triumphant competitor), and

any sexual feeling evokes the original triangle in which a child's first sexual feelings were experienced. Both Othello's passion for and his fears about Desdemona are excited by her role in a triangle that is the precursor of the "network of cuckoldry" that Kahn describes on the adult level. Othello's marriage in fact is staged very much as a public triumph in which he wins the inaccessible woman in a triangle. Onstage, the wedding ceremony is replaced by a trial in which Brabantio is defeated; even the consummation is later publicly announced and celebrated. Though at first Othello's love seems to have little to do with childhood oedipal origins, as the action progresses his "emotional responses" become increasingly those "of a very young boy" reacting to such triangles (Kirsch).

Such oedipal love continually generates new triangles (Othello "won" Desdemona from her father—someone might win her from Othello), and one measure of the primitive quality of oedipal love is its susceptibility to jealousy. When Brabantio disappears as a rival, Othello is ready to replace him with Cassio. And whether the rival is an actual father or a replacement, the intense oedipal love is inseparable from equally strong guilt and disgust at the implicitly incestuous nature of the attachment. In this view Othello's love is doomed to ambivalence—as is his view of Desdemona, whom he speaks of as both "my soul's joy" and "that cunning whore of Venice." The tragedy of Othello is the inevitable tragedy of all men who grow up in families, Kirsch argues. Affection and sensuality are rarely fused in adults, for, as Freud explains, the child splits them apart in order to salvage a pure image of his mother and himself while separating off the sexual and contaminated image. The adult inherits the split: "Who ever is to be really free and happy in love must [reunite love and sex by overcoming] his deference for women and [coming] to terms with the idea of incest with mother or sister. . . . Anyone who . . . subjects himself to serious self-examination will indubitably find that at the bottom of his heart he too regards the sexual act as something degrading, which soils and contaminates not only the body" (Freud). Cassio rationalizes his split between deference and disgust by splitting his love and lust between two women—projecting the one onto "the divine Desdemona" and the other onto Bianca the "monkey" or "fichew." (Neely). Othello has only one woman; so he finds both divinity and animal in

Desdemona when she "changes" from ideal wife to whore. Neither is a perception of the real Desdemona; both images are fueled by fantasies ultimately derived from childhood.

Stanley Cavell (1979) sees Othello's recoil from sexuality not so much as sheer disgust or as a fear of incest but as a recoil from the idea of Desdemona as a violated virgin—that is, as one no longer bearing the magical perfection and immortality of virginity. Othello's rage against Cassio is an attempt to avoid admitting his own guilt at having deflowered her and his anger at discovering that she is flesh and thus that he is mere flesh too. The discovery means that Desdemona is not the perfect creature he had fantasized, and "he cannot forgive her for existing (apart from his fantasies of her), for being separate from him, outside, beyond command, commanding, her captain's captain." The murder is revenge for this as well as for adultery. Othello refuses to acknowledge the violence he has done to Desdemona, though in his dreamlike trance he reenacts it at the murder, re-creating the wedding night (complete with wedding sheets) when he first had made her "die." As Othello watches the sleeping Desdemona before the murder and pauses to say, "When I have plucked the rose, / I cannot give it vital growth again" (V. ii. 13–14), the rose is not only her life but her maidenhead, whose destruction is the "cause" of Othello's guilt and his need to undo the crime. Whatever the source of his recoil, the significant result, Cavell argues, is that Othello denies his relation to Desdemona and refuses to acknowledge her. It is a refusal that turns her to stone ("monumental alabaster," Othello says tenderly just before he kills her) just as Leontes' refusal to acknowledge Hermione transforms her into a statue. Only as stone is Desdemona back in Othello's control, a product of his fantasy again—and only as such can he love her: "I will kill thee, and love thee after" (V. ii. 18–19).

Although Cavell locates the roots of Othello's fantasies in an epistemological concern for perfection, they may have roots in childhood concerns as well. The emphasis on the violence he has done her and on the need for control recalls a preoedipal stage of attachment when sexuality, along with all strong feeling, was not yet separated from aggression; in this stage, "love" is ownership—the loved one is seen almost literally as a possession—and control is the issue. Any adult might emphasize the violence and violation in sex, but Snow describes Othello's feelings as almost a primitive equation of

the two: Othello sees "lust's stains" as "lust's blood," orgasmic discharge as bloody "death" for both partners, and the blood on his wedding sheets becomes equated with the blood he would shed in murdering Desdemona. Like a child, he creates a primitive magic ritual to protect himself from this threatening image; in the ceremonious murder he wants to reenact, he envisions the wedding night without the blood ("yet I'll not shed her blood": V. ii. 3) and thus attempts to undo it. Here, as throughout his jealousy, Othello—again like a child—cannot tolerate ambivalence. "To be once in doubt [of her chastity] is once to be resolved," he says, and he murders Desdemona with the certainty of judge and jury. His quietly mad insistence on doing justice and establishing "cause" suggests that of a child first learning to cope with the clash between his own violent impulses and his parents' rules. In other words, Othello is no more a compulsive anal sadist than a child is. He nevertheless displays the same cluster of associated concerns with violence, domination, certainty, and the law.

Finally, there may be traces of a still earlier form of infantile love in Othello's ambivalence about Desdemona. This is not only preoedipal but presexual, and what is at stake is not sexual satisfaction but survival itself. Othello's dependence on Desdemona is as complete in its way as an infant's total dependence on its mother: when Desdemona is gone, "Othello's occupation's gone." His fear of betrayal is as extreme as an infant's fear that its sustaining mother will desert him, that her "fountain" will dry up or turn poisonous:

> But there where I have garnered up my heart,
> Where either I must live or bear no life,
> The fountain from the which my current runs
> Or else dries up—to be discarded thence,
> Or keep it as a cistern for foul toads
> To knot and gender in.
>
> (IV. ii. 57–62)

Othello thinks of Desdemona in oral terms: she is "sweet Desdemona," "sweeting," and the adulterous intruder's crime was that he "tasted her sweet body" (III. iii. 346). But her maternal qualities are extended beyond nurturance: the Desdemona whom Othello knows is occupied with "house affairs" in her father's home, and she takes the lead in courting Othello and in supporting his boylike image of himself as adventurer. (There is a suggestion, in Othello's biographical tales, of the Prince of Morocco's boyish bravado in *The Merchant of Venice.*)

One danger in Othello's idealizing Desdemona as mother is that she will desert him; but an even greater danger is that she will smother him, eat him up, just as she would "with a greedy ear / Devour up my discourse" (I. iii. 149–150) during their courtship. Maternal virtues can easily become a trap when a child moves toward independence. Othello had supported his claims of royal independence by emphasizing his freedom of choice in marrying Desdemona:

> But that I love the gentle Desdemona,
> I would not my unhousèd free condition
> Put into circumscription and confine
> For the sea's worth.
>
> (I. ii. 25–28)

But he also betrays in these words his image of the danger in marriage. On some level what Othello fears is not only desertion but also encompassment —just what Antipholus fears in *The Comedy of Errors:* a demanding wife who tells him when to be home and with whom to associate. Desdemona's version of these demands seems harmless compared to Adriana's nagging, but it does echo them:

> I'll watch him tame and talk him out of patience;
> His bed shall seem a school, his board a shrift;
> I'll intermingle everything he does
> With Cassio's suit.
>
> (III. iii. 23–26)

Desdemona sounds like an intrusive mother when she begs for Cassio, and her requests take the form of domestic demands:

> Tell me, Othello. I wonder in my soul
> What you could ask me that I should deny
> Or stand so mamm'ring on.
>
> . . .
>
> Why, this is not a boon;
> 'Tis as I should entreat you wear your gloves,
> Or feed on nourishing dishes, or keep you warm.
>
> (III. iii. 68–78)

To all this Othello replies with a typically extravagant "I will deny thee nothing"; but the price of such devotion is suggested, as Snow argues, when he follows with "whereon I do beseech thee grant me this, / To leave me but a little to myself" (III.

iii. 83–85). Othello's "unhousèd free condition" threatens to become the sort of restraint Adriana imposes on Antipholus when she summons a doctor to tie him up for his own good. In The *Comedy of Errors,* Emilia's maternal benevolence corrects the threat, but the Emilia of *Othello* only exacerbates it. Othello smothers the woman who might have smothered him with her affections.

Othello's jealousy and pain at losing Desdemona are only the most conscious of the conflicting attitudes and feelings that recent critics have found implicit in his action and language and that provide new perspectives on the jealousy. What seems to be Othello's purely personal reaction to Desdemona's "betrayal" is also shaped by hidden cultural expectations and prejudices. Even more striking, Othello's feeling about Desdemona and Cassio is fed by a feeling about Desdemona and himself. And what seems to be desire is also fear and guilt.

Othello's case is not unique in the Shakespearean canon. Critics have described similar complexities in Othello's jealous predecessor Claudio in *Much Ado* (Janice Hays, in Carolyn Lenz, ed., *The Woman's Part*), and in a later character, Leontes in *The Winter's Tale* (Schwartz, 1973; Erickson), and such complexities are present in the jealousies of the early *Comedy of Errors.* Nor are these jealous men monstrous anomalies. As Cavell (1979) says, "If such a man as Othello . . . is horrified by human sexuality, in himself and in others, then no human being is free of this possibility." In these analyses, critics are attempting not to label the characters as pathological or to reduce the complexity of conscious behavior to its most primitive components, but rather to suggest the ways in which Shakespeare shows that extraordinary behavior is normal, that seemingly simple passions have complicated and spreading roots in personality.

Character and Shakespeare's Psychology

If *Othello* presents a complex and contradictory set of attitudes toward Desdemona, one might still ask whether they belong solely to Othello or are generated instead by the totality of action and language in the play. In other words, is this Othello's or Shakespeare's fantasy about Desdemona? Are we talking about Othello's psychology or Shakespeare's? Some critics have suggested that throughout the canon Shakespeare distances us from his characters' fantasies by creating worlds that clearly belie those fantasies. But others find Shakespeare at times to be in collusion with his characters' fantasies and sympathetic to their sexual fears. Othello may be wrong about Desdemona's adultery, but Shakespeare also wrote plays, like *Troilus and Cressida,* in which the hero is right. And, right or wrong, the themes of female betrayal and female entrapment recur again and again in the tragedies—and in the comedies as well, though only playfully. Within *Othello* the evidence is mixed. The idea that Desdemona actually committed adultery is Othello's fantasy and not Shakespeare's, but what about the fantasies fueling Othello's feelings about adultery? What about Othello's view of Desdemona as part of a triangle of attractions and jealousies? What about the fantasies that force Desdemona into one of two polarized roles as goddess or whore? Or, even if Shakespeare gives enough external evidence to suggest that such oedipal fantasies are generated by Venetian men rather than being descriptive of Venetian women, how much does Shakespeare collude in Othello's preoedipal fantasies: does Othello see Desdemona as an ideal nurturer who suddenly becomes a nagging wife who will circumscribe him? Or is it Shakespeare who sees her this way? Once again, in considering a character's psychology we must examine the relation between character and Shakespeare's total design, between a character's psychology and the psychological effect of the whole play.

It may finally be impossible to describe that relation in any simple way. But our confusion is in itself one of the ways in which Shakespeare suggests depth of character. *Hamlet* provides an illustrative final example. In that play, on one hand, it is the play, not the prince, that seems to have an oedipus complex. Hamlet does not need to fantasize; the play provides him with the parents every oedipal boy imagines. The slain King (the good father) is almost too good to be true, and Claudius (the bad father) is too conveniently deserving of Hamlet's anger; Gertrude really is the mother of oedipal dreams who needs to be rescued from a bad husband and his wicked ways. In other words, Shakespeare gives Hamlet the kind of world an oedipal child has to invent to rationalize his feelings; Hamlet's feelings about the world are largely corroborated by the facts.

On the other hand, it is not the facts that finally matter. Whether or not Claudius killed Hamlet's father is less interesting than Hamlet's uncertainty about the murder. Claudius' guilt is less interesting than Hamlet's fantasies about it—less interesting than what we might call Hamlet's free associations to the murder, such as his obsessive image of Claudius' new sexual freedom with Gertrude. So too in *Othello* the interesting question is not whether Desdemona was actually unfaithful, but what Othello thinks about the "adultery." A character in a Shakespearean play may demand external "ocular proof" or may set watch on Claudius to see how he reacts to "The Mousetrap." But the whole play encourages us to look instead for something internal, something in the "mind's eye"—the unconscious as well as the conscious mind—where external proof does not matter.

Thus Hamlet may not have invented his world, but he considers it too curiously and responds to it too readily for us to blame it entirely for his ideas. Shakespeare may have provided Hamlet with neatly balanced fathers, but Hamlet saw the ghost in his mind's eye before he saw him on the battlements. His prophetic soul suspected Claudius long before the ghost's accusation, just as his rational mind believes Claudius is innocent long after the ghost's accusation. It is Hamlet who ignores the ghost's emphasis on the politics of the murder and focuses instead on the sex, and Hamlet who generalizes, without the ghost's testimony, from his mother's imagined deeds to Ophelia's. In other words, though Hamlet's view of authority and femininity, of politics and sex, of father and mother, is largely corroborated by Shakespeare, it is also very much his own invention. And it is out of focus just enough for us to see it as such.

Shakespeare presents the duality of experience both as we feel it and as we recognize it in our objective moments. He encourages us to participate in a character's fantasies as if they were real, but he simultaneously suggests the origin of the fantasies in the character's mind. The fantasies are both more real than our own (our father is not a murdered king, our mother not a royal adulteress) and less real (it is easier to see through Hamlet's obsessions than to see through our own). Shakespeare's characters seem so real because our impression of them derives both from inside and outside, from character as well as from design—just as our impression of what it is to be a person derives both from our own internal, private experience and from other people's external images of us and ours of them.

BIBLIOGRAPHY

Janet Adelman, " 'Anger's My Meat': Feeding, Dependency, and Aggression in *Coriolanus,*" in David Bevington and Jay L. Halio, eds., *Shakespeare: Pattern of Excelling Nature* (1978) and "Introduction," in *Twentieth Century Interpretations of King Lear* (1978). W. H. Auden, *The Dyer's Hand and Other Essays* (1962). J. Leeds Barroll, *Artificial Persons* (1974). John Bayley, *Shakespeare and Tragedy* (1981). Ronald S. Berman, "Fathers and Sons in the Henry VI Plays," in *Shakespeare Quarterly,* 13 (1962). Lynda E. Boose, "The Father and the Bride in Shakespeare," in *PMLA,* 97 (1982). Andrew Cecil Bradley, *Shakespearean Tragedy* (1904). Stanley Cavell, "The Avoidance of Love," in *Must We Mean What We Say?* (1976) and "Epistemology and Tragedy: A Reading of *Othello,*" in *Daedalus,* 108 (1979). Cleanth Brooks, "The Naked Babe and the Cloak of Manliness," in *The Well Wrought Urn* (1947). David Cole, *The Theatrical Event* (1975).

Henry Ebel, "Caesar's Wounds: A Study of William Shakespeare," in *Psychoanalytic Review,* 62 (1975). William Empson, *The Structure of Complex Words* (1951). Peter B. Erickson, "Patriarchal Structures in *The Winter's Tale,*" in *PMLA,* 97 (1982) and "Sexual Politics and the Social Structure in *As You Like It,*" in *Massachusetts Review,* 23 (1982). Leslie A. Fiedler, *The Stranger in Shakespeare* (1972). Sigmund Freud, "Contributions to the Psychology of Love: The Most Prevalent Form of Degradation in Erotic Life" (1912), in *Collected Papers,* IV (1925). Erving Goffman, *The Presentation of Self in Everyday Life* (1971). Michael Goldman, "Characterizing Coriolanus," in *Shakespeare Survey,* 34 (1981) and *Acting and Action in Shakespearean Tragedy* (1985). Stephen Greenblatt, *Renaissance Self-Fashioning* (1980). Gayle Greene and Carolyn Ruth Swift, eds., *Women's Studies: An Interdisciplinary Journal,* Special Issue on Feminist Criticism of Shakespeare, 9 (1981–1982).

Sherman H. Hawkins, "*Henry IV:* The Structural Problem Revisited," in *Shakespeare Quarterly,* 33 (1982). Norman N. Holland, *Psychoanalysis and Shakespeare* (1966). Coppélia Kahn, *Man's Estate: Masculine Identity in Shakespeare* (1981). Alvin Kernan, "Introduction," in *Othello,* The Signet Classic Shakespeare (1963). Arthur Kirsch, *Shakespeare and the Experience of Love* (1981). G. Wilson Knight, *The Wheel of Fire* (1930; rev. 1949). L. C. Knights, *How Many Children Had Lady Macbeth?* (1933) and "The Question of Character in Shakespeare," in John Garrett, ed., *More Talking of Shakespeare* (1959). Ernst Kris, "Prince Hal's Conflict," in *Psychoanalytic Explorations in Art* (1952). William Witherle Lawrence, *Shakespeare's Problem Comedies* (1931). Clifford Leech, " 'More Than Our Brother Is Our Chastity,' " in *Critical Quarterly,* 12 (1970). Carolyn Ruth Swift Lenz, Gayle Greene, Carol Thomas Neely, eds., *The Woman's Part: Feminist Criticism of Shakespeare* (1980). J. W. Lever,

ed., *Measure for Measure,* The New Arden Shakespeare (1965).

W. Thomas MacCary, "*The Comedy of Errors:* A Different Kind of Comedy," in *New Literary History,* 9 (1978). Maynard Mack, *King Lear in Our Time* (1965). Louis Adrian Montrose, " 'The Place of a Brother' in *As You Like It:* Social Process and Comic Form," in *Shakespeare Quarterly,* 32 (1981). Maurice Morgann, *Morgann's Essay on the Dramatic Character of Sir John Falstaff* (1912; repr. 1976). Carol Thomas Neely, "Women and Men in Othello, 'What should such a fool / Do with so good a woman?' " in *Shakespeare Studies,* 10 (1978) and "Women and Issue in *The Winter's Tale,*" in *Philological Quarterly,* 57 (1978). Michael Neill, "Shakespeare's Halle of Mirrors: Play, Politics, and Psychology in *Richard III,*" in *Shakespeare Studies,* 8 (1975). Marianne L. Novy, "Giving, Taking, and the Role of Portia in *The Merchant of Venice,*" in *Philological Quarterly,* 58 (1979) and *Love's Argument: Gender Relations in Shakespeare* (1984). A. D. Nuttall, "The Argument About Shakespeare's Characters," in *Critical Quarterly,* 7 (1965). Jocelyn Powell, "Theatrical *Trompe l'oeil* in *Measure for Measure,*" in John Russell Brown and Bernard Harris, eds., *Shakespearian Comedy,* Stratford-Upon-Avon Studies 14 (1972).

Norman Rabkin, *Shakespeare and the Problem of Meaning* (1981). Leo Salingar, "Shakespeare and the Ventriloquists," in *Shakespeare Survey,* 34 (1981). Murray M. Schwartz, "Leontes' Jealousy in *The Winter's Tale,*" in *American Imago,* 30 (1973); "*The Winter's Tale:* Loss and Transformation," *ibid.,* 32 (1975); and "Shakespeare Through Contemporary Psychoanalysis," in *Hebrew University Studies in Literature,* 5 (1977). Murray M. Schwartz and Coppélia Kahn, *Representing Shakespeare: New Psychoanalytic Essays* (1980). Arthur Sewell, *Character and Society in Shakespeare* (1951). Ella F. Sharpe, "From King Lear to The Tempest" (1946), in *Collected Papers on Psycho-Analysis* (1950). Meredith Skura, *The Literary Use of the Psychoanalytic Process* (1981). Edward A. Snow, "Sexual Anxiety and the Male Order of Things in *Othello,*" in *English Literary Renaissance,* 10 (1980). J. I. M. Stewart, *Character and Motive in Shakespeare* (1949). Elmer Edgar Stoll, *Art and Artifice in Shakespeare* (1933). David Sundelson, *Shakespeare's Restorations of the Father* (1983).

Peter Ure, "Character and Role from *Richard III* to *Hamlet,*" in John Russell Brown and Bernard Harris, eds., *Hamlet,* Stratford-Upon-Avon Studies 5 (1963). Robert Weimann, "Society and the Individual in Shakespeare's Conception of Character," in *Shakespeare Survey,* 34 (1981). Barry Weller, "Identity and Representation in Shakespeare," in *ELH,* 49 (1982). Richard P. Wheeler, *Shakespeare's Development and the Problem Comedies* (1981). David Willbern, "Rape and Revenge in *Titus Andronicus,*" in *English Literary Renaissance,* 8 (1978). J. Dover Wilson, ed., *Hamlet,* The New Shakespeare (1934).